MW00667643

Olive Trees and Honey

A Treasury of

Vegetarian Recipes from

Jewish Communities Around the World

GIL MARKS

Houghton Mifflin Harcourt
Boston   New York

This book is printed on acid-free paper. ∞

Copyright © 2005 by Gil Marks

Maps by Roberta Stockwell

Published by Houghton Mifflin Harcourt Publishing Company.
Published simultaneously in Canada

Trademarks: Houghton Mifflin Harcourt and the Houghton
Mifflin Harcourt Publishing logo are trademarks of Houghton
Mifflin Harcourt Publishing Company and/or its affiliates. All
other trademarks are the property of their respective owners.
Houghton Mifflin Harcourt, is not associated with any product
or vendor mentioned in this book.

Library of Congress Cataloging-in-Publication Data
Marks, Gil.
   Olive trees and honey : a treasury of vegetarian recipes from
Jewish communities around the world / by Gil Marks.
      p. cm.
   Includes index.
   ISBN-13: 978-0-7645-4413-2 (hardcover : alk. paper)
   ISBN-10: 0-7645-4413-6 (hardcover : alk. paper)
   1. Vegetarian cookery. 2. Cookery, Jewish. 3. Cookery,
International.   I. Title.
   TX837.M34 2004
   641.5'636'089924—dc22   2004012272

Printed in the United States of America
CW 10 9
4500436225

To my parents,

Beverly and Harold Marks,

for their love and support

❁ • ❁

OTHER BOOKS BY GIL MARKS

The World of Jewish Cooking

The World of Jewish Desserts

The World of Jewish Entertaining

Introduction

❧ · ❧

Food, viewed in Judaism as a source of both physical and spiritual sustenance, is an integral part of the Jewish religion, associated with many rituals and every life-cycle event. It is essential to the observation of the Sabbath and the Jewish festivals, establishing and enhancing the spirit of the day. In addition, the strict segregation of meat and dairy under the dietary laws meant that through history cooks needed to develop a repertoire of nonmeat dishes. In light of this, it is hardly surprising that the many Jewish laws and customs led to the evolution of a wealth of vegetarian recipes, both plain and sophisticated, for every occasion. Whether a person seeks vegetarian dishes for health, philosophical, or gastronomical reasons, Jewish cuisine offers many examples. Yet there exists precious little material exploring traditional Jewish fare.

In *Olive Trees and Honey,* I offer a collection of traditional vegetarian dishes gathered from Jewish communities across the globe. The purpose of this book is not to support or dispute the practice of vegetarianism, but rather to offer an assortment of exciting and possibly unfamiliar recipes that would enliven and enrich any diet. It also provides insights into the origin and evolution of specific vegetarian dishes, as well as the life and history of the communities that created them.

If we are what we eat, then Jews are the accumulation of at least thirty-five hundred years of history. In each of the geographical areas in which Jews found themselves, the local climate, vegetation, traditions, and events transformed their culinary habits. Over the centuries, Jewish customs and cooking continued to evolve, taking on distinct nuances in disparate places and creating diverse cultural communities. As a result, there is no one kind of Jewish cooking, but rather a mosaic of cuisines from Jewish cultural communities of varying sizes and development, each possessing its own unique history and customs. Groups of Jews from Asia, although a very diverse array, are frequently subsumed under the catchall designation Mizrachim (Easterners), which incorporates those from Yemen, Iran (Persia), Georgia, Armenia, Uzbekistan/Bukhara,

Azerbaijan, Afghanistan, Kurdistan, and India (Bombay, Cochin, and Calcutta). In addition, separate Jewish communities emerged and survived for millennia in Italy and Ethiopia. The two largest Jewish cultural communities are Ashkenazim and Sephardim.

Refugees from the original Ashkenaz—a cluster of Jewish communities located on either side of the Rhine River in what is now western Germany and eastern France—gradually spread across most of Europe, eventually becoming the largest and most influential Jewish cultural community. Thus the appellation "Ashkenazim" includes Jews from Alsace, Germany, Poland, Lithuania, Latvia, Estonia, Ukraine, Russia, Belorussia, the Czech Republic, Slovakia, Austria, Hungary, and Romania. These sundry areas exhibit varying degrees of difference in local customs and cooking. The common language of Ashkenazim was Yiddish, a form of Middle High German written in Hebrew and the source of most Ashkenazic recipe names, no matter what their country of origin. The cuisine of the largest Ashkenazic community, arising in the area encompassing Poland, Ukraine, and the Baltic States, is that of the ancestors of the vast majority of American Jews and therefore the one that most Americans commonly associate with "Jewish food."

Following the Expulsion from Spain in 1492 and the mass forcible conversion of Jews in Portugal four years later, Sephardim left Iberia and disseminated throughout the Mediterranean and western Europe (even reaching the North American colony of New Amsterdam), generally arriving in such numbers that they dominated or subsumed any indigenous Jewish populations. Today, there are an estimated 250,000 Sephardim in the United States, a number dwarfed by the five million Ashkenazim who arrived in the nineteenth and twentieth centuries.

Ironically, it was after being exiled and establishing a residence in the domains of the Ottoman Empire that Sephardim found their greatest degree of welcome and economic success. Sultan Bayazid II even thanked the Spanish monarchs for enriching his kingdom while impoverishing their own. Large and important Jewish communities grew up in Ottoman cities of Salonika (now in Greece), for several centuries the city with the world's largest Jewish population, Aleppo (now in Syria), and Istanbul (now in Turkey).

Thus the term "Sephardim" includes Jews from Turkey, Greece, Bulgaria, Yugoslavia, Syria, Iraq, Egypt, Libya, Algeria, Tunisia, Morocco, Holland, and much of France, each with their own traditions and cookery. Nevertheless, wherever they went, the Iberian exiles retained certain aspects of their Spanish heritage: a Sephardic language called Ladino or Judezmo, a dialect of Castilian Spanish written in Hebrew; ancient Sephardic songs, poems, and games; Spanish surnames; and traditional foods. Therefore, most traditional Sephardic recipes bear a Ladino title, although a number employ Arabic, French, Greek, or Turkish terms. The synthesis of Iberian and Ottoman cuisines emerged as the most conspicuous form of Sephardic cooking and the one most closely associated with Sephardic food today.

As a result of two thousand years of Jewish people living in the Diaspora, Jewish cooking constitutes a synthesis of cultures as well as a cross section of much of the world's cuisines. Thus, Jewish cookery encompasses the vegetable-rich fare of the Mediterranean as well as the potato- and buckwheat-laden diet of the shtetls of the Russian Pale. Jewish food connotes the meager fare of the impoverished and isolated Beta Esrael struggling for survival in Ethiopia as well as the rich and elaborate dishes of Marie-Antoine Carême, one of history's most important chefs and the founder of La Grand Cuisine, whose last position was in the Jewish household of Baron de Rothschild in Paris.

CONTENTS

❀ · ❀

ACKNOWLEDGMENTS

⚜ · ⚜

I owe an enormous debt to many people, both in America and abroad. Among those who shared their recipes, ideas, and time with me are Adam and Annie Anik, Suzi Brozman, Dalia Carmel and Hebert Goldstein, Michelle Comet, Lillian Cooper, Rae Dayan, Louise Defez, Poopa Dweck, Julie Goell, Liselotte Gorlin, Phyllis Koegel, Emile de Vidas Levy, Adina Mishkoff, June and Peter Olster, Faye Reichwald, Aaron Rubin, Raquel Sanchez, Stanley Allan Sherman, Mathilde Turiel, Eva Weiss, and Dr. Cynthia and David Zimm.

Very special thanks go to my family—Beverly and Harold Marks, Rabbi William and Sharon Altshul, Efrat Zipporah and Elli Schorr, Moshe Raphael Schorr, Adira Tova Schorr, Meira Bracha Schorr, Anat and Asher Yaakov Altshul, Ora Rivka and Naftali Derovan, Elchanan Matanya Derovan, Esther Chana Altshul, Aryeh Dov Altshul, Eliana Bracha Altshul, Rabbi Jeffrey and Shari Marks, Shlomo Yosef Marks, Miriam Malka Marks, Efrayim Marks, Tehila Marks, Ashira Marks, Rivka Leah Marks, Rabbi Arthur and Aviva Marks, Rivka Marks, Moshe Marks, Leah Marks, Shmuel Marks, Ahron Marks, Yeshai Marks, Yakov Marks, Daniel Marks, Devora Marks, Rachel Marks, Rabbi Labby and Carol Vegh, Chana Tzipora Vegh, Shifra Miriam Vegh, Avrohom Boruch Vegh, Elisheva Vegh, Yisroel Vegh, Adina Rivka Vegh, Moshe Yakov Vegh, Akiva Shabsi Vegh, and Menachem Meir Vegh—who bore the brunt of my culinary development and experimentation.

Very special thanks and appreciation go to my friend and agent Rita Rosenkranz, for her perseverance and counsel.

I want to express my gratitude to all the people at Wiley involved in the production of this book. Most especially I want to thank and acknowledge my editor, Linda Ingroia, and assistant editor, Adam Kowit, for their encouragement, insight, and advice. They were instrumental in transforming a dream into reality. Thank you also to Monique Calello, the production editor; Ava Wilder, the production assistant; Richard Oriolo and Holly Wittenberg, the designers; Roberta Stockwell, who created the wonderful maps; and Gypsy Lovett and Michele Sewell, the publicity managers.

Most archaic Judean fare has long been forgotten. Nor were Jews subsequently responsible for many of the world's culinary discoveries and advances, although there have been some. The principal Jewish contribution to cookery has never been in the creation of new dishes and techniques. Rather it has been in the refinement of local recipes—due to the dietary laws, life-cycle traditions, and personal preferences—and in the dissemination of these foods and ideas to their neighbors and wherever they settled. Through their role in international trade and, all too recurrently, due to exile and flight, Jews served as a primary conveyor of culinary practices from one country to another.

So, what makes a food Jewish? Jewish food is what has been served for centuries on Jewish tables, dishes that evoke the spirit of that community and the generations of Sabbath and holiday dinners as well as the necessities of everyday fare. It is tradition.

Even though Jews were scattered throughout most of the known world, they were generally still able to maintain a degree of unity, both through shared texts and traditions, and sometimes through direct contact. Hence, the cuisines of Jews from Cochin (southern India), Yemen, and Ethiopia, regions separated by the Red and Arabian Seas, reveal discernable similarities, especially in their spice combinations, due to commercial and occasional social interactions.

Even when the people were separated, the various biblical and Talmudic canons, traditions, holidays, and life-cycle events had the same impact on cooking everywhere. The restrictions of the dietary laws excluded certain culinary practices while requiring others. The prohibition against cooking on the Sabbath led to the creation of slow-simmered bean stews (such as *hamin* and *cholent*) and numerous cold salads. The proscription against leavened grain products on Passover resulted in ingenious dishes based on matza. Legends and customs produced a unity of holiday fare, from fried treats on Hanukkah to stuffed foods on Sukkot. The Talmud proffers several items to eat on Rosh Hashanah, Friday night, and other occasions. Thus, while each community developed a unique culinary repertoire, an underlying commonality endured in the various forms of Jewish cooking throughout the centuries.

In modern Israel, Sephardim, Mizrachim, and other non-Ashkenazim make up a majority of the population, and it is their fare, from Israeli salad to falafel, that most American Jews commonly associate with "Israeli food." Notwithstanding the similarities and differences of the various Jewish communities, the modern Israeli diet at its core is not dissimilar from that of ancient Israel, which was, as the Torah described it, "a land of wheat and barley, and grapevines and fig trees and pomegranates; a land of olive trees and honey… you shall eat and be satisfied" (Deut. 8:7–10). During the biblical period, these seven items formed the basis of the diet and the economy of ancient Israel. Almonds, walnuts, carob, capers, lentils, chickpeas, fava beans, and goat's milk cheese and yogurt contributed extra nutrition and flavor. Cabbage, celery, chate melon, lettuce, radishes, and turnips were the predominant vegetables. Onions, leeks, and garlic provided the basic flavorings. In addition, the Levant, the lands bordering the eastern Mediterranean, was rich in indigenous herbs—most notably chervil, cilantro, hyssop, mint, and parsley—and spices, including saffron, anise, caraway, coriander, and cumin. These items remain the basis of the Mediterranean diet today.

The Mediterranean diet, such as that long practiced by Sephardim, has been proven to yield significant health benefits, most notably much lower rates of heart disease, diabetes, and cancer, despite including a significant amount of fat, mostly mono-unsaturated. In 2003, researchers stated that the effectiveness of the Mediterranean diet was attributable not to any single item, but rather to the combination of all its foods: a high intake of olive oil, vegetables, minimally processed grains, legumes, fruits, and nuts; a moderate amount of fish and alcohol; and a low consumption of dairy and meat.

Historically, meat, when consumed, was usually a flavoring agent and, as a rule, a component in a dish reserved for special occasions. Only in the past century has animal flesh assumed such a prominent role in the diet, with meat frequently being served once, sometimes twice, or even three times a day. On the contrary, throughout most of history, cattle and sheep were not regarded as sources of food, but rather sheep were prized for their milk and wool, and cows were valued for plowing, turning the wheels that drew water from rivers and canals, hauling heavy materials, trodding grain for winnowing, powering the millstones for grinding grain, and turning the stone wheel for pressing olives. Flocks and herds served as the principal source of clothing, wealth, and security for our ancestors, something that would have been squandered if eaten. Meat was the exception, not the rule.

Recently, more and more people have begun to reexamine the way they eat, for both physical and spiritual reasons, which in Judaism are intertwined. Deuteronomy instructs, "Be extremely guarding for your lives," an interdiction against doing anything harmful to one's health and life. The linkage of flesh-centered diets to a variety of illnesses and the growing awareness of the preventative and therapeutic roles of numerous vegetables and fruits has focused attention on the value of low-cholesterol and vegetarian foods. Typically, residents of the Mediterranean eat a pound of vegetables a day, twice that of Americans, usually accompanied with olive oil.

And, of course, there are the flavor benefits of the Mediterranean diet as well. Far from limiting one's culinary possibilities, emphasizing vegetables, grains, legumes, and fruits can open a wide world of delicious, exciting, and varied dishes. To be sure, vegetarian cooking does require somewhat more planning and preparation than tossing a steak or hamburger on the grill. The results, however, can be eminently more intriguing and healthful. And not every vegetarian dish requires hours in the kitchen or a host of unusual and expensive ingredients. Some, especially soups, need little more skill than the ability to cut up a few basic ingredients and boil water. For the best flavor, however, vegetarian dishes do require fresh, high quality ingredients.

In that vein, *Olive Trees and Honey* explores traditional Jewish vegetarian dishes and the communities that produced them, as well as the foods used in everyday life and in celebrating special moments. Exploring the foods of diverse cultures is a way to know and experience an array of communities (many of them destroyed or displaced during the course of the twentieth century), for no other aspect of existence more closely touches and reveals a society's life than food.

The recipes in this book, ranging from appetizers to condiments, were selected for their flavor, variety, and cultural legacy. Not surprisingly, in light of environment and history, most of the dishes in this collection derive from the vegetable-loving Mediterranean and southern Asia. Nevertheless, other cultural communities are represented as well, from the steppes of Uzbekistan to the site of the original Ashkenaz in Alsace.

In order to simplify meal preparation, the recipes are often accompanied with ingredient and technique notes, and for inspiration you'll also find historical anecdotes and maps detailing the relevance of a dish or type of food across cultures or as it evolved over time.

Since the recipes reflect cultures from around the world, the foreign language of the recipe titles vary, so you will see Italian, Turkish, Hungarian, Hindi, and languages of many other countries, as well as Arabic and Ladino. If it is not specified, the language of the recipe title is that of the main culture connected to the dish.

For the convenience of those interested in the dairy content of foods, the recipes in this book are designated "P" for pareve (nondairy) or "D" for dairy. All vegetables, fruits, grains, herbs, spices, and eggs are inherently pareve, which, according to kosher laws, means that dishes containing them can be eaten at any meal. Any meat product, however, is strictly proscribed from dairy. In addition, all utensils and dishes used to prepare meat must be different from those used for dairy. Using only olive oil or other vegetable oils for cooking not only eliminates mixing meat and dairy foods, but it also provides a flavorful and healthy alternative to butter and lard. Where there is a choice of ingredients, the recipes are designated "D or P."

Olive Trees and Honey is a collection of vegetarian recipes that honors the creativity, passion, and respect for tradition of Jewish people throughout the world. May it inspire pleasurable meals at your table for years to come.

Food Traditions of a Mosaic of Jewish Communities

❧ · ❧

Alsace

The French province of Alsace, the site of the original area of Ashkenaz, lies between the Rhine River and the Vosges Mountains. Separated historically and geographically from both France and Germany, it has long been claimed and influenced by both countries. After its acquisition by France in 1648, Alsace remained semiautonomous until the French Revolution. Following the expulsion of the Jews from Provençe when the region became part of France in 1481, Alsace was the only part of modern France in which Jews resided until the beginning of the eighteenth century. A government report published in 1784 listed the Jewish population in Alsace at almost twenty thousand. The number increased to fifty thousand by 1970. Today, most of the area's Jewish population live in the cities of Strasbourg, Colmar, and Mulhouse. A large influx of North African Jews in the 1960s altered the makeup of the community. There are now three different Jewish communities: Alsatian, eastern European, and North African.

Alsatian Jewish cuisine, lacking Slavic and eastern Jewish influences, is closer to the original Ashkenazic fare. As in no other area of western Europe, Jewish cuisine has become an integral part of the general Alsatian cuisine: Many dishes even include the term *à la Juive* ("in the Jewish style"). Alsatian Jewish cuisine reflects a strong German influence: Few spices besides cinnamon and pepper are used; cabbage is the predominant vegetable; noodles—Alsatians prefer them very thin—and dumplings enjoy greater popularity here than in the rest of France; and foods are cooked in goose fat or oil, not butter. The soil and climate of Alsace produced grapes for some of the world's best wines, including the elegant Riesling, the spicy Gewürztraminer, and the fresh, floral Pinot Blanc.

Austria

Jews arrived in Austria with the Roman legions, but the country's Jewish community remained insignificant until the end of the twelfth century, when refugees from the Rhineland began pouring into Vienna. After the German scholar Meir ben Baruch ha-Levi established a school in the capital in 1365, Vienna became the spiritual center of central Europe, a position it retained, even in the face of oppression and massacres, until World War II. In the nineteenth century, Austria emerged as the spark of the Zionist movement when an upsurge in anti-Semitism throughout western Europe induced an assimilated Viennese journalist by the name of Theodor Herzl to pen *Der Judenstaat* ("The Jewish State") and found the World Zionist Organization.

Austrian cuisine is a synthesis resulting from thousands of years of conquerors, culture, and food flowing both ways along the banks of the mighty Danube. In the twelfth century, the marriage of several Austrian rulers to Byzantine princesses left a Middle Eastern imprint on the region's cooking. From Germany came thick soups, *wursts* (sausages), Muenster cheese, dark breads, and *kuchen*. From Italy came pasta, dumplings, and pastries. From Hungary came goulash, strudel, and elegant, buttery desserts. Marriages with Italian and French royalty kept the Austrian court abreast of the latest developments in haute cuisine. By the time of the Congress of Vienna (1814–15), held to restructure Europe following Napoleon's defeat, Austrian cuisine, especially its pastries, ranked among the foremost in the world. Austrian Jewry, much of it assimilated

and middle class, enjoyed a synthesis of local cuisine and a refined form of Ashkenazic fare, including caraway-topped dark and sourdough breads, sour cream soup (*steirshe suppe*), apple-and-raisin bread kugel, cheese-filled dumplings (*gefulte topfenknodel*), red cabbage with apples, and, especially, a large repertoire of desserts.

Azerbaijan

Azerbaijan, formerly Persia's northwestern province, lies between the Caucasus Mountains and the Caspian Sea. Its name means the "Land of Flames," referring to its abundant gas and oil reserves, which are perhaps second only to those of Saudi Arabia. Traditional Azerbaijani cooking reflects strong Persian and Turkish influences, seen in such dishes as rice pilafs (*plovs*), stews, soups, and salads.

Jews have lived in Azerbaijan since shortly after the Persian conquest of Babylon. The medieval traveler Benjamin of Tudela noted a chain of hundreds of congregations spread through the region. For centuries, Jews, called Tats, lived in mountain towns, where they developed a distinct culture and cuisine, until marauding bands in the eighteenth century drove them into the cities, bringing their food with them. The main meal is served at noon, with the entire family gathering together. Diners, seated on carpets around a *sofra* (dining cloth), commonly tear pieces from the flat whole-wheat sourdough bread (*sangak*), dip them in broth, and eat them with *turshu* (pickles). Rice is the predominant grain. On a hot summer day, there would be *dovga* (yogurt soup), in the winter *dushbara* (soup with tiny filled pasta). Side dishes might include *salata bahar* (mixed salad) and *badymzhan dolmasi* (stuffed eggplant) or *bibar dolmasi* (stuffed pepper). A combination of numerous spices impart nuance to the cuisine.

In the nineteenth century, Ashkenazic Jews arrived in Azerbaijan, supplementing the Jewish population. Beginning in 1920, the Soviets imposed their own culture on the region, outlawing most spices and forcing the Azerbaijanis to grow alien produce, such as cabbages, beets, and potatoes. The elimination of Soviet control and the subsequent struggles following independence led to more than 27,650 Jews immigrating to Israel. About 20,000 Jews remain in Azerbaijan, living primarily in the capital, Baku, and the city of Kuba.

Ethiopia

For more than two millennia, the land lying to the west of the Red Sea was home to a group of black Jews known to the Ethiopians by the derogatory term of *Falasha* ("Wanderers" in Ge'ez), but calling themselves Beta Esrael ("House of Israel"). Although several medieval Jewish travelers wrote of black Jews living in eastern Africa, the Western world only learned about their existence in a 1790 report by the Scottish explorer James Bruce. Most scholars believe that the Beta Esrael are descendants of native Agau tribes who converted to Judaism by contact with Jews living in Arabia, or by Jewish refugees who arrived in the area from either Egypt or Arabia following the destruction of the First Temple. The Beta Esrael maintained their independence and their own kings and queens until the defeat in the 1620s by Ethiopian Emperor Susenyos, who banished them to the Gondar region adjacent to the Sudanese border and subjected to centuries of persecution.

Before 1977, Ethiopian culture and cookery was obscure outside that country. Then, during the following thirteen years, more than forty thousand Beta Esrael were relocated to Israel, making their ancient traditions accessible to outsiders. Today, the Beta Esrael community in the Holy Land comprises more than eighty thousand members, and their cookery has become a part of the mosaic comprising Israeli cuisine.

Ethiopians traditionally eat two major meals each day: breakfast and dinner. In between, they snack on roasted corn kernels and seeds. The two principal Ethiopian dishes, around which all meals revolve, are injera (a flat batter bread) and *wots* (vegetable- or legume-based stews). The thick injera, fried on round terra-cotta trays and skillets, is usually made in large batches to be stored for up to a week in woven grass sacks. The injera is arranged on a communal plate, and the *wot* is then spooned on top. Each person pulls off a piece of injera while scooping up some of the *wot*, then folds it between his or her fingers to eat. The principal vegetables are cabbage, carrots, corn, potatoes, tomatoes, lettuce, and onions. Chilies, garlic, and mushrooms add variety to dishes. Ethiopian spice mixtures—typically including cardamom, cinnamon, cloves, coriander, allspice, ginger, and turmeric—reflect Arabic and Indian influences.

Georgia

The ancient country of Georgia is situated with the Black Sea to the west, the southern edge of the Great Caucasus Mountains and Russia to the north, and Turkey to the south. The nation's propitious location at the crossroads of the spice and silk trades accounts for the land's once-legendary wealth. Jews are part of Georgia's history. They have lived in the country for more than twenty-five hundred years, mostly inhabiting four cities—Kutaisi, Akhaltsikhe, Batum, and Tiflis (now Tbilisi)—with some settling as farmers scattered about the countryside. Georgia's temperate climate and rich soil yield abundant, high quality vegetables, fruits, and herbs. Georgians are not pasta or rice consumers like their neighbors but instead rely on wheat, in the form of breads, and corn. Arguably, no Old World people have embraced American beans and corn more heartily than Georgians, who use red beans in soups, stews, spreads, salads, and fillings, and enjoy corn fresh (as oil) or as cornmeal (corn bread and mush). Eggplant is the favorite vegetable. Dairy products are found primarily in the form of the ubiquitous *matsoni* (Georgian yogurt) and an array of *khveli* (cheeses). Georgians love sitting around the dinner table, not only eating but talking and singing—indeed, it is the favorite Georgian pastime.

While Georgians prefer their dishes mildly flavored, they are indulgent with fresh herbs, often adding several kinds to one dish, such as red bean soup, beets in cherry sauce, and walnut-stuffed cabbage. Georgian cooks dress up their food with sauces, in particular a walnut sauce called *bazha,* as well as a special spice mixture called *khmeli sumeli* (literally, "mixture of aromas"). The spices going into the mixtures vary (family recipes are jealously guarded), but ground coriander is a constant, and most versions contain fenugreek or ground marigold petals, which contributes a yellow hue. Sour is the favored Georgian flavor, achieved through the use of wine vinegar, pomegranates, or Caucasian sour plums.

Germany

In the wake of Charlemagne's rule, Franco-Germany emerged as a major center of Jewish learning and life. Subsequently, the Jews of the area suffered a series of anti-Semitic attacks, including the Crusades, the Rindfleisch massacres (1298–99), the Armleder massacres (1336–37), and the Black Death massacres (1348–50). Most surviving Ashkenazim relocated to more favorable conditions in the east. A small number, however, remained in Germany, which disintegrated into a collection of small feudal states. When life grew intolerable in one of these states, the oppressed Jews sought haven in another, usually living in small towns. Prohibited from pursuing most occupations, the Jews struggled to earn a livelihood in such fields as money lending and petty trade. Only in the eighteenth century were German Jews able to use their business experience to take advantage of the growing opportunities in the wake of industrialization. Some, most notably the Rothschilds, managed to amass incredible fortunes. A new wave of anti-Semitism in the nineteenth century induced many German Jews to immigrate to America, where quite a few—including families with such famous names as Guggenheim, Strauss, Belmont, Lehman, Warburg, Fleischman, and Schiff—found great success.

German Jewish cookery is stolid but substantial, a synthesis of Teutonic and Ashkenazic sources (without the Slavic dishes of eastern Ashkenazim), including *kugels* (savory puddings), *shalets* (sweet puddings), *knodel/kloese* (dumplings), *nudeln* (noodles), *mandlen* (soup puffs), *tzimmes* (vegetable stews), *gefulte kraut* (stuffed cabbage), *gehakte eier* (egg salad), and *kuchen* (coffeecakes). The food has distinct sweet-and-salty and sweet-and-sour combinations. The principal condiments are mustard and horseradish. Germans enjoy a wide array of soups, including sorrel, green wheat, mushroom, lentil, bean, split pea, and fruit. Legumes play a much larger role in Germany than among Jews of eastern Europe. The predominant vegetables are potatoes, beets, parsnips, onions, cucumbers (dill pickles), and especially cabbage, used to make sauerkraut, cabbage soup, cabbage strudel, cabbage salad, and red cabbage and apples. Beer and wine were common drinks even among the poor.

By force of numbers and affluence, German Jews dominated the American Jewish community until the early twentieth century. They were then overwhelmed by a massive wave of eastern European immigrants; thus it was eastern European culture and cooking rather than German that subsequently most affected the American Jewish community.

Greece

Greece was the first part of Europe in which Jews settled. The first record of a Jew in Greece is an inscription dating to around 300 B.C.E. referring to a slave by the name of Moschos, son of Moschion the Jew. It was only during the Hasmonean period that Jews, primarily Hellenized ones, relocated to Greece in any numbers. The Jews of Byzantium called themselves Romaniote in connection with their pride of having been citizens of the Roman Empire. More than a thousand years of Byzantine rule left the Greek Jewish community depleted and frail. The situation began to change as German Jews arrived in the area in the mid-fifteenth century and many Sephardim at the end of the century, particularly in the port city of Salonika, for many centuries the largest Jewish community in the world.

Each region of Greece boasts its own cooking style and specialties. The north reflects pronounced Slavic and Italian influences, while the south—the Mediterranean and Turkey. Because of the country's pastoral background, dairy products (mostly cheese and yogurt) make up a significant segment of the Greek diet. Modern Greek fare, similar to Turkish cooking, consists primarily of two types of vegetable dishes: *lathera* (literally, "oily," referring to casseroles and stews flavored with olive oil) and *gemista* (stuffed vegetables). Eggplant is far and away the favorite Greek vegetable. Other popular vegetables include spinach, tomatoes, fava beans, and zucchini. Favorite herbs are oregano, dill, thyme, mint, and parsley; spices include cinnamon, allspice, nutmeg, and fennel. Northern Greek cooking generally features a combination of fresh parsley, mint, and dill. As with Asian dining, all the dishes in a Greek meal are commonly served at once, not in the Roman style of individual courses.

Hungary

Jews have lived in Hungary as early as Roman times but in large numbers only since the arrival of German Jewish refugees in the eleventh century. From 1530 until 1687, the Ottoman Turks controlled most of Hungary. During this time, the area attracted a large number of Sephardim and, in the seventeenth century, Ashkenazim fleeing from Poland. After Hungarian resistance led to an Ottoman retreat, Austria immediately moved in to fill the political void, and ironically, the following century of Hapsburg rule proved more oppressive than the earlier era of the Turks.

In many ways, Hungarian cuisine is similar to that of the rest of central Europe: Wheat serves as the primary grain, made into breads, dumplings, and noodles, and cabbage is the most important vegetable. However, Magyar roots, a century and a half of Turkish control, and Austrian domination that lasted for centuries all are reflected in Hungarian cuisine. Lunch—Hungarians eat their main meal at midday—and dinner rarely start without a vegetable or a thick soup/stew called *leves*, usually served with traditional dumplings, croutons, or noodles. Hungarian cooking utilizes few seasonings other than paprika and onions, relying instead on cooking techniques for flavor. Tomatoes—another New World import—and sour cream often accompany paprika in a dish to mellow its sharpness. Unlike northern Ashkenazim, Hungarians enjoy a number of fine wines.

India

Indian Jews fall into three distinct groups situated in three different parts of the country: the Bene Israel of Bombay in the west; the Jews of Cochin on the Malabar coast in the southwest; and, in the east, the Baghdadi of Calcutta. Each of these three groups developed independently and, therefore, manifests significantly different cultural and culinary forms.

The Bene Israel is probably the oldest and certainly the largest Jewish community in India. According to a local legend, a group of Jews fleeing Antiochus Epiphanes (the villain of the Hanukkah story) in 175 B.C.E. were shipwrecked off of the Konkan coast and seven men and seven women reached the shore. For almost two millenia, the Bene Israel had no contact with world Jewry or Jewish developments elsewhere: They were unfamiliar with the Talmud, rabbis, synagogues, or prayer books, all of which originated after the Bene Israel's separation. Only in the mid-1700s, during the British conquest of India, did the outside world become aware of the Bene Israel's existance.

According to one local legend, the Jews of the Malabar coast are descended from Judean exiles fleeing the troops of Babylonian King Nebuchadnezzar. Another legend claims that Jewish sailors in King Solomon's fleet stopped over and remained in the area. The first written mention of a Jewish community existing on the Malabar coast is a pair of copper plates dating to somewhere between 379 and 1000 C.E. Inscribed in a Tamil dialect, the plates record seventy-two special privileges granted to the Jews by the local ruler. Unlike the Bene Israel, the Jews of Cochin remained in contact with other Jewish communities, interacting with the Jews across the Arabian Sea in Yemen and Babylonia.

Although Jewish merchants had been visiting the province of Bengal in northeast India for centuries, it was only after Calcutta became the British capital of India in 1858 and emerged as an important commercial center that the first permanent Jewish settlement was established. The earliest Jewish settlers were jewel merchants from Syria. Soon other Near Eastern Jews arrived, attracted by the economic potential of this foreign location. Within a short time, the city boasted a large and vibrant Jewish community maintaining synagogues, schools, hospitals, and other institutions. Since a large percentage of this growing population came from Iraq, the Jews of Calcutta became known as Baghdadis.

It is only natural that the cuisines of India's many regions are as diverse as the country itself. Still, there are certain characteristics that unite the various forms of Indian cooking. The most profound influence on Indian cuisine was the Hindu religion and its concept of *ahimsa* (a reverence for life), out of which a strong vegetarian tradition developed. The invading Persians, Arabs, Turks, Mongols, and English all left their imprint on Indian culture and cuisine. Everywhere in the country, cooks use an extensive number of home-grown spices, including cardamom, cinnamon, coriander, cumin, fenugreek, ginger, mustard seed, pepper, and turmeric. Traditionally, all the dishes of a meal are served at the same time in small bowls arranged on a metal tray called a *thali*.

Italy

The first Jews known to visit what is now Italy were a delegation sent to Rome by Judah Maccabee in 161 B.C.E. to conduct a treaty between the two countries. Soon, Jews began settling in Rome and regions to the south, including Sicily. Later, Ashkenazim fleeing the massacres in the wake of the Black Death (1348–49) and the French Expulsion (1394) arrived in the Italian city states to the north. By the time of the Italian Renaissance in the fourteenth century, the Jewish population of Italy numbered about fifty thousand. Sephardim arrived in Italy fleeing Spain during the Inquisition, while at the same time Spanish acquisition of the Kingdom of Naples sent most of the Italian Jews to the northern and central states.

Since Italy existed as an assortment of independent states for most of its history, it is only natural that differences in cuisine emerged in each region. The north, which has generally been wealthier, uses much more meat, and the food tends to be more subtly seasoned than the heavily spiced dishes in the south. In the north, pasta generally contains eggs and tends to be fresh and flat (such as fettuccine and cannelloni). In the south, pasta is almost always made from semolina and water and is often dried (such as spaghetti and macaroni). In the Po Valley of the far north, rice serves as the staple grain in the form of risotto. Italian Jewish fare more closely resembles that of Sephardim than of Ashkenazim—in part due to its Mediterranean location and in part to the arrival of Sephardim from Spain. From the ghettos of the Italian cities come some of the most ancient and authentic Jewish dishes.

Morocco

By the time of the Arab conquest in 683 C.E., Morocco hosted a large Jewish community, and several parts of the country were populated solely by Jews. They subsequently built and controlled the gold trade, one of the country's primary sources of economic power, and also played a prominent role in naval operations. Beginning in the late 1300s, northwest Africa experienced an extreme form of Islamic fanaticism and repression, resulting in an economic, scientific, and cultural decline from which it never recovered. By 1438, the situation had deteriorated to such an extent that the Jews of Fez were forced to live in a *mellah* (compulsory Jewish quarter), seventy-eight years before the establishment of Venice's infamous ghetto (the first one in Europe). Many Jews fleeing from Spain in 1492 and Portugal in 1496 came to Morocco, forming the largest Sephardic community in the world, but due to the restrictive climate in the country, few of these immigrants, called *megorashim*, were the better educated. Most Moroccan Jews worked as minor merchants, peddlers, craftsmen, and farmers and, as a result of excessive taxation, subsisted near the poverty level.

Until relatively recently, a typical kitchen in the Maghreb consisted of a hearth fueled by charcoal or dung and a brazier, which served as a heat diffuser—essential to keep *tagines* and other earthenware pots from cracking. The *tagine*, a glazed terra-cotta dish with a tall, conical lid, remains a popular vessel for braising; the slow cooking melds and intensifies the flavors and aromas of the ingredients. Traditionally, Morrocans have eaten one-pot meals cooked in *tagines,* also the name of the stews cooked in them, accompanied with bread or couscous. The arrival of

Sephardim in 1492 added various salads, pastries, and side dishes to the cuisine. Wealthier homes also had a *radaf* (metal warming pan), used to make various sauces and egg dishes.

Over the centuries, a succession of influences (the native Berber, plus the Phoenician, Roman, Jewish, Moorish, Spanish, Turkish, and most recently French) all influenced the cooking of the region. To this day, various parts of Morocco have very different styles of cooking: Fez cuisine has a strong Arab flavor, Marakesh draws on a pronounced Berber heritage, and Tetuan bears a Spanish influence. The bulk of the Moroccan diet consists of wheat (bread and couscous), fava beans, and chickpeas, all of these flavored with onions, garlic, olives, preserved lemons, almonds, dates, figs, and assorted spices. Moroccan cooking relies on the character and combination of ingredients, not on condiments. It liberally mixes seasonings to produce delightful nuances of flavor, aroma, and color—more closely resembling Indian than Middle Eastern cuisine. While the size of portions is generally small, a Moroccan meal almost always contains a large variety of dishes. A meal is not considered a meal unless it contains something hot.

Persia (Iran)

The relationship between Persia and the Jews began in 538 B.C.E., when Cyrus the Great conquered Babylonia and granted the Jews permission to return to Israel and rebuild the Temple. The emergence of the Sasanian dynasty in 226 C.E., whose leaders were Zoroastrians, led to persecutions so intense that the Babylonian scholar Rabina, fearful the oral law would be forgotten, began the process of redacting the Babylonian Talmud. Relief arrived in 642, when the Arabs conquered Persia, ending

twelve hundred years of Persian dominance in western Asia. The position of Persian Jewry deteriorated again with the emergence of the Safawid dynasty in 1502 and the introduction of Shi'ism as the state religion.

Ancient Persians embraced the cuisines of Babylonia, Assyria, and Egypt, added their own distinctive touches, and raised western Asian gastronomy to new heights. Centuries of Persian control of western and central Asia, as well as of India, left its imprint on the cooking of those areas, making Persian cuisine one of the world's most influential. Rice is the predominate grain, and particularly prized is a local variety called *domsiah*. Persian cooking uses a wide variety of vegetables, including cucumbers, beets, celery, cardoons, eggplants, okra, green beans, spinach, squash, and turnips. Citrus fruits—lemons, limes, oranges, and tangerines—and pomegranates are essential to cooking, as Persians prefer a slightly tart taste in their dishes. Persian cuisine uses less spice than that of its neighbors, except for saffron, but, like the Georgians, adds fresh and dried herbs in abundance. While onions are a fundamental seasoning, Persian cuisine is one of the few Jewish cuisines in which garlic is downgraded if not ignored.

Poland and the Baltic States (Eastern Europe)

In desperate need of population and economic growth, the leaders of twelfth- and thirteenth-century Poland and Lithuania invited the persecuted Jews of Franco-Germany to settle in their domains. In return, they allowed the Jews to engage in every form of commerce and even granted them the autonomy to regulate their own communities. Waves of Jewish immigration from the west soon arrived in eastern Europe and from this community developed the largest branch of Ashkenazic Jewry. By the fourteenth century, Poland hosted the world's largest Jewish population, a position it maintained for six hundred years, until World War II. Gradually, eastern European Jewry developed its own distinctive form of Ashkenazic culture.

In Poland, the initial period of prosperity and security came to an end in 1648, when Bogdan Chmielnicki and his Cossack hordes, a peasant uprising against Polish rule in Ukraine, devastated Polish Jewry destroying hundreds of Jewish settlements and taking more than 100,000 Jewish lives. Most Poles, both Jews and gentiles, subsequently eked by on a subsistence level. In the eighteenth century, Poland was partitioned by its neighbors, so many Polish Jews found themselves residents of Lithuania, Germany, Belorussia, Hungary (Galicia), and Ukraine. Following the assassination of Czar Alexander II in 1881, the Russian government sponsored a series of pogroms, inducing more than two million eastern European Jews (at least a third of the total) to immigrate to the United States. The newcomers overwhelmed the smaller Sephardic and German Jewish communities already present, and as a result, the eastern European form of Ashkenazic cooking became what most Americans associate with Jewish food.

The fare of northern Poland and the Baltic states has been strongly affected by Russia to the east and Scandinavia to the northwest, while the southern part of the country reflects the influences of Germany, Ukraine, and Hungary. In addition to claiming its own Slavic dishes, such as knishes, blintzes, and *pirogen*, Polish and Baltic cuisines distinguish themselves from western and central European Ashkenazic cooking by the scarcity of herbs and spices and the presence of regional ingredients, such as buckwheat (*kasha*) and rhubarb. Poland has long boasted an advanced dairy industry; sour cream, butter, and fresh cheeses became staples of the diet and common additions to dishes. Tart foods, such as sour cream, sauerkraut, dill pickles, pickled mushrooms, and pickled beets, enlivened and supplemented a diet overwhelmingly consisting of potatoes and dark bread.

Romania

The mountainous Balkan Peninsula (*Balkan* is Turkish for "mountains") today encompasses the countries of Romania, Yugoslavia (Serbia and Montenegro), the former Yugoslav states (Bosnia and Herzegovina, Croatia, Macedonia, Molova, and Slovenia), Bulgaria, Albania, Greece, and the European part of Turkey. According to legend, the first Jews arrived in the northern Balkan Peninsula during the reign of King Xerxes of Persia (c. 465 B.C.E.). Still, the Jewish community remained small until an influx of refugees arrived, fleeing the repression of the Byzantine Empire. After conquering the Balkans in the fourteenth century, the Turks combined two provinces, Walachia and Moldavia. This de facto union was formalized in 1859, at which time the country adopted its current name Romania. A progression of other refugees further increased the Jewish population of the northern Balkans: Hungarians relocated there after their expulsion in 1367; Sephardim settled here after escaping the Inquisition; Polish Jews came fleeing the Chmielnicki massacres of 1648; and Russians arrived fleeing czarist persecution.

After four centuries of Ottoman rule, the cuisine of the Balkans naturally bears a strong Turkish influence, which mingles with the region's Ashkenazic food traditions. Romanian cooking is primarily peasant fare, differing from its neighbors in its generous use of spices and garlic, plenty of garlic. Horseradish accompanies many dishes to cleanse the palate of garlic and spices. Romania's climate is particularly favorable for legumes and grains, especially corn, which yields the staple food of the Romanian kitchen, cornmeal (generally eaten as *mamaliga*). Common Romanian vegetables include cabbage, bell peppers, potatoes, tomatoes, and, conspicuously, eggplant, the latter being absent in nearby Hungarian and Polish kitchens. Orchards and vineyards dot the Carpathian hillsides, providing abundant wine and a wealth of fresh fruits for the region.

Syria

A strong Jewish presence in Syria, the land to the northest of Israel, dates back to biblical times. Syria, too, was a popular destination for Jews fleeing the Expulsions from Spain and Spanish-controlled southern Italy. During the sixteenth century, Aleppo (*Halab* in Arabic, *Aram Soba* in the Bible), in the northwest of the country, emerged as the center of trade between the Ottoman Empire and Europe, while Damascus became a banking center, with Jews playing major roles in both sectors. The more religious merchants of Aleppo (home of the famous one-thousand-year-old Aleppo Codex, the accepted version of the biblical text; it was partially burned in 1947 by an Arab mob but was rescued and smuggled to Jerusalem where it is now displayed at the Israel Museum's Shrine of the Book) and the more secular artisans of Damascus generally looked condescendingly on one another, including the sphere of cooking.

The cuisine of the Levant—Syria, Lebanon, and Israel—is a blend of Persian, Arabic, Turkish, and Sephardic influences. Wheat (bread, bulgur, and pasta) is the mainstay of the diet. Rice, legumes, and vegetables also feature prominently. Olive oil is used much less frequently in Syria than in much of the region. Many dishes have a sweet-and-sour flavor, commonly provided by citrus fruits, pomegranates, and tamarinds. Dishes are seasoned with cilantro, garlic, allspice, cinnamon, cumin, and Aleppo pepper. The food of Aleppo is known for its delicacy of seasoning and elaborateness.

Tunisia

According to legend, Jews first reached Tunisia, then Carthage, during the reign of King Solomon. The first large, permanent Jewish presence in the area appeared after the destruction of the Second Temple in 70 C.E. The Jewish community grew with the arrival of Sephardim following the Expulsion in 1492 and of Italians from Leghorn (Livorno) in the sixteenth century, who came to negotiate with the numerous pirates operating in the area. In 1946, there were seventy-one thousand Jews in Tunisia. Following Tunisian independence in 1956 and the Six Day War in 1967, much of the ancient Jewish infrastructure was destroyed by the government and most of the Jews fled.

Tunisian cuisine is an amalgamation of diverse influences: Berber, Roman, Arab, Sephardic, Spanish, Turkish, Italian, and French, the latter two yielding a number of elaborate dishes, including *brik* (potato-filled pastry), *ajluk de courgettes* (zucchini relish), *salata mechouiya* (grilled pepper salad), and *shlata djezar metbucha* (cooked carrot salad). The principal grain of the region is wheat, mainly used in breads and to make couscous, the national dish of Tunisia. Other important locally grown foods are dates, grapes, melons, olives, oranges, and tomatoes. Legumes are a mainstay, in dishes such as *lablabi* (chickpea soup). *Harissa*, a fiery chili mixture imported during a forty-year Spanish rule beginning in 1535, is used liberally.

Turkey

Following the split of the Roman Empire, the eastern part—the Byzantine Empire—spent most of its millenium of existence attempting to spread the Greek Orthodox religion while fending off incursions by Persians, Arabs, Huns, and Slavs. More successful than these invaders were the Ottoman Turks, originally from Mongolia, who gradually gained control over western Asia. In 1453, the Turks captured Constantinople (renamed Istanbul), bringing an end to the Byzantine Empire. The Ottoman Empire reached its height under Suleiman the Magnificent (1494–1566), whose domains stretched northwest to Hungary, northeast to Georgia, westward to Algeria, and southeast to the Euphrates River. The number of Jews in Turkey swelled in 1492, as Bayazid II eagerly welcomed the Spanish-Portuguese exiles into his realm. Due to its unique location spanning two continents and the expanse of the former Ottoman Empire, Turkish cooking bears no singular dominant feature; rather, variety is the hallmark of the Turkish kitchen. Eggplant reigns as the monarch of Turkish vegetables, but other favorites include bell peppers, tomatoes, okra, squash, and cucumbers. Turkey is justly renowned for its fruits, both fresh and dried, most notably Smyrna (now Izmir) figs and golden sultana raisins. Yogurt—a Turkish word first used in English in the 1620s—is an essential element of Turkish cooking.

Turkey's strategic location led to its control of the overland spice trade, which ensured a continued supply of seasonings, used subtly in Ottoman cooking. In the palace of the sultan, Ottoman cuisine was raised to special heights, the imperial kitchen employing hundreds of cooks divided into separate groups for the preparation of bread, soup, meat, fish, vegetable dishes, pilafs, pastries, syrups, and confections, many of which found their way into the cuisine of the populace.

Uzbekistan (Bukhara)

Along the fabled Silk Road—starting in China, skirting the northern fringes of the Gobi Desert, passing through Baghdad, and ending in the eastern Mediterranean—a stream of caravans once bore the riches of the Orient to the West, engendering great wealth for legendary central Asian trading towns, most notably Samarkand, Tashkent, and Bukhara—situated in modern-day Uzbekistan and Tajikistan. According to local tradition, the first Jews settled in this area following the Persian king Cyrus's conquest of Babylon in 539 B.C.E. Once a part of the larger Persian Jewish community, the Bukharans split off following the ascendance of the Shiites in Persia in the sixteenth century. The group soon incorporated Jewish refugees arriving from nearby Samarkand following the city's destruction in 1598. Today, the term *Bukharan* refers to all the Jews of Uzbeki and Tajikistan.

Bukharan Jewish cuisine similarly bears the imprint of many cultures, including Persian (kebabs, *palov*, halva, and flat breads), Chinese (pasta and steamed dumplings), Turkish (pastries), Mongolian, Indian, and Russian. Bukharan is a subtle cuisine. The predominant seasonings are onion, garlic, and cilantro; the principal spices are cumin, coriander, and turmeric. In the flat, semiarid land of central Asia, crops must generally be coaxed out of the soil by means of a series of ancient irrigation canals. The result is an assortment of fruit, generally of immense proportions, and vegetables, which Bukharans commonly cook together. Central Asia has long been a pastoral culture, and therefore dairy products and lamb (the fat from lamb tails yielding the predominant cooking fat) make up a significant portion of the diet. Mung bean is the favored legume and wheat, in the form of flat breads and pasta, the principal grain. Rice remains the most costly grain and, consequently, a luxury item generally reserved for special dishes. *Non* (a flat bread) is served at every meal. Hot green tea is enjoyed at the end of meals and frequently in between.

Yemen

Yemen (which is divided into two countries, North Yemen, also called San'a, and South Yemen, also called Aden) stretches along the southwestern tip of the Arabian Peninsula. The first known Jewish settlement there was established after the destruction of the Second Temple in 70 C.E., and for centuries thereafter Jews played a prominent role in the country's economy and politics, dominating the all-important spice trade. The Jewish presence reached its high point when Yusuf As'ar Dhu-Nuwas, a fifth-century Himyar king, and many of his nobles converted to Judaism. This era was brought to an end in 525, when Abyssinian and Byzantine forces conquered the kingdom and killed Dhu-Nuwas. The advent of Islam in the eighth century reduced Yemenite Jews to the lowest rung of the social order and poverty.

It seems that no other country in the Jewish mosaic is more health-conscious in their cuisine than Yemen, and the effects of this are evident in the people's slim, sound physiques and relative longevity. Yemenites who follow their ancient diet are usually free of the afflictions of Western society, most notably high blood pressure, high cholesterol levels, and diabetes. Yemenite cuisine is a spicy one, dominated by cumin, chilies, and fresh coriander. Yemenites contend that the fire in their dishes helps to cleanse the body.

Most Yemenite meals begin with bread—leavened and unleavened flat breads—accompanied with *chilbeh* (a paste made from fenugreek) or, occasionally, *samneh* (clarified butter). The favorite condiment is *z'chug*, a coriander and green chili mixture, or a red chili version called *shatta*. Lentils, fava beans, chickpeas, and bulgur—inexpensive Middle Eastern mainstays—constitute the bulk of the diet. Eggplant is the favorite vegetable. Yemenites borrowed the Persian innovation of stuffing vegetables and fruit (called *memuleh*), an idea that ingeniously stretches limited resources, to create an array of flavorful dishes. Salads or cooked vegetable purées (there is often little distinction between the two in Yemenite cooking) accompany almost every meal. Yemenites love to add pine nuts to dishes for flavor and texture. In accord with their healthful eating habits, desserts traditionally consist of seasonal fresh fruit.

Seasonings and Flavors Important to Jewish Cuisines

❧ · ❧

The ethnic cuisines of Jewish people throughout the world encompass an amazing array of flavors. Many of the cuisines share similar ingredients, such as garlic or chilies, while others feature signature flavors, such as allspice in Syrian dishes and asafetida in Indian dishes. Although the seasonings are not "Jewish," they are prevalent in the foods Jewish people have eaten through history. Here is a brief look at the important ingredients and their relevance to the recipes in this book.

Allspice

Many Syrian dishes are typically seasoned with the country's favorite spice, *bahar* (allspice). Ironically, this berry is native to the West Indies and was only introduced to the Old World by Columbus. Syrians quickly adopted it, because it resembled the area's favorite spice blend—a combination of cinnamon, cloves, and nutmeg. Ever since, it has been impossible to think of Syrian cooking without allspice.

Anise and Fennel

Anise, or aniseed (*Pimpinella anisum*), a member of the Umbelliferae family and native to the Near East, is one of the most ancient spices. Its yellowish brown seeds resemble cumin. Fennel (*Foeniculum vulgare*), another member of the Umbelliferae family, sometimes called sweet cumin, bears light brown-greenish elliptical seeds. Both anise and fennel seeds contain anethol, an essential oil with a licoricelike flavor. However, fennel seeds are milder and less sweet than anise. Because of this, anise tends to be used in sweeter fare, while fennel seed is added to savory dishes, such as breads, sausages, sauces, and liqueurs. Sephardim, however, commonly add anise seeds to their Sabbath and holiday breads.

Asafetida

Asafetida or asfoetida, from the Farsi *aza* (gum) and Latin *foetida* (stinking), is a dried yellowish gum resin made from the rhizomes, or rootlike stems, of a variety of fennel. Raw, it has an unpleasant flavor and a stinking odor; cooked, it develops a garlicky taste and musky trufflelike aroma. Although native to the Middle East and mentioned in the Talmud, today it is primarily found in Indian cooking. Indians believe that asafetida is good for the digestion and add it to legume dishes and cabbage to help their digestibility. Asafetida is available in lump or powdered form: Use it in small amounts to enhance curries, stews, and dried bean dishes.

Basmati

Basmati (literally, "queen of fragrance") is an aromatic Indian long-grain rice with a nutty flavor. When cooked properly, the grains turn out fluffy, yet firmer and longer than those of other long-grain varieties. American-grown basmati transplants, due to differences in soil and climate, generally differ in flavor and aroma from Indian-grown; they are also shorter and less fluffy. Jasmine rice (*kao plow*), a Thai variety of basmati, has a popcorn aroma and a softer texture. Domsiah is a Persian variety of basmati, with a more subtle aroma.

Bay Leaves

The sweet bay laurel tree (*Laurus nobilis*), a native of Asia Minor, produces smooth, glossy green leaves, which add a pungent flavor and aroma to dishes. Since they are so pungent, generally one leaf is sufficient for a dish. Bay leaves from western Turkey tend to be milder but more aromatic, with a greater depth of flavor than American-grown varieties. Fresh bay leaves are a bit more aromatic and much more bitter than dry ones. Bay leaves vary in size from 1 to 3 inches; recipes that call for a bay leaf generally refer to a 2-inch leaf. Look for pale green, supple, unbroken leaves; brittle, brownish leaves have poor flavor.

Berbere

Berbere, the Amharic word for ground dried red chilies, also refers to a spice mixture used to flavor the Ethiopian stews called *wots* and vegetable dishes. It reflects the Arabic and Indian influences on Ethiopian cookery. In this spice blend, cardamom, cinnamon, nutmeg, and allspice add a sweet counterbalance to the fire of the chilies and pepper (from peppercorns).

Capers

Capers are the greenish, unopened buds of a tenacious Mediterranean shrub. Related to mustard and cabbage, the caper shrub grows up to three feet high and sprouts numerous thin, trailing branches. Because its roots can draw nourishment from poor soil or even cracks in a rock, the caper bush grows wild throughout the mountainous regions of the Mediterranean, including Israel. Because the bush so determinedly thrives in the crevices of rocks, stone walls, and in other difficult locales—even growing on the Western Wall—the Talmud compares it to "Israel among the nations." Caper buds bloom into white tulip-shaped flowers when exposed to light; they close at sunset, and so must be picked before sunrise. (In Ecclesiastes, caperberries symbolize the brevity of human life.) The Mishnah considered capers a tithable crop, connoting its usage as an important food two thousand years ago.

Capers have a spicy aroma and piquant, slightly bitter flavor—a combination of mustard and black pepper—that complements other Mediterranean seasonings, most notably basil, chervil, garlic, olives, and oregano. While occasionally used fresh, green capers are more often sun-dried and pickled in vinegar or salt. Some caper buds are allowed to grow into semimature, olive-sized fruits called caperberries, which have a similar but much more intense flavor than the buds.

Capers in vinegar may be used directly or rinsed for a milder taste; capers packed in salt must be rinsed several times or soaked in cold water for at least 30 minutes before being used. Capers are added to a number of salads (such as *michoteta*), dips, relishes (such as caponata), stews (such as *turlu*), and sauces (most notably lemon-wine sauces and tartar sauce). Since intense heat destroys their aroma, capers are generally incorporated into sauces near the end of cooking. Store opened bottles of capers in the refrigerator for up to 6 months; discard if the liquid turns cloudy, indicating the presence of mold.

Cardamom

Cardamom, a member of the ginger family, is the most fragrant of spices (a combination of citrus, camphor, and eucalyptus). Inside the brittle pods are clusters of a dozen or more intensely flavored tiny black-brown seeds, which have a bittersweet taste similar to that of anise, with menthol and lemony undertones. Cardamom follows only saffron among spices in expense, but a little goes a long way. Green pods, preferred in India and the Middle East, have a stronger and sweeter flavor and aroma than the other types. White pods, which are green pods that have been bleached, are considered more aesthetically pleasing and less pungent. Black pods, not true cardamom but a relative, is a staple of African cooking, and have a smoky, nutlike flavor. The pods are used whole, notably added to tea in India and coffee in the Middle East, but the hard outer pod is generally discarded just before using, and the seeds bruised or ground. The seeds begin losing their intensity once crushed. Two pods yield about $1/8$ teaspoon ground cardamom.

Cilantro

Fresh coriander—commonly called cilantro, Chinese parsley, or Mexican parsley—is a member of the Umbelliferae family and probably native to Israel. The leaves, seeds, and roots are all used in cooking for different purposes; the various parts have very dissimilar flavors and should not be substituted for one another. Cilantro has become one of the world's most widely used herbs, a popular component of the cuisines of Asia, Mexico, the Middle East, and the Caribbean. Although cilantro resembles its relative, Italian parsley, the leaves are thinner and a lighter green, and the flavor (musty, peppery, and citrusy) is entirely different. Cilantro and parsley can be interchanged, however, depending on individual preference for a milder or more intense flavor. Unlike parsley, cilantro's soft stems can also be used: simply remove the thicker lower part. Cilantro's refreshing taste complements both cool and hot foods and goes especially well with citrus, mint, ginger, and chilies. It clashes with robust flavors, such as oregano, rosemary, and thyme. Heat dissipates cilantro's flavor and turns it bitter, so the herb is usually added near the end of cooking. With its roots intact, cilantro will last, refrigerated, for up to a week: Cover the leaves with a plastic bag and place the roots in a glass with 1 inch of water. If the roots have been removed, snip the stems on an angle and follow the previous directions, refrigerating for up to 3 days. If cilantro stands for too long, it develops a harsh, unpleasant flavor.

Citrus Fruit

Citrus, evergreen plants with shiny leaves and brightly colored fruit, probably originated in India as a single variety. Over the centuries, through continuous crossing, it has developed into one of the largest fruit families, numbering several thousand varieties. Citrus moved west from its home, through Persia, Asia Minor, and then Greece. Although orange, lemon, and citron (*etrog* in Hebrew) trees were grown in Italy as early as 50 C.E., with the Lombard invasion in 568 and the fall of the Roman Empire, citrus fruit, which requires specialized care, disappeared from Europe and much of the Mediterranean. Jews, however, continued to cultivate citron (for the Sukkot ritual) and other citrus trees. As pointed out by Erich Isaac ". . . it is the antiquity of citrus culture, originally introduced to these regions (Spain, the Maghreb, Sicily, southern Italy, and Egypt, all of which correspond to the large Mediterranean Jewish centers of that time) by Jews, for whom the cultivation of other citrus species was a byproduct of citron cultivation, which explains the persistence of this horticultural specialty." In the eighth century, Jewish traders began spreading citrus fruit to much of the Mediterranean and selling lemons and oranges to eastern and northern Europe, serving as the primary source of citrus for these regions until the late nineteenth century. Not surprisingly, lemons and oranges abound in the cuisine of Mediterranean Jews. Lemon is a high-acid citrus fruit that enhances other foods while adding its own bright flavor. The presence of orange in many venerable Mediterranean dishes is a mark of Sephardic influence.

Cloves

Cloves—from the Latin *clavus,* or "nail," referring to its shape—are the unopened buds of an ever-green tree of the Myrtacae family, which is native to the Molucca Islands in the East Indies. Cloves contain 14 to 20 percent essential oil, most notably eugenol, a chemical that gives the clove its characteristic sweet-hot flavor and peppery aroma. The clove's essential oils dissipate soon after grinding; grind them fresh to maintain the most intense flavor. Cloves complement both sweet and savory foods and are used to flavor pickles, stews, sauces, and desserts. Cloves are rather pungent, so they should be used sparingly.

Cumin

Cumin, the dried fruit of a member of the parsley family, perhaps native to the Nile Valley, is one of the most ancient and important of Middle Eastern spices. Although cumin seeds look somewhat like caraway seeds (oblong and ridged), they are longer, lighter in color (yellowish brown), and straighter, with an acrid fragrance and a warm, bitter-nutty, earthy flavor containing a hint of lemon. Cumin contributes a gentle pungency and warmth to foods, and is used whole or ground. Toasting the seeds enhances their flavor. Cumin contributes a base note that complements more assertive spices, so it frequently appears in spice mixtures.

Black cumin (*Bunium persicum*), a member of the Apiaceae family native to central Asia, is called *katzah/ketzah* in Hebrew and variously as *shahi jeera* ("imperial cumin"), *kala jeera* (black cumin), and *Kashmiri jeera* in Hindi. It is darker, smaller, more intense, and slightly sweeter than the more common cumin (*jeera*). Black cumin has a slightly camphoraceous flavor that turns nutty after the seeds are fried or toasted. Black cumin is not the same as nigella (black onion seeds), with which it is commonly confused. If black cumin is unavailable, substitute cumin or nigella.

Fenugreek

Fenugreek—*hilbeh* in Arabic, *methi* in Hindi, and *rubia* in Hebrew—is a smooth, hard, $1/6$-inch-long yellow-brown member of the pea family native to the Mediterranean. Its celerylike aroma and mellow, slightly bitter flavor (similar to caramelized sugar) emerge when it is lightly heated. Unheated, fenugreek is very astringent; overtoasting gives it a disagreeable bitterness. Fenugreek is particularly popular ground in Yemenite, Ethiopian, Georgian, Moroccan, and southern Indian cuisines, where its bitterness is greatly valued. Its earthy flavor and musky aroma are essential to Yemenite *hilbeh,* Indian curry powders and chutneys, Georgian walnut sauces, and the Ethiopian spice mixture *berbere.* Its principal use in America is in imitation maple syrup and commercial curry powders.

Floral Waters

Floral waters are the result of the distillation process; fresh rose petals produce rosewater, and orange flowers are used to make orange blossom water (also called orange flower water). These are frequently used interchangeably in numerous pastries, puddings, sauces, fruit dishes, salads, and beverages, where they add a flowery complexity and perfume. The process originated in ancient Persia, but because it was so difficult to carry out, the distillations remained rarities until an Arab scholar, Jabir ibn Hayyan, invented a new and easy method of distilling in 800 C.E., revolutionizing not only floral waters but also all distilled spirits. Soon, rosewater (*mai ward*) and orange blossom water (*mai zahr/mai qedda*) became flavorings in Middle Eastern cooking, many families making their own in their basements. Before the advent of vanilla extract in the early twentieth century, Americans and Europeans also flavored their baked goods with these distillates, although their use has since become rare. Orange blossom water and rosewater are available at Middle Eastern and Asian specialty stores. Most commercial varieties come diluted, so their strength may vary; it is best to adjust the amount according your personal tastes.

Garlic

Garlic, the bulb of a member of the lily family, is one of the world's oldest and most important seasonings. The flavor depends on the variety and how it is prepared. Whole cloves of garlic sautéed in oil impart a subtle flavor, baking whole garlic until soft produces a nutty savor, and simmering it in a broth yields a surprisingly delicate, sweet taste. Garlic's distinctive odor and pungent flavor come from a sulfur compound called allicin, which is produced when the garlic cell membranes are broken—through crushing, chopping, or slicing. The more broken up garlic is, the more allicin is released. Heat dissipates allicin, producing a tantalizing pungency in dishes. Whether it is used whole or minced, be careful not to let garlic burn (become dark brown), causing its aromatic oils to turn bitter. Garlic powder has a very different flavor from fresh and should generally not be substituted.

Ginger

Ginger is the knotty rhizome of an orchidlike tropical plant native to the Far East. As international trade expanded, ginger's pungency became an integral part of cuisine and medicine throughout most of the ancient world. Fresh ginger grows in the shape of a hand. White ginger, grown in Jamaica and common to America, is slightly lemony and camphoraceous and more delicate and aromatic than gray ginger, which is grown primarily in India. Ginger's pungency comes from zingerone, gingerol, and shogoal, chemical irritants that activate neurons of the somato-sensory system, making the tongue feel warm. Ginger's flavor mellows as it simmers, developing a hearty warmth. Besides fresh, ginger is available in a variety of forms: dried (ground), crystallized, preserved, and pickled. Ground ginger is powdered dried ginger, which has a different flavor from fresh, and the two do not generally serve as substitutes for each other. Fresh ginger is vital to Indian Jewish cooking, while the ground form is important in Ethiopia, Morocco, and eastern Europe.

Horseradish

HORSERADISH THAT DOES NOT
BRING A PIOUS TEAR TO THE EYE
IS NOT GOD'S HORSERADISH.
—Teyve in Shalom Aleichem's
"Tevye, the Dairyman"

Horseradish, a member of the mustard family, is a fleshy perennial root native to southeastern Europe. The Yiddish name *chrain* is derived from the Slavic *kren* reflecting the Slavic influence on the Ashkenazic pantry. For many people, horseradish is a bottle of sweet red sauce (with beets and sugar added to mellow the taste), but fresh horseradish is neither red nor sweet. The large root is fiery, white, and aromatic. After grating, horseradish loses its volatile oils (primarily allyl isothiocynate) and the bite fades quickly if not preserved, usually in vinegar. Use a (relatively) generous serving for a tangy flavor or just a bit for a subtle taste to spice up a salad, soup, or casserole.

Jaggery

Indian jaggery (*gur*), called *piloncillo* or *panela* in Central America and Mexico, is a brownish-colored raw sugar made by extracting the liquid from sucrose rich plants, such as sugarcane and date palm sap. It is darker and more flavorful than brown sugar. It comes in a cone shape and wrapped in paper, the way Western sugar used to be sold, and is broken into chunks or grated when needed.

Marjoram and Oregano

Members of the Labiatae family, which comprises mint, oregano, and marjoram, crossbreed easily as well as mutate spontaneously, leading to a vast and frequently changing number of varieties and sometimes an unpredictability of flavor. Further adding to the confusion, the English terms *oregano* and *marjoram* are used interchangeably to refer to many Labiatae members, including hyssop and Mexican oregano. The two most common varieties are Greek oregano (*Origanum heracleoticum*), also called winter and wild marjoram, and sweet marjoram (*Origanum majorana*), the latter a frequently overlooked herb with small, woolly gray-green ovate leaves with an earthy flavor and pungent mintiness that most aficionados prefer to oregano. Oregano has a bittersweet flavor and is spicier than marjoram.

Mint

Mint, an aromatic herb that spreads like a weed, may be indigenous to Israel. In any case, it has been a part of Jewish cooking since biblical times. There are many mint varieties, of which spearmint, with smooth pointed leaves and a sweet flavor, is the most common in the kitchen. Although in the West mint is generally associated with lamb and toothpaste, in other parts of the world, especially in Balkan and Persian cooking, it plays many culinary roles in both savory and sweet dishes, complementing delicate flavors and contrasting with fiery and piquant foods. Moroccans use it to make their national beverage, mint tea (*naa naa*). Dried mint adds a refreshing touch to dishes, a trait appreciated in the hot climate of the Middle East. The dried mint found at Middle Eastern and Indian markets is vastly superior to the one in supermarkets.

Mustard

Mustard is a member of the Brassicaceae family, which includes radishes and cabbage, all containing glucocapparin, a volatile oil possessing a peppery flavor. Young, tender mustard leaves, sometimes added to salads, are similar in taste to cress; more mature, sharper leaves are used in cooking. Nonetheless, the plant's enduring value lies in its seeds, which when ground and mixed with a liquid activate an enzyme, releasing its familiar pungency. Whole seeds impart a different, milder flavor to foods. The Talmud refers to mustard seeds as the smallest measure of size.

There are three major species of mustard, each possessing its own distinctive characteristics: white/yellow, brown, and black. The white/yellow mustard seed, the largest type, is milder than the other species but possesses larger amounts of mustard's enzyme. The brown—also called Indian, or Oriental—mustard seed is smaller than white varieties but is more pungent and the most aromatic type. Black mustard seeds are the most pungent of all mustard seeds. Until recently, the black seed was the most prevalent type even in the West. However, the difficulties in harvesting these smaller seeds with machinery led to a marked decrease in their production. Today, most mustards are made chiefly from a mixture of brown and white seeds, with manufacturers mixing various seeds to produce desired qualities and flavors. The yellow color of some brands derives from turmeric.

Olive Oil

Olive oil, one of the world's first oils, has been made in the Levant for more than five thousand years and eventually became the primary fat of most of the Mediterranean region. Neolithic pottery containing olive pits, and remnants of olives, found near Mount Carmel in Israel, reflects the earliest method of oil production: pounding the ripe fruit in small pots. Later virtually every village and many homes possessed at least a small press. Olive oil formed, along with grain and wine, part of a trio constituting the basis of the diet and economy of ancient Israel.

Olives contain 8 to 20 percent oil by weight, which is easily pressed out. As olives ripen on the tree, they darken and develop more oil and sugar. Olives destined for use on the table are generally picked in September or October, while those for making oil are generally left on the tree until January. Olive oil, unlike most other vegetable and seed oils, requires no further processing or refining. Olive oil is generally classified by three grades,

based on the amount of acidity: extra-virgin, virgin, and pure (or simply "olive oil"). Extra-virgin oil is extracted from the first pressing, and virgin oil is generally from the second or third pressing. Pure 100% olive oil, the lowest grade, is a misleading term indicating that it is made only from olives, but it is also chemically refined to reduce acidity and impurities. If the label contains the word *pomace*, the oil is extracted by adding solvents to the pulp. "Light olive oil" is a highly refined version that is lighter in color and neutral in flavor and sometimes is cut with other oils but is not "light" in calories, fat, or other nutrients.

The quality of olive oil, like that of wine, varies according to growing conditions, quality of the fruits, and method of harvesting and processing. Oils range in flavor from bitter to fruity, in color from yellow to vivid green, in texture from light to very thick, and in aroma from dull to intense. Extra-virgin is a better choice for salads, soups, and panfrying. Less expensive oil is generally used for long cooking and frying, since much of the oil's flavor dissipates when subjected to heat.

Onions

Onions are an essential and enduring element of Jewish cooking, and no contemporary form of Jewish cuisine would be complete without them. By the eleventh century, salted raw onions was a common Sabbath dish in Franco-Germany, and they were soon being mixed with other foods, including hard-boiled eggs, fish, and chopped liver,. Onions remained the principal seasoning for Ashkenazim for nearly a millennium, sometimes used both raw and cooked in the same dish to provide different tastes and textures. In some instances, onions constituted a major or even sole component of Ashkenazic dishes.

Onions were equally beloved, if less vital, in the Mediterranean. The Spanish Inquisition considered "making their meat dishes with onions and garlic and cooking them in oil (instead of lard)" to be the sign of a practicing Jew. Sephardim commonly stuff onions, use them for a pastry stuffing, and pickle them. Raw onion salads remain widespread in central Asia and the Caucasus.

The onion is one of the world's most important vegetables, not only because the pungent bulb serves as the base flavor of many dishes, but also for its ability to act on the taste buds, making other foods more flavorful. Onions contain sulfuric compounds, which not only bring a tear to the eyes, but also give the bulbs much of their flavor as well as their keeping ability. There are three predominant onion skin colors: yellow (copper), white, and red (purple). Red onions tend to be sweeter and white onions more pungent than yellow varieties. Onions should be sautéed or cooked in fat rather than water, because fat absorbs the onion's essence while water allows it to dissipate. Store onions in a cool, dark, dry place.

Paprika/Red Pepper

The Spanish began crushing and grinding dried chilies, in the manner of preparing peppercorns, as a substitute for that extremely expensive Indian spice. Crushed red pepper flakes contain the placenta and seeds as well as the flesh. The Ottomans, who probably first discovered the crushed form of chili pods in their dealings with the Portuguese, quickly took a liking to the zest it added to foods. The most popular type of ground chili from Turkey and Syria, commonly called Aleppo pepper, halaby pepper, or Near East pepper, is a deep red, robust, earthy paprika with an ancholike flavor and moderate heat, which becomes more fiery when heated. *Maras*, another Turkish pepper, consists of red pepper flakes with a berrylike flavor and medium heat.

The Turks introduced the brightly colored spice to the Balkans and Hungary during their occupation of the region, which began in 1526. The Hungarians called the spice after the Slavic word for peppercorns, *paparka*, first recorded in 1569. Since paprika was originally much less expensive than peppercorns, it quickly emerged as the predominant seasoning of Hungarian peasants and became an essential part of Magyar cuisine, used to make such classics as *gulyas* (goulash). Paprika ranges in intensity from sweet to hot, depending on the variety of pepper used and how it was ground. The mildest Hungarian paprika is called *rozsa*, "noble sweet rose," ground after the veins and seeds are removed. Hot paprika, called *koenigspaprika* ("king's paprika") and *eros*, is made by grinding the veins and seeds along with the pods. *Feledes* is a mixture of sweet and hot paprika and has a slightly piquant flavor. Spanish paprika, called *pimentón*, is coarser, darker, and more pungent than the Hungarian spice. In Spain, the mature peppers are dried and smoked over oak fires, giving the *pimentón* a smoky flavor. Cayenne is made from a small, deep red pungent variety or a blend of ripe chilies and is even more fiery than hot paprika.

Paprika and other red peppers should have a vibrant red color; pale paprika tends to be bland, while brownish hues are a sign of staleness. Store paprika in the refrigerator to retain freshness. Paprika possesses a high sugar content that caramelizes when it comes into contact with direct heat. This characteristic is an asset when browning, but for the best flavor this spice is usually added near the end of cooking.

Parsley

Parsley, from the Greek *petroselinon* ("growing among the rocks"), has long been an important seasoning in the Middle East and the Mediterranean. Parsley, along with celery, is identified as the *karpas* served at the Passover Seder. The Romans added it to nearly every salad and sauce. Today, it is probably the most commonly used herb. Although many Americans think of parsley as simply a garnish or a breath sweetener, in areas such as the Middle East and Far East, it adds a much-loved grassy flavor to salads, soups, stews, and casseroles. There are two primary types of parsley. The curly-leaf, or French, variety of parsley is the one most available in the United States, but is better as a garnish than in food. The more flavorful flat-leaf, or Italian, variety, with flat, glossy dark green leaves, is preferable for cooking. Dried parsley should not be substituted for the fresh herb.

Pine Nuts

Pine nuts are edible seeds of pine trees. The three most prevalent types are those of the stone pine or umbrella pine from the Mediterranean called *pignoli* in Italian, *snobar* in Arabic, and *camfistigi* in Turkish; the seeds of the Chinese pine; and those from a native American pine tree, which are called piñon nuts. All pine nuts are small, oily kernels, with a soft texture and a delicate flavor that fluctuates greatly, ranging from rich, sweet, and buttery to insipid and plastic. Pine nuts are an important ingredient in Sephardic, Italian, and Middle Eastern cuisines, used in numerous dishes, including pilaf, salads, stuffed vegetables, grape leaves, chicken dishes, omelets, sauces, and pastries.

Toasting pine nuts: Though they can be eaten raw, pine nuts are frequently toasted to enhance their buttery flavor. To toast them, spread the pine nuts on a dry baking sheet and place in a preheated 375°F oven, stirring several times, until golden, 5 to 10 minutes. Or, stir them in a dry heavy skillet over medium heat until golden. Be careful, as pine nuts burn easily.

Pine nuts turn rancid rather quickly, so it is best to purchase them in small amounts. Store in the refrigerator for up to 1 month or the freezer for up to 5 months.

Pomegranate Concentrate

To preserve the tart flavor of pomegranate juice for year-round use, Middle Eastern cooks learned to boil the juice down to a thick syrup the consistency of molasses. Pomegranate juice is widely used in Iran, Iraq, Turkey, and Georgia to give a tart flavor to stews and savory fillings. Add a little to vinaigrettes, marinades, relishes, stuffed vegetables, and even vodka martinis. To make, boil down 2 cups unsweetened pomegranate juice until reduced to $1/2$ cup, about 1 hour. Let cool, then pour into a sterilized jar. It will keep at room temperature for at least a year, and almost indefinitely in the refrigerator. The concentrate, sometimes called pomegranate molasses, is also available in Middle Eastern stores.

Preserved Lemons

Preserved lemons (*hamid m'syiar*), which are pickled in salt, are a unique and essential part of Moroccan cookery. Both the peel and pulp (which soften as they pickle) are used. Preserved lemons marry particularly well with cilantro and ginger.

Saffron

Saffron, the world's most expensive spice, is made from the red-orange or yellowish stigmas of the fall-flowering perennial purple crocus of the Iridaceae family. Each blossom produces three stigmas, and an expert can strip up to twelve thousand flowers a day. More than eighty thousand blossoms and much manual labor are required to produce a single pound of saffron. An acre of land yields only about six pounds of saffron. Most of the ancient Mediterranean civilizations treasured it, including the Hebrews, Egyptians, Greeks, and Romans, not only as a spice, but also in medicine, perfume, and a dye.

Saffron is a key flavoring in numerous rice dishes, fish dishes, and liqueurs. The threads are usually soaked in a little hot liquid before being added to a dish, which helps the spice blend with the other ingredients. Fresh high-quality saffron will immediately color a liquid; stale or poor-quality threads take a long time. A little saffron goes a long way, too much producing a medicinal quality. The more intense the color of the stigma, the better the quality of the spice. It is preferable to purchase saffron threads, since commercially prepared powdered saffron is often adulterated or may contain no genuine saffron at all, but instead such impostors as ground turmeric, achiote, and safflower stamens. Although these impostors do produce a yellowish color (hardly as brilliant as the genuine article), they can not replicate saffron's rich, slightly bitter but honeylike flavor.

Salt

Salt, a crystalline compound, has long been valued as a seasoning as well as a preservative. In Roman times, some people were paid in salt; thus fixed compensation became a *salary* (literally "salt money" in Latin). Processed mine salt is 99 percent sodium chloride, while sea salt is only about 83 percent sodium chloride, with the rest consisting of water and various minerals including iron, magnesium, potassium, sulfur, and zinc. Table salt is finely ground to produce small crystals. Manufacturers may add iodine for nutritional reasons, and other agents (primarily magnesium carbonate or calcium phosphate) to prevent clumping. Kosher salt, sometimes called coarse salt, has coarser crystals. Many chefs prefer using kosher salt because it contains no additives and clings to food.

Scallions

Scallions—also called bunching onions and spring onions—are named for the Israeli seaport of Ashkelon where Europeans first encountered them. Although the terms "scallion" and "green onion" are generally used interchangeably with each other and both refer to immature onions, they are different. Green onions are the green shoots of immature onions, most commonly white ones, which have formed a 1- to 2-inch bulb, but not yet its papery covering. Scallions are varieties harvested before a bulb has formed and, therefore, have a slightly softer texture and milder flavor than green onions. Today, most scallions in the market are actually a separate variety (*Allium fistulosum*), also called Welsh onions (from the German *welsche*, meaning "foreign"), that does not form bulbs, only a small slightly rounded white portion. Both the lower white part and bright green leaves are edible, although the latter is often removed, as it does not braise well. Scallions are eaten raw, used like an herb in salads and soups, or braised to impart a hint of onion to dishes. Generally, the thinner the white bottoms, the sweeter the scallion. Scallions are usually sold in bunches. Avoid purchasing those with wilted tops or white bottoms larger than $1/2$ inch. Remove any rubber band and store, unwashed, in a plastic bag in the refrigerator, away from odor-sensitive foods such as mushrooms for up to 5 days. Rinse under cold water, then trim off the root and any rough tops. Unless otherwise indicated, use both the white and the tender green parts. When using just the white portion, leave about 1 inch of the fairly light green section.

Sesame Seeds

On ripening, the pods of the herbaceous Middle Eastern sesame plant split open to reveal a cache of small oval seeds that have long been an important part of Middle Eastern cooking. There are two basic varieties of sesame, tan and black. The raw tan seeds—which can also be hulled and sold as white seeds—possess a nutty sweet flavor. Black seeds are more pungent. Unless otherwise specified, always use the raw tan seeds. Sesame oil—the seeds are about 50 percent oil—has long been used not only for cooking but also to fuel lamps. Middle Eastern sesame oil is made from raw sesame seeds and is light in color, while Asian sesame oil—which has a dark brown color and strong, nutty flavor—is made from toasted sesame seeds; do not substitute one type for the other. In Sephardic and Middle Eastern cooking, whole sesame seeds add flavor and texture to vegetables and baked goods.

Toasting sesame seeds: Toasting brings out the seeds' attributes: Stir the seeds in a dry skillet over medium heat, shaking the pan occasionally, until lightly golden, 2 to 3 minutes. Or, spread over a baking sheet and heat in a preheated 350°F oven, shaking the sheet several times, until lightly golden, about 12 minutes.

Sour Prunes

A tart dark red plum, called *tkemali* in Georgian and *aloo bukhara* in Farsi, is popular in central Asian and Georgian cooking. Sour plums and sour prunes are generally unavailable in the West. The combination of slightly unripe sweet prunes or unsweetened prune butter and tamarind or lemon juice are traditional substitutes in the role of souring agent by Georgians. Tamarind paste and unsweetened prune butter are available at Middle Eastern specialty shops and natural foods stores. Japanese sour plum paste (*ume shiso*), now generally available in the United States, makes a suitable alternative but tends to be very salty, so reduce the amount of salt in the dish.

Sour Salt

Sour salt is crystallized citric acid, a natural acid known as early as medieval times, but first isolated by the Swedish chemist Carl Wilhelm Scheele in 1784. It is generally extracted from citrus fruits by adding calcium oxide to form calcium citrate, then recovered by treatment with sulfuric acid. Sour salt is solid at room temperature and melts when heated. Before fresh lemons were readily available, eastern European cooks used these crystals, balanced with sugar, to create sweet-and-sour flavors in their cooking. Sour salt is available in most Jewish groceries as well as in the Jewish section of many supermarkets.

Sumac

Before the arrival of lemons and tamarind in the Levant, sumac, the tart red fruit of a Middle Eastern shrub, was the primary way of imparting sourness to dishes. Today, sumac finds its greatest popularity in the Levant, Iran, and Georgia. The tart citrus flavor and light red color add a special touch to eggplant spreads, hummus, kebabs, grilled fish, sauces, salads, soups, and, in its most prominent culinary role, *za'atar* (a spice mixture of sumac, hyssop, and sesame seeds). Sumac berries come dried; they are used whole or ground. A little salt is generally added to facilitate grinding the moist berries.

Tamarind

Tamarind, also called *tamarindo* and Indian date, is a brown 2- to 6-inch-long pod encasing up to ten glossy seeds surrounded by a sticky, tart brown pulp. When the fruit matures, the shell turns brown and brittle. Tamarind follows only dates among fruits in the amount of sugar it contains. However, tamarind is also the most acidic of fruits, with a flavor similar to a combination of apricots and prunes. Before the introduction of lemons, tamarind was the primary souring agent in much of Middle Eastern and Indian cooking, a use it still performs in those regions. The presence of tamarind is one of the few instances of a specifically Jewish practice in Georgian cooking. Although tamarind pods are rarely available in the United States, except at Indian and Latino markets, it is sold as concentrated pulp or in dried blocks, both of which must be softened in liquid before using.

Turmeric

Turmeric, native to southeastern Asia, is the orange-colored rhizome of a member of the ginger family (*Zingiberaceae*). Today, it is grown in India, China, Japan, Java, and Haiti. After harvesting, the rhizome is boiled or steamed, then dried and ground. The resulting golden powder imparts a rich saffronlike color, although it lacks saffron's flavor. The higher the curcumin level, the more intense the orange-yellow color. Turmeric is added to many Persian dishes to mask any unpleasant cooking odors as well as to impart a yellow color, a Middle Eastern symbol of joy. It adds a slightly bitter flavor to curry powder, pickles, soups, poultry, rice, and eggs. Do not overdo it, as turmeric can make a dish too bitter.

Vinegar

Vinegar, whose name is derived from the Old French *vin aigre* ("sour wine"), is among the world's most important condiments as well as one of the earliest preservatives. Its discovery was most certainly a fortunate accident: the result of wine or beer having sat around, exposed to naturally occurring bacteria in the air. Some enterprising and economical cook, not wanting to waste even seemingly spoiled food, must have discovered that the sour yet refreshing liquid was a boon to food preservation. The shelf life of vinegar is nearly indefinite. Vinegar has long held a conspicuous position in the Jewish pantry. In biblical and Talmudic times, vinegar was an important flavoring, condiment, preservative, and medicine. Before the popularization of the lemon in the Mediterranean in the twelfth century, vinegar served as the primary souring agent. It was essential for various Sabbath salads and relishes, ranging from Sicilian caponata to Georgian vegetable salad (*pkhali*), the acid serving to preserve the produce, even in hot climates, long enough to last through the Sabbath.

Vinegar, a mixture of acetic acid and water, is produced when airborne microorganisms metabolize alcohol. While any spirit with less than 18 percent alcohol will turn into vinegar on its own, natural fermentation is a rather inconsistent process. To assist nature, vinegar makers usually add a bacterial starter called a "mother"—it's the slimy film that forms on top—to wine, apple cider, and malt (much as bakers add a yeast mother to help ferment bread dough).

Yogurt

Yogurt has been an important part of the Middle Eastern diet for more than five thousand years. It was originally "discovered" when milk was accidentally fermented with a bacterial culture, thereby curdling into a tangy thick liquid that stayed fresh for days. Yogurt is ubiquitous at Middle Eastern dairy meals: mixed into chopped vegetable salads, spooned over platters of rice and lentils, and drizzled with jam or honey for dessert. Despite its status in the Middle East, yogurt was unknown until recently in most parts of Europe and America. Indeed, yogurt was such a rare food in Europe that it made history when a Turkish Jewish doctor used it to cure King Francis I of France (1494–1547).

Yogurt can be substituted for sour cream in most recipes, but the flavor will be lighter and tangier. Kefir, originally from the Caucasus, is a fermented, effervescent milk product produced from a complex mixture of bacteria and yeast. *Kumiss/koumis* is a similar, thinner relative of yogurt from central Asia.

Vegetarian Foods for Special Occasions and Jewish Holidays

❦ · ❦

There are three basic categories of Jewish holidays: the pilgrim festivals (Passover, Shavuot, and Sukkot), the High Holidays (Rosh Hashanah and Yom Kippur), and the minor festivals (Rosh Chodesh, or the New Moon; Hanukkah; Purim; Tu b'Shevat; Lag b'Omer; and Tisha b'Av, or Fast of the Ninth of Av). Jewish rituals and traditions led to the development of a wide assortment of holiday food, customs, and dishes. *Smachot* (Jewish celebrations) are designed to be observed in public, never in solitude, thereby reinforcing the bonds of community, and they almost always include food, establishing and enhancing the spirit of the occasion. Some of my earliest and fondest memories revolved around the holiday table. I begin by featuring *meze,* served throughout the year.

Meze

In the Middle East, entertaining commonly features mezes, or appetizers (possibly from the Persian word *maza,* meaning "taste"), a practice dating back to ancient Persia. Then, the wealthy would throw lavish parties, such as those recorded in the Scroll of Esther, with copious quantities of wine. To counter any sour or astringent tastes in the wine (an all too frequent occurrence back then), hosts offered various tidbits, such as nuts, dried fruit, and roasted grains, to eat. Eventually, dips, pickles, and salads augmented these hors d'oeuvres. The Ottomans spread the concept and its name throughout their empire and, as a result, variations of the word meze are found from Greece to North Africa.

As most mezes are served at room temperature, they can usually be prepared well in advance. Whether a meze spread constitutes an entire meal or just a starter course, serving meze is always a deeply social ritual, offering the opportunity to share and converse about food in particular and life in general.

FOODS AND FLAVORS: Today, a true *meze* (appetizer assortment), whether modest or elaborate, always features a medley of tastes, textures, aromas, and colors. The dishes are both cooked and uncooked, hot and cold. They are almost always served in small portions, generally accompanied with warm pita bread and chilled ouzo or raki (anise liqueur). Most of the dishes, primarily salads and dips, are relatively simple preparations, and a good meze table relies on the right balance of dishes, and fresh, high-quality ingredients. Due to the region's hot climate, Middle Easterners favor cool salads and fiery condiments, such as the chili sauces *z'chug* and *harissa*. A *meze* table commonly features many of the same ingredients prepared in enticingly different ways. Eggplant, for example, might be served fried, stewed with other vegetables, roasted and puréed into a creamy dip, bathed in spices and herbs, smothered in yogurt or tomato sauce, and wrapped in phyllo and baked. Some *meze* favorites include:

Middle Eastern Eggplant Salad (*Salata de Berengena*), page 101

Syrian Bulgur Relish (*Bazargan*), page 76

Turkish Red Pepper Relish (*Muhammara*), page 77

Tunisian Zucchini Relish (*Ajluk de Courgettes*), page 79

Middle Eastern Chickpea Dip (*Hummus bi Tahina*), page 328

Middle Eastern Mashed Bean Pâté (*Salatet Ful Abiad*) page 311

Turkish Leek Patties (*Keftes de Prassa*), page 255

Sephardic Spinach Patties (*Keftes de Espinaca*), page 284

Middle Eastern Yogurt Cheese (*Labni*), page 47

Turkish Turnovers (*Borekas*), page 176

Moroccan Phyllo Cigars (*Sigares*), page 196

Middle Eastern Pickled Turnips (*Turshi Left*), page 59

Sephardic Chickpea Salad (*Garvansos en Salata*), page 109

Syrian Bulgur Torpedoes (*Kibbe Nayeh*), page 372

Turkish Rice-Stuffed Grape Leaves (*Yaprak Dolmasi*), page 364

Northwest African Grilled Pepper Salad (*Salata Mechouiya*), page 103

Moroccan Fiery Marinated Olives (*Zeitoon al Had*), page 70

Sabbath

From twilight Friday until the appearance of the first three stars on Saturday night, Jews pray, study, reflect, and, in fulfillment of the commandment of *oneg Shabbat* ("enjoyment of the Sabbath"), also socialize, sing, and partake of three meals. The first meal is on Friday night, the second on Saturday following morning prayer services, and late on Saturday afternoon is *shalosh seudot* (the "third meal"). Friday night Sabbath dinner possesses a singular ambience. The table is set with the family's finery.

Candlesticks sprout dancing flames, casting a genial glow over the surroundings. Lively *zemirot* ("traditional songs") are sung intermittently throughout the meal. Thus, a profoundly religious activity and enjoyably gastronomic experience become one and the same.

FOODS AND FLAVORS: Some traditional Friday night dishes are:

Yemenite Flaky Pancake Bread (*Melawah*), page 192

Yemenite Egg Loaf (*Sabaya*), page 193

Yemenite Fenugreek Relish (*Hilbeh*), page 80

Calcutta Fried Whole Potatoes (*Aloo Makalla*), page 276

Indian Rice Pilaf (*Pilau*), page 357

Sephardic Potato Croquettes (*Kioftes de Patata*), page 274

Alsatian Fried Noodles (*Frimsel*), page 393

Ashkenazic Baked Carrot Pudding (*Mehren Kugel*), page 227

Ashkenazic Baked Rice Pudding (*Reis Kugel*), page 366

Ethiopian Vegetable Stew (*Wot*), page 303

Moroccan Vegetable Stew for Couscous (*Légumes pour le Couscous*), page 308

Sephardic Eggplant Pie (*Pastel de Berenjena*), pages 167–168

North African Fried Eggplant "Sandwiches" (*Beitinajn Mi'ili*), page 248

Middle Eastern Yellow Rice (*Arroz con Azafran*), page 346

After-Synagogue Breakfast or Brunch (*Desayuno*)

Historically, morning prayer services were conducted very early in the day, even on the Sabbath and holidays. Thus, when worshippers returned home from synagogue, it was generally too early for lunch, typically the heaviest meal of the day. Instead, following synagogue services, Sephardim enjoyed, and still do, a *desayuno*, which is Spanish for "breakfast," but in the Sephardic sense connoted a brunch.

FOODS AND FLAVORS: *Desayuno* is a casual meal consisting primarily of finger foods, cheeses, olives, fresh fruit, jams, yogurt, rice pudding, ouzo, or raki. Some dishes include:

Middle Eastern Wheat Berry Stew (*Harisa*), page 369

Sephardic Bean Stew (*Hamin*), page 315

Egyptian Slow-Simmered Fava Beans (*Ful Medames*), page 322

Greek Marinated Fried Eggplant (*Melitzanes Tiganites*), page 243

Turkish Eggplant and Cheese Casserole (*Almodrote de Berengena*), page 246

Sephardic "Roasted" Eggs (*Huevos Haminados*), page 425

Sephardic Filled Cheese Pastries (*Boyos*), page 172

Turkish Filled Phyllo Coils (*Bulemas*), page 174

Turkish Turnovers (*Borekas*), page 176

Sephardic Small Pies with Quesada Filling (*Quesadas*), pages 170–171

Yemenite Baked Flaky Rolls (*Jihnun*), page 191

The Third Sabbath Meal
(*Seudat Shlishit*)

The atmosphere at the third Sabbath meal contrasts with that of the others, for the participants are saddened by the imminent departure of the day. The songs are slow and almost mournful. This meal is frequently held in the synagogue between the afternoon and evening services.

FOODS AND FLAVORS: The fare is simple, consisting primarily of challah and a few salads and relishes. Some common dishes are:

Ashkenazic Egg Salad with Fried Onion (*Gehakte Eier mit Tzibbles*), page 424

Russian Cooked Vegetable Salad (*Salat Rousee*), page 96

Italian Eggplant Relish (*Caponata alla Giudea*), page 72

Georgian Vegetable Salad (*Pkhali*), page 75

Hungarian Potato Salad (*Burgonya Salata*), page 97

Indian Cabbage Salad (*Gobi Pachadi*), page 92

Moroccan Raw Carrot Salad (*Shlata Chizo*), page 94

Middle Eastern Mixed Vegetable Salad (*Michoteta*), page 89

Turkish Bulgur Salad (*Kisir*), page 111

"Escorting the Queen"
(*Melaveh Malkeh*)

The Sabbath is viewed metaphorically as a queen. A party following the Sabbath was a symbolic way to escort the Sabbath queen away and, in the process, prolong the special feelings of the day. Following the Havdalah ceremony on Saturday night, it is customary to hold a party called a *melaveh malkeh* (literally "escorting the queen" in Hebrew) by Ashkenazim, *Noche de Alhad* (Nighttime of Sunday) in Ladino by Sephardim, and *Seudat David Hamelek* in Hebrew (Feast of King David) by Moroccans.

FOODS AND FLAVORS: Cakes and cold light dishes prepared before the Sabbath, often dairy, are integral parts of the event. Use any of the leftovers from Seudat Shlishit, Meze, or Desayuno meals and:

Hungarian Wine Soup (*Borleves*), page 144

Persian Yogurt and Cucumber Soup (*Mast Va Khiar*), page 132

Persian Herb Omelet (*Kukuye Sabzi*), page 423

Georgian Vegetable Salad (*Pkhali*), page 75

Syrian Bulgur Relish (*Bazargan*), page 76

Turkish Red Pepper Relish (*Muhannara*), page 77

Romanian Goat Cheese Spread (*Pashtet iz Bryndza*), page 45

Ashkenazic Sweet Noodle Pudding (*Lukshen Kugel*), page 394

Eastern European Filled Pastries (*Knish*), page 150

Hungarian Potato Salad (*Burgonya Salata*), page 97

Italian Cold Pasta in Egg-Lemon Sauce (*Tagliolini con Brodo Brusca*), page 398

Rosh Hashanah

Rosh Hashanah ("Head of the Year"), a two-day holiday falling on the first two days of the month of Tishri, marks the creation of the world. The ten days from Rosh Hashanah through Yom Kippur are called *Yamim Noraim* ("Days of Awe"), a period of concentrated introspection, prayer, and inner transformation. According to tradition, it is during these days that the fate of all people is determined for the coming year. At this time, the performance of symbolic acts is of special significance and food plays a vital role.

FOODS AND FLAVORS: The Talmud mentions five foods to eat on Rosh Hashanah: gourds, black-eyed peas, leeks, beet greens, and dates. Each of these foods was specified because of a similarity between its name and a word signifying a wish for the coming year. The Hebrew word for *gourd* (*kraa*) is similar to *yikara* ("to be called out"), indicating that our good deeds should be called out at this time of judgment. The Aramaic word for *black-eyed peas* is *lubiya*, which is similar to the word for *abundance* and *increase*. The Hebrew word for *leek* (*karti*) is similar to *yikartu* ("to be cut off"), signifying that the Jews' enemies should be cut off. The word for *beet* (*selek*) resembles *she'yistalqu* ("that they will be removed"), which refers to the Jews' enemies. Relatedly, *tamar* (the Hebrew word for *date*) sounds like *yitamu* ("to be removed").

Other Rosh Hashanah foods symbolize fertility and plenty, including seeds and fruits and vegetables containing many seeds. Sephardic homes serve a basket called a *trashkal* full of symbolic fruits and vegetables; the head of the family removes one item at a time and recites an appropriate verse. An ancient custom is to eat a new fruit—one not yet sampled that season—on the second night of Rosh Hashanah after reciting the blessing Shehechiyanu ("Who has preserved us").

Other foods are traditionally avoided on Rosh Hashanah. Eastern Europeans eschew nuts, as well as sour foods, even sweet-and-sour dishes. In North Africa, black foods (the color is associated with mourning), including olives, raisins, eggplant, coffee, and chocolate, are banned from the table, although some people permit these items on the second day.

Food figures so largely on Rosh Hashanah that the holiday has more traditional dishes than any other, including:

Moroccan Pumpkin Soup (*Shorabit Yatkeen*), page 122

Pumpkin Turnovers (*Borekas de Calabaza*), pages 176 and 181

Italian Pumpkin-Filled Pasta (*Tortelli de Zucca*), page 405

Sephardic Black-Eyed Pea Salad (*Salata Lubiya*), page 108

Sephardic Beet Salad (*Salata di Chukundor*), page 99

Central European Cabbage Strudel (*Kroit Strudel*), page 153

Moroccan Raw Carrot Salad (*Shlata Djezar*), page 94

Sephardic Beet Greens (*Silka*), page 211

Sephardic Spinach Patties (*Keftes de Espinaca*), page 284

Italian Rice with Beets (*Riso Rosso*), page 364

Indian Coconut Rice (*Nariyal Chawal*), page 358

Ashkenazic Baked Rice Pudding (*Reis Kugel*), page 366

Yom Kippur

Tradition relates that on the tenth day of the month of Tishri, Moses returned from Mt. Sinai with the second set of tablets of the Ten Commandments and informed the people that they had been forgiven for the incident with the golden calf. Ever since, that day has been Yom Kippur, the Day of Atonement. This twenty-five-hour fast, the culmination of the ten-day period that begins with Rosh Hashanah, is the most profoundly moving day on the Jewish calendar. As it is a fast day, there are obviously no traditional Yom Kippur foods. However, the meals before and after the fast have both developed their own traditions. The eve prior to the fast has a festive character.

FOODS AND FLAVORS: Ukrainian Jews developed the custom of forming the challah for the meal before the fast into images of ascension, either birds (Isaiah 31:5), symbolic of sins flying away and our prayers soaring to the heavens, or ladders, reminiscent of Jacob's dream (Genesis 28:10–22). Dishes in the pre-fast meal are relatively bland so as not to increase thirst during the fast. The meal to break the fast is traditionally a dairy meal, filled with revitalizing fare, including:

Persian Yogurt and Cucumber Soup
(*Mast Va Khiar*), page 132

Persian Spinach and Yogurt Salad
(*Borani Esfanaj*), page 46

Turkish Cucumber and Yogurt Salad (*Toroto*),
page 47

Lebanese Eggplant Spread (*Baba Ghanouj*),
page 101

Italian Cold Pasta in Egg-Lemon Sauce
(*Tagliolini con Brodo Brusca*), page 398

Ashkenazic Sweet Noodle Pudding (*Lukshen
Kugel*), page 394

Sukkot

Four days after Yom Kippur falls the seven-day holiday of Sukkot. This festival represents the trek of the Israelites through the wilderness following the Exodus from Egypt as well as the final harvest of the agricultural year. In remembrance of the Lord's protection during the forty-year transitional period in the desert, the family dines and sometimes sleeps in a *sukkah* (booth), a structure with a temporary roof consisting of branches or other forms of vegetation.

The seventh day of Sukkot, called Hoshanah Rabbah, is regarded as the day on which the verdicts of judgment decided on Yom Kippur are sealed. Therefore, as an extension of the Day of Atonement, foods traditional for the meal before the fast, such as kreplach, are served.

At the conclusion of Sukkot falls a separate series of holidays, Shemini Atzeret and Simchat Torah. Shemini Atzeret is a two-day (one in Israel) biblical festival concluding the extensive holiday period that began nearly a month earlier with Rosh Hashanah.

Simchat Torah ("Happiness over the Torah") is a relatively late creation, its source lying in the ancient and enduring Jewish tradition of publicly reading from a Torah scroll, beginning and ending the cycle of Simchat Torah. It is one of the two, along with Purim, most uninhibitedly joyful occasions on the Jewish calendar, replete with singing, dancing, and feasting.

FOODS AND FLAVORS: The most common Sukkot dishes are filled foods, particularly stuffed vegetables and pastries, symbolizing bounty and the harvest. Many of the dishes are prepared in the form of casseroles or thick stews, which are easy to shuttle outside to the *sukkah*. Preserved vegetable dishes, such as pickles, eggplant spreads, and cucumber salads, representing the harvest, are also traditional Sukkot foods. Simchat Torah fare, similar to that of Sukkot, is intended to reflect the bounty of the harvest and includes thick soups and stews incorporating seasonal produce and filled foods—including filled pastries and stuffed vegetables—symbolizing abundance.

Central European Cabbage Strudel (*Kroit Strudel*), page 153

Ashkenazic Stewed Carrots (*Mehren Tzimmes*), page 226

Romanian Vegetable Stew (*Guvetch*), page 297

Yemenite Eggplant Casserole (*Batinjan bil Firan*), page 247

Syrian Rice-Stuffed Cabbage (*Malfoof Mahshee*), page 218

Sephardic Rice-Stuffed Peppers (*Pimintones Reynados*), page 267

Sephardic Cauliflower in Tomato Sauce (*Carnabeet*), page 234

Italian Braised Fennel (*Finocchi alla Guida*), page 251

Indian Leeks (*Gandana*), page 253

Sephardic Cucumber Salad (*Salata de Pipino*), page 62

Bukharan Stuffed Pumpkin (*Oshee Tos Kadoo*), page 280

Bukharan Turnovers (*Samsa*), page 165

Indian Rice and Vegetable Casserole (*Biryani*), page 360

Persian Rice and Eggplant Casserole (*Tahchin-e Badenjan*), page 361

Hanukkah

In 168 B.C.E., the Hasmonean patriarch Mattathias and his five sons, better known as the Maccabees, launched a revolt against Emperor Antiochus and his Syrian-Greek forces, who sought to obliterate Judaism. Three years later, the Jews chased their oppressors out of Jerusalem. The Temple, desecrated by the enemy, lay in a state of physical and spiritual disarray. Although the priests found but one small vial of untainted olive oil, enough to burn in the candelabra for only one day, the flame lasted for eight days.

Hanukkah ("dedication" in Hebrew) commemorates the rededication of the Temple by the Hasmoneans. Light is the preeminent theme of this eight-day festival, one that is particularly apropos at this time of the year, when daylight once again begins to increase. The central ritual of Hanukkah is the kindling of an eight-branched candelabra—called *hanukkiyah* by Sephardim and *menorah* by Ashkenazim—after sunset each evening. Despite Hanukkah's prominent position in American Jewish life, before this century it was a rather minor festival with no rituals in the synagogue and only a few prayers added to the services. The custom of giving Hanukkah presents is also a modern American phenomenon derived from the Christmas celebration. Hanukkah, perhaps because of its former minor status, never inspired many specific traditional dishes.

FOODS AND FLAVORS: Fried foods, in recognition of the miracle of the oil, became the principal type of Hanukkah fare. In addition, during the Middle Ages, one of the books of the Apocrypha, Judith, which describes events during the Babylonian invasion of Israel, was associated with the Hasmonean revolt. Since the heroine used cheese as a means to get the enemy general thirsty, enabling her to get him drunk and defenseless, dairy dishes became popular Hanukkah fare as well. Dishes include:

Greek Barley Soup (*Sopa de Cebada/ Kritharosoupa*), page 143

Fried Middle Eastern Turnovers (*Sambusak*), page 161

Tunisian Potato-Filled Pastry (*Brik*), page 198

Italian Rice Cake (*Bomba di Riso*), page 362

Georgian Potato Pancake (*Labda*), page 272

Romanian Potato and Vegetable Patties (*Parjoale de Legume*), page 272

Persian Herb Omelet (*Kukuye Sabzi*), page 423

Syrian Omelets (*Edgeh*), page 419

Syrian Pumpkin Patties (*Kibbet Yatkeen*), page 279

Sephardic Cauliflower Patties (*Keftes de Culupidia*), page 236

Sephardic Spinach Patties (*Keftes de Espinaca*), page 284

Turkish Leek Patties (*Keftes de Prassa*), page 255

Yemenite Fried Cauliflower (*Zahra Mi'lee*), page 235

Central European Cheese Dumplings (*Topfenknodel*), page 388

Eastern European Filled Pastries (*Knish*), page 150

Tu b'Shevat

Tu b'Shevat (the fifteenth day of the month of Shevat) is a minor holiday sometimes referred to as the Jewish Arbor Day and referred to in the Talmud as *Rosh Hashanah l'Ilanot* ("New Year for Trees"). In Israel, by early February most of the year's rain has fallen, the sap starts to flow again, and the branches begin to show the first signs of budding. In agrarian ancient Israel, this was a significant occasion, accompanied with singing and dancing.

Sephardim manifested a deep devotion for the day, which they call Las Fructus ("The Fruit"). Among Ashkenazim, on the other hand, Tu b'Shevat was only marginally celebrated, probably because early February is still the dead of winter in northern Europe. Beginning in the late 1800s, when the establishment of agricultural settlements in Israel brought about the need to plant trees to restore the landscape, this holiday took on new significance. The custom of planting trees in Israel on Tu b'Shevat remains a popular one.

FOODS AND FLAVORS: Although there are few specific Tu b'Shevat dishes, a common custom is to serve foods containing fruit, nuts, and wheat or barley.

Hungarian Wine Soup (*Borleves*), page 144

Moroccan Greens with Orange Salad (*Salata Khus w'Portughal*), page 87

Middle Eastern Bulgur-Stuffed Cabbage (*Malfoof Mahshee*), page 217

Bukharan Vegetable and Fruit Stew (*Dimlama*), page 301

Bukharan Baked Rice and Fruit (*Savo*), page 356

Persian Sweet Rice (*Shirin Polo*), page 350

Ashkenazic Barley with Mushrooms (*Gersht und Shveml*), page 375

Persian Carrot Omelets (*Havij Edjeh*), page 422

German Fried Dumplings with Fruit (*Schnitzelkloese*), page 387

Purim

In 586 B.C.E., the Emperor Nebuchadnezzar and his Babylonian forces destroyed Jerusalem and the First Temple, then exiled the upper and middle classes of Judea to Babylon. Forty-seven years later, Babylon was itself conquered by Cyrus, and the Jews suddenly found themselves part of the Persian Empire. It is during this era that the Purim story unfolded, the events recorded in the *Megillat Ester* (Scroll of Esther). Ahasuerus, who ruled the Persian Empire from his capital in Shushan, promoted Haman to the position of prime minister. The new leader conspired to exterminate the entire Jewish population of the Persian Empire on the thirteenth day of the month of Adar. The plot backfired when it turned out that the new queen, Esther, was a Jew, and the villain and his allies were all routed.

In response to Haman's plot to annihilate the Jews, their descendents commemorate Purim through physical enjoyment and riotous celebration. There are four central Purim rituals: reading the *Megillat Ester* (Scroll of Esther), sending *mishloach manot* ("gifts of foods," more commonly pronounced *shalachmanot*) to friends, giving money to the poor, and eating a *seudah* (feast). Children as well as many adults dress up in costumes, an Italian Jewish custom from the fifteenth century, inspired by the masked entertainers of the *commedia dell'arte*. Alcohol is liberally enjoyed, a practice most strongly disapproved of during the rest of the year.

FOODS AND FLAVORS: The *seudah* is traditionally held on Purim afternoon. Ashkenazic feasts begin with a *keylitch*, a large braided challah, symbolizing the rope on which Haman was hung. Many Purim dishes involve a filling, alluding to the many intrigues, secrets, and surprises unfolding in the Purim story. The similarity between the German word for poppy seed (*mohn*) to the villain Haman led to this spice becoming an Ashkenazic Purim food. A triangular shape, such as the hamantashen cookie, came to represent variously Haman's pockets, alluding to the bribes he took; to his ear, which was purported to resemble a donkey's, but reflect a medieval custom of cutting off a condemned man's ear before execution; or his tricornered hat, alluding to his execution although Persians never wore such headwear, a style that became popular in Europe around 1690. Reflecting a legend that Esther ate only vegetable dishes while living in the palace, chickpeas and fava beans became traditional fare.

Kabbalists compare Purim to another, seemingly unrelated holiday: Yom Kippur. The similarity in names was seen as no coincidence and a parallel was drawn between the physical lots of Purim cast by Haman and the metaphysical lots of Yom Kippur. Thus foods served on Yom Kippur eve, especially kreplach, which like the *hamantashen* have three corners, became traditional Purim fare. Other dishes include:

Iraqi Chickpea Turnovers (*Sambusak b'Tawa*), page 161

Venetian Spinach Pasta Roll (*Rotolo di Pasta con Spinaci*), page 407

Persian Sweet Rice (*Shirin Polo*), page 350

Romanian Sweetened Chickpeas (*Tzimmes Nahit*), page 331

Ukrainian Buckwheat and Noodles (*Kasha Varnishkes*), page 377

Passover

Passover is an eight-day holiday (seven in Israel) commemorating the Exodus from Egypt. As with the other pilgrimage festivals, Passover also has an agricultural connection, as it falls at the onset of spring and the barley harvest. In addition, it coincides with the time of year when the shepherds, goatherders, and cowherders would bring their flocks in from winter grazing in the wilderness for the birthing of their lambs, kids, and calves. Therefore, a festival celebrating freedom is perfectly timed for this season of new life and renewed hope.

FOODS AND FLAVORS: A ceremonial dinner called the Seder ("order" in Hebrew) is held on the first two nights of the festival. During the Seder, the Passover story is recounted and relived through a progression of ceremonies and symbolic foods as recorded in the *Haggadah* ("Retelling"). On the table are wine (each person's cup is filled four times), three whole matzas, and six traditional symbols: *maror*, a bitter herb, symbolizing the bitterness of the slavery experience; *charoset*, a fruit mixture devised to blunt the taste of the bitter herbs and symbolizing the mortar used to construct buildings while in slavery; *karpas*, a green vegetable, such as celery or parsley, representing spring and renewal; *chazeret*, lettuce used for the Hillel sandwich with additional matza; *betzah*, a roasted egg, representing the festival sacrifice; and *zeroah*, a roasted shank bone or poultry neck, representing the paschal sacrifice.

Due to its various dietary regulations, Passover fare differs from that of the rest of the year. Over the centuries, creative cooks found ways to adapt some of their everyday dishes as well as creating new ones to meet the special requirements of Passover. To increase matza's utility, it is also ground to make matza meal or finely ground to make matza cake meal. Crumbled and ground matza is used to create an imaginative array of Passover dishes, including stuffings, puddings, casseroles, pancakes, fritters, dumplings, pastries, and cakes. Since matza meal has an intriguing nutty flavor, it is often used for binding and breading throughout the year as well as on Passover.

The Bible forbids the consumption of *chametz* (leavened grain) during Passover. Among Ashkenazim, an interdiction emerged against eating legumes (*kitniyot*) on Passover as well as rice, millet, and some seeds: poppy, sesame, caraway, coriander, and mustard. On the other hand, Sephardim, prolific rice and legume consumers, not only rejected these prohibitions, but frequently featured these foods at the Passover Seder. The restriction of *kitniyot* on Passover remains one of the major differences between Ashkenazim and other Jewish communities. Popular dishes include:

Lag b'Omer

During the time when the Temple in Jerusalem stood, an offering was made on the second day of Passover of an *omer* (a measure) of newly harvested barley. Jews would then count forty-nine days, corresponding to the amount of time from the Exodus until the revelation of the Ten Commandments on Mount Sinai. On the fiftieth day, they celebrated Shavuot and made an offering of two loaves of bread produced from the first of the spring wheat crop. Although the Temple no longer exists, Jews continue the practice of "counting the *omer*."

During ancient times, the months following Passover were once a time of great happiness: The pantry was stocked with the abundance of the early crop and expectations were running high for the next harvest. But over history, several tragedies occurring during this period transformed this span into a very somber one. The Talmud relates that during one of the rebellions against Rome, twenty-four thousand students of Rabbi Akiva died from a plague—some scholars speculate that this plague was actually the Roman army—during the *omer* period. Most of the devastation of the Ashkenazic communities wrought by the Crusades, beginning in 1095, also occurred in the spring.

There is an exception to the melancholy nature of the *omer*: the thirty-third (*lag*) day. The Talmud records that on this day the Roman plague abated. In addition, tradition recounts that this was the day on which the manna first fell, sustaining the Jews during their forty-year stay in the wilderness. Thus, Lag b'Omer became a minor holiday, and primarily a children's holiday, customarily celebrated with bonfires, picnics, and various outdoor activities.

FOODS AND FLAVORS: Carob is a traditional food for this day: Legend has it that Rabbi Shimon and his son were sustained by a carob tree during years of hiding from the Romans. Hard-boiled eggs are another traditional item, associated with mourning and rebirth, or perhaps because they are convenient to carry on picnics. Many America Jews eat Middle Eastern fare on this holiday, such as:

> Yemenite Red Cabbage Salad with Tahini (*Salata Malfoof*), page 93
>
> Sephardic Chickpea Salad (*Garvansos en Salata*), page 109
>
> Northwest African Grilled Pepper Salad (*Salata Mechouiya*), page 103
>
> Syrian Bulgur Torpedoes (*Kibbe Nayeh*), page 372
>
> Middle Eastern Chickpea Spread (*Hummus bi Tahina*), page 328
>
> Middle Eastern Eggplant Salad (*Salata de Berengena*), page 101

Shavuot

The festival of Shavuot (Hebrew for "Weeks") is a two-day Pilgrim Festival (one in Israel) commemorating the giving of the Torah at Mt. Sinai. Also known as Chag ha'Katzir (Festival of the Harvest), Shavuot marks the beginning of the spring wheat harvest. During the time when the Temple stood, two loaves of leavened wheat bread—symbolizing the bounty of the season—were "waved before the Lord" (Leviticus 23:17–20) on Shavuot, besides the Thanksgiving offering, it was the only occasion when leavened bread was used in the Temple.

FOODS AND FLAVORS: Since the bread offering is one of the few biblical rites for this holiday, a special emphasis is placed on the holiday challah. The preeminent Shavuot symbol is dairy food. This custom is partially based on the legend that, after receiving the Torah and the laws of kashrut, the Jews could no longer eat the meat foods they had prepared beforehand or use any of their cooking utensils, which were now unkosher. Therefore, it was necessary to eat dairy dishes on the first Shavuot. Shavuot also corresponds to the time of the year when young ruminants stop suckling; thus, the abundance of milk makes dairy dishes a natural food for the holiday. In addition, dairy products and other white foods such as rice are considered symbols of purity. Commonly eaten dishes include:

Hungarian Green Bean Soup (*Zoldbab Leves*), page 126

Eastern European Sorrel Soup (*Schav*), page 128

Eastern European Filled Pastries (*Knish*), page 150

Eastern European Cheese-Filled Pasta Triangles (*Kaese Kreplach*), page 408

Moroccan Phyllo Cigars (*Sigares*), page 196

Sephardic Filled Pasta (*Calsones*), page 410

Sephardic Baked Noodles with Cheese (*Fila con Queso*), page 399

Italian Pasta Rolls (*Masconod*), page 408

Sephardic Cheese-Stuffed Eggplant (*Berengena Rellenas de Queso*), page 249

Balkan Cheese-Stuffed Peppers (*Pipiritzas con Queso*), page 265

Syrian Artichoke and Cheese Casserole (*Carchof Jiben*), page 205

Greek Spinach and Cheese Casserole (*Sfoungato*), page 285

Persian Beets with Yogurt (*Most Laboo*), page 213

Tisha b'Av

On the ninth day of the month of Av in the year 586 B.C.E., Babylonian forces entered Jerusalem and torched Solomon's Temple and much of the city. Again on the ninth day of the month of Av in 70 C.E., after three years of revolution, Roman forces breached the walls of Jerusalem and laid waste to the Second Temple. Sixty-two years later, a second insurgency met the same fate as the previous one, as once again on the ninth day of Av, the Roman legions defeated the rebel leader Bar Kokhba at the fortress of Betar, resulting in mass death and exile. Thus the most somber span of the Jewish calendar is a three-week period of semimourning, commemorating the national disasters that occurred on this day, including more recently the Expulsion of the Jews from Spain in 1492.

FOODS AND FLAVORS: From the first day of Av, Jews traditionally do not eat meat, except on the Sabbath; some abstain during the entire three-week period. Accordingly, cooks prepare an assortment of dairy and vegetarian fare during this time of year. The meal before the fast also consists of dairy foods and usually contains dishes made from lentils and eggs, both ancient Jewish symbols of mourning. Dishes include:

Sephardic Red Lentil Soup (*Sopa de Lentejas*), page 133

Alsatian Green Lentil Soup (*Soupe de Lentille*), page 135

Sephardic Lentil Salad (*Salata de Lentejas*), page 110

Middle Eastern Lentils and Rice (*Mengedarrah*), page 336

Sephardic "Roasted" Eggs (*Huevos Haminados*), page 425

Cheese and Dairy Spreads

❧ · ❧

According to legend, a Middle Eastern herdsman nearly six thousand years ago stored some milk in a sack made from a calf or lamb's stomach (waterproof animal organs then providing the best portable containers for liquid), only to discover later that the milk had separated. Sampling the coagulated curds—what we call fresh cheese—he realized that it was not only tasty but longer lasting than milk. By 2000 B.C.E., fresh cheese was a common food throughout the area, as attested by the discovery in Middle Eastern archeological digs of numerous small cheese molds replete with holes for draining. Later, the Romans discovered that cooking the milk to produce curds, pressing the curds, soaking the cheese in salt, and aging it for several months produced hard cheeses. Pliny the Elder (c. 77 C.E.) described many of the cheeses favored by Roman gourmets, including ones similar to Swiss and blue. While the basics of cheese making remain relatively unchanged from Roman times, there are now more than two thousand varieties around the globe.

Cheese is created when the solid portion of the milk of a few cloven-hoofed, cud-chewing animals is separated from a liquid called whey. Goat and sheep cheeses are most prevalent in the Middle East and Mediterranean. (When the Bible spoke of "a land flowing with milk and honey," it was referring to goat's milk.) The amazing aspect of cheese making is how small differences in the procedure—including the kind of milk, the amount of salt and other flavorings added, the temperature at which the milk is heated, the pressing, and the length of aging— result in major changes in the cheese's flavor, color, texture, and aroma. Raw milk from cheese-producing animals differs little in taste and color. However, goat's milk cheese has a more

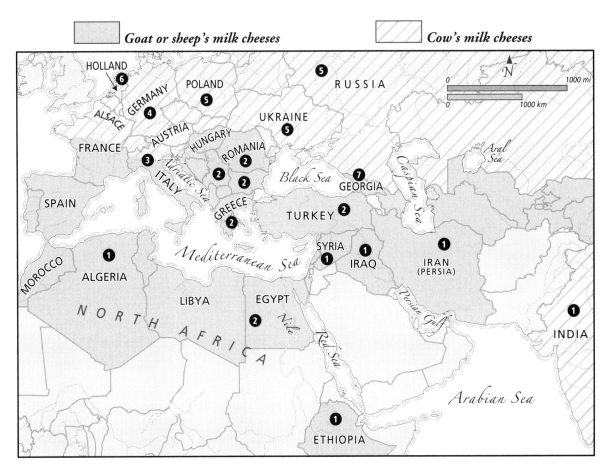

The Predominant Cheeses of the Old World: 1 *soft white cheeses: queso blanco, jibneh, paneer;* **2** *feta, kashkaval;* **3** *Parmesan, mozzarella, ricotta;* **4** *Muenster, topfen, quark;* **5** *farmer cheese;* **6** *Edam, Gouda* **7** *suluguni, imeruli, feta*

piquant flavor and a whiter color than cow's milk cheese. Sheep's milk cheese is also white but carries a distinctly sharp flavor.

To make cheese, a bacterial culture is added to fresh milk to convert the lactose into lactic acid, which balances the pH level; then rennet or an acid is added to coagulate the milk, separating the curds from the whey. The curd is then heated, drained, and salted. Cheese made from these fresh, unripened curds (fresh cheeses), which include cottage cheese, farmer cheese, and chèvre, have a high moisture content and are unripened or only slightly ripened, resulting in a soft texture and a mild, sometimes slightly acidic flavor. The younger the cheese, the milder it will taste. Soaking or boiling a drained soft cheese, such as feta, in brine, stops the ripening process, which allows for longer storage and gives the cheese a saltier flavor. Hard cheeses are made by pressing the curds into molds and leaving them to ripen by the action of microorganisms, allowing for a range of possibilities in flavor and texture much greater than what is found in fresh cheeses.

Hard cheeses require kosher supervision to ensure adherence to Talmudic dictums, which prescribe avoiding unkosher rennet, enzymes, and milk. Therefore, hard cheeses were rarely prominent and frequently nonexistent in most Jewish communities. All of the Jewish cheeses in northern Europe are the curd type, primarily made from cow's milk and occasionally goat's milk. (Each goat produces about one gallon of milk a day, which yields about one pound of cheese.) On the other hand, Ashkenazim in Romania, influenced by the Ottomans during their control of the region, make various soft and hard goat and sheep's cheeses, frequently brined, most notably *bryndza* and *kashkaval*. The principal cheeses of Georgia are *suluguni* (string cheese), imeruli (a fresh, slightly sour cheese), and *bryndza* (a creamy, less salty type of feta). Sephardim, Italians, and Greek Jews, on the other hand, enjoy a variety of fresh and hard cheeses made from cow, sheep, and goat's milk. For centuries, many eastern European meals consisted solely of potatoes or black bread and curd cheese. Ashkenazim, some of whom owned their own cow or goat for providing homemade cheese and sour cream, ate curd cheese on a regular basis, commonly mixed with chopped cucumbers and radishes, mixed into noodles, and as a filling for various pastries, including kreplach, blintzes,

knishes, and strudels. The original Hanukkah latke (pancake) was made from curd cheese; potato latkes did not become popular until the middle of the nineteenth century. In a more elaborate dish, curd cheese was sweetened, fruit sometimes added, and then baked. In Romania, Galicia, and Ukraine, cheese was frequently added to or layered with *mamaliga* (cornmeal mush) for dairy meals.

For millennia, many Mediterranean housewives weekly made their own soft, white fresh cheese, called *queso blanco* by Sephardim and *jiben beida* in Arabic, which went into their everyday cooking. Jews in the Ottoman Empire adopted various local Turkish and Greek cheeses. The cheese variety in the generally mountainous Balkans—Greece, Romania, Bulgaria, and Yugoslavia—was greater than that of eastern Europe, although much less so than that of western Europe. Jews in the Middle East primarily use goat cheese, including feta and labni (yogurt cheese). Goat cheese's intense flavor marries well with many other Middle Eastern foods, especially eggplant, olives, tomatoes, and bell peppers. The simplicity of feta's flavor makes it a perfect complement to bread and olives, as well as an important ingredient in vegetable dishes and pastry fillings. Sephardim used both soft (similar to pot cheese, chèvre, and feta) and hard (similar to kashkaval, Gouda, and Parmesan) kinds of cheeses, which they commonly cooked with vegetables to make dishes such as leek and cheese casserole, spinach and cheese casserole, and cheese-stuffed tomatoes.

What You Should Know: High and prolonged heat causes cheese to become stringy and tough. Therefore, always melt cheese over a low temperature for a very short time. Shred cheese for quick, even blending into sauces.

FAVORITE ASHKENAZIC CHEESES

- **POT CHEESE:** Also called baker's cheese and hoop cheese. A partially drained curd, ideal for filling baked goods. In the Roman manner, the curds were frequently placed in a bread basket to drain.

- **FARMER CHEESE:** A drained curd mixed with a little cream.

- **COTTAGE CHEESE:** A relatively bland fresh cheese with a slightly acidic flavor, historically made by exposing the milk to natural bacteria, which coagulates the protein, separating the curds and whey. Today, this unripe cheese is generally made by adding a bacterial culture to milk to produce lactic acid. Since a creaming mixture is added to store brands, cottage cheese needs to be well drained for use in pastry fillings.

- **BRYNDZA/BRYNZA:** A soft, crumbly white Balkan and Caucasian goat cheese that tends to be milder and less salty than the better-known feta. It is closest to Bulgarian feta. Production was historically from March to October, during grazing season; salting allowed it to be stored through the winter without a loss of quality. Bryndza is the primary Romanian, Slovakian, and Ukrainian cheese, eaten sliced and drizzled with an herb vinaigrette, used in dumplings, or served as an accompaniment to *mamaliga* (cornmeal mush). If substituting a very salty feta for the bryndza, soak it in cold water for a few hours to remove some of the saline.

Favorite Sephardic Cheeses

- **FETA** ("slice" in Greek, as the 10- to 30-pound blocks of cheese are cut into wedges, then brined): A well-known brined cheese common to Turkey and the Balkans. Barreled feta is creamier and milder than the sharper and saltier tinned type. This crumbly cheese is primarily made from sheep's milk, but occasionally from goat's milk as well. Sheep's milk feta has a slightly nutty flavor and a texture that ranges from creamy to dry. Feta made from goat's milk has a slightly tangier flavor and whiter color than sheep's milk feta. Bulgarian feta tends to be creamier and less salty than feta from Greece. Most feta in the West is imported, and the type of milk and brining should be on the label.

- **HALLOUMI:** A Turkish and Balkan full-fat sheep and cow's milk semifirm cheese similar to feta but milder and firmer, so it will not crumble when sliced.

- **JIBEN:** Homemade Middle Eastern white cheese.

- **KASSERI/KASHER** (meaning "kosher" cheese): A firm, slightly piquant but not very flavorful Greek sheep's milk cheese aged for six months to a year. Look for a smooth off-white interior.

- **KASHKAVAL:** Similar to kasseri and based on the Italian caciocavallo. The basic firm cheese in Turkey, Romania, and Bulgaria. It is made from sheep's milk or a combination of sheep and cow's milk. When aged for two to three months, kashkaval is mild and used for the table; more mature cheeses, with the color of straw, are stronger and used for grating.

- **KEFALOTYRI** (*keafalo* means "head" in Greek, referring to the size and shape of this cheese): Made from either sheep or goat's milk, this is a hard, yellow, tangy Balkan cheese used for grating and shredding. Parmesan and Romano, although harder and saltier, or an aged kashkaval make good substitutes.

- **MANOURI:** A soft Greek sheep's milk cheese with a buttery flavor and texture.

- **MITZITHRA:** Made from feta and kefalotyri by-products, this is similar to sheep's milk ricotta.

- **TOULOUMI:** A pungent goat cheese aged in brine.

SOUR CREAM

Back when my mother's Lithuanian grandparents moved to Cleveland, Ohio in 1904, my great grandmother made her own sour cream (*smetane*), similar to the now chic crème fraîche, by mixing some buttermilk into heavy cream and letting it stand at room temperature for a day. Doing this was a necessity, as commercial sour cream was not yet available in many parts of the United States. You can make an approximation using the same method: Heat 2 cups heavy cream (not ultra-pasteurized) to lukewarm (85°F), remove from the heat, stir in 2 tablespoons active-culture buttermilk or yogurt, pour into a sterilized jar or thermos, cover, and let stand at room temperature until thickened, about 8 to 12 hours. The sour cream will keep, refrigerated, for up to 12 days.

In 1882, Lithuanian immigrants Isaac and Joseph Breakstone (Bregstein) opened a small shop on Manhattan's Lower East Side that sold traditional eastern European dairy products, most notably butter, curd cheeses, and sour cream. They would scoop the sour cream out of large barrels into receptacles that the customers would bring from home. By 1912, the brothers were operating two manufacturing plants in New York State, selling wholesale butter, soft cheeses, and sour cream. In 1920, the Breakstone Company began mass marketing cream cheese, which first appeared in New York in 1872, based on France's Neufchatel; it quickly became popular among New York's Jews. When in the 1930s, innovation led to sour cream being sold in small wax-coated paper containers (Breakstone being the first to market consumer-sized packages of sour cream), this Old World ingredient spread across the United States, becoming a standard of the American kitchen. (Even my great grandmother began purchasing sour cream at the store but would occasionally still make her own, preferring its incomparable tang.)

ROMANIAN GOAT CHEESE SPREAD

Pashtet iz Bryndza D

ABOUT 2 CUPS

One popular use for sour cream was this cheese spread. Similar to the Austrian liptauer *and Hungarian* korozot. *It originated as a way to use leftover soft goat cheese. Romanian and Bulgarian feta cheeses tend to be much creamier and less salty, resulting in a smoother texture and milder flavor than those from Greece and Turkey. Serve with* mamaliga *(Romanian Cornmeal Mush, page 379) or slices of Italian or black bread.*

3 tablespoons sour cream or plain yogurt
8 ounces (1 1/2 cups crumbled) *bryndza* (fresh
    goat cheese) or mild, creamy feta cheese
1 hard-cooked egg, chopped
3 tablespoons chopped fresh dill
1 clove garlic, mashed with a pinch of salt
Ground black pepper to taste
Black olives for garnish (optional)

Mix the sour cream into the cheese until smooth. Stir in the egg, dill, garlic, and pepper. Cover and refrigerate for at least 4 hours or up to 1 week. Garnish with the olives.

VARIATION

Central European Cheese Spread (*Liptauer/ Korozott*): This spread was originally made from a soft, white sheep cheese called *lipto*. Omit the egg and dill. Add 1 tablespoon sweet paprika, 2 teaspoons caraway seeds, 1/2 teaspoon dry mustard, 2 chopped scallions or 2 tablespoons minced onion, and, if desired, 1 tablespoon drained capers.

Persian Spinach and Yogurt Salad

Borani Esfanaj

6 TO 8 SERVINGS   D

No Persian dairy meal would be complete without a borani, a yogurt and vegetable dish that is common in Persian cooking and particularly refreshing in hot weather. The name derives from the first woman to rule Persia thirteen hundred years ago: a queen named Poorandikht (or Pouran), who supposedly had a particular fondness for yogurt. Over the centuries, the pronunciation of pooran evolved into boran (the suffix "i" means "with"). Spinach, eggplant, and cucumber are the three favorite types of borani. In this version, the currylike spices complement the tangy yogurt and the slightly bitter, earthy spinach. Other recipes feature mint or fennel. If your yogurt is watery, drain it in a sieve lined with cheesecloth or a coffee filter for about 1 hour. Borani is served as an appetizer, a side dish, or a dip for bread.

3 tablespoons vegetable oil

2 large onions, chopped or thinly sliced

4 to 5 cloves garlic, minced

1 teaspoon ground cumin

1 teaspoon ground turmeric

About 1 teaspoon cayenne or a few drops
    hot sauce

$1/2$ teaspoon ground cinnamon

2 pounds fresh spinach, stemmed, washed,
    and chopped, or 20 ounces thawed frozen
    spinach, squeezed dry

2 cups plain yogurt

About 1 teaspoon table salt or 2 teaspoons
    kosher salt

About $1/4$ teaspoon ground black pepper

1. In a large saucepan, heat the oil over medium heat. Add the onions and sauté until golden, about 15 minutes. Stir in the garlic and sauté for 1 minute. Add the cumin, turmeric, cayenne, and cinnamon and sauté for about 2 minutes. Add the spinach and sauté until wilted, about 5 minutes. Remove from the heat and let cool.

2. In a medium bowl, combine the yogurt, salt, pepper, and, if using, hot sauce. Stir into the spinach. The mixture should be rather thick. Refrigerate for at least 1 hour or up to 1 day to let the flavors meld. Serve cold or at room temperature.

VARIATIONS

Persian *Borani* with Fennel: Omit the cumin, turmeric, cayenne, and cinnamon and add $1/2$ teaspoon fennel seeds.

Persian *Borani* with Mint: Omit the cumin, turmeric, cayenne, and cinnamon and add, with the yogurt, 2 tablespoons minced fresh spearmint or 2 teaspoons dried, about 3 tablespoons fresh lemon juice, and, if desired, $1/2$ cup chopped toasted walnuts.

Persian *Borani* with Eggs: Omit the yogurt. After the spinach is wilted, make 6 indentations in the spinach, break 1 egg into each indentation, and cook over low heat until the eggs are set, about 5 minutes.

TURKISH CUCUMBER AND YOGURT SALAD

Toroto

ABOUT 6 CUPS   D

The classic pairing of yogurt and cucumber yields endless variations in different locales, from the traditional Middle Eastern dill or mint version to Indian pistachio raita. Jewish versions are inevitably flavored with garlic. This recipe calls for English or hothouse cucumbers, which have very few seeds and so do not require seeding. In addition, English cucumbers are not waxed but rather sold shrinkwrapped to inhibit moisture loss; therefore, peeling is optional. If you use regular cucumbers, peel and seed them. Thinly slice or cut up the cucumbers to serve the dish as a salad; grate or dice them to make a delicious dip for toasted pita triangles or naan.

I large English (hothouse) cucumber, coarsely grated, diced for a dip, cut into chunks or thinly sliced for a salad

I small onion, chopped, or 2 to 3 scallions, sliced

About 2 teaspoons table salt or 4 teaspoons kosher salt for sprinkling

2 to 3 cloves garlic

$1/4$ teaspoon table salt or $1/2$ teaspoon kosher salt

3 cups thick yogurt

$1/8$ teaspoon ground white or black pepper

3 tablespoons chopped fresh dill, 2 tablespoons chopped fresh cilantro, or $1/2$ cup chopped watercress

1. Put the cucumber and onion in a colander or large sieve, toss with the salt, weigh down with a plate, and let stand at room temperature for at least 1 hour or up to 3 hours. Drain, then squeeze out the excess moisture. (This keeps the salad from turning watery.)

2. Using the tip of a heavy knife or with a mortar and pestle, mash the garlic and salt into a paste. In a large bowl, combine the yogurt, garlic, pepper, and dill. Add the cucumber and toss to coat. Cover and refrigerate for at least 4 hours or up to 2 days.

VARIATIONS

Turkish Cucumber, Mint, and Yogurt Dip (*Cacik*): Finely chop the cucumber. Substitute 3 tablespoons chopped fresh spearmint or 1 teaspoon dried mint for the dill, and stir in 2 to 3 tablespoons olive oil.

Greek Zucchini and Yogurt Salad (*Kolokithakia Salata*): Blanch 3 pounds whole zucchini in boiling water for 2 minutes, remove with tongs, immerse in ice water to stop the cooking, drain well, thinly slice or chop, then chill. Substitute the zucchini for the cucumber and add 2 tablespoons chopped fresh dill and 2 tablespoons chopped fresh spearmint.

Indian Cucumber and Yogurt Salad (*Cucumber Raita*): Omit the dill and add 1 tablespoon seeded and minced jalapeño chili and 1 teaspoon ground cumin.

Indian Cucumber, Pistachio, and Yogurt Salad (*Cucumber and Pistachio Raita*): In a small, dry skillet over medium heat, stir 2 teaspoons ground cumin, $1/2$ teaspoon celery seeds, $1/2$ teaspoon mustard seeds, $1/2$ teaspoon ground cardamom, $1/2$ teaspoon ground coriander, and $1/4$ teaspoon cayenne until fragrant, about 1 minute. Transfer to a small bowl and let cool. Substitute this mixture for the dill and add 1 cup (5 ounces) coarsely chopped pistachio nuts.

ETHIOPIAN CHEESE SPREAD

Lab

ABOUT 2 CUPS

In Ethiopia, dairy products were generally produced from cow's milk; sheep and goats were reserved for their wool and occasionally their meat. This tangy dip was made with homemade cheese created by naturally occurring bacteria that generated lactic acid, resulting in a tangy taste. Lab is daily fare in an Ethiopian home; several tablespoons are served for each diner on injera (a pancakelike flat bread that doubles as a tablecloth). Since most available fresh cheeses lack the distinct tang of homemade products, you should add a little lemon zest to simulate the original. Serve with injera (Ethiopian pancake bread) or various flat breads.

    1 pound farmer cheese, pot cheese, or mild fresh
        goat cheese (such as fromage blanc or chèvre)
    2 to 4 tablespoons plain yogurt
    3 tablespoons chopped fresh parsley or cilantro
    1 to 3 teaspoons grated lemon zest
    1 tablespoon chopped fresh basil or 1/2 teaspoon
        dried
    1 teaspoon dried oregano
    About 1 teaspoon table salt or 2 teaspoons
        kosher salt
    About 1/4 teaspoon ground black pepper

In a large bowl, combine all the ingredients and stir to blend. The mixture should be moist but thick enough to maintain its shape.

MIDDLE EASTERN YOGURT CHEESE

Labni

ABOUT 1 1/4 CUPS

Labni, a kind of thickened yogurt (from leban, *Arabic for "yogurt"), was developed as a delicious way to extend yogurt's shelf life and utility. Middle Easterners dip flat bread in* labni *sprinkled with chopped fresh dill, mint, or thyme. It also makes a low-fat substitute for cream cheese and sour cream in many recipes, such as Middle Eastern Yogurt Filling (page 163) and Persian Fried Eggplant in Yogurt (page 244). I also use it to make a low-fat cheesecake, substituting it for the cream cheese and sour cream, and as a filling for blintzes.*

    About 3/4 teaspoon table salt or 1 1/2 teaspoons
        kosher salt
    3 cups (1 1/2 pounds) plain yogurt

1. Stir the salt into the yogurt. Line a colander or sieve with a coffee filter or a double layer of cheesecloth and place over a bowl to catch the whey. Pour the yogurt into the prepared colander, cover with plastic wrap, place in the refrigerator, and let drain until thick and firm: After 24 hours, the yogurt will have the consistency of cream cheese; after 48 hours it will be very thick, like a firm goat cheese. (Use the whey in baking and soups.)

2. Gather together the edges of the cheesecloth to form a sack and gently squeeze out the excess whey. Scrape the cheese from the cloth. Store in a covered container in the refrigerator for up to 2 weeks.

Middle Eastern Yogurt with *Za'atar* (*Labni ma Za'atar*): Spread the *labni* over a serving platter, drizzle with olive oil, and sprinkle with *za'atar* (Middle Eastern "Hyssop" Mixture, page 436).

Middle Eastern Yogurt Cheese Balls (*Zanakeel Labni*): Form heaping tablespoons of the *labni* into balls and let them stand at room temperature overnight to firm and ferment. Place in sterilized jars and cover with olive oil. If desired, add 1 dried red chili and a sprig of fresh rosemary to the jar. Makes about 24 balls.

Spinach Dip (*Sabanigh Labni*): Stir in 10 ounces thawed and drained frozen chopped spinach, $1/2$ cup chopped scallions, $1/2$ cup chopped fresh flat-leaf parsley, 3 tablespoons fresh lemon juice, about $1/2$ teaspoon salt, and $1/4$ teaspoon dill. Cover and refrigerate for at least 8 hours before serving.

INDIAN WHITE CHEESE

Panir

ABOUT 1 CUP

Panir is a soft, crumbly, slightly rubbery unripened Indian cheese similar to queso blanco (white cheese). It is not the same as queso freso (fresh cheese). In India, it is generally not eaten by itself but rather incorporated into various dishes, absorbing the flavors. Because it is difficult to make panir with the appropriate elastic texture from pasteurized milk, you can approximate the results by substituting fresh mozzarella. Serve panir with vegetables, pasta, and in stir-fries.

> 4 cups whole goat or cow's milk
> 2 tablespoons fresh lemon juice
> $1/2$ cup plain yogurt

1. In a large, heavy nonreactive saucepan, bring the milk to a boil, stirring frequently to prevent scorching. Reduce the heat to low and stir until the milk reaches about 185°F.

2. Stir the lemon juice into the yogurt. Add to the milk and stir in one direction for about 10 seconds. Remove from the heat and stir until the curds separate and the whey turns yellow, about 1 minute. If the curds fail to form within 1 minute, briefly return to the heat and add a little more lemon juice. Remove from the heat, cover, and let stand for 10 minutes.

3. Line a colander with a triple layer of cheesecloth and set over a large bowl to catch the whey. Gently pour in the milk mixture and let stand for several minutes. When most of the whey has drained, bring the corners of the cloth together, tie them, hang the bag over a bowl, and let the mixture drain for 1 to 3 hours. The curds should be soft and moist. Panir keeps in the refrigerator for up to 2 weeks.

Pot Cheese: Substitute $11/2$ tablespoons distilled white vinegar for the lemon juice and yogurt.

Kneaded *Panir*: Knead the drained curds into a firm, round ball, about 7 minutes, then pat into a $1/2$- to $3/4$-inch-thick disk, tie in cheesecloth, and weight with a heavy object for about 2 hours.

Fried *Panir*: Cut the *chonti panir*, above, into $1/2$- to $3/4$-inch chunks. In a large heavy skillet, heat $1/4$-inch vegetable oil over medium heat to 350°F. In batches, fry the cheese chunks, turning, until golden brown on all sides, about 30 seconds per batch. Drain. The fried chunks are cooked with sugar and condensed milk (*chanar payesh*), in sugar syrup, coated in a chickpea flour batter and deep-fried (*panir pakora*), with peas in spicy tomato sauce (*matar panir*), with spinach (*palak panir*), and added to various vegetable dishes.

Syrian White Cheese

Jiben

ABOUT 1 POUND   Ⓓ

Among the first interviews that I conducted for Kosher Gourmet Magazine *was one with Rae Dayan at her home in Flatbush, Brooklyn. She generously gave me instructions for a variety of enticing Syrian dishes, including this surprisingly simple homemade cheese, also called queso fresco (fresh cheese) in Ladino. The drained and pressed cheese was also cut into large chunks and rubbed with kosher salt or soaked in a brine to make feta. Syrian housewives commonly made white cheese on a weekly basis, using it in numerous dishes, including* bulgur pilavi *(Turkish Bulgur Pilaf, page 371),* keskasune *(Syrian Tiny Pasta with Chickpeas, page 401),* calsones *(Sephardic Filled Pasta, page 410), and* edgeh *(Syrian Omelets, page 419). Rennet separates the curds from the whey; it comes in liquid and tablet form made from animal or vegetable sources. Store liquid rennet in the refrigerator for up to two years; dilute in water before using.*

> 8 cups whole milk, preferably unhomogenized
> 1 teaspoon kosher liquid rennet dissolved in
>   1/3 cup distilled water
> 2 tablespoons kosher salt

1. In a medium saucepan, heat the milk until lukewarm (88°F); maintain at this temperature for about 10 minutes. Remove from the heat, stir in the rennet, and let stand at room temperature without disturbing until the mixture congeals, about 2 hours.

2. Gently stir the mixture until the whey separates from the curds. Let stand at room temperature for about 30 minutes. (The mixture will look like a thin yogurt with the curds below and a yellowish liquid surrounding it.) Pour off as much liquid (whey) as possible. (Reserve the whey to use in soups and other dishes.)

3. Line a colander or basket with a double thickness of cheesecloth, pour in the curds, and sprinkle with 1 tablespoon of the salt. Let stand at room temperature to drain for 12 to 20 hours.

4. Gather the ends of the cloth together and squeeze the remaining liquid from the curds, about 5 minutes. The curds will amass into a firm ball.

5. Sprinkle 1 1/2 teaspoons of the salt into a shallow bowl, place the cheese on top, and sprinkle with the remaining 1 1/2 teaspoons salt. Cover and refrigerate for 1 hour. Wrap the cheese in plastic wrap and store in the refrigerator for up to 1 week.

INDIAN CLARIFIED BUTTER

Ghee

ABOUT ¹/₂ CUP

Ghee and samneh *(see Variations) are essential ingredients in many forms of cookery throughout parts of Asia and Africa, especially in central and northern India, where a little is spooned over legumes for flavor and smoothness, utilized as a bread spread, and used for frying in dishes such as Indian Split Pea Soup (page 136), Cochini Mixed Vegetable Soup (page 124), Calcutta Curried Potatoes (page 275), and Indian Curried Spinach (page 283).*

It is advisable to clarify butter in large batches: Preparing ghee *or* samneh *with less than 1 pound of butter may cause it to burn. Also, while it takes a long time to prepare,* ghee *lasts indefinitely. The larger the amount of fresh butter used and more water it contains, the longer the cooking time. For those who do not have the time or patience to make their own* ghee, *several companies sell brands with kosher certification.*

1 pound (4 sticks) unsalted butter, preferably organic, cut into pieces

1. In a heavy 4-cup saucepan, melt the butter over medium-low heat, about 10 minutes. The butter will bubble, crackle, and foam. Using a dry spoon, skim the foam from the surface. (At this stage, the yellow liquid could be poured off from the whitish solids on the bottom into a container, yielding European clarified, or drawn, butter.)

2. To make the ghee: Reduce the heat to very low. If any ripples appear on the surface of the butter during cooking, reduce the heat. Continue cooking, without stirring or moving the pan, occasionally skimming off the foam, until the butter turns a clear golden color, the white solids sink to the bottom of the pan, and the butter stops crackling (indicating the absence of water), about 45 minutes. When skimming the foam, make sure the spoon is dry, as you do not want to introduce any water. At this stage, all the water has been removed, yielding ghee, but many Indians prefer to cook the butter longer, developing a nutty flavor. (For a lighter, clearer clarified butter, skip to Step 4.)

3. To make nutty ghee: A heat diffuser is helpful in preventing burning but is not essential. Continue cooking over very low heat until the white sediment on the bottom turns golden brown, about 30 additional minutes. Do not overcook (watch closely) or the solids will burn, imparting a bitter flavor.

4. Remove from the heat, skim off any crust from the surface, and let stand until all the solids have settled to the bottom but the ghee is still warm, about 10 minutes. Pour the clear golden liquid (ghee) through a double layer of cheesecloth or a coffee filter into a dry, clean glass jar or a crock, leaving the solids on the bottom or the cloth. The leftover solids go well with vegetables, rice, and bread. Cover the ghee and store in a cool, dry place for up to 4 months or in the refrigerator for up to a year. The ghee will solidify but not harden.

VARIATIONS

Middle Eastern Clarified Butter (*Samneh*): After skimming off the foam in Step 1, cook the butter over medium-low heat until it stops crackling (indicating the absence of water) and turns a clear golden color, about 45 minutes. For a fresh flavor, place in the refrigerator. For a pungent flavor, let stand in a cool, dry place for 1 to 2 weeks, then store in the refrigerator. For Yemenite *samneh*, after skimming off the foam in Step 1, add 2 tablespoons fenugreek seeds, then strain after cooking. With the exception of clarified butter, Yemenites ate few dairy products, even yogurt. In Israel, traditionalists still use only *samneh* but many adopted yogurt into their diet.

Ethiopian Spiced Clarified Butter (*Niter Kebbeh*): After skimming off the foam in Step 1, add $1/4$ cup minced onion, $1 1/2$ tablespoons minced garlic, 2 teaspoons minced fresh ginger, 2 to 3 crushed green cardamom pods or $1/4$ teaspoon ground cardamom, 1 (2-inch) stick cinnamon, 2 to 3 whole cloves, $3/4$ teaspoon ground turmeric, $1/8$ teaspoon freshly grated nutmeg, and, if desired, $1/4$ teaspoon ground fenugreek. For a nondairy *niter kebbeh*, vegetable oil is substituted for the butter, simmered with the spices for 45 minutes, then strained. *Niter kebbeh* along with *berbere* (chili powder) are the two essential flavorings of Ethiopian cookery and are used in most *wots* (stews) and vegetable dishes.

DEGREES OF SEPARATION

Long before recorded history, and, of course, the advent of refrigeration, the principal way to preserve very perishable butter was to remove the water and milk solids, a process called clarifying. The cooking process destroys bacteria and deactivates enzymes, while the elimination of the water prevents microbial growth, which keeps the butter from going rancid. It also lets the clarified butter reach higher temperatures without burning. Numerous cultures have developed methods of clarifying butter. European clarified butter, also called drawn butter and usually made from cow's milk, is heated for only a few minutes, then strained to eliminate most of the milk solids, without any significant cooking, keeping the flavor mild and leaving only pure liquid butter with a small amount of water. Both *samneh* (also called *samna* or *smen*), the Middle Eastern clarified butter, historically made from sheep or goat's milk, and Indian ghee (from the Sanskrit "bright"), frequently made from water buffalo butter, are cooked much longer and more slowly, eliminating more solids and water, enabling these butters to be stored for several months even without refrigeration. In fact, some people store *samneh* in a cool, dry place (traditionally in earthenware crocks) for several weeks or sometimes for more than a year, so that it can develop a characteristic fermented nutty aroma and flavor. A teaspoon of fermented *samneh* is generally sufficient to flavor dishes. Most Jews did not cook with the fermented type, preferring the milder version; in this book, the unfermented *samneh* is called for.

PICKLES, MARINATED VEGETABLES, AND RELISHES

❧ · ❧

Before the advent of refrigeration and canning in the nineteenth century, most foods had to be consumed rather quickly or be lost to spoilage. (Practical commercial canning began in 1861, when Isaac Solomon of Baltimore added calcium chloride to canning water, thereby reducing the processing time from six hours to thirty minutes.) It was therefore vital for people to find ways to conserve limited resources. At least four thousand years ago, before the advent of the first cultivated vegetables and long before the detection of bacteria, people discovered several substances that forestalled spoilage. The two most effective natural preservatives, which date back to the ancient world, are salt and vinegar, used individually or in conjunction with each other.

Simply sprinkling foods with salt or an acid can preserve food, but for only a few days. One of the most popular and widespread of the ancient methods for long-term preservation was pickling (a term derived from *pokel*, a German word for salt), *kavush* in Hebrew: a process of infusing foods with acid, thereby creating an environment hostile to dangerous microorganisms. Pickling keeps produce for several months or even longer without refrigeration or canning. It can be accomplished by blanching vegetables in water or briefly brining them to extract excess moisture, then submerging them in vinegar, as with Polish Pickled Mushrooms (page 58), Middle Eastern Pickled Turnips (page 59), and Calcutta Pickled Okra (page 61). A more complicated method is brining, also called fermenting, which consists of soaking foods in brine for an extended period under controlled conditions to produce acid from naturally occuring bacteria, as used in making Ashkenazic Kosher Dill Pickles (page 55) and sauerkraut.

To our ancestors, pickles were no trifling matter but rather a fundamental part of the diet. Besides contributing valuable nutrition, they enlivened meals consisting primarily of coarse breads and other starches, and made them more palatable. Pickled foods were essential, from Moroccan preserved lemons to the ubiquitous Indian chutneys.

Throughout most of recorded history, both the elite and the impoverished masses relied on pickles and relishes. Pickled turnips, radishes, cabbage, celery, and grapes were standard fare in ancient Mesopotamia and Egypt. Persians and Arabs spread their pickles throughout the Middle East. Romans pickled everything from olives to fish; by the second century they were importing additional pickles, including capers and onions, from Spain. Later, Sephardim and Italians began pickling even more vegetables, such as artichokes and cauliflower.

Until recently, sauerkraut (pickled, fermented cabbage) served as the principal vegetable across central and eastern Europe and as a staple of the Ashkenazic diet. Ashkenazim annually filled crocks or barrels with cabbages, cucumbers, and beets, then left them to ferment in root cellars or other cool places, to provide zest to dining for much of the year.

Technically, all of the recipes in this chapter are pickles, as they are cured with salt or vinegar. However, some are simply marinated—soaked in a seasoned liquid for a relatively short time. Marinating was done to impart extra flavoring and to extend a dish's shelf life for a few days, such as from Friday until Sabbath lunch. Relishes are similar to pickles and marinated vegetables, except that the ingredients are chopped into small pieces to serve as a salad, dip, or condiment. Larger pickle pieces and marinated vegetables are used for appetizers or side dishes.

Salt, acids, and sugar inhibit the growth of bacteria, and therefore foods containing relatively large amounts of them do not require extended processing at high temperatures and need not be stored in entirely sterile conditions. Salt plays many roles in pickling: It enhances taste, including removing raw flavors; it deters bacteria; and it extracts water from vegetables, which not only keeps the vegetables crisp, but also prevents the water from seeping out later and diluting the preservative effect of the vinegar. Use kosher salt or another additive-free salt, because table salt contains anticaking agents that cause cloudiness in the brine, and sometimes iodine, which darkens pickles and can leave a bitter aftertaste, and dextrose, which alters the proportions of salt to water. For extended storage, acid, in the form of lactic and acetic acids derived from naturally occurring bacteria or vinegar, is also necessary to forestall the growth of bacteria. Any type of vinegar containing at least 5 percent acetic acid can be used for pickling, while any vinegar or citrus juice is suitable for marinating.

The seasonings employed in pickling and marinating vary greatly. Sugar imparts sweetness and acts as an additional preservative. Allspice and coriander seeds contribute a more rounded sweet flavor. Mustard seeds hinder the development of bacteria and molds, and thus are often added as a preservative as well as a flavoring agent. (These should be used sparingly, to avoid an undesirable pronounced mustard flavor.) Chilies add a kick. Other traditional pickling spices include bay leaves, cardamom seeds, cinnamon sticks, celery seeds, cloves, dill heads and seeds, and peppercorns. Whole spices give a fuller flavor than ground ones and do not cloud the liquid. Packaged commercial "pickling spices" are intended for sweet pickles.

What You Should Know: Without heat processing and eliminating air with a vacuum—a Western technique dating back only to the nineteenth century and one generally not applicable to traditional Jewish home cooking—bacteria will develop within a few days or weeks in most salt-brined foods unless the pH of the brine is 4.6 or higher. To help forestall spoilage, it is advisable to wash storage containers in hot, soapy water. (For information on preserving in jars and sterilization, see the Ashkenazic Kosher Dill Pickles recipe below.) One pound of vegetables will fill a 1-quart jar.

 CLASSIC PICKLES

ASHKENAZIC KOSHER DILL PICKLES

Marinierte Ugerkehs/Saure Ugerkehs

ABOUT 4 QUARTS

English translations of the Bible record that cucumbers (kishuim) *were among the Egyptian foods the Israelites wandering in the wilderness yearned for. That "cucumber," however, was actually a chate melon* (Cucumis melo, *var.* chate), *also called an Armenian cucumber or, in Arabic,* faqqus. *The chate melon is a long, slender light green–skinned, ribbed member of the muskmelon family native to North Africa, already utilized as a food in Egypt four thousand years ago. The cucumber* (khiar *in Farsi and Arabic), a native of India, has been cultivated for more than three thousand years, but did not reach Europe or Africa until much later.*

About the time that the cucumber was first cultivated, people in Egypt and India were eating chate melons and cucumbers fresh in salads and pickled. During the early medieval period, Arabs spread the Indian cucumber throughout the southern Mediterranean and into Spain, gradually supplanting the chate melon in most areas. On reaching medieval Europe, cucumbers, at that time small, curved, prickly, and bitter, were considered an unhealthy food, for the compounds that made them bitter also made them hard to digest—often resulting in burps. The British, considering them fit only for animal feed, called them "cowcumbers." Before gardeners bred out much of the bitterness, most Europeans would only eat cucumbers fermented in brine, leading to the immense popularity of the pickled form.

Pickled cucumbers achieved great popularity in many parts of Europe and the Middle East, but arguably nowhere more than among eastern European Jews, who ate them with black bread and later potatoes as the bulk of their diet. Because vinegar was extremely rare and expensive in northern Europe, salt alone was generally used for pickling, resulting in fermented pickles. It has become popular in many parts of the world to use vinegar to prevent the growth of bacteria (called fresh-pack and quick-process pickles), but at the expense of the pickle's character by eliminating the lactofermentation. Nevertheless, traditional Jewish pickles contain no vinegar.

Too much salt renders pickles inedible and destroys the desirable bacteria necessary for fermentation. Yet enough salt must be added to prevent the growth of undesirable bacteria, while allowing the survival of the bacteria that feed on sugars in the vegetables and produce lactic acid, which in turn creates conditions for other microorganisms to produce acetic acid; the two sources of acid help to form the brine, an acid bath that cures the vegetables, and creates a characteristic tangy, yet mellow flavor. In eastern Europe, the heel of a loaf of sour rye bread was sometimes added to the brine to kick start the fermentation process. Olives and sauerkraut were also historically pickled using the same fermentation process. Lactic acid fermentation can be rather tricky, and bad batches occasionally occur, even among experienced pickle makers.

What You Should Know: The Kirby is the most common pickling variety; gherkins (not a variety but rather any small cucumber bred for solid, crisp flesh) are also used for pickling. Use firm cucumbers free of spoilage or blemishes. Avoid those with waxed skin, which prevents absorption of the brine (waxed cucumbers have an unnatural sheen). Wash the cucumbers well because any dirt can ruin the entire jar. Using garlic to flavor salt brine is a longtime eastern European practice, popularized in America by Jewish immigrants. Thus, this type of pickle became known as a "kosher dill." Even American government standards state that the term "kosher pickle" or "kosher style" can only be used by the brands containing garlic. According to Jewish law, of course, pickles don't need garlic to be kosher. Authentic kosher dills get their distinctive taste not only from garlic, but also from dill and the special brine. Vary the other seasonings according to your personal tastes.

The temperature in the pickling room should be neither too hot nor cold; a temperature between 65°F and 72°F allows for the growth of the desirable bacteria and lactic acid fermentation, which softens the vegetables as well as producing natural bacteroicins (substances that kill bacteria).

For storage of four months or longer, pickles should be sealed in a canning jar. There are three types of jars: those with two-piece lids with a thin rubber ring bonded to the metal cap, those with one-piece metal caps, and those with a glass lid secured by a spring wire clip ("lightening jars"). The first kind, currently the predominant type in America and the most reliable, requires heat processing, which also softens the cucumbers and is not desirable for fermented pickles.

For the latter two types, the lids should be used with a flat rubber ring to create an airtight seal. In any case, do not use if the rim of the jar is chipped. To store pickles for more than a month, you need to first sterilize the jars, thereby destroying any bacteria or other substances that could spoil the food. To sterilize, bring a large pot of water to a boil, submerge the jars, lids, and rings and boil for 10 minutes, turn off the heat, and let the jars stand in the hot water until ready to fill. (My sister sterilizes the jars by washing them in a dishwasher. She also stopped looking for rings for her jar lids and omits them, simply placing a plastic bag on top before securing the lids. However, her pickles are generally consumed within a week or two and are not intended for months on the shelf. My sister also adjusts the amount of kosher salt from batch to batch, adding between 2 to 4 tablespoons for every quart of water.)

For millennia, our ancestors safely fermented pickles in large stoneware crocks and wooden barrels before the advent of preserving jars, and some people still prefer this way. Large glass jars and food-grade plastic containers make suitable modern substitutes. Arrange the cucumbers vertically in the crock, close together so that they are secured in place, add the seasonings, and fill completely with brine. (This assures that there are no air pockets.) It is vital that all of the cucumbers be completely submerged in the brine, preferably by at least two inches, as some of the water evaporates. Therefore weigh the cucumbers down with a large plate (not metal or plastic) topped with a heavy weight. (A sterilized rock was once traditional, but I prefer a large bottle filled with water or a sealed food-grade plastic bag filled with additional brine.) Cover the crock with a double thickness of cheesecloth, a clean kitchen towel, or pillowcase to keep out mold and insects. Fermented pickles can be stored in the original crock for at least three months, provided that any white or gray scum is periodically removed from the surface.

Ashkenazim commonly serve dill pickles as an appetizer or side dish, or chop them into a relish to serve as garnish or add to salads, such as egg salad and potato salad. American delis must have both "sours" and "half-sours" on the table before the customer sits down. In Europe, the leftover pickle juice (kvas) was never thrown out, but used as a tangy base for various soups.

For this recipe, use the freshest cucumbers possible, preferably within 24 hours of picking; older ones produce pickles with hollow centers.

About 24 very fresh 4-inch-long pickling cucumbers
(4 pounds total)
8 cups soft water (see Notes)
1/2 cup kosher salt
8 fresh dill heads (see Notes), well washed,
12 to 16 sprigs fresh dill, or 1 to 2 teaspoons
dill seeds
8 cloves garlic
16 whole peppercorns
4 bay leaves
1 to 2 teaspoons mustard seeds
1/2 teaspoon coriander seeds (optional)
1/2 teaspoon red pepper flakes
4 small dried red chilies or a small piece of fresh
horseradish (optional)

1. Soak the cucumbers in ice water for at least 1 or up to 8 hours. This enhances the crispness. Drain. Snip off the bitter-tasting tip of the blossom end (the end not attached to the vine).

2. To make the brine: In a nonreactive saucepan, such as stainless steel or an enameled pan (do not use iron, copper, brass, zinc, galvanized metal, or aluminum, except hard-anodized aluminum), combine the water and salt. Bring to a simmer stirring to dissolve the salt, about 4 minutes. Remove from the heat and let cool.

3. Sterilize four 1-quart jars, metal lids, and new rubber rings, or one 1-gallon jar, or a large nonreactive crock. Divide all the seasonings evenly among the jars. Pack about 6 cucumbers upright—without squashing—into each jar.

4. Pour the cooled brine over the cucumbers to cover, leaving 1/2 inch of headroom. Tightly cover the jars and shake well. This is the "new green" stage. Place upside down on a towel (in order to detect any leaks) and let stand overnight. If any liquid has seeped from a jar, tighten the lid. Otherwise place the jars lid side up in a dark place, like a cupboard or pantry, at room temperature (68°F to 72°F is best) to ferment. After 2 to 3 days, tiny bubbles will begin rising in the liquid, a sign of fermentation. After 4 to 5 days from the beginning, the bacteria will gradually begin to sour the cucumbers, but at this point they will remain bright green outside and white inside and very crisp. This is the "half-sour" stage. If you prefer "half-sours," refrigerate them at this point to slow down the fermentation; the longer they stand at room temperature, the more intense the sour flavor and softer the texture become. After 2 to 3 weeks, the tiny bubbles will stop rising, a sign that fermentation has ceased. The pickles will turn a greenish-brown outside and translucent inside and develop a tangy flavor and softer, but not mushy, texture. This is the "sour" or "full-sour" stage. Once the pickles become sours, store them in the refrigerator or a cool place, which slows down the fermentation, for up to 6 weeks. (They are usually devoured sooner.)

If there is any indication of spoilage, such as mold, an off odor, sliminess, or mushiness, do not taste, but discard the entire bottle. Don't worry if the brine turns cloudy or a little white scum floats to the surface, these are by-products of fermentation.

5. Use a clean fork or tongs to remove the pickles, as your fingers will contaminate the brine. (Professional pickle handlers now use plastic gloves.) Once the jar is opened, store in the refrigerator.

VARIATION

Ashkenazic Pickled Green Tomatoes (*Marinierte Tomaten*): Substitute about 24 small, firm green (immature) tomatoes (no larger than a plum tomato) for the cucumbers and increase the kosher salt to ³/4 cup. The tomatoes will take 2 to 3 weeks to become "half-sours" and about 5 weeks for "full-sours."

N O T E S   The minerals in hard water tend to hinder the pickling process by reducing brine acidity. If you do not have soft water in your area, boil tap water for 15 minutes, cover, and let cool for 24 hours, discarding any scum that forms on the surface, then pour off the water, leaving any sediment on the bottom.

Dill heads are the flower buds, not the green fronds, of the dill plant, and are usually picked before they open. It is preferable to use soft dill heads, before they mature and dry. Dill flower heads are often in season before cucumbers are available from July to August, but they can be frozen until you are ready to make pickles. Do not wash them before freezing.

The traditional manner for determining the right amount of salt in the brine is to place a raw egg in a pot of water and add enough salt until the egg rises to the surface and protrudes above the water by the diameter of a dime.

POLISH PICKLED MUSHROOMS

Marinierte Shveml

ABOUT 2 CUPS

A favorite among my mother's repertoire of appetizers is this dish of flavorful pickled mushrooms, which requires little fuss. Pickling is the most common way of preparing mushrooms in Poland: The mushrooms are cooked and then preserved in a vinegar brine. (Marinated mushrooms, by contrast, soak in an oil-based marinade—something once generally too expensive for most eastern Europeans.) In the United States, pickled and marinated mushrooms are usually made from the inexpensive button variety, while in Poland they are made with the local borowik *(called* cèpes *in French,* porcini *in Italian, and* boletus *in Greek), the most common variety in Europe, gathered wild from the woods for millennia.*

The fragrant borowik *is shaped like a button mushroom, but has a round cap and a fat stem that flares at the base. Rather than gills,* borowik *have a pale, spongy underlayer consisting of tiny tubes and pores. When cooked, they have a silky texture and a rich beefy, wine flavor. Since much of the flavor in this dish derives from the brine, mild-flavored white button mushrooms make an acceptable substitute, but you can certainly use* borowik *or* cremini. *The flavor of the mushrooms can be varied by adding 8 coarsely chopped dill sprigs to the cooled brine, or adding 2 whole cloves and 2 allspice berries with the peppercorns. These flavorful morsels make delicious hors d'oeuvres, solo or as part of a relish tray. My mother occasionally garnished the bowl with thin strips of red pepper and served the mushrooms with individual toothpicks. In Poland, pickled mushrooms, sometimes garnished with chopped parsley, are commonly served with black bread and plenty of well-chilled vodka.*

1 pound small, firm white or brown mushrooms

1 teaspoon table salt or 2 teaspoons kosher salt

BRINE:

1 cup distilled white, cider, or red wine vinegar

³/₄ cup water

2 bay leaves

1 teaspoon table salt or 2 teaspoons kosher salt

3 to 4 black peppercorns or ¹/₈ teaspoon ground
black pepper

¹/₂ teaspoon sugar

2 cloves garlic, minced

1 tablespoon vegetable oil or olive oil

1. Clean the mushrooms with a dampened sponge or paper towels. Cut off the tough ends of the mushroom stems. If any of the mushrooms are large, cut them in half lengthwise. Place in a medium saucepan and add water to cover. Bring to a boil, add 1 teaspoon salt, reduce the heat to low, and simmer until tender, about 10 minutes. Drain and let cool.

2. To make the brine: In a medium, nonreactive saucepan, combine the vinegar, water, bay leaves, salt, peppercorns, and sugar. Bring to a boil, remove from the heat, add the garlic, and let cool.

3. Place the mushrooms in a sterilized jar, pour the marinade over top, and drizzle with the oil to form a protective coating. Cover and refrigerate for at least 24 hours. The flavor will mellow as the mushrooms stand; they are best after a week. Store in the refrigerator for up to 1 month. Serve at room temperature.

MIDDLE EASTERN PICKLED TURNIPS

Turshi Left

ABOUT 2 QUARTS

Middle Eastern pickles, made with vinegar, tend to be much less salty than European ones. Some versions of turshi, *intended to last for up to a year, are first brined for a brief period to extract the excess moisture in the vegetable, then pickled in a mixture of half vinegar and half brine, resulting in an intense vinegar flavor. This recipe, intended for a shorter period of storage, contains a much smaller proportion of vinegar and, to my mind, a better taste. Whereas the cucumber is Europe's most popular pickle, the Middle East favors the turnip, the most common pickle in the region and possibly the original pickle. Pickled turnips, variously called* turshi left, mkhelal lifet, *and* navets sales, *are a mainstay of mezes. They are also mixed into salads and served as a condiment at most meals and as a side dish to rice dishes, vegetable stews, and* kukuye sabzi *(Persian Herb Omelet, page 423). Turnips may be pickled alone or as part of a mélange of vegetables. Before the advent of the beetroot in the sixteenth century, saffron was sometimes added to tint the turnips yellow. The beet imparts a traditional light pink hue; omit it if you prefer white turnips.* Turshi, *symbolizing the harvest, is a common sight on Sukkot tables in the Middle East.*

2 pounds (about 6 small) white turnips,
    peeled and cubed, sliced, or julienned
1 small beet, peeled and sliced
3 to 5 cloves garlic, halved
$^3/_4$ teaspoon ground ginger (optional)
1 small fresh hot red chili or $^1/_4$ teaspoon
    red pepper flakes (optional)
2 tablespoons chopped fresh celery leaves
    (optional)

BRINE:

3 cups water
1 cup distilled white, cider, or white wine vinegar
2 tablespoons kosher salt

$^1/_2$ teaspoon olive oil (optional)

1. In a sterilized 2-quart jar, combine the turnips, beet, garlic, and, if using, ginger, chili, and celery leaves.

2. To make the brine: In a medium nonreactive saucepan, combine the water, vinegar, and salt. Bring to a simmer and stir with a wooden spoon until the salt is dissolved, about 4 minutes.

3. Pour the hot brine over the turnips to cover. If desired, drizzle the oil over the top to seal, keeping out unwanted bacteria. Let cool, then tightly cover. Let stand in a cool, dark place for at least 3 or up to 10 days. The vegetables will develop a mellow, tangy flavor, but will still be rather crisp. The longer the vegetables are left at room temperature, the softer they will become. Store in the refrigerator for up to 3 months. Serve chilled or at room temperature. Use tongs or a slotted spoon to remove the pickles from the jar.

Middle Eastern Pickled Cabbage (*Turshi de Kol*): Substitute 1 shredded head (about 2 pounds) cabbage for the turnips.

Middle Eastern Pickled Cauliflower (*Turshi de Culupidia*): Substitute 1 medium-large head (about 2$^1/_4$ pounds) cauliflower, cut into florets, for the turnips.

Persian Pickled Peppers (*Filfel Makboos*): Substitute 6 bell peppers of any color for the turnips. Cut off and reserve the tops; discard the seeds and ribs. Mix together 3 cups (about 8 ounces) shredded cabbage and 1 chopped celery stalk and stuff into the peppers. Place the tops on the peppers and tie with kitchen twine to secure.

Middle Eastern Pickled Mixed Vegetables (*Turshi Khodar*): Use only 6 ounces (2 small) turnips. Add 8 ounces sliced carrots, 8 ounces cauliflower cut into florets, 4 ounces sliced zucchini, 1 or 2 seeded, deribbed (white removed), and sliced green or red bell peppers, 2 sliced stalks celery, and 1 cup (about 4 ounces) shredded cabbage or 4 to 5 gherkin cucumbers.

CALCUTTA PICKLED OKRA

Bamia Pickle

ABOUT 2 CUPS

This is a synthesis of Middle Eastern and Indian styles. Okra, usually called lady's fingers or bhindi, is popular in India when prepared properly. As the Indian woman who gave me this recipe noted, "When cooked improperly, it turns out soggy and stringy." Indians believe that water spoils okra, so they generally cook it in other liquids. To avoid too much water, they even clean the pods with a slightly moist towel rather than directly in or under running water. If there is any sign of spoilage, such as discoloration or off odor, discard the okra. (Acid, with a pH of 4.6 or higher, usually deactivates any Clostridium botulinum, *but this dangerous bacteria can survive and become productive.) Serve with any Indian dish, such as Indian Rice Pilaf (page 357), cucumber raita (Indian Cucumber and Yogurt Salad, page 47), and Indian breads.*

1 1/2 cups cider or malt vinegar, plus more as needed

2 tablespoons sugar

1 tablespoon kosher salt

2 to 4 small green chilies (optional)

8 ounces small okra (about 40 pods)

4 teaspoons chopped fresh cilantro or parsley

4 teaspoons minced garlic

4 teaspoons minced fresh ginger

1. In a nonreactive saucepan, bring the 1 1/2 cups vinegar, the sugar, and salt to a simmer, stirring with a wooden spoon until the sugar and salt dissolve, about 4 minutes. If using, add the chilies and simmer for 2 more minutes. Let cool.

2. Trim off the tops of the okra and cut a 1-inch lengthwise slit in each pod. Mix together the cilantro, garlic, and ginger and stuff about 1/4 teaspoon into each pod.

3. Pack the okra and chilies into a sterilized 1-quart jar. Pour the vinegar mixture over the top to cover, leaving 1/2-inch headroom. If there is not enough liquid to cover the okra, add some additional vinegar. Close the jar and let stand in a cool, dark place for at least 24 hours, then refrigerate for at least 1 week or up to 1 month.

VARIATION

Easier Pickled Okra: Instead of stuffing the okra, in Step 1, add the cilantro, garlic, and ginger to the pickling liquid. If desired, substitute 1 teaspoon dill seeds or 1 teaspoon mustard seeds for the cilantro.

VINEGAR FOR PICKLING Vinegars vary little in their acidity, but small variances translate into noticeable differences in flavor and usage. The acidity level of 5 percent is necessary for home canning and long-term preservation, while less-acidic vinegars are fine for marinating. Cider, malt, and distilled white vinegar, generally with 5 percent acidity, are preferable for pickling. Cider vinegar is an amber-colored, sharp, fruity vinegar made from fermented apple cider; it is ideal for pickling fruits and flavoring marinades and chutneys but too intense for dressing green salads. Malt vinegar, made from malted barley, is slightly sweet and pairs well with fried foods and chutneys. Distilled white vinegar is made from ethyl alcohol distilled from grain. Its clarity and strong flavor make it the favorite for pickling vegetables, but it is too assertive for most cooking.

SEPHARDIC CUCUMBER SALAD

Salata de Pipino

6 TO 8 SERVINGS

Until the development of more easily digestible and less bitter cucumbers in the eighteenth century, these vegetables were rarely eaten raw but instead were marinated or pickled. This cool marinated salad appears in Jewish cooking from India to Spain, with only slight variations. Serve as a salad or side dish; its refreshing taste complements a variety of spicy and fiery dishes.

> 4 regular cucumbers (about 2¹/₂ pounds total), halved lengthwise, seeded, and thinly sliced, or 2 large English (hothouse) cucumbers, thinly sliced
>
> About 1 tablespoon table salt or 2 tablespoons kosher salt
>
> 1 small onion, chopped or sliced
>
> ¹/₂ cup cider or distilled white vinegar
>
> 1 tablespoon sugar
>
> About ¹/₄ teaspoon ground white or black pepper

1. Put the cucumbers in a colander or large sieve, toss with the salt, weigh down with a plate, and let stand at room temperature for at least 1 or up to 3 hours. Rinse with cold water, drain, and pat dry. (This removes excess water, which would turn the salad watery.) Transfer the cucumbers to a large bowl.

2. In a small bowl, mix together the onion, vinegar, sugar, and pepper. Pour the dressing over the cucumbers and toss to coat. Taste and, if necessary, add a little more salt. Cover and refrigerate for at least 3 hours. Serve chilled or at room temperature.

VARIATIONS

Ashkenazic Cucumber Salad (*Marinirte Ugerkeh*): Add ¹/₄ cup chopped fresh dill.

Hungarian Cucumber Salad (*Uborka Salata*): Add 2 teaspoons sweet paprika. If desired, drain the salad after it has marinated 3 hours in the refrigerator and add 1 to 1¹/₂ cups sour cream.

Indian Cucumber Salad (*Kachumber*): Substitute ¹/₂ cup fresh lemon or lime juice for the vinegar and add 1 cup chopped cilantro or ¹/₄ cup fresh spearmint, 1 to 2 seeded and minced small hot chilies, and 1¹/₂ cups diced tomatoes.

Indian Cucumber Salad (*Zalatta*): Substitute ¹/₂ cup fresh lemon or lime juice for the vinegar and add 1 julienned green or red bell pepper, 2 to 3 teaspoons minced fresh ginger, and, if desired, 1 to 3 seeded and minced fresh green chilies.

Romanian Cucumber Salad (*Uborkasalata*): Add 1 tablespoon chopped fresh or 1 teaspoon dried tarragon.

Yemenite Cucumber Salad (*Khiar Salata*): Substitute ¹/₂ cup fresh lemon or lime juice for the vinegar and add ¹/₄ to ¹/₃ cup chopped fresh fennel fronds.

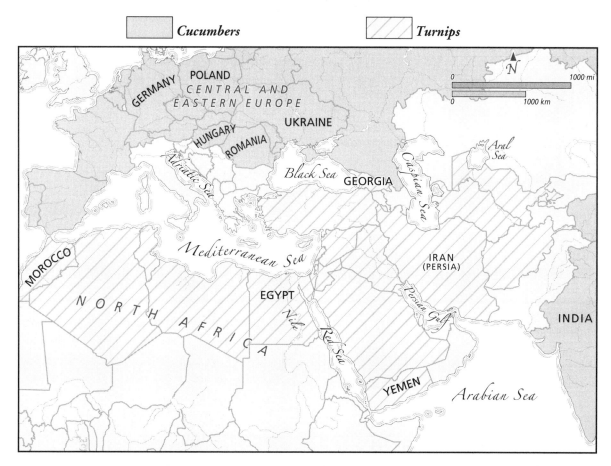

Two Principal Pickles of the Old World: *Countries from Persian and Arabic regions tended to favor pickled turnips, while most Europeans primarily pickled cucumbers.*

ITALIAN MARINATED ARTICHOKE HEARTS

Carciofi Marinati

6 TO 8 SERVINGS   Ⓟ

A favorite Italian way of preparing and thereby storing artichokes is to marinate the tender hearts. Slightly tangy homemade marinated artichokes have a fresher flavor than store-bought ones, and the flavor can be adapted to your own preferences. The artichokes can be mixed into salads and other dishes, eaten alone as an appetizer, or served as part of an antipasto platter. A typical antipasto platter features various crudités, olives, tiny marinated mushrooms in olive oil, marinated roasted bell peppers, marinated artichokes, and at dairy meals, Italian cheeses.

1 lemon

12 fresh artichokes or 30 ounces unthawed frozen artichoke hearts

3 tablespoons olive oil

1 large onion, chopped

2 1/2 cups water

1/2 cup red wine vinegar

1 tablespoon table salt or 2 tablespoons kosher salt

DRESSING:

1 cup extra-virgin olive oil

1/4 cup fresh lemon juice (about 1 1/2 lemons)

3 tablespoons chopped fresh parsley

2 to 3 cloves garlic, minced

About 1/2 teaspoon table salt or 1 teaspoon kosher salt

Ground black pepper to taste

2 tablespoons red pepper flakes or 2 teaspoons dried oregano (optional)

1. To prepare the artichokes: Squeeze the lemon into a large bowl of cold water. Working with one artichoke at a time, cut off the stem, slice off the top half, and trim all the dark green areas (this will remove all of the thorny tips as well). Scoop out the fuzzy choke (a grapefruit spoon or melon baller works well). Place in the lemon water until ready for use.

2. Heat the oil in a large nonreactive saucepan over medium heat. Add the onion and sauté until soft and translucent, about 5 minutes. Add the artichokes and sauté until coated, about 2 minutes. Add the water, vinegar, and salt. Bring to a boil, cover, reduce the heat to low, and simmer until tender, about 25 minutes for fresh artichokes, 15 minutes for frozen. Drain.

3. To make the dressing: In a small bowl, combine all the ingredients and whisk until blended. Drizzle over the artichokes and toss to coat. Refrigerate, stirring about every hour for 4 hours. Store in the refrigerator for up to 3 weeks.

VARIATIONS

Italian Artichoke Salad (*Insalata di Carciofi*): Cut the marinated artichokes into quarters or sixths and mix with 4 ounces cubed mozzarella cheese and 2 tablespoons chopped fresh basil or 1 tablespoon dried oregano.

Italian Marinated Artichoke Hearts with Mushrooms (*Carciofi Marinati con Funghi*): Reduce the artichokes to 8 fresh or 20 ounces frozen and add 1 pound thickly sliced mushrooms with the dressing.

WINE VINEGAR FOR MARINADES Red wine vinegar is tangy and full-bodied, the flavor and quality varying according to the wine used, usually Pinot Noir. White wine vinegar is generally made from Sauvignon Blanc and Chardonnay. Wine vinegar ranges from 5 to 7.5 percent acidity, with more acidic ones preferred for marinades and deglazing, milder ones for salads and pickling.

TURKISH SWEET-AND-SOUR ARTICHOKES

Anjinaras

6 TO 8 SERVINGS

This is a Turkish Jewish style of preparing artichokes. Since artichokes begin appearing in the early spring, they are a common Sephardic Passover food. This one, featuring a combination of citrus, olive oil, and capers, makes a delicious appetizer or side dish.

3 lemons, halved

8 large artichokes

3 cups water

1 1/2 cups fresh orange juice

3/4 cup olive oil

About 1/2 cup fresh lemon juice (about 3 lemons)

1/3 cup distilled white or cider vinegar

1 teaspoon table salt or 2 teaspoons kosher salt

3 tablespoons capers, drained

About 2 tablespoons sugar or honey

1. To prepare the artichokes: Squeeze the lemons, reserving the juice for the cooking liquid. Place the lemon rinds in a bowl of cold water. Working with one artichoke at a time, trim the stem, leaving 2 to 3 inches of the stem attached. Cut off the top third of the artichoke and pull off all the dark green outer leaves, including those with a thorny tip, leaving the edible inner part. Peel off the dark-colored fibers from the stem and the base of the artichoke. Scoop out the fuzzy choke (a grapefruit spoon or melon baller works well). Leave whole or cut in half lengthwise. Place the artichoke, stem-side up, in the lemon water while preparing the remaining artichokes.

2. In a large nonreactive saucepan, combine the water, orange juice, oil, lemon juice, vinegar, and salt. Bring to a boil over medium heat. Add the artichokes, stem-side up, cover, reduce the heat to low, and simmer until tender, 30 to 40 minutes. Transfer the artichokes to a bowl.

3. Add the capers and sugar to the cooking liquid and boil until reduced by half, to about 3 cups. Pour over the artichokes. Serve warm, at room temperature, or chilled as an appetizer or side dish. Store in the refrigerator for up to 3 days.

VARIATION

Sephardic Artichokes with Lemon (*Inginaras con Limón*): Omit the orange juice, vinegar, and capers and reduce the sugar to 1/2 teaspoon and the oil to 2 tablespoons. Greeks sometimes add 1 to 2 tablespoons chopped fresh dill and/or 16 peeled pearl onions to the lemon artichoke cooking liquid; Balkan cooks add 2 thinly sliced carrots.

BALKAN MARINATED BEETS

Chukundor

ABOUT 4 CUPS, OR 6 TO 8 SERVINGS

Although beets have a long shelf life, they are sweetest and most tender when young and fresh, becoming woody and losing flavor as they mature and grow larger. Many cultures pickle beets, both to preserve young ones at their tasty peak and to perk up those past their prime. Middle Eastern marinated beets tend to be much tangier than the sweet-and-sour European versions. Serve as part of a meze *(appetizer assortment) or as a side dish. Among many Sephardim, marinated beets are a common Sukkot and Passover dish.*

The first time I made these, my hands ended up stained bright red. I was able to return to normal by rubbing my hands, as well as the cutting board, with salt, rinsing, washing with soap, then repeating. Of course, rubber gloves prevent the problem.

> 2 pounds (about 8) unpeeled beets, stems
>   trimmed to 1 inch (see Note)
> 1 cup cider, red wine, or distilled white vinegar
> 1 cup water
> 3 tablespoons cumin seeds
> 1 tablespoon sugar
> About $^1/_2$ teaspoon table salt or 1 teaspoon
>   kosher salt

1. Put the beets in a large pot of boiling water, cover, reduce the heat to a simmer, and cook until tender, 30 to 50 minutes. Or, cook over 1 inch of boiling water in a covered steamer, adding more water when necessary, until tender, 50 to 60 minutes. Or, wrap the beets in aluminum foil and bake in a 375°F oven until tender, about 1 hour. When cool enough to handle, cut off the stem and root, slip off the skins, and cut the beets into $^1/_4$-inch-thick slices. Let cool.

2. In a small nonreactive saucepan, combine the vinegar, water, cumin seeds, sugar, and salt. Bring to a simmer and stir until the sugar and salt dissolve, about 4 minutes.

3. Put the beets in a glass or ceramic bowl and pour the hot marinade over the top. Let cool. Cover and refrigerate for at least 12 hours or up to 2 weeks. The beets will become increasingly sour as they stand. Drain before serving.

NOTE When trimming beets for cooking, cut off most but not all of the stems, and do not cut off the root, or the color and nutrients will bleed away.

VARIATIONS

Eastern European Pickled Beets (*Marinirte Burekehs*): Omit the cumin, increase the sugar to $^3/_4$ to 1 cup, and add 1 halved and thinly sliced red or white onion in Step 3.

German Pickled Beets (*Gepikilti Burik*): Substitute 2 teaspoons caraway seeds or 12 whole cloves for the cumin, increase the sugar to $^1/_3$ to $^1/_2$ cup, and add 1 to 2 halved and thinly sliced onions in Step 3. Some Germans also like to add 6 to 8 peeled whole hard-boiled eggs in Step 3.

SEPHARDIC SWEET-AND-SOUR CELERY

Apio

6 TO 8 SERVINGS

During the Passover Seder, Jews in Turkey and the Balkans have long eaten the celery leaves as karpas (a green vegetable on the Seder plate representing spring and renewal); they then use the stalks in this sweet-and-sour dish. In Italy, celeriac, or celery root—first cultivated by Italian gardeners during the Renaissance—is a frequent substitute. Be sure to use fresh lemon juice; it makes a major difference in taste. Serve warm as a side dish, or at room temperature or chilled as an appetizer.

I cup water
About $1/3$ cup fresh lemon juice (about 2 lemons)
$1/4$ cup olive oil
About I tablespoon sugar
About I teaspoon table salt or 2 teaspoons kosher salt
2 large bunches celery, leaves removed, cut into I $1/2$-inch-long pieces
3 tablespoons chopped fresh parsley for garnish

In a large pot, combine the water, lemon juice, oil, sugar, and salt. Bring to a boil over high heat. Add the celery, reduce the heat to low, partially cover, and simmer, stirring occasionally, until tender, about 30 minutes. Transfer to a serving dish. Sprinkle with the parsley.

Italian Sweet-and-Sour Celery Root (*Cavessas de Apio*): *Cavessas* is is Ladino for "knobs." Substitute 3 celery roots (about 14 ounces each—choose roots that feel heavy for their size), peeled and cut into $1/4$-inch-thick slices, for the celery. Celeriac will be tender in about 20 minutes.

Sephardic Celery with Carrots (*Apio con Safanorias*): Reduce the celery to 1 large bunch. Add 1 pound carrots cut on the diagonal into $1/4$-inch-thick oval slices, and cook with the celery.

Middle Eastern Celery with Fennel (*Apio con Fenouils*): Reduce the celery to 1 large bunch. Cut 1 large bulb fennel in half lengthwise, then crosswise into 1-inch-thick slices, and cook with the celery.

Pretty good - I halved recipe

OLIVES: THE FIRST PICKLES?

Olives have played an enduring and important role in Jewish life and lore from the start. The Bible included olives among the seven agricultural species with which the land of Israel is blessed (hence the name of this book). Since then, olives have been an endless source of symbolism and meaning. Olive oil symbolizes light and sanctity. Because the roots of felled olive trees sprout suckers that grow into new trees, olive trees represent renewal and fertility. The story of the dove bringing Noah an olive branch led to the tree's association with peace. Some scholars believe that the olive's hard, gnarled roots served as the original plow. The trees also symbolize longevity and endurance, for although it takes at least five years before olive trees bear fruit, they live an incredible length of time, thriving in poor soil and resisting long periods of drought. The Garden of Gethsemane (Hebrew for "olive press"), lying at the base of the Mount of Olives in Jerusalem, contains olive trees possibly more than two thousand years old.

Long before they were eaten, olives were treasured for their oil. (Oleuropein, the chemical that makes raw olives inedibly bitter, separates naturally from the pressed oil.) People picked olives where they grew wild in regions around northern Israel and southern Syria before first cultivating them nearly six thousand years ago.

THE CURED OLIVE: According to legend, the discovery that brining would make olives edible happened one day thousands of years ago, when someone noticed a few olives that had fallen into in the sea and, being sufficiently hungry, tasted one—and found it deliciously pickled by the salt water.

The hard flesh of most green olives withstands brine for an extensive period, so the fruit is commonly first soaked in a lye solution (about 1/4 cup sodium hydroxide for every gallon of cold water) for 12 hours to 2 weeks. This removes most of the oleuropein and breaks down the flesh so the brine can more easily permeate the center and lactic acid fermentation can take place. The more intense the lye solution and the longer the soaking, the more flavor is extracted from the fruit. In the Mediterranean, partially lye-treated olives, which retain more of the olive's pungent taste, are more common than completely treated ones. An even green color, as opposed to a mottled color, is a sign of lye processing.

After soaking in lye, olives are then wet cured in brine or, occasionally, dry cured in rock salt. A tangy, yet mellow flavor develops through lactic acid fermentation. Cracking the olive's flesh allows the brine to penetrate more easily, which shortens the curing process to about 6 weeks; curing can take up to a year if the olives are not cracked. Brine curing olives without soaking in lye or cracking, rarely done today, can take up to two years.

There are hundreds of types of olives, which are classified in any number of ways: by variety, size, color, origin, or the type of cure used. Olive flavors ranges from bland to strong, and from simple to complex. Both texture and flavor are determined by the variety, the growing conditions (climate and soil), the degree of ripeness of the olive, the subsequent processing, and the method of storage. Green olives, the unripe fruit, are picked in early fall; black/purple olives have been allowed to tree ripen until November, darkening from reddish brown to purple or black. People who live around olive trees tend to favor shriveled brine-cured black olives, sometimes called Greek-style olives, which possess a smoky flavor. These are the high-quality olives available in gourmet shops and some delis. Most American canned black olives were actually not tree ripened at all, but rather are green olives that derive their dark color from aeration and exposure to ferrous gluconate; they tend to be sweet and juicy but are bereft of any genuine olive flavor.

Cured Olive Varieties

- **AMFISSA**: A large, mild purple Greek variety. The brine may contain vinegar.
- **BARNEA**: Pale green or black, elongated, and medium-sized, with strong herbal flavors. An Israeli olive reminiscent of the Kalamata. It produces a mild, fruit-flavored oil.
- **GAETA**: Small, purple to brownish-purple olives from central Italy, with a good balance of fruit, salt, and bitterness. The flavor is similar to that of the Kalamata. Salt cured, packed in brine or oil.
- **KALAMATA**: Purple-black, medium-large, almond-shaped, mild, vinegar-cured olives with a fruity flavor. The world's best known olive, ubiquitous to Greek salads.
- **LIGURIAN**: A purple to black, medium-sized, rich, and bitter brine-cured Italian olive.
- **MANZANILLO**: Yellowish-green or black, round, juicy, mild, lye treated. Also called Spanish olive. Usually stuffed with pimientos or occasionally almonds or capers. Produces an almost neutral-flavored oil. Originally from Spain, the Manzanillo is now a major variety in Israel.
- **MOROCCAN**: Black, medium-sized, and wrinkled, with a smoky, salty flavor. Baked, then oil cured.
- **NABALI**: Tan or pale green, medium sized. A meaty, juicy, brine-cured Israeli olive. Produces an almost neutral-flavored oil.
- **NIÇOISE**: Dark brown to purple, very small. Brine cured and packed in oil, with a nutty, slightly bitter flavor. The most popular French olive.
- **PICHOLINE**: Pale green, medium to small, elongated, and firm. Nutty but mild in flavor.
- **SEVILLANA**: Green, large, meaty, and mild; usually salt cured. Also called Queen's olive or Gordal.
- **SOURI**: Beige or black, small, elongated, juicy, brine cured. Produces a peppery, honey-flavored oil. The name means "Syrian," but this is now the principal variety in Israel.

MOROCCAN FIERY MARINATED OLIVES

Zeitoon al Had

ABOUT 3 CUPS, OR 50 TO 60 OLIVES

Cured olives are a ubiquitous accompaniment at Middle Eastern meals; they are frequently marinated in various aromatics to acquire layers of flavor. These olives are spiced in a traditional Moroccan style, with a kick from hot chilies. Mediterraneans believe that excess brine hides the true flavor of olives, so they usually soak or blanch olives in water before marinating them. Serve at room temperature as an appetizer or as a salad (if serving as a salad, pit the olives before blanching).

1 pound (about 60 small olives, or 3 cups)
    brined-cured green olives, drained

¹/₄ cup olive oil or vegetable oil

5 to 6 cloves garlic, crushed (about 2 tablespoons)

1 tablespoon tomato paste

About 14 ounces plum tomatoes, peeled, seeded,
    and chopped (2 cups); see page 291

¹/₂ cup water

3 (¹/₄-inch-thick) lemon slices

¹/₂ to 1 teaspoon cayenne or *harissa* (Northwest
    African Chili Paste, page 433)

¹/₂ teaspoon ground cumin or 1 branch fresh
    thyme

Pinch of salt

Ground black pepper to taste

1. Put the olives in a medium saucepan, add water to cover, and bring to a boil; drain and set aside.

2. In a large skillet or saucepan, heat the oil over medium heat. Stir in the garlic, then the tomato paste, and sauté until the paste begins to darken, 2 to 3 minutes. Add the tomatoes, water, lemon slices, cayenne, cumin, salt, and pepper and bring to a low boil.

3. Stir in the olives, reduce the heat to medium-low, and simmer, stirring frequently, until the liquid evaporates, about 5 minutes. Remove from the heat. Discard the lemon slices and let cool. Cover and refrigerate for at least 24 hours or up to 1 week. Serve at room temperature.

Syrian Sweet-and-Sour Olives

Zeitoon bi Hamod

1 1/2 CUPS, OR ABOUT 25 OLIVES

These olives, flavored with tangy pomegranate concentrate or tamarind paste, are customarily served in a small, pretty ceramic bowl as part of a meze *(appetizer assortment).*

> 1 1/2 cups (about 8 ounces) small to medium brine-cured unpitted green olives
> 1/2 cup extra-virgin olive oil
> 1/3 cup pomegranate concentrate (see page 22) or 3 tablespoons Syrian Mock Tamarind Sauce (page 434)
> 1/3 cup water
> 1 to 2 cloves garlic, minced
> 1 tablespoon packed brown sugar
> About 1/4 teaspoon kosher salt
> 10 whole black peppercorns

Rinse the olives and drain. If the olives are uncracked, lightly crush by pressing on them gently with the palm of your hand. In a medium bowl, combine all the remaining ingredients. Put the olives in a sterilized 1-quart jar, drizzle the marinade over them, cover tightly, and shake to coat the olives. Let stand at room temperature for 3 hours, then refrigerate for at least 3 days or up to 3 months. Serve at room temperature.

VARIATION

Syrian Olives and Red Peppers (*Zeiton bi Felfel*): Add 1 cup seeded, deribbed (white removed), and chopped red bell peppers and substitute 1/4 teaspoon red pepper flakes for the peppercorns.

RELISHES

From the onset of civilization until fairly recently, a single food comprised the bulk of the diet of most Western people: bread. Typical loaves were coarse and hard, often made from barley and other rough grains rather than wheat. Fine wheat flour was usually available only to the rich or for special occasions. As a result, various flavorsome relishes—anything from minced vinegared vegetables to spiced purées—were developed to be used as dips and spreads to make the breads easier to chew by adding flavor and moisture. (The Talmud, which contains five different words for relishes, states: "One who is about to recite the *hamotzi* [blessing over bread] is not permitted to do so before salt and relish are placed before him.") Dips that could be eaten cold were particularly useful during the Sabbath, as cooking and reheating were prohibited.

Although contemporary breads are generally soft enough to enjoy on their own, the Middle East in particular retains an affection for a wide range of chopped and puréed relishes, frequently serving assortments of them as *meze* (pages 27–28) or with bread. The wide range of relishes found on contemporary Jewish tables, present at everyday meals as well as during periods of celebration, reflects the different tastes and experiences of various communities. The principal eastern European relish is the pungent *chrain* (grated horseradish in vinegar), while Germans prefer the flavor of mustard. The fire in Yemenite relishes derives from chilies. Indians use various fresh and cooked chutneys. Eggplant relishes, such as the Moroccan *zaalouk* and Italian caponata, and other chopped vegetable salads are popular in the Mediterranean.

Italian Eggplant Relish

Caponata alla Giudea

ABOUT 3 CUPS, OR 5 TO 6 SERVINGS P

Packed with the heady flavors of the Mediterranean—sweet tomatoes, meaty eggplant chunks, salty capers, and aromatic olive oil—this sweet-and-sour relish is highly addictive. For the best flavor, buy high quality olives and pit them yourself. Adjust the amount of vinegar and sugar to personal preference. Caponata is served with bread as an appetizer, alone as a side dish, or as a pasta sauce, but it also makes a delicious filling for phyllo and other pastries. One of my favorite ways to use caponata is to spoon it onto crostini (garlic-rubbed toasted bread) or toasted pita triangles.

2 medium eggplants (about 1 pound each),
    peeled and cut into $^3/_4$-inch cubes
2 tablespoons kosher salt plus 1 teaspoon,
    or 1 tablespoon table salt plus $^1/_2$ teaspoon
$^3/_4$ cup olive oil
2 large onions, coarsely chopped
3 to 4 inner stalks celery, coarsely chopped
2 to 3 cloves garlic, minced
1$^1/_4$ pounds plum tomatoes, peeled, seeded, and
    chopped (about 3 cups); see page 291
$^3/_4$ cup green olives, pitted and coarsely chopped
$^1/_4$ cup chopped fresh parsley
4 to 6 tablespoons red wine vinegar
2 to 3 tablespoons sugar
About $^1/_4$ teaspoon ground black pepper
$^1/_4$ cup capers, drained
$^1/_4$ cup (1$^1/_2$ ounces) pine nuts, toasted
    (see page 22); optional

1. Put the diced eggplant in a colander, sprinkle with the 2 tablespoons kosher salt or 1 tablespoon table salt, and let stand for 1 hour. Rinse with water and press between several layers of paper towels until dry.

2. In a large saucepan, heat $^1/_2$ cup of the oil over medium heat. Add the eggplant and sauté until golden brown and tender but still firm, about 10 minutes. Transfer the eggplant to a plate and drain off any oil.

3. In the same pan, heat the remaining $^1/_4$ cup oil. Add the onions, celery, and garlic and sauté until softened, about 10 minutes. Add the tomatoes, olives, parsley, vinegar, sugar, the remaining salt, and the pepper. Cover and simmer over low heat, stirring occasionally, until the tomatoes break down into a thick sauce, about 15 minutes.

4. Add the eggplant and capers and cook, stirring occasionally, until all the vegetables are tender, about 10 minutes. Taste and adjust the seasoning. If using, stir in the pine nuts. Caponata keeps well in the refrigerator for up to 4 days; the flavors will meld as it stands.

CAPONATA

Jews lived on Sicily since Roman times. While developing ways to prepare vegetables a day or more ahead to serve for the cold Sabbath lunch, they came on a delicious solution: *cappone*, a venerable Latin term for sweet-and-sour dishes. The vinegar component preserved the food; the honey or sugar also acted as a preservative and tamed the acid. *Cappone* became an integral component of Sicilian-Jewish cookery. In addition to vinegar and sugar, these dishes commonly contained capers, olives, and raisins or prunes, in the Arabic style. The Arabs controlled parts or all of Sicily from 827 to 1061, during which time they introduced their cooking techniques and favorite foods to the island, including the eggplant. Although most non-Jewish Sicilians initially ignored this alien food, the Jews readily embraced eggplant, using it to create various dishes, including caponata. When Sicily fell under the rule of Spain, which in 1492 expelled nearly forty thousand Jews, most of this ancient community settled in central and northern Italy, bringing with them their dishes, including caponata, which was eventually further refined to include tomatoes. Today in Italy, this dish is commonly designated *alla giudia* (the name of the Roman ghetto), connoting its Jewish origins.

MOROCCAN EGGPLANT RELISH

Zeilouk d'Aubergines

6 TO 8 SERVINGS ⓟ

Moroccan cooking relies on combining seasonings to produce nuances of flavor, color, and aroma. This dish reflects the synthesis of Andalusian vegetable stews and Moroccan spices, most notably cumin. This fusion resulted when Jews fleeing Spain in 1492 settled in Morocco, bringing their cooking techniques with them. Although initially Moroccan Jews scorned the newcomers' eating habits, especially their much-loved vegetable stews and casseroles, the Sephardim were so numerous and economically successful that Sephardic traditions eventually supplanted many local ones— which greatly increased the popularity and versatility of the eggplant. Since then, eggplant has been a constant presence at the Moroccan table, frequently appearing mashed into a delicious tangy paste, as here.

2 medium-large eggplants (about 1¹/₂ pounds each), peeled

1 tablespoon table salt plus ¹/₂ teaspoon, or 2 tablespoons kosher salt plus 1 teaspoon

About ³/₄ cup vegetable oil or olive oil for frying

2 onions, finely chopped

3 to 5 cloves garlic, minced

2 green bell peppers, seeded, deribbed (white removed), and coarsely chopped (optional)

1³/₄ pounds plum tomatoes, peeled, seeded, and chopped (4 cups); see page 291

³/₄ cup tomato juice or 3 tablespoons tomato paste

2 teaspoons sweet paprika

1 teaspoon ground cumin

Ground black pepper to taste

1 teaspoon red wine vinegar

¹/₄ cup chopped fresh cilantro or parsley

1. Cut the eggplants crosswise into ¹/₂-inch-thick slices, then into ¹/₂-inch-wide sticks, then into ¹/₂-inch dice. Place in a colander or on a wire rack, sprinkle lightly with the 1 tablespoon table salt or 2 tablespoons kosher salt, and let stand for at least 1 hour. (Moisture will appear on the surface, and the eggplant will become more pliable.) Rinse the eggplant under cold running water, then repeatedly press between several layers of paper towels until the slices feel firm and dry. The eggplant can be stored, covered, in the refrigerator for up to 4 hours.

2. In a large heavy saucepan, heat about 3 tablespoons of the oil over medium heat. In about 3 batches, fry the eggplant, adding about 3 tablespoons more oil with each new batch, until lightly browned, 3 to 5 minutes on each side. Transfer to paper towels to drain.

3. In the same pan, heat the remaining 3 tablespoons oil over medium heat. Add the onions, garlic, and, if using, bell peppers, and sauté until softened, 5 to 10 minutes. Add the tomatoes, tomato juice, paprika, cumin, the remaining salt, and the pepper and bring to a boil.

4. Return the eggplant to the pan and simmer over medium heat, stirring occasionally, until the eggplant is tender and the tomatoes have broken down, about 20 minutes. Leave the relish chunky, or mash to a smooth texture. Stir in the vinegar and cilantro. Serve warm or at room temperature.

GEORGIAN VEGETABLE SALADS

Pkhali

ABOUT 4 CUPS, OR 6 TO 8 SERVINGS

A pkhali, *a cross between a salad and a relish, is made from one kind of chopped cooked vegetable tossed with Georgian walnut sauce. The secret to making a good* pkhali *is allowing it to stand long enough, at least 6 hours, for the flavors to meld and the ample garlic to mellow. For special occasions, Georgians offer several kinds of* pkhali, *the walnut sauce highlighting, rather than overwhelming, the qualities of each vegetable to create many distinctive flavors.* Pkhali *is garnished with fresh herbs or pomegranate seeds and served with* deda's puri *(flat bread),* mchadi *(Georgian Corn Cakes; page 379), and Georgian cheeses:* suluguni *(string cheese),* imeruli *(a fresh, slightly sour cheese), and* bryndza *(a creamy, less salty type of feta).*

> 1 cup *bazha* (Georgian Walnut Sauce, page 432)
> About 3 cups cooked chopped vegetable
>   (see Variations)

1. To make the sauce: Using a mortar and pestle or a food processor, grind the walnuts, onion, and garlic, and salt into a paste. Blend in the vinegar, cilantro, coriander, cayenne, turmeric, fenugreek, and the chili, if using. Add enough water to make a sauce the consistency of heavy cream. Let stand at room temperature for 1 hour.

2. Mix the vegetable and walnut sauce together. Cover and refrigerate for at least 6 hours or up to 3 days. To serve, spread the pkhali over a plate, smoothing the top. The traditional Georgian practice is to score a diamond pattern in the surface.

VARIATIONS

Georgian Beet Salad (*Charkhalis Pkhali*): Use 3 cups finely chopped cooked beets (about 1 1/2 pounds, or 6 to 8 beets). This is often served with the following dish, made from the beet greens.

Georgian Beet Green Salad (*Charkhalis Pkhali*): Six beets yield about 1 pound of greens. Cook 1 pound young beet leaves in 1 cup hot water over low heat until tender, about 30 minutes. Drain, let cool, then pat dry and coarsely chop. (You should have about 3 cups of cooked greens.) Use for the vegetable.

Georgian Red Bean Salad (*Lobio Pkhali*): Use 3 cups cooked red beans, mashing half of the beans to blend with the walnut sauce.

Georgian Green Bean Salad (*Mtsvani Lobio Pkhali*): Use 1 1/2 pounds green beans, trimmed, cooked until crisp-tender, patted dry, and chopped. If desired, add 1 to 2 tablespoons chopped fresh dill.

Georgian Cabbage Salad (*Kombosta Pkhali*): Use 3 cups shredded cabbage (about 8 ounces), sautéed in 3 tablespoons olive oil until tender, about 10 minutes.

Georgian Eggplant Salad (*Badrijani Pkhali*): Use 1 large (about 1 3/4 pounds) eggplant, roasted, peeled, and mashed. (See page 246, Step 1, for instructions on how to roast eggplant.)

Georgian Spinach Salad (*Isanakhi Pkhali*): Use 3 cups finely chopped cooked spinach (2 pounds raw).

SYRIAN BULGUR RELISH

Bazargan

ABOUT 2 CUPS, OR 5 TO 6 SERVINGS

The name of this spicy dip means "of the bazaar," because the ingredients are historically common in Syrian international marketplaces. Serve as an appetizer with pita bread or crackers, or as a side dish. The fruity, tart flavor may be a bit intense for those accustomed to mild spreads. Use less tamarind sauce or pomegranate concentrate for a milder relish. You can transform bazargan *into a salad by adding chopped bell peppers or dried fruit and stirring in the optional onion.*

1 cup (6 ounces) fine-grain bulgur wheat
2 cups cold water

DRESSING:
$^1/_2$ cup finely chopped walnuts or pistachio nuts
$^1/_4$ to $^1/_2$ cup Syrian Mock Tamarind Sauce
   (page 436); 2 tablespoons prune butter and
   2 tablespoons apricot butter; or 3 tablespoons
   pomegranate concentrate (see page 22)
$^1/_4$ cup fresh lemon juice
3 tablespoons tomato paste
2 tablespoons olive oil
2 tablespoons chopped fresh parsley
1 to 2 teaspoons ground cumin
About 1 teaspoon table salt or 2 teaspoons
   kosher salt
About $^1/_4$ teaspoon ground black pepper or cayenne

1 small onion, finely chopped or grated or
   1 tablespoon pine nuts for garnish (optional)

1. Put the bulgur in a medium bowl, pour in the water, and let stand until tender, about 30 minutes. Drain in a sieve, pressing out any excess water with the back of a large spoon. Transfer to a medium bowl.

2. In a small bowl, combine all the dressing ingredients. Pour over the bulgur and toss to coat. Cover and refrigerate for at least 2 hours to let the flavors meld. Store in the refrigerator, without the onion, for up to 5 days, or in the freezer for 3 months. Serve chilled or at room temperature. Mix well before serving. If desired, sprinkle with the onion or pine nuts.

Turkish Red Pepper Relish

Muhammara

ABOUT 3 CUPS, OR 6 TO 8 SERVINGS

Originally, this tangy bell pepper spread was pounded in a mortar with a pestle; a food processor now makes the task much easier. There are several variations of this meze *favorite, most containing walnuts and bread. Serve as an appetizer with pita bread or crackers.*

2¹/₂ pounds (about 5 large) red bell peppers

1¹/₂ cups (6 ounces) chopped walnuts

¹/₂ cup fine fresh bread crumbs, fine fresh whole-
   wheat pita crumbs, or wheat cracker crumbs

About ¹/₂ cup extra-virgin olive oil

2 to 3 tablespoons pomegranate concentrate
   (see page 22)

1 tablespoon fresh lemon or lime juice

1 to 2 cloves garlic, minced

1 to 3 small hot red chilies, minced,
   or ¹/₄ to ¹/₂ teaspoon red pepper flakes

¹/₂ to 1 teaspoon ground cumin

1 teaspoon sugar

About ³/₄ teaspoon table salt or 1¹/₂ teaspoons
   kosher salt

¹/₄ cup chopped fresh cilantro or parsley for garnish

2 tablespoons toasted pine nuts (see page 22)
   for garnish

1. To roast the peppers: Place a wire rack over the top of a gas burner and place the peppers on the rack over the fire, or hold the pepper with tongs. Turn the pepper until the skin blackens and blisters, about 3 minutes. Or, place the peppers under a broiler 2 inches from the heat, turning every 4 to 5 minutes, until charred, about 15 minutes. Wrap in paper towels, enclose in a brown paper bag, or place in a bowl and cover. Let stand until the skin peels off easily, about 15 minutes. Rub off the skin. Do not rinse under water, which removes much of the flavor. Discard the stems and seeds.

2. In a food processor or a mortar, grind the nuts and bread crumbs until smooth. Add the peppers, oil, pomegranate concentrate, lemon juice, garlic, chili, cumin, sugar, and salt and process into a thick, creamy paste, adding a little more oil, if necessary, to thin it to the desired consistency. Cover and refrigerate overnight or up to 1 week. Sprinkle with the cilantro and pine nuts.

MOROCCAN EGGPLANT RELISH

Kahrmus

ABOUT 3 CUPS, OR 5 TO 6 SERVINGS   P

In this spicy version of eggplant spread, the ingredients are cooked until thickened. This relish is good warm, but even better after mellowing for several hours. Serve with bread or crackers.

2 eggplants (about 1 pound each)

1/4 cup olive oil

1 large onion, chopped

2 to 3 cloves garlic, minced

About 1 pound plum tomatoes, peeled, seeded, and chopped (2 cups); see page 291

2 tablespoons red wine vinegar or fresh lemon juice

1 to 2 teaspoons ground cumin

1/2 teaspoon sweet paprika

About 1/8 teaspoon cayenne

About 1/2 teaspoon table salt or 1 teaspoon kosher salt

About 1/2 teaspoon ground black pepper

Pinch of sugar or drop of honey

Black olives for garnish (optional)

1. To roast the eggplant: Light a fire in a charcoal grill, preheat the broiler, or preheat the oven to 400°F. Cut several slits in the eggplants. Roast over hot coals or 5 inches from the heat source of the broiler, turning occasionally, until charred and tender, about 40 minutes. Or place on a baking sheet and roast in the oven until very tender, about 50 minutes. Let cool until able to handle. Peel the eggplants, being careful not to leave any skin. Coarsely chop the eggplant, place in a colander, and let drain for about 30 minutes.

2. In a large saucepan, heat the oil over medium heat. Add the onion and garlic and sauté until soft and translucent, about 5 minutes.

3. Stir in the eggplant, tomatoes, vinegar, cumin, paprika, cayenne, salt, pepper, and sugar. Cook over medium-low heat, stirring frequently, until thickened, about 10 minutes. Serve warm or at room temperature. If desired, garnish with the olives.

TUNISIAN ZUCCHINI RELISH

Ajluk de Courgettes

ABOUT 3½ CUPS, OR 4 TO 5 SERVINGS

An ajluk *is a northern Tunisian relish made from boiled vegetables highly seasoned with lemon juice, spices, and chili. The result is reminiscent of an Indian chutney. Zucchini (*qura *in Arabic and* courgettes *in French) is a particular favorite for this dish, as is eggplant, zucchini-and-eggplant, and pumpkin. Moroccans enjoy a similar dish called* zaalouk, *which is seasoned with cumin and paprika instead of caraway and coriander. These relishes are traditional on Sukkot as a symbol of the harvest, and on other special occasions as part of a Tunisian* meze, *served with pita bread or crackers, or as an accompaniment to couscous.*

1½ pounds small or medium zucchini

DRESSING:

3 to 4 cloves garlic

About 1 teaspoon table salt or 2 teaspoons
   kosher salt

2 teaspoons caraway seeds, ground

1 to 2 teaspoons coriander seeds, ground

About 3 tablespoons fresh lemon juice
   (about 1 large lemon)

1 to 2 teaspoons *harissa* (Northwest African
   Chili Paste, page 433)

About 3 tablespoons extra-virgin olive oil for
   drizzling

1. Bring a large pot of lightly salted water to a boil, add the zucchini, and boil until very soft, about 15 minutes. There should be no crispness left in the squash. Drain, place in a colander, and gently press out the excess moisture. Transfer the zucchini to a bowl and coarsely mash.

2. To make the dressing: Using the tip of a heavy knife or with a mortar and pestle, mash the garlic and salt into a paste. In a small bowl, combine the garlic, caraway, and coriander. Stir in the lemon juice and harissa.

3. Stir the dressing into the zucchini. Cover and refrigerate for at least 3 hours or up to 3 days. Spoon onto a serving plate and drizzle with the oil.

VARIATIONS

Tunisian Eggplant Spread (*Ajluk de Aubergines***):** Substitute 2 pounds peeled and cubed eggplant for the zucchini, boiling it until very soft, about 25 minutes.

Tunisian Pumpkin Spread (*Ajluk de Potiron***):** Substitute 2 pounds peeled, seeded, and cubed pumpkin for the zucchini.

Yemenite Fenugreek Relish

Hilbeh

ABOUT ¹/₂ CUP

Yemenites enjoy the spicy, balsamiclike bitter flavor and jellylike texture of hilbeh, *arguably the source of their longevity and good health (fenugreek purportedly lowers cholesterol, reduces inflammation, and soothes the throat and gastrointestinal lining), at every meal of the day.* Hilbeh *has an almost gelatin-like consistency, with an odor and flavor reminiscent of caramelized sugar and vanilla. It is always made fiery—the intensity as well as the color determined by the amount of green chilies and the optional addition of tomato.* Hilbeh *is used as an all-purpose condiment, much in the manner of salsa or Indian chutney; as a dip and bread spread; and to add texture and flavor to soups and stews. Serve with pita bread,* melawah *(Yemenite Flaky Pancake Bread, page 192),* jihnun *(Yemenite Baked Flaky Rolls, page 191),* kubaneh *(overnight Sabbath bread),* falafel *(Middle Eastern Chickpea Fritters, page 325), hard-boiled eggs, and various light dishes.*

> 3 tablespoons fenugreek seeds or 2 tablespoons ground fenugreek
>
> 2 cups cold water, plus more if needed
>
> 1 to 2 teaspoons *z'chug* (Yemenite Chili Paste, page 438) or 1 to 3 small hot green chilies
>
> About ¹/₂ teaspoon table salt or 1 teaspoon kosher salt
>
> 2 to 4 tablespoons fresh lemon juice
>
> About ¹/₄ cup water

1. If using fenugreek seeds, grind them to a fine powder in a mortar. Put the ground fenugreek in a large bowl, add the 2 cups water, stir well, and let soak for at least 3 hours or preferably overnight. The fenugreek will expand and develop a jellylike consistency. Soaking removes some of the bitterness. Carefully pour off the water. The fenugreek gelatinizes, so the water will pour off rather easily.

2. With a mortar and pestle or in a small food processor, process the fenugreek, chili paste, and salt into a paste. Transfer to a medium bowl and, using a wooden spoon, gradually beat in the lemon juice and enough water to produce a smooth mixture with the consistency of mayonnaise, 5 to 10 minutes. Or in the food processor with the machine on, gradually add the juice and water. Cover and store in the refrigerator for up to 1 week. If it becomes too firm, beat in a little more water.

VARIATIONS

Spicy Fenugreek Relish (*Hilbeh*): Omit the lemon juice and ¹/₄ cup water. Grind with the fenugreek 4 black cardamom pods or 8 green cardamom pods, 1 teaspoon caraway seeds, ¹/₂ teaspoon coriander seeds, and 2 to 3 cloves garlic. Add 1 cup plum tomatoes puréed in a food processor or blender and strained.

Indian Fenugreek Relish (*Halba*): Yemenite Jews introduced *hilbeh* to the Jews of southern India. The Indian Jews, of course, added their own special touches. Add ¹/₄ to ¹/₂ cup chopped cilantro, 1 teaspoon grated fresh ginger, and 1 to 3 minced cloves garlic.

SALADS

❦ · ❦

Few vegetables were eaten raw by peoples of the ancient Middle East. Those that were, such as lettuce, chate melons (similar to cucumbers), onions, and black radishes—initially always eaten separately from each other—would first be sprinkled with salt or brine to tame the bitterness and add flavor. The Roman term for these raw lettuce dishes, *herba salata* ("salted greens"), gave rise to the English word *salad*. By the time of imperial Rome, the lettuce was also being moistened and flavored with olive oil and wine vinegar. Further innovation was inevitable, as people devised new ways of flavoring greens with various herbs, spices, and nuts and increasingly adding other raw vegetables. During the Middle Ages, the number of cold vegetable dishes in the Mediterranean greatly expanded because of the widespread medieval belief that eating cool, moist foods counteracted unpleasant digestive effects created by hot, dry weather. The components of what was considered a salad, therefore, changed to incorporate a wide array of vegetables, legumes, and sometimes fruit.

The Romans introduced the idea of a set order of courses, including small portions of foods at the beginning of a meal to arouse the appetite and, at the end, lettuce to aid digestion—still a common practice in European countries such as France and Italy. Eventually, lettuce developed the reputation of being an appetite stimulator and, during the reign of Domitian (81–96 C.E.), the Romans switched all salads to the start of the meal. In the Middle East and Far East, however, salads were (and still are) commonly served as an accompaniment to the meal itself, or as part of a *meze* (appetizer assortment) at the beginning of the meal, not as a separate course. Usually, the salad appetizers remained on the table during the meal as side dishes, further blurring the distinction between salads and other vegetable dishes.

Because of prohibitions against cooking and heating on the Sabbath, cold vegetable salads, made without raw leafy greens, which easily wilted, and commonly flavored with vinegar as a preservative and a touch of honey or sugar to counteract the acid, became prevalent among Mediterranean and Middle Eastern Jews. Because hospitality was always an integral part of Jewish life, a host had to have plenty of cold dishes on hand during the Sabbath, for both invited and unexpected guests. No Sephardic meal is considered complete without at least one and generally several salads, consisting not only of greens, but also of various raw and cooked vegetables, legumes, and grains.

On the other hand, Ashkenazic cookery, which developed in a northern climate, eschewed raw leafy greens—any that grew there were generally cooked—and featured very few raw vegetable dishes, except for those made with black radishes or cucumbers. Most Polish "salads" and appetizers were based on eggs and fish or made from cooked or pickled vegetables, such as beets and cabbage. Ashkenazim living further south, in Hungary, Romania, and Ukraine, enjoyed a much wider variety of salads, including those made with bell peppers, tomatoes, and eggplant.

There is some overlap as to what is called a salad and what is a dip, relish, or spread. Often, the same foods appear in different guises: Sliced cucumbers in yogurt constitutes a salad, but if the cucumbers are finely chopped, it serves as a relish or a dip. A Sephardic cook would not be concerned with such classifications; what was important on the Sabbath and other special occasions was to have a variety of chopped, marinated, mashed, and pickled dishes that would complement each other when eaten together. Likewise, a salad, relish, or dip would go equally well with bread for a simple, everyday meal. On the other hand, Ashkenazim historically tended to feature a single salad per meal, called a *forspeis* (Yiddish for "before food").

What the salads in this book share is the presence of oil and vinegar or lemon juice, usually in the form of a dressing, which flavors and melds the disparate ingredients. Sephardic dressings typically consist of olive oil and lemon juice or wine vinegar, sometimes spiced with ground cumin. Other main ingredients in Sephardic dressings reflect an Arabic influence, including tahini, yogurt, and chilies. Ashkenazim, for dairy meals, frequently dress the vegetables with sour cream; on other occasions they would sprinkle vegetables with salt and maybe vinegar but rarely with oil, which until recently was scarce and expensive in northern Europe.

Unlike the pickles and relishes (covered in the preceding chapter), these salads are eaten either fresh or within a day or two of preparation. This chapter's salads are organized by their main ingredients: leafy greens, raw vegetables and fruit, cooked vegetables, legumes, and grains.

LETTUCE AND OTHER LEAFY GREENS

The Talmud lists five items that could be used for the bitter herb (*maror*) of the Passover Seder: *chazeret* (romaine lettuce), *ulshin* (endive or chicory), *tamchah* (horehound or another type of lettuce), *charchevina* (possibly *eryngo*, a perennial herb thistle that grows up to 3 feet in the dry soils of fields and rocky places around the Mediterranean), and *maror* (possibly a type of cilantro or a wild lettuce). The Talmud enumerates the characteristic features that any bitter herb possesses—"white sap and . . . a pale (grayish) green appearance"—and concludes that the five forms are listed in order of preference, romaine lettuce being the most preferable vegetable. The Sages explain, "Just as lettuce is first sweet (when young), then bitter (as it matures), so was the behavior of the Egyptians to our ancestors."

Throughout history, most cultures praised the digestive benefits of eating leafy greens, particularly lettuce, which was originally culled wild from the fields during the spring and first cultivated in ancient Egypt.

Rudimentary lettuce consisted of an elongated central stalk sporting loose, prickly red-tinged dark green leaves. The ribs contained a considerable amount of white latex sap, hence the plant's Latin name, *lactuca* (milky). At first, lettuce was favored as much for the oil obtained from its seeds as for the leaves, which were bitter, particularly when mature, sometimes requiring boiling to be edible.

Even after the advent of lettuce cultivation, the vegetable was difficult and costly to grow out of season and remained a luxury for most people except during the spring. It was the Romans who developed the now-common head lettuce, as well as several less bitter varieties, which they spread through much of the empire. The Romans also discovered methods to grow lettuce and some other favorite vegetables throughout the year, turning salads into a daily component of the Mediterranean diet.

Sephardim and Italians used romaine lettuce and other leafy greens not only for the Seder, but also in seasonal salads. In a 1513 trial of the Spanish Inquisition, one of the allegations of continued practice of Judaism by a former maid against the accused was that "she gave us lettuce and radishes and cheese and cress."

Raw vegetables, especially greens, were viewed far less favorably in northern Europe. Although lettuce was among the vegetables grown in Charlemagne's gardens, it was rarely sold in the markets of that time; watercress was the more common green and was generally eaten cooked. Beginning in the medieval period, the conventional wisdom in much of Europe was that raw greens were for animals and not only lacked nutrition, but rotted in the intestines like a compost heap. Indeed, one seventeenth-century English cookbook was called scandalous for promoting the consumption of salads. This debate was often a matter of mere rhetoric, for lettuce was rarely available in those northern climates for much of the year, if at all. Thus, Ashkenazim were generally forced to substitute readily available horseradish root, although its taste was fiery rather than bitter, for the bitter green at the Seder.

Lettuce

The hundreds of varieties of lettuce (an annual plant) are divided into four groups: loose leaf, butterhead, crisphead, and romaine. Loose-leaf lettuces (such as green oak leaf and red leaf), like their rudimentary ancestor, have leaves that do not form a head but grow loosely from the stem; their mild-flavored leaves may be large and smooth or narrow and frilly. Butterheads (such as Boston and Bibb), as the name indicates, possess a delicate and buttery flavor, with soft leaves formed into loose heads, which are whitish-green near the center and dark green near the outside. Crisphead lettuce, called Batavian lettuce in England, forms compact heads of crisp leaves; its most notable variety is iceberg, first introduced in 1894. The Moors brought lettuce to Spain and were credited with developing the modern form of romaine, with its loose head of milder, elongated, upright leaves.

Other Greens

Arugula, also called roquette and rocket, was popular in salads as far back as Roman times and is probably the wild plant mentioned in 2 Kings 4:39. Although never very popular in the Arabic world, arugula is well loved in western Europe and especially among Sephardim. The elongated emerald green leaves and the four-petaled white flowers have a slightly piquant, mustardlike flavor that mixes well with milder greens. The flavor is stronger in the summer than in springtime. Look for smooth, young leaves whose edges are not yet fully notched, preferably with the roots attached. Avoid leaves that show traces of yellow.

Dandelion leaves (from the Latin *dens leonis,* or "lion's teeth," referring to the jagged edges of the leaves) have long been used in cooking throughout Asia and Europe; the young leaves are crisp, slightly bitter, and very nutritious. Choose small, thin-stemmed organic leaves with a bright green color. Avoid wilted or yellow leaves. Unlike most greens, dandelion greens should be stored in a plastic bag in the refrigerator for several days before using, which mellows their bitterness slightly. Dandelion may be substituted for chicory, endive, escarole, or arugula in most recipes. It is generally available from March through May and September through October.

Chicory and endive, two close relatives, have long been confused with each other. The original chicory, which still grows wild in parts of Israel, is much like wild lettuce in appearance. Endive, although very similar to chicory, was developed into a distinct species during prehistoric times. Modern chicory forms loose heads of narrow, ragged-edged dark green leaves that become white near the heart; these center leaves are milder than the slightly bitter outer ones. In addition to the original wild endive plant, two subspecies of endive have developed: curly endive and escarole. Curly endive, which has loose, narrow, curly, light-green leaves, is also called frisée (French for "curly"). Escarole, also called scarole, broadleaf endive, and Batavian endive, has flat, broad, dark-green leaves that form a loose head. The least bitter member of the chicory family, it has a milder flavor and coarser texture than curly endive, and Europeans use it in soups as well as salads. Belgian endives are the yellow shoots of chicory grown in darkness.

Radicchio, also called red chicory, is another member of the chicory family, with a slightly bitter flavor similar to escarole. The Verona variety, most common in America, has a small head of roundish leaves with a deep-red color. Domestically grown radicchio is generally more bitter than Italian. The small, tight heads have red and white leaves that are a favorite for salads and may be used as elegant serving bowls and for garnishes. In central Italy, this chicory is used to stuff ravioli or to mix into risotto. Raddicchio becomes sweeter during cooking, but loses much of its color. Adding a little red wine helps to maintain the redness.

Borage, a native of the eastern Mediterranean, is primarily used in stews and salads, as well as medicinally. The name derives from the Arabic *abu buraq* ("father of sweat"), referring to its diaphoretic properties. The wrinkled green leaves, which grow up to 4 inches in length, have a cucumberlike taste. Use only the young leaves in salads and cooking.

Mâche has small, round, smooth, dark green leaves. It is a favorite of grazing sheep, thus its other name, lamb's lettuce. Mâche has gained great popularity in Europe because of its firm texture and mild, nutty flavor. Due to its mild flavor, it is best served with a mild dressing.

Watercress, possibly a native of Turkey, is not a true cress but a member of the Cruciferae family. Generally sold by the bunch, it has small, dark green leaves that give a peppery flavor to salads, sandwiches, and soups.

ITALIAN MIXED GREENS

Insalate Verde/Misticanza

6 TO 8 SERVINGS

For centuries, southern Europeans made salads from mixed lettuces and tender, small-leafed greens of various shapes, colors, and flavors (piquant, bitter, peppery, and mild). The Italians call this combination mista *("mixed") or* misticanza, *and it generally consists of about five parts lettuce to four parts other greens, including green chicory and radicchio. The French version is called* mesclun *(Provençal for "mixed"), and it typically combines two parts lettuce (including Red Salad Bowl or oak leaf, romaine, and Lollo Rossa and Lollo Biondo) to one part bitter greens, such as arugula, frisée, mizuna, and tatsoi. Mesclun niçoise is a sharper mix made up of equal parts lettuce and bitter greens, arugula, curly endive, dandelion leaves, broadleaf cress, and spadona chicory.*

This basic Italian green salad can be varied by availability of the greens and personal preference. Plan on 3 to 4 ounces (about $1^1/3$ cups) of mixed leafy greens per person as a first course. For 8 cups of greens, use a 4-quart salad bowl. Italians prefer a pronounced flavor of olive oil in the dressing with only a note of acid, about 1 part vinegar to 3 parts oil, unlike the Arabic style favoring a larger proportion of acid. For freshness, always dress salad greens just before serving. In addition, Italians lightly dress, not drench, the salad, allowing the flavor of the greens to prevail. Misticanza would typically be part of a Sabbath lunch with riso del sabato *(Sabbath saffron rice) and onion focaccia.*

Leaves from I small head (about 8 ounces) butterhead lettuce, such as Boston or Bibb, torn into bite-sized pieces

Leaves from I small head (about 8 ounces) escarole or curly endive, torn into bite-sized pieces

Leaves from I small head (about 8 ounces) romaine or red leaf lettuce, torn into bite-sized pieces

I bunch (about 8 ounces) arugula or watercress, torn into bite-sized pieces

$^1/2$ cup chopped mixed fresh herbs, such as basil, chervil, chives, dill, parsley, and tarragon

VINAIGRETTE:

I small clove garlic

About $^1/2$ teaspoon table salt or I teaspoon kosher salt

About $^1/8$ teaspoon ground black pepper

2 teaspoons Dijon mustard or $^1/2$ teaspoon dry mustard (optional)

3 tablespoons red or white wine vinegar or 2 tablespoons red wine vinegar and I tablespoon fresh lemon juice

I shallot, minced

$^1/2$ cup extra-virgin olive oil or $^1/4$ cup olive oil and $^1/4$ cup vegetable oil

In a large bowl, mix together the greens and herbs. To make the vinaigrette: Using the tip of a heavy knife or with a mortar and pestle, mash the garlic and salt into a paste. In a small bowl, combine the garlic, pepper, and mustard, if using. Stir in the vinegar and shallot. In a slow, steady stream, whisk in the oil. Drizzle the vinaigrette over the greens and toss well to coat.

VARIATIONS

Italian Escarole and Orange Salad (*Scarola a Insalata*): Omit the butterhead lettuce, romaine lettuce, arugula, and herbs and increase the escarole to 4 bunches. Add 4 to 5 peeled and segmented large seedless oranges and garnish the salad with ¹/₂ cup toasted sliced almonds.

Sephardic Arugula Salad (*Salata de Rocca*): Omit the butterhead lettuce, escarole, and romaine lettuce, increase the arugula to 3 bunches (about 24 ounces), and use 1 cup chopped parsley or watercress for the herbs. Add 1 large red onion, cut into rings.

Egyptian Arugula Salad (*Salata al-Girgir*): Follow the directions for Sephardic Arugula Salad, but substitute 6 quartered plum tomatoes for the onion.

MIDDLE EASTERN DANDELION SALAD

Salata Hindba

6 TO 8 SERVINGS   Ⓟ

Although fresh spinach salads have become widespread in America, many other traditional Old World greens are still ignored, including dandelion greens. In parts of the Mediterranean, dandelion salad is a common spring or late-summer dish; the leaves must be picked before the plant flowers and turns overly bitter. Italians and Greeks use the leaves in salads during the Passover holiday. Raw dandelion, a diuretic, is considered excellent for internal cleansing. Lemon juice is commonly used in dandelion salads, as it mellows some of the bitter taste.

Some people cook the leaves, which remove much of the bitterness, but I enjoy combining the dandelion's slightly bitter raw leaves with milder greens

such as mâche or romaine lettuce. Dandelion salad is frequently garnished with foods that provide contrasting flavors, most notably sliced hard-boiled eggs, black olives, or grapefruit or mandarin orange segments.

- 1¹/₂ pounds (about 14 cups) young dandelion leaves, or 12 ounces dandelion leaves and 12 ounces mâche or romaine lettuce, torn into bite-sized pieces
- 1 to 2 cups coarsely chopped tomatoes
- 1 red onion, halved and thinly sliced

DRESSING:

- 1 clove garlic
- About ¹/₂ teaspoon table salt or 1 teaspoon kosher salt
- 2 to 4 tablespoons fresh lemon juice or red wine vinegar
- Ground black pepper to taste
- 1 small chili, seeded and minced (optional)
- ¹/₄ cup extra-virgin olive oil

In a large bowl, combine the dandelion greens, tomatoes, and onion. To make the dressing: Using the tip of a heavy knife or with a mortar and pestle, mash the garlic and salt into a paste. In a small bowl, combine the garlic, lemon juice, pepper, and the chili, if using. In a slow, steady stream, whisk in the oil. Drizzle over the vegetables and toss to coat. Serve immediately.

VARIATIONS

Greek Dandelion Salad (*Horta*): Add 16 to 18 black olives and 1¹/₂ cups marinated artichoke hearts or 8 ounces crumbled feta or goat cheese.

Iraqi Dandelion with Yogurt Salad (*Salata Hindba ma Laban*): Omit the tomatoes. Add 3 to 4 cups plain yogurt and 1 cup chopped fresh cilantro. Chill before serving.

Italian Dandelion, Fennel, and Radish Salad (*Insalata di Cicoria*): Omit the tomatoes and onion and add 2 small fennel bulbs cut into thin slices, 6 to 8 sliced red radishes, and ¼ cup chopped fresh basil or chives.

Romanian Dandelion Salad (*Salata de Papadie*): Add 1 tablespoon chopped fresh dill.

Syrian Spinach Salad (*Salata Sabanigh*): Substitute 1½ pounds stemmed spinach for the dandelion. If desired, substitute 1 cup coarsely chopped walnuts and ½ cup pomegranate seeds for the tomatoes.

Moroccan Greens with Orange Salad

Salata Khus w'Portughal

5 TO 6 SERVINGS

This delicate salad is just lightly dressed orange slices with greens, but the dressing gives the dish a unique and very Moroccan flavor. (Combining oranges with greens is an old Sephardic practice.) Sephardim typically serve this as a refreshing end to a rich meal, most notably the Passover Seder.

Blood oranges look especially stunning on the plate. I like to arrange the orange slices in an overlapping circle, but you can also toss them with the greens. Moroccans also prepare the salad without the greens, accenting the oranges with a sprinkling of black olives, radishes, or dates.

Leaves from 1 head romaine lettuce, torn into pieces, or 1 bunch arugula or stemmed watercress, or any combination

4 blood oranges or navel oranges, chilled, peeled, excess pith removed, and sliced crosswise

DRESSING:

¼ cup fresh orange juice

2 tablespoons fresh lemon juice

1 teaspoon grated orange zest

About 1 teaspoon table salt or 2 teaspoons kosher salt

1 to 3 tablespoons honey or sugar (optional)

1 tablespoon orange blossom water (optional)

1 teaspoon ground cinnamon, ¼ cup chopped fresh spearmint, or ¼ cup chopped fresh cilantro (optional)

½ cup argan oil (see Note), or ¼ cup olive oil and ¼ cup peanut oil

1. Arrange the greens on chilled individual serving plates or on a platter. Divide the orange slices among the serving plates or arrange in overlapping sections on the platter.

2. To make the dressing: In a small bowl, combine the juices, zest, salt, and optional honey, orange blossom water, and cinnamon. In a slow, steady stream, whisk in the oil. Drizzle the dressing over the oranges. Let stand for about 10 minutes before serving.

VARIATIONS

Israeli Orange, Red Onion, and Avocado Salad (*Salat Tapuz*): An Israeli adaptation of the Moroccan standard: Add 2 thinly sliced red onions and 2 peeled, pitted, and sliced avocados.

Moroccan Orange and Radish Salad (*Salata Latsheen wa Fijil*): Omit the sugar and add 2 bunches (about 12 ounces) red radishes, coarsely grated or thinly sliced.

Moroccan Orange and Black Olive Salad (*Salata Zeitoon*): Omit the sugar. Add to the dressing 2 to 3 minced cloves garlic, 1 teaspoon ground cumin, and a pinch of cayenne or 2 teaspoons sweet paprika. Scatter 1 cup pitted and halved oil-cured black olives and, if desired, 1 chopped red onion over the oranges.

Moroccan Orange and Date Salad (*Salata Latsheen wa Tamir*): Add 1$^1/_2$ cups coarsely chopped pitted dates and $^1/_2$ cup coarsely chopped toasted almonds or $^1/_4$ cup chopped pistachio nuts.

N O T E The thorny evergreen argan tree (*Argania spinosa*, also called ironwood), which grows only in southwestern Morocco, bears almond-shaped nuts containing a dark amber-colored oil rich in antioxidants and flavonoids. Used in cosmetics and medicine as well as cooking, argan oil has a long shelf life (at least 18 months) and high smoking point (420°F). It has a uniquely subtle, nutty, slightly fruity flavor and a rich, velvety texture, and is used as a dip for bread as well as a traditional flavoring in many Moroccan salads, soups, *tagines*, and vegetable dishes. Argan oil is usually paired with lemon juice, which enhances its distinctive flavor. Imported argan oil, unrefined and cold-pressed, is available from specialty stores and distributors. Look for it in Middle Eastern grocery stores or well-stocked ethnic markets.

ORANGES

During much of the Middle Ages, Sephardim and other Jewish communities were the primary growers of citrus fruit in the Mediterranean—a situation that developed out of the need for *etrogs* (citron) for the Sukkot ritual. As a result, oranges found their way into Sephardic cooking early on.

Today, there are more than two thousand orange varieties, of which about one hundred are cultivated on a major scale. Sweet oranges (*Citrus sinensis*) are divided into three types: common (including Valencia and Jaffa), navel, and blood. Blood, or pigmented, oranges have long been prized in the Mediterranean, where they comprise one-third of all cultivated oranges, for their intense color and deep flavor. They are generally small, seedless oranges with a deeper flavor and redder color than other sweet oranges. Full blood oranges have red skin and red flesh; semiblood oranges have orange skin and red flesh. The degree of redness depends on the variety and climate, with hotter climates producing deeper colors and a sweeter flavor.

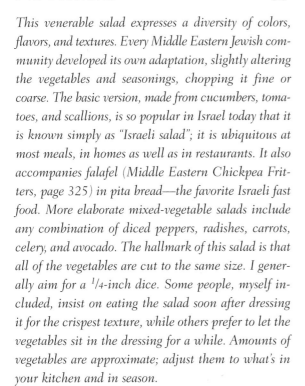

RAW VEGETABLE AND FRUIT SALADS

MIDDLE EASTERN MIXED VEGETABLE SALAD

Michoteta

5 TO 6 SERVINGS   Ⓟ

This venerable salad expresses a diversity of colors, flavors, and textures. Every Middle Eastern Jewish community developed its own adaptation, slightly altering the vegetables and seasonings, chopping it fine or coarse. The basic version, made from cucumbers, tomatoes, and scallions, is so popular in Israel today that it is known simply as "Israeli salad"; it is ubiquitous at most meals, in homes as well as in restaurants. It also accompanies falafel (Middle Eastern Chickpea Fritters, page 325) in pita bread—the favorite Israeli fast food. More elaborate mixed-vegetable salads include any combination of diced peppers, radishes, carrots, celery, and avocado. The hallmark of this salad is that all of the vegetables are cut to the same size. I generally aim for a ¼-inch dice. Some people, myself included, insist on eating the salad soon after dressing it for the crispest texture, while others prefer to let the vegetables sit in the dressing for a while. Amounts of vegetables are approximate; adjust them to what's in your kitchen and in season.

2 regular cucumbers or 6 Kirby cucumbers, diced (about 3 cups)

21 ounces ripe but firm plum tomatoes, diced (about 3 cups)

1 each green, red, and yellow bell pepper, seeded, deribbed (white removed), and diced

8 to 10 scallions, sliced, or 1 red or white onion, diced

1 cup peeled and diced white radish, such as daikon or icicle, or 6 to 8 red radishes, diced (optional)

¼ cup extra-virgin olive oil

2 to 3 tablespoons fresh lemon juice or red wine vinegar

3 tablespoons chopped fresh parsley or spearmint, or *za'atar* (Middle Eastern "Hyssop" Mixture, page 436) to taste

1 clove garlic, minced (optional)

About ½ teaspoon table salt or 1 teaspoon kosher salt

Ground black pepper to taste

1 head romaine lettuce or 1 pound fresh spinach, washed, dried, stemmed, and torn into bite-sized pieces for garnish (optional)

1 cup brine-cured black olives, such as Kalamata, pitted (optional)

3 tablespoons capers, drained (optional)

1. In a large bowl, mix together all the ingredients except the lettuce, olives, and capers. Serve immediately or let it sit at room temperature for up to 1 hour. (Do not refrigerate, as cold temperatures destroy the flavor and texture of fresh tomatoes.)

2. If using, arrange the lettuce on a large serving platter and spread the salad over the lettuce. If desired, sprinkle with the olives or capers.

Calcutta Mixed Vegetable Salad (*Michoteta*): Add 1 seeded and minced fresh green chili and about 1 teaspoon minced fresh ginger.

Greek Mixed Vegetable Salad (*Horiataki Salata*): Add about 10 ounces (2 cups) crumbled feta cheese.

Azerbaijani Mixed Vegetable Salad (*Salata Bahar*): This is the most popular salad on the Azerbaijani Jewish table. Cooks are rated on how finely and evenly they chop the vegetables, transforming the salad into an art. In America, Azerbaijani immigrants adopted the practice of garnishing the salad with a rose-shaped red radish. To make *salata bahar*, finely chop all the vegetables. Garnish with red onion slices and quartered hard-boiled eggs.

MIDDLE EASTERN SALADS

The *michoteta* (diced mixed salad) is so popular that Middle Easterners have enjoyed it on almost a daily basis for millennia. Originally, since few vegetables were eaten raw and vegetables were highly seasonal, salads could only be made at certain times of the year, primarily the spring and summer. The Romans developed methods to produce some of these vegetables out of season, but it was the medieval Arabs whose agronomic improvements first made several growing seasons in a single year possible for the average farmer, allowing many fresh vegetables to be available year-round. Since then, the Middle Eastern *suq* (marketplace) has been continuously filled with a wide variety of fresh produce, which inevitably goes into mixed salads—called *salatat al-khudra* ("salad of the vegetable market") in Syria and, in Greece, variously *angourodomatosalata* ("salad of the vegetable market"), *horiataki salata* ("country salad"), and *elleniki salata* ("Greek salad"). The first such salad consisted of chate melons, onions, and radishes and dates back to the time of the pharaohs. The Indian cucumber then arrived in the early medieval period and supplanted the chate melon. Later, the arrival of American bell peppers and tomatoes in the Middle East led to their inclusion and, in many areas, substitution for some of the classic vegetables.

BUKHARAN TOMATO SALAD

Banadora

5 TO 6 SERVINGS

I only make this salad between June and October, when locally grown vine-ripened tomatoes are abundant. When possible, I buy tomatoes at a farmers' market; the difference in flavor is well worth any extra effort. (If you grow your own, even better.) As a Bukharan cook from Queens, New York once explained to me when I asked why her tomato salad was so much more flavorful than most: "Ripe tomatoes are meant to burst to release their seeds, which is not the state in which stores want them." Because ripe tomatoes get damaged or become moldy during transportation and storage, the tomatoes available in most American stores are picked when green, then sprayed with ethylene gas, which induces them to turn red, but without acquiring a ripe flavor. In addition, during handling, tomatoes are frequently subjected to temperatures below 55°F, which destroys the ripening enzyme, and results in a woolly textured, flavorless tomato. Don't purchase tomatoes that have been chilled, and don't store this salad in a refrigerator. In fact, this salad is best when the tomatoes are sliced just before serving. Banadora might be served as a side dish or as part of a summer lunch, along with hard cheese and flat bread.

2 pounds ripe but firm tomatoes, seeded and diced (about 5 cups); see page 291
2 green bell peppers, seeded, deribbed (white removed), and diced
6 to 8 scallions, sliced, or 1 white or red onion, finely chopped
2 to 4 tablespoons chopped fresh parsley or cilantro
3/4 cup vegetable oil or extra-virgin olive oil
1/3 cup red wine vinegar or fresh lemon juice
About 1/2 teaspoon table salt or 1 teaspoon kosher salt
Ground black pepper to taste
1 clove garlic, minced (optional)

In a large bowl, combine all the ingredients. Serve immediately or let stand at room temperature for up to 1 hour. Do not refrigerate.

VARIATIONS

Indian Tomato Salad (*Kuccha*): Substitute 1 to 2 seeded and minced hot green chilies for the bell peppers.

Moroccan Tomato Salad (*Shlata bi Matesha*): Omit the bell peppers and add 3/4 to 1 cup coarsely chopped green olives and 2 tablespoons capers.

Israeli Tomato Salad (*Salat Ahgvaniyah*): Add 1 peeled, pitted, and diced ripe avocado, 2 tablespoons chopped fresh basil, and 1 minced clove garlic.

INDIAN CABBAGE SALAD

Gobi Pachadi

6 TO 8 SERVINGS

India's salads primarily consist of nonleafy vegetables because most of the country's leafy greens (grown naturally) contain many insects, making it bothersome to prepare to eat raw. Cabbage is one exception, as bugs can be removed more easily from its thick, wide leaves.

Pachadi is a southwest Indian vegetable salad, generally served raw, with a unique dressing made from peanut oil, lemon juice, ground peanuts, and grated coconut. The flavor of this cabbage pachadi from Cochin (popular during the winter when fresh vegetables are scarce), is very different from European coleslaw; its piquant blend of spices and lemon juice is complemented by the sweetness of brown sugar to create a characteristic sweet-and-sour effect. It is generally eaten with Coconut Rice (Indian Coconut Rice, page 358) or rice flour flat breads.

I small head (about I pound) green cabbage, cored and thinly shredded (about 5 cups)

21 ounces ripe tomatoes, diced, or 12 ounces carrots, shredded (about 3 cups either)

³/4 cup grated fresh coconut or packaged unsweetened coconut

³/4 cup peanut powder (see Note)

¹/2 cup chopped fresh cilantro or parsley

I¹/2 teaspoons jaggery, brown sugar, or honey

¹/3 cup peanut oil or vegetable oil

³/4 teaspoon mustard seeds

³/4 teaspoon cumin seeds or ground cumin

I tablespoon seeded and minced hot green chilies

¹/2 teaspoon ground turmeric

Pinch of asafetida (optional)

I to 2 tablespoons fresh lemon juice

About I teaspoon table salt or 2 teaspoons kosher salt

1. In a large bowl, combine the cabbage, tomatoes, coconut, peanut powder, cilantro, and jaggery.

2. Heat the oil in a kadai (woklike Indian pan), wok, or medium, heavy skillet over medium heat. Add the mustard seeds and sauté until they begin to pop, about 2 minutes. Stir in the cumin. Add the chilies, then the turmeric and asafetida, and sauté until the chilies begin to color but do not burn.

3. Pour the dressing over the cabbage mixture and toss to coat. Let stand for at least 3 hours to allow the flavors to meld. Just before serving, stir in the lemon juice and salt.

NOTE Peanut powder, used by Indians to thicken curries and as an ingredient in *raitas* and chutneys, is available in Indian markets and other specialty stores. To make your own, spread unshelled peanuts in a single layer on a baking sheet and roast in a 350°F oven, shaking the pan occasionally, until light brown, about 25 minutes. While still warm, shell and skin the peanuts. Let cool. Working with a small amount at a time, use a mortar and pestle, a nut grinder, or a food processor to grind the peanuts into a fine powder. Be careful not to overwork them or you will have peanut butter. If the powder looks oily, squeeze it in a paper towel for several minutes. Four ounces of unshelled peanuts yield 1 cup peanut powder.

YEMENITE RED CABBAGE SALAD WITH TAHINI

Salata Malfoof

6 TO 8 SERVINGS

The venerable cabbage has remained widespread throughout Europe and the Mediterranean, where it is still generally the most common vegetable in the garden. In the Middle East, however, the cabbage lost some of its appeal toward the end of the Middle Ages as eggplants, spinach, cauliflower, and other vegetables began to proliferate. Yemenites, most of whom lived in abject poverty and had fewer fresh vegetables at their disposal, still tend to use a good deal of cabbage, stuffed, pickled, cut in salads, and cooked in stews. This cool salad makes a perfect counter to the hot climate of Yemen. The red cabbage, more strongly flavored than green, stands up to the tahini, which takes the place of oil. Yemenites also make a slightly fiery version with chilies, but I prefer this more subtle flavoring. You can add some grated onion and black or daikon radish for a zesty touch. Serve as a side dish or stuff into pita bread.

1 small head (about 1 pound) red cabbage, cored and shredded (about 5 cups)
1 large carrot, shredded (about 1 cup)
1 green bell pepper, seeded, deribbed (white removed), and shredded or thinly sliced
1 red bell pepper, seeded, deribbed (white removed), and shredded or thinly sliced

DRESSING:
3/4 cup tahini (sesame seed paste)
About 1/3 cup water
1/4 cup chopped fresh cilantro or parsley
3 tablespoons fresh lemon juice
About 1 teaspoon table salt or 2 teaspoons kosher salt
About 1/8 teaspoon ground black pepper

In a large bowl, combine the cabbage, carrot, and peppers. In a small bowl, stir together all the dressing ingredients to make a pourable consistency. Toss the dressing with the salad and let stand for at least 15 minutes before serving but not more than a day, or the cabbage's vibrant color will bleed out.

[handwritten notes: 14·15 Excellent & quick. Try with zhoug! Excellent with zhoug cut salt a bit.]

Moroccan Raw Carrot Salad

Shlata Chizo

5 TO 6 SERVINGS   Ⓟ

Carrot salads are a relatively new dish, especially raw ones. Until well into the twentieth century, most Europeans ate only cooked carrots, primarily in stews and soups. In the Middle East, people also used them as a component of cooked dishes, but sometimes added grated or minced raw carrots as a minor ingredient to various salads. It was in northwestern Africa that carrots, both cooked and raw, became the featured component of salads—typically an accompaniment to couscous or part of an assortment of salads.

Moroccans brought carrot salads to Israel in the 1940s, and they quickly became ubiquitous. These salads are a traditional Rosh Hashanah dish in Israel, a symbol of a sweet and fruitful year to come. At many Israeli restaurants, cooked carrot salad automatically appears on the table with the bread, pickles, and hummus. The carrots are usually flavored with charmoula, a characteristic Moroccan marinade of oil, lemon juice, garlic, cumin, and salt. Most cooks add heat with chilies, sometimes in dangerous proportions. I have tasted some that left me gasping and others that proved a lively appetizer, so adjust the amount of chilies to your own preference and that of your guests. For a fancy presentation, Israelis serve raw carrot salad, commonly called gezer chai ("live carrots"), in quartered avocados or on a bed of lettuce leaves, garnished with a sprig of mint.

1 pound carrots, coarsely grated (about 4 cups)

1/4 cup vegetable oil or extra-virgin olive oil

3 to 4 tablespoons fresh lemon juice

1/4 cup chopped fresh cilantro or parsley

2 to 4 cloves garlic, mashed or minced

1 teaspoon ground cumin or 1/2 teaspoon ground cumin and 1/4 teaspoon ground cinnamon

1 teaspoon sweet paprika

Pinch of salt

About 1/2 teaspoon *harissa* (Northwest African Chili Paste, page 433), 1 tablespoon minced green chilies, or 1/4 to 1/2 teaspoon cayenne (optional)

In a large bowl, mix together all the ingredients. Cover and let marinate in the refrigerator for at least 2 hours or up to 2 days to allow the flavors to meld and permeate the carrots. Serve chilled or at room temperature.

VARIATIONS

Moroccan Cooked Carrot Salad (*Shlata Chizo Metbucha*): Do not grate the carrots, but cut them on the diagonal into 1/4-inch-thick slices. Cook in gently boiling water until crisp-tender, about 10 minutes. Drain, rinse under cold water, and drain again. Toss with the dressing as above.

Moroccan Carrot-Orange Salad (*Shlata Chizo*): Omit the cumin and add 1 1/2 teaspoons orange blossom water or 1/2 cup fresh orange juice, 1/4 cup chopped fresh spearmint, and, if desired, 1 tablespoon sugar or honey.

Turkish Carrot Salad with Yogurt (*Havuc Salatasi*): Substitute 1 cup plain yogurt for the lemon juice.

Eastern European Radish Salad

Ritachlich

5 TO 6 SERVINGS   Ⓟ

Ritachlich was one of my grandfather's favorite dishes, and I remember him methodically shredding the elongated black radishes using an old-fashioned box grater to achieve the desired coarseness, then eating the pungent salad with chunks of black bread or hot boiled potatoes. It was a nostalgic nod to his mother's kitchen in Lyubavichi, which he left as a teenager, coming alone to America. He sometimes added cucumbers, turnips, carrots, and other vegetables to tone down the sharpness of the radishes. He insisted that the leaves extracted moisture from the radishes and would only buy those already trimmed of the greens. Black radishes are rare these days, but check better fruit and vegetable stores. Black radishes are frequently salted to mellow their bite; if you prefer a stronger kick, omit the salting.

1 pound (about 2 large) winter radishes, preferably black radishes or daikon, peeled and coarsely grated (about 3 cups)
3 tablespoons kosher salt
1 onion, chopped, or 4 to 5 scallions, thinly sliced
6 tablespoons vegetable oil
2 tablespoons distilled white or cider vinegar
About 1 teaspoon sugar
Table or kosher salt to taste
Ground black pepper to taste

1. Put the radishes in a colander or large sieve, toss with the salt, weigh down with a plate, and let stand at room temperature for 30 minutes or in the refrigerator overnight. Rinse in cold water, then press out the excess moisture.

2. In a medium bowl, combine the radishes with all the remaining ingredients. Let stand for at least 1 hour.

VARIATION

Substitute $1^{1}/_{2}$ to 2 cups sour cream for the dressing.

BLACK RADISHES

The most ancient type of radish and the most common one in eastern European cookery is the black radish, a soot-colored root with a crisp ivory interior. Black radishes are either cylindrical, like a turnip, or oval and stretching up to a foot in length. Mature autumn black radishes can reach the potency of horseradish. The more available and milder daikon, a similarly shaped white radish, can be substituted for the black radish. In eastern Europe, black radishes were a major ingredient, used in salads, mixed with sour cream or schmaltz, coarsely shredded and fried, and even cooked with honey and ground ginger into radish preserves. Almost the entire American black radish crop, primarily from New Jersey and California, is sold immediately before Passover and Rosh Hashanah and used in traditional Ashkenazic dishes.

COOKED VEGETABLE SALADS

RUSSIAN COOKED VEGETABLE SALAD

Salat Rousee

6 TO 8 SERVINGS   Ⓟ

Salads were unknown in Russia until French chefs began to settle here in the nineteenth century, including Lucien Olivier. He opened the Hermitage restaurant in Moscow in 1864 for which he created this fancy potato salad, called "Salad Olivier." Olivier later opened a restaurant in Wiesbaden, Germany, where he offered "salade à la Russe." Following the Russian Revolution, immigrants spread the dish far and wide, including Iran, where it is called olivieh. *In most countries, including Italy, France, Germany, Turkey, and Morocco, it is known as Russian Salad.*

The predominant Russian vegetables—potatoes, beets, carrots, and cucumbers—all made their way into this salad, either cooked or pickled. Russians commonly add plenty of meat, poultry, and fish to the dish, but Jews make a vegetarian version and sour cream is sometimes used in the dressing. Mediterranean Jewish variations use a vinaigrette for the sour cream and mayonnaise.

Because this salad can be prepared well ahead of time, it became popular Sabbath and holiday fare. Italians typically serve it for the third Sabbath meal on Saturday afternoon with cold zuppa di verdura *(mixed vegetable soup) and crusty bread. Russians in Israel commonly serve this on a bed of soft lettuce, accompanied with dark bread and chilled vodka.*

3 to 4 unpeeled beets

4 boiling potatoes, about 1 pound total (see Note)

8 ounces green beans, trimmed and cut into $^1/_2$-inch pieces

4 carrots, cut into $^1/_2$-inch cubes

1 pound green peas, shelled (1 cup), or 1 cup thawed frozen peas

2 onions, coarsely chopped

4 dill pickles, cut into $^1/_2$-inch cubes

4 scallions, sliced

DRESSING:

$^1/_4$ cup white wine vinegar or distilled white vinegar

1 teaspoon dry mustard or 1$^1/_2$ teaspoons Dijon mustard

$^3/_4$ teaspoon sugar

About $^1/_4$ teaspoon table salt or $^1/_2$ teaspoon kosher salt

Ground white or black pepper to taste

$^1/_2$ cup vegetable oil

2 hard-boiled eggs, sliced, for garnish (optional)

1. Preheat the oven to 375°F. Wrap the beets in aluminum foil and bake until tender, about 1 hour. Or put the beets in a large pot of boiling water, cover, reduce the heat to a simmer, and cook until tender, 30 to 50 minutes. When cool enough to handle, peel and cut into $^1/_2$-inch cubes.

2. Meanwhile, cook the potatoes in lightly salted boiling water until tender but not mushy, about 40 minutes. Drain and, when cool enough to handle, peel and cut into $^1/_2$-inch cubes.

3. Steam or boil the beans, carrots, peas, and onion until crisp-tender, about 2 minutes.

4. In a large bowl, combine the beets, potatoes, beans, carrots, peas, onions, pickles, and scallions. To make the dressing: In a small bowl, stir

together the vinegar, mustard, sugar, salt, and pepper. In a slow, steady stream, whisk in the oil. Pour over the vegetables and toss to coat. Cover and refrigerate for at least 30 minutes or up to 2 days to let the vegetables absorb the dressing. Serve chilled or at room temperature, garnished with the hard-boiled eggs, if desired.

<hr />

VARIATIONS

Creamy Dressing: Omit the oil, reduce the vinegar to 1 tablespoon, and add 1 cup mayonnaise or $^1/_2$ cup mayonnaise and $^1/_3$ cup sour cream.

Italian Cooked Vegetable Salad (_Insalata Russa_): This dish was once ubiquitous at many Italian holiday meals, but has since lost much of its prominence. Recently, however, it has experienced somewhat of a revival among some younger Italians. Substitute 8 ounces steamed diced cauliflower for the beets and 2 to 3 tablespoons tiny capers for the pickles.

<hr />

NOTE Boiling (waxy) potatoes, which are low in starch and hold their shape after cooking, are preferred for salads, as high-starch russet (baking) potatoes tend to fall apart and also absorb too much of the dressing, resulting in a dry salad. Yukon Gold and Red Bliss are excellent varieties for salads. Boiling the potatoes with the skins on prevents them from absorbing too much water. A serrated knife works best for cutting cooked potatoes.

<hr />

HUNGARIAN POTATO SALAD

Burgonya Salata

6 TO 8 SERVINGS

Beginning in the nineteenth century, with the general acceptance of the potato in Europe, most countries developed some form of salad based on cooked potatoes. This creamy version, also called krumpli salata, _contains the Hungarian favorite, paprika._

> 3 pounds (about 16 small new or 8 medium) boiling potatoes (see Note)
> 3 tablespoons distilled white, cider, or red wine vinegar
> About 1 cup sour cream or $^1/_2$ cup sour cream mixed with $^1/_2$ cup mayonnaise
> $^1/_3$ cup chopped fresh parsley
> 1 to 2 tablespoons sugar
> 1 to 1$^1/_2$ teaspoons sweet paprika
> About 1 teaspoon table salt or 2 teaspoons kosher salt
> About $^1/_4$ teaspoon ground black pepper

1. Put the potatoes in a large pot and add water to cover. Bring to a boil, cover, reduce the heat to low, and simmer until the potatoes are knife-tender but still firm, about 20 minutes for small potatoes and 30 minutes for medium potatoes. Drain.

2. While still warm, cut the potatoes into $^3/_4$-inch cubes and drizzle 2 tablespoons of the vinegar over the warm potatoes. Let cool.

3. In a large bowl, combine the sour cream, the remaining 1 tablespoon vinegar, the parsley, sugar, paprika, salt, and pepper. Add the potatoes and toss to coat. Refrigerate until ready to serve (up to 1 day).

MIDDLE EASTERN POTATO SALAD

Salata Batata

6 TO 8 SERVINGS

While Americans love creamy potato salads, people in the Middle East like tangy versions with a lemon dressing. This is a popular Sabbath dish, generally accompanied with lots of different pickles.

3 pounds (about 16 small or 8 medium) boiling potatoes (see Note, page 97)

DRESSING:

$^1/_3$ cup fresh lemon juice

3 tablespoons chopped fresh cilantro or parsley

1 teaspoon sugar

About 1 teaspoon table salt or 2 teaspoons kosher salt

About $^1/_4$ teaspoon ground black pepper

$^2/_3$ cup extra-virgin olive oil or vegetable oil, or $^1/_3$ cup each

$^3/_4$ cup sliced scallions or chopped white or red onions

1 cup chopped celery (optional)

1. Put the potatoes in a large pot and add water to cover. Bring to a boil, cover, reduce the heat to low, and simmer until the potatoes are knife-tender but still firm, about 20 minutes for small potatoes and 30 minutes for medium potatoes. Drain. When cool enough to handle, about 10 minutes, peel. While still warm, cut the potatoes into large cubes or thin slices. Place in a large bowl.

2. To make the dressing: In a small bowl, combine the lemon juice, cilantro, sugar, salt, and pepper. In a slow, steady stream, whisk in the oil. Drizzle the dressing over the warm potatoes and toss to coat. Add the scallions and celery, if using. Let stand at room temperature for 30 minutes to allow the potatoes to absorb the dressing. Cover and refrigerate for several hours or overnight. Serve chilled or at room temperature.

VARIATIONS

Moroccan Potato Salad (*Salade de Pommes de Terre*): Add $1^1/_2$ to 2 rinsed and chopped preserved lemons, $^1/_3$ cup capers, drained, and 6 to 8 quartered marinated artichoke hearts or about 4 dozen small brine-cured olives (black or green).

Syrian Potato Salad (*Salata Batata*): Add 1 to $1^1/_2$ teaspoons ground allspice. Garnish with quartered hard-boiled eggs and 8 to 12 brine-cured black olives.

Tunisian Potato Salad (*Tourchi Batata*): Add 1 tablespoon ground cumin, 1 teaspoon sweet paprika, $^1/_2$ to 1 teaspoon caraway seeds or 1 to 2 teaspoons ground caraway, and 2 to 3 teaspoons *harissa* (Northwest African Chili Paste, page 433) or about $^1/_2$ teaspoon hot sauce.

Tunisian Sabbath Potato Salad (*Salade du Shabbat*): Tunisians commonly serve fancier versions of potato salad on Friday night. Follow the directions for the main recipe (above), reducing the potatoes to $1^1/_2$ pounds, and cook along with them 8 ounces (about 4) carrots cut into chunks, 1 small head cauliflower cut into florets, 4 celery stalks cut into chunks, and 3 to 4 peeled turnips cut into chunks.

SEPHARDIC BEET SALAD

Salata di Chukundor

6 TO 8 SERVINGS   D OR P

While Europeans may season beets with dill or mix them with sour cream, Middle Easterners generally prefer them in tangy and spicy salads. This beet salad is popular Sabbath fare and a traditional Rosh Hashanah dish, because it is a symbol of a sweet year to come and because the Hebrew word for beet, silka, *connotes that our enemies should be removed.*

Save the beet greens to use separately (Sephardic Beet Greens, page 211), cook the greens with white beans (Italian Beet Greens and White Beans, page 211), or toss them with walnut sauce (Georgian Walnut Sauce, page 432).

Do not cut off the root of the beets before cooking or the color and nutrients will bleed away.

2 pounds 2-inch beets, about 8 total,
    stems trimmed to 1 inch
1 red or white onion, thinly sliced

DRESSING:
3 tablespoons fresh lemon juice or red wine
    vinegar
3 tablespoons chopped fresh cilantro or parsley
2 to 3 teaspoons sugar
About $1/2$ teaspoon table salt or 1 teaspoon
    kosher salt
Ground black pepper to taste
6 tablespoons olive oil or vegetable oil
1 cup (5 ounces) crumbled feta cheese (optional)

1. Preheat the oven to 375°F. Wrap the beets in aluminum foil and bake until tender, about 1 hour. Or, put the beets in a large saucepan, add water to cover, bring to a boil, cover, reduce the heat to low, and simmer until fork-tender, about 35 minutes. When cool enough to handle, peel and cut into $1/2$-inch cubes. You should have about 4 cups.

2. In a large bowl, combine the beets and onion. To make the dressing: In a small bowl, combine the lemon juice, cilantro, sugar, salt, and pepper. In a slow, steady stream, whisk in the oil. Drizzle over the beets, toss to coat, cover, and refrigerate for at least 3 hours or up to 2 days. Serve chilled or at room temperature. Sprinkle with feta cheese just before serving, if desired.

VARIATIONS

Syrian Beet Salad (*Salata Shawandar*): Reduce the oil to 2 tablespoons and add 2 to 3 tablespoons *temerhindi* (Syrian Mock Tamarind Sauce, page 434) and 2 teaspoons ground cumin.

Moroccan Beet Salad (*Shlata Barba*): This beet salad contains seasonings characteristic of the Maghreb; at a Moroccan meal, it would accompany several other salads of different vegetables and dressings. Increase the lemon juice to 5 to 6 tablespoons, decrease the oil to 3 tablespoons, and add 1 tablespoon orange blossom water, $1/2$ teaspoon ground cinnamon, and $1/4$ teaspoon ground cumin. Or, substitute 10 chopped fresh mint leaves for the cilantro and add 2 peeled and segmented navel oranges.

Middle Eastern Cauliflower Salad with Tahini

Salatet Zahra bil Tahina

6 TO 8 SERVINGS   D

Middle Easterners and Sephardim historically used cauliflower, flavored with tomatoes, lemon juice, or tahini dressing, as a cooked or pickled vegetable, but not raw.

I head cauliflower, about 2 pounds; or I small head cauliflower and I head broccoli, cut into florets (about 6 cups total)

I small onion, chopped or cut into crescents

About I pound tomatoes, chopped (2 cups) or 6 to 8 red radishes, trimmed and quartered (optional)

DRESSING:

3 to 4 cloves garlic

I teaspoon table salt or 2 teaspoons kosher salt

$^1/_2$ cup extra-virgin olive oil or vegetable oil

$^1/_2$ cup fresh lemon juice

$^1/_2$ cup tahini (sesame seed paste)

$^1/_2$ cup plain yogurt

$^1/_2$ cup chopped fresh parsley

1. Steam the cauliflower over boiling water or cook in lightly salted boiling water until crisp-tender, 8 to 10 minutes. Rinse under cold water, drain, and pat dry with a towel.

2. In a large bowl, combine the cauliflower, onion, and, if using, the tomatoes. Using the tip of a heavy knife or with a mortar and pestle, mash the garlic and salt into a paste. In a small bowl, combine all the dressing ingredients. Drizzle over the salad and toss to coat. Refrigerate for at least 1 hour or up to 2 days. Serve chilled or at room temperature.

VARIATIONS

Middle Eastern Orange-Cauliflower Salad (*Salatet Zahra bil Bortugal*): Omit the olive oil and lemon juice, reduce the tahini to $^1/_4$ cup, increase the yogurt to $^3/_4$ cup, and add 1 tablespoon fresh orange juice and 1 teaspoon grated orange zest.

Nondairy Middle Eastern Cauliflower Salad (*Karnabet bi Taratour*): Omit the oil and yogurt and add $^1/_2$ cup water.

MIDDLE EASTERN EGGPLANT SALAD

Salata de Berengena

ABOUT 4 CUPS, OR 6 TO 8 SERVINGS   P

Following the introduction of the Indian eggplant by the Persians to regions around the Middle East about the fourth century C.E., this dish became the most popular mashed vegetable salad and was eventually spread by the Arabs as far west as the Atlantic. Subsequently, the Ottomans, during their occupation of the Balkans and Hungary, introduced their favorite vegetable, eggplant, to Europe, which in due course reached Ukraine and Russia, emerging as a favorite type of ikra *(vegetable "caviar"). Hence, versions of eggplant salad, also called* salata batinjan *and* caviare d'aubergines *(eggplant caviar) in the Middle East, are common from India to Morocco.*

Arguably, the most famous variation, made with tahini (sesame seed paste), is the Lebanese baba ghanouj—baba *is the Arabic word for "father" as well as a term of endearment;* ghanouj *means "indulged." Roasting the eggplant imparts a pleasing smoky flavor. Do not overwhelm the eggplant's subtle flavor with excessive seasonings. Serve with pita, crackers, crudités, and on Passover, matza.*

2 eggplants (about 1¼ pounds each), roasted
   (see page 246, Step 1)
About 5 tablespoons fresh lemon juice
About ¼ cup extra-virgin olive oil
¼ cup chopped fresh parsley
3 to 4 cloves garlic
1¼ teaspoons table salt or 2 teaspoons
   kosher salt
Ground black pepper to taste

1. Peel the roasted eggplants, being careful not to leave any skin. Put in a colander, and let drain for about 30 minutes.

2. Chop the eggplant with a sharp knife or mash with a fork; there should still be small chunks. If you prefer a smoother texture, process the pulp in a food processor.

3. Using the tip of a heavy knife or with a mortar and pestle, mash the garlic and salt into a paste. In a medium bowl combine all the ingredients. Let stand at room temperature for at least 30 minutes to allow the flavors to meld, or refrigerate for up to 3 days. Serve at room temperature or slightly chilled.

VARIATIONS

Calcutta Eggplant Spread (*Brinjal Bharta*): Add 1 to 2 minced small green chilies.

Greek Eggplant Spread (*Melintzano Salata*): Add 1 teaspoon ground cumin and 2 tablespoons chopped fresh oregano or 1 tablespoon dried oregano.

Israeli Eggplant Spread (*Salat Chatzilim*): Omit the lemon juice and oil and add ½ cup mayonnaise or 1 cup plain yogurt.

Lebanese Eggplant Spread (*Baba Ghanouj*): Substitute 6 to 8 tablespoons tahini (sesame seed paste) for the oil.

Persian Eggplant Spread (*Nazkhatun*): Add 4 teaspoons dried mint and ½ teaspoon ground cinnamon.

Romanian Eggplant Spread (*Putlejela*): Substitute 3 tablespoons distilled white vinegar for the lemon juice. Add 1 chopped onion, 1 seeded, deribbed (white removed), and chopped green bell pepper, and 1 to 2 tablespoons sugar.

Yemenite Eggplant Spread (*Salata Batinjan*): Omit the lemon juice and oil and add 2 cups seeded and chopped tomatoes (see page 291) and 2 to 3 teaspoons *z'chug* (Yemenite Chili Paste, page 438).

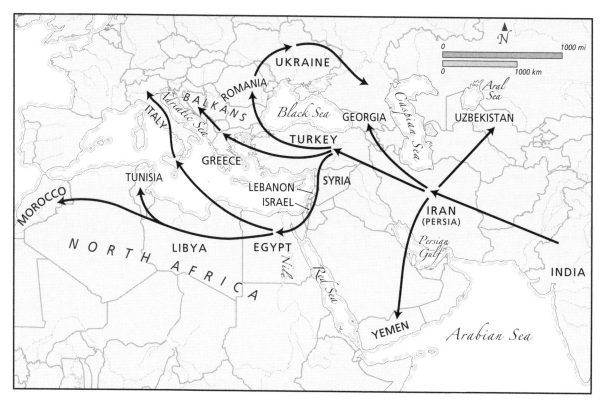

The Spread of Eggplant Salad: *Eggplant salad originated in India and spread through the Ottoman Empire, northern Africa, and into Europe, each country flavoring it with its own popular seasonings.* **India:** *green chilies;* **Iran (Persia):** *mint, cinnamon;* **Yemen:** *tomatoes, chilies, coriander;* **Uzbekistan:** *just onions and salt;* **Turkey:** *yogurt;* **Romania:** *green bell peppers, garlic;* **Ukraine:** *tomatoes, garlic;* **Georgia:** *walnut sauce;* **Greece:** *oregano, cumin;* **Balkans:** *peppers, tomatoes, lemon juice;* **Italy:** *olives, raisins;* **Syria:** *pine nuts;* **Lebanon:** *tahini;* **Israel:** *mayonnaise;* **Egypt:** *paprika, cumin, tomato paste;* **Tunisia:** *olives, artichokes;* **Morocco:** *cumin, paprika*

Northwest African Grilled Pepper Salad

Salata Mechouiya

6 TO 8 SERVINGS

Although the practice of grilling and marinating vegetables as a way of extending their shelf life and enhancing their flavor dates back thousands of years, all of the major ingredients of this popular northwest African grilled salad are imports: bell peppers and tomatoes from South America, garlic from western Asia, and the sometimes-used eggplant from India. Adding chili peppers to the bell peppers is a Tunisian touch. Moroccan Jews brought salata mechouiya *(pronounced "mesh-WE-yah" and, therefore, sometimes also spelled* mishweeye *or* meshwiya*) to Israel, where it became a standard Sabbath and holiday dish, generally accompanied with pita bread. It also appears at breakfast; for this, the dressing is omitted and the grilled peppers are topped with yogurt and a sprinkling of salt and fresh mint.*

6 to 8 plum tomatoes
1 small head garlic, unpeeled
2½ pounds (about 8) assorted green, red, and
    yellow bell peppers; or 7 bell peppers and
    2 to 4 jalapeño chilies; or 4 bell peppers and
    6 to 8 Anaheim or poblano chilies
Olive oil for coating

DRESSING:

2 to 3 tablespoons fresh lemon juice or red wine
    vinegar
2 tablespoons chopped fresh parsley
½ teaspoon ground cumin or pinch of ground
    anise or ground coriander
About ½ teaspoon table salt or 1 teaspoon
    kosher salt
Ground black pepper to taste
¼ cup extra-virgin olive oil

1 to 2 tablespoons tiny capers for garnish
    (optional)

1. Light a fire in a charcoal grill or preheat the broiler. Coat the tomatoes, garlic, and peppers with oil and place on an oiled rack over the coals or 5 inches from the heat source under the broiler. Grill or broil the vegetables: the tomatoes, turning frequently with tongs, until the skins wrinkle and slip off, about 5 minutes, or use the tomatoes raw; the garlic, turning occasionally, until softened, 10 to 15 minutes; the peppers, turning every 3 to 4 minutes, until the skin cracks and blisters, 15 to 25 minutes. (Or, impale the peppers with a long-handled fork and roast directly over a gas flame, turning, for 3 to 4 minutes.)

2. Place the peppers in a large covered bowl or plastic bag and let steam for about 15 minutes. Starting from the stem end, peel off the skin from the peppers. Do not rinse. Remove and discard the stems and seeds, then quarter or coarsely chop. Save any juice from the peppers to add to the dressing.

3. Peel the grilled tomatoes, remove the seeds, and coarsely chop. (If using raw tomatoes, seed them but don't peel.) Peel the garlic and mash.

4. In a large bowl, combine the peppers, tomatoes, and garlic and let stand for at least 1 hour to allow the flavors to meld or cover and store in the refrigerator for up to 3 days; let stand at room temperature for at least 30 minutes before serving.

5. Just before serving, make the dressing: In a small bowl, combine the lemon juice, parsley, cumin, salt, and pepper. In slow, steady stream, whisk in the oil. Drizzle over the salad and toss to coat. If desired, sprinkle with the capers.

VARIATIONS

Moroccan Grilled Vegetable Dip (*Salata M'Tayibeh*): Using a fork or in a food processor, coarsely mash the peppers, chilies, tomatoes, and garlic, then whisk in the dressing and sprinkle with the capers.

Romanian Eggplant, Pepper, and Tomato Dip (*Pindzur*): This salad, also called *ajvar*, is popular in the Balkans. Roast 2 medium eggplants (see page 246, Step 1). Peel the eggplants, being careful not to leave any skin. Place in a colander and let drain for about 30 minutes. Using a fork or in a food processor, coarsely mash together the eggplants, peppers, tomatoes, and garlic, and whisk in the dressing.

YEMENITE ROASTED BELL PEPPER SALAD

Salata Felfel

6 TO 8 SERVINGS

After the Spanish brought chilies back from America, the pepper spread along the Mediterranean, where farmers developed newer and sweeter varieties, most notably the bell pepper. Early on, the favorite way of eating peppers, both fiery and sweet, was to roast them first. Roasting peppers dramatically changes the vegetable: It softens the texture, caramelizes the sugar, brings out the capsicum flavor—which imparts a smoky note—and makes the thin skin easy to remove. The result is a sweet, earthy flavor quite different from that of a raw pepper. Green peppers, which are actually immature red, yellow, or purple peppers, are also enhanced by roasting, but will be less sweet since they contain little sugar to caramelize.

The intensified flavor of roasted peppers marries well with many Mediterranean ingredients, including olive oil, goat cheese, garlic, basil, and capers. In this version of pepper salad, the roasted peppers are added to a tangy tomato sauce to produce an interesting contrast of flavors and textures.

2 pounds (about 6) assorted red, yellow, and
green bell peppers, roasted and peeled
(see page 267)
Olive oil for coating

TOMATO SAUCE:
1/4 cup olive oil or vegetable oil
2 large onions, chopped
3 to 4 cloves garlic, minced
1 to 2 teaspoons ground cumin
2 teaspoons sweet paprika
1 pound plum tomatoes, peeled, seeded, and
chopped (about 2 1/2 cups); see page 291
About 1 teaspoon table salt or 2 teaspoons
kosher salt
Ground black pepper to taste

3 tablespoons cider or distilled white vinegar
1 tablespoon fresh lemon juice

1. Slice the peppers in half lengthwise and
remove the seeds and stem. Cut the peppers into
3/4- to 1-inch-wide lengthwise strips.

2. To make the sauce: In a large saucepan,
heat the oil over medium heat. Add the onions and
garlic and sauté until soft and translucent, 5 to 10
minutes. Stir in the cumin and paprika. Add the
tomatoes, salt, and pepper and simmer, stirring frequently, until softened, about 15 minutes.

3. Add the peppers and any of their juice.
Remove from the heat and stir in the vinegar and
lemon juice. Let cool.

VARIATION

Yemenite Fiery Roasted Bell Pepper Salad
(*Salata Felfel*): Omit the tomatoes, cumin, and
paprika and stir about 2 teaspoons *shatta* (Yemenite
Red Chili Paste, page 438) into the softened onions.

LEGUME AND
GRAIN SALADS

ITALIAN GREEN BEAN SALAD

Fagiolini Conditi

6 TO 8 SERVINGS

*Italian cooking—straightforward, adaptable, and
inexpensive—focuses on pulling the most flavor possible from fresh, basic ingredients. A favorite Italian
way of enjoying green beans is as an antipasto salad,
in which the nutty sweet flavor of the beans is
enhanced with a basic vinaigrette and a hint of herbs.
Cooking the beans in boiling salted water helps to
maintain a uniform green color. Steaming the beans
retains more nutrients and a fresher flavor.*

2 pounds green beans, trimmed and cut into
1-inch pieces
1 onion, thinly sliced
1 small red bell pepper, seeded, deribbed
(white removed), and chopped
1/2 cup chopped fresh basil, 3 tablespoons
chopped fresh tarragon, or 3 tablespoons
chopped fresh parsley

DRESSING:
2 tablespoons red wine vinegar or fresh
lemon juice
2 to 3 cloves garlic, minced
About 3/4 teaspoon table salt or 1 1/2 teaspoons
kosher salt
Ground black pepper to taste
Pinch of sugar
1/4 cup extra-virgin olive oil

1. In a large pot of salted boiling water, cook the green beans until crisp-tender, 4 to 6 minutes. Or, steam them in a covered steamer over boiling water for 6 to 8 minutes. Do not overcook. Drain and keep warm.

2. In a large bowl, combine the beans, onion, bell pepper, and basil. To make the dressing: In a small bowl, combine the vinegar, garlic, salt, pepper, and sugar. In a slow, steady stream, whisk in the oil. Drizzle over the beans and toss to coat. Some people prefer the beans freshly dressed, while others like to marinate them in the dressing for at least 4 hours. Serve at room temperature.

VARIATIONS

This simple salad can be easily enhanced by adding any of the following: 2 cups cooked red beans, 2 cups cooked chickpeas, 8 quartered cooked artichoke hearts, 1 pound julienne carrots cooked until crisp-tender, 12 ounces thinly sliced mushrooms, 2 cups cooked cheese tortellini, 1 pound coarsely chopped toasted and skinned hazelnuts, or 2 tablespoons drained tiny capers.

Greek Green Bean Salad (*Fasolakia Salata*): Omit the bell pepper and substitute 2 tablespoons chopped fresh dill for the basil. If desired, add 1 cup (5 ounces) crumbled feta cheese.

SEPHARDIC WHITE BEAN SALAD

Avicas en Salata

6 TO 8 SERVINGS

Sephardim have always been bean-lovers, relying on them for their primary source of protein. For centuries, Sephardic cooks made cold fava bean salads for the Sabbath and other meals as well as using fava beans as the basis for their Sabbath stews. With the arrival of American beans in the sixteenth century, white beans quickly became the basis of most Sephardic meals in Turkey and the Balkans, in the form of soups, stews, and salads. For some families, this salad (also called salata di fijones blanco), augmented with olives and hard-boiled eggs, constituted a meal in itself. For a portable meal, serve the bean salad in pita bread. Typically, white bean salads are mildly seasoned so as not to overwhelm the delicate flavor of the beans.

I pound (about 2^1/$_3$ cups) cannellini, navy, or
   other dried white beans, picked over, soaked
   for 8 hours in cold water, and drained
12 whole peppercorns
I bay leaf
I large red onion, chopped, or 4 to 5 scallions, sliced
^{1}/$_4$ to ^{1}/$_2$ cup chopped fresh parsley or cilantro

DRESSING:
^{1}/$_4$ to ^{1}/$_2$ cup red wine vinegar or fresh lemon
   juice, or ^{1}/$_4$ cup fresh lemon juice and
   2 tablespoons red wine vinegar
About I teaspoon table salt or 2 teaspoons
   kosher salt
Ground black pepper to taste
About ^{3}/$_4$ cup olive oil or vegetable oil

Tomato wedges and sliced hard-boiled eggs for
   garnish (optional)

1. Put the beans in a stockpot and add cold water to cover by 2 inches. Tie the peppercorns and bay leaf in a piece of cheesecloth and add to the pot. Bring to a boil, cover, reduce the heat to medium-low, and simmer until tender but not mushy, about 1 hour. Drain. Discard the cheesecloth.

2. In a large bowl, combine the beans, onion, and parsley. To make the dressing: In a small bowl, combine the vinegar, salt, and pepper. In a slow, steady stream, whisk in the oil. Drizzle over the beans and toss to coat. Refrigerate for several hours or overnight to let the flavors meld. Serve at room temperature as part of a meze or as the basis for a light meal. For the latter, bean salads are commonly garnished with tomato wedges and sliced hard-boiled eggs and accompanied with plenty of fresh bread.

VARIATIONS

Italian White Bean Salad (*Fagioli Conditi*): Make the dressing with vinegar. Include 1 whole clove garlic and 2 teaspoons chopped fresh sage or 1 teaspoon dried sage in the cheesecloth. Add 8 to 12 Italian Marinated Artichoke Hearts (page 64) or 1 sliced bulb fennel to the salad. This salad makes a delicious topping for Italian bruschetta: Cut French or Italian bread on the diagonal into $3/4$-inch-thick slices, place on a wire rack set on a baking sheet, and bake in a preheated 350°F oven until golden and crisp, about 10 minutes. Brush the tops lightly with olive oil and top with some of the bean salad.

Moroccan White Bean Salad (*Shlata Lubiya*): Make the dressing with lemon juice. Add 1 to 2 seeded and minced hot red chilies with the parsley.

Romanian White Bean Salad (*Fasole Salata*): Add 1 mashed clove garlic to the dressing with the salt and pepper and garnish the salad with $3/4$ cup (4 ounces) crumbled feta cheese and 15 to 16 brine-cured black olives.

Turkish White Bean Salad (*Piyaziko/Piyaz*): Substitute $1/2$ cup chopped fresh dill and $1/2$ cup chopped fresh spearmint for the parsley. If desired, add 3 to 4 chopped plum tomatoes.

N O T E   Bay leaves, reputed to help the digestion of beans, are commonly cooked with them.

SEPHARDIC BLACK-EYED PEA SALAD

Salata Lubiya

6 TO 8 SERVINGS   Ⓓ OR Ⓟ

The sweet, earthy flavor of black-eyed peas is complemented by a wide variety of robust foods and flavors, so this salad can consist simply of the beans topped with a basic vinaigrette or augmented with various tastes and colors. Serve with pita or Italian bread.

- 1 pound (about 2¹/₃ cups) dried black-eyed peas, picked over, soaked in cold water to cover for at least 4 hours, and drained
- 1 tablespoon fresh lemon juice
- About 1 teaspoon table salt or 2 teaspoons kosher salt
- 1 red onion, chopped, or 5 to 6 scallions, thinly sliced

DRESSING:

- 5 tablespoons fresh lemon juice or red wine vinegar
- About 1 teaspoon table salt or 2 teaspoons kosher salt
- Ground black pepper to taste
- 2 cloves garlic, mashed (optional)
- 1 to 3 teaspoons sugar or honey (optional)
- ¹/₂ teaspoon ground cumin or ¹/₄ teaspoon ground allspice (optional)
- ¹/₂ cup extra-virgin olive oil or vegetable oil

pretty good

- ¹/₄ cup chopped fresh parsley
- 1 tablespoon chopped fresh dill (optional)
- 1 green or red bell pepper, seeded, deribbed (white removed), and diced (optional)
- 1 cup brine-cured black olives, pitted and chopped (optional)
- 5 to 6 plum tomatoes, chopped, or ¹/₂ cup chopped drained oil-packed sun-dried tomatoes (optional)
- 1¹/₂ to 2 cups (8 to 10 ounces) crumbled feta cheese (optional)

1. Put the black-eyed peas in a stockpot and add water to cover by 2 inches. Add the lemon juice. (It helps maintain the color of the peas.) Bring to a boil, cover, reduce the heat to low, and simmer until tender, about 45 minutes. About 5 minutes before the end of cooking, add the salt. Drain.

2. In a large bowl, combine the black-eyed peas and onion. To make the dressing: In a small bowl, combine the lemon juice, salt, pepper, and, if using, garlic, sugar, or cumin. In a slow, steady stream, whisk in the oil. Drizzle over the warm black-eyed peas and toss to coat. Let cool. Refrigerate for several hours or overnight to allow the flavors to meld. Just before serving, add the parsley and, if desired, one or more of the remaining ingredients and toss to combine. Serve at room temperature.

Sephardic Chickpea Salad

Garvansos en Salata

6 TO 8 SERVINGS

This venerable salad, one of the easiest and most popular ways in the Middle East and Mediterranean to utilize chickpeas, is a meze favorite, served on an everyday basis as well as at important occasions. Some Sephardim serve this salad on Rosh Hashanah and Sukkot, when it represents the abundance of the harvest and the year. In a salad, the chickpea's nutty flavor is generally allowed to stand on its own, dressed with a little oil and lemon juice or vinegar and usually not augmented with a lot of additions and seasonings. A Sephardic friend revealed that she frequently uses canned chickpeas instead of dried, but to enhance their flavor she first brings them to a boil in a large pot of water, then drains them. For a light meal, serve chickpea salad in pita breads, accompanied with lettuce.

I pound (about 2¹/₂ cups) dried chickpeas, picked over, soaked in cold water to cover for 12 hours, drained, and rinsed

I red onion, coarsely chopped, or 3 to 4 scallions, sliced

I green bell pepper, seeded, deribbed (white removed), and chopped

I red bell pepper, seeded, deribbed (white removed), and chopped (optional)

DRESSING:

2 to 3 cloves garlic

I teaspoon table salt or 2 teaspoons kosher salt

4 to 6 tablespoons fresh lemon juice, red wine vinegar, or cider vinegar

¹/₂ cup chopped fresh parsley or cilantro

Ground black pepper to taste

¹/₂ cup extra-virgin olive oil or vegetable oil

1. Put the chickpeas in a stockpot and add water to cover by 2 inches. Bring to a boil, cover, reduce the heat to low, and simmer until tender, about 1¹/₂ hours. Drain.

2. In a large bowl, combine the chickpeas, onion, and bell peppers. To make the dressing: Using the tip of a heavy knife or with a mortar and pestle, mash the garlic and salt into a paste. In a small bowl, combine the garlic, lemon juice, parsley, and pepper. In a slow, steady stream, whisk in the oil. Pour the dressing over the chickpeas and toss to coat. Cover and refrigerate for at least 1 hour or up to 3 days to allow the flavors to meld. Serve at room temperature.

VARIATIONS

Expand the basic chickpea salad into a more substantial dish with various additions, such as some chopped fresh tomatoes, about 1 cup (5 ounces) crumbled feta cheese, some Italian Marinated Artichoke Hearts (page 64), 1 pound diced or coarsely grated carrots, or 1 head of cauliflower cut into florets and steamed until crisp-tender.

Indian Chickpea Salad (*Chholar dal*): Omit the oil, use lemon juice, and add 1 seeded and minced hot green chili and about ¹/₄ teaspoon cayenne.

Moroccan Chickpea Salad (*Shlata H'mes*): Omit the bell peppers and add 1 teaspoon ground cumin and 2 teaspoons sweet paprika or ¹/₂ teaspoon cayenne.

Turkish Chickpea Salad (*Nohut Salatasi*): Add 1 seeded and minced small red chili, ¹/₄ cup drained capers, and 2 tablespoons chopped fresh spearmint or 2 teaspoons dried oregano.

Sephardic Lentil Salad

Salata de Lentejas

6 TO 8 SERVINGS

For much of history, lentils served as inexpensive regular fare throughout parts of Asia, Africa, and Europe. To vary the flavor, cooks commonly added fresh herbs and spices. Although the practice is not typically Sephardic, I generally cook 2 to 3 chopped carrots with the lentils to provide both flavor and color. Among my other favorite nontraditional adjustments is to substitute 1/2 cup walnut oil for the olive oil, add 2 teaspoons dried thyme, and, just before serving, stir in 1 cup coarsely chopped walnuts. For a light lunch, accompany lentil salad with bread and plain yogurt. Or, serve on a bed of trimmed spinach leaves or mixed salad greens and sprinkle with crumbled mild goat cheese.

1 pound (about 2 1/4 cups) brown or green lentils, picked over and rinsed

8 cups water

1 bay leaf

1/2 teaspoon dried thyme (optional)

DRESSING:

About 1/3 cup fresh lemon juice or red or white wine vinegar

1/3 cup chopped fresh parsley, cilantro, or spearmint

About 1 teaspoon table salt or 2 teaspoons kosher salt

About 1/2 teaspoon ground black pepper

1 to 2 cloves garlic, minced (optional)

1/2 teaspoon ground cumin (optional)

2/3 cup extra-virgin olive oil

1 red onion, chopped, or 4 to 6 scallions, sliced

1 large tomato, seeded and chopped (optional); see page 291

1. In a large saucepan, combine the lentils, water, bay leaf, and thyme, if using. Bring to a boil, cover, reduce the heat to medium-low, and simmer until tender but not mushy, about 25 minutes. Drain.

2. Put the warm lentils in a large bowl. To make the dressing: In a small bowl, combine the lemon juice, parsley, salt, pepper, and, if using, garlic and cumin. In a slow, steady stream, whisk in the oil. Drizzle over the lentils and toss to coat. Just before serving, stir in the onion and, if using, tomato. Serve warm or at room temperature.

VARIATIONS

Ethiopian Lentil Salad (*Yemiser Selatta*): Heat 3 tablespoons vegetable oil in a large skillet over medium heat, add 2 chopped red or yellow onions and 2 to 4 seeded and minced jalapeño chilies, and sauté until softened, about 5 minutes. Add to the salad.

Greek Lentil Salad (*Salata Faki*): Add 3/4 to 1 1/2 cups (4 to 8 ounces) crumbled feta cheese, 1/3 cup chopped green olives, and 2 tablespoons chopped fresh spearmint.

Yemenite Lentil Dip (*Salata Adas*): Add 1 cup tahini (sesame seed paste) and increase the lemon juice to 1 cup and the parsley to 2 cups. Using a large mortar and pestle, potato masher, or a food processor, mash the combined salad into a paste.

TURKISH BULGUR SALAD

Kisir

4 TO 5 SERVINGS

Westerners have become familiar with tabbouleh (the flavorful bulgur salad with tomatoes and lots of parsley), but there are several other popular Middle Eastern bulgur salads, such as the Syrian bazargan *(Syrian Bulgur Relish, page 76) and one of the most important Ottoman salads,* kisir, *a piquant mixture from southern Turkey.*

The red peppers give this former peasant salad a dramatic red color, while the pomegranate molasses and lemon juice provide a fruity tartness. Hot red chilies add a zesty kick. Typically, cooks let the bulgur soak while cutting the vegetables. Kisir is usually served with turshi *(Middle Eastern Pickled Turnips, page 59) and plenty of pita bread or on a bed of romaine or Bibb lettuce leaves. Either is customarily used to scoop up the salad.*

- I cup (6 ounces) fine or medium bulgur wheat (not cracked wheat)
- I cup boiling water
- I cup chopped fresh parsley
- 3 to 4 plum tomatoes, seeded and diced (see page 291)
- 1/2 cup sliced scallions (6 to 8 total) or I large onion, finely chopped
- 2 green bell peppers, seeded, deribbed (white removed), and chopped (optional)
- I cucumber, peeled, seeded, and chopped (optional)

DRESSING:

- 2 large red bell peppers, seeded, deribbed (white removed), and chopped
- I small red chili, seeded and chopped
- 2 tablespoons water
- I tablespoon pomegranate concentrate (see page 22)
- I to 3 teaspoons hot Hungarian paprika or ground Aleppo or Maras pepper
- 1/4 cup fresh lemon juice
- 1/4 cup extra-virgin olive oil
- About I teaspoon table salt or 2 teaspoons kosher salt
- About 1/4 teaspoon ground black pepper
- 1/2 to I teaspoon ground cumin (optional)

1. Put the bulgur in a medium bowl, pour the boiling water over the top, and let stand until the water is absorbed, about 20 minutes, depending on the age and type of bulgur. Fluff with a fork. Add the parsley, tomatoes, scallions, green peppers, and, if using, cucumber.

2. Meanwhile, make the dressing: In a food processor or blender, purée the bell peppers, chili, and water until smooth. Scrape into a small saucepan and cook over medium heat, stirring frequently, until thickened and reduced to about 2/3 cup, about 10 minutes. Remove from the heat and add the pomegranate concentrate and hot paprika. Stir in the lemon juice, oil, salt, pepper, and, if using, cumin.

3. Drizzle the dressing over the salad and toss to coat. Cover and refrigerate for several hours to let the flavors meld and the bulgur absorb the dressing. Serve chilled or at room temperature.

Easy Turkish Bulgur Salad: In this version, the salad dervies its red tint from tomato paste instead of red peppers, while sumac gives the fruity tartness. Substitute the following dressing: Combine $1/4$ cup olive oil, 2 tablespoons fresh lemon juice, 2 tablespoons tomato paste, 2 teaspoons red pepper flakes, $1/2$ teaspoon table salt or 1 teaspoon kosher salt, $1/8$ teaspoon ground black pepper, and $1/2$ to 1 teaspoon ground sumac or ground cumin.

Middle Eastern Bulgur Salad (*Tabbouleh*): The name of this classic dish derives from the Arabic word for "to spice." Omit the dressing and add $1/3$ cup extra-virgin olive oil, 2 to 5 tablespoons fresh lemon juice, $1/4$ to $1/2$ cup chopped fresh spearmint, about 1 teaspoon table salt or 2 teaspoons kosher salt, and $1/4$ teaspoon ground black pepper.

Soups

❦ · ❦

After humans first mastered fire, they initially used it in cooking to roast meat and grains. The invention of earthenware vessels (which happened around the same time as the domestication of animals and plants) led to the advent of stews and soups. Until the use of metal pots spread during the Roman period, soups continued to be cooked in wide-bottomed terra-cotta kettles, arranged at first on rocks and later on clay stands over the fire. Even after the advent of metal kettles, many cooks persisted in using earthenware for making soups and stews, including the northwest African *tagine* and the modern crockpot, as pottery, a poor conductor of heat, proved to be ideal for slow cooking, which was necessary to soften and intensify the flavor of hard grains, dried legumes, and tough roots. Soon, barley stews led to the creation of both bread and beer, and when some spilled into the fire to form the first rudimentary loaves and leftover gruels fermented into an alcoholic beverage, which quickly became the mainstays of the diet. Also of great importance were legume soups, generally made from lentils, fava beans, split peas, and chickpeas and flavored with onions and garlic, supplementing and enlivening the diet. This grain trio of gruels, bread, beer along with legume stews provided the eight essential amino acids necessary to build protein and fuel civilization. Adding to the basic fare were assorted dairy products and a few fruits and vegetables.

At first, the only dining utensil was the right hand; the left was exclusively reserved for sanitation purposes. Middle Easterners generally used small pieces of flat bread to scoop up gobs of thick soup, or tore a loaf into bite-sized pieces, spread it over a wooden or earthenware platter, and heaped stew on top. The saturated bread pieces were then picked up, with the right hand, and popped into the mouth.

In the medieval kitchen, a metal kettle could usually be found hanging to the side of the hearth. There, legumes, vegetables, various scraps and leftovers, a few bones, and, when available, pieces of meat were simmered into a savory concoction known in French as *pot-au-feu*, literally "pot on the fire." (This is also the origin of the English phrases "potluck" and "gone to pot.") In most instances, these soups were not replaced but simply added to each day—a perpetually replenished food. For many families, the contents of the soup kettle, along with bread, constituted the main or sometimes the only meal of the day. The British called their evening meal, consisting of *pot-au-feu*, sup or supper, from the German *sop* (meaning "to soak"), referring to the bread that was inevitably dipped into the stew, or over which the liquid was served, which probably also gave rise to the word *soup*. Until 1700 and the invention of the ladle in France, European diners dipped their bowls directly into the kettle. The only dining utensil would be a wooden spoon (knives were generally unnecessary at the table for all but the upper classes, who ate more meat, while forks were an Italian Renaissance invention whose use spread slowly).

Few Westerners are familiar with the Persian *ash* or Hungarian *leves,* as well as many other international soups, which is unfortunate, for there exists a world of soups to spice up and add nourishment to any supper table. Most regions boast at least one ubiquitous local favorite: Russian *borscht,* Italian *minestrone,* Spanish gazpacho, Slavic *krupnik* (mushroom barley), Moroccan *hareera* (chickpea and lentil), and Uzbekistani *lagman* (noodle). Many of these made their way into Jewish cookery, generally with the addition of a Jewish touch. Substance and flavor are the enduring hallmark of Jewish soups. They tend to fall within four categories: basic vegetable soups that have only water or stock as their base; creamy vegetable soups that are thickened by dairy, whether sour cream or yogurt; legume and grain soups, flavorful and naturally hearty concoctions harkening back to the earliest soups; and fruit soups. Some soups require little or no *potchke* ("hassle") and many entail only chopping the ingredients and an occasional stir. Soup provides an ideal first course for a spring or summer meal and a hearty repast for the fall and winter. Hot or cold, thick or thin, simple or complex—nothing is as comforting, nourishing, or enduring as a bowl of soup.

VEGETABLE STOCK

ABOUT 2¹/₂ QUARTS

Vegetable stock has a delicate flavor, which will vary slightly from batch to batch even if you always use the same vegetables. You can add other vegetables than those listed, but do not overdo strongly flavored ones, particularly members of the cabbage family, such as broccoli, Brussels sprouts, cauliflower, kale, and kohlrabi. Avoid adding bell peppers, which impart an off flavor. For a more delicate taste, do not sauté or roast the vegetables. If you don't have time to make stock, use vegetable bouillon cubes, but beware of the extra sodium and MSG in some brands.

Use vegetable stock as a base for other soups, or serve it by itself with noodles, matza balls, or rice.

- 3 tablespoons vegetable oil
- 3 onions, coarsely chopped (for a darker stock, do not skin)
- 3 carrots, scrubbed and coarsely chopped
- 3 stalks celery with leaves, coarsely chopped
- 2 leeks (white and light green parts only), washed and coarsely chopped
- 3 quarts water
- 1 to 2 parsnips or turnips, peeled and coarsely chopped
- 1 cup peelings from well-scrubbed potatoes, or ¹/₄ cup brown lentils, or 2 sweet potatoes, peeled and quartered (optional)
- 5 to 6 cloves garlic
- 10 to 12 sprigs fresh parsley
- 2 sprigs fresh thyme or ¹/₂ teaspoon dried thyme
- 2 bay leaves
- About 2 teaspoons table salt or 1 tablespoon kosher salt (optional)
- 6 to 8 whole black peppercorns

1. In a large pot, heat the oil over medium-high heat. Add the onions, carrots, celery, and leeks and sauté until lightly browned, about 15 minutes. Or, combine those ingredients in a roasting pan and bake, uncovered, in a preheated 450°F oven for 1 hour, then transfer to a large pot.

2. Add all the remaining ingredients. Bring to a boil, partially cover, reduce the heat to low, and simmer for 1 hour. Remove from the heat and let stand for 30 minutes.

3. Strain the stock through a colander, pressing out any liquid, then discard the solids. Store in the refrigerator for up to 4 days or freeze for up to 3 months.

NOTES   For extra richness, save the water after cooking vegetables and use it as part or all of your vegetable stock's cooking liquid. You can also save vegetable scraps and trimmings (onion skins, carrot tops and peels, potato skins, celery leaves, and so on) in the freezer and add them to enhance your stock. In fact, some restaurants use only scraps to make stock, about 2 cups for every 4 cups of water—but at a loss of flavor.

A general rule of thumb when seasoning stock is, for every 4 cups of water, use 2 tablespoons fresh herbs or 2 teaspoons dried herbs, and ¹/₄ to ¹/₂ teaspoon table salt (¹/₂ to 1 teaspoon kosher salt), 1 tablespoon soy sauce, or 3 tablespoons miso (fermented soy paste). Stock reduces as it simmers, intensifying its flavors, so it is best not to add too much salt at the beginning of cooking. If you use stock as the base for a soup, be careful about adding additional salt called for in the soup recipe. If the soup tastes too salty, try adding a peeled raw potato and cook until enough excess salt is absorbed, then discard the potato.

Ukrainian Beet Soup

Borscht

6 TO 8 SERVINGS   Ⓓ OR Ⓟ

Beets come into season in June and are picked through October. In northern Europe, much of the harvest was once stored in cellars or beneath mounds of dirt to last through the winter. Before the onset of winter, some of the beets were fermented in large earthenware crocks to make russel *(the Slavic word for "brine"), a process similar to pickled cucumbers, which was then used to flavor horseradish, preserves, kugels, and other dishes, as well as being the flavorful pickling liquid served as a vinegary borscht. A second kind of borscht was made from raw beets chopped and simmered into a simple soup, frequently flavored with a little vinegar and sugar. For centuries, these two beet soups were among the principal foods of Ukrainian Jews. In my parents and grandparents' homes, every Passover meant purchasing jars of this sparkling red soup—made from fresh beets; the fermented type is extremely rare these days. The leftover bottles provided borscht for months to come.*

At dairy meals, the chilled soup is generally paired with two other traditional eastern European mainstays, boiled potatoes and sour cream, during Passover, constituting with some matza and butter a full meal. Sour cream adds a tangy note to the soup as well as a creamy, thicker texture, while the potatoes contribute a textural and flavor contrast. Or, it is drunk straight as a rich sweet-and-sour nectar.

2 1/2 pounds beets, peeled and diced or coarsely grated

I large onion, skinned and left whole

8 cups water

2 to 4 tablespoons fresh lemon juice or cider vinegar, or about 2 large pieces sour salt (citric acid crystals)

I to 4 tablespoons sugar

About 2 teaspoons table salt or I tablespoon kosher salt

Ground black pepper to taste

16 ounces (2 cups) sour cream (optional)

In a large pot, combine the beets, onion, and water. If using the sour salt, add it now, too. Bring to a boil, reduce the heat to low, cover, and simmer until the beets are tender, about 45 minutes. Stir in the lemon juice, if using, then the sugar, salt, and pepper and simmer for 10 minutes. Remove and discard the onion. Serve hot or cold. Top with a liberal dollop of sour cream, if desired.

VARIATIONS

Polish Beet and Cucumber Soup (*Chlodnik*): Serve this soup chilled. Chop the onion before cooking and leave it in the soup. Just before serving, stir in 2 cups seeded and chopped cucumbers and 1/2 teaspoon grated horseradish or 2 tablespoons chopped fresh dill.

Polish-Style Beet Soup (*Borscht*): You can use eggs to thicken the borscht without sour cream; the result is a lighter color and a more viscous texture. Gradually stir 2 cups of hot borscht into 3 lightly beaten eggs, then stir the egg mixture into the soup and simmer over low heat, stirring constantly, until slightly thickened, about 5 minutes. Do not boil.

Excellent ?
Super easy!
Try less sugar
A bit less cider vinegar

BORSCHT

WAIT UNTIL YOU HAVE TASTED OUR BORSCHT TONIGHT,
THEN YOU'LL KNOW WHAT GOOD FOOD IS.

—*Tit for Tat* by Sholom Aleichem

For centuries, eastern Europeans made soup from a stout, whitish root related to carrots and parsnips, called *borshch* in Slavic areas and cow parsnip in England. Although the root's somewhat acrid flavor hardly made the most flavorsome soups, even with the addition of meat and bones, it was one of the few vegetables available to peasants during the winter. That is, until the modern-day beetroot was developed in the sixteenth century. Beets were inexpensive, flavorful, and easily grown. Soon, people began adding beetroots to their soup, which quickly supplanted the *borshch* entirely, though the new soup retained its familiar name. Since the erstwhile Russian name for beet soup was *malorossisky* (the former name for Ukraine) *borshch*, it is probable that beet *borshch* was first made in Ukraine. Beet soup quickly spread throughout much of eastern Europe.

In Ukraine, the predominant beet-growing region of eastern Europe, borscht was everyday fare. Farther north, where beets were often less accessible, this soup was generally reserved for special occasions, such as Passover, the third meal of the Sabbath, or the festivities immediately following the Sabbath. Although non-Jews added meat or bones to borscht as flavoring, Jews developed a vegetarian version in order to enjoy the soup enriched with sour cream.

To improve the taste (following the establishment of the first sugar beet refineries in the early 1800s, which first made inexpensive sugar accessible in the region), they started adding sugar, turning borscht into a sweet-and-sour dish. Polish Jews tend to add a large amount of sugar, while most Ukrainians use more vinegar. When eastern European Jews emigrated to America, they brought vegetarian borscht with them; at one point it was featured in the many Jewish resorts that once flourished in the Catskill Mountains of eastern New York, giving rise to the region's nickname, the Borscht Belt.

GERMAN CABBAGE SOUP

Krautsuppe

6 TO 8 SERVINGS

Cabbage has been the most important vegetable in northern Europe as well as the Mediterranean from time immemorial. Cabbage soup was the most common dish in medieval Europe. Although non-Jews commonly flavored their cabbage soup with pork or sausages, Jews used beef flanken (a section of the short ribs) or frequently opted for a vegetarian version. Slavs commonly added some sauerkraut for a tart flavor, but sour salt or lemon juice better serve that role. With the spread of the sugar beet in the early nineteenth century, sweet-and-sour versions of cabbage soup also became popular.

This simple, inexpensive soup, called krautsuppe *in Teutonic regions and* shchi *or cabbage borscht, in Slavic areas, provided the basis for many meals, especially in the fall and winter, sometimes topped with sour cream and accompanied with a chunk of dark bread, boiled potatoes, or* piroshki *(turnovers).*

> 3 tablespoons vegetable oil
>
> 2 onions, chopped
>
> 2 carrots, chopped (optional)
>
> I large head (about 2 pounds) green or savoy
>   cabbage, cored and shredded
>
> 8 cups Vegetable Stock (page 115) or water
>
> I 1/2 pounds plum tomatoes, peeled, seeded,
>   and chopped (about 3 1/2 cups; see page 291);
>   or 1/2 cup tomato paste
>
> 2 boiling potatoes, peeled and coarsely grated
>
> I bay leaf
>
> I teaspoon caraway seeds (optional)
>
> About 2 teaspoons table salt or I tablespoon
>   kosher salt
>
> Ground black pepper to taste

In a large pot, heat the oil over medium heat. Add the onions and, if using, the carrots and sauté until softened, 5 to 10 minutes. Add the cabbage and stir to coat. Add the remaining ingredients, cover, and simmer until tender, about 1 hour. Serve hot. Cabbage soup tastes even better reheated the following day. Store in the refrigerator for up to 3 days.

VARIATIONS

Ashkenazic Sweet-and-Sour Cabbage Soup (*Zeesih-Zoyirih Krautsuppe*): When the soup is done, add 1/2 cup granulated sugar, 1/4 cup packed brown sugar, 1 teaspoon sour salt (citric acid crystals) or about 1/3 cup fresh lemon juice, and, if desired, 1/2 cup golden raisins and simmer for another 10 minutes.

Hungarian Cabbage Soup (*Krautzip*): Omit the tomatoes and potatoes. Melt 1/4 cup butter or heat 1/4 cup oil in a medium saucepan over medium heat, add 1/4 cup unbleached all-purpose flour, and stir until bubbly, 2 to 3 minutes. Stir in about 1 cup hot cabbage cooking liquid, whisk until smooth, then add to the soup and simmer, stirring constantly, until slightly thickened, about 5 minutes.

Italian Cabbage Soup (*Minestra di Cavolo*): Omit the tomatoes and use olive oil. Add 3 to 4 cups cooked white beans or 1 cup brown rice with the stock or 1 cup white rice after cooking the cabbage for 30 minutes. If desired, add 2 leaves fresh sage with the onions. For dairy meals, sprinkle with grated provolone or Parmesan cheese or add some cheese rinds near the end of cooking.

Russian Cabbage Soup (*Shchi*): Add 1 teaspoon fresh dill weed or 1/2 teaspoon dried dill weed and 1/2 teaspoon celery salt. If desired, add 2 cups peeled and julienned celery root with the cabbage.

EGYPTIAN POTATO SOUP

Batata Lamoun

6 TO 8 SERVINGS

Egypt's brightly colored potato soup omits the milk, butter, and cream common in European versions, instead flavoring the dish with lemon. Anita Abraham, who prepared this dish for me, mentioned while cutting the potatoes that when she had a headache as a young girl growing up in Egypt, her mother would fasten a slice of potato to her forehead. Although she remains uncertain as to the efficacy of this practice, she does know that this potato soup always cures the blues for her.

3 tablespoons olive oil

3 large leeks (white and light green parts only), washed and chopped, or 3 onions, chopped

2 to 3 stalks celery with leaves, chopped

2 to 3 cloves garlic, minced

$1/4$ teaspoon ground turmeric

2 pounds boiling potatoes, peeled and coarsely chopped

$6^{1}/2$ cups water

1 bay leaf

About 2 teaspoons table salt or 1 tablespoon kosher salt

Ground white pepper to taste

About $1/4$ cup fresh lemon juice

In a large pot, heat the oil over medium heat. Add the leeks, celery, garlic, and turmeric and sauté until softened, 5 to 10 minutes. Add the potatoes, water, bay leaf, salt, and pepper. Bring to a boil, cover, reduce the heat to low, and simmer until the potatoes are very soft, about 45 minutes. Leave as is, or, using a wooden spoon or potato masher, mash the potatoes. Just before serving, stir in the lemon juice.

VARIATION

Ashkenazic Potato Soup (*Kartoffel Zup*): Omit the turmeric and lemon juice, use butter, reduce the water to 4 cups, and add 3 cups milk. If desired, just before serving stir in 1 cup sour cream and simmer over low heat until heated through.

NOTE Baking (russet) potatoes break down during cooking, while waxier boiling potatoes hold their texture. Therefore, use boiling potatoes for chunkier soups, and baking potatoes for smoother soups.

HUNGARIAN ASPARAGUS SOUP

Sparga Leves

6 TO 8 SERVINGS D OR P

Hungarians rarely start a lunch or dinner without soup (leves), many of which make ample use of seasonal produce. Hungary has long been Europe's largest producer of asparagus, in season from late February to early July, and much of the harvest goes into delicate soups, which they prepare both simply and elaborately. This colorful soup, for example, could be glamorized with shaved truffles or black truffle oil for a special occasion—or simply topped with a dollop of sour cream or a sprinkling of chopped chives.

3 tablespoons unsalted butter or vegetable oil
(see Note)

1 pound leeks (white and light green parts only),
washed and chopped; or 2 onions, chopped;
or about 1 cup of each

1 cup high-acid white wine, such as dry Tokaj,
Sauvignon Blanc, Chenin Blanc, or Soave

8 cups water

2 pounds asparagus, trimmed, tips cut off and
reserved, stalks chopped

2 baking (russet) potatoes, peeled and diced,
or 1/2 cup long-grain white rice

1 tablespoon sweet paprika, 1 tablespoon fennel
seeds, 1 tablespoon chopped fresh tarragon,
dash of hot sauce, or pinch of freshly grated
nutmeg

About 1 teaspoon table salt or 2 teaspoons
kosher salt

Ground white or black pepper to taste

1. In a large pot, melt the butter over medium heat. Add the leeks and sauté until soft and translucent, about 5 minutes. Add the wine and cook until reduced by half. Add the water and bring to a boil.

2. Add the asparagus tips and cook until just tender, about 3 minutes. Using a slotted spoon, transfer the tips to a bowl of cold water to stop the cooking. Drain and set aside.

3. Add the potatoes or rice to the cooking liquid, reduce the heat to low, cover, and simmer until very tender, about 30 minutes.

4. Add the chopped asparagus stalks, paprika, salt, and pepper. Cover and simmer until the asparagus is very tender, about 8 minutes.

5. Strain the soup, returning the cooking liquid to the pot. In a blender or food processor, purée the solids, then press through a sieve with the back of a large spoon, discarding the thick fibers. Stir the asparagus purée into the cooking liquid. Serve warm or chilled, garnished with the asparagus tips.

VARIATION

Hungarian Cream of Asparagus Soup (*Sparglecremsuppe*): Omit the potatoes and wine. After puréeing the soup, add 1 cup light cream or plain yogurt and, if desired, 1 tablespoon fresh lemon juice.

N O T E For soups to be served chilled, use oil instead of butter, as the latter solidifies when cold.

ITALIAN ARTICHOKE SOUP

Minestra di Carciofi

6 TO 8 SERVINGS   D OR P

Minestra is the Italian word for a thick soup in which the ingredients stand apart from the broth, while zuppa *is more uniform in texture. This chunky, refreshing* minestra *makes use of seasonal artichokes, available in late spring and summer. It can be enhanced with 2 cups cooked fava beans, 1 pound asparagus trimmed and cut into 1-inch pieces, or 1 sliced fennel bulb—add them about 5 minutes before the artichokes are tender. For extra flavor, serve with grated Parmesan cheese.*

1 lemon, halved

8 to 10 large artichokes

3 tablespoons olive oil or unsalted butter

2 onions, chopped, or 2 leeks (white and light green parts only), washed and chopped

2 to 3 large cloves garlic, minced; or 1 small dried red chili, seeded and minced

8 cups Vegetable Stock (page 115)

7 ounces plum tomatoes, peeled, seeded, and chopped (1 cup); see page 291

1 bay leaf

About 2 teaspoons table salt or 1 tablespoon kosher salt

About 1/4 teaspoon ground white or black pepper

1/3 cup pine nuts, toasted (see page 22), or 1 lemon, thinly sliced, for garnish

1. To prepare the artichokes: Squeeze the juice from the lemon and add to a large bowl of water along with the empty lemon shells. Working with one artichoke at a time, cut off the top half, occasionally dipping the artichoke into the lemon water while you work to prevent discoloration. Pull all the dark green outer leaves. Peel off the dark-colored fibers from the stem and base of the artichoke. Cut the artichoke in half lengthwise and dig out the fuzzy choke with a grapefruit spoon, melon baller, or teaspoon. Coarsely chop the heart and stem. Store the artichokes in the lemon water. Drain before using.

2. In a large nonreactive pot, heat the oil over medium heat. Add the onions and garlic and sauté until soft and translucent, about 5 minutes. Stir in the artichoke pieces and sauté until shiny, 2 to 3 minutes.

3. Add the stock, tomatoes, bay leaf, salt, and pepper. Bring to a boil, cover, reduce the heat to low, and simmer until the artichokes are tender, about 30 minutes. Discard the bay leaf. Garnish with pine nuts. Store any leftover soup in the refrigerator for up to 5 days.

VARIATIONS

Italian Artichoke Soup with Egg (*Minestra di Carciofi e Uova*): Gradually whisk about 1 cup of the hot soup into 3 lightly beaten large eggs, then stir the egg mixture into the soup and simmer, stirring constantly, until slightly thickened, about 3 minutes. Do not boil.

Creamy Italian Artichoke Soup (*Minestra di Carciofi*): Omit the tomatoes, add 1 cup milk or heavy cream, and heat through for about 5 minutes.

Italian Smooth Artichoke Soup (*Zuppa di Carciofi*): Omit the tomatoes. Add 1 peeled and chopped large baking (russet) potato or 1/2 cup long-grain white rice with the stock. When the ingredients are tender, purée the soup in a blender or food processor until smooth.

Italian Artichoke and Pea Soup (*Minestra di Carciofi e Bisi*): When the artichokes are almost tender, add 1 cup fresh or frozen green peas and 8 to 10 ounces small dried pasta such as rotini and simmer, uncovered, until the peas are tender and the pasta is al dente (tender but firm to the bite), about 8 minutes.

MOROCCAN PUMPKIN SOUP

Shorabit Yatkeen

6 TO 8 SERVINGS

During cooking, much of the pumpkin breaks down, thickening the soup, but some chunks remain, along with the chickpeas and onion, providing a hearty, comforting texture. Most Moroccans prefer this soup savory, with a subtle blend of spices, adding only a touch of sugar to bring out the earthy flavor of the pumpkin.

Since the pumpkin (because of its many seeds), chickpeas, and split peas are all traditional symbols of fertility and abundance, this soup is a common sight on Rosh Hashanah and Sukkot, a period which happens to correspond to the Moroccan pumpkin harvest. Some holiday versions of the soup, known as sopa de la siete veruras/soupa aux sept légumes, *contain seven traditional symbolic vegetables, including pumpkin, onions, carrots, turnips, cabbage, zucchini, and chickpeas. I like to serve the soup in a white porcelain bowl to display the orange color. The soup becomes yellowish when split peas are used.*

$1/4$ cup vegetable oil

2 leeks (white and light green parts only), washed and chopped, or 2 onions, chopped

8 cups Vegetable Stock (page 115) or water

2 to 3 pounds pumpkin, butternut squash, or other winter squash, peeled, seeded, and cut into 1-inch cubes (5 to 6 cups)

3 cups cooked chickpeas or 1 cup dried yellow split peas

2 carrots, cut into chunks (optional)

1 to 4 tablespoons packed brown or granulated sugar

2 (3-inch) cinnamon sticks or about 1 teaspoon ground cinnamon

$1/4$ teaspoon ground ginger

$1/4$ teaspoon ground turmeric or saffron thread

$1/8$ teaspoon ground allspice or freshly grated nutmeg

About $1^1/2$ teaspoons table salt or $2^1/2$ teaspoons kosher salt

Ground black pepper to taste

$1/4$ cup chopped fresh parsley or cilantro, $1/2$ cup toasted pumpkin seeds (see Note) or pine nuts (see page 22), or 1 cup sautéed mushrooms for garnish

1. In a large pot, heat the oil over medium heat. Add the leeks and sauté until soft, about 5 minutes. Add the stock, pumpkin, chickpeas, optional carrots, sugar, spices, salt, and pepper. Bring to a boil, cover, reduce the heat to low, and simmer until the pumpkin is very soft, about 50 minutes. Discard the cinnamon sticks.

2. To serve, garnish with the parsley or pumpkin seeds, or top each bowl with a little mound of sautéed mushrooms.

Creamy Pumpkin Soup (*Shorabit Yatkeen*): Omit the chickpeas. In a blender or food processor, purée the cooked soup until smooth. Or, substitute 4 cups canned pumpkin purée for the fresh pumpkin. Return to the pot, add 1 cup light cream or milk, if desired, and reheat.

Fiery Pumpkin Soup (*Shorabit Yatkeen*): Omit the cinnamon, ginger, and allspice. Add, with the onion, 1 minced clove garlic and 1 minced small hot green chili or Scotch bonnet chili, or add about 1 teaspoon cayenne and 1/2 teaspoon ground cumin with the pumpkin.

Bukharan Pumpkin and Mung Bean Soup (*Mosh Kovok*): Omit the chickpeas, cinnamon, ginger, and allspice. Add, with the pumpkin, 2 cups cooked white beans, 6 ounces raw mung beans, and 2 peeled and diced boiling potatoes. Serve topped with a dollop of yogurt.

NOTE   To toast pumpkin seeds: Wash the pumpkin seeds under cold running water and spread over paper towels to dry. Preheat the oven to 250°F. Spread the seeds over a baking sheet, sprinkle with salt, if desired, and bake, stirring every 15 minutes, until dry, about 1 hour. Increase the heat to 500°F and bake until lightly browned, about 5 minutes. Let cool and store in an airtight container at room temperature for up to 3 months.

1·11·15
Excellent!
Easy to make →
I used 7 onions)
and Dutch Oven
Very Authentic

PERSIAN ONION SOUP

Eshkaneh

6 TO 8 SERVINGS

Persian cooking uses herbs, both fresh and dried, and minimal blends of a few spices, keeping flavors understated. In accord with the Persian philosophy of duality, meals contain both hot and cold dishes and individual dishes often contain sweet-and-sour flavors. In this dish, onions provide the primary flavoring, enlivened with the tartness of fresh lemon or lime juice and a note of dried mint, a staple of the cuisine. The result is a unique golden soup with a sweet-and-sour flavor and creamy texture.

According to legend, this soup dates back to around 250 B.C.E. and the successful revolt of the Persian King Arsaces I against Antiochus II of Syria, when fresh foods were scarce. Eshkaneh is generally accompanied with lavash or pita bread and a bowl of mixed chopped fresh basil, cilantro, and mint. The soup is customarily garnished with fenugreek leaves, but parsley is a more available substitute.

5 tablespoons vegetable oil
8 yellow or red onions (about 4 pounds),
   thinly sliced
About 1/2 cup sugar
2 tablespoons unbleached all-purpose flour
8 cups water
1/2 teaspoon ground turmeric
About 1 1/2 teaspoons table salt or 2 1/2 teaspoons
   kosher salt
1/4 teaspoon ground black pepper
3/4 to 1 cup fresh lemon or lime juice, or 1/2 cup each
About 1 tablespoon dried mint, crushed
1/2 teaspoon ground cinnamon
3 large eggs, lightly beaten
Chopped fresh parsley for garnish

1. In a large pot, heat the oil over medium heat. Add the onions and sauté until translucent, about 10 minutes. Sprinkle with 1 tablespoon of the sugar and sauté until golden, about 5 minutes. Stir in the flour and cook, stirring, for about 3 minutes. Gradually stir in 2 cups of the water, scraping to loosen any browned bits.

2. Add the remaining 6 cups water, the turmeric, salt, and pepper. Bring to a boil, cover, reduce the heat to low, and simmer, stirring occasionally, until the flavors blend, about 40 minutes.

3. Add the lemon juice and the remaining sugar, tasting to adjust the tartness, and simmer for 10 minutes. Stir in the mint and cinnamon.

4. Just before serving, gradually whisk 1 cup of the hot soup into the eggs. Stir the egg mixture into the soup and simmer, stirring constantly, until slightly thickened, about 3 minutes. Do not boil. Serve warm, garnished with the parsley.

COCHINI MIXED VEGETABLE SOUP

Rasam

5 TO 6 SERVINGS   Ⓓ OR Ⓟ

Most countries boast some form of mixed vegetable soup. The seasonings clearly mark this one's Indian origins, in this instance from Kerala in the south. Rasam ranges from a simple but spicy tomato soup to this more elaborate variation. It is served to start the meal or as the second course, commonly accompanied with steamed rice or papadams (wafer bread) and various curries. An elderly gentleman from Cochin now living in Israel told me that his Indian

Jewish mother gave him rasam *whenever he had a bad cold, claiming that it removed heat from the body; she added extra cilantro to pacify the fever. Hence,* rasam *is the Indian Jewish "penicillin."*

SOUP:

3 tomatoes, peeled, seeded, and diced
   (about 2 cups); see page 291
1 cup sliced carrots
1 cup peeled, seeded, and cubed pumpkin
   or winter squash
1 cup sliced green beans
1 cup peeled and diced beets or turnips
1 cup sliced zucchini
1 cup peeled and cubed boiling potatoes
1 cup shredded stemmed spinach
3 tablespoons chopped fresh cilantro
1 tablespoon *ghee* (Indian Clarified Butter,
   page 51) or vegetable oil
1 teaspoon honey or 1 tablespoon jaggery
1 teaspoon ground coriander
1 to 4 small green chilies, seeded and minced
$1/2$ teaspoon ground turmeric
$1/2$ teaspoon minced fresh ginger
About $1/2$ teaspoon table salt or 1 teaspoon
   kosher salt
3 cups water

SPICE MIXTURE:

1 tablespoon *ghee* or vegetable oil
$1/2$ teaspoon black mustard seeds
$1 1/2$ teaspoons cumin seeds
$1/2$ teaspoon black cumin seeds or 2 teaspoons
   coriander seeds
1 bay leaf, crushed
$1/8$ to 1 teaspoon ground black pepper

About 1 teaspoon fresh lemon juice
   or 2 teaspoons tamarind pulp
$1/2$ cup chopped fresh cilantro

1. In a large pot, combine all the soup ingredients except the spice mixture. Bring to a boil, cover, reduce the heat to low, and simmer until the vegetables are tender, about 20 minutes.

2. To make the spice mixture: In a ladle or small skillet over high heat, melt the ghee. Add the mustard seeds and sauté until they begin to pop, about 30 seconds. Add the cumin seeds, bay leaf, and pepper and sauté until golden, 1 to 3 minutes.

3. Stir the spice mixture into the soup and simmer until the flavors meld, about 5 minutes. Stir in the lemon juice. Serve warm, garnished with the cilantro.

❧ CREAMY SOUPS ❧

HUNGARIAN CREAM OF MUSHROOM SOUP

Gomba Leves

6 TO 8 SERVINGS

 D

The nomadic Magyars, from whom the country of Hungary received its name, carried cauldrons with them called bogracs, *which were convenient for preparing hearty soups and slow-simmering stews over open fires. This tradition endures in the myriad of soups and stews that remain standards of Hungarian cuisine.*

The forests of Hungary boast over seventy varieties of edible mushrooms. For centuries, Hungarians from most every walk of life headed to the nearby woods in the fall and early spring to gather mushrooms for flavoring numerous dishes and making pots of this luscious soup. When cooking with mushrooms, it is best to avoid intense seasonings and complicated preparations that mask the mushroom's delicate flavor. Hungarian cooking utilizes few spices other than paprika—occasionally a little marjoram, dill, caraway, or pepper. This light but filling soup captures the mushroom's earthy essence, balanced by a little hot paprika and the tang of sour cream. Use whatever wild mushrooms are available to create a diversity of flavors. Along with crusty bread, a green salad, and perhaps a bottle of Sauvignon Blanc or Pinot Noir, this soup serves as a complete meal.

1/4 cup unsalted butter or olive oil,
    or 2 tablespoons each
1 large onion or 6 to 8 shallots, chopped
2 tablespoons sweet paprika
1 to 2 tablespoons hot Hungarian paprika
    or cayenne
1/4 cup unbleached all-purpose flour
6 cups Vegetable Stock (page 115) or water,
    at room temperature
2 pounds mixed fresh wild mushrooms of any
    kind, or a mix of wild and button mushrooms,
    thickly sliced
About 1 1/2 teaspoons table salt or 2 1/2 teaspoons
    kosher salt
Ground white or black pepper to taste
1/4 cup chopped fresh dill or 1 sprig fresh thyme
2 cups sour cream or 1 cup heavy cream,
    at room temperature

1. In a large pot, melt the butter over medium heat. Add the onion and sauté until soft and translucent, about 5 minutes. Stir in both paprikas. Stir in the flour to form a paste and cook over low heat, stirring constantly, until smooth and bubbly, 3 to 5 minutes.

2. Gradually whisk in the stock, whisking until smooth. Add the mushrooms, salt, pepper, and, if using, the thyme. Bring to a boil, reduce the heat to

low, and simmer, stirring frequently, until the soup thickens and the mushrooms are tender, about 20 minutes. For a smoother consistency, purée half or all of the soup in a blender or food processor. At this point, the soup can be stored in the refrigerator for up to 3 days and reheated.

3. To serve, add the dill, if using. Stir in the sour cream, $1/2$ cup at a time, and stir over low heat until heated through, about 5 minutes. Do not boil. Serve warm.

N O T E For a more intense flavor, in a glass measuring cup, soak 1 ounce dried mushrooms of any type in hot water to cover for 30 minutes, then remove and chop. Add the dried mushrooms and soaking liquid (being careful not to pour in the sediment at the bottom) to the soup with the fresh mushrooms.

HUNGARIAN GREEN BEAN SOUP

Zoldbab Leves

5 TO 6 SERVINGS

Until the late Middle Ages, bread served as a crude thickener for soups. Even today, many peasant soups call for bread crumbs or torn bread. Flour thickens liquids better and more quickly than bread; however, until the Hungarian invention in the 1840s of rollers to grind wheat, the relatively coarse flour used left a gritty texture in soups. Fine white flour produces a smoother texture. One way to add flour to soups without creating lumps is by dispersing it in a cold liquid, called a slurry. The slurry is usually added near the end of the cooking, but must be cooked for several minutes to remove the raw flour taste. Raw flour thickens more quickly than cooked, as in a roux. In this soup, the lactic acid in the sour cream causes the proteins in the flour to coagulate, increasing its thickening ability.

This soup is adapted from a recipe that appeared in the June 1987 issue of my Kosher Gourmet Magazine, *contributed by Kathy Rosenbluh, who had known only Hungarian cooking until the age of eighteen. Years later, after experimenting with and discovering other cuisines, she still asserts that nothing beats her family's home cooking. Kathy's mother regularly served this soup for Shavuot dinner, along with* turos derelve *(cheese kreplach), always made from scratch.*

During hot weather, Hungarians serve most soups cold. This early summer soup, rich but light, is a way to display the new crop of tender young green beans. There are few other ingredients or seasonings in the soup, which captures the essence of the freshest vegetables and allows the delicate sweetness and herbal flavor of the beans to shine in harmony with the soothing sour cream and slight zing from the vinegar. Since this recipe relies primarily on the flavor of the beans, older beans or frozen ones will result in a less desirable taste. If you don't have access to a farm or vegetable plot, look for a farmers' market or a good vegetable store.

4 cups water

1 small onion, chopped

About 1 teaspoon table salt or 2 teaspoons
    kosher salt

1 pound young, slender green beans, trimmed and
    chopped into pea-sized pieces

3 tablespoons unbleached all-purpose flour

1 cup sour cream, at room temperature

1 to 3 teaspoons distilled white or tarragon
    vinegar or fresh lemon juice

Pinch of sugar or drop of honey (optional)

Chopped fresh chives or dill, or sweet paprika,
    for garnish

1. In a large pot, combine the water, onion, and salt. Bring to a boil, reduce the heat to low, cover, and simmer for 15 minutes. Add the beans and simmer, uncovered, until very tender but not mushy, about 15 minutes for fresh young beans. Remove from the heat.

2. In a medium bowl, stir the flour into the sour cream. Gradually stir 1 cup of the hot bean mixture into the sour cream. Add the sour cream mixture to the soup, beating constantly. Simmer, stirring constantly, over low heat without boiling until heated through and slightly thickened, about 5 minutes.

3. Stir in the vinegar to taste. If too tart, add a little sugar. The soup should be tart, not sweet and sour. Let cool to room temperature, then refrigerate until chilled, at least 3 hours. Ladle into chilled bowls and garnish with a sprinkle of chives, if desired.

N O T E Acid or high heat can cause milk and some other dairy products to curdle. Since sour cream contains a significant amount of lactic acid, boiling it in a soup or cooking it for too long will coagulate the proteins, resulting in curds. If the soup curdles, combine an additional $1/2$ cup sour cream with 1 tablespoon flour, then slowly stir in a little of the hot liquid and gradually stir into the soup and heat through.

EASTERN EUROPEAN SORREL SOUP

Schav

6 TO 8 SERVINGS   D OR P

Sorrel (sour grass), called schav in Slavic areas, is a member of the buckwheat family. Its English name is derived from the Old French for "sour," due to its distinctively striking but pleasant tart taste. The arrow-shaped dark green sorrel leaves, which look like spinach, are primarily used in soups and sauces, but small young ones with a delicate tang go raw into salads, adding an interesting contrast to bitter and sweet greens.

Sorrel is still picked wild in eastern Europe from April through June and, combined with potatoes, makes a simple peasant soup. Since sorrel appears around Passover and flourishes through Shavuot even in much of northern Europe, sorrel soup, commonly thickened with potatoes stored through the winter, became a widespread Ukrainian and Polish holiday dish. Jews would make a vegetarian version, so as to use sour cream, resulting in a cleaner-tasting soup than those made with meat or chicken stock. Some Poles will add a little sugar for an unorthodox sweet-and-sour taste. Spinach is frequently added, not only because it is cheaper and more readily available, but also for color—spinach remains green after cooking, while sorrel turns a grayish green. (I've tried making it with spinach and adding lots of lemon, but the results were hardly the same.) Wealthier people enriched their soups with a few eggs, sometimes indulging in both eggs and sour cream.

Fresh sorrel makes all the difference in this soup. Now, at least once every spring, I head to the farmers' market on a quest for sorrel to make a pot of schav and savor its unique flavor.

If you can find it, use the variety called French, or buckler, sorrel. For this soup, older, tougher sorrel actually works better than the younger, higher-priced leaves. Look for bright green leaves with no sign of yellowing. Store in a plastic bag in the refrigerator for up to 5 days. Sorrel is frequently covered with grit, so repeatedly immerse the leaves in a big bowl of cold water until no grit remains on the bottom of the bowl. Serve schav with dark bread as the main part of a light lunch or as the first course of a special dinner.

8 cups water

1 1/2 pounds sorrel, washed, stemmed, and chopped (about 8 cups)

1 pound boiling potatoes, peeled and diced

5 to 6 scallions, chopped

About 1 1/2 teaspoons table salt or 2 1/2 teaspoons kosher salt

About 1/2 teaspoon ground white or black pepper

1 to 4 tablespoons fresh lemon juice

2 large eggs or 4 large egg yolks, lightly beaten (optional)

1 to 2 cups sour cream (optional)

Any combination of chopped celery, cucumbers, radishes, and scallions, for garnish (optional)

1. In a large pot, combine the water, sorrel, potatoes, scallions, salt, and pepper. Bring to a boil, reduce the heat to low, partially cover, and simmer for 20 minutes. Add the lemon juice and continue simmering, uncovered, until the potatoes are very tender, about 10 minutes. The sorrel will begin to disintegrate. Leave the soup with a chunky texture or purée in a blender or food processor until nearly smooth. Adjust the lemon juice and reheat.

2. For a richer, thicker soup, gradually whisk 1 cup of the hot soup into the eggs, then stir the egg mixture back into the soup. Stir over low heat until slightly thickened, about 5 minutes. Do not boil.

3. Serve warm or chilled. For the latter, refrigerate for at least 4 hours. The soup can be stored in the refrigerator for up to 2 days, or, if made without the eggs, for up to a week. Garnish with a dollop of sour cream or stir it into the soup and sprinkle with various chopped vegetables.

SYRIAN SPINACH SOUP

Shoorbah Sabanekh

6 TO 8 SERVINGS   D OR P

Spinach soup is a light spring and early summer treat in many parts of the Middle East and Mediterranean. This Syrian version is accented with mint, but a little ground ginger or nutmeg is a tasty alternative. The soup is sometimes called labaneya, *from the Arabic word for "yogurt." It is always made without meat or chicken stock so that it can be served with plenty of yogurt, but for a nondairy soup use pomegranate concentrate or lemon juice for a touch of tartness. Some cooks stir the yogurt into the soup, while others spoon a large dollop over each serving for the individual diners to stir in. Spinach soup is commonly served with pita bread.*

1/4 cup vegetable oil or unsalted butter

2 onions, chopped

3 to 4 cloves garlic, minced

2 pounds fresh spinach or Swiss chard, washed, stemmed, and coarsely chopped, or 20 ounces thawed frozen spinach, squeezed dry

7 cups Vegetable Stock (page 115) or water

3/4 cup basmati or other long-grain white rice

2 teaspoons dried mint, crushed, or 1/2 cup chopped fresh mint

About 1 teaspoon table salt or 2 teaspoons kosher salt

Ground black pepper to taste

2 to 4 cups plain yogurt or 2 tablespoons pomegranate concentrate (see page 22) or 2 to 4 tablespoons fresh lemon juice

1. In a large pot, heat the oil over medium heat. Add the onions and garlic and sauté until soft and translucent, 5 to 10 minutes. Gradually add the spinach, stirring until wilted, about 5 minutes.

2. Add the stock, rice, dried mint, if using, salt, and pepper. Bring to a boil, cover, reduce the heat to medium-low, and simmer until the rice is tender, about 20 minutes. If using fresh mint, add it after cooking for 15 minutes, then simmer another 5 minutes.

3. Leave the soup with a chunky texture or process in a blender or food processor until nearly smooth. If too thick, add a little more stock. Top each portion with several dollops of yogurt or stir it into the soup. If reheating after adding the yogurt, be careful not to boil. Serve hot or chilled.

VARIATIONS

French Spinach and Pea Soup (*Potage au Épinards et Petits Pois*): Omit the rice, reduce the spinach to 1 pound, and add 20 ounces fresh or frozen green peas.

Greek Spinach Soup (*Spanakosoupa*): Substitute ⅓ cup chopped fresh dill for the mint and 1 cup orzo (rice-shaped pasta) for the rice, cooked in boiling water until al dente, adding the dill, pasta, and 2 to 4 tablespoons fresh lemon juice about 5 minutes before serving.

Persian Spinach Soup (*Pshal Dueah*): Substitute 2 tablespoons chopped fresh dill for the mint, and add 1 teaspoon ground turmeric when the rice is tender.

Indian Spinach Soup (*Palak Shorva*): Omit the mint. In Step 1, before adding the spinach, stir in 1 teaspoon ground cumin, ½ teaspoon ground turmeric, and ⅛ teaspoon ground cinnamon or 1 teaspoon ground fenugreek. Add 1 tablespoon fresh lemon juice with the spinach. If desired, substitute 2 cups canned coconut milk for the yogurt and garnish with toasted unsweetened shredded coconut.

AZERBAIJANI KEFIR AND GREENS SOUP

Dovga

6 TO 8 SERVINGS

Azerbaijan boasts about thirty national soups. All are distinctive for being very thick, and the creamy dovga is one of the favorites. Although similar creamy spinach soups are popular in Persia and Turkey, the large amount of fresh herbs, the yellow split peas, and the kefir in this version mark its Caucasian roots. Kefir (the word is derived from the Turkish keif, meaning "feeling good"), called matsoni in Georgia, is an effervescent milk product made from small, complex clumps of bacteria and yeast (called "grains") that have been grown together, then added to milk to ferment. Kefir has a refreshing, mild, slightly tart flavor reminiscent of buttermilk, which varies according to the type of milk used, the grains (each colony of yeast and bacteria is slightly different), and the incubation period.

For generations, to ferment kefir Caucasians would place milk and some kefir grains in a sack made from animal hide and hang it near the front door. People were expected to prod the sack whenever they entered or left the house—a practical way to ensure the contents were continually mixed to assist fermentation. Kefir grains were regarded as part of the family's wealth and were passed down from one generation to the next. The curd size of kefir is smaller than that of its distant cousin, yogurt, and, therefore, is easier to digest. Kefir has recently become available in most natural foods stores, but yogurt can be substituted in recipes.

Since kefir provides a third of the liquid in this recipe, it gives the soup a creamy texture, a slight fizz from natural carbonation, and a pleasant, yeasty aroma. The addition of bitter spinach and tart sorrel and the fresh herbs creates an interesting balance of flavors. Dovga, considered good for the digestion, is usually served after the main course or plov (rice pilaf), the latter generally offered after the main course at an Azerbaijani feast. It is best served fresh and warm.

3 tablespoons vegetable oil or unsalted butter

I large onion, chopped

6 cups Vegetable Stock (page 115) or water

1/2 cup yellow split peas, soaked for 4 hours
    and drained

1/3 cup long-grain rice

2 tablespoons unbleached all-purpose flour

3 cups plain kefir or yogurt

I large egg, lightly beaten

8 ounces stemmed, washed, and chopped spinach,
    about 5 cups, or 3 cups stemmed and chopped
    sorrel or watercress and 1 1/2 cups chopped
    stemmed spinach

About I teaspoon table salt or 2 teaspoons
    kosher salt

Pinch of sugar

4 to 5 scallions (white and light green parts only),
    chopped

3 tablespoons chopped fresh cilantro

3 tablespoons chopped fresh dill

3 tablespoons chopped fresh mint
    or I tablespoon dried mint

Ground sumac for garnish

1. In a large pot, heat the oil over medium heat. Add the onion and sauté until soft and translucent, about 5 minutes. Add the stock and bring to a boil. Add the split peas, reduce the heat to low, and simmer for 30 minutes. Add the rice, partially cover, and simmer for 15 minutes.

2. Stir the flour into the kefir. Add the egg. Gradually whisk 2 cups of the hot soup into the kefir, then stir the kefir mixture into the pot. Add the spinach, salt, and sugar and simmer over low heat until the rice is tender, about 10 minutes. Do not boil.

3. Add the scallions, cilantro, dill, and mint and simmer, stirring constantly, for 1 minute. Remove from the heat. Serve warm. Sprinkle a little sumac over each serving.

VARIATION

Instead of sumac, heat 2 tablespoons vegetable oil in a ladle or small saucepan over medium-low heat and stir in 1/4 teaspoon cayenne or 1 tablespoon sweet paprika. Drizzle a little of this mixture over each serving.

Persian Yogurt and Cucumber Soup

Mast Va Khiar

6 TO 8 SERVINGS   D

This easy, tasty soup, also called dueh, *makes a refreshing start to a summer meal. Yogurt lightly diluted with a little milk provides a tart, creamy base enhanced by the cool sweetness of cucumbers and the pungency of raw garlic. The amount and types of herbs and garlic are a matter of availability and preference. Cooks in some areas augment the basic recipe by adding seedless grapes, raisins, pickled cucumbers, scallions, or ground nuts. A splash of olive oil contributes a fruity or slightly pungent note. For a tarter flavor, add a squeeze of fresh lemon juice. Serve with crusty bread or pita.*

    2 to 5 cloves garlic

    1 teaspoon table salt or 2 teaspoons kosher salt

    4 cups plain yogurt

    1 cup milk or $^1/_2$ cup buttermilk and $^1/_2$ cup water

    1 to 2 tablespoons extra-virgin olive oil (optional)

    1 $^1/_3$ pounds cucumbers, peeled, seeded, and diced
       or grated (about 4 cups)

    $^1/_2$ cup chopped scallions

    $^1/_4$ to $^1/_2$ cup chopped fresh dill, cilantro, or mint;
       or 6 tablespoons chopped fresh tarragon and
       3 tablespoons fresh dill

    2 hard-boiled eggs, chopped; or $^1/_2$ cup chopped
       walnuts for garnish (optional)

Using the tip of a heavy knife or a mortar and pestle, mash the garlic and salt into a paste. In a large bowl, blend together the yogurt, milk, and, if using, oil. Stir in the garlic, cucumbers, and scallions. Refrigerate for at least 1 hour. About 5 minutes before serving, stir in the herbs. Pour into serving bowls and sprinkle with the eggs.

VARIATIONS

Bulgarian Yogurt and Cucumber Soup (*Tarator*): Omit the scallions, reduce the dill or mint to 1 tablespoon, and add 1 cup ground walnuts and $^3/_4$ cup raisins.

Iraqi Yogurt and Cucumber Soup (*Shorabit Laban Barida*): Add $^1/_2$ cup finely ground blanched almonds and a pinch of cayenne.

NOTE Yogurt serves as a primary ingredient in numerous Persian dishes, including soups, sauces, and salads. If you find that yogurt is too tart for your taste, in any recipe blend in a little nonfat dry milk—the lactose sweetens it.

BEAN, LEGUME, AND GRAIN SOUPS

SEPHARDIC RED LENTIL SOUP

Sopa de Lentejas

6 TO 8 SERVINGS

Mild-tasting red lentils are an excellent canvas for other flavors. Spices ranging from cumin to ginger, herbs, chili paste, fruit, and various grains all contribute their personalities to versions of the classic red lentil soup. Middle Eastern Jews commonly serve red lentil soup—sometimes mixed with rice, bulgur, or noodles—with simple salads, boyos (cheese pastries), and olives every Thursday night as the traditional vegetarian meal before the Sabbath. Even the poor would not eat lentils on the Sabbath, as this legume was considered a common food. Garnish with lemon wedges or top with a dollop of yogurt.

3 tablespoons olive oil or vegetable oil

2 white or red onions, chopped

4 to 5 cloves garlic, minced

1 teaspoon ground cumin or 1/2 teaspoon ground cumin and 1/2 teaspoon ground coriander

2 cups red lentils, picked over, rinsed, and drained

14 ounces plum tomatoes, peeled, seeded, and chopped (2 cups); see page 291

8 cups water

2 bay leaves

About 2 teaspoons table salt or 1 tablespoon kosher salt

Ground black pepper to taste

2 to 4 tablespoons fresh lemon juice or wine vinegar

Olive oil for drizzling

Handwritten note (Instant Pot version): Instapot Version 2 cups Red lentils, 3 smashed garlic, 3 cups water, salt/pepper, cumin

1. In a large pot, heat the oil over medium heat. Add the onions and garlic and sauté until soft and translucent, 5 to 10 minutes. Stir in the cumin, then the lentils, and sauté until coated, about 1 minute. Add the tomatoes and sauté for 1 minute.

2. Add the water, bay leaves, salt, and pepper. Bring to a boil, cover, reduce the heat to low, and simmer until the lentils break down, about 40 minutes. Discard the bay leaves.

3. If the soup is too thick, add a little more water. For a smoother consistency, purée the soup in a blender or food processor. The soup will keep, refrigerated, for up to 3 days. Before serving, stir in the lemon juice. Drizzle each serving with a little olive oil.

VARIATIONS

Armenian Red Lentil Soup (*Vospapur*): Add 1/2 cup chopped dried apricots and 1/2 teaspoon dried thyme with the water.

Calcutta Red Lentil Soup (*Massor Dal*): Add 2 teaspoons grated fresh ginger, 1 teaspoon turmeric, and 2 to 3 minced small dried red chilies or 1/4 teaspoon cayenne with the cumin. Serve over rice and sprinkle with fresh dill or cilantro.

Egyptian Lentil and Noodle Soup (*Adas bi Rishta*): Omit the tomatoes. The cooking time will be about 30 minutes. Do not purée the soup. Add, with the lemon juice, 5 to 6 ounces noodles or vermicelli broken into small pieces and cooked until tender.

Handwritten note: Good & easy add salt & lemon

Moroccan Red Lentil and Chickpea Soup (*Shorabit Adas*): Omit the lemon juice and cumin. Add 2 teaspoons sweet paprika, 1 teaspoon ground cinnamon, 1 teaspoon ground turmeric, and 1/2 teaspoon ground ginger with the cumin. After puréeing, add 1 1/2 cups cooked chickpeas or wheat berries and heat through.

Handwritten note: Good, but try others & original.

Handwritten note: Excellent, Yemeni version. Good way to use Zhoug

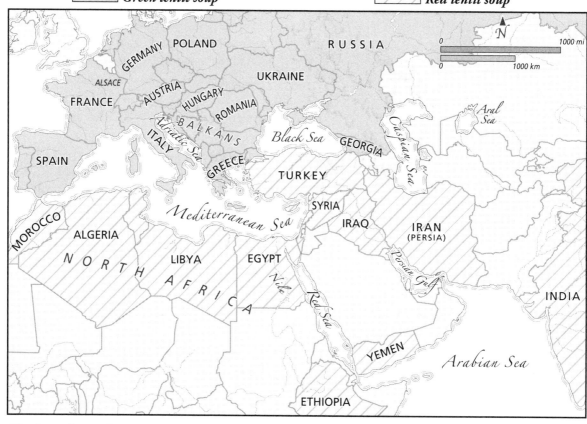

The Prevalence of Green and Red Lentil Soup: *Europeans prefer the textural feel of firmer green lentils in their soup, while Middle Easterners favor the smoother consistency of red lentils.*

My own version 2/7/16

3 cloves garlic
1 tsp cumin
1 tsp tabil
2 tsp curry
1/2 tsp tumeric
2 tsp + salt
2c lentils / 8c water

Saute garlic
add spices
add lentils
add water
Simmer covered one hour
Blend 3/4 in vitamix

Syrian Red Lentil and Bulgur Soup (*Calca*):
Omit the tomatoes and cumin. Add 3 chopped carrots
and 2 chopped stalks celery with the onions and 1 cup
coarse bulgur with the lentils. The cooking time will be
about 30 minutes. Some people serve the soup with
plenty of lemon and orange wedges, squeezing them
alternately on successive spoonfuls of soups for
sequential sour and sweet tastes.

Yemenite Red Lentil Soup (*Adas Ahnar*): Omit
the lemon juice and cumin and add 1 to 3 teaspoons
z'chug (Yemenite Chili Paste, page 438) with the water.

↑ *Excellent*

JACOB'S RED LENTIL SOUP

The world's all-time most famous lentil
dish is unquestionably Jacob's red pot-
tage (Genesis 25:30), reflecting the antiquity
of this still-popular soup. (French cuisine calls
this dish *potage d'Esau*—Esau was Jacob's
twin, who sold his birthright for a bowl of
red lentil soup.) Red lentils, which are actually a salmon color, tend to turn pink or
golden as they cook, suggesting that Jacob's
stew was underdone when Esau wanted
to "swallow it." Today, numerous variations
of red lentil soup exist from the Maghreb
to India.

ALSATIAN GREEN LENTIL SOUP

Soupe de Lentille

6 TO 8 SERVINGS

*This is a sturdy Alsatian soup, loaded with vegetables
and accented with thyme. Unlike red lentils that disintegrate during cooking, green and brown lentils
hold their shape and are, therefore, best for salads and
soups where you want texture. Green lentils have a
slightly nutty, peppery taste. Adding a little vinegar
helps to break down the lentils, giving the soup a
smoother texture and rounder flavor.*

3 tablespoons vegetable oil
2 onions, chopped
3 carrots, chopped
2 turnips or 1 small rutabaga, peeled and chopped
2 stalks celery, diced, or 1 small celery root,
    peeled and diced
2 to 3 cloves garlic, minced
8 cups water
2 cups green or brown lentils, picked over, rinsed,
    and drained
1 tablespoon chopped fresh thyme or 1 teaspoon
    dried
1 bay leaf
About 2 teaspoons table salt or 1 tablespoon
    kosher salt
Ground black pepper to taste
2 to 3 tablespoons cider or red wine vinegar
    (optional)

1. In a large pot, heat the oil over medium
heat. Add the onions, carrots, turnips, and celery
and sauté for 10 minutes. Add the garlic and continue sautéing until the vegetables are softened,
about 5 minutes.

2. Add the water, lentils, thyme, bay leaf, salt, pepper, and, if using, vinegar. Bring to a boil, cover, reduce the heat to low, and simmer until the lentils are tender, about 50 minutes. Discard the bay leaf. For a thicker soup, purée 3 to 4 cups of the soup in a blender or food processor and return to the pot. Serve warm.

INDIAN SPLIT PEA SOUP

Chana Dal

6 TO 8 SERVINGS D OR P

I never particularly liked split pea soup, having been accustomed to the English style, dense and one-dimensional. Then, while dining at one of the many kosher Indian restaurants on Lexington Avenue in New York, my companion insisted that I try her soup. It was creamy and alive with a multitude of flavors, with a pleasant lemony undertone. Since the restaurant was virtually empty of other patrons, the chef meandered over to chat. In explaining how to make this dish, he cautioned me to be careful when adding the spice mixture to the soup, as the ghee tends to bubble. This soup is commonly served over hot basmati rice; accompanied with fresh tomato salad (Indian Tomato Salad, page 91) or plain yogurt, it becomes a one-dish meal.

3 tablespoons *ghee* (Indian Clarified Butter, page 51) or vegetable oil
2 onions, chopped
2 carrots, chopped (optional)
2 to 3 cloves garlic, minced
1 tablespoon minced fresh ginger
1 to 2 teaspoons minced small green chilies
1 teaspoon ground coriander
9 cups Vegetable Stock (page 115) or water
2 cups dried yellow split peas, picked over, soaked in cold water to cover for at least 5 hours, and drained
1/4 cup fresh lemon or lime juice
1 tablespoon honey or packed brown sugar
2 bay leaves
1 teaspoon ground turmeric
About 1 1/2 teaspoons table salt or 2 1/2 teaspoons kosher salt
About 1/4 teaspoon ground black pepper

SPICE MIXTURE:
3 tablespoons ghee or vegetable oil
2 teaspoons black mustard seeds
2 teaspoons cumin seeds
1/4 teaspoon fenugreek seeds or 1/8 teaspoon ground fenugreek (optional)

3 tablespoons chopped fresh cilantro or parsley

1. In a large pot, melt the ghee over medium heat. Add the onions and, if using, the carrots and sauté until softened, 5 to 10 minutes. Add the garlic, ginger, chilies, and coriander and sauté for 1 minute.

2. Add the stock, peas, lemon juice, honey, bay leaves, turmeric, salt, and pepper. Bring to a boil, cover, reduce the heat to low, and simmer, stirring occasionally, until the peas are very tender, about 1 hour and 45 minutes. For a smoother consistency, purée the soup in a blender or food processor, then return to the pot. If too thick, add a little additional water.

3. To make the spice mixture: In a ladle or small saucepan, melt the ghee over medium-high heat. Add the mustard seeds and fry until they begin to pop, about 30 seconds. Add the cumin and, if using, the fenugreek and fry until golden, about 1 to 3 minutes. Stir the spice mixture into the soup and simmer until the flavors meld, about 5 minutes. Stir in the cilantro. Serve warm.

VARIATIONS

Indian Curried Split Pea Soup (*Chana Dal*): Omit the mustard seeds, cumin seeds, and fenugreek seeds, and, with the turmeric, add 1 teaspoon ground cumin, $^1/_2$ teaspoon ground cinnamon, and $^1/_4$ teaspoon ground cloves.

Indian Split Pea and Pumpkin Soup (*Chana Dal*): After cooking for $1^1/_2$ hours, add about $1^3/_4$ cups peeled, seeded, and cubed pumpkin and cook until tender, about 15 minutes.

Indian Split Pea and Spinach Soup (*Chana Dal*): Omit the lemon juice and honey. After cooking the peas for 45 minutes, add $1^1/_2$ cups chopped stemmed spinach and cook an additional 30 minutes.

GEORGIAN RED BEAN SOUP

Lobiani

6 TO 8 SERVINGS

The Georgian love of walnuts manifests itself most especially in various walnut sauces, which they add to almost everything. Rather than the walnut sauce persistently dominating, its flavor interacts with the other ingredients, creating a different taste and character in every dish. Here, walnut sauce complements another Georgian favorite, red beans. As is typical of Georgian cuisine, plenty of fresh herbs help to balance the taste. I find this soup comes in handy during the winter when I am preoccupied with some project; served over rice, it provides several meals. Georgians, however, usually accompany this soup with various breads instead of rice.

I pound (about $2^1/_3$ cups) dried small red beans, picked over, soaked for 8 hours in cold water to cover, and drained

WALNUT SAUCE:

$^1/_2$ cup walnuts

2 to 3 cloves garlic

2 teaspoons coriander seeds or I teaspoon ground coriander

$^1/_4$ cup red wine vinegar

$^1/_4$ cup olive oil or vegetable oil

2 large onions, chopped

About 2 teaspoons table salt or I tablespoon kosher salt

About $^1/_4$ teaspoon ground black pepper

$^1/_3$ cup chopped fresh cilantro

$^1/_3$ cup chopped fresh dill

$^1/_3$ cup chopped fresh parsley

I tablespoon chopped fresh mint

1. Put the beans in a large pot and add water to cover by 2 inches. Bring to a boil, cover, reduce the heat to low, and simmer until the beans are very tender, about 1 1/2 hours.

2. Meanwhile, make the sauce: Using a mortar and pestle or a food processor, grind together the walnuts, garlic, and coriander. Add the vinegar and blend until smooth. Set aside.

3. Roughly mash the beans with the cooking liquid, using the back of a wooden spoon or a potato masher. Or, strain the beans, reserving the cooking liquid, and pulse briefly in a food processor to coarsely mash them—do not purée—and return the beans and liquid to the pot.

4. In a large skillet, heat the oil over medium heat. Add the onions and sauté until golden, about 15 minutes. Stir the onions and any oil into the soup. Add the salt and pepper and simmer for 1 minute.

5. Stir in the walnut sauce and simmer over very low heat, stirring frequently, until the flavors meld and the soup thickens slightly, about 10 minutes. Add a little more water if the soup is too thick. (At this point, the soup can be stored in the refrigerator for up to 2 days; it will thicken as it sits, so add a little liquid to reach the desired consistency.)

6. To serve, stir in the herbs and simmer for 5 minutes. Serve warm.

VARIATION

Lobiani: This is a popular Georgian flavor variation: Omit the dill and mint. Add with the water 1 tablespoon chopped fresh thyme, 2 teaspoons chopped fresh rosemary, and 1 teaspoon chopped fresh sage or 1/4 teaspoon dried sage.

N O T E You can cook the beans without presoaking by increasing the amount of water to about 12 cups and the cooking time to at least 2 hours.

PERSIAN WHITE BEAN AND NOODLE SOUP

Ashe Reshte

6 TO 8 SERVINGS

Soup holds a special place in Persian cooking. Indeed, the Farsi word for "cook" is ash-paz ("soup maker"), and the word for "kitchen" is ash-paz-khaneh ("room of the soup maker"). Full of protein-rich beans, vegetables, and noodles, this hearty cold-weather soup— a favorite Persian comfort food—is a meal in itself.

3 tablespoons olive oil or vegetable oil

2 onions, chopped

1/2 teaspoon ground turmeric

8 cups Vegetable Stock (page 115) or water

1 pound (2 1/3 cups) navy, cannellini, or other small dried white beans, picked over, soaked for 8 hours in cold water to cover, and drained

8 to 16 ounces fresh spinach or Swiss chard, stemmed and chopped; or thawed frozen chopped spinach

1/2 cup sliced scallions

2 turnips or beets, peeled and chopped (optional)

About 2 teaspoons table salt or 1 tablespoon kosher salt

Ground black pepper to taste

1 pound fresh egg noodles (Egg Noodle Dough, page 392) or dried wide egg noodles

1/2 cup chopped fresh parsley

2 tablespoons dried mint, crushed

1/2 teaspoon ground cinnamon

Lemon wedges or yogurt for garnish

1. In a large pot, heat the oil over medium heat. Add the onions and sauté until golden, about 15 minutes. Stir in the turmeric.

2. Add the stock and beans. Bring to a boil, partially cover, reduce the heat to low, and simmer, stirring occasionally, for 1 hour. Add the spinach, scallions, and, if using, the turnips. Simmer until the beans are tender, about 30 minutes. Season with the salt and pepper. The soup can be prepared to this point up to 2 days ahead, stored in the refrigerator, and reheated.

3. Add the noodles and parsley and cook over medium heat, uncovered and stirring occasionally, until tender, about 3 minutes for fresh noodles, 8 to 12 minutes for dried. Stir in the mint and cinnamon. Serve warm, with lemon wedges alongside. Top with a dollop of yogurt if desired.

VARIATIONS

Persian White Bean and Noodle Soup (*Ashe Reshte*): Omit the mint and cinnamon and add 1/2 cup chopped cilantro and 1/2 cup chopped fresh dill with the parsley.

Persian White Bean and Noodle Soup (*Ashe Reshte*): For a creamy bean soup: In Step 3, after adding the mint, gradually stir about 1 cup hot soup into 1 cup plain yogurt, then stir the yogurt mixture into the soup and heat through. Do not boil.

Persian White Bean, Lentil, and Noodle Soup (*Ashe Reshte*): Reduce the beans to 1 cup and, after cooking for 45 minutes, add 1 cup brown lentils, then continue cooking another 30 minutes before adding the noodles.

TUNISIAN CHICKPEA SOUP

Lablabi

6 TO 8 SERVINGS

Lablabi is a filling chickpea soup—nearly a stew—from Tunisia and eastern Algeria, full of vegetables and flavored with characteristic Maghrebi seasonings of cumin, chilies, and lemons. My Tunisian friends tell me it is primarily eaten at breakfast, typically garnished with savories like capers, olives, diced red pepper, chopped hard-boiled eggs, or a whole soft-boiled egg. I prefer it for lunch or dinner. Serve with lemon wedges or yogurt.

1/4 cup olive oil or vegetable oil

1 large onion, chopped

3 carrots, chopped

1 small (about 10 ounces) celery root, peeled and chopped; or 2 stalks celery, chopped

2 to 4 cloves garlic, minced

About 10 cups water

1 pound (2 1/3 cups) dried chickpeas, picked over, soaked for 12 hours in cold water, and drained

2 bay leaves

1 tablespoon cumin seeds or 1 1/2 teaspoons ground cumin

1 to 2 tablespoons *harissa* (Northwest African Chili Paste, page 433) or 1 teaspoon cayenne

About 1 teaspoon table salt or 2 teaspoons kosher salt

Ground black pepper to taste

1/2 cup chopped fresh cilantro, mint, or parsley

2 to 3 tablespoons fresh lemon juice or 1 cup plain yogurt

3 to 4 cups French bread cubes or pita bread triangles (optional)

Olive oil for drizzling

1. In a large pot, heat the oil over medium heat. Add the onion, carrots, celery root, and garlic and sauté until softened, about 10 minutes.

2. Add the water, chickpeas, and bay leaves. Bring to a boil, cover, reduce the heat to low, and simmer until very tender, about 1 1/2 hours.

3. Meanwhile, toast the cumin seeds, if using, in a dry skillet over medium heat until lightly browned, 1 to 3 minutes, shaking the skillet or stirring the seeds to prevent burning. Grind into a powder using a mortar and pestle or a spice grinder. Add the ground cumin, harissa, salt, and pepper to the soup. Cover and simmer for 15 minutes. Discard the bay leaves.

4. Using a wooden spoon or potato masher, coarsely mash the chickpeas in the pot. Or, pulse the soup briefly in a blender or food processor, return to the pot, and reheat. The soup can be stored in the refrigerator for up to 3 days and reheated before serving.

5. To serve, add the cilantro and lemon juice and heat through. If desired, before serving the soup, place about 1/2 cup bread pieces in the bottom of each serving bowl and ladle the soup over the top. Drizzle with olive oil.

VARIATIONS

Tunisian Fava Bean Soup (*Bissara*): Substitute 1 pound skinless dried fava beans for the chickpeas. Mature fava beans, both fresh and dried, have a tough skin that needs to be removed. The children in the family were commonly drafted for this tedious step, rubbing the beans to loosen the skin. Today, skinless dried beans are available in Middle Eastern markets.

Moroccan Chickpea and Spinach Soup (*Potakhe*): *Potakhe* is derived from the common Sephardic practice of cooking legumes and vegetables together. Omit the cumin and *harissa*. After coarsely mashing the chickpeas, stir in 2 pounds stemmed and chopped fresh spinach or Swiss chard, or frozen spinach thawed and squeezed dry, and the lemon juice, cover, and simmer until the spinach is tender, 2 to 4 minutes.

LABLABI

Lablabi, the sound of a seed rattling in a dried pod, is the Arabic name for the hyacinth bean, as well as for a venerable hyacinth bean soup once popular in the region. An Indian native and a longtime resident of the Mediterranean, the hyacinth bean's white, yellowish, or black pea-shaped seeds are toxic and must be boiled in several changes of water to be safe; consequently, the chickpea is generally substituted in the popular Maghrebi soup. *Lablabi* was regular fare among many in the Maghreb, the poor omitting the vegetables and relying only on chickpeas, fava, or hyacinth beans. Spooning the soup over bread transforms it into an inexpensive vegetarian meal.

Turkish Mixed Legume and Bulgur Soup

Tandir Corbasi

6 TO 8 SERVINGS

This is a response I received to a weekly e-mail column I wrote several years ago: "I love all of your recipes but particularly the mixed-bean soup. It reminded me of a soup called makhlouta *my Lebanese grandmother used to make on a weekly basis.*" My recipe actually came from a Turkish grandmother. Cooking grains and legumes together, often as a soup, is a common, efficient way of supplying all the major nutrients in one dish. The name tandir *is derived from the Persian word for a clay oven* (tandor), *which is where this soup was traditionally cooked. The Turkish word* corba *is derived from* shurba, *a Persian word for "soup";* corba *also means "tangy," which is the principal flavor of* corba *soups.*

In this soup, the red lentils break down and blend with a little tomato paste to create a thick sauce frequently brightened with hints of mint and chili. You can omit the chickpeas and beans for a simpler dish. In Turkey, this soup would start off dinner—the main meal of the day—followed with an entrée accompanied with salads, turshi *(pickles), and rice pilaf or* dolma *(rice-filled vegetable). More simply, serve this cold-weather soup with a salad, pita bread, and yogurt.*

¹/₄ cup olive oil

2 onions, chopped, or 3 leeks (white and light green parts only), washed and chopped, or 1 cup each

2 to 4 cloves garlic, minced

1 tablespoon tomato paste

About 8 cups Vegetable Stock (page 115) or water

³/₄ cup dried chickpeas, picked over, soaked for 12 hours in cold water, and drained

³/₄ cup dried small white beans or black-eyed peas, picked over, soaked for 8 hours in cold water, and drained

2 bay leaves

³/₄ cup red lentils

³/₄ cup (4¹/₂ ounces) coarse bulgur wheat

1 teaspoon sweet paprika

About 1 teaspoon table salt or 2 teaspoons kosher salt

Ground black pepper to taste

¹/₂ to 1 teaspoon red pepper flakes or cayenne pepper (optional)

1 tablespoon dried mint, crushed (optional)

¹/₂ cup chopped fresh parsley or cilantro (optional)

1. In a large pot, heat the oil over medium heat. Add the onions and garlic and sauté until soft and translucent, 5 to 10 minutes. Add the tomato paste and stir until slightly darkened, about 1 minute.

2. Add the stock, chickpeas, beans, and bay leaves. Bring to a boil, cover, reduce the heat to low, and simmer for 1¹/₂ hours.

3. Add the lentils, cover, and simmer for 30 minutes.

2/9/05

Excellent! Good, hearty soup. Very easy, but takes long to cook - 2+ hours

4. Add the bulgur, paprika, salt, pepper, and, if using, the pepper flakes. Simmer, stirring occasionally and adding more water if necessary, until the chickpeas, beans, and bulgur are tender, about 30 minutes. If using, add the mint and/or parsley right before serving. The soup can be stored in the refrigerator for up to 2 days and reheated before serving. If too thick, add a little more water.

VARIATIONS

Turkish Mixed Legume and Rice Soup (*Tandir Corbasi*): Substitute 1 cup long-grain rice for the bulgur, adding it with the lentils and covering the pot for the final 20 minutes of cooking. Or, reduce the bulgur to ¹/₂ cup and add ¹/₂ cup long-grain rice.

Lebanese Mixed Legume and Bulgur Soup (*Makhlouta*): Omit the tomato paste, chili, and mint and add 2 teaspoons ground cumin or 1 tablespoon chopped fresh thyme or 1 teaspoon dried thyme.

Syrian Mixed Legume and Bulgur Soup (*Alajah*): Omit the tomato paste, chili, and mint and add about 1 tablespoon fresh lemon juice with the parsley.

Syrian White Bean and Bulgur Soup (*Shorabit Ful Abiad wa Bourgul*): Omit the tomato paste, chickpeas, and lentils. Increase the white beans to 1 pound (2¹/₃ cups) and add 1 tablespoon chopped fresh thyme or 1 teaspoon dried thyme.

SEPHARDIC EGG AND BULGUR SOUP

Sopa de Huevos y Bulgur

6 TO 8 SERVINGS · D OR P

Egg-and-lemon soups (sopa de huevo y limón), *creamy and refreshingly tart, are prevalent in the eastern Mediterranean, particularly during the summer. Many versions contain chicken; this one instead combines the soup with a bulgur (called* trahanas *in Greek) to make a thick, hearty vegetarian dish perfect for a soothing winter dinner. The bright lemon balances the earthy flavor of the bulgur; the eggs add a touch of richness.*

> ¹/₄ cup olive oil or vegetable oil
> 2 cups (about 12 ounces) coarse bulgur
>   or cracked wheat
> 8 cups Vegetable Stock (page 115) or water
> About 1¹/₂ teaspoons table salt or 1 tablespoon
>   kosher salt
> 1³/₄ pounds plum tomatoes, peeled, seeded,
>   and chopped (about 4 cups); see page 291
> About ¹/₄ teaspoon ground black pepper
> ¹/₄ to ¹/₃ cup fresh lemon juice
> 4 large eggs, lightly beaten
> ¹/₄ cup chopped fresh parsley or dill
> ¹/₄ cup grated kefalotyri, Parmesan, or other hard
>   cheese for sprinkling (optional)

1. In a large pot, heat the oil over medium-low heat. Add the bulgur and sauté until well coated and lightly colored, about 5 minutes.

2. Add 4 cups of the stock and ¹/₂ teaspoon of the table salt or 1 teaspoon of the kosher salt. Bring to a boil, cover, reduce the heat to low, and simmer until the liquid is absorbed and the bulgur is tender, about 20 minutes.

3. Add the remaining 4 cups stock, the tomatoes with their juices, the remaining salt, and the pepper. Bring to a boil, reduce the heat to low, and simmer, stirring occasionally, until the tomatoes are tender, about 5 minutes. Remove from the heat.

4. Whisk the lemon juice into the eggs. Gradually whisk 1 cup of the hot soup into the eggs, then stir the egg mixture into the pot. Place over a low heat and simmer, stirring constantly, until the soup begins to thicken, about 5 minutes. Do not boil or it will curdle. Serve hot, sprinkled with the parsley and, if using, the cheese.

GREEK BARLEY SOUP

Sopa de Cebada/Kritharosoupa

6 TO 8 SERVINGS

For millennia, barley, in the form of soups, bread, and beer, served as the predominant food of much of Asia, Africa, and Europe. Then, with the widespread introduction of common wheat around two thousand years ago, the more venerable grain gradually lost much of its luster. Barley remained a minor component of the eastern European diet, while Sephardim only consumed it in circumstances of severe want. Among the few barley dishes enduring in the Mediterranean are a cold sweetened dessert (sleehah) *and several thick hearty soups—wonderful cold-weather fare. Whereas mushrooms are the predominant partner of barley in northern Europe, Greeks commonly enhance their barley soup with fresh herbs, cheese, and milk or yogurt, giving it a creamy texture.*

3 tablespoons unsalted butter or vegetable oil

2 onions, chopped

1 clove garlic, minced

2 tablespoons chopped fresh marjoram
or 2 teaspoons dried marjoram

3 tablespoons chopped fresh parsley,
plus more for garnish

2 sprigs fresh rosemary or 1 teaspoon dried
rosemary

7 cups Vegetable Stock (page 115) or water

1 cup (7 ounces) pearl barley

1 large boiling potato, peeled and diced

2 to 3 carrots, chopped (optional)

1 bay leaf

About 1 teaspoon table salt or 2 teaspoons
kosher salt

Ground black pepper to taste

2 cups milk

2 large egg yolks, lightly beaten

1/4 cup grated kefalotyri or Parmesan cheese

1. In a large pot, melt the butter over medium heat. Add the onions and sauté until soft and translucent, about 5 minutes. Add the garlic, marjoram, the 3 tablespoons parsley, and the rosemary and sauté for 1 minute.

2. Add the stock, barley, potato, carrots, bay leaf, salt, and pepper. Bring to a boil, cover, reduce the heat to low, and simmer until the barley is tender but still slightly chewy, about 50 minutes. Discard the rosemary sprigs. Add the milk and heat through.

3. Remove the soup from the heat. Gradually stir 1 cup of the hot soup into the egg yolks, then stir the yolk mixture and cheese into the soup. Place over low heat and simmer, stirring constantly, until slightly thickened, about 3 minutes. Do not boil. Serve warm. Garnish with a sprinkle of additional chopped parsley.

Armenian Barley and Yogurt Soup (*Spas*):
Omit the milk, Parmesan, marjoram, and rosemary.
Add 3 tablespoons chopped fresh mint or 1 tablespoon
dried mint. Stir the egg yolks (or 1 large egg) into 2 cups
plain yogurt or sour cream and continue as above. Serve
hot or cold.

FRUIT SOUPS

HUNGARIAN WINE SOUP

Borleves

6 TO 8 SERVINGS

*Hungary and Romania—the two major wine-growing
regions of central and eastern Europe—are particularly well known for their elegant soups made from a
range of fruits cooked with local wines. Fresh fruits
are used during the summer and fall, dried fruits at
other times. Wine soups are elegant, aromatic treats
eaten on special occasions, usually either at the start
of a meal or for dessert. Wine soups are not merely
fruit juice or fruit in wine, but should possess added
nuances of flavor and texture. In wine soup, the color
and most pronounced flavor derives from the type of
wine used, with added elements contributed by citrus
juice and the types of fruit. Immigrants brought wine
and fruit soups to Israel, where they became a popular part of the developing cuisine.*

*This soup is meant to taste somewhat tart, with only
enough sugar to enhance the fruit and balance the
acidity in the fruit and wine. It is lightly thickened
with tapioca (which won't detract from the soup's
color or flavor) just to create a little body, not to be
gelatinous or syrupy. Do not use a poor-quality wine,
as the inferior flavor will affect the soup.*

*The soup is delicious using either whole or puréed
fruit. At dairy meals, sour cream is sometimes added
for a creamy texture and added richness, but I prefer
the more pure taste of the wine and fruit. A little
spoonful swirled into each bowl, however, is attractive.*

4 cups dry red or rosé wine or 2 cups fruity dry
  white wine and 2 cups dry red wine
4 cups (about I pound) any combination of fresh
  or frozen fruit, such as blueberries, cherries,
  orange slices, sliced peaches, sliced plums,
  raspberries, and strawberries
1 1/2 cups fresh orange juice
1/2 cup fresh lemon juice
1/2 to I cup sugar
6 tablespoons quick-cooking tapioca
2 (3-inch) sticks cinnamon
3 to 4 whole cloves, or I vanilla bean,
  split lengthwise (optional)
1/2 cup light cream or sour cream for garnish
  (optional)
Mint sprigs for garnish (optional)

In a large nonreactive pot, combine the wine, fruit,
juices, sugar, tapioca, cinnamon, and, if using, the
cloves or vanilla bean. Bring to a gentle boil, stirring
occasionally. Reduce the heat to low and simmer
until the fruit is tender, about 10 minutes. Discard
the cinnamon sticks and cloves or vanilla bean. Serve
warm or chilled. Garnish with a swirl of cream
and/or a mint sprig, if desired.

To thicken fruit with cornstarch: Omit the tapioca and reserve $1/2$ cup of the orange juice. When the fruit is tender, dissolve $1/4$ cup cornstarch or potato starch in the reserved orange juice to form a smooth paste, then stir into the hot soup and cook, stirring constantly, over medium-low heat until slightly thickened, about 4 to 5 minutes.

HUNGARIAN WINE

Hungary is justly renowned for its fruit trees and preserves, including apples, apricots, berries, cherries, peaches, and plums. Cherries are particularly popular in Hungary, but due to a very short growing period in early summer their enjoyment is restricted. On the other hand, there are two types of cultivated raspberries: summer bearing, which produce one crop a year beginning in June and running till August, and ever bearing, yielding one crop around late June and another in late September. Unlike the rest of central Europe, where beer is king, wine—both dry and semidry—is the preferred alcoholic beverage of Hungary. The Romans planted vineyards in the area around 280 C.E., and its wine was soon being praised and exported throughout Europe. Today, with seventeen wine regions, Hungary is one of the world's largest wine-growing countries. From the hills of the northeast comes Tokay, a golden, sweet dessert wine. Harslevelu is a high-quality dry white. The eastern town of Eger is famous for Egri, a full-bodied dry red wine. These and other wines have an important place in Hungarian dining.

SAVORY PASTRIES

❦ • ❦

The advent of the Middle Ages led to a dramatic decline in European baking. The breads and cakes of the upper class were rather crude and limited, and the poor made do with much less and had to use coarse maslin flour and other inferior ingredients. Quite the opposite situation held sway in many medieval Islamic regions, which experienced a golden age of agronomy and gastronomy. The Arabs were the first to learn how to refine the sugarcane from the Far East, and for centuries the Nile River Valley was the home of the world's finest *sukkar* ("sugar" in Arabic), the sugar industry there primarily controlled by Egyptian Jews.

Wheat flourished in North Africa, Turkey, and Spain and was ground into white as well as high quality whole-wheat flour. Cooks in Moorish Spain developed many notable baking techniques, including the method of leavening batters with beaten egg whites, leading to dishes like the classic sponge cake (*pan de España*). Medieval Arabs also learned to raise cakes with the first chemical leavening, wood ash, resulting in a light texture without the need for yeast or beaten eggs, although plenty of spices were needed to mask its bitter aftertaste. Adding to the growing sophistication of Moorish baking were rudimentary forms of puff pastry and cream puff pastry. Further east, from central Asia came the paper-thin dough later called *phyllo* in Greek, which bakes into a crisp, flaky, multilayered pastry.

Drawing from all these innovations, the Sephardic Jews of the Iberian Peninsula developed a sophisticated baking tradition encompassing an assortment of refined pastries. Included in the Sephardic repertoire were *pasteles* (pies), *pastelitos* (small pies), *tapadas* (large pies), *minas* (layered pies), *panisicos dulces* (sweet rolls), *boyos* (cheese pastries), and empanadas (turnovers, at first only deep-fried, but later also baked). Medieval Sephardic cuisine was so highly regarded that a widespread Arab maxim advised: "Wear the clothing of Arabs (more comfortable), sleep in the beds of Christians (softer), and eat the food of Jews."

The relocation of Sephardim following the Expulsion of 1492 led to the dissemination of their respective cuisines throughout much of the Mediterranean, Balkans, and Near East. Therefore, there exists a similarity in Jewish pastries, especially in the fillings (most notably spinach, eggplant, and cheese), in all the areas that became new homelands of the Sephardim, although each area introduced local seasonings and preferences. Once these foods reached the Balkans, some filtered farther northward, where they were filled with northern ingredients such as cabbage, mushrooms, or mashed potatoes.

Although much of the Roman culinary tradition was lost with the fall of the empire, medieval Italians regained their interest in baking sophisticated pastries when Arabs and later Turks conquered nearby parts of Europe, including the Balkans, Spain, and especially Sicily, introducing their fare to those areas. The dishes then found their way into Italy—across the straight of Messina connecting Sicily with the Italian Peninsula, and along the northern Mediterranean from Spain and Greece. More directly, waves of Crusaders returning to Italy from the Middle East brought back with them the culinary wealth of that region.

Influenced by Arabic and Ottoman gastronomy, Italian cuisine exploded during the Renaissance, including the development or refinement of many baked goods, including cream puffs and macaroons. Renaissance Florentines developed the first puff pastry, which spread throughout the Roman Catholic world (see map). Other pastries were developed in Italian Jewish ghettos before spreading throughout the country, including *buricches* (turnovers) and *crostate* (covered tarts). Italians even adapted the Arabic maxim, "*Vesti da Turco e mangia da Ebreo*" ("Dress like a Turk and eat like a Jew"), referring to the high quality of culinary skills in the scattered Jewish ghettoes of Italy.

The Italian innovations in baking and pastry spread to other parts of Europe with varying degrees of impact. France and Austria incorporated and in many ways soon surpassed the achievements of Renaissance Italy. Northern Europeans, with little high quality wheat at their disposal, benefited less from these culinary advancements. Nevertheless, Ashkenazic cooks made do, ingeniously transforming buckwheat, barley, cabbages, potatoes, and other available ingredients into satisfying dishes, especially knishes, piroshki (turnovers), and strudels.

Most cultures developed some characteristic type of pastry stuffed with a savory filling. For much of history, except for the wealthy, these were generally reserved for special occasions, as delicate pastry requires finely milled and sifted flour. Then, in the wake of the Industrial Revolution came vastly improved types of wheat and larger and better milling capabilities. In the 1840s, a new type of mill that replaced rotary millstones with smooth steel rollers was introduced in Hungary, resulting in standardized high quality germless white flour. Hungarians soon began using porcelain rollers, which yielded even finer flour at a much lower cost. Suddenly, any competent home cook could produce high quality yet inexpensive baked goods.

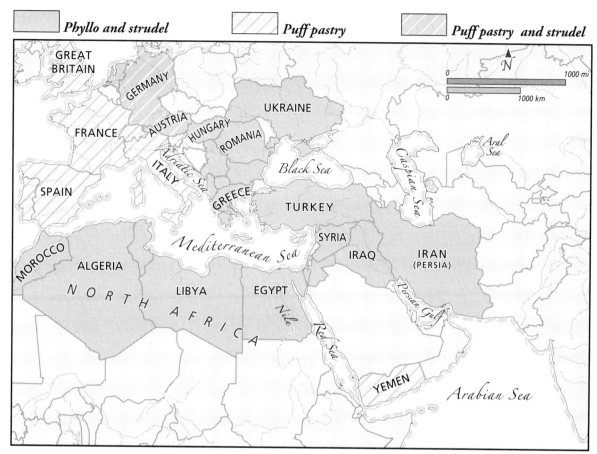

Legend:
Phyllo and strudel | Puff pastry | Puff pastry and strudel

Prevalence of Puff Pastry and Phyllo: *Phyllo dough, which emerged in Persia, generally spread to the farthest stretches of the Muslim world (the Turks brought it to central Europe, where it was called strudel). Puff pastry, which probably originated in Spain, was perfected in Renaissance Italy and spread through the domains of the Holy Roman Empire. Yemen's rudimentary form of puff pastry was transformed by Sephardim, who carried the tradition with them from Spain.*

Knishes

The original knishes (the name is derived from *knysz,* a Slavic fried cake) were Polish and Ukranian fried patties, most often made from kasha or mashed cooked turnips (the potato did not yet reach Europe). These patties commonly accompanied soup, the two frequently constituting the entire meal. Inspired cooks developed the practice of stuffing the patties with sautéed mushrooms, onion, or chopped meat, and eventually began adding flour to the mashed turnips or kasha, transforming it into a rudimentary dough that could be stretched to allow less dough to hold more filling without falling apart.

When the potato became popular in eastern Europe in the mid-nineteenth century, it was commonly substituted for turnips and kasha in knishes, often being added both to the flour pastry and to the filling. Later, a basic pastry dough made without potatoes emerged as the most widespread knish wrap. Soon, professional bakers began making knishes and, with the popularization of the home oven, so did many housewives, and the resulting flavorful treat emerged as the preeminent Ashkenazic filled pastry. As the knish became more of an undertaking to prepare, however, requiring rolling out and shaping the pastry dough, it was also transformed into fare for special occasions.

Immigrants brought the knish to America at the end of the nineteenth century, where initially it remained Jewish fare, peddled from pushcarts in Brooklyn and on the Lower East Side of Manhattan; later it was also sold at delis and specialty stores and could be found on the menu in kosher resorts. Knishes were always small in the Old World, but in typical American fashion, they grew to mammoth proportions in the United States. On the other hand, miniature versions became a staple at weddings and bar mitzvahs. Soon the knish emerged as a favorite nosh for the entire population of New York City. A rule of thumb in American comedy is that K is a funny-sounding letter; thus, the knish found its way into various vaudeville routines and eventually the American consciousness. Today, it is produced at stores and factories across the country.

EASTERN EUROPEAN FILLED PASTRIES

(Knish)

ABOUT 12 KNISHES   D or P

A few venerable New York City institutions, some in business for nearly a century, are famous for their knishes. Recently, however, I have been disappointed by what I've tasted there, finding the fillings insipid and the pastry soggy and lacking flakiness. We had better knish makers in my synagogue in Richmond, Virginia, and I am sure the situation was similar in other towns throughout America. By observing great home cooks and relatives preparing knishes over the years, I was able to pick up valuable techniques. My Lithuanian grandmother preferred a mashed-potato pastry dough for its moistness, while my Romanian grandmother insisted on an oil pastry dough, which remains tender even after repeated handling. The first grandmother cut them from rolls to save time and effort, while the other hand-formed individual knishes. I retain nostalgic feelings for both styles, as long as the filling is flavorful and the pastry tender.

Potato is the most popular knish filling, followed by kasha *and cheese. For the wrapping, old-fashioned potato pastry dough is more fragile and less crisp than standard flaky pastry dough and tends to split during baking, but the authentic flavor and moistness the potatoes add compensates for any difficulties. For a sturdier and crispier pastry, use oil pastry dough or standard flaky pie dough.*

Ashkenazic Potato Pastry Dough (page 156),
   Ashkenazic Sour Cream Pastry Dough (page
   155), or Ashkenazic Oil Pastry Dough (page 154)
Choice of Ashkenazic pastry filling (pages 156–159)
1 large egg beaten with 1 tablespoon water

1. Preheat the oven to 350°F. Line a large baking sheet with parchment paper or lightly grease it.

2. Divide the dough in half or thirds for easier handling. On a lightly floured surface, roll each piece out into a rectangle $1/4$ inch thick. Cut into 4-inch squares. Drop about $1/4$ cup filling in the center of each square, bring the edges together over the filling, and pinch to seal. Place on the prepared baking sheet, seam-side down, and brush with the egg mixture.

3. Bake until golden brown, 30 to 40 minutes. Serve warm or at room temperature. The knishes can be frozen, then covered loosely with aluminum foil and reheated in a preheated 375°F oven until warmed through, about 15 minutes.

VARIATION

Knish Rolls: Divide the pastry into thirds. Roll each piece into a 10-inch square. Along one side, spread about 1 cup of filling in a 7-inch-long strip. Starting from the filling side, roll up jelly-roll style, then tuck the ends under. Place on a greased baking sheet, seam-side down, and brush with the egg mixture. Bake until golden brown, about 40 minutes. Using a serrated knife, cut into 1- or $1^{1}/2$-inch pieces.

Piroshki

Following the Rindfleisch massacres in Germany in 1298 and the massacres in western and central Europe surrounding the Black Death in 1348, the majority of surviving Ashkenazim relocated eastward to Poland, Ukraine, and the Balkan States. For the following six centuries, the majority of the world's Jews would call eastern Europe home, numbering about five million by the start of the fifteenth century. Poland emerged as the country with the world's largest Jewish population. As a result, most Americans associate Polish fare, a synthesis of Franco-German and Slavic influences, with Jewish cooking.

The eastern European climate and long winters, particularly in the Balkan States and northern Poland, was not conducive for growing most vegetables and fruits. Black breads and other starches constituted the bulk of the diet. Wrapping vegetables, meats, and even other grains in dough proved an economical and tasty way to stretch limited resources and utilize leftovers. Among these filled foods are a variety of Russian, Polish, and Ukrainian pastries and pastas, all of whose names derive from the Slavic word *pir* ("feast"), connoting the original occasion of their uses. *Piroghi* (the singular is *pirog*) are large Russian pies, usually made from a yeast dough and rectangular in shape. They are not the same as the filled pasta called *pierogi* in Poland and *pyrohy* in Ukraine. (Russians and Poles use a G, while Ukrainians substitute an H and vice versa.) To further complicate matters, filled pasta is known as *vareniki* in Russia, from the Slavic *var*, meaning "to boil."

Most important to Jewish cooking are piroshki, the Yiddish equivalent of the Slavic *pirozhki*, which are small half-round Russian and Ukrainian turnovers, derived from the Turkish *borek*. The original *pirozhki* (singular *pirozhok*) were deep-fried, but the baked version became increasingly popular with the spread of home ovens in the nineteenth century. These ubiquitous Slavic pastries have long been hawked by vendors on street corners and at train stations in Russia and Ukraine, but also appear on the menu in upscale cafes, usually as an accompaniment to soups. Non-Jewish Russians enjoy various sizes of *pirozhki*, some large enough to feed six, while Jews tend to favor diminutive ones. Most Russians make their *pirozhki* with the original yeast dough, while Jewish cooks prefer sour cream pastry dough or, for nondairy meals, oil pastry dough. Piroshki make delicious *zakouski* (appetizers) as well as an accompaniment to borscht and other soups, the duo commonly constituting a Russian lunch.

Russian Turnovers

(*Piroshki*)

ABOUT 36 SMALL TURNOVERS D or P

Several of the women in my parents' former synagogue were incredibly proficient piroshki makers, capable of churning out trays of beautiful pastries in a matter of minutes, using only a wooden dowel and a glass. It takes me longer and my piroshki are never quite as attractive, but they are just as tasty, the burst of flavorful filling complementing the tender pastry. I like to serve them with soup or simply accompanied with sour cream.

Ashkenazic Sour Cream Pastry Dough (page 155),
   Ashkenazic Oil Pastry Dough (page 154),
   Ashkenazic Yeast Pastry Dough (page 155),
   or Ashkenazic Potato Pastry Dough (page 156)
Any Ashkenazic pastry filling (pages 156–159)
1 egg white, lightly beaten, for brushing
1 large egg beaten with 1 teaspoon water

1. Preheat the oven to 350°F. Line 2 large baking sheets with parchment paper or lightly grease them.

2. Divide the dough in half or thirds for easier handling. On a lightly floured surface, roll out the pastry ⅛ inch thick. Using a 3-inch biscuit cutter or an upturned drinking glass, cut into rounds. Reroll any excess pastry. Place 1 heaping teaspoon filling in the center of each round. Brush the edges with a little egg white, fold over to form a half-moon, and pinch the edges or press with the tines of a fork to seal. The piroshki may be prepared to this point and frozen for up to 4 weeks; do not thaw before baking.

3. Place the piroshki on the prepared baking sheets and brush the tops with the egg mixture. Bake until golden brown, about 30 minutes for fresh, 40 minutes for frozen. Serve warm or at room temperature.

Strudel

The Turks, who occupied Hungary (from 1526 to 1687) and Romania (from 1601 to 1878), brought their famously thin phyllo dough into the heart of central and eastern Europe. Almost immediately, the Hungarians began substituting this thin dough in some of their pastries, most notably strudel (from the German word for "whirlpool," referring to the dish's characteristic swirl of filling and pastry). Strudel had originally consisted of savory mixtures or fruit preserves rolled up in a relatively thick dough. Soon, not only Hungarians but also Austrians, Germans, and Romanians were fanatic about these revamped "whirlpools" and phyllo dough strudel became the norm across Europe. Thus, what's considered "strudel" dough in Europe today is really no different from the phyllo dough used in Greece and the Middle East (except that strudel dough is left as one large piece, while phyllo is cut into smaller sheets).

Classic savory fillings for strudel include mushrooms, onions, mashed potatoes, and cabbage. Since traditional strudel was such a demanding process owing to the difficulty of making the dough, many housewives limited it to special occasions, sometimes preparing it only once or twice a year—most notably for Rosh Hashanah or Sukkot. Today, making strudel is not at all difficult or time-consuming, as phyllo dough (also spelled filo and fila) is available frozen in Middle Eastern markets and most groceries as well as fresh from specialty bakeries. Many markets, however, let the frozen packages thaw and then refreeze them, resulting in dough that sticks, tears, and crumbles. So if your phyllo reacts that way, purchase it at another store in the future.

A 1-pound box contains 20 to 25 leaves, each about 17 by 12 inches. Thaw the phyllo in the refrigerator—never at room temperature—for at least 8 hours, then remove it from the refrigerator about 2 hours before using. To prevent the delicate sheets from drying out, unroll the sheets onto a flat surface and cover with a slightly damp (not wet) cloth. Work with only one sheet at a time, keeping the rest covered. Do not refreeze; reroll and tightly wrap any leftovers in plastic wrap and store in the refrigerator for at least a week.

CENTRAL EUROPEAN CABBAGE STRUDEL

(*Kroit Strudel*)

8 TO 10 SERVINGS

To tell the truth, when I make strudel, I usually use commercial phyllo dough. It is, of course, easier and a lot quicker than preparing homemade. There are occasions, however, when I actually start from scratch, making and stretching my own dough, the latter stage taking only about 15 minutes, not including the time to clean up. Even the first time I tried stretching phyllo dough, tearing more than a few holes in the sheets and scattering plenty of flour on the table and floor, the finished product tasted good enough to warrant the effort. I subsequently met a German baker who, with his assistant, easily manipulated the dough paper thin in a matter of minutes, leaving no holes or spilled flour even. Although I never mastered his proficiency, I did learn some of his filling recipes.

Cabbage is the standard central European savory strudel. However, potato-filled strudel is also quite good. A few bread crumbs can be sprinkled on the dough to absorb the excess liquid released during cooking.

8 sheets thawed frozen phyllo dough

$^1/_2$ cup (1 stick) unsalted butter or margarine, melted

About $^1/_2$ cup fresh bread crumbs (optional)

Ashkenazic Cabbage Filling (page 158), Cabbage and Apple Filling (page 158), or Ashkenazic Potato Filling (page 156)

1. Position a rack in the center of the oven. Preheat the oven to 375°F. Line a large baking sheet with parchment paper or lightly grease it.

2. Lay a cloth or piece of parchment paper on a flat surface. Place a phyllo sheet on top and brush with butter. Sprinkle lightly with bread crumbs, if using. Continue layering with the remaining phyllo, butter, and bread crumbs, brushing the top of each sheet of phyllo with butter.

3. Mound the filling in a 3-inch-wide strip along one long side of the phyllo rectangle, leaving a 1-inch border along the end and the sides. Fold in the 1-inch sides of the phyllo over the filling, then fold the short end of the pastry over the filling. Lifting the cloth from the filling end (the cloth supports the phyllo and prevents it from breaking), roll the phyllo jelly-roll style. The strudel can be prepared ahead of time to this point and frozen; do not thaw before baking.

4. Place the strudel, seam-side down, on the prepared baking sheet and brush with butter. Bake until golden brown, about 35 minutes; about 45 minutes for frozen. Let cool for at least 10 minutes before serving. Using a serrated knife, cut into serving portions and serve warm. The strudel may be reheated in a preheated 400°F oven.

VARIATION

Cabbage and Feta Strudel (*Kroit Strudel mit Kaese*): Add $^1/_2$ to $^3/_4$ cup (3 to 4 ounces) crumbled feta cheese to the cabbage filling.

ASHKENAZIC OIL PASTRY DOUGH

(*Beimel Teig*)

MAKES ENOUGH DOUGH FOR ABOUT THIRTY-SIX 3-INCH TURNOVERS OR 12 KNISHES

This is actually a variation of strudel dough, used for making a thin, crisp crust for knishes and piroshki.

3 cups unbleached all-purpose flour

$^3/_4$ teaspoon baking powder

$^1/_2$ teaspoon table salt or 1 teaspoon kosher salt

6 tablespoons vegetable oil

$1^1/_2$ large eggs, lightly beaten ($4^1/_2$ tablespoons)

9 tablespoons lukewarm water (80°F to 90°F)

$1^1/_2$ teaspoons distilled white vinegar

In a medium bowl, combine the flour, baking powder, and salt. In another bowl, beat together the oil and eggs, then stir in the water and vinegar. Stir into the flour mixture until a soft, smooth dough is formed. Do not overwork. Cover and let stand at room temperature for 1 hour.

ASHKENAZIC SOUR CREAM PASTRY DOUGH

(Smeteni Teig)

MAKES ENOUGH DOUGH FOR ABOUT
THIRTY-SIX 3-INCH TURNOVERS,
12 KNISHES, OR TWO 9-INCH PIES

- 3 cups unbleached all-purpose flour
- $3/4$ teaspoon table salt or $1 1/2$ teaspoons kosher salt
- $1/2$ teaspoon baking powder
- $3/4$ cup ($1 1/2$ sticks) unsalted butter, chilled
- $2/3$ cup sour cream
- 2 large egg yolks, lightly beaten

In a medium bowl, combine the flour, salt, and baking powder. Using a pastry cutter or 2 dinner knives, cut in the butter to form coarse crumbs. In a small bowl, combine the sour cream and egg yolks; stir to blend. Stir into the flour mixture to form a soft dough. Add a little water if too dry. Divide in half, shape into balls, flatten, wrap in plastic wrap, and refrigerate for at least 30 minutes.

ASHKENAZIC YEAST PASTRY DOUGH

(Teig)

MAKES ENOUGH DOUGH FOR
ABOUT 42 TURNOVERS   D OR P

- 1 package ($2 1/4$ teaspoons) active dry yeast or 1 cake fresh yeast
- $1/4$ cup warm water (105°F to 115°F for dry yeast; 80°F to 85°F for fresh yeast) plus $2/3$ cup warm water or milk
- 3 teaspoons sugar or honey
- 2 large eggs
- $1/4$ cup butter or vegetable shortening, melted
- $1 1/2$ teaspoons table salt or 1 tablespoon kosher salt
- About $3 1/2$ cups unbleached all-purpose flour

1. In a large bowl, dissolve the yeast in $1/4$ cup of the water. Stir in 1 teaspoon of the sugar and let stand until foamy, 5 to 10 minutes. Stir in the remaining water, the remaining 2 teaspoons sugar, the eggs, butter, salt, and 2 cups of the flour. Gradually add enough of the remaining flour to make a workable dough.

2. Knead the dough until smooth and elastic, 10 to 15 minutes. (To knead in a food processor, combine the flour, eggs, butter, and salt in the work bowl of a food processor and add the yeast mixture. With the machine on, gradually add enough warm water until the dough forms a ball, then process around the bowl about 25 times.) Place in a greased large bowl, turning to coat. Cover loosely with plastic wrap or a damp towel and let rise in a warm, draft-free place until nearly doubled in bulk, about $1 1/2$ hours. Punch down the dough, knead briefly, cover, and refrigerate for 8 hours or up to 24 hours.

ASHKENAZIC POTATO PASTRY DOUGH

(Kartoffel Teig)

MAKES ENOUGH DOUGH FOR
THIRTY-SIX 3-INCH TURNOVERS
OR 12 KNISHES

  1 cup mashed potatoes

  3 large eggs, lightly beaten

  1 tablespoon vegetable shortening or margarine,
    softened

  1/2 teaspoon table salt or 1 teaspoon kosher salt

  1/4 teaspoon ground turmeric (optional)

  3 cups unbleached all-purpose flour, plus more
    if needed

In a medium bowl, combine the potatoes, eggs, shortening, salt, and, if desired, the turmeric. (The turmeric produces a bright yellow color favored by some cooks.) Gradually add the 3 cups flour to form a smooth, soft dough. If the dough is too soft or sticky, add a little extra flour. Do not overwork the dough or it will be tough. Cover and refrigerate for 30 minutes.

ASHKENAZIC POTATO FILLING

(Kartoffelfullung)

MAKES ABOUT 3 CUPS,
ENOUGH FOR 48 TURNOVERS
OR 12 KNISHES  OR

  3 tablespoons vegetable oil

  2 onions, chopped

  2 1/2 cups mashed potatoes or 2 cups mashed
    potatoes mixed with 1 cup (8 ounces) farmer
    or pot cheese

  1 large egg, lightly beaten

  About 3/4 teaspoon table salt or 1 1/2 teaspoons
    kosher salt

  Ground white or black pepper to taste

In a large skillet, heat the oil over medium heat. Add the onions and sauté until lightly golden, about 15 minutes. Stir into the potatoes and let cool. Stir in the egg, salt, and pepper.

ASHKENAZIC CHEESE FILLING

(Kaesefullung)

MAKES ABOUT 3 CUPS, ENOUGH FOR
48 TURNOVERS OR 12 KNISHES

- 3 cups (1 1/2 pounds) farmer cheese or 2 cups
  (1 pound) pot cheese and 1 cup (8 ounces)
  cream cheese, at room temperature
- 3 tablespoons sour cream, at room temperature
- 1 large egg, slightly beaten
- About 3/4 teaspoon table salt or 1 1/2 teaspoons
  kosher salt
- 3 tablespoons chopped fresh dill or parsley
  (optional)
- About 1/4 teaspoon ground white or black pepper
  (optional)

In a medium bowl, combine all the ingredients and beat until smooth.

VARIATION

Sauté 1 chopped large onion or 10 to 12 sliced scallions in 3 tablespoons butter until soft, 5 to 10 minutes. Add to the above mixture.

ASHKENAZIC KASHA FILLING

(Kashafullung)

MAKES ABOUT 3 CUPS, ENOUGH FOR
48 TURNOVERS OR 12 KNISHES

- 2 large eggs
- 1 1/2 cups toasted coarse or whole kasha
- 2 tablespoons vegetable oil or margarine
- 2 onions, chopped
- 3 cups boiling water
- About 3/4 teaspoon table salt or 1 1/2 teaspoons
  kosher salt
- Ground black pepper to taste

1. In a small bowl, lightly beat 1 egg, then add the kasha and stir until all the kernels are evenly coated. Stir in a dry skillet over medium heat until each grain is dry and separated, about 3 minutes.

2. In a large skillet, heat the oil over medium heat. Add the onions and sauté until soft and translucent, 5 to 10 minutes. Add the water, salt, and pepper and bring to a boil. Add the kasha, cover, reduce the heat to low, and simmer until the liquid is absorbed, about 20 minutes. Let cool. Lightly beat the second egg and stir into the kasha mixture.

ASHKENAZIC CABBAGE FILLING

(Kroitfullung)

MAKES ABOUT 3 CUPS,
ENOUGH FOR 48 TURNOVERS
OR 12 KNISHES   D OR P

The cabbage filling, sans the pastry, is also served, warm or cooled, as a side dish.

> I small green cabbage, cored and finely shredded (about 6 cups)
> I¹/₂ teaspoons table salt or I tablespoon kosher salt, for sprinkling
> ¹/₄ cup unsalted butter or vegetable oil
> I onion, chopped
> I teaspoon sugar
> Salt to taste
> About ¹/₄ teaspoon ground black pepper
> I to 2 teaspoons caraway seeds (optional)
> I tablespoon chopped fresh dill (optional)

1. Put the cabbage in a colander, toss with the salt, and let stand for about 30 minutes. Squeeze out the excess liquid. If the cabbage fails to release a lot of liquid, rinse under water to remove the excess salt, then squeeze. Or, bring a large pot of slightly salted water to a boil, add the cabbage, blanch for 3 minutes, and drain in a colander. When cool, squeeze the cabbage to extract any excess liquid.

2. In a large skillet, melt the butter over medium heat. Add the onion and sauté until soft and translucent, about 5 minutes. Add the cabbage and sauté until wilted, about 15 minutes. Drain off any liquid. Add the sugar, salt, pepper, and, if using, caraway or dill. Let cool.

VARIATION

Cabbage and Apple Filling: Omit the pepper, caraway, and dill. Reduce the cabbage to 4 cups and increase the sugar to 2 to 3 tablespoons. After cooling the cabbage, add 2 to 3 peeled and coarsely chopped tart apples, ¹/₂ cup raisins or chopped dates, and 3 tablespoons lemon juice or ¹/₂ cup sour cream.

ASHKENAZIC MUSHROOM FILLING

(Shvemlfullung)

MAKES ABOUT 3 CUPS, ENOUGH FOR
48 TURNOVERS OR 12 KNISHES   D

> 3 tablespoons unsalted butter or vegetable oil
> 3 shallots or I large onion, minced
> I¹/₄ pounds button mushrooms, finely chopped
> ¹/₂ cup heavy cream
> ¹/₄ cup fresh bread crumbs or wheat germ
> 3 tablespoons minced fresh parsley or I teaspoon dried thyme
> About ¹/₂ teaspoon table salt or I teaspoon kosher salt
> Ground black pepper to taste
> 2 large egg yolks, lightly beaten

1. In a large skillet, melt the butter over medium heat. Add the shallots and sauté until soft and translucent, about 2 minutes. Add the mushrooms, increase the heat to medium-high, and cook, stirring frequently, until the mushrooms release their moisture and it evaporates, about 15 minutes.

2. Add the cream and cook, stirring frequently, until thickened, about 2 minutes. Remove from the heat and stir in the bread crumbs, parsley, salt, and pepper. Stir in the egg yolks. Let cool.

Omit the cream and egg yolks. After adding the bread crumbs, add ¼ cup sour cream and 1 mashed hard-boiled egg yolk. Or, add 2 cups (1 pound) pot cheese.

ASHKENAZIC CARROT FILLING

(Mehrenfullung)

MAKES ABOUT 3 CUPS, ENOUGH FOR
48 TURNOVERS OR I LARGE PIE

This very sweet filling is used especially for small pastries, such as piroshki, which are commonly brushed with honey when hot from the oven.

> 2½ pounds carrots, grated (about 9 cups)
> 3 cups sugar
> ¼ cup water
> ½ teaspoon ground ginger

In a large saucepan, combine the carrots, sugar, and water and bring to a boil over medium heat. Cook, stirring frequently (especially near the end) until the carrots are soft and the mixture thickened, about 20 minutes. If the mixture looks as if it will scorch, add a little more water. Stir in the ginger. Remove from the heat and let cool.

VARIATION

Italian Carrot Filling (*Sostanzioso*): Reduce the sugar to 2 cups and substitute 7 tablespoons minced candied ginger for the ground ginger. Use to fill a typical 9-inch double-crust tart (*Torta di Carote*).

MIDDLE EASTERN PASTRIES

SYRIAN MINIATURE LENTIL PIZZAS

(*Lahamagine*)

ABOUT 28 SMALL PIES

The first time I attended a Syrian function was in Flatbush, Brooklyn and I was looking forward to sampling the ethnic specialties. I found it odd that there were no lahamagine, *generally ubiquitous at Syrian affairs. Only toward the end of the evening did a Syrian friend inform me that experienced partygoers always station themselves near the kitchen door to have a chance at the hot* lahamagine, *which quickly vanish. Maneuvering myself nearer to the kitchen, I finally managed to snag one, which was well worth the effort. Although the name of these miniature pizzas, a contraction of the Arabic* lahem bil ajin, *means "meat with dough," this is a Jewish vegetarian variation.*

> **TOPPING:**
> ¾ cup red lentils
> 3 cups water
> I onion, grated
> 3 tablespoons *temerhindi* or mock *temerhindi* (Syrian Mock Tamarind Sauce, page 434)
> 3 tablespoons tomato paste
> 3 tablespoons vegetable oil
> Pinch of cayenne
> About ¾ teaspoon table salt or 1½ teaspoons kosher salt
>
> Middle Eastern Yeast Dough (page 162)
> ½ cup pine nuts (optional)
> Olive oil or vegetable oil for brushing (optional)

1. To make the topping: In a medium saucepan, combine the lentils and water. Bring to a boil, reduce the heat to low, and simmer, uncovered, until soft, about 30 minutes. Drain. Mash the lentils with a spoon or a potato masher (do not purée). Add the onion, temerhindi, tomato paste, oil, cayenne, and salt. Let cool.

2. Preheat the oven to 375°F. Line 2 large baking sheets with parchment paper or lightly grease them.

3. After letting the dough rise until doubled in bulk, punch it down, knead briefly on a lightly floured surface, divide into fourths, form into balls, cover, and let stand for 15 minutes. Roll out each ball $1/8$ inch thick. Using a 3-inch biscuit cutter or an upturned drinking glass, cut out rounds. Reroll and cut the scraps. Or, divide the dough into 1-inch balls and roll into $1/8$-inch-thick rounds.

4. Place the dough rounds on the prepared baking sheets. Spread each with 1 heaping tablespoon of the filling and, if using, sprinkle with a few pine nuts. Lightly press down on the topping with the back of a spoon or your fingers.

5. Bake until the edges are golden but not crisp, about 15 minutes. If desired, after baking brush the edges with olive oil to keep them soft. To prepare the lahamagine ahead, bake for only 10 minutes, let cool, then freeze for up to 1 month; bake, unthawed, in a 375°F oven until golden brown, about 15 minutes. Serve warm.

Sambusak

The *sambusak*, an early filled pastry, is probably the forerunner of the Iberian empanada (from the Spanish "to cover with bread") as well as the Italian calzone. The first written record of *sambusak* dates back to ninth-century Iraq; the dish eventually became ubiquitous at most Middle Eastern celebrations. The name *sambusak* (also called *sanbusak*) derives from the Farsi *sanbusa* ("triangular"), connoting the original shape of the pastry and its Persian origin. *Sambusak* appeared in Spain by the thirteenth century and, soon thereafter, became a traditional part of the Sephardic Sabbath meal.

The original *sambusak* consisted of pieces of bread dough filled with chopped meat, folded over the filling into a triangle, and fried in sesame oil—a form that predominated well into the fourteenth century. Eventually, the easier-to-fashion half-moon emerged as the prevailing shape, while newer forms of pastry were frequently substituted for the yeast dough. Yeast-dough versions, however, remain extremely popular in Syrian, Lebanese, and Iraqi communities. Although some yeast-dough turnovers continue to be cooked in hot oil, most *sambusak* are now baked. Cheese has long been the most common vegetarian filling, but vegetables, particularly spinach, pumpkin, and squash, are popular in season. Some Syrians refer to meat-filled turnovers as *sambusak* and vegetarian and cheese-filled versions as *bastel* (from the Ladino "*pastel*"). Iraqi Jews specialize in chickpea fillings. Leeks, onions, and potatoes are all used individually or paired with other flavors. Small *sambusak* make a tasty appetizer, while large ones are a meal in themselves.

MIDDLE EASTERN TURNOVERS

(*Sambusak*)

ABOUT 36 PASTRIES　　　　Ⓓ or Ⓟ

I know a Syrian businessman whose work requires that he travel on a regular basis. His wife always packs a large supply of frozen sambusak, *which defrost by the time he reaches his destination, providing a taste of home and his cure for jet lag. Semolina adds an interesting crunch to the pastry. The oil pastry is heavier, but more malleable than the semolina pastry; the yeast dough is the lightest.*

Middle Eastern Yeast Dough (page 162), Middle
　　Eastern Semolina Pastry Dough (page 162),
　　or Sephardic Oil Pastry Dough (page 177)
Choice of Middle Eastern Pastry filling
　　(pages 163–164)
I large egg beaten with I teaspoon water
¹/₄ cup raw sesame seeds for sprinkling (optional)

1. Preheat the oven to 375°F. Line 2 large baking sheets with parchment paper or lightly grease them.

2. Divide the dough into fourths and shape into balls. On a lightly floured surface, roll out each ball to a ¹/₈-inch thickness and, using a 3-inch biscuit cutter or an upturned drinking glass, cut the dough into rounds. Reroll and cut the scraps. Or, divide the dough into 1-inch balls and roll into 3-inch rounds ¹/₈ inch thick.

3. Spoon 1 heaping teaspoon of filling into the center of each dough round. Fold the edge over the filling and press down firmly to seal. Place the sambusak 2 inches apart on the prepared baking sheets, brush the tops with the egg mixture and, if desired, sprinkle lightly with sesame seeds. If using yeast dough, prick with the tines of a fork to vent the steam. The pastries can be frozen at this point for up to 3 months; do not thaw before baking

4. Bake until lightly golden, but not browned, 15 to 20 minutes for fresh, about 25 minutes for frozen. Serve warm or at room temperature.

VARIATIONS

Large *Sambusak*: Cut the dough into 4- or 5-inch rounds and fill each with 2 tablespoons of the filling.

Fried *Sambusak*: In a large, heavy pot, heat at least 1 inch vegetable oil to 350°F and fry the *sambusak* in batches, turning once, until golden, about 2 minutes per side.

Iraqi Chickpea Turnovers (*Sambusak b'Tawa*): This version of the Middle Eastern classic is made for Purim in honor of Queen Esther who, according to tradition, ate no meat after marrying King Ahasuerus. *Tawa* is the Arabic name of the heavy skillet in which these pastries were originally fried. Follow the directions for *sambusak*, but use the Middle Eastern Semolina Pastry Dough (page 162) or Sephardic Oil Pastry Dough (page 177) and Iraqi Chickpea Filling (page 164).

MIDDLE EASTERN YEAST DOUGH

MAKES ENOUGH DOUGH FOR ABOUT
FORTY-EIGHT 3-INCH TURNOVERS   Ⓟ

This is the classic sambusak *dough—essentially a bread dough enriched with olive oil.*

> I package (2^1/$_4$ teaspoons) active dry yeast
>   or I cake fresh yeast
> I cup plus 2 tablespoons warm water
>   (105°F to 115°F for dry yeast; 80°F to 85°F
>   for fresh yeast)
> I teaspoon sugar or honey
> ^{1}/$_4$ cup olive oil or vegetable oil
> 2 teaspoons table salt or I tablespoon kosher salt
> About 4 cups unbleached all-purpose flour

In a large bowl, dissolve the yeast in ^{1}/$_4$ cup of the water. Stir in the sugar and let stand until foamy, 5 to 10 minutes. Add the remaining water, the oil, salt, and 2 cups of the flour. Gradually add enough of the remaining flour until the mixture just holds together. On a lightly floured surface, knead the dough until smooth and elastic, 10 to 15 minutes. (To knead in a food processor, combine the flour, oil, and salt in the work bowl of a food processor and add the yeast mixture. With the machine on, gradually add enough warm water until the dough forms a ball, then process around the bowl about 25 times.) Cover with a large bowl and let rise in a warm place until doubled in bulk, about 2 hours, or in the refrigerator overnight.

MIDDLE EASTERN SEMOLINA PASTRY DOUGH

(Masa Smead)

MAKES ENOUGH DOUGH FOR
ABOUT THIRTY-SIX 3-INCH
TURNOVERS   Ⓓ OR Ⓟ

Before the popularization of modern bread flour by the Romans, semolina was the preferred variety of wheat throughout the Middle East and the type mandated by the Bible for use in the Temple. Middle Easterners still retain a fondness for this coarse, hard wheat, which adds a yellow color and interesting crunch to pastry dough. You can buy semolina flour, which is more granular than wheat flour, in Middle Eastern and natural foods markets. Using baking powder produces a lighter pastry.

> 2 cups unbleached all-purpose flour
> I cup semolina flour
> ^{1}/$_4$ teaspoon table salt or ^{1}/$_2$ teaspoon kosher salt
> I teaspoon baking powder (optional)
> I^1/$_4$ cups (2^1/$_2$ sticks) unsalted butter
>   or margarine, softened
> About ^{1}/$_4$ cup water

In a medium bowl, combine the flour, semolina, salt, and, if using, the baking powder. Stir with a whisk to blend. In a large bowl, beat the butter until smooth. Using a wooden spoon or electric mixer gradually work in the flour mixture. Add enough water to make a soft, moist dough that clears the sides of the bowl. Cover with plastic wrap or a damp towel and let stand at room temperature for at least 1 hour. The dough will firm as it rests.

MIDDLE EASTERN CHEESE FILLING

MAKES ABOUT 2 CUPS, ENOUGH FOR
36 TURNOVERS

- 2 cups (8 ounces) shredded kashkaval or
  Muenster cheese; or 1 cup (4 ounces)
  shredded Muenster and 1 cup (3 ounces)
  grated kefalotyri; or 1 1/3 cups Parmesan
  cheese
- 1 large egg, lightly beaten
- 1/8 teaspoon baking powder
- Pinch of salt

In a medium bowl, combine all the ingredients and
stir to blend.

VARIATIONS

Potato-Cheese Filling: Reduce the cheese to 1 cup
(4 ounces), omit the baking powder, and add 1 cup
mashed potatoes.

Spinach-Cheese Filling: Reduce the cheese to
1 cup (4 ounces), omit the baking powder, and add
1 cup cooked, squeezed dry, and chopped spinach.

MIDDLE EASTERN YOGURT FILLING

MAKES ABOUT 2 CUPS, ENOUGH FOR
36 TURNOVERS

- 2 cups *labni* (Middle Eastern Yogurt Cheese,
  page 48)
- 1 large egg, lightly beaten
- 1 onion, chopped (optional)
- 1/2 cup chopped fresh parsley or cilantro
- About 1/2 teaspoon table salt or 1 teaspoon
  kosher salt
- About 1/4 teaspoon ground black pepper

In a medium bowl, combine all the ingredients.
Stir well to blend.

MIDDLE EASTERN SPINACH FILLING

MAKES ABOUT 2 1/2 CUPS, ENOUGH FOR
36 TURNOVERS

- 3 tablespoons olive oil or vegetable oil
- 2 onions, chopped
- 1 pound stemmed fresh or 10 ounces defrosted frozen spinach or chard, cooked, squeezed dry, and chopped
- 3 to 4 tablespoons pine nuts
- 1 large egg, lightly beaten
- 1 to 3 teaspoons ground sumac or 2 tablespoons fresh lemon juice
- About 1/2 teaspoon table salt or 1 teaspoon kosher salt
- Ground black pepper to taste

In a large skillet, heat the oil over medium heat. Add the onions and sauté until soft and translucent, about 5 to 10 minutes. Stir in the spinach and cook until dry. Remove from the heat, stir in the pine nuts, and let cool. Stir in the remaining ingredients.

VARIATIONS

Omit the sumac and increase the lemon juice to 1/4 cup or add 1/2 cup pomegranate seeds. Pomegranates are traditional on Rosh Hashanah; the many seeds are symbolic of fertility and abundance of good deeds.

Add 4 to 8 ounces crumbled feta cheese.

IRAQI CHICKPEA FILLING

MAKES ABOUT 2 CUPS, ENOUGH FOR
36 TURNOVERS

- 3 tablespoons regular sesame oil or vegetable oil
- 1 large onion, chopped
- 1/2 to 1 teaspoon ground cumin
- 1/2 teaspoon ground turmeric
- About 1/2 teaspoon table salt or 1 teaspoon kosher salt
- Ground black pepper to taste
- 2 cups cooked chickpeas, mashed (about 6 ounces dried)
- 1/4 cup chopped fresh cilantro or parsley (optional)

In a large skillet, heat the oil over medium heat. Add the onion and sauté until soft and translucent, about 5 minutes. Stir in the cumin, turmeric, salt, and pepper. Add the chickpeas and cook until dry. If desired, add the cilantro. Remove from the heat and let cool.

Bukharan Turnovers

(Samsa)

ABOUT 20 PASTRIES   Ⓓ OR Ⓟ

While Bukharans (Jews from the Uzbekistan region) take great pride in the variety and quality of their breads and savory pies, the unquestionable national favorite is samsa. *In Uzbekistan,* samsa *are a common street food, customarily baked on the inner wall of a tandoor (a cone-shaped clay oven), hawked by vendors throughout the cities and sold at every* chaykhana *(teahouse), which can be found on practically every other block.*

Samsa are best right out of the tandoor, the way Bukharans prefer them. At home, samsa *are commonly served as an accompaniment to soup, followed by* plov *(pilaf) and salads. When guests visit a household, they are presented with a* dastarkhan *(offering tray) laden with* samsa *and other favorites. Meat pervades in this land once filled with nomads, and it is the most common filling in these golden crisp half-moons, but Jews frequently substitute a squash or potato filling for use at dairy meals and to serve with* kaymak, *a local form of rich clotted cream. Bukharans use* ghee, *cottonseed oil, or corn oil in the dough, but not olive oil; that is generally reserved for dressing salads. Unlike the vibrant spices of Georgian and Indian fare, Bukharan seasonings are rather simple, primarily a touch of cumin, turmeric, and coriander.*

PASTRY:

1 cup warm water (105°F to 115°F)

2 tablespoons cottonseed oil, corn oil, or melted *ghee* (Indian Clarified Butter, page 51)

1 teaspoon table salt or 2 teaspoons kosher salt

About 3 cups unbleached all-purpose flour

SQUASH FILLING:

¼ cup vegetable oil

2 large onions, chopped

2 pounds butternut other winter squash, or pumpkin (such as cheese or sugar pumpkin), peeled, seeded, and shredded

About ½ teaspoon ground cumin

½ teaspoon ground turmeric

About ½ teaspoon table salt or 1 teaspoon kosher salt

About ½ teaspoon ground black pepper

1. To make the pastry: In a medium bowl, combine the water, oil, and salt. Stir in 1 cup of the flour. Gradually stir in enough of the remaining flour to make a soft dough that comes away from the sides of the bowl and is not sticky. On a lightly floured surface, knead the dough until smooth, about 2 minutes. Form into a ball, cover with plastic wrap, and let stand at room temperature for 1 hour.

2. To make the filling: In a large saucepan, heat the oil over medium heat. Add the onions and sauté until soft and translucent, 5 to 10 minutes. Add the squash and spices and cook, stirring frequently, until the squash breaks down and forms a uniform mass, about 15 minutes. Let cool.

3. Preheat the oven to 375°F. Line 2 large baking sheets with parchment paper or lightly grease them.

4. On a lightly floured surface, roll out the dough into a ¹/₁₆-inch-thick rectangle, flouring frequently to prevent sticking. Cut into 4-inch squares. Place 1 heaping tablespoon of filling in the center of each square. Bring one end over the filling to form a triangle and press the edges to seal.

5. Place on the prepared baking sheet. Bake until golden brown, about 20 minutes. Serve warm or at room temperature.

SEPHARDIC PASTRIES

Pasteles

Double-crust pastries with a savory filling are a Sabbath treat with roots stretching back to Persia at least two thousand years ago. Originally, the crust was devised not so much for eating, but as an efficient way of keeping the filling fresh and moist during the Sabbath and—in an age before the advent of tableware—conveying the soft food to the mouth. Eventually the double crust took on symbolic meaning as the double portion of manna, which the Israelites, during their forty years of wandering in the wilderness, found protected by a lower and upper layer of dew.

Early on, Sabbath pies appeared in both Spain and Italy. Every Friday morning, housewives in medieval Spain assembled a *pastel* (Spanish for "pastry"), consisting of a bottom and top layer of a rudimentary puff pastry encasing a savory filling and placed in a special large earthenware dish with a cover. After the lid was secured, the *pastel* was placed in the family oven or taken to the communal bakery to partially cook. Before the onset of the Sabbath, the pie was retrieved, while the family's *hamin* (Sabbath stew) was placed in the oven to cook overnight. Meanwhile, the *pastel* was usually hung on a metal rack over the family's hearth to finish cooking and stay warm for Sabbath dinner.

Over time, the pastry crust grew more delicate and tender. During Passover, two layers of moistened matza replaced the pastry. Fillings became more varied as well, with seasonal vegetables, commonly mixed with cheese, frequently substituted for the original meat filling. After the concept of the smaller turnover, or empanada, reached Iberia

and entered the Sephardic consciousness, large pies lost some, but hardly all, of their prominence.

In Italy, Sabbath meat or fish pies were first recorded in the eleventh century and from at least that time have been an important part of Italian Jewish cuisine, now variously called *pasticcio*, *torta*, and *pizza ebraica* ("Jewish pie"). The arrival of Sephardim in the area following the Expulsion led to the introduction of assorted vegetable and cheese fillings.

Early in the Middle ages, these Sephardic and Italian pies made their way into Jewish communities further north. Provençal Jews adopted the pie from the Sephardim, calling it *pashtet*, while those in Austria, where the pie probably came from nearby Italy, first referred to the pie as *brietling*, a name probably derived from the Teutonic *brot* (bread). In any case, by the twelfth century, Azhkenazic French, Alsatian, and German Jews had embraced the Sephardic and Italian pies, slightly revamping and renaming it *pashtida*. So integral was this pie to the medieval Ashkenazic Sabbath that a contemporary story told of a German Jewish child kidnapped by thugs, who, on the Sabbath, cried so incessantly for his *pashtida* that his location was soon discovered. Nevertheless, partially due to a meat shortage in Europe in the fifteenth century as well as to the expense of white flour, Sabbath pies eventually disappeared from the Ashkenazic repertoire.

Pasteles followed the Sephardim everywhere they migrated, becoming a traditional Sabbath dish as far away as India. In Morocco, with phyllo substituted for the traditional pastry dough, it became the classic dish *pastilla* or (since Arabic does not have a P equivalent) *bistilla*. Over the course of time, Sephardim around the world developed a variety of savory pies—large, small, and miniature. Small pies, both open-faced and covered, called *pastelitos* or, in

Greece, *pastelikos,* became the pride and joy of Sephardic housewives. Two-crust pastries—variously known as *pasteles,* *tapadas* (from the Spanish *tapar,* "to cover"), *mina* ("mine" in Spanish), *megina* (from the Spanish *migas,* "crumbs"), and *inchusa,* as well as *borekitas* in Turkey and pita in Greece—are still popular Sephardic dishes, appearing weekly on many Sabbath tables.

SEPHARDIC PIE

(*Pastel*)

6 TO 8 SERVINGS   D OR P

Americans, who are primarily accustomed to pies being sweet, frequently fail to realize that until relatively recently all pies were savory. Indeed, one of the most distinctive and ancient aspects of Sephardic cuisine is its assortment of savory pies, the largest of which is the double-crust pastel.

Sephardic Oil Pastry Dough (page 177), Sephardic
    Oil-Butter Pastry Dough (page 177), or
    Sepahrdic Yogurt Pastry Dough (page 178)
Choice of *pastel* filling (pages 168–170)
1 large egg beaten with 1 tablespoon water
2 tablespoons raw sesame seeds (optional)

1. Preheat the oven to 375°F. Grease a 12-inch tart or pie plate, an 8-inch-square baking pan, a 9-inch quiche pan, or a shallow 8-cup baking dish.

2. Form a large ball out of two-thirds of the pastry and a smaller ball out of the remaining third. On a lightly floured surface, roll out the larger ball into a $1/4$-inch-thick round and fit it into the prepared dish. Spoon in the filling. Roll out the remaining pastry and place it over the filling, crimping the edges to seal. Cut several slits in the top to vent the steam. Brush with the egg mixture and, if using, sprinkle with the sesame seeds.

3. Bake until the crust is golden brown and the filling is set, about 40 minutes. Let stand for at least 10 minutes before serving. Serve warm or at room temperature.

VARIATIONS

Double the recipe and bake in a 9-by-13-inch pan.

Sephardic Passover Pie (*Mina*): Soak 4 matzas in milk or water until pliable but not soggy, about 3 minutes. Drain and pat with paper towels. Line the bottom and sides of the prepared dish with a single layer of matza, fill, cover with the remaining matza, and brush with the egg mixture or melted butter. Bake as above.

The following fillings, more custardlike than those used for turnovers, are the favorite for making large pies. Sephardim commonly use mashed potatoes to add body to the filling, as a binder, and as a substitute for cheese.

EGGPLANT PASTEL FILLING

(*Gomo de Berenjena*)

MAKES ENOUGH FOR 1 LARGE PIE

Among the most popular pastel *fillings is eggplant, which I first sampled on a summer Saturday afternoon in Jerusalem. I immediately fell in love with it. The cheese enhances the flavor of the slightly tangy, smoky eggplant, and adds body. Some cooks even bake the filling by itself to serve as a side dish or light entrée. Eggplant is a particularly favorite* pastel *in Turkey.*

2 pounds eggplants

3/4 cup (4 ounces) crumbled feta cheese or
    1/2 cup (4 ounces) farmer cheese

1/2 to 1 cup (2 to 4 ounces) shredded kashkaval,
    Gouda, Gruyère, or Muenster cheese

3 large eggs, lightly beaten

About 1/2 teaspoon table salt or 1 teaspoon
    kosher salt

Ground black pepper to taste

1/8 teaspoon freshly grated nutmeg (optional)

Light a fire in a charcoal grill, preheat the broiler, or preheat the oven to 400°F. Cut several slits in the eggplants. Roast over the hot coals or broil 3 to 4 inches from the heat source under the broiler, turning occasionally, until charred and tender, about 20 minutes. Or, place on a baking sheet and bake in the oven until very tender, about 50 minutes. Let stand long enough so that you can handle them. Peel the eggplants, being careful not to leave any skin. Coarsely chop the pulp, put in a colander, and let drain for about 30 minutes. Stir in the cheeses, eggs, salt, pepper, and, if using, nutmeg.

VARIATION

Pareve Eggplant Filling: Omit the cheeses and add 1 cup mashed potatoes, 2 tablespoons matza cake meal or flour, and 1 large onion chopped and sautéed in 3 tablespoons olive oil until soft and translucent.

CHEESE PASTEL FILLING

(Gomo de Queso)

MAKES ENOUGH FOR 1 LARGE PIE

1 cup (5 ounces) crumbled feta cheese

$^3/_4$ cup (6 ounces) cream cheese or farmer
  cheese, at room temperature

$^3/_4$ to 1 cup (3 to 4 ounces) shredded kashkaval,
  Gouda, Gruyère, or Muenster cheese

1 cup mashed potatoes

5 large eggs, lightly beaten

About $^1/_2$ teaspoon table salt or 1 teaspoon
  kosher salt

About $^1/_2$ teaspoon ground white or black pepper

In a medium bowl, combine all the ingredients and
stir to blend.

LEEK PASTEL FILLING

(Gomo de Prasa)

MAKES ENOUGH FOR 1 LARGE PIE

$2^1/_4$ pounds leeks, white and light green parts
  only, cut into $^1/_4$-inch-thick slices, washed,
  and drained

$^1/_4$ cup unsalted butter or olive oil

1 large onion, chopped

1 cup (4 ounces) shredded kashkaval, Gouda,
  Gruyère, or Muenster cheese; or 1 cup
  (5 ounces) crumbled feta cheese; or $^1/_2$ cup each

1 cup heavy cream

3 large eggs, lightly beaten

About 1 teaspoon table salt or 2 teaspoons
  kosher salt

Ground black pepper to taste

Put the leeks in a large pot and add cold water to
cover. Bring to a boil, reduce the heat to low, and
simmer until tender, about 20 minutes; drain. In a
large skillet, melt the butter over medium heat.
Add the leeks and onion and sauté until soft, about
5 to 10 minutes. Remove from the heat and let cool.
Stir in the cheese, cream, eggs, salt, and pepper.

VARIATIONS

Substitute 1 cup mashed potatoes for the cream and
increase the eggs to 4.

Sephardic Greens Filling (*Gomo Verde*): Omit
the cream, increase the eggs to 5, and reduce the leeks
to about 12 ounces. Add 1 pound stemmed and chopped
spinach, 1 chopped small head romaine lettuce, 3 chopped
scallions, and 2 tablespoons chopped fresh dill.

SPINACH PASTEL FILLING

(Gomo de Espinaca)

MAKES ENOUGH FOR I LARGE PIE

9 cups fresh spinach, stemmed (about 2 pounds
total); or a mixture of stemmed beet greens,
chard, and sorrel; or 20 ounces thawed frozen
spinach, squeezed dry

$^1/_4$ cup unsalted butter or olive oil

10 to 12 scallions, sliced, or I large onion,
chopped

I cup (5 ounces) crumbled feta cheese

$^3/_4$ cup (6 ounces) farmer cheese or cream
cheese, at room temperature

$^3/_4$ cup (3 ounces) shredded kashkaval, Gouda,
Gruyère, or Muenster cheese

3 large eggs, lightly beaten

$^1/_4$ teaspoon freshly grated nutmeg or $^1/_4$ cup
chopped fresh dill

$^1/_8$ teaspoon cayenne (optional)

About $^3/_4$ teaspoon table salt or I $^1/_2$ teaspoons
kosher salt

Ground black pepper to taste

1. In a large saucepan, cook the spinach with
just the water clinging to it until wilted. Squeeze
out the excess moisture and finely chop.

2. In a large skillet, melt the butter over medium
heat. Add the scallions and sauté until softened,
about 5 minutes. Stir in the spinach. Remove from
the heat and let cool. Stir in the cheeses, eggs, nutmeg, optional cayenne, salt, and pepper.

VARIATIONS

Omit the kashkaval, increase the farmer cheese to 1 cup
(8 ounces), and add $^1/_2$ cup (1 $^1/_2$ ounces) grated kefalotyri or Parmesan cheese. Or, omit the feta and add
1 cup (3 ounces) grated kefalotyri or Parmesan cheese.

Pareve Spinach Filling: Omit the cheeses and use
olive oil. After sautéing the scallions, stir in 2 tablespoons
unbleached all-purpose flour and cook, stirring constantly,
for about 3 minutes. If desired, add $^1/_2$ cup dried currants, soaked in water to cover for 20 minutes and
drained, and $^1/_4$ cup toasted pine nuts (see page 22).

SEPHARDIC SMALL PIES

(Pastelitos)

24 SMALL OPEN-FACED PIES
OR 18 COVERED PIES

*I was sitting next to a woman at a Sephardic engage-
ment party, and she mentioned how her Greek grandmother served these petite pies for brunch, but in America
and Israel they have also become hors d'oeuvres for parties. She recounted how her grandmother, well into
her eighties, deftly shaped and filled scores of these dainty
fluted pastries, and envied her ability to produce such
uniform tartlets by hand. Many contemporary cooks
form and bake* pastelitos *(*pastelikos *in Greek) and a
cheese version called* quesadas *in a greased muffin
pan. Accomplished cooks mold uniform little pastry
cups in the palm of their hand, breaking off egg-sized
pieces and cupping the hand while pressing and hollowing out the dough with two fingers of the other
hand to form little pots about $^1/_8$ inch thick.*

*Yogurt pastry and oil-butter pastry complement
fillings containing cheese.*

Sephardic Oil Pastry Dough (page 177),
    Sephardic Yogurt Pastry Dough (page 178),
    or Sephardic Oil-Butter Pastry Dough (page 177)
Quesada Filling (page 171) or choice of *pastel*
    filling (pages 168–170)
Raw sesame seeds for sprinkling (optional)
1 large egg beaten with 1 tablespoon water

1. Preheat the oven to 375°F. Lightly grease a
9-by-13-inch baking pan or 2 standard muffin pans.

2. For open-faced pies, form the dough into
twenty-four 1-inch balls; for covered pies, form
about two-thirds of the dough into eighteen 1-inch
balls. On a floured surface, roll the balls out into
$1/8$-inch-thick rounds, then form into $1^1/2$- to 2-inch-
deep cups with $1^1/2$- to 2-inch-wide mouths. Place
on the prepared pan or in the muffin pans. Refrigerate for at least 30 minutes or up to 2 days.

3. Fill the cups with the filling. If desired, for
the quesada filling, sprinkle the tops with sesame
seeds and narrow the opening slightly. For the vegetable fillings, leave uncovered or roll out the
remaining dough and, using a 2-inch biscuit cutter,
cut out dough rounds for top crusts, place over the
filled pastries, and crimp the edges to seal. Brush
the tops with the egg mixture.

4. Bake until golden brown, about 30 minutes. Serve warm or at room temperature.

QUESADA FILLING

(*Gomo de Queso*)

24 SMALL OPEN-FACED PIES   D

*Small pies filled with cheese, related to the Spanish
cheese turnover* quesadilla, *are variously written* quesadas, kezadas, *or* guizadas, *all names derived from the
Spanish word* queso *("cheese").*

$1/4$ cup unsalted butter
2 tablespoons unbleached all-purpose flour
2 cups milk
2 cups (8 ounces) shredded kashkaval, Gouda,
    Gruyère, Monterey jack, Muenster, or white
    Cheddar cheese
2 large eggs, lightly beaten
About $3/4$ teaspoon table salt or $1^1/2$ teaspoons
    kosher salt
About $1/2$ teaspoon freshly grated nutmeg

In a medium saucepan, melt the butter over medium
heat. Add the flour and stir until bubbly, 2 to 3 minutes. Gradually whisk in the milk. Bring to a boil
and cook, stirring constantly, until slightly thickened, 3 to 5 minutes. Remove from the heat, add
the cheese, and stir until melted. Stir in the eggs,
salt, and nutmeg.

Boyos, Bulemas, and Borekas

It has been several years since I had the good fortune of attending a considerable *desayuno* (Sephardic Sabbath breakfast) replete with an assortment of traditional dishes. Today, many Sephardim limit the fare at their *desayuno* to yogurt and maybe a single pastry or omit the meal altogether. Fortunately, some people cling to the tradition, preparing dishes that have been passed down for centuries. As the wife of a Sephardic rabbi told me, "Handing down recipes is not only a nicety, but an obligation."

Ubiquitous at these traditional meals, which are always dairy, are a trio of pastries that have been made since Ottoman times and some even longer: *boyos*, *bulemas*, and *borekas*. In texture, *boyos* fall in between the very thin, very crisp pastry of *bulemas* and the slightly thicker, less crisp casing used for *borekas*. At least one, and frequently all three of these pastries, are proudly displayed for the enjoyment of family and guests.

BOYOS

Sephardim generally made bread—for much of history an arduous, time-consuming process—only twice a week, on Mondays and Fridays. After a few days, the bread would become stale and innovative cooks would seek tasty ways to utilize it. *Boyos* (from *bollo*, Spanish for "balls"), one of the oldest extant Sephardic dishes, originated when cooks soaked dry bread in water or milk, seasoned the mixture with cheese and spices, then fried dollops of the batter in hot oil. Over the centuries, more sophisticated variations of *boyos de pan* ("balls of bread") developed, most using dough in lieu of bread, but always incorporating cheese, including cheese-filled squares, cheese pinwheels, and classic cheese puffs.

SEPHARDIC FILLED CHEESE PASTRIES

(Boyos)

ABOUT 24 PASTRIES   D

In this version of boyos, *the yeast dough is left to rise in oil and then brushed with more oil, which results in a very flaky pastry. The classic filling for* boyos *is cheese, but other popular fillings include eggplant, leek, onion, potato, pumpkin, and spinach.*

DOUGH:
1 teaspoon active dry yeast
1 cup warm water (105°F to 115°F)
1/2 teaspoon sugar
1 teaspoon melted unsalted butter or olive oil
1 teaspoon table salt or 2 teaspoons kosher salt
About 3 cups unbleached all-purpose flour

About 1 1/3 cups vegetable oil
1/2 cup unbleached all-purpose flour
1/4 cup finely grated kefalotyri, Parmesan, Romano, or other hard cheese
About 1 1/2 cups any Sephardic pastry filling (pages 178–181)
1 large egg beaten with 1 teaspoon water
Additional grated kefalotyri, Parmesan, or Romano cheese or raw sesame seeds for sprinkling (optional)

1. To make the dough: In a medium bowl, dissolve the yeast in 1/4 cup of the water. Stir in the sugar and let stand until foamy, 5 to 10 minutes. Add the remaining water, butter, and salt. Stir in 1 cup of the flour. Gradually add enough of the remaining flour until the mixture holds together. On a lightly floured surface, knead until smooth

and elastic, 10 to 15 minutes. (To knead in a food processor, combine the flour, butter, and salt in the work bowl of a food processor and add the yeast mixture. With the machine on, gradually add enough warm water until the dough forms a ball, then process around the bowl about 25 times.) Cover with an inverted large bowl and let stand at room temperature for about 30 minutes.

2. On a floured surface, divide the dough into 4 equal pieces, knead each piece until smooth, and form into a ball. Add about ¼ inch of the oil to a baking pan or casserole that will just fit the balls without touching. Place the balls in the pan and turn to coat in the oil. Cover the pan with plastic wrap and let stand at room temperature for about 30 minutes.

3. Preheat the oven to 400°F. Line a large baking sheet with parchment paper or lightly grease it.

4. In a small bowl, combine the flour and cheese. Stir to blend. On a lightly oiled surface, such as a countertop or large cutting board, roll out each ball of dough into a 15-inch square. Lightly brush with oil. Sprinkle 3 tablespoons of the cheese mixture over each dough square. Roll up jelly-roll style, then cut the rolls crosswise into six 2½-inch-long pieces. Flatten each piece, roll into a 5-inch square, and brush with oil. Spoon about 1 tablespoon of the filling into the center of each dough square. Bring the corners of the dough together in the center, slightly overlapping, and press the edges to seal in the filling.

5. Place the boyos, seam-side down, on the prepared baking sheet. Brush with the egg mixture and, if using, sprinkle with the cheese or sesame seeds.

6. Bake until golden brown, 20 to 25 minutes. Serve warm or at room temperature.

SEPHARDIC CHEESE PINWHEELS

(Boyikos)

ABOUT 36 PASTRIES

This is a variation of boyos *in which the dough does not contain yeast but does include some of the cheese.*

DOUGH:
1 cup vegetable oil
⅔ cup water
¾ cup (2¼ ounces) finely grated kefalotyri, Parmesan, Romano, or other hard cheese
1 teaspoon table salt or 2 teaspoons kosher salt
About 4½ cups unbleached all-purpose flour

1 large egg beaten with 1 teaspoon water
1⅓ cups (5 ounces) finely grated kefalotyri, Parmesan, Romano, or other hard cheese

1. To make the dough: In a large bowl, combine the oil, water, the ¾ cup cheese, and the salt. Gradually add enough flour to make a soft dough. Form into a ball, wrap in plastic wrap, and let stand at room temperature for 20 minutes.

2. Preheat the oven to 375°F. Line 2 large baking sheets with parchment or lightly grease them.

3. Divide the dough into thirds. On a lightly floured surface, roll out each third into a 12-by 6-inch rectangle ¼ inch thick. Sprinkle each rectangle with ⅓ cup cheese. Starting from one short side, roll up jelly-roll style. Cut crosswise into ½-inch slices.

4. Place on the prepared baking sheet, cut-side up, and flatten slightly. Brush with the egg mixture and lightly sprinkle with the remaining cheese.

5. Bake until golden brown, about 20 minutes. Serve warm or at room temperature.

TURKISH FILLED PHYLLO COILS

(Bulemas)

ABOUT 24 MEDIUM ROLLS   Ⓓ OR Ⓟ

Bulemas, or bolemas (from bilmuelos, Ladino for fritters), also called rodanchas ("roses"), as their coiled form resembles a flower, are another ancient Sephardic treat that developed newer and more sophisticated forms during the Ottoman Empire. They also evolved from a fried food to a baked one. This is the easy version of these coiled pastries, made with commercial phyllo dough.

I pound (about 24 sheets) frozen phyllo dough
1½ cups (3 sticks) melted unsalted butter
    or olive oil
About 4 cups any Sephardic pastry filling
    (pages 178–181)
Grated kefalotyri, Romano, or Parmesan cheese
    for sprinkling (optional)

---

1. Thaw the phyllo in the refrigerator for at least 8 hours; it must be thawed completely before using or it will crumble. Do not thaw at room temperature, or the sheets will stick together. Unopened, phyllo will keep for almost a month in the refrigerator. Remove it from the refrigerator about 2 hours before using.

2. Preheat the oven to 350°F. Line 2 large baking sheets with parchment paper or lightly grease them.

3. Lay the phyllo sheets on a flat surface and cover with a slightly damp towel. Working with 1 sheet at a time, place it on a flat surface and lightly brush with butter. Fold in half lengthwise and lightly brush with butter. Spoon about ¼ cup filling in a thin strip along one long side, leaving a 1-inch border on both short ends. Fold the short ends over by 1 inch. Starting from the filling side, roll up jelly-roll style.

4. Holding the roll at both ends, gently push the roll toward the center to crimp. (Crimping makes the roll more flexible, allowing it to be coiled.) Brush with butter. Starting at one end of the roll, gently curl it into a coil. The coils can be frozen at this point for up to 3 months; do not thaw before baking. Place on the prepared baking sheet, leaving 1 inch between coils. Brush with butter, and, if desired, lightly sprinkle with the cheese.

5. Bake until crisp and golden brown, about 25 minutes for fresh, 40 minutes for frozen. Serve warm or at room temperature.

VARIATIONS

For the traditional version of *bulemas* made with yeast dough, which is easier to coil without tearing, substitute the dough for *boyos* (Sephardic Filled Cheese Pastries, page 172). Divide the dough into eighteen 1-inch balls, place in ½ cup oil, turning to coat, cover with plastic wrap, and let stand in the oil for 30 minutes. Place the dough balls on an oiled surface, flatten, then roll and stretch into very thin 5½-by-10-inch rectangles. Proceed as above, but do not crimp as in Step 4.

Small *Bulemas*: Cut the phyllo in half lengthwise and spoon 1 to 2 tablespoons filling in a thin strip about 1 inch from a narrow end. Roll up and coil as above. Pack the coils close together on the baking sheet to prevent them from uncoiling. Makes about 48.

Large *Bulemas*: Do not fold the phyllo sheets in half. Brush a sheet with butter and spread the filling in a 1¼-inch-wide strip along one long side, leaving a 1-inch border on both sides. Roll up and coil as above. Bake in a preheated 350°F oven for about 45 minutes, or until crisp and golden brown.

BOREKAS

The Turks were a nomadic people who originated in Mongolia, eventually shaking off Chinese domination and making their way to the steppes of central Asia. In the tenth century, the Turks converted to Islam and began moving westward. In 1299, Osman I (1259–1326) emerged as the most powerful Turkish leader, establishing the Ottoman dynasty, which gradually eroded the Byzantine Empire. Finally in 1453, the Ottoman Turks captured the capital of Byzantium itself, and the land thereafter bore their name. The Ottoman Empire reached its height of power under Suleiman the Magnificent (1494–1566), his domain stretching in Europe as far north as Hungary and Romania, westward to Algeria, northeast to Georgia, and southeast to the Euphrates River.

Among the foods that the Turks brought with them from central Asia was a deep-fried filled dumpling called *bugra*, which by the fifteenth century evolved into an assortment of filled and layered pastries, both baked and fried, collectively known as *borek*, the cornerstone of Turkish cuisine. These treats were so highly regarded that the head *borek* baker held one of the most important positions in the Ottoman imperial household. Around the same time that the modern Turkish *borek* was developing, Sephardic exiles escaping the Expulsion of 1492 arrived in the realm of the sultan, the two cultures symbiotically enriching one another's culture and cuisine. Since it was primarily in the Ottoman Empire that the Spanish-Portuguese Jews found haven, the cuisine that arose synthesizing Middle Eastern, Iberian, and the local Ottoman cooking emerged as the most conspicuous form of Sephardic cuisine and is still the one most closely associated with them.

By the eighteenth century, the Iberian empanada (turnover) merged with the Ottoman *borek* to form the *boreka*. Classic Jewish *borekas* (called *bourekakia* in Greece) call for a heavier, thicker dough than the Turkish *borek*, which is made with a thick form of phyllo called *yufka* or occasionally puff pastry. *Borekas* can be large or small; popular savory fillings include cheese, potato, spinach, and eggplant. Turnovers with cheese or cheese-and-vegetable fillings, sometimes called *borekitas*, are popular for *desayuno* (Sephardic Sabbath brunch) and other dairy meals, while *borekas* with pareve fillings are served at meat meals.

Since homemade turnovers require a bit of effort to prepare, they are usually reserved for special occasions. It is not uncommon, however, for hosts to offer as many as five different varieties of *borekas* at a meal. Many cooks use different toppings, such as grated cheese or sesame seeds, or make border designs to differentiate between the different fillings. In modern Israel, triangular *borekas*—frequently made from puff pastry or phyllo—follow only falafel in popularity as a street snack food.

TURKISH TURNOVERS

(Borekas)

ABOUT TWENTY-FOUR 4-INCH
PASTRIES D OR P

*The approximately thirty thousand Sephardim who
arrived in New York City between 1890 and 1924 were
outnumbered by the more than two million Ashkenazim
who also immigrated during that period. Many subsequently adopted the more prevalent Ashkenazic practices, forgetting their culture and customs. Similarly,
European culture dominated the State of Israel during
its early years. I was discussing this with a Sephardic
rabbi from Israel who fears for the future of the Sephardic culture, but did note that he had recently visited
the island of Mallorca and found fellow Sephardim
preparing many of the same dishes as his own family,
including boyos, quesadas, and borekas. For many
Sephardim, eating a boreka provides a sense of Jewish
identity in the way that a blintz or a bagel does for
eastern Europeans.*

Sephardic Oil-Butter Pastry Dough (page 177),
   Sephardic Cheese Pastry Dough (page 177),
   or standard flaky pastry dough
About 2 cups any Sephardic pastry filling
   (pages 178–181)
1 large egg beaten with 1 tablespoon water
Grated kefalotyri, Parmesan, or other hard
   cheese; or raw sesame seeds for sprinkling
   (optional)

1. Preheat the oven to 375°F. Line 2 large baking sheets with parchment paper or lightly grease
them.

2. Form the dough into 1½-inch balls. Place
the dough balls on a flat surface and, using your
fingertips, flatten and press them into 4-inch rounds.

3. Spoon 1 tablespoon filling into the center
of each round. Fold the round in half over the filling to form a half-moon shape and press the rounded
edge with the tines of a fork to seal. The pastries
can be frozen for up to 3 months; do not thaw
before baking.

4. Place the borekas 1 inch apart on the prepared
baking sheets. Brush the tops with the egg mixture
and, if desired, sprinkle with grated cheese. Bake
until golden, about 20 minutes for fresh, 30 minutes
for frozen. Serve warm or at room temperature.

VARIATION

Small *Borekas*: Divide the dough into 1-inch balls,
roll into 3-inch rounds, and fill with 1 heaping teaspoon
filling. Makes about 32.

SEPHARDIC OIL PASTRY DOUGH

(*Masa Aceite*)

MAKES ABOUT THIRTY-TWO
3-INCH TURNOVERS OR 1 LARGE
TWO-CRUST PIE

This is the standard Sephardic pastry dough, which yields a crisp, tender, and flaky crust.

> $^1/_2$ cup lukewarm water (80°F to 90°F)
> $^1/_2$ cup vegetable oil
> $^3/_4$ teaspoon table salt or 1$^1/_2$ teaspoons kosher salt
> About 2$^1/_2$ cups unbleached all-purpose flour

In a medium bowl, combine the water, oil, and salt. Stir in 1 cup of the flour. Gradually stir in enough of the remaining flour to make a soft dough that comes away from the sides of the bowl. Wrap in plastic wrap and let stand at room temperature for 30 minutes.

VARIATION

Sephardic Cheese Pastry Dough: Add $^1/_3$ to $^1/_2$ cup grated kefalotyri, aged kashkaval, Parmesan, Romano, or Swiss cheese with the flour.

SEPHARDIC OIL-BUTTER PASTRY DOUGH

(*Masa Fina*)

MAKES ABOUT THIRTY-TWO
3-INCH TURNOVERS OR 1 LARGE
TWO-CRUST PIE

In this dough, a little acid is substituted for an equal amount of water, to help keep the gluten relaxed. This makes the dough easier to handle and the pastry more tender.

> $^1/_4$ cup vegetable oil
> $^1/_2$ cup (1 stick) unsalted butter, melted
> $^1/_4$ cup lukewarm water (80°F to 90°F)
> 2$^1/_2$ teaspoons distilled white vinegar
> $^3/_4$ teaspoon table salt or 1$^1/_2$ teaspoons kosher salt
> About 2$^1/_2$ cups unbleached all-purpose flour

In a medium bowl, beat together the oil, butter, water, vinegar, and salt. Gradually work in enough flour to make a soft dough that pulls away from the sides of the bowl. Do not overwork it. Wrap in plastic wrap and refrigerate for 1 hour.

Sephardic Yogurt Pastry Dough

(Otra Masa Afrijaldada)

MAKES ABOUT THIRTY-TWO
3-INCH TURNOVERS OR I LARGE
TWO-CRUST PIE

This rich dough is especially complementary to cheese, a major component of many pastel *fillings. A pastry made from either yogurt or sour cream, due to the acid and milk solids, is light and tender and does not get tough. Yogurt pastry is less tangy than one made from sour cream.*

3/4 cup (1 1/2 sticks) unsalted butter or margarine, softened
1/4 cup yogurt or sour cream
I large egg, lightly beaten
1/2 teaspoon table salt or I teaspoon kosher salt
About 2 1/2 cups unbleached all-purpose flour

In a medium bowl, combine the butter, yogurt, egg, and salt. Gradually stir in enough flour to make a soft dough. Form into a ball, cover with plastic wrap, and let stand in a cool place for 1 hour or in the refrigerator for up to 2 days.

VARIATION

Omit the egg and increase the butter to 3/4 cup plus 2 tablespoons (1 3/4 sticks) and the yogurt or sour cream to 1/2 cup. This pastry, due to the absence of the egg, will appear drier while mixing, so work it with your hands to form into a ball and, if necessary, add a little milk.

Sephardic Cheese Filling

(Gomo de Queso)

MAKES ABOUT 4 CUPS, ENOUGH FOR
FORTY-EIGHT 3-INCH TURNOVERS

I cup (4 ounces) shredded kashkaval, Gouda, Gruyère, or Muenster cheese
I cup (5 ounces) crumbled feta cheese; or I cup (3 ounces) grated kefalotyri, Parmesan, or Romano cheese
2 cups mashed potatoes or 1/2 cup (4 ounces) farmer or ricotta cheese
2 tablespoons softened unsalted butter or vegetable oil
4 large eggs, lightly beaten
About 1/2 teaspoon table salt or I teaspoon kosher salt
Ground white or black pepper to taste
1/4 cup chopped fresh parsley or 2 chopped scallions (optional)

In a large bowl, combine all the ingredients and stir to blend.

VARIATION

This is a basic Sephardic cheese filling, but there are numerous versions that vary the types and proportions of cheese. For a more intense cheese flavor but a heavier texture, omit the mashed potatoes.

SEPHARDIC EGGPLANT FILLING

(Gomo de Berenjena)

MAKES ABOUT 4 CUPS, ENOUGH FOR
FORTY-EIGHT 3-INCH TURNOVERS

- 2 (about 1 pound each) eggplants
- 2 cups (8 ounces) shredded cheese,
  such as kashkaval, kasseri, Gouda, Gruyère,
  Monterey jack, or Muenster; or 1 cup
  (4 ounces) shredded cheese and 3/4 cup
  (4 ounces) crumbled feta cheese
- About 1/4 teaspoon table salt or 1/2 teaspoon
  kosher salt
- Ground black pepper to taste

Light a fire in a charcoal grill, preheat the broiler, or preheat the oven to 400°F. Cut several slits in the eggplants. Roast over hot coals or broil 3 to 4 inches from the heat source under the broiler, turning occasionally, until charred and tender, about 20 minutes. Or, place on a baking sheet and bake in the oven until very tender, about 50 minutes. Let stand long enough so that you can handle it. Peel the eggplants, being careful not to leave any skin. Coarsely chop, put in a colander, and let drain for about 30 minutes. Mash the eggplant into a pulp. There should be about 2 cups. Stir in the remaining ingredients.

VARIATION

Pareve Eggplant Filling: Omit the cheese, increase the salt to about 1/2 teaspoon, and add 2 lightly beaten eggs, 2 tablespoons olive oil, and about 1/4 to 1/2 cup matza meal or fresh bread crumbs, adding more if necessary, to make a thick filling.

TURKISH EGGPLANT AND TOMATO FILLING

(Gomo de Handrajo)

MAKES ABOUT 4 CUPS, ENOUGH FOR
FORTY-EIGHT 3-INCH TURNOVERS

- 2 eggplants (2 pounds total), peeled
- About 1 tablespoon table salt or 2 tablespoons
  kosher salt
- 1/4 cup olive oil or vegetable oil
- 2 onions, chopped
- 3 plum tomatoes, peeled, seeded, and chopped
  (see page 291), about 1 cup
- Ground black pepper to taste

1. Cut the eggplants crosswise into 1/2-inch-thick slices, then into 1/2-inch-wide sticks, then into 1/2-inch cubes. Put in a colander or on a wire rack, sprinkle lightly with the salt, and let stand for at least 1 hour. (Moisture will appear on the surface, and the eggplant will become more pliable.) Rinse the eggplant under cold water, then press between several layers of paper towels, repeatedly pressing several times until the pieces feel firm and dry. The eggplant can be stored in the refrigerator for up to 4 hours.

2. In a large saucepan, heat the oil over medium heat. Add the onions and sauté until lightly golden, about 15 minutes. Add the eggplants, tomatoes, and pepper and cook, stirring frequently, until the eggplant is soft and the liquid evaporates, about 15 minutes. Mash, then let cool.

VARIATION

Reduce the eggplant to 1 pound and add 1 pound shredded zucchini.

SEPHARDIC LEEK FILLING

(Gomo de Prassa)

MAKES ABOUT 4 CUPS, ENOUGH
FOR FORTY-EIGHT 3-INCH
TURNOVERS

3 tablespoons unsalted butter or olive oil

12 ounces leeks (white and light green parts only), washed and chopped (about 3 cups)

1 onion, chopped

$1/4$ cup water

3 large eggs, lightly beaten

$3/4$ cup matza meal or fresh bread crumbs

About $1/2$ teaspoon table salt or 1 teaspoon kosher salt

Ground black pepper to taste

In a large skillet, melt the butter over medium heat. Add the leeks and onion and sauté until slightly softened, about 5 minutes. Add the water, cover, and cook until the leeks are tender, about 5 minutes. Uncover and cook, stirring frequently, until the liquid evaporates. Let cool, then stir in the remaining ingredients.

VARIATION

Leek and Cheese Filling: Reduce the matza meal to $1/4$ cup and add 1 cup (8 ounces) farmer cheese or 1 cup (3 ounces) grated kefalotyri cheese.

SEPHARDIC POTATO FILLING

(Gomo de Patata)

MAKES ABOUT 4 CUPS, ENOUGH FOR
FORTY-EIGHT 3-INCH TURNOVERS

$1^{1}/2$ pounds baking (russet) potatoes, peeled and cut into chunks

2 cloves garlic, mashed (optional)

3 tablespoons olive oil or vegetable oil

2 onions, chopped

About $1/2$ teaspoon table salt or 1 teaspoon kosher salt

2 large eggs, lightly beaten

1. Put the potatoes and, if using, the garlic in a large pot and add cold water to cover. Bring to a boil, reduce the heat to low, and simmer until tender, 15 to 20 minutes. Drain and mash. You should have about 3 cups.

2. In a large skillet, heat the oil over medium heat. Add the onions and sauté until golden, about 15 minutes. Stir into the potatoes and add the salt. Let cool. Stir in the eggs.

VARIATIONS

Potato and Cheese Filling: Omit the onions (add the oil to the potatoes) and add 2 cups (10 ounces) creamy feta or goat cheese or 2 cups (8 ounces) shredded kashkaval, Gouda, Gruyère, Monterey jack, or Muenster cheese.

Potato and Squash Filling: Omit the onions, reduce the potatoes 1 pound (2 cups mashed), and add 1 cup cooked and mashed butternut squash (about 12 ounces raw) and 1 cup (5 ounces) creamy feta or goat cheese.

SEPHARDIC PUMPKIN FILLING

(Gomo de Calabaza)

MAKES ABOUT 3 CUPS, ENOUGH
FORTHIRTY-SIX 3-INCH
TURNOVERS

2 pounds pumpkin (such as cheese or sugar
  pumpkin) or winter squash, peeled, seeded,
  and diced (about 4 cups)
1 cup (4 ounces) grated kashkaval or 1 cup
  (5 ounces) crumbled feta cheese
1/2 cup (1 1/2 ounces) grated kefalotyri, Romano,
  or Parmesan cheese (optional)
1 large egg, lightly beaten
About 1/2 teaspoon table salt or 1 teaspoon
  kosher salt

Steam the pumpkin until tender, about 10 minutes,
or cook, covered, in simmering water for about
20 minutes. Place in a colander, set a plate on top,
weigh down, and let drain for at least 30 minutes.
Transfer to a bowl and mash. There should be
about 2 cups. Stir in all the remaining ingredients.

VARIATIONS

Substitute 2 cups (16 ounces) canned pumpkin purée
for the fresh pumpkin.

Sweet Pumpkin Filling: Omit the cheese and
add 1/3 cup packed brown or granulated sugar, about
1 teaspoon ground cinnamon or 1 tablespoon anise
seeds, and 1 teaspoon vanilla extract.

Sweet Potato Filling: Substitute 1 pound peeled
sweet potatoes for the pumpkin, steaming them for
about 20 minutes and omitting the draining process.

SEPHARDIC SPINACH FILLING

(Gomo de Espinaca)

MAKES ABOUT 4 CUPS, ENOUGH
FOR FORTY-EIGHT 3-INCH
TURNOVERS

2 pounds (about 8 cups packed) stemmed fresh
  spinach or chard; or 30 ounces thawed
  chopped frozen spinach, squeezed dry
3 tablespoons olive oil or vegetable oil
1 large onion or 8 scallions, chopped
2 to 3 tablespoons chopped fresh parsley,
  cilantro, or dill
2 large eggs, lightly beaten
1 cup (4 ounces) shredded kashkaval, kasseri,
  Gouda, Gruyère, Monterey jack, or Muenster
  cheese; or 1 cup (5 ounces) ricotta cheese
1 cup (5 ounces) crumbled feta or 1 cup
  (8 ounces) farmer cheese
About 1/2 teaspoon table salt or 1 teaspoon
  kosher salt
About 1/2 teaspoon ground black pepper
About 1/8 teaspoon freshly grated nutmeg, ground
  cumin, or paprika

1. If using fresh spinach, put it, with the water
clinging to the leaves, in a heavy pot over medium
heat, cover, and cook until wilted. Drain and chop.

2. In a large skillet, heat the oil over medium
heat. Add the onion and sauté until soft and translucent, about 5 minutes. Add the spinach and parsley and stir until the liquid evaporates. Remove
from the heat and let cool.

3. Stir in all the remaining ingredients.

VARIATION

Pareve Spinach Filling: Substitute 1 cup mashed
potatoes for the cheeses and add 1 tablespoon fresh
lemon juice.

Buricche

A rudimentary form of puff pastry called *ojaldre* or *hojaldre* was popular in Moorish Spain. *Ojaldre* was rather thick and difficult to manipulate, however, and its use faded during the Renaissance when some ingenious Florentine bakers invented the modern puff pastry, called *pasta sfoglia* in Italian and *pâte feuilletée* in French. The bakers had found a way to produce a layered pastry that was much thinner and flakier than the prevalent rudimentary types, yet without having to use the time-consuming and skilled art of hand stretching the dough to paper thinness necessary for phyllo.

Instead, numerous thin layers of butter are folded between layers of dough, so that during baking the water present in the butter will steam and puff the dough up, resulting in numerous crisp, flaky layers. Bakers from western Europe, including Italy, gravitated to the buttery puff pastry, while those from central and eastern Europe overwhelmingly adopted phyllo dough to produce flaky pastry, most notably in strudel.

When Sephardim from the Ottoman Empire arrived in Italy in the sixteenth century, they introduced *borekas* and pumpkin fillings. Italians combined these with their puff pastry to create small puff pastry turnovers called *buricche*, a name probably derived from *borekas*.

ITALIAN TURNOVERS
(*Buricche*)

ABOUT 20 PASTRIES

You can substitute store-bought puff pastry or standard flaky pie pastry for the buricche *pastry.*

DOUGH:
¹/₂ olive oil or vegetable oil
¹/₂ cup lukewarm water (80°F to 90°F)
¹/₂ teaspoon table salt or I teaspoon kosher salt
About 2¹/₂ cups unbleached all-purpose flour, sifted, plus more for sprinkling

About ¹/₂ cup (I stick) plus 2 tablespoons unsalted butter or margarine, softened
Choice of *buricche* filling (pages 183–184)
I large egg beaten with I tablespoon water

1. To make the dough: In a medium bowl, combine the oil, water, and salt. Stir in 1 cup of the flour. Gradually stir in enough of the remaining flour to make a soft dough that comes away from the sides of the bowl. Wrap in plastic wrap and let stand at room temperature for 30 minutes.

2. On a piece of waxed paper or plastic wrap or on a lightly floured surface, roll out the dough into a 6-by-9-inch rectangle about ¹/₃ inch thick.

Brush with the 2 tablespoons butter and lightly sprinkle with flour. With the narrow end facing you, fold over the top third of the dough, then fold over the uncovered bottom third, forming a 3-by-6-inch rectangle. Wrap in plastic wrap and refrigerate for about 30 minutes.

3. Roll the dough, seam-side up, into a $1/4$-inch-thick rectangle. Brush with 2 tablespoons butter, lightly sprinkle with flour, and fold in thirds as above. Repeat rolling, brushing, and folding 3 more times. Cover in plastic wrap and refrigerate for at least 2 hours or overnight. Let stand at room temperature for about 15 minutes before rolling.

4. Preheat the oven to 400°F.

5. On a piece of waxed paper or plastic wrap or on a lightly floured surface, roll out the dough $1/8$ inch thick. Cut into 3-inch squares or rounds. Spoon 1 tablespoon of the filling in the center of each piece, fold over to form a triangle or half-moon, and press the edges to seal. Place on an ungreased baking sheet, 1 inch apart, and brush with the egg mixture.

6. Bake until golden brown, 15 to 20 minutes. Serve warm or at room temperature. Store in an airtight container at room temperature for up to 2 days or in the freezer for up to 6 months.

ITALIAN SPINACH BURICCHE FILLING

(*Spinaci*)

MAKES ABOUT 2 1/2 CUPS, ENOUGH FOR
TWENTY-FOUR 3-INCH TURNOVERS

1 pound stemmed fresh spinach or 10 ounces
    thawed frozen spinach, squeezed dry
2 tablespoons olive or vegetable oil
1 onion or 6 scallions, chopped
1 large egg, lightly beaten
$1/2$ to $3/4$ cup (2 to 3 ounces) shredded Provolone,
    kashkaval, Muenster, Monterey jack, or Swiss
    cheese
About $1/2$ teaspoon table salt or 1 teaspoon
    kosher salt
Dash of ground black pepper
Dash of freshly grated nutmeg or cayenne
    (optional)

1. If using fresh spinach, put it, with the water clinging to the leaves, in a heavy pot over medium heat, cover, and cook until wilted. Drain and chop.

2. In a large skillet, heat the oil over medium heat. Add the onion and sauté until soft and translucent, about 5 minutes. Add the spinach and stir until dry. Let cool. Stir in all the remaining ingredients.

ITALIAN EGGPLANT BURICCHE FILLING

(Melanzane)

MAKES ABOUT 2¹/₂ CUPS, ENOUGH FOR
TWENTY-FOUR 3-INCH TURNOVERS

1 medium-small (14 ounces) eggplant, peeled
About 2 teaspoons table salt or 4 teaspoons
   kosher salt
3 tablespoons olive oil
1 onion, chopped
2 plum tomatoes, peeled, seeded, and chopped
   (see page 291)
1 tablespoon chopped fresh parsley
Ground black pepper to taste

1. Coarsely grate or dice the eggplant. Put in a colander, sprinkle lightly with the salt, and let stand for at least 1 hour. (Moisture will appear on the surface, and the eggplant will become more pliable.) Rinse the eggplant under cold water, then press between several layers of paper towels, repeatedly pressing several times until the pieces feel firm and dry. The eggplant can be stored in the refrigerator for up to 4 hours.

2. In a large skillet, heat the oil over medium heat. Add the onion and sauté until golden, about 15 minutes. Add the eggplant and tomatoes, reduce the heat to low, and cook, stirring frequently, until soft, about 10 minutes. Increase the heat to medium-high and cook until the liquid evaporates, about 2 minutes. Coarsely mash, using a wooden spoon or potato masher. Put in a colander and let cool. Stir in the parsley and pepper.

ITALIAN PUMPKIN BURRICHE FILLING

(Zucca)

MAKES ABOUT 2¹/₂ CUPS, ENOUGH FOR
TWENTY-FOUR 3-INCH TURNOVERS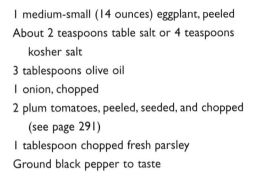

2 pounds pumpkin (such as cheese or sugar
   pumpkin) or winter squash, peeled, seeded,
   and diced (about 4 cups)
³/₄ cup fine dried bread crumbs
8 small amaretti cookies, crushed
1 large egg, lightly beaten
1 teaspoon grated lemon zest
Pinch of freshly grated nutmeg
Pinch of salt

Steam the pumpkin in a covered steamer over boiling water until tender, about 10 minutes, or cook, covered, in simmering water for about 20 minutes. Put in a colander, set a plate over top, weigh down, and let drain for at least 30 minutes. Transfer to a bowl and mash with a wooden spoon or potato masher. There should be about 2 cups. Stir in all the remaining ingredients.

AMARETTI AND MACAROONS

The word "macaroon" comes from the Italian *maccarone* ("paste"), referring to a paste made from crushing and then mashing almonds. The Italian name for this cookie, *amaretti* ("little bitter ones"), refers to the macaroon's original ingredients, primarily bitter almonds and a little honey. When sugar became more accessible, amaretti evolved into the sweeter version known today. Since most macaroons contain no flour, they became a natural addition to the Passover pantry. Although in America, Passover macaroons became associated with the insipid, chewy canned variety, the fresh-baked ones—crispy on the outside and slightly moist and chewy in the center—make delicious treats.

❖ KHACHAPURI ❖

Due to centuries of Persian rule and cultural domination, Georgian cooking displays a pronounced Persian influence, including the cone-shaped clay oven Georgians use to bake their largely Persian-inspired bread, a *tone*, the Georgian name for the Persian *tanor*.

The principal Georgian bread is *deda's puri*, literally meaning "mother's bread," which is similar to pita but has a hole in the center to prevent it from puffing up and forming a pocket. Because the bread was until recently baked on the hot inner wall of the *tone* or on a pan over an open fire, the breads had to be thin so that the center would bake before the outside burned. For centuries, hungry Georgians in need of a snack would wrap a plain piece of soft *deda's puri*, hot from the oven, around a chunk of *suluguni* (string cheese) or other cheese; the fresh bread and melting cheese made an irresistible combination. At some point, perhaps inspired by the Persian *sambusak*, cooks started baking the cheese directly inside the bread, producing what has become the Georgian national dish, *khachapuri* (pronounced "kah-chah-POOR-ee").

The original *khachapuri* used bread dough, but cooks have since made them with phyllo (*penovani*), puff pastry, flaky pastry, and quick-bread dough. So far I have collected recipes for a dozen different types of *khachapuri*, two of which I have included as my favorites. The arrival of the modern oven allowed bakers to bake bread at lower heats and produce thicker, larger, and more sophisticated versions of the pastry, including *khachapuri* made from phyllo packages and puff pastry bundles. Bean and potato fillings were introduced by Georgian Jews—who could not eat the cheese-filled breads at meat meals—and subsequently became adopted by their non-Jewish neighbors. Still, cheese *khachapuri* remain the classic and most popular. *Khachapuri* are sold at special cafes throughout Georgia, while proficient home cooks prepare their own for special occasions. No Georgian feast is considered complete without trays of small *khachapuri*; a large one constitutes a meal in itself. They are eaten as an appetizer, part of breakfast or lunch, and with tea as a snack.

GEORGIAN FILLED FLAT BREAD

(*Khachapuri*)

4 PASTRIES   D OR P

My cousin David Zimm, who was born in Odessa in the former Soviet Union and immigrated to Boston as a boy, admits that he is generally not a very good cook. However, he did spend several years during college working in a bakery, and in the process became quite proficient at making bagels and breads. Trying to re-capture some of the dishes from his childhood, David began mastering khachapuri, *whose popularity has spread north from Georgia to Ukraine and Russia (Odessa lies across the Black Sea from Georgia). Although David rarely finds time to bake these days, thanks to his advice I can now whip up a batch of* khachapuri *when I want a bread pie different from pizza. Cheese* khachapuri *are best when warm.*

DOUGH:

1 package (2¼ teaspoons) active dry yeast or 1 cake fresh yeast

1 cup warm water (105°F to 115°F for dry yeast; 80°F to 85°F for fresh yeast) or ¼ cup warm water and ¾ cup warm milk

1 teaspoon granulated sugar or honey

½ cup (1 stick) unsalted butter or margarine, softened

1½ teaspoons table salt or 1 tablespoon kosher salt

About 3½ cups unbleached all-purpose flour

Choice of *khachapuri* filling (pages 188–189)
1 large egg beaten with 1 teaspoon water

1. Line 2 large baking sheets or four 8-inch round cake pans with parchment paper or lightly grease them.

2. To make the dough: In a large bowl, dissolve the yeast in ¼ cup of the water. Stir in the sugar and let stand until foamy, 5 to 10 minutes. Add the remaining water, the butter, and salt. Stir in 2 cups of the flour. Gradually add enough of the remaining flour so that the mixture holds together. On a floured surface, knead the dough until smooth and elastic, about 10 minutes. (To knead in a food processor, combine the flour, butter, and salt in the work bowl of a food processor and add the yeast mixture. With the machine on, gradually add enough warm water until the dough forms a ball, then process around the bowl about 25 times.) Shape into a ball, place in a large oiled bowl turning to coat, cover, and let rise until nearly doubled in bulk, about 1½ hours.

3. Punch down the dough and divide into 4 equal pieces. On a lightly floured surface, roll each piece into a 12-inch round and spread a generous ¾ cup filling in the center, leaving a 6-inch border

on all sides. Begin folding the edges of the dough toward the center over the filling, with each fold overlapping the previous one, then twist the excess dough in the center into a knot. Place on the prepared baking sheets, at least 2 inches apart. Cover and let rise until puffy, about 30 minutes.

4. Meanwhile, preheat the oven to 375°F.

5. Brush the khachapuri with the egg mixture. Bake until golden brown, about 40 minutes. Transfer to a wire rack and let stand for at least 10 minutes. Serve warm or at room temperature.

VARIATIONS

Small *Khachapuri*: Divide the dough into 8 equal pieces, roll into 8-inch rounds, and heap about ²/₃ cup filling into the center. Or place into 8 greased jumbo muffin pans. Bake for 25 to 30 minutes. Makes 8.

Miniature *Khachapuri*: Form the dough into 1-inch balls and roll into thin 3-inch rounds. Spoon 1 tablespoon filling into the center of each round, bring the sides together in the center to enclose the filling, and pinch the seams to seal. Bake for 15 to 20 minutes. Makes about 24.

Diamond *Khachapuri*: Roll the dough into an 8-by-24-inch rectangle and cut it into twelve 4-inch squares. Spoon about 2 tablespoons filling into the center of each square and bring the edges together over the filling to form a diamond shape, pinching the seams to seal. Bake for about 20 minutes. Makes 12.

Large *Khachapuri*: Roll the dough into a 20-inch round about ¹/₄ inch thick. Fit the dough into a greased 9-inch round springform pan, letting the excess drape over the sides. Spoon in the filling. Gather the edges together to meet in the center, pleating the dough as evenly as possible into overlapping folds. Twist the dough ends that meet in the center to form a knob. Cover and let stand for about 30 minutes. Bake until golden, about 1 hour, then remove the sides and bottom of the pan and bake on a baking sheet for an additional 5 minutes. Let cool for at least 30 minutes before slicing. Makes 1 large loaf.

GEORGIAN PIES

(*Khachapuri*)

6 PASTRIES

This version of khachapuri uses a nonyeast dough but has an almost breadlike consistency. Until recently, these pies were cooked in a covered pottery dish called a ketsi *over an open fire, but today an oven is the more common means of baking. Using yogurt or sour cream gives the pastry a light texture and buttery flavor and makes the dough easier to roll.*

DOUGH:

About 3 cups unbleached all-purpose flour

³/₄ teaspoon baking soda

1 teaspoon table salt or 2 teaspoons kosher salt

³/₄ cup plain yogurt or sour cream

3 tablespoons melted unsalted butter or vegetable oil

1 large egg, lightly beaten

Choice of *khachapuri* filling (pages 188–189)
1 large egg beaten with 1 teaspoon water

1. To make the dough: Sift the flour, baking soda, and salt together onto a sheet of waxed paper. In a large bowl, combine the yogurt, butter, and egg. Stir in the flour mixture to make a soft dough that is no longer sticky. On a floured surface, knead until smooth, about 3 minutes, adding a little flour if too sticky. Form into a ball, cover with plastic wrap, and let stand at room temperature for 1 hour.

2. Preheat the oven to 350°F. Line a large baking sheet with parchment paper or grease it.

3. Divide the dough into 6 equal pieces. On a lightly floured surface, roll out each piece into a 9-inch round about ¹/₈ inch thick. Mound about ²/₃ cup filling in the center of each round. Gather

the edges of each round together to meet in the center, then press down to expel any air and slightly flatten the filling. Pinch the edges to seal.

4. Place the khachapuri on the prepared baking sheet, at least 1½ inches apart, brush with the egg mixture, and poke a hole in the center to vent the steam. Bake until golden brown, about 30 minutes. Serve warm or at room temperature. Using a serrated knife, cut into wedges.

VARIATIONS

Skillet *Khachapuri*: This is the old-fashioned way of preparing these pastries. At the end of Step 3, slightly flatten each *khachapuri* into a 7-inch round. For each pastry, in a large, heavy skillet, melt 1 tablespoon butter over low heat. One at a time, place the *khachapuri*, seam-side down, in the skillet, cover, and cook, occasionally shaking the pan, until golden brown on the bottom, about 12 minutes. Turn, adding another tablespoon of butter, cover, and cook until golden brown, about 12 minutes.

Small *Khachapuri*: Divide the dough into 24 equal pieces. Roll each piece into a 6-inch round and spoon about 2 tablespoons filling in the center of each round. Form as in Step 3. Bake for about 8 minutes. Makes 24.

Large *Khachapuri*: Divide the dough into 4 equal pieces. Roll each dough piece into a ¼-inch thick round about 12 inches in diameter. Spread about 1 cup filling in the center of the dough, leaving a 6-inch border on all sides. Form as in Step 3. Bake for about 35 minutes. Makes 4.

GEORGIAN CHEESE FILLING

(Khveli)

MAKES ABOUT 5 CUPS

The following is an equivalent of the combination of Georgian cheeses most commonly used in khachapuri: sulguni *(string cheese),* imeruli *(a fresh, slightly sour cheese), and* bryndza *(similar to mild creamy feta). A little butter is added for creaminess. If the feta is very salty, soak in cold water for an hour, then drain well, before crumbling.*

> 2½ cups (10 ounces) shredded mozzarella or Gruyère cheese
> 1½ cups (8 ounces) crumbled creamy feta cheese
> ¾ cup (6 ounces) farmer or pot cheese
> ¼ cup unsalted butter, softened
> 1 large egg, lightly beaten
> About ¼ teaspoon table salt or ½ teaspoon kosher salt
> ¼ teaspoon ground white pepper (optional)

In a large bowl, combine all the ingredients and stir to blend.

VARIATIONS

Omit the feta and farmer cheeses, increase the butter to ½ cup (1 stick), reduce the mozzarella to 2 cups (8 ounces), and add 2 cups (8 ounces) shredded white Cheddar, Monterey jack, or Muenster cheese.

Omit the mozzarella and feta, increase the farmer cheese to 1 cup (8 ounces), and add 4 cups (1 pound) shredded Muenster cheese.

GEORGIAN BEAN FILLING

(Lobiani)

$^1/_4$ cup olive oil or vegetable oil

2 onions, chopped

4 cups cooked and mashed red beans
   (about 13 ounces dried)

About 1 teaspoon table salt or 2 teaspoons
   kosher salt

Ground black pepper to taste

$^1/_2$ cup chopped fresh cilantro, $^3/_4$ teaspoon
   ground coriander, or $^1/_4$ teaspoon red pepper
   flakes

In a large skillet, heat the oil over medium heat. Add the onions and sauté until golden, about 15 minutes. Add the beans, salt, and pepper and cook, stirring frequently, until dry, 5 to 10 minutes. Remove from the heat and stir in the cilantro. Let cool.

GEORGIAN POTATO FILLING

(Kartopilani)

MAKES ABOUT 5 CUPS

$^1/_4$ cup olive oil or vegetable oil

2 onions, chopped

4 cups mashed potatoes

2 tablespoons chopped fresh parsley

1 tablespoon chopped fresh dill

About 1 teaspoon table salt or 2 teaspoons
   kosher salt

Ground black pepper to taste

In a large skillet, heat the oil over medium heat. Add the onions and sauté until golden, about 15 minutes. Add the potatoes, parsley, and dill and cook, stirring frequently, until dry, about 2 minutes. Season with the salt and pepper. Let cool.

VARIATION

Potato and Cheese Filling: Omit the onions and oil. While still warm, mash the potatoes with $^1/_4$ cup butter, then stir in $1^1/_2$ cups (6 ounces) shredded mozzarella cheese, $^3/_4$ cup (4 ounces) crumbled feta cheese, and $^1/_2$ cup (4 ounces) farmer cheese or pot cheese.

❧ AJIN ❧

Taimani (Hebrew for "Yemenite") Jewish cookery is remarkable for the ways it developed in spite of a history of oppression and poverty. Working with few resources, cooks had to be creative, and they developed an assortment of humble flat breads, which along with various inexpensive legumes formed the basis of almost every meal. For the Sabbath and other special occasions, cooks fried or baked breads from *ajin,* a rich dough made enticingly flaky by repeatedly folding it in a manner similar to puff pastry. *Ajin* is uncharacteristic of Yemenite food, probably adapted from the Sephardic *ojaldre,* a rudimentary puff pastry, after Iberian exiles arrived in the Ottoman Empire in the later fifteenth century. However it migrated into the cuisine, it became the pinnacle of Yemenite pastry.

Following the mass immigration of Yemenites to Israel beginning in 1949, this pastry became extremely popular among many non-Yemenite Israelis, and can now be found frozen in most Israeli supermarkets. But making your own dough is actually not as complicated as it may seem, although it does require some time to sporadically refrigerate. The various dishes made from the pastry are commonly accompanied with *z'chug* (Yemenite Chili Paste, page 438), *hilbeh* (Yemenite Fenugreek Relish, page 80), chopped or puréed tomatoes, and baked eggs, or are drizzled with a little honey.

YEMENITE FLAKY PASTRY DOUGH

(*Ajin*)

6 PIECES   Ⓓ OR Ⓟ

Historically, ajin *was leavened by wild yeast as it sat out, so its rising always depended a little on chance. Most modern versions, however, incorporate a little baking powder into the dough. Searching for the best* ajin *recipe and perfecting my technique required making many versions over the course of months. When I finally demonstrated the results to a proficient Yemenite cook, I was elated when she approved of its flaky dough and bronzed crust. I also enjoyed the fruits of my research—Yemenite pastries for breakfast and dinner.*

- 4 cups unbleached all-purpose flour
- 1 tablespoon sugar
- ¹/₂ teaspoon baking powder
- ¹/₄ cup *samneh* (Middle Eastern Clarified Butter, page 51), margarine, or vegetable oil, plus 6 tablespoons *samneh* or margarine, softened
- About 1¹/₄ cups water
- 1¹/₂ teaspoons table salt or 2¹/₂ teaspoons kosher salt
- 2 teaspoons distilled white vinegar or fresh lemon juice (optional)
- Vegetable oil for rolling

1. Combine the flour, sugar, and baking powder. Using a pastry cutter or two dinner knives, cut in the ¹/₄ cup samneh to produce fine crumbs. In a small bowl, combine the water, salt, and, if using, the vinegar. (A little acid helps to relax the gluten in the dough.) Add this to the flour mixture and stir just until the dough holds together and clears the sides of the bowl. On a floured surface, knead the

dough until smooth, about 3 minutes. Divide the dough into 6 equal pieces, wrap in plastic wrap, and refrigerate for at least 30 minutes or overnight.

2. On a lightly oiled surface, press each piece of dough into a small square, then roll into a 9-inch square. Spread with 1 tablespoon of the softened samneh. Fold the top third of the dough over the center third, then fold up the bottom third to form a rectangle 9 by 3 inches. Bring the short ends of the rectangle together to meet in the center to form a 3-inch square. Repeat with the remaining dough. Cover with plastic wrap and refrigerate for at least 30 minutes and up to 2 hours. (If too hard, the butter will splinter and puncture the dough and the dough will not roll out easily. If the butter hardens, let stand at room temperature for about 10 minutes.)

3. Place each dough package, seam-side-up, on a lightly floured surface and roll into an 8-inch square. Fold the top third of the square over the center third, then fold the bottom third over to make a rectangle. Wrap and refrigerate the rectangles for 30 minutes. Remove and repeat rolling the dough into 8-inch squares, folding in rectangles, and refrigerating twice more, for a total of four folds. At this point *ajin* can be wrapped in plastic wrap and frozen for up to 3 months, then thawed before using.

VARIATIONS

For a sweeter pastry, increase the sugar to $1/4$ cup.

To make the dough in a food processor: Put the flour and baking powder in a food processor. Cut the butter into small pieces and scatter it over the flour. Process for several seconds until the butter becomes fine particles. In a medium bowl, combine the sugar, water, salt, and vinegar and stir. With the machine running, gradually add the water mixture until the dough forms a ball, about 40 seconds. On a floured surface, briefly knead until smooth. Divide into pieces and proceed as in the main recipe.

YEMENITE BAKED FLAKY ROLLS

(Jihnun)

6 LARGE ROLLS   D OR P

These flaky cylindrical spiraled pastries (also spelled jachnoon *and* jachnun*) are traditionally baked overnight and served for Sabbath breakfast. Whole eggs in the shell are commonly nestled in between the dough spirals, to be removed and eaten alongside them the following morning, accompanied with standard Yemenite condiments—z'chug (Yemenite Chili Paste, page 438) and* hilbeh *(Yemenite Fenugreek relish, page 80)—crushed tomatoes, or honey.*

> Yemenite Flaky Pastry Dough (page 190),
> 2 tablespoons *samneh* (Middle Eastern Clarified Butter, page 51) or margarine, softened
> 6 to 7 eggs in shells (optional)

1. Preheat the oven to 200°F. Grease an 8-inch square baking pan or 9-inch ovenproof pot.

2. Spread each dough rectangle with 1 teaspoon samneh. Starting from the narrow end, roll up the dough rectangles jelly-roll style into tight cylinders.

3. Place the dough cylinders in the prepared pan, wedging the eggs, if using, standing on end in between them with 1 egg in the center. Cover with a lid or heavy-duty aluminum foil. Bake for about 12 hours. The jihnun should be golden brown. Serve warm or at room temperature.

VARIATION

For a slightly quicker version, bake at 250°F for about 6 hours.

Yemenite Flaky Pancake Bread

(Melawah)

  D OR P

While consulting on a bar mitzvah in Philadelphia for a family with a Yemenite father, I supervised the making of hundreds of melawah, *which resemble flaky, delicate pitas. The Yemenite grandmother, thinking that we had used a Yemenite cook, was shocked to meet the non-Yemenite crew who had carefully crafted each bread.*

While learning how to make melawah *and eating the experiments, I came to understand why these pastries are so popular in Israel today: When not overworked or burnt, they are gloriously flaky and irresistibly moist and delicious.* Melawah, *also spelled* melawach *and* miloach, *also go by the name* tawa, *the Arabic name for the heavy skillet in which they are cooked. Yemenites say to flatten the dough to fit it into your skillet. If the pastry is thicker than 1/4 inch, it will not cook through; if too thin, it loses its flakiness. When served with a little honey,* melawah *also constitutes dessert.*

Yemenite Flaky Pastry Dough (page 190)

1. Starting from the narrow end, roll up the dough rectangles jelly-roll style, into tight cylinders. Place the cylinders, spiral-side up, on a lightly greased or oiled surface and flatten into 1-inch-thick rounds. Wrap in plastic wrap and refrigerate for at least 4 hours and up to 3 days. If very hard, let stand at room temperature until pliable but not soft, about 20 minutes.

2. Place a disk on a lightly greased or oiled surface and, using lightly oiled hands, press into a round 1/8 to 1/4 inch thick and about 7 inches in diameter. At this point, the melawah can be placed between sheets of waxed paper and frozen for up to 3 months, then thawed before using.

3. Heat a large, dry cast-iron or heavy nonstick skillet over medium-high heat. Place a dough round in the skillet and cook for 30 seconds. Reduce the heat to medium-low and cook until the bottom is golden brown, about 3 minutes. Turn and cook until golden, about 5 minutes. If the melawah threatens to burn before the interior cooks, remove from the skillet and place in a 375°F oven for a few minutes until cooked through. Serve warm or at room temperature.

VARIATION

If you do not have a seasoned cast-iron or nonstick skillet, melt 1 teaspoon *samneh* (Middle Eastern Clarified Butter, page 51) or margarine in a large, heavy skillet. You do not have to replenish the fat before cooking each *melawah*.

Yemenite Egg Loaf

(*Sabaya*)

6 TO 8 SERVINGS D OR P

Sabaya, a rich bread loaf, is traditionally slow cooked for Friday night dinner, sliced, and served with a hearty soup or drizzled with honey. In Yemen, the layers were simply stacked one on top of the other free-form and baked in the backyard clay oven, but a loaf pan is more convenient and stable. A family that could not afford the eggs would simply spread a little samneh (clarified butter) between the layers. Some cooks like to sprinkle a little black cumin between each layer, as the seed's warm nutty pungency contrasts with the slightly caramelized flaky pastry.

4 pieces Yemenite Flaky Pastry Dough, folded in
   rectangles (page 190)
3 large eggs, lightly beaten
2 to 3 teaspoons black cumin seeds

1. Starting from the narrow end, roll up the dough rectangles jelly-roll style, into tight cylinders. Place the cylinders, spiral-side up, on a lightly greased or oiled surface and flatten into 1-inch-thick rounds. Wrap each round in plastic wrap and refrigerate for at least 4 hours or up to 3 days. If very hard, let stand at room temperature until pliable but not soft, about 20 minutes.

2. Preheat the oven to 250°F. Grease a 9-by-5-inch loaf pan.

3. On a lightly floured surface, roll out each disk of dough to fit the loaf pan. Press a dough rectangle in the bottom of the pan and spread with about 3 tablespoons of egg. Repeat layering, ending with a dough rectangle. Sprinkle with the cumin seeds.

4. Bake, uncovered, until golden brown, about 3 hours. Let cool slightly or completely before cutting into slices using a serrated knife.

PHYLLO/YUFKA

Phyllo ("leaf" in Greek), called *fila* in Arabic, *yufka* in Turkey, and *penovani* in Georgia, is a mixture of flour, water, and oil that has been stretched paper thin. When these delicate sheets are layered with melted fat and baked, they produce a crisp, flaky pastry used in a wide variety of savory and sweet treats. Although many Westerners associate this dough with the Greeks, they did not invent it; the Turks were responsible for bringing phyllo to the Balkans, but this innovation seems to have originated in Persia, where it was first mentioned in the early fifteenth century. The name of the preeminent phyllo treat baklava, pronounced *baglava* in many areas, probably derived from the word *balg* (Farsi for "leaf"), indicating the dish's Persian origin and possibly the source of the dough as well.

Whenever phyllo dough was invented, its fame had been established by the commencement of the Ottoman Empire, for it was a favorite ingredient in the imperial kitchens of Istanbul, where it was called *yufka*, a word derived from *yuvga*, or "folded bread" in Turkish. Vast guilds of professional pastry makers once provided a steady supply of the dough to the inhabitants of Istanbul and Salonika, a Greek city that for centuries as part of the Ottoman Empire was home to the world's largest Jewish community.

Turkish *yufka* comes both paper thin like modern phyllo and slightly thicker, and usually in rounds rather than rectangular sheets. The Turks and Arabs eventually spread the dough throughout the Middle East and North Africa as well as to the Balkans and central Europe. Due to the efforts of Greek immigrants, beginning in the 1960s, commercial phyllo dough began appearing frozen in American supermarkets, making it accessible to everyone. Frozen *yufka*, both the phyllolike and the thicker varieties, has recently begun appearing in Israel as well as in some specialty stores in the West, but phyllo can usually be substituted.

N O T E   Thaw frozen phyllo in the refrigerator for at least 8 hours; it must be thawed completely before using or it will crumble. Do not thaw at room temperature, or the sheets will stick together. Unopened, phyllo will keep for almost a month in the refrigerator. Remove it from the refrigerator about 2 hours before using. Work with one sheet at a time, keeping the remainder covered with plastic wrap or a damp towel.

SEPHARDIC ONION PHYLLO PIE

(Mina de Zeboiya)

8 TO 10 SERVINGS   D OR P

Small phyllo pastries provide an attractive appetizer, while large ones make a tempting main course or side dish. Moist fillings are suitable for large pastries but require six or more phyllo layers to stay crisp and keep from breaking apart. In this dish, a few standard ingredients are transformed into an elegant presentation. The mina *(Ladino for "mine") takes a little work to create, but the end result—layered creamy onion and sweet almond filling sandwiched between delicate layers of crisp, flaky pastry—is well worth the effort.*

ONION LAYER:

2 pounds whole yellow or white onions, peeled

3 tablespoons unsalted butter or vegetable oil

1/2 cup unbleached all-purpose flour

2 cups milk or almond milk (see Notes)

6 large eggs, lightly beaten

1 teaspoon ground cinnamon

About 1 teaspoon table salt or 2 teaspoons
    kosher salt

ALMOND LAYER:

1 cup (5 ounces) whole raw almonds

1/2 teaspoon ground cinnamon

2 to 4 tablespoons sugar (optional)

10 sheets thawed frozen phyllo or *yufka* dough

3/4 cup (1 1/2 sticks) unsalted butter or margarine,
    melted

1. To make the onion layer: In a large pot of boiling water, add the onions, reduce the heat to medium-low, and simmer until soft, about 30 minutes. Drain, reserving the cooking liquid. Chop the onions coarsely and purée them in a blender or food processor. In a medium saucepan, melt the butter over medium heat. Whisk in the flour and cook, stirring constantly, until bubbly, 2 to 3 minutes. Gradually whisk in the milk and 1 cup of the reserved onion cooking liquid. Cook over medium-low heat, stirring constantly, until thick and bubbly, about 5 minutes. Remove from the heat and gradually stir into the eggs. Add the cinnamon and salt. Let cool. The filling may be prepared up to 3 days ahead and refrigerated.

2. To make the almond layer: In a food processor, finely grind the almonds, cinnamon, and, if using, the sugar.

3. Preheat the oven to 375°F. Butter a 10- or 11-inch round baking dish or a 9-by-13-inch baking dish.

4. To assemble, working with 1 phyllo sheet at a time, line the prepared dish with a sheet of phyllo, draping the excess over the edges. Lightly brush with butter. Repeat layering and brushing with 5 more sheets, draping each phyllo sheet in a different direction if using a round dish. Sprinkle half the almond mixture over the phyllo, spread with the onion mixture, and sprinkle with the remaining almond mixture. Fold in the draped excess. Top with the 5 remaining dough sheets, brushing each with butter and tucking in the edges. Score the top of the pastry in 2- or 3-inch squares or diamond shapes.

5. Bake until golden brown, about 40 minutes. Let stand at least 10 minutes before cutting into squares or diamonds.

NOTES Bake phyllo and *yufka* until crisp and golden brown. Underbaking results in soggy phyllo; overbaking toughens the pastry. Since the pastry is so thin, the top layers generally crack during baking and cooling. Cutting the pastry can, of course, cause further cracking. Scoring the top layers of a large phyllo dish before baking makes it easier to cut into serving pieces. Use a serrated knife to cut.

For easy application, place the melted butter or oil in a spritzer bottle and spray onto the pastry.

To clean a pastry brush, wash well and shake dry, cover the bristles with kosher salt to draw out any moisture, then rub out the salt.

To make almond milk: Pour 3 cups boiling water over 1 cup (5 ounces) ground raw almonds, cover, and let soak for at least 2 hours. In a blender, purée the almonds and soaking liquid until smooth. Strain through several layers of cheesecloth, squeezing out any liquid.

❧ WARKA ❧

When *yufka* reached the Maghreb, cooks developed their own form—frequently using semolina flour—called *warka* or *ouarka* ("leaf") in Morocco, *malsuqa* or *malsouka* in Tunisia, and *diyul* in Algeria. These thin, round sheets, slightly thicker but more flexible than phyllo, require great skill to prepare and, therefore, are rarely made by home cooks. In Morocco, every marketplace has at least one *warka* maker, inevitably a woman, deftly plying her trade. A small piece of soft dough is placed on a special large, round heated copper dish resembling an inverted wok and gradually worked into a very thin round about 10 inches in diameter. When the *warka* is dry, it is removed from the pan, piled on top of other sheets, and wrapped to keep the dough fresh and soft. *Warka* is not available in American groceries, but frozen *yufka* and phyllo dough are good substitutes.

Small *warka* pastries make an attractive appetizer. Among the most popular are rolls variously called *dedos* ("fingers" in Spanish), *asabia* ("fingers" in Arabic), and *sigares, cigares,* and *garros* ("cigars" in Morocco). Algerians call potato-filled *sigares,* now prevalent in Israel, *beztels.* Frying yields the crispest pastry, but many people now prefer baking them.

MOROCCAN PHYLLO CIGARS

(*Sigares*)

ABOUT 48 SMALL ROLLS   D OR P

Before getting into the writing and food businesses, I prepared fancy meals for friends, each time trying to outdo myself and eventually earning a reputation as a gourmet. Michelle Comet, then a respected kosher caterer in New York City, asked if I would like to moonlight for her as a baker and I readily agreed. By observing Michelle and her crew, I learned a tremendous amount about cooking, including the preparation of cigars and many other phyllo shapes. When properly done, the contrast of the crisp pastry and soft filling is simply delectable, and the shape makes these ideal finger foods. Favorite fillings include potato, cheese, and spinach.

1 pound (about 24 sheets) thawed frozen phyllo
   dough, *yufka,* or *warka*
About 1¹/₂ cups (3 sticks) unsalted butter, melted,
   or light olive oil
About 3 cups any Sephardic pastry filling
   (pages 178–181)

1. Preheat the oven to 375°F. Grease a large baking sheet.

2. Lay the stack of phyllo sheets on a flat surface and cut in half lengthwise. Work with 1 strip at a time, covering the remaining phyllo with a damp towel.

3. To assemble, place 1 phyllo strip on a flat surface and lightly brush with butter. Spoon 1 tablespoon of the filling in a thin strip about 1 inch from one narrow end, leaving a 1-inch border on both sides. Fold the bottom 1 inch of phyllo over the filling, then fold in the 1-inch border on the long sides. From the filling end, roll up jelly-roll style. The rolls can be refrigerated for up to 1 day or frozen for up to 3 months. Do not thaw before baking.

4. Place the rolls, seam-side down, on the prepared baking sheet and brush with butter. Bake until crisp and golden brown, about 20 minutes for fresh, 30 minutes for frozen. Serve warm or at room temperature.

N O T E   To reheat phyllo pastries, place a wire rack on a large baking sheet, arrange the pastries in a single layer on top, and place in a preheated 300°F oven until heated through, 8 to 10 minutes.

VARIATIONS

Fried *Sigares*: After rolling up, brush the outer edge with lightly beaten egg white to seal. In batches, fry the rolls in at least 2 inches of peanut oil or vegetable oil heated to 365°F until golden on all sides, about 4 minutes.

Turkish Phyllo Squares (*Borek*): In Step 3, mound the filling about 1 inch from a narrow end in the center of the buttered strip. Fold the uncovered border over the filling, then fold over the border on the long sides. From the filling end, continue folding (not rolling) to the end of the strip.

Sephardic Phyllo Triangles (*Ojaldres/ Hojaldres*): In Step 3, mound the filling about 1 inch from a narrow end in the center of the buttered strip. Fold a corner of the phyllo diagonally over the filling, forming a triangle. Brush the corner flap with butter and continue folding, maintaining the triangular shape, flag style, to the end of the strip.

OJALDRES

Among the dishes in the Sephardic culinary repertoire before the Expulsion in 1492 was *ojaldres* (sometimes spelled *hojaldre*, derived from the Spanish *hoja*, or "leaf"), a rich unleavened dough that was the predecessor to puff pastry. To make *ojaldres*, bread dough was rolled out to about a half-inch thick, spread with fat, rolled into a cylinder, and cut into slices. The slices were then rolled out—several slices combined for forming larger sheets—filled, and fried or baked (the latter basted with melted fat during baking to help separate the layers). This rudimentary puff pastry yielded relatively thin layers, although they were thicker and less crisp than either phyllo or modern puff pastry.

After Sephardim arrived in the Ottoman Empire and eventually adopted *yufka* into their pantry, the term *ojaldres*, or *hojaldres*, took on new meaning to refer to filled phyllo triangles, a dish popular throughout the Middle East and Mediterranean (the best known is the spinach-filled Greek version, *spanakopites*). In modern Spanish, *ojaldres/hojaldre* refers to actual puff pastry.

❧ BRIK ❧

When the Turkish *yufka* and *borek* reached the Maghreb, the residents readily adapted them to local cooking, deep-frying the filled pastry packages, calling them *burak* in Algeria, *bureka* in Libya, *briwat*, *biouat*, or *briate* in Morocco, and *brik* in Tunisia. *Brik* emerged as the Tunisian national snack food, today sold from stands and street vendors throughout the country. In Tunisia, *brik* are made with *malsuqa*, the Tunisian semolina-based form of *yufka*. The dish was brought from Morocco to Israel, but most Israelis substitute *yufka* or, more recently, commercially made Chinese egg roll wrappers or, preferably, since they are thinner, Filipino spring roll wrappers called *lumpia*.

Tunisians fill *brik* with a wide array of fillings, but Jewish versions tend to favor mashed potatoes. In Tunisia, *brik* makers customarily put an uncooked egg in the filling; the egg becomes soft-boiled, still deliciously runny, during frying.

TUNISIAN POTATO-FILLED PASTRY

(Brik)

12 PASTRIES   Ⓟ

The first time I sampled a brik*, I ended up with streaks of egg yolk on my shirt, as no one warned me that it was fluid and would spurt. It was delicious nonetheless. Fry these dough packages just before serving to ensure a crisp pastry. And be careful if you include a traditional egg inside the pastry.*

2 tablespoons olive oil or vegetable oil

I large onion, chopped

2 to 3 cloves garlic, minced

$^1/_3$ cup chopped fresh parsley

I$^1/_2$ cups mashed potatoes

I large egg, lightly beaten

About $^1/_4$ teaspoon table salt or $^1/_2$ teaspoon kosher salt

12 (6- to 8-inch) square or round *brik* sheets, thick *yufka* sheets, *lumpia* (Filipino spring roll wrappers), or Chinese egg roll wrappers

$^1/_4$ cup *harissa* (Northwest African Chili Paste, page 433), optional

12 small eggs or yolks (optional)

I egg white, lightly beaten

Vegetable oil for frying

1. To make the filling: In a large skillet or wok, heat the oil over medium heat. Add the onion and sauté until golden, about 15 minutes. Add the garlic and sauté for 1 minute. Add the parsley and sauté for an additional minute. Let cool. Stir in the potatoes, egg, and salt.

2. Working with 1 brik sheet at a time (cover the remaining sheets with a damp towel), place a brik sheet on a flat surface and spoon a heaping tablespoon of the potato filling in the center. If using, top with 1 teaspoon harissa and/or break an egg into the center. Fold the sides over the filling, slightly overlapping, then fold over the top and bottom. Brush the inside edges with a little egg white and press to seal. The rolls can be prepared to this point up to 2 hours before frying.

3. Heat at least 1 inch of oil in a skillet over medium heat to 350°F.

4. In batches, add the brik and fry, turning once, until golden brown, about 1$^1/_2$ minutes per side. Remove with a slotted spoon, drain on a wire rack for a minute, then serve immediately. Brik are customarily a finger food.

COOKED VEGETABLE DISHES

❦ · ❦

In biblical times, most vegetables of the Mesopotamian region were still gathered wild. Prevalent wild plants of the day included arugula, capers, cardoons, celery, chicory, lettuce, mallow, and mushrooms. The eventual cultivation of more vegetables along with foreign interactions came an increased quantity and diversity of vegetables. Because of its strategic location at the crossroads between Asia, Africa, and Europe, the land of Israel came into routine contact with numerous nations and their foods. After the Persian Empire spread eastward into India, Asian produce became part of the Mesopotamian diet, including such staples as citrus fruits, cucumbers, rice, eggplant, ginger, and sugarcane. The Romans introduced not only new vegetables and dishes, but also their methods of agriculture and system of aqueducts, guaranteeing a more constant, nonseasonal supply of produce. During the Roman period, the residents of the Levant enjoyed a variety of cultivated vegetables, including beet greens, chard, cabbage, cress, fennel, lettuce, mustard, purslane, radishes, and turnips.

After the fall of the Roman Empire in the fifth century C.E., European agriculture and cooking, even among the upper classes, regressed to a rather primitive level. In Islamic lands, on the other hand, the Arabs not only preserved Greek, Roman, and Persian agricultural techniques and culinary practices, but greatly improved on them. During the six centuries following the death of Muhammad in 632, Arab merchants introduced new plants from all over Asia, while their farmers developed higher-yielding and better-tasting varieties and greatly increased the productivity of the land. Arabic hydrological innovations also meant that farmers were no longer solely reliant on yearly rainfall to produce crops, resulting in a vegetable boom around the southern shores of the Mediterranean.

The Arabs brought their favorite plants and innovations to Iberia, transforming the Islamic part of Spain into a garden paradise. By the eleventh century, Islamic Spain was the world's botanical capital. Sephardim capitalized on the bounty available to them to develop a highly sophisticated and distinctive cuisine, full of vegetables and fruits, and redolent with the flavors and fragrances of garlic, onions, cilantro, mint, parsley, cinnamon, coriander, cumin, saffron, lemons, oranges, pine nuts, and almonds. Perhaps no feature is as immediately noticeable in Sephardic cooking as the abundance of four particular vegetables: eggplants, tomatoes, spinach, and leeks, which have pervaded their cooking for a full millenium. A characteristic Sephardic way of preparing these vegetables was to mix them with cheese and with eggs. Since even after the Expulsion of 1492 Sephardim have tended to inhabit countries with warm climates, primarily in the Mediterranean region, fresh produce, often available year-round, has continued to predominate the cuisine.

Due to Muslim encroachments into Europe, Arabic scientific advances and cooking techniques gradually began making their way northward into Provençe, Italy, and the Balkans. By the twelfth century, the cooking in these southern European areas already reflected a more pronounced use of vegetables and an affinity for Arabic, Moorish, and Turkish cuisines, an influence that would continue to grow over the ensuing centuries. During the late Middle Ages (c. 1100–1400), the Arabic gastronomic sway grew even stronger, helping to spur a new European appreciation of the pleasures of eating. However, the Mediterranean diet, emphasizing olive oil, vegetables, grains, legumes, and fruit and utilizing only a small amount of meat, found resistance farther north, where such practices were viewed as unhealthy and abnormal. In addition, the cooler climates and harsher conditions of northern

Europe meant that less fresh produce was generally obtainable, even after farmers began adopting some of the new agricultural techniques. Thus, Ashkenazim relied primarily on grains and starches for their sustenance, and essentially used onions and salt for the majority of their flavoring.

The sixteenth century witnessed some of the most monumental changes in vegetable cooking in Jewish-inhabited regions, as indigenous South American produce reached the Old World by way of Spain and Portugal, most notably haricot or common beans, chilies, chocolate, corn, white potatoes, sweet potatoes, pumpkins, squash, and tomatoes. Converso (forcibly converted Spanish Jews) merchants soon spread these vegetables through their mercantile contacts with exiled Sephardim in North Africa, Italy, France, and the Ottoman Empire. In turn, Sephardic traders attempted to interest their Ashkenazic contacts in these foods, meeting with only mixed success in most instances. Sephardim, however, readily adapted these new ingredients to their cooking, generally with more enthusiasm than their non-Jewish neighbors.

Raw tomatoes and peppers joined the classic cucumber to become the basis for most Mediterranean salads, while the onion, an ancient Jewish favorite, was now sautéed and cooked with tomatoes to provide what has become the distinctive Sephardic base for numerous vegetable dishes. On the other hand, the vegetables of the Ashkenazim, almost always eaten pickled or cooked to the point of mushiness, consisted primarily of cabbage, cucumbers, and a few root vegetables, most notably beets, carrots, parsnips, radishes, turnips, and, beginning in the mid-1800s, the potato.

One notable feature of vegetarian fare is that almost any dish can serve as a main course or a side dish depending on the portion size and the nature of the presentation. Braised vegetables, for example, could be served alone, as an accompaniment to another dish, or over couscous or tossed with pasta as a main course. Because various cultures never adopted the Roman preoccupation with set courses, a meal in many Jewish communities consisted of various dishes served together with no one predominant dish around which others revolved. Nevertheless, some dishes by their nature are more substantial than others, making them more practical to serve as a main course, while other dishes lend themselves to being side dishes. In addition, many of these vegetable dishes are as delicious at room temperature as they are hot, making them perfect for the Sabbath or any occasion where hot food is not an option.

COOKING VEGETABLES

A vegetable can be simply steamed and drizzled with a little olive oil or be part of an elaborate concoction with a host of other vegetables and flavorings. The simpler the dish, the greater the need to prepare it correctly.

In general, heat and acid destroy the chlorophyll and break down green vegetables—too much of either will cause discoloration and a mushy texture. The best way to maintain a vegetable's color and texture is to cook it uncovered—allowing the acid to dissipate into the air—in as little water as possible or to steam it. For green vegetables to be served cold or reheated, blanch them in boiling water, then immediately place in cold or ice water to halt the cooking process and preserve the bright color.

The cells of fresh vegetables are packed with water, which gives them their crisp texture. While vegetables are still in the ground, this moisture is replaced by the roots soaking up water. In order stay crisp and not to wilt, harvested vegetables also need a water source to replenish the moisture that continually seeps out of the plant cells. Therefore, soak limp vegetables in a bowl of cold water for at least 10 minutes to revive them.

Soaking vegetables in ice water stiffens them, as the water, attracted by the salt inside the vegetable, enters the cells. The reverse happens when vegetables come into contact with exterior salt (through salting or in a dressing); in this case, the water is drawn out of the plant cells, resulting in a limp vegetable. Although this is detrimental in the case of crisp greens like lettuce, it can be desirable in vegetables with a high water content, such as cabbage, cucumbers, eggplants, and zucchini. Extracting excess water before cooking keeps them firm and, if they are to be fried, prevents them from absorbing too much oil.

❧ ARTICHOKES ❧

Much of the unforested terrain of the Levant was once covered with fields of wild thistles, which farmers would set ablaze to make space for more desirable plants. Somehow, an adventurous eater long ago managed to figure out that two kinds of these unwelcoming plants were actually edible, and even very tasty: the cardoon (see page 222) and the artichoke, its close relative or, according to some, its descendent.

Although artichoke cultiavation dates back to Roman times, it was the Moors who first fell in love with the vegetable, beginning to cultivate it in Spain around 800, eventually developing new and improved varieties. It subsequently became an often used ingredient in Sephardic cooking, prepared in countless recipes. Meanwhile, in medieval Europe, the artichoke was absent from the table, possibly entering Italy in the twelfth century by way of Sicilian Jews. The Italians spoke disparagingly of it as "the Jewish vegetable." Nevertheless, its popularity spread outside the Jewish ghettos, reaching even the Medicis of Florence. It was Catherine de Medici who popularized the artichoke in France, bringing artichoke recipes with her—along with with the rest of fine Florentine cooking and her retinue of private chefs—after her marriage to Henry II of France in 1533. By the late sixteenth century, this once-reviled thistle constituted an important part of Mediterranean cuisine. Because of the Arabs' role in the popularization of artichokes, the English, French, and Italians all derive their words for artichoke (*artichaut* and *cariofo*, respectively) from the Arabic *al-kharshuf* rather than the Latin *cynara*.

The part of the artichoke we eat is the unopened bud of the plant's flower. Although there are more than fifty varieties of artichoke, by far the most popular in the United States is the Green Globe, an Italian cultivar with large globular flower buds bearing thick, fleshy scales; it resembles a gray-green pine cone 3 to 5 inches in diameter. The central branch produces the largest artichokes, the middle branches medium ones, while baby artichokes grow on the lower branches, which receive the least sunlight.

What You Should Know: Choose artichokes with tightly closed inner leaves, which indicates they are still young (spring artichokes have tightly closed leaves; by the summer they will have opened a bit). A bronze color on the outside is the result of frost and does not affect the taste. Store in a plastic bag in the refrigerator for no more than 5 days.

Only the heart (the meaty base), the interior portion of the stem, the soft yellowish immature inner leaves, and the fleshy base of the outer leaves (called a bract) can be eaten in a large Green Globe artichoke. In the center of the heart lies an inedible fuzzy core called the choke that must be removed before serving. Small "baby" globes, however, rarely have developed chokes, and are tender enough to be eaten with only the outer leaves and tips trimmed.

Artichoke hearts (also called bottoms), trimmed of all leaves and stems, resemble 2- to 3-inch cups, making them ideal for stuffing or as a base on which to serve other foods. To cook artichoke hearts, boil them gently in lightly salted water until tender, 15 to 20 minutes. Most commercial frozen or marinated artichoke hearts, usually packaged halved or quartered, also include the edible inner leaves and sometimes a little stem, making them perfect for use in salads and stews. Middle Eastern specialty stores sell frozen whole artichoke bottoms with all the leaves removed.

Artichokes contain a unique organic acid called cynarin, which for most people enhances the flavor of other foods that are eaten with or after eating artichokes. To test your response to cynarin, eat a piece of artichoke, then take a sip of water. If the water tastes somewhat sugary, you are cynarin sensitive. Cynarin also causes certain wines (very dry, acidic wines, such as Sauvignon Blanc, Pinot Blanc, and brut Champagne, hold up best) to taste metallic, making artichokes a very difficult food to pair with wine.

Around the Mediterranean, artichokes have long been plentiful and inexpensive, which helps explain their popularity among Italian and Sephardic Jewish cooks, who often lived in poverty. Today, Israel has emerged as one of the world's leading growers of artichokes, and this vegetable has become an important component of the country's emerging cuisine. Because the first artichokes appear in early spring, they are a Passover favorite. Sephardim usually cook young artichokes whole, trimming older, tougher ones for their edible hearts.

JERUSALEM ARTICHOKE

The Jerusalem artichoke, despite its name, is not an artichoke at all and has nothing to do with the Holy Land nor does it taste like an artichoke. This tuber, with its lumpy knobs, a brownish skin, and white flesh, is a member of the sunflower family (it is also known as a sunchoke) and is one of the few native North American vegetables. It has a slightly sweet-nutty flavor and crunchy texture when raw, and is firm with a sweetly earthy flavor when cooked.

ITALIAN FRIED ARTICHOKES

(Carciofi Fritti)

6 TO 8 SERVINGS P

The generally impoverished Jews of medieval Italy utilized the most inexpensive produce, especially vegetables considered "Jewish"—eggplant, fennel, and artichokes—to create incredibly flavorful fare. Because of governmental restrictions limiting ovens, Roman Jews became specialists at frying. Arguably the most famous of these dishes is carciofi *alla Giudia (*Giudia *was the name of the Roman ghetto), deepfried flattened whole baby artichokes without a batter, best made with a variety of artichoke generally unavailable outside of the Mediterranean.*

Carciofi fritti is another traditional Jewish friedartichoke dish, this one coated with a batter. Baby globe artichokes, about the size of an egg, are not immature, but rather grow in the shade near the bottom of the plant. The inner leaves are completely edible. Using matza meal turns this into a traditional Italian Passover side dish, when it might be served during the first Seder along with minestra di riso *(soup with rice) and* spinaci salatai *(Italian Spinach with Garlic, page 283).*

> 1 lemon, halved, plus 2 lemons cut into wedges for garnish
> 12 baby artichokes (no larger than 2 inches in diameter) or 20 ounces thawed frozen artichoke hearts
> About 1 teaspoon table salt or 2 teaspoons kosher salt
> 2 to 3 cloves garlic, minced (optional)
> Olive oil for frying
> About 1 cup flour or matza meal for dredging
> 3 large eggs, lightly beaten
> Salt for sprinkling
> 1/4 cup tiny capers for garnish (optional)

1. Squeeze the lemon halves into a large bowl of cold water and add the lemon shells. Working with one artichoke at a time, cut off the tip and peel the stems, occasionally dipping the artichokes into the lemon water while you work to prevent discoloration. Remove the tough dark green outer leaves and trim off any tough or pointy tips. Do not remove the pale inner leaves. Cut in half or quarters lengthwise, as desired. Most small artichokes have not developed any fuzzy choke, but if you spot any, scoop it out. Store the artichokes in the lemon water. (If using frozen artichokes, begin at Step 2.)

2. In a large nonreactive saucepan, combine the water, lemon juice, salt, and, if using, garlic. Add the artichokes. Bring to a boil, cover, reduce the heat to medium, and cook until knife-tender, about 20 minutes for halves, 15 minutes for quarters. Drain. (At this point, the artichokes can be served plain, with a vinaigrette, or tossed with fettuccine and a light sauce.)

3. In a large, heavy skillet, heat at least $^1/_2$ inch oil to about 365°F.

4. Dredge the artichokes in the flour, shaking off any excess, then dip in the egg to coat. Fry in batches, turning until golden brown on all sides, 2 to 3 minutes total. Drain on paper towels. The artichokes can be briefly kept warm in a low oven while preparing the remaining artichokes. Sprinkle lightly with the salt. Serve warm, with the lemon wedges and, if using, the capers.

VARIATION

Double-Fried Artichokes: Omit Step 2. Instead, remove the raw artichoke pieces from the lemon water, dry (a salad spinner helps), then fry in the oil until lightly colored, about 15 minutes. Remove from the oil and let cool. Just before serving, dredge the artichokes in flour, omitting the eggs, and fry again until golden brown.

SEPHARDIC BRAISED ARTICHOKES AND FAVA BEANS

(Anjinaras con Ful)

6 TO 8 SERVINGS

Artichokes and fava beans, ubiquitous on many Sephardic Passover tables, are often cooked together. In many areas, hawkers went door to door selling crates of artichokes and beans, while smaller amounts could be found at open-air markets.

Although many Sephardim cook the dish until very tender, I prefer a firmer texture. The original dish was cooked in olive oil and sometimes white wine; tomatoes were a relatively late but popular addition, their acidity showing off the artichoke's mild flavor. The use of dill in this dish is a Balkan variation. When you find young fava beans (3 to 5 inches long), you can cut up and cook their velvety pods, too. On Friday nights in the spring and summer, many Sephardim from the Mediterranean serve this dish over rice, recreating a taste of twelfth-century Moorish Spain.

I lemon, halved

8 large globe artichokes

3 tablespoons olive oil or vegetable oil

I large onion, chopped

2 pounds fresh fava beans, shelled and peeled (see page 321), about 2 cups; or 10 ounces frozen fava beans

I cup tomato purée or seeded and crushed plum tomatoes (see page 291)

I cup water

About I teaspoon sugar or honey

About I teaspoon table salt or 2 teaspoons kosher salt

$^1/_2$ to I cup chopped fresh dill to taste (optional)

1. Squeeze the lemon halves into a large bowl of cold water and add the lemon shells. Working with one artichoke at a time, cut off the top half, occasionally dipping the artichokes into the lemon water while you work to prevent discoloration. Pull off all the remaining leaves. Cut off the stem or leave 2 to 3 inches attached. Peel off the dark-colored fibers from the stem and base of the artichoke. Cut the artichoke lengthwise into quarters and remove the fuzzy choke (a grapefruit spoon or melon baller works well). Store the artichokes in the lemon water.

2. In a large nonreactive saucepan, heat the oil over medium heat. Add the onion and sauté until soft and translucent, about 5 minutes. Add the artichokes and sauté for another 5 minutes. Stir in the beans and continue cooking for 2 minutes. (The beans will retain a bright green hue, while the artichokes will develop an olive-green color.)

3. Add the tomato purée, water, sugar, salt, and, if using, the dill. Bring to a boil, reduce the heat to low, and simmer, uncovered, until the artichokes and beans are tender and most of the liquid has evaporated, about 45 minutes for fresh beans, 30 minutes for frozen. Serve warm or at room temperature.

VARIATIONS

Sephardic Artichoke Hearts with Fava Beans and Lemon (*Anjinaras con Limón*): Omit the tomatoes, increase the water to 1$^{1}/_{2}$ cups, and add about $^{1}/_{4}$ cup fresh lemon juice and 2 to 3 mashed cloves garlic. If desired, substitute 3 chopped sprigs of mint for the dill.

Greek Artichokes with Fava Beans in Egg-Lemon Sauce (*Anginares me Koukia*): Omit the tomatoes, increase the water to 2 cups, and add about $^{1}/_{4}$ cup fresh lemon juice and 2 to 3 mashed cloves garlic. After cooking, strain the cooking liquid into a saucepan and add $^{1}/_{2}$ cup milk. Gradually beat the milk mixture into 1 lightly beaten egg, then stir over low heat until thickened, pour over the vegetables, and serve warm.

Greek Artichokes with Peas (*Anginares me Arakes*): Substitute 2 cups fresh or frozen green peas for the fava beans, adding them after cooking the fresh artichokes for about 30 minutes.

SYRIAN ARTICHOKE AND CHEESE CASSEROLE

(*Carchof Jiben*)

6 TO 8 SERVINGS

This dish, related to the fritada, *reflects the common Sephardic practice of cooking vegetables with cheese and eggs. Artichokes and cheese, which have a delightful affinity, here are bound together in a casserole with a firm, custardlike texture. The casserole is commonly accompanied with pita bread. I like to add a few drops of hot sauce or stir in some chopped spinach.*

  1 lemon, halved
  8 large globe artichokes or 20 ounces thawed
    frozen artichoke hearts
  3 tablespoons olive oil or unsalted butter
  1 large onion, chopped
  6 cloves garlic, minced (optional)
  3 cups (12 ounces) shredded Muenster or other
    mild firm white cheese
  6 large eggs
  About 1 teaspoon table salt or 2 teaspoons
    kosher salt
  Ground black pepper to taste
  3 tablespoons chopped fresh parsley for garnish

1. Squeeze the lemon halves into a large bowl of cold water and add the lemon shells. Working

with one artichoke at a time, cut off the top half, occasionally dipping the artichokes into the lemon water while you work to prevent discoloration. Pull off all the remaining leaves. Cut off the stem or leave 2 to 3 inches attached. Peel off the dark-colored fibers from the stem and base of the artichoke. Cut the artichoke lengthwise into quarters and remove the fuzzy choke (a grapefruit spoon or melon baller works well). Store the artichokes in the lemon water.

2. Preheat the oven to 350°F. Grease a shallow 8-cup casserole.

3. In a large, heavy saucepan, heat the oil over medium heat. Add the onion and, if using, the garlic and sauté until soft and translucent, about 5 minutes. Add the artichokes and, again, sauté for about 5 minutes.

4. In a large bowl, stir together the cheese, eggs, salt, and pepper. Stir in the artichokes and onions.

5. Spoon into the prepared casserole. Bake until golden brown, about 40 minutes. Place on a wire rack and let cool for 5 minutes to set. Serve warm, sprinkled with the parsley.

VARIATION

Fava Bean and Cheese Casserole (*Ful Jiben*): Substitute 4 cups skinned and cooked fresh or frozen fava beans for the artichokes (to skin and cook fava beans, see page 321).

SEPHARDIC STUFFED ARTICHOKES

(*Anjinaras Reyenados*)

4 SERVINGS

Stuffed artichokes are commonplace throughout the Mediterranean region. Since the artichokes are cooked whole, the preparation method is slightly different from that of baby artichokes or sectioned large ones. This dish can serve as either a hearty appetizer or the main course for a light meal. The stuffing can also be used for artichoke bottoms.

1 lemon, halved
4 large globe artichokes

STUFFING:
1 1/2 cups fresh bread crumbs
1/4 cup chopped fresh parsley
1/4 cup chopped fresh dill, 1/2 cup (1 1/2 ounces) grated Parmesan or kefalotyri cheese, or 1/2 cup chopped mushrooms
2 to 3 cloves garlic, minced
About 1/2 teaspoon table salt or 1 teaspoon kosher salt
Ground black pepper to taste
2 tablespoons olive oil
1 tablespoon fresh lemon juice

2 cups water or 1 cup water and 1 cup crushed tomatoes
3 tablespoons olive oil for drizzling

1. Squeeze the lemon halves into a large bowl of cold water and add the lemon shells. Cut off the stems at the base so the artichokes stand upright. If you like, you can peel off the tough stringy skin from the stems and cook the stems with the artichokes. Remove the loose, tough outer leaves. Cut about 1 inch off the top of each artichoke, then with scissors snip off the thorny tips of the leaves individually. Scoop out the fuzzy chokes (a grapefruit spoon or melon baller works well). After trimming, store the artichokes in the lemon water. Drain well before stuffing.

2. To make the stuffing: In a medium bowl, combine all the stuffing ingredients and stir to blend. If the artichokes are very tightly closed, bang the top of each one on a flat surface. Beginning at the top of each artichoke, spread the leaves open with your fingers as much as you can, then gently pack the stuffing between the leaves, then into the center of the artichokes. (If you stuff the artichokes inside the stuffing bowl, the excess conveniently falls inside.)

3. Pour the 2 cups water into a nonreactive saucepan (do not use aluminum or iron) large enough to hold the artichokes in a single layer. Place the artichokes upright in the saucepan, add the stems, if using, and drizzle with the oil. Cover, bring to a boil, reduce the heat to low, and simmer, adding more water as needed, until the artichokes are tender and the outer leaves pull off easily, about 50 minutes. Or, place the artichokes and water in an oven-proof saucepan or deep casserole and bake in a preheated 350°F oven for 30 to 35 minutes. Remove from pan and serve warm or at room temperature.

ITALIAN PASTA-STUFFED ARTICHOKES

(Carciofi Ripieni)

6 SERVINGS

This dish combines several Italian favorites: artichokes, pasta, and Parmesan cheese. The addition of mint reveals its Roman origins. Roman cooking is quite simple, relying on olive oil, garlic, pepper, parsley, and mint, which grows like a weed in limited space and poor soil. Fettuccine is the basic Roman pasta, most often used fresh. The combination of artichoke, mint, and garlic makes for an impressive and sensuous antipasto. As a Roman chef counseled me, "Never overwhelm artichokes with strong flavors. You want to taste the artichoke." Parboiling the artichokes makes them easier to stuff.

I lemon, halved
6 globe artichokes, about 10 ounces each

STUFFING:
I pound fresh egg noodles cut into ¹/₄-inch-wide strips (Egg Noodle Dough, page 392) or dried fettuccine, broken into 2-inch pieces
3 to 4 tablespoons olive oil
2 to 3 cloves garlic, minced
3 to 4 tablespoons chopped fresh mint
¹/₂ cup (I¹/₂ ounces) grated Parmesan or Romano cheese

Olive oil for drizzling

1. Squeeze the lemon halves into a large bowl of cold water and add the lemon shells. Cut off the stems at the base so that the artichokes stand upright. If desired, you can peel off the tough

stringy skin from the stems and cook the stems with the artichokes. Remove the loose, tough outer leaves. Cut about 1 inch off the top of each artichoke and, using scissors, snip off the thorny tips of the leaves individually. Scoop out the fuzzy chokes in the center (a grapefruit spoon or melon baller works well). After trimming, store the artichokes in the lemon water.

2. Put the artichokes in a nonreactive pot (do not use aluminum or iron) large enough to hold the artichokes in a single layer. Add 1 inch of water. Cover, bring to a boil, reduce the heat to low, and cook the artichokes until tender and a leaf pulls out easily, about 30 minutes. Remove the artichokes from the water and let cool.

3. Preheat the oven to 350°F. Grease a casserole large enough to hold the artichokes in a single layer with olive oil.

4. In a large pot of salted boiling water, cook the fettuccine until just al dente (firm to the bite), about 3 minutes for fresh noodles, 8 minutes for dried. Drain.

5. In a large skillet, heat the oil over medium-low heat. Add the garlic and sauté until fragrant, about 1 minute. Remove from the heat, stir in the pasta, then stir in the mint and Parmesan. Stuff into the center and between the leaves of the artichokes.

6. Arrange the artichokes in the prepared casserole and drizzle with olive oil. Cover with aluminum foil and bake until heated through, 15 to 20 minutes. Serve warm.

ASPARAGUS

The appearance of the first stalks of asparagus is one of the earliest signs of spring. This member of the lily family, native to Greece or Turkey, has long grown wild throughout much of southern and middle Europe. The Romans, who cultivated this vegetable as well as picked the more intensely flavored perennial wild stalks, considered asparagus an aphrodisiac—a sentiment shared by many cultures over the centuries. After the collapse of the Roman Empire, cultivated asparagus (like so many other foods) disappeared from Europe and, until the eighteenth century, was primarily found wild, much of each year's growth being consumed by wild boars. Fortunate diners enjoyed whatever was protected or salvaged.

The situation was different in the Islamic regions of the Mediterranean, where asparagus continued to be cultivated and was customarily prepared by boiling in water, then briefly sautéing. Asparagus has long been served in Italy, Hungary, and the Balkans, enjoyed in soups and salads, as a side dish, or topped with a delicate sauce. These stalks are also used in the Sephardic kitchen, added to a salad or a *fritada* (omelet).

What You Should Know: The asparagus season runs from late February to early July. Although stalks range from toothpick thin (for wild young asparagus) to over an inch thick, size does not affect quality. White asparagus, favored in parts of western Europe, is from the same plant as the green, but are grown shielded from the sun under soil, which prevents activation of the chlorophyll, the source of pigment. Choose asparagus with firm, straight stalks and compact, closed tips. Asparagus toughens after harvesting, so plan on cooking it within a day or two of purchase. To store, arrange the stalks vertically in a jar with about an inch of water on the bottom and refrigerate.

ITALIAN ASPARAGUS IN EGG-LEMON SAUCE

(*Asparagi di Salsa*)

5 TO 6 SERVINGS

This classic dish of asparagus, made with a sauce that predates the modern hollandaise, is from the Jewish community in Tuscany. It is typical of Italian-Jewish fare, utilizing a few basic and inexpensive ingredients to create a delicacy. The sauce is also wonderful with other vegetables and eggs.

$^{1}/_{2}$ cup olive oil

I to 2 cloves garlic

2 pounds asparagus, trimmed and cut into
   I$^{1}/_{2}$-inch pieces

About I teaspoon table salt or 2 teaspoons
   kosher salt

Ground black pepper to taste

$^{1}/_{2}$ cup water

2 teaspoons unbleached all-purpose flour

2 large eggs, lightly beaten

5 tablespoons fresh lemon juice

1. In a large skillet, heat the oil over medium heat. Add the garlic and sauté until fragrant, about 1 minute. Add the asparagus, salt, and pepper and sauté for 2 minutes. Discard the garlic.

2. Add the water and bring to a boil. Cover, reduce the heat to medium-low, and cook until the asparagus is tender but not mushy, 4 to 5 minutes for thin spears and 8 to 10 minutes for very thick ones. Transfer the asparagus to a serving platter, leaving the cooking liquid in the skillet.

3. In a medium bowl, gradually whisk the flour into the eggs, then beat in the lemon juice. In a slow, steady stream, gradually whisk in the reserved hot cooking liquid. Pour the egg mixture back into the skillet and cook over low heat, stirring constantly, until thickened to the consistency of hollandaise sauce, about 3 minutes. Pour the sauce over the asparagus and serve warm or at room temperature. If serving cooled, press a piece of plastic wrap against the surface to prevent a film from forming.

VARIATION

Italian Leeks in Egg-Lemon Sauce (*Porri di Salsa*): Substitute for the asparagus 2$^{1}/_{2}$ pounds leeks, white and light green parts only, washed and cut into 3-inch lengths; cook for 25 to 35 minutes.

BEETS AND BEET GREENS

The modern world knows the beet, a member of the Chenopodiaceae family and a native of the eastern Mediterranean, primarily for the characteristic red color of its root. Developing the size, flavor, and lovely color of today's red beet, however, took centuries of cultivation: The original beet was a thin, white-rooted plant picked not for its root but rather for its large leaves, which resemble those of chard and spinach (both close relatives of the beet). In fact, beet greens were so highly regarded in ancient Israel, Greece, and Rome that farmers devised methods of growing this plant throughout much of the year. Among the responses to the question, "Wherewith does one show delight in the Sabbath?" the Talmud responds, "With beet [greens], a large fish, and garlic," which were all considered aphrodisiacs.

The contemporary garden beetroot was developed in Italy in the sixteenth century, but it failed to make a culinary impact on most of the world for another two centuries. Eventually, people in many parts of the world recognized its delightful flavor: The beet possesses more sucrose than any other vegetable. In northern Europe, where the beet was one of the few vegetables available throughout the winter, the beetroot became a staple, used in soups, salads, and pickles. Eastern European Passover standards include borscht (beet soup), *russel tzikel* (fermented beets), and *eingemachts* (beet preserves). While beet greens remained a seasonal food, the roots could be stored in root cellars or dirt piles for an extended period. The beetroot eventually became popular in the Middle East as well, most notably in salads, relishes, and soups. A beet is typically added to the Middle Eastern pickles called *turshi* to produce a pink hue.

What You Should Know: The best season for beets is May through October. Choose firm, deep-colored beets up to 2 inches in diameter; larger ones tend to be woody and flavorless. If possible, buy beets with the stems and leaves still attached: You can examine the freshness of the stems to tell the quality of the roots. However, since the leaves continue to extract moisture from the roots, remove them as soon as possible. Beet greens are rarely sold by themselves even though they are delicious cooked. Store the greens in a plastic bag in the refrigerator for up to 3 days and cook separately. While the beetroots have a long shelf life, their tenderness and sweetness deteriorate during storage. Store the roots in a plastic bag in the crisper for up to 3 weeks. Cook the beets unpeeled, with the roots and about 1 inch of the stems attached to prevent color and nutrients from bleeding away. Adding a few tablespoons of lemon juice or vinegar to the cooking water results in a brighter color.

NOTE To remove beet stains from hands or wooden cutting boards, rub them with salt and rinse. Repeat if necessary.

Italian Beet Greens and White Beans

(Bietola con Fagioli)

6 TO 8 SERVINGS

This is another flavorful dish popular in Tuscany. Ancient Romans had commonly paired beet greens with lentils or dried fava beans in dishes similar to this one, but the arrival of white beans from South America in the sixteenth century halved the dish's cooking time and yielded a more delicate, balanced flavor.

Beet greens, with their slightly bitter, earthy flavor, become quite tender after cooking for only about 10 minutes, but in this recipe they are simmered for a long time under and over the beans to meld the flavors. White beans are generally seasoned sparingly not to overpower their delicate flavor. You can substitute chard for the beet greens.

    3 tablespoons olive oil
    2 red or yellow onions, chopped
    2 pounds beet greens
    Ground black pepper to taste
    1¼ cups dried cannellini, Great Northern, or
        other small white beans, picked over, soaked
        for 8 hours in water to cover, and drained
    1 pound plum tomatoes, peeled, seeded, and
        chopped (see page 291), about 2½ cups
    About 3 cups Vegetable Stock (page 115) or water
    Salt to taste

1. In a large pot, heat the oil over medium heat. Add the onions and sauté until soft and translucent, 5 to 10 minutes. Remove from the heat and stir in the greens and pepper to coat.

2. Remove and reserve half of the greens. Spoon the beans over the remaining greens in the pot, then top with the reserved greens. Spread the tomatoes over the top and add enough stock to cover by about 1 inch.

3. Bring to a boil, cover, reduce the heat to low, and simmer, without stirring, until the beans are tender, about 1½ hours. After cooking for about 1 hour, add the salt. Serve warm.

Sephardic Beet Greens

(Silka)

3 TO 4 SERVINGS

Among many Sephardim, beet greens are used much like spinach and are even more popular than beetroots. Sephardim either prepare this salad as is, or mix in a little egg and flour and make keftes, *or fried patties. Syrians might serve silka for Rosh Hashanah dinner, or make* edgeh *(Syrian Omelets; page 419) with it, serving it alongside leek* keftes, lubiya *(black-eyed peas),* yerba *(stuffed cabbage, celery, or carrots), and lemon pilaf for a deliciously varied holiday meal.*

    Greens (leaves and stems) from about 16 medium
        beets
    3 tablespoons olive oil or vegetable oil
    2 to 4 cloves garlic, minced
    2 to 3 tablespoons fresh lemon juice
    About ½ teaspoon table salt or 1 teaspoon
        kosher salt

1. Wash the greens well and cut into bite-sized pieces. Put the greens in a large saucepan and

add water to cover. Bring to a boil, reduce the heat to low, and simmer until tender, about 5 minutes. (This extracts some of the bitterness.) Drain and squeeze out the excess liquid. You should have about 2 cups of greens.

2. In a large skillet, heat the oil over medium heat. Add the garlic and sauté for 1 minute. Add the greens and sauté until tender and dry, about 5 minutes. Remove from the heat and stir in the lemon juice and salt. Serve warm or at room temperature.

VARIATIONS

Italian Beet Greens (*Biete da Orta*): Add 1 tablespoon pine nuts and 1 tablespoon yellow raisins in Step 2 after adding the garlic and before adding the greens.

Moroccan Beet Greens (*Silka*): Add $^1/_2$ teaspoon sweet paprika with the lemon juice.

Russian Beet Greens (*Svyokli*): Omit the lemon juice. Combine $^1/_2$ cup sour cream or plain yogurt, 1 tablespoon grated horseradish, and 1 teaspoon prepared mustard and stir into the cooked greens.

Syrian Beet Greens (*Silka*): Add $^1/_2$ teaspoon dried oregano and $^1/_2$ teaspoon dried thyme in Step 2 with the greens.

Sephardic Beet Green Patties (*Keftes de Silka*): Let the beet green mixture cool, then mix in $^1/_2$ cup unbleached all-purpose flour or matza meal and 1 large egg. Shape into patties 3 inches long and 1 inch wide, with tapered ends. In a large skillet, heat a thin layer of olive oil and fry the patties, turning, until golden brown, about 3 minutes per side.

GEORGIAN BEETS IN CHERRY SAUCE

(*Charkhalis Chogi*)

6 TO 8 SERVINGS   Ⓓ OR Ⓟ

Georgians love to purée fruits to make a variety of sauces—not only dessert sauces, but also tart sauces to pair with vegetables. When I first tried this recipe, I used fresh Bing cherries (which are sweet) but found the dish lacking flavor. One Georgian cook I questioned explained that only sour cherries would do, and that in Georgia they always used Cornelian cherries. Although Cornelian cherries are nearly impossible to find in America, sour cherries, including Morello, Montmorency, and Early Richmond, can sometimes be found at farmers' markets in June and July. The tartness of the cherries provides an interesting contrast to the beets. Another cook suggested I use tart dried cherries instead, which allowed her to make this dish any time of the year.

Roasting the beets tends to give them the sweetest and best flavor. Cooking them uncovered gives them a more intensely "roasted" flavor, while wrapping them in foil partially steams them, making them moister.

8 beets (2 pounds total without the greens), stems trimmed to 1 inch

Olive oil or vegetable oil for coating (if roasting uncovered)

CHERRY SAUCE:
$^2/_3$ cup dried tart cherries (see Note)

$1^1/_4$ cups water

2 tablespoons unsalted butter or vegetable oil

2 onions, chopped

$^1/_4$ cup chopped fresh cilantro or dill

$^1/_4$ cup chopped fresh parsley

About $^1/_4$ teaspoon table salt or $^1/_2$ teaspoon kosher salt

1. Preheat the oven to 375°F.

2. Coat the beets with the oil or wrap each in aluminum foil. Place in a single layer in a baking pan. Roast until knife-tender, about 1 hour. Let cool slightly, then trim, peel, and thinly slice.

3. To make the sauce: While the beets are roasting, combine the cherries and water in a small saucepan and bring to a boil. Reduce the heat to low and simmer, uncovered, until very tender, about 20 minutes. Purée in a blender or food processor.

4. Meanwhile, melt the butter in a large skillet over medium heat. Add the onions and sauté until soft and translucent, 5 to 10 minutes. Stir into the cherry purée. Add the cilantro, parsley, and salt.

5. Pour the sauce over the beets. Serve warm or at room temperature.

NOTE There are more than six hundred varieties of sweet cherries and three hundred varieties of sour cherries, varying in color from yellow to bright red to dark purple. Sweet cherries are primarily eaten fresh; sour cherries, such as the small, pale red Morello, are most often used in cooking, baking, and making liqueurs. Dried cherries, made from tart cherries, are frequently infused with sugar before drying and sprayed with oil afterward; unsweetened ones are preferable but not mandatory for this recipe.

PERSIAN BEETS WITH YOGURT

(Most Laboo)

6 TO 8 SERVINGS

Variations of this simple dish, called shawandar bil leban *in Arabic, abound throughout the Middle East. The yogurt's tartness contrasts wonderfully with the sweetness of the beets. Some of the yogurt will take on a pink color. If the yogurt is very watery, drain it in a coffee filter or cheesecloth-lined sieve until thickened.*

8 beets (2 pounds total without the greens),
    stems trimmed to 1 inch
1 to 2 cloves garlic
$^1/_2$ teaspoon table salt or 1 teaspoon kosher salt
$^1/_4$ cup chopped fresh mint or 1 red or white
    onion, thinly sliced (optional)
2 cups plain yogurt

1. Put the beets in a large saucepan and add water to cover. Bring to a boil, cover, reduce the heat to low, and simmer until the beets are fork-tender, about 35 minutes. Let cool to the touch, then trim and peel the beets and cut into $^1/_4$-inch-thick slices or julienne. You should have about 4 cups.

2. Using the tip of a heavy knife or with a mortar and pestle, mash the garlic and salt into a paste. Stir the garlic paste and, if using, the mint into the yogurt. Add the beets. Cover and refrigerate for at least 1 hour. Alternatively, arrange the beets on a serving platter, spread the yogurt-garlic mixture on top, and sprinkle with the mint.

VARIATION

Persian Beet and Yogurt Dip (*Borani Laboo*): Finely chop or mash the cooked beets before stirring them into the yogurt. Serve with pita bread.

❧ CABBAGE ☙

One of the oldest cultivated foods, cabbage has been the most widely eaten vegetable in history, a food of the poor and, in some areas, often the only vegetable available. The original cabbage was a loose head of leaves, similar to its close relative, kale. It was also very bitter, as the plant contained a significant amount of mustard oil. The leaves and even more often the stalk were consumed, but sometimes required pickling or several boilings to be palatable. From this wild ancestor, agronomists developed nearly five hundred varieties of cabbage, including flowering varieties like broccoli and cauliflower. The now-familiar green cabbage, consisting of a firm, light green head with mild-flavored, smooth leaves, first appeared in Germany around the middle of the twelfth century.

The Talmud considers the cabbage healthful, noting "cabbage for sustenance." Cabbage certainly played that role among Ashkenazim, serving as northern Europe's predominant vegetable until the acceptance of the potato in the mid-1800s. Cabbage was pickled and fermented to make sauerkraut, boiled, braised, and stuffed; it also provided the basis for numerous soups and fillings for savory pastries, including knishes, blintzes, and strudel. Boiled cabbage was the most common cooking odor of the *shtetlach* across eastern Europe. In many instances, an Ashkenazic lunch consisted solely of black bread and sauerkraut.

A common central European way of preparing cooked cabbage was to mix it with noodles, frequently flavoring the dish with caraway. Germans traditionally served cabbage on Rosh Hashanah and Hoshanah Rabbah (the end of Sukkot), since the vegetable's Teutonic name, *kohl*, sounds like the prominent holiday prayer *kol mevasar* ("a voice announcing"). Stuffed cabbage became typical Ashkenazic holiday fare, especially on Sukkot, when it symbolized the harvest. Although less vital to other Jewish communities than to Ashkenazim, cabbage has remained important, especially in India and Ethiopia, where it goes into intensely spiced salads and braises. On the other hand, the residents of the Mediterranean and Middle East, with so many vegetables at their disposal, relied much less on cabbage, occasionally using it pickled, stuffed, or stewed.

What You Should Know: Do not cut cabbage with a high-carbon knife; the knife will discolor. Adding a little sugar to the cooking water keeps cabbage crunchy. Adding a whole walnut in the shell to the cooking water eliminates an overly "cabbagey" odor, while adding a few caraway seeds to braised cabbage enhances its flavor and aroma.

ETHIOPIAN BRAISED CABBAGE

(Tikil Gomen)

6 TO 8 SERVINGS   Ⓓ OR Ⓟ

In Ethiopia, many families grew cabbages outside their hut to provide a regular supply. The carrots are a recent addition to this lightly spiced dish, giving it color and a note of sweetness. Cooking cabbage in fat gives it extra flavor and a firmer texture. This dish is customarily served over injera (Ethiopian flat bread).

1/4 cup *ghee* (Indian Clarified Butter, page 51)
    or vegetable oil
I onion, chopped
I small green bell pepper, seeded, deribbed
    (white removed), and finely chopped
I to 3 jalapeño chilies, seeded and minced
I tablespoon mustard seeds
I head (2 pounds) green or savoy cabbage,
    cored and coarsely shredded
I to 3 carrots, coarsely grated (optional)
1/2 cup water
About I teaspoon table salt or 2 teaspoons
    kosher salt
Ground black pepper to taste

1. In a large, heavy pot, melt the ghee over medium-high heat. Add the onion, bell pepper, and chilies and sauté until softened, 5 to 10 minutes. Stir in the mustard seeds.

2. Add the cabbage and, if using, the carrots and sauté until the cabbage is slightly wilted, about 5 minutes. Add the water, salt, and pepper. Bring to a boil, cover, reduce the heat to medium, and simmer, adding more water if necessary, until just tender but still slightly crunchy, about 15 minutes. Serve warm or at room temperature.

GERMAN RED CABBAGE WITH APPLES

(Rote Kroit mit Apfles)

6 TO 8 SERVINGS   Ⓓ OR Ⓟ

This German dish, also popular in Alsace, Austria, Holland, and Hungary. It is usually served with boiled or mashed potatoes. The slight peppery flavor of the red cabbage, which is mellower than that of green varieties, is enhanced by the apples and acid; the sugar and vinegar contribute a sweet-and-sour dimension. Many older versions call for braising the cabbage for hours, but most people prefer a firmer texture in the cabbage. Some insist that the dish is even better when left to stand in the refrigerator for a day and then reheated. The German grandmother who shared this recipe with me insisted that only tart apples should be used. She also advised, "Choose a cabbage that feels firm and heavy."

1/4 cup vegetable oil or unsalted butter
3 to 4 tart cooking apples, such as Granny Smith,
    Greening, Macoun, Macintosh, or Pippin,
    peeled, cored, and sliced
2 onions, thinly sliced
I head (about 2 pounds) red cabbage, cored,
    tough outer leaves discarded, and shredded
I teaspoon caraway seeds, 5 whole cloves,
    or I tablespoon chopped fresh dill (optional)
1/2 cup dry red wine, such as Pinot Noir
    or Burgundy
1/2 cup water
I tablespoon red wine vinegar or cider vinegar
About 1/4 cup granulated or packed brown sugar
I bay leaf
About 1 1/2 teaspoons table salt or I tablespoon
    kosher salt
About 1/8 teaspoon ground black pepper

1. In a 4-quart nonreactive saucepan, heat the oil over medium heat. Add the apples and onions and sauté until they begin to soften, about 5 minutes. Add the cabbage and optional spices and sauté until slightly wilted, about 5 minutes.

2. Stir in the wine, water, vinegar, sugar, bay leaf, salt, and pepper. Bring to a boil, cover, reduce the heat to low, and simmer, stirring occasionally, until tender but not mushy, about 30 minutes. Serve warm or at room temperature. The cabbage can be prepared 1 day ahead, refrigerated, and reheated before serving.

VARIATIONS

Red Cabbage with Cherries (*Rote Kroit mit Kirschen*): Add 8 ounces pitted and poached fresh sour cherries to the cooked cabbage. Or, add ¹/₄ cup dried tart cherries and ¹/₄ cup dried currants with the wine.

Red Cabbage with Chestnuts (*Rote Kroit mit Kastanie*): About 10 minutes before serving, add 12 to 16 parboiled and peeled whole chestnuts and heat through.

Romanian Baked Red Cabbage with Apples (*Varza*): The long baking time of this dish produces a mellow-flavored cabbage. A little rice helps to slightly thicken the cooking liquid. Combine all the ingredients in a large casserole, add 2 tablespoons white rice, cover, and bake in a preheated 400°F oven for about 2 hours.

NOTE Red cabbage and apples are natural partners, not only because both can survive the winter. Tart apples possess acid, which preserves the cabbage's red color during cooking (the vinegar and wine in this recipe help with this as well). Cabbage's red color comes from a pigment called anthocyanin, which gives many red and purple foods their hue, including berries, apples, grapes, and eggplant. The pigment in any plant fades during cooking unless preserved by the presence of acid.

INDIAN BRAISED CABBAGE

(*Bundgobi*)

6 TO 8 SERVINGS Ⓓ OR Ⓟ

Elezar Grafstein, who spent several years serving as a rabbi in Bombay, was indispensable in my search to locate Indian Jews living in the United States. Most of the Bombay Jews I contacted were reluctant to discuss their community, perhaps because of their former position in India as outcastes. Indeed, it required a bit of persuasion to convince one Indian woman I located in New Jersey to meet with me, let alone to share recipes for some of her favorite vegetable dishes. She told me that when she was a child, one of her most beloved bedtime stories concerned a sumptuous meal consisting of thirty-three vegetable dishes as well as thirty-two varieties of sweets.

During the week, most Indians prepare only one or two vegetables, besides the ubiquitous dal *(legumes), for lunch and dinner, while on the Sabbath and holidays there will likely be at least three or four. Indians prepare two primary types of fried vegetables, gobi and* bhaji/subji. *The former is braised (a "wet" method), prepared by first frying the vegetables, then adding liquid, while the latter is a "dry" method using only ghee or oil to cook the vegetables.*

This recipe is a spicy Indian-Jewish version of braised cabbage, prepared by the "wet" method, commonly served during the winter when other fresh vegetables are scarce, and usually accompanied with Indian flat breads.

¹/₄ cup *ghee* (Indian Clarified Butter, page 51) or vegetable oil

¹/₂ teaspoon cumin seeds

¹/₂ teaspoon fennel seeds

¹/₄ teaspoon brown mustard seeds

4 fenugreek seeds

1 onion, chopped

1 head (2 pounds) green or savoy cabbage, cored,
 tough outer leaves discarded, and coarsely
 shredded

About 1 cup water

2 cloves garlic

1 1/2 teaspoons table salt or 1 tablespoon
 kosher salt

3 plum tomatoes, peeled, seeded, and chopped
 (see page 291), about 1 cup

1 tablespoon fresh lemon juice

2 teaspoons minced fresh ginger

1 teaspoon seeded and minced jalapeño or other
 hot green chili

1 teaspoon garam masala

1/2 teaspoon ground turmeric

1. In a large nonreactive pot, melt the ghee over medium-high heat. Add the cumin, fennel seeds, mustard, and fenugreek and sauté until fragrant, about 30 seconds. Add the onion and sauté until soft and translucent, about 5 minutes. Add the cabbage and sauté until slightly wilted, about 5 minutes.

2. Add the water. Bring to a boil, cover, reduce the heat to medium, and simmer until just tender but still slightly crunchy, about 15 minutes.

3. Using the tip of a heavy knife or with a mortar and pestle, mash the garlic and salt into a paste. Combine the garlic, tomatoes, lemon juice, ginger, garlic, chili, garam masala, and turmeric in a medium saucepan. Simmer over medium heat, stirring occasionally, until the tomatoes begin to soften, about 10 minutes.

4. Add to the cabbage and heat through, about 5 minutes. Serve warm.

MIDDLE EASTERN BULGUR-STUFFED CABBAGE

(Malfoof Mahshee)

ABOUT 9 LARGE ROLLS

Unlike central European renditions of stuffed cabbage, which usually contain some kind of meat, Middle Eastern stuffed-cabbage dishes use a number of vegetarian fillings. This one is made with a bulgur mixture. Skillful cooks carefully scrutinize each cabbage, squeezing to see if the leaves are firm, yet moist and, therefore, tender. I like to serve this dish with Cucumber and Yogurt Salad (page 47).

STUFFING:

3 tablespoons olive oil or vegetable oil

1 large onion, chopped

1 to 2 cloves garlic, minced

1 1/3 cups (8 ounces) medium or fine bulgur

2 cups water

About 1 teaspoon table salt or 2 teaspoons
 kosher salt

1/4 cup chopped fresh parsley

2 tablespoons minced fresh ginger or 1 teaspoon
 dried thyme

1/2 cup dried currants, raisins, chopped dried figs,
 or toasted sliced almonds

1 head (about 2 pounds) green or savoy cabbage,
 cored and tough outer leaves discarded,
 but left whole

About 1/2 teaspoon table salt or 1 teaspoon
 kosher salt

Ground black pepper to taste

2 cups tomato juice, 2 cups water, or 1 cup
 tomato sauce and 1 cup water

1. To make the stuffing: In a large saucepan, heat the oil over medium heat. Add the onion and garlic and sauté until soft and translucent, about 5 minutes. Add the bulgur and stir until coated, about 2 minutes. Add the water and salt and bring to a boil. Remove from the heat and stir in the parsley, ginger, and currants. Cover and let stand for 30 minutes.

2. Bring a large pot of water to a boil. Place the whole cabbage head in the pot and parboil until the leaves can be removed easily and are supple enough to roll, about 10 minutes. Remove the cabbage and let stand long enough so that you can handle it. Remove 16 to 18 large leaves, cut out the tough part of the center rib of each leaf, and reserve the leaves. Remove the remaining leaves. Line the bottom of a deep pot or baking dish with half of the remaining leaves.

3. Spoon about $^1/3$ cup stuffing into the center of each reserved cabbage leaf. Fold the stem end over the stuffing, fold in the sides, and roll up.

4. Place the cabbage rolls, seam-side-down, in the pot or dish. Sprinkle with the salt and pepper. Top with the remaining cabbage leaves. Add the tomato juice.

5. Cover the pot with a lid and simmer over low heat until tender, about 1 hour, or cover the baking dish with aluminum foil and bake in a preheated 350°F oven for about $1^1/2$ hours. (Baking intensifies the flavors.) Serve warm.

VARIATION

Sweet-and-Sour Sauce: Use the tomato sauce, and add to the sauce 2 to 4 tablespoons lemon juice, 1 tablespoon sugar, and, if desired, $^3/4$ cup raisins and $^1/2$ teaspoon ground cinnamon.

SYRIAN RICE-STUFFED CABBAGE

(Malfoof Mahshee)

ABOUT 12 LARGE ROLLS

Smell often has a stronger impact on memory than sight. For a Syrian friend, the aroma of this dish wafting through the house was a sign of Sunday dinner, when his family enjoyed it as a main course nearly every week. Stuffed cabbage tastes even better the second day, reheated. It freezes well, too.

I head (about 2 pounds) green or savoy cabbage, cored and tough outer leaves discarded, but left whole

STUFFING:
3 tablespoons olive oil or vegetable oil
I large onion, chopped
I cup long-grain white or brown rice
2 cups water
About I teaspoon table salt or 2 teaspoons kosher salt
$^1/4$ teaspoon ground black pepper
About I $^1/2$ cups dried chickpeas, picked over, soaked in water to cover for 12 hours, drained, rinsed, and cooked (see page 329, Step I)
$^1/2$ cup chopped fresh cilantro
$^1/2$ cup chopped fresh mint
$^1/2$ cup chopped fresh parsley

SAUCE:
2 tablespoons olive oil or vegetable oil
I to 2 cloves garlic, minced
3 cups tomato juice, 3 cups water, or 2 cups water and I cup tomato sauce
About $^3/4$ teaspoon table salt or I $^1/2$ teaspoons kosher salt
Ground black pepper to taste

1. Bring a large pot of water to a boil. Put the whole cabbage in the pot and parboil until the leaves can be removed easily and are supple enough to roll, about 10 minutes. Remove the cabbage and let stand long enough so that you can handle it. Remove 12 large leaves, cut out the tough part of the center rib of each leaf, and reserve the leaves. Remove the remaining leaves. Line the bottom of a deep pot or baking dish with half of the remaining leaves.

2. To make the stuffing: In a medium saucepan, heat the oil over medium heat. Add the onion and sauté until soft and translucent, about 5 minutes. Add the rice and stir until it is coated and turns glossy, about 3 minutes. Stir in the water, salt, and pepper. Bring to a boil, cover, reduce the heat to low, and simmer until the rice is almost tender, about 15 minutes for white rice, 35 minutes for brown rice. Remove from the heat and stir in the chickpeas, cilantro, mint, and parsley. The stuffing can be prepared up to 2 days ahead and stored in the refrigerator.

3. Spoon about $1/3$ cup stuffing in the center of each reserved cabbage leaf. Fold the stem end over the stuffing, fold in the sides, and roll up. Place the cabbage rolls, seam-side down, in the pot or dish. Top with the remaining cabbage leaves.

4. To make the sauce: In a medium saucepan, heat the oil over medium heat. Add the garlic and sauté until just golden, about 1 minute. Add the tomato juice, salt, and pepper. Bring to a boil, reduce the heat to low, and simmer, stirring occasionally, for 5 minutes. Pour over the cabbage rolls.

5. Cover the pot with a lid and simmer over low heat until tender, about 1 hour, or cover the dish with aluminum foil and bake in a preheated 350°F oven, about $1^1/2$ hours. Baking intensifies the flavors. Serve warm.

VARIATIONS

Syrian Spiced Stuffed Cabbage (*Malfoof Mahshee*): Omit the cilantro, mint, and parsley from the filling and add, with the water, $1^1/2$ teaspoons ground allspice, $1/2$ teaspoon ground cinnamon, $1/2$ cup dried currants or raisins, and, if desired, $1/4$ to $1/2$ cup slivered almonds, pistachios, or pine nuts.

Syrian Sweet-and-Sour Stuffed Cabbage (*Malfoof Mahshee*): Use the tomato juice or sauce. Add $1/2$ cup raisins, 3 to 4 tablespoons granulated or packed brown sugar, $1/4$ cup fresh lemon juice, and 1 tablespoon *temerhindi* (Syrian Mock Tamarind Sauce, page 434) or 2 teaspoons prune butter and 2 teaspoons apricot butter.

Georgian Walnut-Stuffed Cabbage

(*Kombostos Nigozit Satenit*)

6 SIDE-DISH SERVINGS

OR 2 TO 3 ENTRÉE SERVINGS

This dish is not a conventional stuffed cabbage, but rather a roulade, artfully made by rolling a characteristically Georgian pungent walnut sauce in overlapping blanched cabbage leaves, without any further cooking. Individual leaves may also be filled and rolled like a cigar. Some cooks like to mix the pomegranate seeds into the filling, adding a crunch and fruity tartness. These roulades make a delightfully different side dish or appetizer. (You can also prepare fried eggplant slices in this manner: Spread about 1 tablespoon walnut sauce on each slice and roll up.)

2 small stalks celery, finely chopped,
    or 3 tablespoons chopped celery leaves
Georgian Walnut Sauce (page 432)
6 large green cabbage leaves
2 tablespoons pomegranate seeds for garnish
    (optional)

1. Stir the celery into the Georgian Walnut Sauce. Let stand at room temperature for at least 30 minutes. The mixture can be stored in the refrigerator for up to 3 days. Taste and adjust the seasoning and thickness. It should have a spreadable consistency.

2. Cut the ribs from the cabbage leaves and discard. Blanch the leaves in a pot of lightly salted boiling water until pliable, about 2 minutes. Drain, pat dry, and let cool.

3. On a flat surface, arrange the leaves in single file stem to stem, overlapping the edges slightly. Spread evenly with the walnut sauce mixture, leaving a 1/2-inch border on all sides. Starting from a narrow side, roll up jelly-roll style. The roll should be about 6 inches long. Cover with plastic wrap and let stand at room temperature or in the refrigerator for several hours or up to 3 days, so the leaves can absorb some of the sauce.

4. To serve, using a serrated knife, cut the roll crosswise into 1-inch-wide slices. Garnish with the pomegranate seeds.

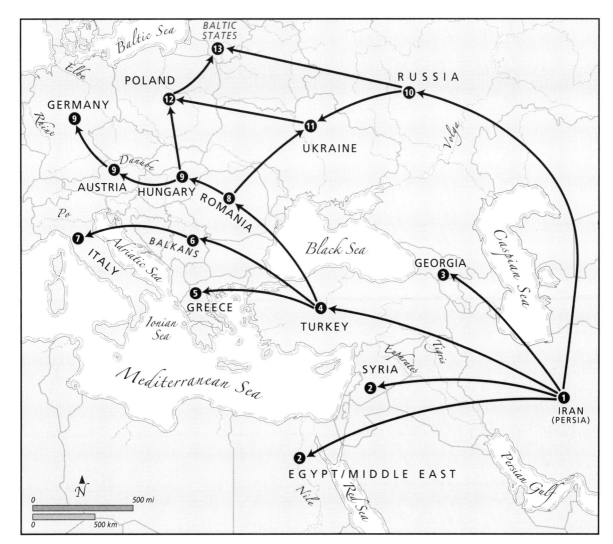

The Spread of Stuffed Cabbage: *Stuffed cabbage originated in Iran (formerly Persia) and became a favorite dish in Jewish communities throughout Asia, Europe, and North Africa. Note the similarity of terms for stuffed cabbage, which offers evidence of the paths along which the dish migrated.* **1** *mishee malfoof;* **2** *malfoof mahshee;* **3** *tolma;* **4** *samas de kol or dolmas kalam;* **5** *dolmas de kol;* **6** *yaprakes di kol;* **7** *cavoli ripieni;* **8** *sarmali;* **9** *gefulte kraut;* **10** *praakes or galuptze;* **11** *holoptsche;* **12** *holishikes ("little doves") or teibelekh;* **13** *holishkes or prakkes*

❧ CARDOONS ❧

The succulent stalks of the cardoon—a thistle, possibly native to Israel, that grows in bunches somewhat like celery—were once a treasured indulgence in parts of the Mediterranean region and in Persia. Millennia ago, someone discovered that cooking this tough, monstrous-looking plant for an extended time tenderized it and gave it a unique bittersweet flavor reminiscent of artichoke hearts (artichokes are a close relative of cardoons). Cardoons are still eaten in these regions; Tunisians and Moroccans make a beloved Passover soup with a mixture of cardoons, carrots, and kohlrabi mixed with crumbled matza, and they use cardoons in stews to top couscous. Persians smother the stalks in a garlicky yogurt sauce. Italians have a particular fondness for the vegetable, preparing it stewed, baked, and fried. In northern Italy, cardoon soup is claimed to keep away colds in the winter. The cardoon is little known in much of the rest of the world, which is a shame, as it is a tasty and interesting vegetable with a long history.

What You Should Know: Cardoon stalks—wider and flatter than celery stalks, with a silvery gray color—vary highly in flavor and texture, even within a single plant. The inner stalks are generally more tender than the outer ones. Choose pale stalks with deep green leaves. Avoid plants with bruises or signs of wilting. (It is okay, however, if the tops look brown from where the flowers were cut off; the heads are cooked or used as a vegetable substitute for rennet in cheese making.) Cardoons are usually available from October through May, and they are at their best in the cooler months, as warm weather tends to toughen them and make them overly bitter. To store, wrap in plastic wrap and refrigerate for up to 1 week. Discard any remaining leaves before using.

STEWED CARDOONS

6 TO 8 SERVINGS   P

Cardoon stalks can be substituted for celery in many recipes. Cardoons are commonly boiled to remove excess bitterness before being stewed, baked, or fried. A little flour or lemon juice is frequently added to the cooking liquid to lighten the color and keep the cardoons from discoloring.

- I lemon, halved, or 2 tablespoons distilled white vinegar
- 2 bunches cardoons (4 pounds total)
- I tablespoon table salt or 2 tablespoons kosher salt
- I tablespoon unbleached all-purpose flour dissolved in I cup cold water, or ¼ cup plain lemon juice

1. Squeeze the lemon halves into a large bowl of water and add the lemon shells. Cut off the stem end of each cardoon bunch, leaving the individual stalks. Discard any woody outer stems. Trim the tips and jagged edges and peel off the thick outer fibers, occasionally dipping the cut edges into the lemon water while working. Cut the stalks into 3- or 4-inch-long pieces. Place in the lemon water and let soak for 30 minutes.

2. Bring a large pot of water to a boil. Add the salt, then the flour-water mixture and return to a boil.

3. Drain the cardoons and add to the pot. Return to a boil, reduce the heat to medium-low, and simmer, uncovered, until tender, about 30 minutes. Drain, rinse under cold running water, and drain again. The cardoons can be prepared to this point up to 1 day ahead; store in the refrigerator.

NOTE   Phytochemicals in cardoons give wine a bitter taste, so they are usually not served with wine.

ITALIAN CARDOONS IN THE SKILLET

(Cardi al Tegame)

6 TO 8 SERVINGS   P

Cardi al tegame is common at Italian Purim feasts, alongside ravioli and Carciofi Fritti *(Italian Fried Artichokes, page 203). Top the cardoons with Egg-Lemon Sauce (page 431), add to omelets, or serve as a side dish.*

    Stewed Cardoons (page 222)
    2 cups water
    3 tablespoons olive oil
    3 tablespoons chopped fresh parsley
    I to 2 cloves garlic, sliced
    About ¹/₂ teaspoon table salt or I teaspoon
       kosher salt
    Ground black pepper to taste

Put the cardoons in a medium saucepan and add all the remaining ingredients. Cover and simmer over low heat, stirring occasionally, until the cardoons are very tender and the liquid evaporates, about 1 hour. Serve warm.

ITALIAN CARDOONS WITH CHEESE

(Cardi al Formaggio)

4 TO 5 SERVINGS

    ¹/₂ recipe Stewed Cardoons (page 222)
    Salt to taste
    ¹/₂ cup (I¹/₂ ounces) grated Parmesan cheese
    ¹/₄ cup unsalted butter, melted

1. Preheat the oven to 350°F. Grease a 9-by-13-inch baking dish.

2. Sprinkle the cardoons with the salt. Scatter half of the cardoons in the prepared dish and sprinkle with half the cheese. Arrange the remaining cardoons over top and sprinkle with the remaining cheese. Drizzle with the butter.

3. Bake until the cheese melts, about 25 minutes. Serve warm.

ITALIAN FRIED CARDOONS

(Cardi Fritti)

6 TO 8 SERVINGS

Olive oil or vegetable oil for frying
Stewed Cardoons (page 222)
1 cup unbleached all-purpose flour
2 large eggs, lightly beaten
Salt to taste
Lemon wedges

1. In a medium skillet, heat at least $1/2$ inch oil over medium heat. In batches, dredge the cardoon pieces in the flour, then dip into the eggs. Fry, turning once, until golden brown, about $1^1/2$ minutes per side.

2. Using a slotted spoon or wire-mesh skimmer, transfer the cardoons to paper towels to drain and sprinkle lightly with salt. The cardoons can be transferred to a wire rack set on a baking sheet and kept warm in low oven while preparing the remaining batches. Serve very hot, accompanied with lemon wedges.

PERSIAN CARDOONS WITH YOGURT

(Borani Kangar)

6 TO 8 SERVINGS

Stewed Cardoons (page 222)
$1/4$ cup unsalted butter
3 cups plain yogurt
About 1 teaspoon table salt or 2 teaspoons kosher salt
Ground black pepper to taste

Using a fork or potato masher, mash the stewed cardoons to a coarse consistency. In a large skillet, melt the butter over medium heat. Add the cardoons and cook, stirring constantly, until heated through. Remove from the heat and stir in the yogurt, salt, and pepper. Serve warm or chilled, as a side dish, or as a dip for flat bread.

❧ CARROTS ❧

The carrot, a member of the Umbelliferae family, is a native of southern Afghanistan. The original wild carrot had a purple color and was small, fibrous, woody, and not particularly tasty. One kind of wild carrot still around today is called Queen Anne's lace; it gives a sense of what early carrots looked like. In the fifteenth century, horticulturists bred out the antyocyanin pigment that gave early carrots their purple coloring, producing varieties with yellow and whitish roots, which were preferable because they no longer colored soups and stews. Subsequently, the carrot and its close relative the parsnip became frequently confused with each other, although the parsnip was at the time more common. Indeed, the carrot's root was not widely eaten at first; instead carrots were used primarily as medicine and for their seeds, which were treated as spices, used similarly to its various relatives, anise, caraway, coriander, and cumin.

In the twelfth century, the Moors introduced the carrot to Spain, and the Spanish eventually brought new varieties to their territories in Holland, where they then spread eastward. The now-common orange carrot, colored by high levels of carotene, emerged in Holland around 1600. The carrot's now-familiar sweetness, too, was developed in Holland around that time, the root's sugar content having been increased steadily through cultivation by Greeks, Romans, Arabs, and finally the Dutch, who produced a carrot that ranked second only to beets in the amount of sugar it contained.

Historically, carrots were utilized as part of a stew or soup rather than as the primary component of a dish. When carrots were featured, they were usually simply prepared and seasoned. In the Middle East, the roots, both cooked and raw, are used in salads as well as in soups, stews, pickles, and omelets. Fat carrots are stuffed and braised for holiday meals.

Carrots thrive even in poor soil and can be left in the ground or a root cellar through the winter. Therefore, as their flavor improved through cultivation over the centuries, they became one of the most important eastern European vegetables. Beginning in the late medieval period, partially due to its name—in Yiddish, *mehren* ("multiply" or "increase')and, in Hebrew, *gezer* ("tear"), indicating that any unfavorable decrees should be torn up—the carrot became an important part of Rosh Hashanah tradition. The carrot's sweetness fits in well with the theme of the holiday; in addition, carrot slices resemble gold coins. Ashkenazim commonly complemented the carrot's sweetness by cooking it with honey in stews, soups, preserves, puddings, cakes, and candy. Eastern Europeans, viewing raw carrots as unhealthy, ate them only cooked, usually to the point of mushiness.

What You Should Know: Carrots have a tender outer layer surrounding a tough core that becomes increasingly fibrous as it matures. A carrot's flavor depends on the variety, soil, climate, and degree of maturity. Choose firm, well-formed roots. Avoid carrots that are split, blemished, or show signs of rotting at either end.

ASHKENAZIC STEWED CARROTS

(Mehren Tzimmes)

8 TO 10 SERVINGS   P

Among eastern European Jews, tzimmes *is a delicacy enjoyed on the Sabbath and holidays. My Romanian grandmother made a complex* tzimmes, *replete with a variety of vegetables and fruits as well as meat; this one-dish meal was called* gahntze tzimmes. *My Lithuanian grandmother's* tzimmes, *on the other hand, consisted sparely of carrots, prunes, and sometimes sweet potatoes, the latter a substitute for the parsnips used in the Old Country.*

Tzimmes is a late-medieval slow-simmered stew, its name playfully derived from two different German words for eat: zum *and* essen. *At some point, the word also began to mean a "fuss," due to all the chopping, stirring, and stewing involved in making the dish.* Tzimmes *recipes vary widely but always include at least one root vegetable, usually carrots. In fact, it was in the late-medieval period, when carrots were first used in* tzimmes, *that the dish first became a popular Ashkenazic Rosh Hashanah food probably as a result of the carrots and honey. Other traditional vegetables include parsnips, rutabagas, sweet potatoes, and turnips. Whatever the ingredients, the main requirement for a good* tzimmes *is a long cooking time over low heat to blend and intensify the flavors.*

3 tablespoons vegetable oil

2 onions, chopped or sliced

2¹/₂ to 3 pounds carrots, sliced

3 tart apples, peeled, cored, and sliced; or 1 pound dried apricots or prunes; or 1 cup raisins; or 1 cup chopped dried figs; or a combination (optional)

1¹/₂ cups Vegetable Stock (page 115) or water, or ³/₄ cup stock and ³/₄ cup orange juice

¹/₄ to ¹/₂ cup honey, packed brown sugar, or granulated sugar

2 bay leaves

1 teaspoon ground cinnamon (optional)

¹/₄ teaspoon ground ginger

About 1 teaspoon table salt or 2 teaspoons kosher salt

Ground black pepper to taste

1. Preheat the oven to 350°F. Grease a 3-quart casserole.

2. In a large saucepan, heat the oil over medium heat. Add the onions and sauté until soft and translucent, about 5 to 10 minutes. Add the carrots and stir to coat, about 3 minutes. Add the remaining ingredients and simmer, stirring occasionally, for 10 minutes.

3. Spoon into the prepared casserole, cover with a lid or foil, and bake until tender and most of the liquid is absorbed, 1 to 1¹/₂ hours. Uncover and bake until the top is golden brown, about 10 minutes. Serve warm. Tzimmes can be stored in the refrigerator for up to 2 days, then reheated.

VARIATIONS

Carrot and Parsnip *Tzimmes*: Reduce the carrots to 1¹/₂ pounds and add 1¹/₂ pounds peeled and sliced parsnips.

Carrot and Sweet Potato *Tzimmes*: Reduce the carrots to 1¹/₂ pounds and add 1¹/₂ pounds peeled and sliced sweet potatoes.

Carrot and Rhubarb *Tzimmes*: Omit the apples, reduce the carrots to 1 1/2 pounds, and add 3 cups (about 1 pound) rhubarb, peeled and cut into 2-inch pieces.

ASHKENAZIC BAKED CARROT PUDDING

(Mehren Kugel)

6 TO 8 SERVINGS   D OR P

The origin of baked carrot pudding, or kugel, *a sweet, moist, cakelike dish, is in the seventeenth century, when Germans began adding root vegetables to baked grain puddings then common. Also around that time, these savory puddings, which resembled the English plum pudding, started becoming sweeter, thanks to the increasing affordability of sugar (first from Caribbean plantations, and later from European sugar beets). Because of their natural sweetness, carrots became the preferred root to use in these new baked sweet puddings.*

Ashkenazic cooks soon began adapting these puddings for the Sabbath and holidays. As central European cookery grew more sophisticated in the nineteenth century, carrot puddings evolved into carrot cakes. With the advent of solid vegetable shortening in 1911, an inexpensive nondairy substitute for butter and schmaltz, Ashkenazic carrot puddings also acquired an even more cakelike nature, although they were a bit on the heavy side compared to modern carrot cakes. Thus, long before carrot cake became an American food, my Lithuanian grandmother made a rich and moist baked carrot pudding.

Mehren kugel, although sweet and cakelike, was not a dessert, but rather a side dish for a Sabbath or holiday meal, commonly baked in a ring shape to make sure that the center would not be raw or the outside overdone. Some versions call for 3/4 cup or more of sugar, resulting in an intensely sweet dish. I have also seen recipes calling for 2 cups shortening. On the other side of the scale, my mother substitutes applesauce for part or all of the butter to reduce the fat, and sometimes substitutes whole-wheat flour for the white flour, which yields a heavier texture but is more healthful. My grandmother insisted that hand-grated carrots are superior to "those overly coarse ones from a food processor."

1 1/2 cups unbleached all-purpose flour

1 teaspoon baking powder

1/2 teaspoon baking soda (see Note)

1/2 teaspoon table salt or 1 teaspoon kosher salt

1/2 teaspoon ground cinnamon

1/4 teaspoon freshly grated nutmeg or ground ginger

1/2 cup (1 stick) unsalted butter, vegetable shortening, or margarine, softened

1/2 cup packed brown sugar

1 large egg

3 tablespoons fresh lemon or orange juice

1 to 2 teaspoons grated lemon or orange zest

2 cups grated carrots, or 1 cup grated carrots and 1 cup grated sweet potato

1/2 to 3/4 cup raisins, snipped dried figs, chopped nuts, or a combination (optional)

1. Preheat the oven to 350°F. Grease a 9-inch tube pan or Bundt pan, or a 9-by-5-inch loaf pan.

2. Sift the flour, baking powder, baking soda, salt, and spices together onto a sheet of waxed paper. In a large bowl, cream together the butter and sugar, beating until light and fluffy, about 5 minutes. Beat in the egg. Add the flour mixture, lemon juice, and zest. Stir in the carrots and, if using, the raisins.

3. Spoon into the pan. Bake until golden, about 45 minutes for a tube pan or Bundt pan, 1 hour for a loaf pan. Serve warm or at room temperature.

Substitute 2 cups mashed cooked carrots for the grated carrots, omit the baking soda, and increase the baking powder to 1$^{1}/_{2}$ teaspoons and the eggs to 2.

N O T E When heated, the baking soda, an alkali, reacts with the acid in the carrots to break down their cell walls, leaching out water. Without it, the carrots would become crisp and the kugel would be dry.

Bukharan Braised Baby Carrots

(*Sabzi Piez*)

6 TO 8 SERVINGS

One of the Soviet Union's earliest projects was to transform Uzbekistan into a major cotton producer, in the process destroying both the area's traditional agriculture as well as its ecosystems, including the Aral Sea, which was drained. Among the other results, cotton seeds became a more important source of oil in the region. (In America, many oils labeled "vegetable" or "cooking" are actually cottonseed oil.) Cottonseed oil has a slightly nutty, buttery flavor, and serves as a flavor enhancement for other foods. Savory, firm braised carrots are a much-devoured side dish among central Asian Jews, and they are frequently eaten with plov (Azerbaijani Rice Pilaf, page 352).

$^{1}/_{4}$ cup cottonseed oil or vegetable oil

2 large onions, coarsely chopped

2 pounds baby carrots, or julienned regular carrots (see Note)

3 to 4 cloves garlic, minced

1$^{1}/_{4}$ teaspoons cumin seeds

$^{3}/_{4}$ teaspoon sweet paprika

About $^{1}/_{4}$ teaspoon hot paprika or cayenne

1 tablespoon tomato paste

$^{1}/_{2}$ cup water

About $^{1}/_{2}$ teaspoon table salt or 1 teaspoon kosher salt

1. In a large saucepan, heat the oil over medium heat. Add the onions and sauté until soft and translucent, 5 to 10 minutes. Add the carrots and sauté until they begin to brown, about 15 minutes.

2. Stir in the garlic and spices. Add the tomato paste and sauté for 1 minute. Stir in the water and salt, cover, reduce the heat to medium-low, and simmer until the carrots are just tender, about 7 minutes for julienned carrots and 10 minutes for baby carrots.

3. Uncover and cook, stirring constantly, until the liquid is reduced and thickened, 2 to 3 minutes. Serve warm.

N O T E Genuine baby carrots have been cultivated to grow to a small size; they are not immature. Most of the bagged "baby carrots" in stores, however, are actually regular carrots cut and trimmed to a small size. You can use either type in this and many other recipes calling for baby carrots.

[handwritten note] Excellent!! Make as is. Including cook times. Slightly sweet. (I used 1 lb carrot and cut in half.

ITALIAN BRAISED CARROTS

(Carote Sofegae)

6 TO 8 SERVINGS   Ⓓ OR Ⓟ

Carrots are less prevalent in vegetable-loving Italy than in most other parts of Europe; however, since they are easy to grow and inexpensive, they have been utilized there to provide economical dishes. Many Italian recipes call for soaking whole carrots in cold water for 30 minutes before parboiling them in their skin; they are then peeled and sliced, which they claim results in moister, more flavorful carrots. The word sofegae *in the name of this recipe means "suffocated," referring to vegetables that are cooked over a very low heat for a long time, resulting in mushy vegetables.*

This version, involving braising, speeds up the process a bit and produces firmer carrots. Braising, a method of cooking using a relatively small amount of liquid, merges and intensifies flavors, while producing a thick sauce. The sweet-and-sour flavor and the use of raisins and pine nuts in this Venetian dish denote its Jewish origins, as these flavor combinations were brought north by Sicilian Jews.

1/4 cup sweet red wine or 2 tablespoons cream
    sherry and 2 tablespoons sweet vermouth

2 tablespoons red wine vinegar

1/2 to 3/4 cup dried currants or raisins

1/4 cup olive oil or unsalted butter

2 pounds carrots, diagonally sliced

Pinch of ground cinnamon

Pinch of freshly grated nutmeg

1/2 cup water

1/4 cup pine nuts, toasted (see page 22)

About 1/2 teaspoon table salt or 1 teaspoon
    kosher salt

Ground black pepper to taste

1. In a small bowl, combine the wine, vinegar, and currants and let soak for 15 minutes.

2. In a large saucepan, heat the oil over medium heat. Add the carrots, cinnamon, and nutmeg and sauté until well coated, about 5 minutes.

3. Add the currant mixture, water, pine nuts, salt, and pepper. Bring to a boil, cover, reduce the heat to medium-low, and cook, stirring occasionally, until the carrots are tender, about 20 minutes. Serve warm or at room temperature.

VARIATION

Italian Braised Cauliflower (*Cavolfiore Affogato***):** Substitute 1 head (about 2 pounds) cauliflower cut into florets for the carrots; simmer until tender, about 8 minutes.

Moroccan Glazed Carrots

(Dsjada)

6 TO 8 SERVINGS   P

*My family made glazed carrots with a simple season-
ing of honey and occasionally orange. When I visited
Israel, I met Jews who prepared the basic dish of glazed
carrots in vastly different ways. This spicy Moroccan
version, redolent with the earthiness of caraway and
cumin and given a slight kick of chilies, contrasts
markedly with the simple Ashkenazic style of cooking
carrots. Serve this as a side dish, salad, or appetizer.*

2 pounds carrots, diagonally sliced

I cup water

$^{1}/_{4}$ teaspoon table salt or $^{1}/_{2}$ teaspoon kosher salt

GLAZE:

$^{1}/_{4}$ cup vegetable oil

2 onions, halved and thinly sliced

3 to 4 cloves garlic, minced (optional)

$^{1}/_{2}$ teaspoon caraway seeds

$^{1}/_{2}$ teaspoon ground cumin

$^{1}/_{2}$ teaspoon sweet paprika

About $^{1}/_{4}$ teaspoon cayenne pepper
    or $^{1}/_{2}$ teaspoon red pepper flakes

About $^{1}/_{8}$ teaspoon table salt or $^{1}/_{4}$ teaspoon
    kosher salt

Ground black pepper to taste

2 to 4 tablespoons fresh lemon juice

3 tablespoons chopped fresh parsley, cilantro,
    or mint for garnish

1. In a medium saucepan, combine the carrots, water, and salt. Bring to a boil, cover, reduce the heat to low, and simmer until fork-tender, 10 to 15 minutes. Drain, reserving $^{1}/_{4}$ cup cooking liquid. (You can add the remaining cooking liquid to a vegetable stock or soup.)

2. To make the glaze: In a large skillet, heat the oil over medium-high heat. Add the onions and, if using, the garlic and sauté until soft and translucent, 5 to 10 minutes. Stir in the caraway and cumin. Add the carrots and sauté until coated, about 2 minutes.

3. Add the $^{1}/_{4}$ cup reserved cooking liquid, the paprika, cayenne, salt, and pepper. Cook, uncovered, stirring frequently, until the liquid evaporates and the carrots are coated, about 5 minutes. Just before serving, stir in the lemon juice and sprinkle with the parsley. Serve warm or at room temperature.

VARIATIONS

For slightly sweet glazed carrots: Omit the caraway seeds, paprika, and lemon juice and add 2 tablespoons packed brown or granulated sugar, $^{1}/_{4}$ to $^{1}/_{2}$ teaspoon ground cinnamon, and $^{1}/_{4}$ teaspoon ground coriander with the cayenne.

Moroccan Glazed Carrots with Artichokes (*Dsjada bi Kharshoof*): In Step 2, add 1 to 2 cups cooked artichoke hearts.

Moroccan Glazed Carrots with Asparagus (*Dsjada bi Kishkalmaaz*): In Step 2, add 1 pound asparagus cut into $1^{1}/_{2}$-inch pieces, simmered in water until tender, about 4 minutes, refreshed in cold water, and drained.

Egyptian Carrots with Yogurt

(Djezar ma Leban)

6 TO 8 SERVINGS

This simple but flavorful preparation makes a refreshing salad or light addition to a meal.

2 pounds carrots, sliced, or baby carrots
   (see Note, page 228)
1/4 cup unsalted butter
3 to 4 cloves garlic, minced
About 1/2 teaspoon table salt or 1 teaspoon
   kosher salt
Ground white or black pepper to taste
1 1/2 cups plain yogurt
1/4 cup chopped fresh cilantro or parsley

1. In a large pot of lightly salted boiling water, cook the carrots until fork-tender, or steam them over boiling water in a covered streamer, about 15 minutes. Drain.

2. In a large skillet, melt the butter over medium heat. Add the carrots and garlic and sauté until heated through, about 2 minutes. Season with the salt and pepper.

3. Transfer the carrots to a serving platter, top with the yogurt, and sprinkle with the cilantro. Serve warm.

❧ CAULIFLOWER ❧

As its name indicates (the word cauliflower is derived from the Italian *caoli fiori,* from the Latin *caulis floris*, or "cabbage flower"), cauliflower is a cabbage developed for its head of thousands of immature flower buds called "curds." Cauliflower appeared relatively late in history; it was first recorded in Asia Minor in the thirteenth century and soon found its way to Moorish Spain, where it was originally called "Syrian cabbage." It was introduced to Italy in 1490 and to the rest of Europe in the sixteenth century. Sephardim, in particular, retain a fondness for this vegetable, preparing it in many forms, including in tomato sauce, fried, and pickled. It is also popular in Italian and Indian cooking. Cauliflower is not historically an Ashkenazic food, except among Hungarians and Romanians, but recently cauliflower *kugels* and *latkes* have gained popularity.

Although available year-round, cauliflower is at its best from September through November. Choose unblemished, creamy-white heads with compact florets and bright green leaves. Old heads have a strong odor, while young ones have a faint cabbage smell. Refrigerate in a plastic bag for up to 5 days. To prepare, remove the outer green leaves and cut off the woody stalk. Soak the cauliflower, head down, in cold water for 30 minutes to refresh. For extra crispness, mix 1 teaspoon vinegar and 1 teaspoon salt into the soaking water.

What You Should Know: Some people have had a bad experience with mushy, overcooked cauliflower. Cooked properly, however, these compact white heads are delicious. If baking cauliflower, first parboil the head whole for about 10 minutes, which averts a bitter taste.

INDIAN BRAISED CAULIFLOWER

(*Gobi*)

5 TO 6 SERVINGS D OR P

Cauliflower is one of the most popular vegetables in India, especially in Jewish kitchens, where it is a culinary remnant of immigrants arriving from the Middle East. Jews in Calcutta adapted cauliflower to Indian cooking methods and seasonings, resulting in this lively, bright yellow dish. It is commonly cooked with spices and potatoes (aloo gobi), *which absorb the vegetable's flavor and extends the dish. Peas add an interesting contrast* (aloo gobi aur mater). *Be careful not to overcook the cauliflower, or it will take on an unpleasant aroma and texture. Serve with warm Indian breads, rice, and yogurt.*

1/4 cup *ghee* (Indian Clarified Butter, page 51)
   or vegetable oil
2 teaspoons black or yellow mustard seeds
   or 1 teaspoon mustard seeds and 1 teaspoon
   cumin seeds
2 teaspoons minced fresh ginger
1/2 teaspoon ground turmeric
1 head (about 2 pounds) cauliflower, cut into
   bite-sized florets
2 to 3 boiling potatoes, cut into 1/2-inch pieces
   (optional)
1/4 cup water
1 1/2 to 2 cups green peas (optional)
About 1/4 teaspoon table salt or 1/2 teaspoon
   kosher salt
Ground black pepper to taste
1/4 to 1/2 teaspoon cayenne pepper or red pepper
   flakes
About 2 tablespoons fresh lemon or lime juice
1/2 cup chopped fresh cilantro or parsley for garnish

1. In a karai (woklike Indian pan), wok, or large heavy skillet, melt the ghee over medium heat. Add the mustard seeds and sauté until they begin to pop, about 30 seconds. Add the ginger and turmeric and sauté until fragrant, about 30 seconds. Add the cauliflower and, if using, the potatoes and sauté until lightly browned, about 5 minutes.

2. Add the water, optional peas, salt, pepper, and cayenne. Cover, reduce the heat to medium-low, and cook, stirring occasionally, until just tender, 5 to 10 minutes. Remove from the heat and sprinkle with the lemon juice and, if using, the cilantro. Serve warm.

ITALIAN CAULIFLOWER PÂTÉ

(*Pasticcio di Cavolfiore*)

5 TO 6 SERVINGS   D OR P

Vegetable pâtés became the rage in America in the 1980s but have been commonplace in Italy for centuries. When I want to add a special touch to a meal, I will make a vegetable pâté, sometimes even a three-vegetable loaf with layers of carrots, broccoli, and cauliflower. This Italian cauliflower pâté is light, with a slightly pungent, nutlike flavor. Serve warm or at room temperature as a side dish or appetizer.

1 head (about 2 pounds) cauliflower, cut into florets

$1/4$ cup unsalted butter or olive oil

2 large eggs

2 tablespoons unbleached all-purpose flour

About $1/2$ teaspoon table salt or 1 teaspoon kosher salt

Ground white or black pepper to taste

$1/4$ teaspoon freshly grated nutmeg or pinch of cayenne (optional)

$1/2$ cup ($1 1/2$ ounces) grated Parmesan or Romano, or $1/2$ cup (2 ounces) Swiss cheese (optional)

1. Preheat the oven to 400°F. Grease a 6-cup baking dish or an 8-by-4-inch loaf pan, line the bottom with waxed paper, and grease again.

2. Bring a large pot of salted water to a boil and cook the cauliflower, uncovered, until tender but not at all mushy, about 12 minutes. Do not overcook. Drain.

3. In a blender or a food processor, purée the cauliflower and butter. Let cool, then blend in the eggs, flour, salt, pepper, and, if using, the nutmeg and Parmesan.

4. Pour into the prepared pan. Bake until golden, about 30 minutes. Serve warm or at room temperature. Invert onto a serving platter, remove the paper, and cut into wedges or slices.

VARIATIONS

Melt $1/2$ to 1 cup (2 to 4 ounces) shredded fontina, Gouda, Gruyère, or crumbled blue cheese in the top of a double boiler and spoon a little over the top of each slice of *pasticcio*.

Italian Cauliflower Custard (*Sformato di Cavolfiore*): Add 1 cup milk and increase the eggs to 4. Grease an 8-cup baking dish or 9-by-5-inch loaf pan, line the bottom with waxed paper, regrease, pour in the cauliflower mixture, and cover with a piece of greased waxed paper. Place the dish in a larger baking pan, add boiling water to reach halfway up the dish, and bake in a preheated 350°F oven until set, about 50 minutes.

SEPHARDIC CAULIFLOWER IN TOMATO SAUCE

(*Carnabeet*)

5 TO 6 SERVINGS   P

Sometimes both recipes and communities can be discovered in unexpected places. Seattle, Washington, boasts a significant Sephardic population, the third largest in America, numbering more than three thousand. By 1914, the city had three Sephardic congregations based on the members' distinct geographic origins: Turkey, Rhodes, and the Balkans. Each of these groups manifested distinct customs and forms of Sephardic cooking. Among the dishes still shared by the various Sephardic communities there is carnabeet, made using a classic Sephardic technique of simmering vegetables in tomato sauce. With cauliflower, sometimes the florets are deep-fried first to create additional layers of flavor. All of these variations are popular Rosh Hashanah and Sukkot fare.

1 head (about 2 pounds) cauliflower, cut into florets

SAUCE:

2 tablespoons olive oil or vegetable oil

1 onion, chopped

2 to 3 cloves garlic, minced (optional)

2 plum tomatoes, peeled, seeded, and crushed
   (see page 291), about $^1/_2$ cup; or $^1/_2$ cup
   crushed canned tomatoes

1 cup water

Pinch of salt

2 tablespoons fresh lemon juice

$^1/_4$ cup chopped fresh parsley for garnish
   (optional)

1. In a large pot of salted boiling water, cook the cauliflower, uncovered, until just crisp-tender, about 8 minutes. Do not overcook. Drain.

2. To make the sauce: In a large, heavy saucepan, heat the oil over medium heat. Add the onion and optional garlic and sauté until soft and translucent, about 5 minutes. Stir in the tomatoes, water, and salt and bring to a boil.

3. Add the cauliflower, cover, reduce the heat to low, and simmer until tender, about 10 minutes. Stir in the lemon juice. Serve warm or at room temperature. If desired, garnish with the parsley.

VARIATIONS

Syrian Cauliflower in Tomato Sauce (*Zahra bi Salsa*): Add $^1/_2$ teaspoon ground cumin with the tomatoes.

Sephardic Fried Cauliflower in Tomato Sauce (*Culupidia Frita con Salsa*): Follow Steps 1 to 4 for fried cauliflower (see page 235); add it to the tomato sauce, cover the saucepan or transfer to a greased 8-cup casserole, and bake in a preheated 350°F oven for 30 minutes. Serve warm.

Yemenite Fried Cauliflower

(*Zahra Mi'lee*)

5 TO 6 SERVINGS   P

Whenever I eat these deep-fried florets, I am transported back to Israel and the first time I tried them in a Yemenite restaurant. The tender cauliflower in this dish makes an interesting contrast to the crisp yellow coating, while frying imparts a slightly smoky flavor. A variation is to coat the cauliflower in lightly beaten eggs, then in flour or matza meal. To be sure, this dish has its roots in the Arabian Peninsula, but it was adapted by Yemenite Jews who brought it to the Promised Land and, like much of the rest of their cooking, influenced the Israeli culinary scene. It is served accompanied with lemon wedges or tahini.

1 head (about 2 pounds) cauliflower,
   cut into large florets

BATTER:
$^1/_2$ cup unbleached all-purpose flour

1 teaspoon ground cumin

$^1/_4$ teaspoon ground turmeric

$^1/_2$ teaspoon table salt or 1 teaspoon kosher salt

Dash of ground black pepper

2 large eggs, lightly beaten

2 tablespoons water

Vegetable oil for deep-frying

Table salt or kosher salt for sprinkling (optional)

Lemon wedges or tahini (Middle Eastern Sesame
   Sauce, page 430), optional

1. In a large pot of salted boiling water, cook the cauliflower, uncovered, until crisp-tender, about 5 minutes. Do not overcook. Drain and let cool slightly.

2. To make the batter: In a large bowl, combine the flour, cumin, turmeric, salt, and pepper. Add the eggs and water and blend until smooth and not runny. This can also be done in a blender. If necessary, adjust the consistency by adding a little flour or liquid. (A well-blended batter should literally hop off the spoon when dropped into the oil, not disintegrate or run off in a stream.) Let stand for 45 minutes.

3. In a large, heavy skillet or saucepan, heat about 2 inches oil over medium heat to 375°F until almost smoking.

4. Dip the florets into the batter, letting the excess drip off. In batches, fry until golden brown on all sides, 2 to 3 minutes. Using a slotted spoon, transfer to paper towels to drain. Sprinkle with the salt, if desired. Serve warm, with lemon wedges if you like. The cauliflower can be transferred to a wire rack set on a baking sheet and kept warm in 300°F oven while preparing the remaining batches.

SEPHARDIC CAULIFLOWER PATTIES

(Keftes de Culupidia)

5 TO 6 SERVINGS   P

Fried patties are another distinctive Sephardic way of preparing vegetables. The coating can be omitted, but the patties will be less crisp. This is a popular Passover and Hanukkah dish, commonly served with yogurt, lemon wedges, agristada (Egg-Lemon Sauce, page 431), or tomato sauce.

> 1 medium-large head (about 2^{1}/$_{4}$ pounds)
>   cauliflower, cut into florets
> 3 large eggs, lightly beaten
> 1 onion, minced
> ^{1}/$_{3}$ cup chopped fresh parsley
> About ^{3}/$_{4}$ teaspoon table salt or 1^{1}/$_{2}$ teaspoons
>   kosher salt
> Ground white or black pepper to taste
> About 1 cup fresh bread crumbs or matza meal
>
> COATING:
> 1 large egg, lightly beaten
> Flour for dredging
>
> Olive oil or vegetable oil for frying

1. In a large pot of salted boiling water, cook the cauliflower, uncovered, until tender but not mushy, about 12 minutes. Do not overcook. Drain. Finely chop or mash with a fork.

2. In a medium bowl, combine the cauliflower, eggs, onion, parsley, salt, and pepper. Add bread crumbs until the mixture is thick enough to mold.

3. Shape the cauliflower mixture into oval patties 3 inches long and 2 inches wide, with tapered ends. To coat: Dip the patties into the beaten egg, then dredge in the flour.

4. In a large, heavy skillet over medium heat, heat a thin layer of oil. In batches, add the patties and fry, turning, until golden brown, about 3 minutes per side. Keep warm in a low oven while preparing the remainder. Serve warm. Or, reheat in a 250°F oven for about 20 minutes.

VARIATION

Italian Cauliflower Patties (*Fritelle de Cavolfiore*): Add ^{1}/$_{4}$ cup grated Parmesan or Romano cheese and omit the coating.

❧ CELERY ❧

Celery, a member of the Umbelliferae family, originated in marshy areas along the shore of the eastern Mediterranean, where uncultivated rudimentary celery, also called smallage or water parsley, can still be found. Wild celery, which is inedible when raw, was valued primarily for its flavorful seeds and leaves. Celery seeds, possessing a warm, pungent flavor, were used medicinally for a variety of ailments, including colds, indigestion, hangovers, arthritis, gout, and liver problems. The leaves, similar in appearance and usage to those of its relative parsley, were utilized as an herb, sometimes eaten raw but primarily cooked. The Romans incorporated the leaves and stalks in everything from appetizers to dessert, adding it profusely to nearly every salad and sauce.

Even when the celery plant was cultivated more than two thousand years ago, it remained bitter and intensely flavored. Our familiar contemporary celery—crisp, sweet, and succulent, with overlapping stalks relatively free of strings—was developed in late-seventeenth-century Italy and barely resembles its wild ancestor, which had hollow, woody, spreading stalks with inedible fibrous strings. There are two types of cultivated stalk celery: self-blanching (yellow) and green (Pascal). Most western celery is the Pascal type, bright green, crisp, and sweet. Pascal is sometimes grown with the stalks shielded from direct sunlight, to produce a white, softer stalk.

Celery found its way into Jewish ritual as *karpas* (likely related to the Farsi *karafs*, "green"), the fresh green herb at the Passover Seder representing spring and renewal, probably in accord with the Greek custom of eating celery leaves or parsley at the start of the meal to stimulate the appetite. *Karpas* is dipped into saltwater or vinegar at the start of the Seder to stimluate the children's curiosity, as neither dipping food nor serving appetizers were at that point a Jewish practice. Otherwise, in Jewish cooking, celery has been primarily a flavoring component for soups, stews, stuffings, and salads. In the Middle East, however, it sometimes serves as the main ingredient, and may be stuffed, pickled, or cooked in a vinaigrette until limp. A venerable Sephardic dish features stewed celery in a cumin-accented chickpea sauce. Persians combine it with a few seasonings to create a tasty stew for topping rice.

PERSIAN CELERY STEW

(Khoreshe Karafs)

6 TO 8 SERVINGS

This dish was developed as a way of turning inexpensive ingredients into a filling and satisfying meal. Wild celery is known in the Talmud as "karpas of the rivers," a distinction from its close relative parsley, which is called "karpas of the mountains." Celery gives this dish a clean herbal and mineral flavor with a suggestion of pepper, while the parsley adds a pleasing, grassy note. Using smallage, sometimes available in Italian markets, or Chinese celery produces a more aggressive flavor than the subtle, more common Pascal celery.

An Iranian cook once told me that the outer celery stalks have more flavor than celery hearts. Do not use blanched celery, which is white Pascal grown in trenches, as it is too mild. This stew can be served simply, focusing on the celery, or made more complex with the addition of carrots, artichoke hearts, fava beans, or other common Middle Eastern vegetables. Like other Persian stews, it is customarily served with rice. For a tarter flavor, add the lime or lemon juice.

1/4 cup vegetable oil

1 large onion, chopped

2 bunches smallage or green celery (3 pounds total), cut into 1-inch pieces, including leaves

2 cups Vegetable Stock (page 115) or water

1 1/2 cups chopped fresh flat-leaf parsley

3 tablespoons dried mint, crushed

Salt to taste

Ground black pepper to taste

1/4 to 1/3 cup fresh lime or lemon juice (optional)

1. In a large saucepan, heat the oil over medium heat. Add the onion and sauté until soft and translucent, about 5 minutes. Add the smallage and sauté for about 5 minutes.

2. Add the stock and bring to a boil. Cover, reduce the heat to low, and simmer until nearly tender, about 30 minutes.

3. Add the parsley, mint, salt, pepper, and, if using, the lime juice. Cook, uncovered, until the celery is tender and the sauce thickened, about 10 minutes. Serve warm.

VARIATION

Sweet-and-Sour Celery Stew (*Khoreshe Karafs*): Add 2 to 3 tablespoons sugar with the lime juice.

CHARD

Chard, a native of the eastern Mediterranean, is also called Swiss chard, blette, leaf beet, spinach beet, white beet, and silverbeet. This member of the Chenopodiaceae (goosefoot) family is so closely related and linked to the beet that they share the same name in Hebrew (*selek*), Aramaic (*silka*), and Arabic (*silq*). The English word *chard* in fact derives from the French name for cardoon (*carde*), perhaps because chard's white stems, which are generally detached from the leaves, resemble a peeled and cut cardoon. Some people took to calling it Swiss chard (the vegetable was not popular in Switzerland; rather, the botanist who gave chard its scientific name was Swiss), to distinguish it from cardoons. Unlike the beet, chard never developed a large edible root; its culinary usage has remained its leaves.

Swiss chard grows best in coastal areas with plentiful rainfall, and it is in those countries around the Mediterranean where it is primarily used. Easy to grow, chard (its leaves regenerate after cutting) tolerates both heat and cold, and so it was historically among the few greens available in winter.

What You Should Know: Crinkled chard leaves range in color from dark green to red; the stalks are white or red. Avoid chard with any browning on the stalks or yellowing on the leaves. Store in plastic bags in the refrigerator for up to 3 days. Chard has an earthy flavor with a bitter undertone. Young chard leaves can be used fresh in salads. Older leaves are used like spinach, while the tougher stalks are cooked like asparagus and celery or puréed. The stalks are usually detached and cooked separately or in stages.

Chard is generally prepared simply, rounded out by a basic olive oil dressing. It is also added to stews, used as a filling for pastry or pasta, or stuffed like cabbage leaves. Italians add it to winter lentil and white bean soups. Syrians use it in pancakes, omelets, dips, and stews. Like the closely related beet greens, chard is a traditional Rosh Hashanah food.

TUNISIAN BRAISED CHARD

(*Silka*)

6 TO 8 SERVINGS   Ⓟ

Tunisians manifest a particular love of chard, alone, in stews with chickpeas or lentils, or added to rishta *(fettuccine). As one Tunisian explained to me, "The leaves can be cooked for a long time without falling apart like most greens do." I find the best way to season this dish is simply with a little olive oil, lemon juice, and pepper flakes. Adding the pepper flakes early in the cooking disperses the heat evenly through the dish; adding them near the end results in scattered spots of heat. Serve this as a side dish, accompanied with couscous or rice, or toss with fettuccine.*

2 pounds chard, soaked in a large bowl of cold
     water several times and drained

$1/4$ cup extra-virgin olive oil

1 large onion, chopped

1 to 2 cloves garlic, minced

$1/4$ to $1/2$ teaspoon red pepper flakes

2 plum tomatoes, peeled, seeded, and chopped
     (see page 291), optional

About 2 tablespoons fresh lemon juice

About $1/4$ teaspoon table salt or $1/2$ teaspoon
     kosher salt

1. Separate the chard leaves from the stems. Cut the stems into $1/2$-inch-wide pieces and the leaves into 1-inch pieces. There should be about 8 cups.

2. In a large saucepan, heat the oil over medium heat. Add the onion and garlic and sauté until soft and translucent, about 5 minutes. Add the chard stems, cover, reduce the heat to low, and simmer for 3 minutes.

3. Add the leaves, pepper flakes, and, if using, the tomatoes and sauté for 1 minute. Cover and cook until tender, about 10 minutes. (Some cooks add the pepper flakes to cook only for the last minute.) Stir in the lemon juice and salt. Serve warm.

VARIATIONS

Sephardic Pastry Filling (*Gomo de Silka*): Stir 1 large beaten egg into the cooked greens. Use to fill *sigares* (Moroccan Phyllo Cigars, page 196), *borekas* (Turkish Turnovers, page 176), or other filled pastries.

Moroccan Chard Salad (*Shlata Silka*): Substitute 2 teaspoons sweet paprika and 1 teaspoon ground cumin for the pepper flakes.

Syrian Chard with Chickpeas (*Silka bi Hummus*): This dish combines two Rosh Hashanah symbols in one dish. Omit the pepper flakes and add $1 1/2$ cups cooked chickpeas with the chard leaves.

❧ COLLARD ❧

Collard (also called collard greens or collards) and its close relative kale are both primitive nonheading cabbages native to the eastern Mediterranean or Asia Minor, cultivated since prehistoric times. Consisting of a large stalk with broad, loose oval leaves similar to those of the original wild cabbage, collard is milder than the crinkly leaved, bitter kale. In many early cultures, the collard stalk was the preferred part of the plant to eat. Both the Greeks and Romans consumed a good deal of collard (and kale; the two were then rarely distinguished), as it was an extremely easy plant to grow. However, as milder, more versatile varieties of cabbage emerged, the use of collard steadily declined, and today it is best known as an African food or American soul food; in America it is traditionally accompanied with hot sauce and vinegar. In Ethiopian cuisine, collard greens remain part of the Jewish culinary tradition, following only cabbage and onions in importance among vegetables.

What You Should Know: Collard and kale are extremely nutritious. Collard is a winter crop, best from January to April; cool weather produces a higher sugar content and an interesting, almost smoky flavor. Look for firm deep green leaves with no sign of wilting, yellowing, or browning. Store unwashed greens in plastic bags in the refrigerator for up to 5 days. The leaves' bitter taste will increase during storage.

To prepare, remove the stem and tough central rib from the leaves—approximately half of the collard's weight. Tough, assertive greens like collard require a relatively long cooking time and a lot of liquid to soften and remove the bitterness. The greens are commonly mixed with white beans or black-eyed peas. Ethiopians usually add plenty of spices, particularly chilies.

ETHIOPIAN COLLARD GREENS

(*Yeabesha Gomen*)

4 TO 5 SERVINGS

Growing up in the South, I certainly heard of collard greens, but I never actually ever saw any until years later when I was dining at the home of an Ethiopian family in Israel. I watched the grandmother systematically pull the large, dull green leaves from the central stalk, inspect them for signs of yellow or decay, wash them well, and finally shred them with a knife. Unlike the western African style of slow cooking greens "down to a low gravy," Ethiopians first boil the greens in salted water to remove the excess bitterness, then, after draining, stew, cream, or purée them, the way that primitive cabbages were prepared in the ancient Middle East.

These cooked collard greens have a slightly bitter, vaguely cabbagelike flavor, accented by chilies and a little ginger. Ethiopians customarily serve collard greens as an accompaniment to a wot *(Ethiopian Vegetable Stew, page 303) and injera (Ethiopian flat bread).*

> 1 pound collard greens, stemmed and coarsely chopped (about 7 cups)
> 3 tablespoons *niter kebbeh* (Ethiopian Spiced Clarified Butter, page 52), *ghee,* or vegetable oil
> 2 red or yellow onions, chopped
> 1 to 2 cloves garlic, minced
> 1/2 teaspoon grated fresh ginger (optional)
> 3 to 4 large green chilies, such as Anaheim, seeded and chopped or sliced, or 1 to 3 small hot green chilies, seeded and minced, or about 1/2 teaspoon cayenne
> 1 cup water
> Salt to taste
> Ground black pepper to taste

1. In a large pot of salted boiling water, cook the collard greens, covered, until tender but not mushy, about 10 minutes. Older leaves may require a longer cooking time. Drain. Plunge into cold water, drain, and press out the excess liquid.

2. In a large skillet, melt the niter kebbeh over medium heat. Add the onions and sauté until golden, about 15 minutes. Add the garlic and, if using, the ginger and sauté until fragrant, about 1 minute. Add the chilies and sauté for 2 minutes.

3. Add the greens, water, salt, and pepper. Reduce the heat to low and simmer, stirring occasionally, for 15 minutes. Serve warm or at room temperature.

VARIATIONS

Ethiopian Collard Greens in Tomato Sauce (*Yeabesha Gomen*): Use the minced small chilies and omit the ginger. After sautéing the chilies in Step 2, add 4 peeled, seeded, and chopped plum tomatoes (see page 291), but do not add the water yet. After cooking the tomatoes for 15 minutes, dissolve 1 tablespoon unbleached all-purpose flour in 3 tablespoons fresh lemon juice in a small bowl, stir in 1 cup water, add to the pot, and simmer until the sauce thickens, about 3 minutes.

Ethiopian Collard Greens with Cheese (*Ayib be Gomen*): Spiced butter is added to soft fresh cheese in this dish for flavor and texture. Combine 1 pound farmer or pot cheese, 1/4 cup *niter kebbeh* (Ethiopian Spiced Clarified Butter, page 52), 2 to 3 mashed cloves garlic, and about 1/2 teaspoon table salt or 1 teaspoon kosher salt and spoon over the top of or mix into the greens. To replicate *niter kebbeh*, combine 1/4 cup *ghee* or softened butter, 1/2 teaspoon ground cardamom, 1/4 teaspoon ground ginger, 1/8 teaspoon ground cinnamon, and 1/8 teaspoon ground cloves.

❧ EGGPLANT ❧

In a popular Ladino folksong, "Si Savesh la Buena Djente" ("Dear People, Do You Know of the Battle of the Vegetables," page 242), the eggplant and tomato argue over which is the superior food. Judging by the import and variety of eggplant recipes in the Sephardic repertoire, it might just be the winner, or perhaps the answer is that both vegetables are at their best when married with each other. Jewish exiles fleeing southern Spain following the arrival of the fanatical Almohads in 1146, and again fleeing from Spain and Spanish-controlled Sicily and southern Italy in 1492, helped to popularize the eggplant throughout much of the Mediterranean, spreading the vegetables and numerous dishes made with it. This strikingly beautiful vegetable eventually became a staple of the light and varied cookery of the Mediterranean, beloved today by every level of society.

Originally eggplant was a native of India, where it has been cultivated for more than four thousand years. The plant's path from its homeland can be traced backward through its French name, *aubergine*, which is derived from the Catalan *alberginia*, which comes from the Arabic *al-batinjan* by way of the Persian word *badenjan*, which itself comes from the Sanskrit *vatin-ganah* ("antiflatulence vegetable"). By the fourth century C.E., the eggplant arrived in Persia, where it quickly became a favorite vegetable. In the eighth century, the Arabs began spreading the plant westward; it probably reached Spain in the late ninth century, where it was enthusiastically received and soon appeared in numerous Moorish and Sephardic recipes. The attitude was very different, however, in the rest of Europe, where eggplant was considered poisonous and utilized only as a garden ornament.

A member of the nightshade family, the eggplant is actually a very large berry. It was originally small, white, and ovate, hence its American name (the French name *aubergine* supplanted the name *eggplant* in Britain in the eighteenth century). Since the white type bruises easily, the more familiar purple hybrid has become the most widespread, although white eggplants are available in some markets.

The rich, meaty texture of the versatile eggplant makes it an ideal meat substitute. Eggplants are very porous and therefore absorb a copious amount of oil. Indeed, a lack of concern over the amount of olive oil used to fry eggplant was once a sign of wealth in the Middle East.

Cooked eggplant has a subtle flavor that is deliciously complemented by a large variety of assertive vegetables and seasonings. In addition, it soaks up spices, marinades, and toppings so that the flavors meld into the flesh of the eggplant. Eggplant can be prepared in an endless variety of ways—Turks claim more than thirty different basic methods—including fried, roasted, grilled, boiled, stuffed, marinated, pickled, and stewed. Eggplant is certainly the most popular vegetable in its native India, where numerous varieties, in various shapes and colors, are sold at almost every market, large or small. And it has long been a mainstay from central Asia through north Africa. Georgians incorporate it into a myriad of stews, salads, and relishes. Syrians love stuffed eggplants and pickled baby eggplants. Moroccans serve it in *tagines* with couscous and make it into eggplant jam. Sephardim serve plain or marinated fried eggplant slices cold as part of a Sabbath lunch and *meze* (appetizer assortment) or warm as a side dish, usually accompanied with a tomato sauce or *labni* (yogurt cheese). They also use it in casseroles, stews, salads, omelets, pickles, as a pastry filling, and even for confections.

SI SAVESH LA BUENA DJENTE

(DEAR PEOPLE, DO YOU KNOW OF THE BATTLE OF THE VEGETABLES?)

translated from the Ladino

Dear people, do you know of the battle of
the vegetables?
All is put before you.
The tomato rises up from the center:
"My food is famous, better than the eggplant!"

The eggplant responds:
"Be quiet, tomato.
You are not worth a penny.
Two days in the basket,
you are ready for the garbage!"

The tomato responds:
"Be quiet, eggplant.
You are not worth a penny.
Many mouths are holding themselves in
wait for me.
From the fish at the beginning,
in the rice I am submerged.
If you speak of appetite,
the salad is me."

The eggplant responds:
"Be quiet, tomato.
You are not worth a penny.
When the best people come down,
using the most expensive oil,
alburnia* is the result!
My food is the most praised,
better than the tomato!"

Alburnia is a popular eggplant relish similar to kahrmus *(Moroccan Eggplant Relish, page 78), named after the large earthenware vessel in which it was originally cooked.*

What You Should Know: The globe eggplant is the largest eggplant variety, growing up to 10 inches long, and the most common in the West, with a thick, deep-purple skin and many large seeds. Although its diameter is best for slicing into cutlets, the globe is less flavorful than some other, smaller, varieties, such as Japanese eggplants, Sicilian eggplants, and white eggplants. Eggplants with a round bottom, sometimes called males, contain fewer seeds and are less bitter than those with a deep indentation on the bottom, called females. Choose firm, blemish-free eggplants with dark, glossy skin and a bright green calyx (cap). Eggplants should feel heavy for their size; puffy or overly soft eggplants tend to be bitter. Store in the warmest part of the refrigerator, uncovered, for up to 5 days. Eggplant increases in bitterness the longer it is stored. If the temperature is too cold, the insides will darken.

Salting, which has little effect on the eggplant's bitterness, does extract excess moisture and limits the amount of oil the eggplant can absorb. When cooked without salting, the result is usually greasy, mushy, and bland. (Baby eggplants do not require salting.) For those on a low-salt diet, omit the salting and steam the sliced or cubed eggplant before other cooking until tender but not mushy, about 4 minutes, then gently press between several layers of paper towels to extract the moisture. A Sephardic method of frying eggplant without absorbing too much oil is to dip it into egg first.

GREEK MARINATED FRIED EGGPLANT

(*Melitzanes Tiganites*)

6 TO 8 SERVINGS

It is impossible to be served an Israeli meze *(appetizer assortment) that does not contain at least one and frequently a myriad of eggplant dishes. It is inspiring as well as a bit intimidating to watch a professional* meze *chef adeptly carve, salt, and cook crates of eggplants, all the while keeping a watchful eye on a host of other dishes. Fried eggplant slices are among the most widespread Middle Eastern appetizers and side dishes, eaten warm from the skillet or marinated, and, since they can be prepared well ahead and served cold, they are common on the Sabbath. A typical Sephardic Sabbath morning breakfast includes assorted salads, cheese pastries, brown eggs, and marinated eggplant, the tender and strongly seasoned disks stimulating the taste buds.*

> 2 medium-large eggplants (about 1 1/2 pounds each), peeled
> About 1 tablespoon table salt or 2 tablespoons kosher salt
> Olive oil or vegetable oil for frying
>
> **MARINADE:**
> 1/4 cup red wine vinegar
> 2 to 3 tablespoons fresh lemon juice
> 1/4 cup chopped fresh parsley or cilantro
> 2 to 3 cloves garlic, minced
> Pinch of salt
> Ground black pepper to taste
> 1 teaspoon dried thyme or marjoram (optional)
> 1/4 cup extra-virgin olive oil

1. Cut the eggplants into ½-inch-thick crosswise slices, then into ½-inch-wide sticks. Put in a colander or on a wire rack, sprinkle lightly with the salt, and let stand for at least 1 hour. (Moisture will appear on the surface, and the eggplant will become more pliable.) Rinse the eggplant under cold water, then repeatedly press between several layers of paper towels until the slices feel firm and dry. The eggplant can be stored in the refrigerator for up to 4 hours.

2. In a large skillet, heat about 3 tablespoons oil over medium heat. In several batches, adding about 3 tablespoons more oil between batches, fry the eggplant, turning, until fork-tender and dark brown, but not burnt, 3 to 5 minutes per side. Using a slotted spatula, transfer to paper towels to drain.

3. To make the marinade: In a small bowl, combine the vinegar, lemon juice, parsley, garlic, salt, pepper, and optional thyme. In a slow, steady stream, whisk in the oil. Drizzle over the warm eggplant slices. Let cool to room temperature. Refrigerate, turning occasionally, for at least 2 hours or up to 2 days to allow the eggplant to absorb the marinade. Serve chilled or at room temperature.

Georgian Fried Eggplant in Walnut Sauce (*Badrijani Nigozit*): Substitute 1 cup *bazha* (Georgian Walnut Sauce, page 432) for the marinade and refrigerate for at least 6 hours.

Indian Fried Eggplant (*Brinjal*): Omit the marinade. Before frying, sprinkle the eggplant slices with about 1 teaspoon ground coriander and 1 teaspoon ground cumin. Afterwards, toss with 2 cups plain yogurt. Store in the refrigerator for up to 1 day.

Moroccan Fried Eggplant and Pepper Salad (*Salade d'Aubergines et Poivrons*): Roast, peel, and slice 5 to 6 red, yellow, or green bell peppers into strips (see page 267, Step 1). In Step 3, toss with the eggplant slices. If desired, add 2 to 3 rinsed and chopped preserved lemons.

Persian Fried Eggplant in Yogurt (*Badenjan Mfassakh*): This *meze* favorite, also called *borani badenjan*, usually contains mint as well as yogurt, both ingredients proving refreshing contrasts to the frequently torrid Persian climate. In place of the marinade in the main recipe, combine 2 cups thick plain yogurt or *labni* (Middle Eastern Yogurt Cheese, page 48), 1 tablespoon crushed dried mint or ½ cup chopped fresh mint, 1 to 2 cloves garlic mashed with a pinch of salt, and ⅓ cup chopped fresh cilantro or parsley. Store in the refrigerator for up to 1 day.

Sephardic Fried Eggplant (*Berengena Frita*): Before frying, dredge the eggplant sticks in flour, then dip into a lightly beaten egg. Or, dip the eggplant sticks in beaten eggs, then in bread crumbs or matza meal.

INDIAN CURRIED EGGPLANT

(Brinjal Kari)

In this southern Indian one-dish meal, eggplant is enhanced by a thick sauce, full of rich spices and seasonings. Frying mustard seeds, chilies, and curry leaves together is typical of southern Indian cooking. Curried eggplant is generally accompanied with rice and yogurt. I have also used it in a strudel.

2 eggplants (about 1 1/2 pounds total), peeled

About 2 teaspoons table salt or 4 teaspoons
    kosher salt

1/4 cup peanut oil or vegetable oil

1/2 teaspoon black mustard seeds

1 large onion, chopped

1 tablespoon minced fresh ginger

1 teaspoon minced small hot green chili

2 cloves garlic, minced

1 1/2 teaspoons cumin seeds

10 to 12 curry leaves (see Note)

3 bell peppers, or 1 each green, red, and yellow
    bell pepper, seeded, deribbed (white removed),
    and cut into 1-inch pieces

1/2 cup water

About 1/2 teaspoon table salt or 1 teaspoon
    kosher salt

1 teaspoon dried oregano or 2 teaspoons
    chopped fresh basil

1 pound plum tomatoes, peeled, seeded, and
    quartered (see page 291), about 2 1/2 cups

2 cups dried chickpeas, picked over, soaked in
    water to cover for 12 hours, drained, rinsed,
    and cooked (see page 329, Step 1)

2 teaspoons honey

1 teaspoon ground turmeric

8 ounces spinach, washed, drained, stemmed,
    and chopped (about 4 cups)

2 tablespoons chopped fresh cilantro or parsley

1. Cut the eggplants crosswise into 1-inch-thick slices, then into 1-inch-wide sticks, then into 1-inch cubes. Put in a colander or on a wire rack, sprinkle lightly with the salt, and let stand for at least 1 hour. (Moisture will appear on the surface, and the eggplant will become more pliable.) Rinse the eggplant under cold water, then repeatedly press between several layers of paper towels until the slices feel firm and dry. The eggplant can be stored in the refrigerator for up to 4 hours.

2. In a karai (woklike Indian pan), wok, or large heavy pot, heat the oil over medium heat. Add the mustard seeds and sauté until they begin to pop, about 30 seconds. Stir in the onion, then the ginger, chili, garlic, and cumin and sauté until the onion is softened, about 5 minutes. Add the curry leaves and sauté until crisp. Add the eggplant and bell peppers and sauté until softened, about 5 minutes.

3. Stir in the water, salt, and oregano. Cover and simmer over low heat or cook in a preheated 350°F oven, stirring occasionally, until the eggplant is tender, about 30 minutes.

4. Add the tomatoes, chickpeas, honey, and turmeric. Cover and heat through, about 5 minutes. Uncover and cook 5 minutes, or until most of the liquid evaporates. Add the spinach and cilantro and simmer until tender, about 5 minutes. Serve warm.

NOTE Curry leaf, *kari patta* or *meetha neem* in Hindi, is a small shiny, aromatic green leaf native to southern India. It resembles but does not taste like a bay leaf. The curry leaf lent its name to curry powder, to which it is occasionally added. The leaf imparts a sharp, spicy flavor (hints of lemon, pepper, and sage) to foods. Dried and sometimes even fresh curry leaves are available in Indian markets. If you don't have any curry leaves, then make the dish without them.

Turkish Eggplant and Cheese Casserole

(*Almodrote de Berengena*)

6 TO 8 SERVINGS Ⓓ

In the Ottoman Empire, Sephardic vegetable-egg-and-cheese casseroles became known as almodrote *or* almudroti, *Ladino for "hodgepodge." The three favorite types used eggplant, spinach, and zucchini, or a combination. Eggplant has a great affinity for cheese, which actually bolsters the vegetable's flavor while helping to bind the casserole and blend with the eggs to create a custardy texture. For a more pungent flavor, use feta; for a milder, creamier consistency, use farmer or cream cheese. This venerable dish is served warm as an appetizer for Friday night dinner and a main course at various dairy meals, as well as at room temperature as part of a* desayuno, *a Sabbath brunch.*

2 eggplants (about 2¹/₂ pounds total)

1 cup (5 ounces) crumbled feta or 1 cup
    (8 ounces) farmer or cream cheese

1 cup (4 ounces) shredded kashkaval, Gruyère,
    or yellow Cheddar cheese

3 large eggs, lightly beaten

³/₄ cup fresh bread crumbs, matza cake meal,
    or mashed potatoes

About ¹/₂ teaspoon table salt or 1 teaspoon
    kosher salt

Ground black pepper to taste

Pinch of sugar

About 1 tablespoon olive oil for drizzling

1. Light a fire in a charcoal grill or preheat the broiler. Cut several slits in the eggplants. Roast over the hot coals or 5 inches from the heat source of the broiler, turning occasionally, until charred and tender, about 40 minutes. Or, place on a baking sheet and bake in a preheated 400°F oven until very tender, about 50 minutes. Let stand long enough so that you can handle. Peel the eggplant, being careful not to leave any skin. Place in a colander and let drain for about 30 minutes. Coarsely chop; do not purée.

2. Preheat the oven to 350°F. Oil a shallow 8-cup baking dish, such as an 8-inch square or a 7-by-11-inch dish.

3. In a large bowl, combine the feta cheese, ¹/₂ cup of the shredded cheese, the eggs, bread crumbs, salt, pepper, and sugar. Stir in the eggplant. Pour into the prepared dish and drizzle with a little oil.

4. Bake for 20 minutes. Sprinkle with the remaining shredded cheese and bake until golden brown, about 25 minutes. Let stand for at least 5 minutes before serving. Serve warm or at room temperature.

VARIATION

Sephardic Eggplant, Zucchini, and Cheese Casserole (*Almodrote de Berengena y Kalavasa*): Use only 1 eggplant. Cut 1¹/₂ pounds zucchini into chunks and simmer until just tender; drain, coarsely mash, and add with the eggplant.

Yemenite Eggplant Casserole

(Batinjan bil Firan)

6 TO 8 SERVINGS   P

During one of my stints studying in Israel, the evening cook at my school was a Yemenite woman, who six days a week single-handedly whipped up a range of Middle Eastern vegetarian fare for dinner, showing a particular fondness for eggplant. One of her tastiest dishes was a relatively simple but flavorful eggplant casserole layered with a lightly spicy tomato sauce. Unlike meat sauces, which require a long cooking time to meld the flavors, tomato sauce should be cooked just long enough to thicken it and mellow the acid in the tomato, but not too long to impair the fruity flavor. Good-tasting raw tomatoes produce good sauces, but canned tomatoes are preferable when fresh ones are out of season. If the sauce lacks verve, add a little mild wine vinegar, a few drops of hot sauce, or a pinch of red pepper flakes near the end of cooking. This dish is generally accompanied with flat bread.

3 eggplants (about 3³/₄ pounds total), peeled

About 1 tablespoon table salt or 2 tablespoons
    kosher salt

Olive oil or vegetable oil for frying

SAUCE:

¹/₄ cup olive oil or vegetable oil

2 onions, chopped

4 to 5 cloves garlic, minced

2 to 3 teaspoons ground cumin

¹/₂ teaspoon ground turmeric

2¹/₄ pounds plum tomatoes, peeled, seeded, and
    chopped (see page 291), about 6 cups

About 1 teaspoon table salt or 2 teaspoons
    kosher salt

¹/₂ teaspoon sweet paprika

About ¹/₈ teaspoon cayenne

Ground black pepper to taste

1. Cut the eggplants crosswise into ¹/₂-inch-thick slices. Put in a colander or on a wire rack, sprinkle lightly with the salt, and let stand for at least 1 hour. (Moisture will appear on the surface, and the eggplant will become more pliable.) Rinse the eggplant under cold water, then repeatedly press between several layers of paper towels until the slices feel firm and dry. The eggplant can be stored in the refrigerator for up to 4 hours.

2. In a large, heavy skillet, heat about 3 tablespoons oil over medium heat. In batches, fry the eggplant, turning and adding 3 tablespoons more oil between batches, until lightly browned and fork-tender, 3 to 5 minutes per side. Using a slotted spatula, transfer to paper towels to drain.

3. To make the sauce: Heat the oil in a large saucepan over medium heat. Add the onions and sauté until soft and translucent, 5 to 10 minutes. Add the garlic, cumin, and turmeric and sauté for 30 seconds.

4. Add the tomatoes, salt, paprika, cayenne, and pepper. Bring to a boil, reduce the heat to low, and simmer, uncovered, stirring occasionally, until the tomatoes break down to a sauce, about 30 minutes. The sauce may be cooled and stored in the refrigerator for up to 3 days.

5. Preheat the oven to 350°F. Oil a 7-by-11-inch or 9-by-13-inch casserole.

6. Arrange a layer of eggplant slices in the prepared casserole and spread with a layer of sauce. Repeat layering until all the eggplant is used, ending with a layer of sauce.

7. Bake until heated through, about 30 minutes. Serve warm or at room temperature.

North African Fried Eggplant "Sandwiches"

(Beitinajn Mi'ili)

5 TO 6 SERVINGS

Among many Jews from North Africa, no Sabbath would be considered complete without eggplant "sandwiches." More than a simple and tasty dish eaten for generations, this traditional treat (called mafroum *in Libya) featuring a meat, mushroom, or cheese filling sandwiched between layers of eggplant, represents the biblical manna, which fell between layers of dew—adding a mystical element to each bite.*

2 medium-large eggplants (about 1 1/2 pounds
    each), peeled
About 1 tablespoon table salt or 2 tablespoons
    kosher salt
Olive oil or vegetable oil for frying

FILLING:

1 cup (8 ounces) creamy feta cheese
    or cream cheese, softened
1 large egg yolk
1/2 cup (2 ounces) shredded haloumi
    or mozzarella cheese
Salt to taste

Unbleached all-purpose flour for dredging
2 large eggs, lightly beaten
Fresh bread crumbs or matza meal
Vegetable oil for deep-frying

1. Cut the eggplants crosswise into 1/2-inch-thick slices. Put in a colander or on a wire rack, sprinkle lightly with the salt, and let stand for at least 1 hour. (Moisture will appear on the surface, and the eggplant will become more pliable.) Rinse the eggplant under cold water, then press repeatedly between several layers of paper towels until the slices feel firm and dry. The eggplant can be covered and stored in the refrigerator for up to 4 hours.

2. In a large skillet, heat about 3 tablespoons oil over medium heat. In batches, fry the eggplant slices, turning and adding 3 tablespoons oil between each batch, until golden brown but still slightly undercooked, 2 to 3 minutes per side. Using a slotted spatula, transfer to paper towels to drain.

3. To make the filling: In a medium bowl, beat together the feta cheese and egg yolk until smooth. Stir in the shredded cheese and salt.

4. Using a knife, spread the stuffing over half of the eggplant slices and top with the remaining slices to form sandwiches. Dredge the sandwiches in the flour, dip in the egg, then coat with the bread crumbs.

5. In a large skillet, heat at least 1 inch of oil in a large skillet over medium heat to about 370°F. Fry the sandwiches, turning, until golden brown, 2 to 3 minutes per side. Drain on paper towels. Serve warm or at room temperature.

VARIATIONS

Mushroom-Cheese Stuffing: Omit shredded cheese. Sauté 2 minced shallots in 2 tablespoons vegetable oil until soft, about 2 minutes; add 8 ounces chopped mushrooms; sauté until the liquid evaporates, about 10 minutes. Purée if desired. Stir into feta mixture.

Potato-Cheese Stuffing: Substitute 3/4 cup mashed potatoes for the feta cheese and increase the shredded cheese to 1 cup (4 ounces).

Baked Eggplant "Sandwiches" (Beitinajn bil Firan): After frying the eggplant slices and making sandwiches, do not coat and fry. Instead, arrange in a single layer in a large oiled baking dish, pour 2 lightly beaten eggs over the top, drizzle with 1 tablespoon olive oil or vegetable oil, and bake in a 350°F oven until golden brown, about 50 minutes.

SEPHARDIC CHEESE-STUFFED EGGPLANT

(Berengena Rellenas de Queso)

4 SERVINGS   Ⓓ

The first time I made stuffed eggplant, following a different recipe from this one, I was enormously disappointed in the results, as the vegetable tasted insipid and too firm, even after baking for an extended period. Then, an informative Sephardic grandmother advised to parboil the eggplant to give it a creamy texture. Other cooks panfry the eggplant rather than parboiling it, but I find that frying requires more effort and adds extra calories. There are numerous versions of stuffed eggplant, adapted to whatever ingredients are available in the pantry. This cheese-filled version makes a savory entrée for a light meal or a delicious side dish.

2 eggplants (about 1 pound each), halved lengthwise

4 tablespoons olive oil or vegetable oil

1 onion, chopped

2 to 3 cloves garlic, minced

2 tablespoons chopped fresh parsley

1 cup fine fresh bread crumbs

1 tablespoon chopped fresh chives or 1 teaspoon
    dried oregano and $1/2$ teaspoon dried basil

About $1/2$ teaspoon table salt or 1 teaspoon
    kosher salt

Ground black pepper to taste

1 cup (5 ounces) crumbled feta, 1 cup (4 ounces)
    shredded Cheddar or Muenster cheese,
    or 1 cup (8 ounces) ricotta cheese

1 large egg, lightly beaten

$1/4$ cup toasted pine nuts (see page 22), $1/4$ cup
    coarsely chopped capers, $1/2$ cup chopped pitted
    black olives, or any combination (optional)

1 to 2 tablespoons olive oil for drizzling

1. Scoop out the cores of the eggplant (a melon baller or grapefruit knife works well) leaving a $1/2$-inch-thick shell and reserving the pulp. In a large pot of salted boiling water, cook the shells until tender but not soft, about 3 minutes. Drain.

2. Coarsely chop the reserved eggplant pulp. (It might appear like a lot, but it will cook down.) In a large skillet, heat 2 tablespoons of the oil over medium heat. Add the onion and garlic and sauté until soft and translucent, about 5 minutes. Add the remaining 2 tablespoons oil, then the eggplant pulp and parsley and sauté until softened, about 10 minutes. Remove from the heat and stir in the bread crumbs, chives, salt, and pepper. Add the cheese, egg, and, if using, the pine nuts.

3. Preheat the oven to 350°F. Oil a large baking pan.

4. Lightly salt the insides of the eggplant shells and stuff with the pulp mixture. Arrange in the baking pan and drizzle with a little oil. Cover with the lid or aluminum foil and bake for 20 minutes. Uncover and bake until golden, about 10 minutes. Serve warm.

VARIATIONS

After sautéing the eggplant pulp, add 2 cups peeled, seeded, and chopped plum tomatoes (see page 291), about 14 ounces, and simmer, stirring frequently, for 10 minutes.

Pareve Stuffed Eggplant: Substitute 2 cups cooked rice or bulgur for the cheese and bread crumbs.

Italian Stuffed Eggplants: Substitute $1/4$ cup chopped basil or mint for the chives and 1 cup shredded mozzarella, provolone, caciocavallo, or Parmesan cheese for the feta. If desired, reduce the cheese to $1/4$ cup and add about 1 cup chopped brine-cured black olives and 3 tablespoons chopped drained capers.

STUFFED EGGPLANT BY ANY OTHER NAME

Stuffed eggplant is so widespread throughout the Middle East and Balkans that it is known by numerous names, including the Sephardic *berengena rellenas* and *medias de berengena* (literally, "eggplant halves"), Turkish *patlican dolmasi*, Persian *dolma badenjan*, Arabic *batinjan mahshi*, Bulgarian *merendjen a inchidos*, and Italian *melanzane ripiene*. Arguably, nowhere are stuffed eggplants more popular than in Greece, where they are called *dolmas de melitzanes*. Stuffed thin slices of eggplant are called *yaprakites*, from the Turkish word for "leaf." And when Greeks stuff baby eggplants, they call the dish *papoutsakia* ("booties"), a whimsical reference to the shape of the small fruits. There are even more variations in the fillings than in the names.

Fennel, a member of the Umbelliferae family and a relative of dill and carrots, is one of the most ancient cultivated plants. The feathery green and bronze fennel leaves went raw into salads, the young succulent shoots were cooked in various dishes, and the thin roots were brewed into a remedy for indigestion. But fennel's real importance was in its green-yellow seeds, used both as a spice and as a medicine. Possibily a native of Israel, fennel still grows wild through much of the Mediterranean. The Greeks called it *marathon* (from *maraino*, "to grow thin"), referring to its use in weight loss, as the seeds were believed to be an appetite suppressant and aide to the digestion of fat. The Romans called it *foeniculum* ("fragrant hay") and spread fennel to all parts of the empire. Following the fall of the Roman Empire, fennel cultivation (like that of many plants) disappeared from most of Europe, continued primarily by enlightened farmers in Moorish Spain.

The fennel bulb found in markets today is actually a subspecies of the ancient plant, often going by the names finocchio (from the Italian), Florence fennel, bulbing fennel, or mistakenly, anise. Grown for its bulbous base of leaves, which is eaten as a vegetable, it resembles celery with a round bottom. The other subspecies, called sweet fennel, is grown for its seeds and leaves.

Sociologists have coined the term "conservatism of cuisine," which reflects the idea that few people are adventurous when it comes to food, preferring to rely on that to which they are accustomed. Thus, it has generally taken many years for an alien dish or vegetable to seep into some countries, even when the newcomer is delicious or superior to native food. Finocchio is a good example of this syndrome. In the sixteenth century, Jews from Sicily popularized bulb fennel among Jews in the middle and northern sections of Italy, and for centuries they incorporated it into numerous dishes. Meanwhile, finocchio was ignored by many non-Jewish Italians. As late as 1891, finocchio, along with eggplant, was considered by many Italians, in the words of the famed Florentine cookbook writer Pellegrino Artusi (*La Scienza e L'Arte di Mangiar Bene*) as "the vile food of the Jews." Only in the late nineteenth century did Italians at large come to adore what Italian Jews had loved for centuries.

Fennel is an amazingly versatile vegetable. The crisp fennel bulb and its stalks, with a mild licorice flavor, are ideal for eating raw in salads or with dips. Fennel salad (*bisbas*) with olives and *harissa* (chili sauce) is a specialty of the Tunisian island of Djerba. Sautéing and roasting fennel caramelizes its natural sugars, yielding a deep flavor. Braising or adding fennel to sauces or soups marries the vegetable's flavor with that of the cooking liquid.

What You Should Know: Fennel is a winter vegetable, best from October through April. Look for firm very white bulbs tinged with a little green. Fennel is generally sold with the stalks trimmed and only a few leaves remaining. The fronds should show no brown. Fennel bulbs differ between male and female: the males are rounded, the females flatter, with some cooks claiming that female bulbs are more flavorful. Store fennel in the refrigerator for up to 5 days.

ITALIAN BRAISED FENNEL

(*Finocchi alla Giuida*)

6 SERVINGS

During fennel season, I enjoy incorporating fennel bulbs raw into salads and cooked in various dishes, most notably this ubiquitous Italian Jewish braised fennel, brought to mainland Italy by Sicilian Jews and initially popularized in the Roman ghetto. Braising is a two-way process, first panfrying, then simmering in liquid; the flavor of the vegetable thus infuses the sauce, and the sauce brings out the flavor of the fennel. This dish, also called finocchiin tegame, *is served as an entrée or side dish, accompanied with Italian bread to mop up the sauce.*

3 medium-large fennel bulbs (about 1 pound each)
1/4 cup olive oil or vegetable oil
2 to 3 whole cloves garlic
2 cups Vegetable Stock (page 115) or 1 1/2 cups water and 1/2 cup dry white wine
About 1/2 teaspoon table salt or 1 teaspoon kosher salt
Ground black pepper to taste

1. Trim the root ends of the fennel but do not remove them entirely, so that the stalks remain attached, and cut off the leaves. Cut the bulbs lengthwise into quarters. Place in a large bowl of cold water and let soak for 30 minutes. Drain and pat dry.

2. In a large skillet or heatproof casserole, heat the oil over medium heat. Add the garlic and sauté until golden but not burnt, about 2 minutes. Discard the garlic. Add the fennel and fry, turning frequently, until golden and a little soft, about 10 minutes.

3. Add the stock, bring to a boil, cover, reduce the heat to low, and simmer until tender but not mushy, about 25 minutes. If the cooking liquid is thin, remove the fennel, boil the liquid for 1 or 2 minutes, and pour over the fennel. Sprinkle with the salt and pepper. Serve warm or at room temperature with the broth.

VARIATIONS

Italian Fennel in Vinaigrette (*Finocchi alla Giuida*): Drain the cooked fennel. Combine 2 tablespoons red wine vinegar, about $1/8$ teaspoon table salt or $1/4$ teaspoon kosher salt, and ground black pepper to taste. Whisk in $1/4$ cup extra virgin olive oil and drizzle over the fennel.

Italian Fennel Gratin (*Finocchi Gratinati*): Drain the cooked fennel and place in a baking pan. Combine $1/4$ cup extra-virgin olive oil, $1/4$ cup chopped fresh parsley, and 2 to 3 minced cloves garlic and drizzle over the fennel. Combine $1/3$ cup fresh bread crumbs and, if desired, $1/4$ cup grated Parmesan or Romano cheese; sprinkle over the fennel and bake in a preheated 375°F oven until golden, about 18 minutes.

Italian Braised Fennel and Artichokes (*Finocchi e Carciofini*): Reduce the fennel to 2 medium bulbs and, in Step 2, add 12 baby artichokes, trimmed and halved lengthwise with the fennel.

LEEKS

Leeks, which look like large scallions, have oblong white bulbs and long, flatish dark green leaves. This native of the eastern Mediterranean was among the most common plants depicted in ancient Egypt, and their remains were found in excavations of Bronze-Age Jericho. The leek was one of the foods that the Israelites yearned for after leaving Egypt and has been a part of Jewish cooking from the onset. They are among the vegetables that the Talmud suggests eating on Rosh Hashanah, since its Aramaic name *karti* is the same as the Hebrew word "cut off" (signifying cutting oneself off from one's enemies as a way of preparing for the new year).

The Romans loved leeks and disseminated them throughout Europe. Charlemagne so cherished leeks that he ordered them planted throughout his realm, and as a result, they held a prominent place in early Ashkenazic cooking, though somewhat less so after Ashkenazim relocated from France and Germany to eastern Europe. Among Sephardim, on the other hand, the leek was consistently among the most important vegetables, used solo or combined with other vegetables in various soups, stews, casseroles, patties, and savory pastries. In the Ottoman Empire, leeks were commonly paired with beans or rice. During periods of severe poverty, the leek was the only regular vegetable on the Sephardic table.

The leek is the mildest member of the onion family, with a sweeter taste than onions have. When cooked, they have a silky texture and subtle flavor, a combination of shallots, scallions, and garlic. Large pieces of leek are commonly braised or grilled to serve as a side dish, either hot or cold. Slices and small pieces provide an essential element in many venerable dishes, including soups, sauces, salads, and casseroles. Leeks have a particular affinity for olive oil, potatoes, cream, Parmesan cheese, white wine, fennel, tarragon, and thyme.

What You Should Know: Leeks vary in size from less than $1/2$ inch to more than 2 inches in diameter; there is no difference in flavor or texture between large and small bulbs. Choose firm bulbs with unblemished leaves and dark green tops. Avoid those with either wilted leaves or those that are too tough to bend, connoting that the plant had gone to seed and has a flavorless core.

Leeks are usually sold in a bunch of 4 to 5 medium or 2 to 3 large. Place in plastic bags and store in the refrigerator for up to 2 weeks. Do not trim until just before using, then trim off the root at the base. Most recipes utilize only the white and light green sections.

Leeks grow underground and usually contain a significant amount of dirt and sand between their layers, which must be thoroughly cleaned. To wash, cut the leeks crosswise into rings or halve the leeks lengthwise, place in a bowl of cold water to soak for at least 15 minutes and up to two hours, then rinse under cold running water, separating the leaves slightly. Repeat, if necessary.

INDIAN LEEKS

(*Gandana*)

5 MAIN OR 10 SIDE SERVINGS

By adding a few spices and a lemon dressing, newly emerged fall leeks are transformed into a lightly spiced side dish. This variation, traditional for Rosh Hashanah in Calcutta, provides both the side dish as well as the soup. The meal commences with an apple compote and a series of symbolic fruits and vegetables. Other holiday dishes include pilau (Indian Rice Pilaf; page 357), vegetable curries, and winter squash or pumpkin.

About $2^{1}/_{2}$ cups water

5 to 6 cloves garlic, crushed

3 (3-inch-long) strips lemon zest

2 bay leaves

1 (2-inch-long) cinnamon stick

Pinch of freshly grated nutmeg

2 pounds (about 10) leeks, white and light green parts only, halved lengthwise and washed

DRESSING:

6 tablespoons fresh lemon juice

About 1 teaspoon table salt or 2 teaspoons kosher salt

$1/4$ teaspoon cayenne

$1/4$ teaspoon ground white or black pepper

Pinch of saffron or ground turmeric

1 tablespoon vegetable oil

1. In a pot or roasting pan large enough to hold the leeks in a single layer, bring the water to a

low boil. Add the garlic, zest, bay leaves, cinnamon, and nutmeg and simmer for about 10 minutes.

2. Add the leeks, cover, and simmer until tender, about 15 minutes. Drain. (Reserve the cooking liquid for soup.) Place the leeks on a serving platter and prick with a fork.

3. To make the dressing: Combine the lemon juice, salt, cayenne, pepper, and saffron. In a slow, steady stream, whisk in the oil. Drizzle the dressing over the leeks and refrigerate overnight.

TURKISH BRAISED LEEKS WITH TOMATOES

(*Prassa Yahnisi*)

4 TO 6 SERVINGS   P

In most cultures, leeks are generally employed as a flavoring component, but Sephardim frequently feature this much-beloved vegetable as the focus of a dish, using it in various stews, croquettes, and pastry fillings. Several Sephardic cooks declared that winter and spring leeks have the strongest flavor and are the tastiest. Braising is a popular method of preparing large pieces of leeks, as it caramelizes some of the sugar and develops the flavors. In this characteristic Turkish dish, tomatoes and olive oil accent the mild flavor of the leeks. A little lemon juice is commonly added to the sauce to impart tartness. Serve chilled as an appetizer, or warm with lots of fresh bread to mop up the sauce.

1 pound (about 5) leeks, white and light green parts only
¼ cup olive oil
1 pound plum tomatoes, peeled, seeded, and chopped (see page 291), about 2½ cups
About 1 teaspoon table salt or 2 teaspoons kosher salt
Ground black pepper to taste
Pinch of sugar
1 cup water
2 to 3 tablespoons fresh lemon juice (optional)

1. Cut the leeks crosswise into 3-inch lengths. Make a 1-inch cut through the center of each end, leaving the central 1 inch whole. Carefully spread the leaves on each end. Soak the leeks in cold water to cover for 10 minutes. Remove (do not drain), then hold under cold running water to remove any remaining dirt. Pat dry with paper towels.

2. In a large skillet or heavy saucepan, heat the oil over medium heat. Add the leeks in a single layer and fry, turning occasionally, until lightly browned on all sides, about 15 minutes. Transfer the leeks to a plate.

3. Add the tomatoes, salt, pepper, and sugar to the pan and simmer for 5 minutes. Stir in the water and bring to a boil.

4. Add the leeks to the tomato sauce, cover, reduce the heat to medium-low, and simmer until the leeks are very soft, about 20 minutes. (The cooking time will vary according to the diameter and age of the leeks. Overcooking will toughen them.) If using, stir in the lemon juice and simmer for an additional 5 minutes.

Substitute ¹/4 cup tomato sauce for the tomatoes and add with the water.

Greek Braised Leeks with Tomatoes (*Yahni de Prassa*): Add 2 tablespoons chopped fresh dill with the water. Omit the lemon juice.

Greek Braised Leeks in Egg-Lemon Sauce (*Prassa con Agristada*): Omit the tomatoes, adding the fried leeks to the water. When the leeks are soft, remove them from the liquid. Beat together 2 large eggs and about 5 tablespoons fresh lemon juice, stir into the saucepan, and keep stirring until thickened. Pour over the leeks and let cool.

Balkan Braised Leeks with Olives (*Prassa con Azeitunas*): Omit the tomatoes. In Step 4, before returning the fried leeks to the pan, add 12 to 16 pitted and halved black olives. As the olives are salty, reduce the amount of salt.

Turkish Braised Leeks with Beans (*Prassa con Avicas*): Omit the lemon juice. The tomatoes are optional. Add 1¹/2 cups cooked white beans with the water.

Turkish Braised Leeks with Rice (*Prassa Zeytinyagli*): Omit the tomatoes and lemon juice. Before adding the water, add 3 tablespoons long-grain rice to the softened leeks and sauté until coated, about 3 minutes. If desired, add 2 cups thinly sliced carrots with the leeks.

TURKISH LEEK PATTIES

(*Keftes de Prassa*)

ABOUT 24 SMALL PATTIES D OR P

Many of my Turkish and Balkan friends cannot imagine Passover or Rosh Hashanah without leek patties, also called prasafuchies *and* fritas de prasa. *Leeks are associated with Passover because the Israelites in the wilderness complained about no longer having them to eat. According to a legend, the Israelites fleeing Egypt ate leek patties on the very first Passover in Egypt (though of course these did not contain mashed potatoes or packaged matza meal). Patties made with matza meal yield a purer leek flavor than those made with ground meat. Many hosts make the patties in advance, then reheat them for the meal, while others prefer frying them just before serving.*

Serve these delicate patties as either a main course or side dish. These might be part of a Turkish Rosh Hashanah dinner with spinach and pumpkin patties, as well as borekas de calabaza *(pumpkin turnovers),* lubiya *(black-eyed peas), and rice. For Passover, they would be accompanied with* apio *(sweet-and-sour celery),* anjinaras *(sweet-and-sour artichokes),* calabasa *(braised zucchini), and* minas *(matza pies). A common warning from my Sephardic friends is to always take a patty or two when the platter is nearby, as they tend to go very quickly.*

> 2 pounds (about 10) leeks, white and light green
>   parts only, cut into thin lengthwise slices
>   and washed
> 2 to 5 cloves garlic
> 1¹/2 teaspoons table salt or 1 tablespoon
>   kosher salt
> 1 cup mashed potatoes
> About ¹/2 cup matza cake meal, fresh bread
>   crumbs, or finely ground walnuts

3 large eggs, lightly beaten

1 tablespoon vegetable oil or melted butter

About $1/2$ teaspoon ground black pepper

$1/4$ to $1/2$ teaspoon freshly grated nutmeg
   or cayenne (optional)

$1/3$ to $2/3$ cup (1 to 2 ounces) grated aged
   kashkaval, Parmesan, or Romano cheese
   (optional)

$1/3$ cup pine nuts, toasted (see page 22), optional

About 2 cups vegetable oil for frying

Lemon wedges

1. Add the leeks to a large pot of lightly salted boiling water. Cover, reduce the heat to low, and simmer until very tender, about 30 minutes. Drain and let cool. Squeeze out the excess liquid.

2. Using the tip of a heavy knife or with a mortar and pestle, mash the garlic and salt into a paste. In a large bowl, combine the leeks, potatoes, and matza meal. Add the eggs, oil, garlic, pepper, and, if using, the nutmeg, cheese, and pine nuts. If the mixture is too soft to form into patties, add a little more matza meal. Shape the mixture into patties 3 inches long, 2 inches wide, and $3/4$ inch thick, with tapered ends.

3. In a large skillet, heat about $1/2$ inch oil over medium-high heat. In batches, fry the patties, turning, until golden brown, about 3 minutes per side. Using a slotted spatula, transfer to paper towels to drain. Serve hot or at room temperature accompanied with the lemon wedges. The keftes can be stored in the refrigerator for 1 day, then reheated in a 250°F oven or in a tomato sauce.

VARIATIONS

Greek Leek Patties (*Keftikes de Prassa*): Substitute $1/2$ cup chopped fresh dill for the nutmeg.

Sephardic Leek Pâté (*Prasifouchi*): Omit the matza meal. In a blender or food processor, purée all of the ingredients together until smooth. Grease an 8-cup baking dish or loaf pan, line the bottom with wax paper, regrease, pour in the leek mixture, and bake in a 375°F oven until set, about 45 minutes.

SEPHARDIC LEEK AND CHEESE CASSEROLE

(*Quajado de Puerro con Queso*)

6 TO 8 SERVINGS   D

A classic example of the Sephardim's love of vegetables mixed with cheese and eggs, this comforting casserole goes by many names: quajado/cuajada ("coagulated"), sfongato de puerro ("leek sponge"), and almodrote de prassa ("hodgepodge of leeks"). Quajado also refers to a Spanish white sheep cheese. The type of cheeses and seasonings used in the dish depends on availability and personal preference. Quajado is a popular Passover dish in Spain, Greece, and Turkey; soaked, crumbled matza is frequently added. This is commonly garnished with a dollop of yogurt.

1/4 cup olive oil or vegetable oil

3 pounds leeks (about 15 medium or 12 large), white and light green parts only, cut into thin lengthwise slices and washed

1 large onion, chopped (optional)

1 cup water

2 teaspoons table salt or 4 teaspoons kosher salt

1 cup (5 ounces) crumbled feta, 1 cup (8 ounces) farmer or pot cheese, or 1 cup (3 ounces) grated kefalotyri or Parmesan cheese, or a combination

1 cup (4 ounces) shredded kashkaval, Gouda, Muenster, or Cheddar cheese

5 large eggs, lightly beaten

2 tablespoons olive oil or vegetable oil

About 1/2 teaspoon table salt or 1 teaspoon kosher salt

Ground black pepper to taste or 1/2 teaspoon cayenne

1/4 cup chopped fresh dill or 1/2 teaspoon freshly grated nutmeg (optional)

1. Preheat the oven to 350°F. Oil a 9-inch square or 8-by-11-inch baking dish or two 9-inch pie plates.

2. In a large saucepan, heat the oil over medium heat. Add the leeks and, if using, the onion and sauté until softened, about 10 minutes. Add the water and 1 1/2 teaspoons of the table salt or 3 teaspoons of the kosher salt, cover, and simmer until the leeks are tender, about 15 minutes. Drain.

3. In a large bowl, combine the cheeses, eggs, oil, the remaining 1/2 teaspoon table salt or 1 teaspoon kosher salt, pepper, and, if using, the dill. Stir in the leeks.

4. Spoon into the prepared baking dish. Bake until set and golden brown, about 50 minutes. Serve warm or at room temperature.

VARIATIONS

Sephardic Leek and Potato Casserole (*Quajado de Puerro y Patata*): Omit the cheese and cook 2 pounds peeled and diced russet potatoes with the leeks, mashing them together after draining. If desired, add 1/2 cup grated kashkaval or Parmesan cheese.

Sephardic Leek, Zucchini, and Cheese Casserole (*Quajado de Puerro y Calavasa con Queso*): Use only 1 1/2 pounds leeks and add 2 cups (about 1 pound) grated zucchini with the water.

MUSHROOMS

Mushrooms have fed and mystified humans since time immemorial. In ancient Israel, mushrooms, especially the genus *Boletus* (also known as cèpe or porcini), were gathered by the masses, particularly after a major rainfall. In the modern Middle East, mushrooms play a minor culinary role; in certain areas they are sautéed to make salads and are added to various omelets, rice dishes, and vegetable stews. In eastern Europe, on the other hand, mushrooms, among the few ingredients available to the poor, were particularly important, sautéed with onions, pickled, or added to soups, stews, and kasha dishes and used to fill pastry and pasta.

The French became the first to commercially cultivate mushrooms in 1650. Until World War II, brown buttons, today called cremini, were the most prevalent cultivated mushrooms, then white buttons supplanted them in the United States. Today, there is a widening range of cultivated mushrooms, including many formerly exotic species. Mature mushrooms contain glutamic acid, which imparts an intense flavor and acts as a flavor enhancer. Wild mushrooms contain a large amount of glutamic acid and therefore have an even deeper flavor than cultivated ones.

What You Should Know: Choose firm, heavy mushrooms without blemishes. Fresh mushrooms should have a sweet earthy smell and feel slightly damp. Avoid those with an ammonia or musty odor, that feel sticky or slimy, or that have a number of holes under the cap or in the stem (a sign of bugs). As soon as mushrooms are picked, a natural enzymatic breakdown begins, so they are best used within 3 to 5 days of picking. Store white button mushrooms in a paper bag in the refrigerator. Or, arrange the mushrooms in a single layer in a large basket and cover with a towel. Do not wash before storing. Store different species of mushrooms separately, as some break down more quickly than others. Never soak mushrooms in water, or they will absorb too much moisture. Button mushrooms, however, can be rinsed, shortly before cooking, under cold running water without absorbing any appreciable amount of liquid. Mushrooms can also be wiped with a dampened towel, sponge, or pastry brush. Trim off any tough part of the stem. Mushrooms are 90 percent water and therefore shrink by up to 40 percent during cooking.

GEORGIAN MUSHROOMS IN SOUR CREAM

(Soko Arajanit)

6 TO 8 SERVINGS

Since ancient times, Georgians have been masterful shepherds and herdsmen as well as mushroom gatherers. As a result, dairy products constitute a major component of the Georgian diet, transformed into an array of cheeses, butter, and sour cream. Mushrooms, abundant in the forests and mountains, are generally seasoned with wine vinegar or, as in this case, sour cream, contrasting the tangy sauce with the meaty flavor of the mushrooms. Since there were no cultivated mushrooms in Georgia, the residents had to wait for a rainfall to enjoy this dish. This is served as a main course, with mamaliga *(Romanian Cornmeal Mush, page 379) or bread.*

1/4 cup unsalted butter or vegetable oil

2 pounds mushrooms, rinsed and thickly sliced

3/4 cup sour cream, at room temperature

1/4 cup milk

2 tablespoons unbleached all-purpose flour

About 1/2 teaspoon table salt or 1 teaspoon
   kosher salt

Ground black pepper to taste

1/4 cup chopped fresh parsley for garnish

1. In a large skillet, melt the butter over medium heat. Add the mushrooms and sauté until they begin to release their liquid, about 3 minutes. Cover and simmer until tender, about 5 minutes.

2. In a medium bowl, combine the sour cream, milk, and flour. Gradually stir into the cooked mushrooms and simmer, stirring constantly, until thickened, about 5 minutes. Season with the salt and pepper. Serve warm or at room temperature as a side dish or on toast as an appetizer. Sprinkle with the parsley.

VARIATIONS

Georgian Mushrooms in Walnut Sauce (*Soko Nigozit*): Omit the sour cream sauce and stir the cooked mushrooms into 1 cup *bazha* (Georgian Walnut Sauce, page 432). If desired, rather than sautéing, grill the whole mushrooms until soft, then chop.

Romanian Mushrooms in Sour Cream (*Ciuperci in sos de Smintina*): Add 2 teaspoons chopped fresh dill with the salt.

HUNGARIAN MUSHROOM STEW

(*Gomba Paprikás*)

4 TO 5 SERVINGS   Ⓓ OR Ⓟ

Hungary's location, southerly enough to have a relatively temperate climate and in proximity to the cultural influences of Austria and the Ottoman Empire, led to the development of an exceptional cuisine. Hungarians created many ways of using mushrooms, from filling puff pastries to topping toast. This lively tomato sauce provides an interesting and characteristically Hungarian contrast to the moist, full-flavored, somewhat earthy mushrooms. It is served as a main course, accompanied with noodles or rice.

1/4 cup vegetable oil

1 large onion, chopped

1 red bell pepper, seeded, deribbed (white
   removed), and chopped

2 to 3 cloves garlic, minced

1 pound plum tomatoes, peeled, seeded, and
   chopped (see page 291), about 2 1/2 cups

About 1 teaspoon table salt or 2 teaspoons
   kosher salt

1/2 cup Vegetable Stock (page 115) or water

2 tablespoons sweet Hungarian paprika

Ground black pepper to taste

Pinch of sugar

1 pound button or other meaty mushrooms,
   cleaned and sliced (about 5 1/2 cups)

1/4 cup sour cream at room temperature
   (optional)

1. In a large saucepan, heat the oil over medium heat. Add the onion, bell pepper, and garlic and sauté until softened, about 10 minutes. Add the

tomatoes and salt and cook, stirring occasionally, until softened, about 10 minutes.

2. In a food processor or blender, process the tomato mixture. Add the stock, paprika, pepper, and sugar and process until smooth.

3. Return the mixture to the saucepan. Add the mushrooms and cook over medium-high heat, stirring frequently, until the mushrooms are tender and the sauce thickens, about 20 minutes. Remove from the heat and, if using, stir in the sour cream. Serve warm.

VARIATION

Romanian Mushrooms in Tomato Sauce (*Guvetch de Ciuperci*): Omit the bell pepper and sour cream. Substitute $^1/_2$ cup dry red wine for the stock, reduce the paprika to 1 teaspoon, and add $^1/_2$ teaspoon dried oregano and $^1/_4$ to $^1/_2$ teaspoon red pepper flakes. If the sauce is a little flat, stir in a little red wine vinegar or hot sauce. Serve as an accompaniment to *mamaliga* (Romanian Cornmeal Mush, page 379) or pasta.

ROMANIAN STUFFED MUSHROOMS

(*Ciuperci Umplute*)

ABOUT 24 HORS D'OEUVRES   D OR P

Every culture has its idiosyncrasies. Among those of Romanian cookery is garlic and typically plenty of it. To me, it is sometimes overdone. Then again, seasoning is always a subjective matter. Mushroom caps are a popular and versatile base for hors d'oeuvres; the Romanian version, of course, contains garlic. Romanians serve these hot or at room temperature as part of a meze (appetizer assortment) or as a side dish.

1 pound (about 24) large button mushrooms, rinsed

$^1/_4$ cup vegetable oil

8 to 10 scallions (white and light green parts only), thinly sliced, or 1 large onion, finely chopped

1 to 3 cloves garlic, minced

$^1/_4$ cup fresh bread crumbs or matza meal

2 tablespoons chopped fresh parsley

1 tablespoon chopped fresh dill

About 2 teaspoons table salt or 1 tablespoon kosher salt

About 1 teaspoon ground black pepper

$^1/_4$ cup unsalted butter, melted, or vegetable oil

$^3/_4$ cup grated aged kashkaval, kefalotyri, or Parmesan cheese (optional)

$^1/_3$ cup dry white wine

1. Remove the stems from the mushroom caps and finely chop them.

2. In a large skillet, heat the oil over medium heat. Add the scallions and garlic and sauté until soft, about 5 minutes. Add the chopped stems and sauté until the mushrooms release their liquid and it evaporates, about 5 minutes. Stir in the bread crumbs, parsley, dill, salt, and pepper. Let cool. Store in the refrigerator for up to 3 days.

3. Preheat the oven to 350°F. Grease a large shallow casserole or baking sheet.

4. Place the mushroom caps in the prepared baking dish and drizzle the butter over top. Bake, uncovered, for 10 minutes.

5. Fill the mushrooms with the stuffing and, if using, sprinkle with the cheese. Bake until browned, about 20 minutes. Drizzle with the wine. Serve warm.

STUFFED VEGETABLES

No one can pinpoint exactly where or when the practice of stuffing vegetables started, although Persia might be the place of origin, but it certainly caught on, spreading throughout the ancient world. Stuffed vegetables—called *dolma* in Persian, *dolmathes* in Greek, *mehshi* or *mahshi* in Arabic, *yenas* in the Balkans, *reyenadas* in Ladino, and *memulaim* in Hebrew—became an important dish in nearly every Jewish community, a delicious way to stretch limited resources. Stewing was the old-fashioned way of preparing stuffed vegetables before home ovens became widespread.

In the Middle East, almost any vegetable is stuffed, including beets, carrots, celery, chard stalks, onions, and turnips. Indigenous Syrian Jews derisively referred to the Sephardic exiles settling in Syria as *medias* ("halves"), a reference to the way the newcomers cut their vegetables in half to be stuffed, in contrast to the Middle Eastern technique of hollowing out the whole vegetable. For special occasions, Middle Easterners serve a medley of stuffed vegetables, usually consisting of bell peppers, zucchini, and small eggplants, each vegetable imparting some of its flavor into the filling and sauce. For large crowds, the vegetables are stacked in the pot, with the firm ones on the bottom and the more delicate ones on top.

While Ashkenazim generally use some meat in their fillings for stuffed vegetables, purely vegetarian fillings abound in the Middle East. Cheese-stuffed vegetables are customarily served warm, while rice-stuffed vegetables are appropriate either hot or cold. Stuffed vegetables can be served as a tasty side dish, an appetizer, or even an entrée. A platter of several stuffed vegetables makes a colorful addition to a *meze* (appetizer assortment). Since stuffing vegetables is time consuming, Sephardim generally serve stuffed vegetables at special occasions, including bar mitzvahs and weddings. Stuffed foods symbolize harvest and abundance, and so are particularly prominent during the holidays of Sukkot and Purim.

❧ OKRA ❧

Okra, a member of the mallow family and a relative of cotton, is probably a native of Ethiopia. Its first recorded appearance was in twelfth-century C.E. Egypt. Shortly thereafter, the Moors introduced okra to Spain, where, like other vegetables, it gained wide acceptance among Sephardim. It is also popular in many communities around the southern Mediterranean and in India.

Okra's mucilaginous nature—it becomes slimy when overcooked—makes it unappetizing to many, although this characteristic makes it a desirable thickener in stews. Soaking it in vinegar water or blanching and frying it lessen this attribute. Cutting okra releases the chemical compounds that cause the sliminess, so experienced cooks leave them intact or, if chopping, fry them. Okra is often paired with tomatoes or lemon juice, as their acid helps to counteract the sliminess.

What You Should Know: For best flavor, use pods less than 4 inches long. Mediterranean cooks prefer even smaller pods. Larger, mature pods require a slightly longer cooking time. Although okra can be found year-round, it is best between May and October. If your fingernail cannot easily pierce the pod, it is too old. Store in a plastic bag at room temperature—cold causes it to deteriorate—for no more than a day or two. Rinse just before cooking, as the water increases the sliminess. Do not cook in an iron or aluminum pot.

SEPHARDIC OKRA WITH TOMATOES

(*Bamia con Domates*)

6 TO 8 SERVINGS

Most Sephardim have been brought up on okra and use methods handed down over the generations to produce a tender, succulent vegetable. One of these methods is to simmer the pods in a sweet-and-sour tomato sauce. This recipe is a starting point, with each community adding its own touch. Frying okra in a little oil until browned before cooking enhances the flavor. For a tangier flavor, use less sugar; for a sweet-and-sour flavor, use a larger amount. Bamia is usually accompanied with rice or flat bread. For a fancy presentation, some cooks arrange the okra in a concentric circle.

> 2 pounds small okra, caps removed
> 8 cups cold water mixed with $^1/_2$ cup distilled white or cider vinegar
> 5 tablespoons olive oil
> 2 onions, chopped
> 2 to 3 cloves garlic, minced
> 1$^3/_4$ pounds plum tomatoes, peeled, seeded, and chopped (see page 291), about 4$^1/_4$ cups, or 6 ounces tomato paste dissolved in 2 cups water
> 2 to 4 tablespoons fresh lemon juice
> 1 to 2 tablespoons granulated or packed brown sugar or honey
> About 1 teaspoon table salt or 2 teaspoons kosher salt
> Ground black pepper to taste

1. Soak the okra in the vinegar water for 1 hour. Drain and pat dry.

2. In a large skillet or heavy saucepan, heat the oil over medium heat. Add the onions and sauté until soft and translucent, 5 to 10 minutes. Add the garlic and sauté for 1 minute. Add the okra and sauté until lightly golden, about 5 minutes.

3. Add the tomatoes, lemon juice, sugar, salt, and pepper. Bring to a boil, cover, reduce the heat to low, and simmer until the okra is tender, about 30 minutes. Serve warm or at room temperature.

VARIATIONS

Sephardic Okra with Lemon (*Bamia con Limón*): Substitute 1 cup water for the tomatoes and increase the lemon juice to ¹/₂ cup.

Ethiopian Okra with Tomatoes (*Bamya Aleecha*): Omit the lemon juice and sugar. Add 1 tablespoon minced fresh ginger and ³/₄ teaspoon ground cardamom with the tomatoes. After cooking the okra for 25 minutes, add 1 to 3 seeded and minced jalapeño peppers and cook for 5 additional minutes.

Greek Okra with Tomatoes (*Bamyes*): In Step 3, when the okra is tender, add 2 tablespoons chopped fresh dill. Or, add 1¹/₂ teaspoons ground coriander before adding the tomatoes.

Indian Okra with Tomatoes (*Bindi Bhaji*): Okra is also called "ladies fingers" in India. Omit the sugar and add ¹/₂ teaspoon ground turmeric and ³/₄ teaspoon red pepper flakes or several drops hot sauce with the lemon juice. If desired, reduce the tomatoes to 2 cups and substitute ¹/₄ cup tamarind paste dissolved in 2 cups water for the lemon juice.

Syrian Okra with Tomatoes (*Bamia bil Benadora*): Add with the tomatoes ¹/₄ teaspoon ground allspice and 2 tablespoons *temerhindi* (Syrian Mock Tamarind Sauce, page 434), or 1 tablespoon apricot butter and 1 tablespoon prune butter. If desired, add ³/₄ cup (4 ounces) pitted prunes.

PEPPERS

The capsicum pepper, a relative of the potato and tomato, is a native of South America. By the time Columbus stumbled onto the New World, members of the capsicum family—what the Nahutals of the Caribbean called *chilli*—had already spread throughout most of Central and South America. On sampling the fiery pods, Columbus, who thought he was in the Spice Islands of India, assumed capsicum to be the source of peppercorns and called them *pimienta* (Spanish for "pepper," thus the source of the misleading but enduring name). The Portuguese and Spanish brought these plants to the Old World. Chilies were virtually ignored in most of Europe, their fiery charms being most warmly appreciated in areas with hot climates, such as Africa, Yemen, Turkey, and the Far East.

Capsicums interbreed with relative ease, producing an ever-increasing array of chili varieties, now numbering more than two hundred. All capsicums start out green, then, as they mature on the vine, turn into an array of colors, including red, yellow, orange, brown, and black.

Chili flavors range from mild to fire-alarm hot. Determining a chili's piquancy is no easy matter, since even chilies of the same variety can differ in intensity. A general rule of thumb is that the smaller the chili, the hotter it tends to be, and chilies with pointed tips and broad shoulders tend to be hotter than those with rounded, blunt tips. Color is also a sign: Yellowish-orange veins are another indication of fire, brighter colors are more fiery, and reds are milder than greens. Of course, there are always exceptions, and experience is the best teacher.

The heat in chilies is due to the chemical compound capsaicin, a unique alkaloid and volatile oil that produces a stinging sensation in the mouth as well as in other areas of the body. It does not burn the stomach or cause stomach problems, but does increase stomach acid. This reddish-brown substance is so potent that it can still be tasted if only one part in a million.

In the eighteenth century, European horticulturists cultivated milder forms of capsicum (*grossum*), most notably the bell pepper, named for its squarish shape with two to four lobes. Green peppers—again, the unripe version of any bell pepper—are more bitter and slightly firmer than ripe ones. Bell peppers, raw and cooked, became an important part of cooking in sections of Europe and Asia, particularly in the more moderate climes of the Mediterranean and Balkans. They are routinely added to salads, casseroles, and stews and, due to their boxlike structure, are perfect for stuffing.

What You Should Know: To get the flavor from chilies without all of the fire, first remove the ribs and seeds. When working with chilies, never touch your eyes or an open cut. It is advisable to wear rubber gloves, but in any case, afterward wash your hands and utensils well with hot, soapy water. If the chilies in a dish begin to burn your mouth, do not reach for a beer or a glass of water—alcohol and water actually intensify and spread the heat of capsaicin. On the other hand, dairy products mute the capsaicin and starches, such as bread, decrease its effects.

HUNGARIAN PEPPER RAGOUT

(*Lecsó*)

4 TO 5 SERVINGS

The Turks introduced chilies to the Balkans by the mid-sixteenth century and, within a hundred years, the ground form, paprika, had become the most important spice in Hungary. Sweet red peppers arrived in the 1700s, supplanting the fiery chilies and becoming essential for a myriad of stews called paprikás *and* gulyás. *The most important pepper variety in Hungary is* pierprzyca, *a large, dark red heart-shaped pepper. Hungarians love peppers not only in the ground form of paprika, but also fresh and stewed. Lecsó, pronounced and frequently called* lecho *in Russia and Israel, is among the most popular Hungarian dishes, a sweetish or piquant mélange of peppers and tomatoes. Hungarians insist that* lecsó, *which is prepared in a number of varieties, must not be cooked in a hurry, but requires slow simmering to meld and develop the various components. Serve as a side dish, dip, or accompaniment to omelets, rice, crusty bread, or matza. Hungarians enjoy a little red Egri wine with their* lecsó.

3 tablespoons vegetable oil

2 onions, halved and sliced

2 pounds (6 large) red bell peppers, yellow banana peppers, Italian peppers, or any combination, seeded, deribbed (white removed), and sliced

About 1 tablespoon sweet Hungarian paprika

1 1/2 pounds plum tomatoes, peeled, seeded, and chopped (see page 291), about 4 cups

1 teaspoon sugar

About 1/2 teaspoon table salt or 1 teaspoon kosher salt

Ground black pepper to taste

About 1/4 cup tomato purée (see page 291) or water, if needed

1. In a large saucepan, heat the oil over medium heat. Add the onions and sauté until soft and translucent, 5 to 10 minutes. Add the peppers and sauté until softened but not browned, about 10 minutes. Stir in the paprika.

2. Add the tomatoes, sugar, salt, and pepper. Cover and cook for 10 minutes. If the vegetables have not released sufficient liquid to make a thin layer on the bottom, add the tomato purée. Cover, reduce the heat to low, and cook, stirring occasionally and adding more liquid if necessary, until the peppers are very tender and the sauce thickened, about 20 minutes. Serve warm or at room temperature.

VARIATIONS

When the peppers are tender, add 2 lightly beaten eggs and gently stir until they scramble. Serve warm. Or, at the end of Step 2, top each serving of *lecsó* with a fried egg.

Relish style: When the peppers are tender, remove from the heat and stir in about 1 1/2 tablespoons red wine vinegar. Serve at room temperature.

BALKAN CHEESE-STUFFED PEPPERS

(*Pipiritzas con Queso*)

8 SERVINGS

Thin-fleshed varieties of peppers, known as Italian or frying peppers, have a long, tapered pod usually picked when yellowish-green. Varieties include Corno di Toro ("bull's horn"), Cubanelle, gypsy, Sweet Hungarian, Italia, and Sweet Banana. They have thinner walls and less water than bell peppers and are therefore ideal for frying. These peppers, once the most common type of sweet pepper in central Europe, have become more common and less expensive in American markets during the past few years. Cheese-stuffed peppers are particularly popular in Italy, Hungary, and the Balkans. The use of feta marks this distinctive treatment of peppers, also called piperies yemistes *in Greece, as Balkan.*

8 large Italian frying peppers

STUFFING:

1 1/4 cups (6 ounces) crumbled feta cheese
1 cup (8 ounces) farmer cheese or 1/2 cup
   (4 ounces) farmer cheese and 1/2 cup
   (2 ounces) shredded kashkaval cheese
1 large egg, lightly beaten
1 tablespoon fresh lemon juice
Pinch of dried oregano or marjoram (optional)

About 2 tablespoons olive oil or vegetable oil
   for coating

1. Cut a small slit partway down one side of each pepper, starting from the cap end. Blanch the peppers in a pot of lightly salted boiling water for

5 minutes. Drain and let stand long enough so that you can handle them. Under cold running water, remove the seeds and ribs, being careful to leave the peppers intact. Pat dry with paper towels.

2. Combine all the stuffing ingredients. Stuff into the peppers. The stuffed peppers may be stored in the refrigerator for 1 day; let stand at room temperature for at least 30 minutes before cooking.

3. Preheat the broiler.

4. Coat the peppers with the oil. Place about 5 inches from the heat source of the broiler and broil, turning once, until the skin blisters and begins to blacken, about 6 minutes per side. Rub off the blackened skin. Serve immediately.

VARIATION

Balkan Fried Stuffed Peppers (*Pipiritzas Inchidos Fritos*): In Step 1, grill the peppers over coals or broil, turning, until blackened, about 6 minutes per side, rub off the blackened skin, cut an incision along the side of the peppers, remove the seeds, and stuff. Roll the peppers in flour and fry in a little oil, turning, until browned on all sides.

NOTE   Cheese-filled peppers are served warm, while rice-filled peppers can be eaten either warm or at room temperature.

ROMANIAN CHEESE-STUFFED PEPPERS

(*Pipiruchkas Reynados con Queso*)

6 SERVINGS

Many cooks use only mature red and yellow peppers to stuff, for a sweeter flavor. Others prefer the more pronounced, herbal taste of green peppers. In any case, choose peppers with a vivid color and a glossy exterior. In this version, the filling is a simple slice of cheese, but it is enlivened with a tomato sauce. For a zestier dish, use poblano or Anaheim chilies. Serve as a side dish or appetizer, accompanied with plenty of bread for the sauce.

6 red or yellow bell peppers, or 3 of each,
    or 6 poblano or Anaheim chilies
6 large slices teleme (telemasa), haloumi,
    Monterey jack, or mozzarella cheese

SAUCE:
2 tablespoons olive oil or vegetable oil
1 onion, chopped
2 to 3 cloves garlic, minced
2 pounds plum tomatoes, peeled, seeded,
    and chopped (see page 291), about 5 cups
1 teaspoon sugar
About 1 teaspoon table salt or 2 teaspoons
    kosher salt
Ground black pepper to taste

1. Arrange a wire rack over the top of a gas burner or on a baking sheet 3 inches from the heat source of the broiler. Place the peppers on the rack over the fire or under the preheated broiler, turning until the skin begins to blacken and blisters, about 3 minutes. Do not burn. Place in a paper bag or in a bowl and cover. Let stand until the skin peels easily, about 15 minutes. Rub off the blackened skin. A paper towel makes this easier, as the skin sticks to it. Do not rinse under water, which removes flavor and adds liquid. Cut a small slit down one side starting from the cap, then remove and discard the stem, ribs, and seeds, leaving the peppers intact. Insert a piece of cheese into each pepper.

2. To make the sauce: In a medium saucepan, heat the oil over medium heat. Add the onion and garlic and sauté until soft and translucent, about 5 minutes. Add the tomatoes, sugar, salt, and pepper. Bring to a boil, reduce the heat to low, and simmer, stirring frequently, until the tomatoes soften, about 15 minutes.

3. Preheat the oven to 350°F. Oil a large baking dish.

4. Arrange the peppers on their sides in a single layer in the prepared dish and pour the sauce over the top. Bake until the cheese melts, about 30 minutes. Serve warm.

SEPHARDIC RICE-STUFFED PEPPERS

(*Pimintones Reynados*)

6 SERVINGS

Bell peppers are the easiest vegetable to prepare for stuffing, due to their large interior and firm walls. This vegetarian rice-stuffed version originated in Turkey before spreading throughout much of the Arab world, as well as to India and the Balkans, the seasonings varying from region to region. Sephardim generally season the filling simply with tomatoes, letting the flavor of the baked peppers shine. Others add complementary seasonings.

Pimintone, the Sephardic word for peppers, is *also employed as slang for a "grouch," but anyone served these stuffed peppers could never be grumpy. My mother recommends choosing peppers with a relatively flat, wide bottom that will stand on their own.*

6 green, red, or yellow bell peppers (about 5 ounces each), or any combination

STUFFING:
3 tablespoons olive oil or vegetable oil
1 large onion, chopped
1 1/4 cups white or brown long-grain rice
2 1/2 cups water
6 ounces plum tomatoes, peeled, seeded, and chopped (see page 291), about 3/4 cup, or 2 tablespoons tomato paste
3 tablespoons chopped fresh parsley
1 teaspoon sugar or honey
1/2 teaspoon table salt or 1 teaspoon kosher salt
About 1/4 teaspoon ground black pepper

1 tablespoon olive oil or vegetable oil for drizzling

1. Slice off and reserve the tops of the peppers. Discard the ribs and seeds. If the peppers do not stand upright, carefully trim the bottoms, without puncturing the pepper. In a large pot of salted boiling water, blanch the peppers for 3 minutes. Remove and drain, cut-side-down, for 1 minute, then invert.

2. To make the stuffing: In a medium, heavy saucepan, heat the oil over medium heat. Add the onion and sauté until soft and translucent, about 5 minutes. Add the rice and sauté until opaque, about 3 minutes. Add the water, tomatoes, parsley, sugar, salt, and pepper. Bring to a boil, cover, reduce the heat to low, and simmer until the water is absorbed, about 15 minutes for white rice, 40 minutes for brown rice. Remove from the heat and let stand, covered, for at least 10 minutes.

3. Preheat the oven to 350°F.

4. Fill each pepper with the rice mixture and replace the tops. Place the peppers closely together in a casserole standing upright and drizzle with the oil. Cover and bake until the peppers are tender but still firm and the stuffing is heated through, about 30 minutes. Serve warm or at room temperature.

VARIATIONS

Romanian Rice-Stuffed Peppers (*Pipirnchkas Reynados*): At the end of Step 2, add 1 cup (4 ounces) shredded halumi, Monterey jack, mozzarella, or Cheddar cheese. If desired, reduce the rice to 1 cup and the water to 2 cups and add 1 cup cooked red or black beans and $^1/_2$ teaspoon red pepper flakes or $^1/_4$ teaspoon cayenne pepper.

Greek Rice-Stuffed Peppers (*Pipiruchkas Yenos*): In Step 2, add with the water $^1/_4$ cup dried currants or raisins, $^1/_4$ cup pine nuts or slivered almonds, 3 tablespoons chopped fresh dill, and $1^1/_2$ teaspoons chopped fresh thyme or $^1/_2$ teaspoon dried thyme.

POTATOES

SUNDAY POTATOES, MONDAY POTATOES,
TUESDAY AND WEDNESDAY POTATOES,
THURSDAY AND FRIDAY POTATOES,
BUT SHABBOS, FOR A CHANGE, A POTATO KUGEL.
—An Old Yiddish Song

The white potato is now such an intrinsic part of Ashkenazic cooking it is difficult for many to comprehend that this tuber is a relatively recent addition to the Jewish pantry. A member of the nightshade family, the white potato flourished in the difficult conditions and poor soil of the higher elevations of the Andes in Chile, a trait that would eventually make it the world's predominant vegetable. During its initial period of cultivation, however, this knobby tuber ran a distant second to the sweet potato in popularity. When the white potato (a misnomer, as its color can range from yellow to purple) finally reached Spain around 1570, it was regarded as a source of leprosy or as poisonous. Indeed, fifteenth-century Europeans, with their ingrained eating habits, rejected many of the culinary American imports. Only in the face of abject poverty, most notably in Ireland after 1780, did potatoes find their way into the European diet.

The potato subsequently proved a vital crop, cooked in stews, when famine and hunger swept France in the 1790s in the wake of the Revolution. The Germans soon joined the bandwagon and by the end of the eighteenth century were using potatoes to make a variety of dishes, such as *kloese* (dumplings), salads, soups, pancakes, and breads, as well as flour. Even here, however, this new attitude was primarily on the part of the masses. Upper-class Germans still viewed the potato as "poor man's food" and would not deign to eat them. The potato took even longer to gain acceptance in eastern Europe, even among the poor. It was not until a series of crop failures in Ukraine and Poland in 1839 and 1840 that potatoes were for the first time planted in large numbers in that part of the world.

But within a very short period, these hearty tubers supplanted buckwheat and barley and emerged as the staple of the eastern European diet. In particular, potatoes provided an inexpensive way to fill the hungry stomachs of the exploding Jewish population. At the time of the partition of Poland between Austria, Prussia, and Russia in 1815, the Jewish population of Russian Poland numbered about one and a quarter million. By the census of 1897, that number, despite massive emigration of Jews to America and Israel beginning in 1880, grew to about five million (15 percent of the total population of Poland). Not coincidentally, this Jewish population explosion, happening at a rate more than twice that of their non-Jewish neighbors, corresponded with the popularization of the potato in eastern Europe.

Many eastern European families ate potatoes, often seasoned with onions, three times a day. Potatoes were used to create new dishes, such as *potatonik* (a cross between kugel and bread), and were incorporated into various traditional dishes, most notably *cholent* (Sabbath stew), *knaidlach* (dumplings), knishes (pastry), borscht (soup), kreplach (filled pasta), and kugel (baked pudding). The potato latke (pancake) emerged as the prototypical Ashkenazic Hanukkah food.

What You Should Know: The hundreds of varieties of white potatoes are generally classified as baking (russet), boiling (waxy), and new—groupings based on starch content, shape, and age. The potato is the starchiest of all vegetables, with starch making up 65 to 80 percent of its dry weight. The amount of sugar increases and the amount of water decreases during storage.

The Russet Burbank variety, also called baking, mealy, and Idaho, was developed by horticulturist Luther Burbank in 1871. Long and oblong, with a thick brown skin, russets are high in starch and low in sugar and moisture. In high-starch potatoes, the starch cells are nearly filled with starch granules and split apart during cooking to produce a fluffy flesh that is best for baking, frying, and making pancakes. In addition, due to their low moisture content, mealy potatoes can absorb butter, milk, or other liquids without becoming gummy, a quality preferred for mashing and making dumplings.

Waxy potatoes, sometimes called boiling, Eastern, or Maine, have a smooth, thin skin and a round or elliptical shape. These potatoes are lower in starch and contain more water and sugar than russet potatoes, which gives them a waxy appearance. Waxy potatoes hold their shape during cooking and absorb flavors, so are best for salads, stews, and soups. The preferred cooking methods for waxy potatoes are boiling and roasting; the high sugar content causes them to brown too quickly to be suitable for frying.

New potatoes are waxy potatoes harvested before maturity and shipped directly from the field to market without the usual storage period. Thus, skin color (red, white, or brown) and size (some new potatoes are as large as mature potatoes) are not necessarily signs of "newness."

> According to an old Yiddish saying, "*Yichus* [notable ancestry] is like a potato—they are both in the ground."

ASHKENAZIC POTATO PUFFS

(Bilkas)

ABOUT 8 PUFFS   P

After the potato became an integral part of the eastern European diet, Ashkenazim primarily ate them boiled, perhaps with some butter, sour cream, or schmaltz. More adventuresome cooks soon began using leftover potatoes to make various dumplings, including halkes, kartoffel kloeses, *and* shlishkes. Bilkalach, *once particularly popular on Passover in the time before many other foods were available to Ashkenazim, are the baked form of dumpling, transforming a simple dish into an elegant presentation. The potato mixture (after Step 2) can also be spread or dropped over various casseroles before baking, to serve as a dumpling garnish. Do not overcook the* bilkas, *or they will dry out and be better suited for a paperweight or doorstop.*

2 pounds unpeeled baking (russet) potatoes,
    scrubbed

2 teaspoons table salt or 4 teaspoons kosher salt

1 tablespoon vegetable shortening or oil

2 large eggs

Ground white or black pepper to taste

Garlic powder or onion powder to taste
    (optional)

1/4 cup matza cake meal

1 large egg beaten with 1 tablespoon water

1. Put the potatoes in a large pot and add cold water to cover by 1 inch and 1 teaspoon of the table salt or 2 teaspoons of the kosher salt. Bring to a low boil, reduce the heat to medium-low, and simmer, uncovered, until fork-tender, about 25 minutes. Drain. Peel the potatoes and, while still warm, run through a food mill or ricer. Or, return the peeled potatoes to the warm cooking pot, add the shortening, and mash with a potato masher, a heavy whisk, or a pastry blender over a low heat, being careful not to overmix. You should have about 4 cups.

2. Blend in the eggs, the remaining salt, the pepper, and optional garlic powder. Add the matza meal. Refrigerate until firm, at least 1 hour.

3. Preheat the oven to 375°F. Grease a large baking sheet.

4. Moisten your hands with water and shape 1/4 cupfuls of the potato mixture into ovals. Place on the prepared baking sheet and use a wet finger to make a small indentation in the center of each. Brush with the egg mixture.

5. Bake until golden, about 30 minutes. Serve warm.

VARIATIONS

Omit the matza meal and increase the vegetable shortening to 1/4 cup. Drop mounds of the mixture by spoonfuls onto the baking sheet and proceed as above.

Caramelized-Onion-Filled *Bilkas*: Sauté 2 chopped large onions in 3 tablespoons oil until golden, about 15 minutes. Place about 1 tablespoon onions in the center of the mashed potatoes and mold the mixture around them to enclose them. Proceed as above.

Fried Mini *Bilkas*: Heat a thin layer of oil in a large skillet over medium-high heat, drop the potato mixture into the pan by heaping tablespoonfuls, and fry, turning, until golden brown, about 2 minutes per side.

MOROCCAN MASHED POTATO CASSEROLE

(Batata bil Firan)

6 TO 8 SERVINGS   Ⓟ

Middle Easterners, rarely content with plain boiled or mashed potatoes, frequently add various spices and vegetables and usually bake or fry the mixture. In this casserole, which is popular Moroccan Passover fare, the various ingredients lend complexity to basic mashed potatoes.

> 2 pounds unpeeled baking (russet) potatoes, scrubbed
>
> 2 teaspoons table salt or 4 teaspoons kosher salt
>
> 3 tablespoons vegetable oil
>
> 3 onions, chopped
>
> 1 to 2 cloves garlic, mashed (optional)
>
> 6 large eggs
>
> About $^1/_2$ teaspoon ground white or black pepper
>
> $^1/_4$ teaspoon ground turmeric
>
> 1 carrot, diced and cooked until tender
>
> 1 cup green peas or 4 scallions, sliced
>
> $^1/_3$ cup chopped fresh parsley or cilantro

1. Put the potatoes in a large pot and add cold water to cover by 1 inch and 1 teaspoon of the table salt or 2 teaspoons of the kosher salt. Bring to a low boil, reduce the heat to medium-low, and simmer, uncovered, until fork-tender, about 25 minutes. Drain. Peel the potatoes and, while still warm, run them through a food mill or ricer. Or, return the peeled potatoes to the warm cooking pot and mash with a potato masher, heavy whisk, or pastry blender over low heat, being careful not to overmix.

2. Preheat the oven to 350°F.

3. In a large skillet, heat the oil over medium heat. Add the onions and sauté until lightly golden, about 15 minutes. If using, add the garlic and sauté for 1 minute.

4. Beat the eggs into the potatoes, one at a time. Stir in the remaining salt, the pepper, and turmeric. Add the onions, carrot, peas, and parsley.

5. Generously oil a shallow 8-cup baking dish, such as an 8-inch square or 7-by-11-inch dish, then heat in the oven until hot, about 3 minutes. Carefully spoon the potato mixture into the baking dish. Bake until golden and set, about 50 minutes. Serve warm or at room temperature.

VARIATION

Dairy Potato Casserole: Reduce the eggs to 2 and add 1 cup (8 ounces) cream cheese or 1 cup sour cream, or $^3/_4$ cup (6 ounces) cream cheese and $^1/_2$ cup ($1^1/_2$ ounces) grated Parmesan cheese. Bake the casserole for about 40 minutes, sprinkle with $^1/_2$ cup grated Parmesan or shredded Cheddar cheese, and continue baking for about 10 minutes.

GEORGIAN POTATO PANCAKE

(*Labda*)

5 TO 6 SERVINGS D OR P

Most Westerners celebrate Hanukkah with traditional Ashkenazic potato latkes, typically made from grated raw potatoes. Georgians make their own version of potato pancake with mashed potatoes mixed with the ubiquitous national ingredient, the walnut. In addition to Hanukkah, this dish is eaten daily during Passover, providing a filling substitute for bread. Accompaniments might include pkhali (Georgian Vegetable Salads, page 75) and soko arajanit (Georgian Mushrooms in Sour Cream, page 258). Although Georgians generally serve labda *plain, I like a little sour cream or yogurt with it.*

>   1 pound boiling potatoes
>   1¹/₂ teaspoons table salt or 3 teaspoons
>   kosher salt
>   1 cup (4 ounces) ground walnuts
>   3 large eggs, lightly beaten
>   2 tablespoons chopped fresh parsley
>   Ground white or black pepper to taste
>   4 tablespoons *ghee* (Indian Clarified Butter,
>   page 51) or vegetable oil

1. Put the potatoes in a large pot add cold water to cover by 1 inch and 1 teaspoon of the table salt or 2 teaspoons of the kosher salt. Bring to a low boil, reduce the heat to medium-low, and simmer, uncovered, until fork-tender, about 25 minutes. Drain. Peel the potatoes and, while still warm, run through a food mill or mash. Stir in the walnuts, eggs, parsley, the remaining salt, and the pepper.

2. In a 10-inch skillet, melt 2 tablespoons of the ghee over medium heat.

3. Spoon all of the potato mixture into the skillet to form one large pancake, leveling the surface with a spatula. Fry until golden brown on the bottom, about 4 minutes. Slide the pancake onto a large plate.

4. Add the remaining 2 tablespoons ghee to the skillet. Invert the pancake into the skillet and fry until golden brown, about 4 minutes. Slide onto a plate and cut into wedges. Serve warm or at room temperature.

ROMANIAN POTATO AND VEGETABLE PATTIES

(*Parjoale de Legume*)

ABOUT 24 SMALL PATTIES D OR P

My Romanian grandmother noted that "Man can't live on potatoes alone," and it is true that Romanian Jews historically consumed fewer potatoes than Jews to the north, where potatoes constituted the bulk of the diet. Romania, due to extended domination by the Turks as well as a warmer climate, benefited from the culinary wealth of both Europe and Asia and developed a unique repertoire of dishes. From the Sephardim, who arrived in the Balkans with the Ottomans, Ashkenazic Romanians adopted the concept of fried vegetable patties. Besides the pervasive carnatzlach *(meat patties), Romanians transformed mashed potatoes and various leftovers into this flavorful dish. These vegetable-packed patties can be a simple presentation or embellished with a dollop of yogurt or tomato sauce.*

1 pound boiling potatoes

2¼ teaspoons table salt or 4½ teaspoons kosher salt

4 tablespoons unsalted butter or olive oil

2 tablespoons milk or reserved potato cooking water

Ground black pepper to taste

½ teaspoon ground turmeric

3 large eggs, lightly beaten

2 tablespoons chopped fresh cilantro or fresh parsley

½ cup coarsely chopped carrots

½ cup coarsely chopped cauliflower or celery

½ cup coarsely chopped green beans

½ cup fresh or frozen green peas

1 onion, chopped

2 to 3 cloves garlic, minced

½ to 1 teaspoon ground cumin (optional)

About ½ cup unbleached all-purpose flour for dredging (optional)

Vegetable oil for frying

TOMATO SAUCE (OPTIONAL):

1 tablespoon olive oil or vegetable oil

1 teaspoon unbleached all-purpose flour

2 cups puréed tomatoes (see page 291)

About 1 teaspoon table salt or 2 teaspoons kosher salt

½ teaspoon sugar

1. Put the potatoes in a large pot and add cold water to cover by 1 inch and 1 teaspoon of the table salt or 2 teaspoons of the kosher salt. Bring to a low boil, reduce the heat to medium-low, and simmer, uncovered, until fork-tender, about 25 minutes. Drain. Peel the potatoes and, while still warm,

mash in a large bowl with 2 tablespoons of the butter. Stir in the milk, the remaining salt, the pepper, and turmeric. Let cool slightly, then stir in the eggs and cilantro.

2. Steam the carrots, cauliflower, beans, and peas in a covered steamer over boiling water until just tender, about 3 minutes. Stir into the potato mixture.

3. In a medium skillet, melt the remaining 2 tablespoons butter over medium heat. Add the onion and garlic and sauté until soft and translucent, about 5 minutes. If using, add the cumin and stir for 1 minute. Stir into the potato mixture.

4. Form the potato mixture into patties, 3 inches long, 1½ inches wide, and about ¾ inch thick. If the mixture is sticky, dredge the patties in the flour to facilitate shaping. The patties can be stored in the refrigerator for up to 1 day.

5. In a large skillet, heat a thin layer of oil over medium-high heat. In batches, fry the patties, turning once, until golden brown, about 4 minutes per side. Serve warm or at room temperature.

6. To make the sauce: In a medium saucepan, heat the oil over medium heat. Add the flour and stir for 2 minutes. Add the puréed tomatoes, salt, and sugar and cook, stirring constantly, until thickened, about 5 minutes. Drizzle over the patties.

VARIATION

Romanian Potato and Spinach Patties (*Kartofel Chremslach*): Omit the carrots, cauliflower, beans, and peas. After sautéing the onion in Step 3, add 1 pound chopped stemmed spinach and sauté until wilted, about 2 minutes.

SEPHARDIC POTATO CROQUETTES

(Kioftes de Patata)

ABOUT 48 CROQUETTES   Ⓟ

Potato croquettes, also called bimuelos de patata, constitute a light meal, commonly accompanied with poached eggs and a salad, but they also are popular as an appetizer, sometimes mixed with cooked leeks, for Friday night dinner. At dairy meals, they are usually accompanied with yogurt.

> 3 pounds unpeeled baking (russet) potatoes,
>   scrubbed
> 2 teaspoons table salt or 4 teaspoons kosher salt
> 6 large eggs, lightly beaten
> $^1/_2$ cup unbleached all-purpose flour or
>   matza cake meal
> $^1/_2$ cup chopped cilantro, fresh parsley,
>   or cooked spinach
> Ground white or black pepper to taste
>
> COATING:
> Unbleached all-purpose flour for dredging
> 1 large egg beaten with 1 teaspoon water
> About 2 cups fresh bread crumbs or matza meal
>
> Vegetable oil for frying

1. Put the potatoes in a large pot and add cold water to cover by 1 inch and 1 teaspoon of the table salt or 2 teaspoons of the kosher salt. Bring to a low boil, reduce the heat to medium-low, and simmer, uncovered, until fork-tender, about 25 minutes.

Drain. Peel the potatoes and, while still warm, run through a food mill or ricer. Or, return the peeled potatoes to the warm cooking pot and mash with a potato masher, a heavy whisk, or a pastry blender over medium-low heat, being careful not to overmix. You should have about 6 cups of mashed potatoes.

2. In a large bowl, combine the potatoes, eggs, flour, cilantro, the remaining salt, and the pepper. Stir to blend. Shape the potato mixture into 1-inch balls. To coat: Roll in the flour, dip in the egg wash, then roll in the bread crumbs to coat evenly. This gives the kioftes a thick crust.

3. In a large saucepan, heat at least $^1/_2$ inch oil to 370°F over medium-high heat.

4. In batches, fry the potato balls without crowding the pan, turning until golden brown on all sides, about 4 minutes. Using a slotted spoon, transfer to paper towels to drain. Serve warm.

VARIATIONS

Sephardic Potato Pancakes (*Keftes de Patata*): Omit the breading. Form the potato mixture into patties 3 inches long and 1 inch wide, with tapered ends, and fry in a thin layer of olive oil or vegetable oil over medium-high heat until golden brown, about 2 minutes per side.

Greek Potato Croquettes (*Fritas de Kartof*): Add 1 to $1^1/_2$ cups (4 to 6 ounces) shredded kashkaval or Muenster cheese or 1 to $1^1/_2$ cups (3 to $4^1/_2$ ounces) grated Parmesan cheese and, if desired, a pinch of grated nutmeg.

Iraqi Potato Croquettes (*Batata Charp*): Add $^1/_2$ teaspoon ground allspice and $^1/_8$ to $^1/_4$ teaspoon cayenne.

CALCUTTA CURRIED POTATOES

(Aloo Bhaji)

5 TO 6 SERVINGS   D OR P

Bhaji is a dry curry combining an intriguing blend of sweet, spicy, and sour flavors, usually made with potatoes, which absorb flavors well. In India, Jewish curries like this one tend to be fresher tasting and less spicy and oily than non-Jewish versions. Do not cook tomatoes over too high a heat, which will evaporate the water before the acid dissipates.

Indians warn against the Western habit of drinking beer with curries, because the gas and hops react to the spices, resulting in a very bitter flavor and upsetting the carefully balanced spicing. The preferable beverages are water, tea, lassi (sweet or savory yogurt drinks), milk, or coconut milk.

3 tablespoons *ghee* (Indian Clarified Butter, page 51) or vegetable oil

I onion, sliced

I teaspoon minced fresh ginger

I to 2 cloves garlic, minced

$^1/_2$ teaspoon ground turmeric

2 whole cloves or cardamom pods

I bay leaf

$^1/_2$ teaspoon minced chili or $^1/_4$ teaspoon cayenne (optional)

2 pounds new or medium boiling potatoes, peeled and cut into large chunks

4 tomatoes (about 6 ounces each), peeled, seeded, and chopped (see page 291)

I cup water

About $^3/_4$ teaspoon table salt or I$^1/_2$ teaspoons kosher salt

Ground black pepper to taste

2 tablespoons chopped fresh cilantro or parsley

1. In a karai (woklike Indian pan) or large saucepan, melt the ghee over medium heat. Add the onion and sauté until soft and translucent, about 5 minutes. Add the ginger, garlic, turmeric, cloves, bay leaf, and, if using, the chili and sauté for about 2 minutes. Add the potatoes and sauté until lightly colored, about 2 minutes.

2. Add the tomatoes, water, salt, and pepper. Cover and cook over medium-low heat, stirring occasionally, until the potatoes are tender, about 30 minutes. Or, bake, covered, in a preheated 425°F oven, stirring occasionally, for about 1 hour.

3. Uncover and cook until most of the liquid has evaporated. Sprinkle with the cilantro. Serve warm or at room temperature.

VARIATIONS

Calcutta Curried Green Beans and Potatoes (*Loobia Bhaji*): Add 2 pounds sliced green beans with the tomatoes. This dish, popular among Jews from Calcutta, is customarily made with Chinese long beans, also called yard-long beans and asparagus beans, a close relative of black-eyed peas. The pods, more tender and sweeter than those of haricot beans, grow from 12 to 30 inches in length. Pick smooth pods before the seeds mature. Indians frequently sell long beans in bundles containing a dozen pods.

Calcutta Curried Cauliflower and Potatoes (*Phulgobi Bhaji*): Add 1 head cauliflower cut into florets and, if desired, $^1/_2$ cup fresh or frozen green peas, $^1/_2$ cup sliced green beans, and/or 1 chopped carrot with the tomatoes.

Calcutta Curried Okra and Potatoes (*Bindi Bhaji*): Soak 1 pound trimmed okra in 8 cups cold water mixed with $^1/_2$ cup distilled white or cider vinegar for 1 hour. Drain and pat dry with paper towels. Add the okra with the potatoes.

CALCUTTA FRIED WHOLE POTATOES

(Aloo Makalla)

6 TO 8 SERVINGS   Ⓟ

In this wonderful, unique recipe, whole potatoes are simmered in oil for a long time, developing a splendidly firm crust that keeps the interior moist and not at all oily. Aloo makalla is the most famous Jewish dish in India—a synthesis of Arab and Indian cooking traditions that evolved as Middle Eastern Jews relocated to Calcutta in the wake of the British Empire (aloo is Hindi for "potatoes"; makalla is Arabic for "fried").

In Calcutta, a Jewish table was judged by the quality of its aloo makalla. Most of the Jews of Calcutta employed at least one person to do their cooking, although the woman of the household planned and supervised the menus. Thus, many non-Jews learned how to prepare this classic Jewish dish, and even though most of Calcutta's Jewish community has emigrated, aloo makalla remains popular in India.

The distinct cooking method gives the potatoes a moist interior and a very hard surface, so firm that they are a bit difficult to cut, requiring stealthy securing with a fork, which frequently causes the inside to "jump" out. Despite the long time in the oil, the potatoes do not become soggy. Aloo makalla is traditionally served every Friday night, and on holidays, at weddings, and other special occasions, accompanied with bhaji *(curried potatoes and vegetables),* khutta *(vegetable dishes), and* pilau *(rice pilaf).*

2 teaspoons table salt or 4 teaspoons kosher salt
$^1/_2$ teaspoon ground turmeric
3 pounds small boiling potatoes, peeled and pricked on all sides with a fork
About 4 cups peanut oil or vegetable oil

1. Bring a large pot of water to a boil and add the salt and turmeric. Add the potatoes, return to a boil, and parboil for 5 minutes. Drain. Let the potatoes cool, then pat dry.

2. Put the potatoes in a karai (woklike Indian pan), wok, or large saucepan and add enough oil to cover. Bring to a boil over medium-high heat and cook for about 15 minutes. Do not stir. Reduce the heat to low and simmer, shaking the pan occasionally, until the potatoes are crusty and lightly golden, about 1 hour. At this point, the pan can be removed from the heat, and the potatoes can sit in the oil for up to 3 hours.

3. To finish: Heat the pan with the oil and potatoes over medium-high heat and fry the potatoes until the crust is crisp and golden brown, about 5 minutes. Using a slotted spoon, transfer to paper towels to drain. Serve hot.

SEPHARDIC FRIED POTATO SLICES

(Kartofis)

6 TO 8 SERVINGS   Ⓓ OR Ⓟ

I learned this simple but flavorful side dish from a former cook in the Israeli army. These crisp potatoes redolent with garlic and olive oil, remind him of his childhood.

4¹/₂ pounds baking (russet) potatoes, peeled

4 cloves garlic

About 2¹/₂ teaspoons table salt or 5 teaspoons
    kosher salt

¹/₄ cup olive oil, or 2 tablespoons olive oil
    and 2 tablespoons unsalted butter

1. Put the potatoes and 2 cloves garlic in a large pot and add cold water to cover and 1 teaspoon of the table salt or 2 teaspoons of the kosher salt. Bring to a boil, reduce the heat to low, and simmer until the potatoes are tender but not mushy, 20 to 25 minutes. Drain and let cool. Cut the potatoes into ¹/₄-inch-thick slices.

2. In a large skillet, heat the oil over medium-low heat. Add the remaining 2 cloves garlic and sauté until golden but not burnt, about 3 minutes. Discard the garlic.

3. Increase the heat to medium-high. In batches, adding more oil if necessary, sauté the potato slices until golden on both sides, about 3 minutes per side. Sprinkle with the remaining salt.

VARIATION

Sephardic Golden Potatoes with Onions (*Kartofis con Sevoyas*): Heat ¹/₄ cup olive oil or vegetable oil in a large skillet, add 4 large onions cut into rings, and sauté until golden, about 15 minutes. When serving, arrange the onions on top of the fried potatoes.

HUNGARIAN FRIED POTATOES

(Patatas Bravas)

5 TO 6 SERVINGS   Ⓟ

Hungarians accompany their cube-shaped version of "fierce" fried potatoes—the Spanish name revealing the dish's origins—with paprika-flavored tomato sauce instead of ketchup. It is similar in texture to American hash browns. To make them really fierce, add ¹/₂ to 1 teaspoon red pepper flakes or a little Hungarian hot paprika to the sauce. These potatoes are also delicious seasoned simply with salt and pepper.

2 pounds baking (russet) potatoes, peeled and
    cut into 1-inch cubes

SAUCE:

3 tablespoons olive oil or vegetable oil

1 large onion, chopped

2 cloves garlic, minced

2 tablespoons unbleached all-purpose flour

1 cup Vegetable Stock (page 115) or water

8 ounces plum tomatoes, peeled, seeded, and
    chopped (see page 291), about 1¹/₄ cups

2 tablespoons Hungarian sweet paprika

About ³/₄ teaspoon table salt or 1¹/₂ teaspoons
    kosher salt

Ground black pepper to taste

About 1 cup vegetable oil

1. Soak the potatoes in ice water to cover for at least 1 hour or in the refrigerator for up to 3 days. This removes the surface starch and chills the potatoes, which will prevent the exterior from burning before the interior is cooked.

2. To make the sauce: In a medium skillet, heat the oil over medium heat. Add the onion and

garlic and sauté until soft and translucent, about 5 minutes. Add the flour and cook, stirring, for 3 minutes. Gradually stir in the stock. Add the tomatoes, paprika, salt, and pepper and cook, stirring occasionally, until the tomatoes are tender, about 10 minutes. Bring to a boil, reduce the heat to low, and simmer until thickened and reduced to about 2 cups, about 8 minutes. In a blender or food processor, purée until smooth.

3. Drain the potatoes and pat dry with paper towels. In a large skillet or heavy saucepan, heat the oil over medium heat. Add the potatoes and stir until well coated. Reduce the heat to medium-low and cook, stirring occasionally, until golden and tender, about 20 minutes. If the potatoes have browned but are not yet done inside, carefully add a few tablespoons of water to the pan, cover, and cook until tender.

4. Pour the tomato sauce over the cooked potatoes. Serve at once.

VARIATION

Hungarian Potatoes in Sour Cream (*Paprikásburgonya*): Omit the sauce. If desired, add 2 seeded, deribbed (white removed), and sliced green or red bell peppers to the oil before adding the potatoes. After frying, remove potatoes from the skillet, stir in 2 teaspoons sweet paprika, then 1 cup sour cream (at room temperature) and about $1/2$ teaspoon table salt or 1 teaspoon kosher salt, and heat through. Do not boil. Pour over the potatoes.

N O T E   Older potatoes are better for frying than fresh, as potatoes lose moisture during storage, which makes them brown better.

❧ PUMPKIN ❧

The pumpkin, a large orange fruit, has been widely cultivated throughout the Americas since ancient times and was among the first New World foods introduced to Europeans by Native Americans. Still, it is a much-neglected food, in North America primarily relegated to pies. Yet the orange-colored flesh with an earthy overtone offers many culinary possibilities: It can be baked, boiled, steamed, or stuffed.

Sephardim and Italian Jews adopted pumpkin into their pantry earlier—in the beginning of the sixteenth century—and more vigorously than their non-Jewish neighbors. Therefore, the presence of pumpkin in many Mediterranean dishes is a sign of Sephardic influence. Sephardim use it to make soups, stews, puddings, jams, cakes, and pancakes, and to fill pastries. The pumpkin, due to its many seeds, is a symbol of fruitfulness and bounty, and, therefore, traditional Rosh Hashanah and Sukkot fare. Stuffed pumpkins are common on the latter holiday. The Bene Israel of Bombay use it to make a curried stew and a puddinglike confection. Pumpkin-filled ravioli is a signature dish of Italian Jews.

What You Should Know: Although the flesh of the bright orange-colored common field pumpkin can be used, it tends to be very stringy and lacking in flavor. A better choice is the sweeter cheese pumpkin—so named because its tan skin resembles the color of cheese—or the small orange-skinned sugar pumpkin, sometimes called a pie pumpkin. Choose a firm, bright pumpkin that weighs 4 to 5 pounds. Avoid very large pumpkins, which are full of fibers. Make sure the stem is still on and the skin is not soft or broken. Store in a cool, dry place for up to 1 month.

To cook a pumpkin, cut it into eighths, remove the seeds and fibers, place in a large pot of lightly salted boiling water, cover, and simmer over low heat until tender, about 15 minutes. Drain, cut off the peel, and mash. Put the flesh in a sieve and gently press on it with the back of a large spoon to remove the excess liquid.

Pumpkin is one of the few foods whose canned version is usually equal or superior to the home-made product. If you find that canned pumpkin has a metallic taste, simmer it in a saucepan over medium-high heat, stirring, for about 5 minutes.

SYRIAN PUMPKIN PATTIES

(Kibbet Yatkeen)

ABOUT 12 PATTIES

These flavorful patties, which contain no eggs, are denser and more healthful than typical Western pancakes. In Syria, bulgur supplies the body in these patties, but in America some cooks discovered that oats make a suitable substitute. Of course, traditionalists insist on bulgur. Syrians tend to prefer their pumpkin pancakes savory and somewhat spicy, while Sephardim from Turkey and Greece generally like them slightly sweet. These might be served at a Syrian Hanukkah meal alongside bazargan *(Syrian Bulgur Relish, page 76),* yerba *(stuffed grape leaves), spinach salad, and rice with pine nuts.*

1 cup fine bulgur

2 cups warm water

2 cups mashed cooked pumpkin (about 2¹/₂ pounds raw) or 16 ounces pure-pack canned pumpkin

1 cup whole-wheat or unbleached all-purpose flour

¹/₂ cup cold water

1 onion, chopped

3 to 4 cloves garlic, minced

About ¹/₂ teaspoon table salt or 1 teaspoon kosher salt

¹/₂ teaspoon ground coriander

¹/₂ teaspoon ground black pepper

¹/₄ teaspoon ground allspice

¹/₄ teaspoon ground cumin

Pinch of Aleppo or cayenne pepper

Vegetable oil for frying

1. Put the bulgur in a medium bowl, add the warm water, and let soak for 30 minutes. Drain.

2. Transfer the bulgur to a food processor. Add all of the remaining ingredients except the oil and process until smooth. If the mixture is too thin, add a little more flour. Using floured hands, shape into oval patties about 2 inches long, 1 inch wide, and ¹/₂ inch thick, tapering the ends.

3. Heat ¹/₄ inch oil in a large skillet over medium heat. In batches, fry the patties, turning once, until golden brown, about 2 minutes per side. Serve warm or at room temperature.

VARIATIONS

Sephardic Pumpkin Patties (*Fritadas de Calabaza*): This batter is looser than the bulgur version and is dropped from a spoon. Omit the bulgur, the ¹/₂ cup cold water, the onion, garlic, coriander, pepper, allspice, cumin, and Aleppo pepper. Add 3 large eggs, 2 to 8 tablespoons granulated or packed brown sugar, 2 teaspoons ground cinnamon, ¹/₂ teaspoon freshly ground nutmeg, and a pinch of ground ginger.

Syrian Baked Pumpkin Casserole (*Kibbet Yatkeen bi Seniyeh*): Spread the pumpkin mixture in an oiled 9-inch square baking pan. Cut into diamonds or 1½-inch squares, drizzle with ¼ cup vegetable oil, and bake in a preheated 375°F oven until golden brown, about 45 minutes.

BUKHARAN STUFFED PUMPKIN

(*Oshee Tos Kadoo*)

6 TO 8 SERVINGS

Many residents of Uzbekistan maintain a vegetable plot in which, among other things, they grow pumpkins, usually enough to store for several months after the harvest. Pumpkins, which are capable of being kept throughout the winter, historically provided an ideal source of nutrition when other vegetables were scarce. They also make an attractive presentation, served whole, without needing to be cut up before cooking.

Bukharans are renowned for stuffed pumpkin, one of the grandest of all the stuffed vegetables in their repertoire, usually reserved for very special occasions in the autumn, such as Sukkot and the Sabbath. The local pumpkins can grow to prodigious proportions, and the largest are often sold by the chunk to be cooked and mashed or added to stews. For this elegant recipe, however, smaller whole pumpkins are necessary. The seeds can be toasted for the perfect winter snack.

This vegetarian version of stuffed pumpkin is filled with another local Bukharan favorite, palov *(rice pilaf).*

STUFFING:

3 tablespoons vegetable oil

1 large onion, chopped

1¼ cups long-grain white rice

2 cups Vegetable Stock (page 115) or water

About 1 teaspoon table salt or 2 teaspoons kosher salt

Ground black pepper to taste

Pinch of saffron threads or ¼ teaspoon ground turmeric

1 tablespoon hot water

¼ cup dried currants or raisins

¼ cup chopped fresh cilantro or parsley

½ cup cooked chickpeas (optional)

1 tart apple, peeled, cored, and coarsely chopped (optional)

1 quince, peeled, cored, and diced (optional)

1 small pumpkin (4 to 5 pounds)

1 teaspoon sugar

Pinch of salt

1 cabbage leaf (optional)

1. To make the stuffing: In a medium, heavy saucepan, heat the oil over medium heat. Add the onion and sauté until soft and translucent, about 5 minutes. Add the rice and sauté until well coated, about 3 minutes. Add the stock, salt, and pepper, bring to a boil, cover, reduce the heat to low, and simmer until the liquid is absorbed but the rice is still slightly underdone, about 15 minutes.

2. Dissolve the saffron in the hot water and stir into the rice. Add the currants, cilantro, and any combination of chickpeas, apples, and/or quince, if desired.

3. Cut out a disk from the stem end of the pumpkin about 4 inches in diameter. Scoop out and discard the seeds and loose fibers. Sprinkle the insides with the sugar and salt.

4. Pack the stuffing into the pumpkin and put on the lid. Arrange the cabbage leaf, if using, in the bottom of a deep baking pan or large pot to prevent the bottom of the pumpkin from burning. Place the pumpkin in the pan and add enough water to reach about 1 inch up the sides. Bring to a boil, cover, reduce the heat to low, and simmer, or bake in a preheated 375°F oven until the pumpkin is tender, about 2 hours. Cut into wedges or scoop out the filling and pulp. Serve warm.

VARIATION

Substitute 3 acorn squash for the pumpkin, dividing the stuffing between them, and cook for about 45 minutes.

✤ SPINACH ✤

Spinach, a relative of the beet, is a Central Asian herb with dark green leaves. The derivation of the word *spinach* from the Farsi *isfanakh* ("thorn"), referring to its prickly seeds, reflects the plant's Persian origins. It appeared rather late on the culinary scene, developed in Persia around the sixth century, introduced to Europe, by way of the Moors in Spain, only around 1100 C.E., where it quickly became a Sephardic favorite, generally supplanting the much-used beet green and chard. According to the Sephardic sage Solomon Almoli (c. 1485–1542), to dream of spinach signifies happiness, riches, and honor. Spinach arrived in Italy in the thirteenth century, and subsequently the Italians, Arabs, and Sephardim helped to spread it across most of the Mediterranean.

Spinach can withstand a heavy frost and, therefore, was generally available until rather late in the year and frequently was the first vegetable planted for the spring. Because spinach makes its initial appearance near the onset of spring, it became traditional Passover and Shavuot food. The plant does not fare well in hot temperatures, going to seed when the temperature surpasses 75°F. However, after the nights begin to cool again, in late August or early September, the fall spinach crop matures, just in time for Rosh Hashanah.

Fall spinach tends to be a bit tougher than that of spring. The prickly seeded variety, sometimes called winter spinach, yields crinkled, lobed leaves with a robust flavor. The smooth-seeded variety, however, bears up better in warmer weather; its smooth leaves make it easier to clean and thus preferable for commercial use. Modern cultivars often possess the best traits of both varieties.

Spinach has a delicate, slightly bitter flavor that stands alone and also provides an excellent base for many other foods. It has a particular affinity to goat cheese, eggs, lemon, garlic, nutmeg, basil, dill, and oregano. By the thirteenth century, Persians were already pairing fresh spinach with yogurt, garlic, and various spices. Once Italians caught on, they became fervid spinach lovers, especially in Florence, where they even used it in desserts. Turks and Greeks commonly cook spinach with rice, stuff it like grape leaves, and use it to fill *boreks* and various phyllo pastries. In North Africa, it is frequently flavored with olive oil, lemon juice, cumin, and chilies. Sephardim use spinach (both the name and the vegetable) interchangeably with chard in many recipes, including salads, stews, soups, patties, casseroles, omelets, pies, pastry fillings, and even a Sabbath soup utilizing spinach or chard stems. Many traditional spinach recipes call for extensive cooking, which reduces its acidity, but contemporary cooks generally favor a short cooking time.

What You Should Know: Choose crisp, dark green leaves with no sign of yellowing or limpness. Store in a plastic bag in the refrigerator for up to 3 days. Spinach toughens and wilts as it ages. Spinach has a high water content and thus shrinks considerably during cooking; 1 pound (6 to 8 cups) fresh spinach yields about 1½ cups cooked. Frozen spinach is a convenient and acceptable alternative to fresh, although less flavorful and, at times, somewhat bitter.

ITALIAN SPINACH WITH PINE NUTS AND RAISINS

(*Spinaci Pinoli e Passerine*)

6 TO 8 SERVINGS

When spinach reached Italy around the thirteenth century, it supplanted cabbage as the favorite vegetable. The use of pine nuts and raisins in this dish is an Arabic convention, signifying Arabic influence on this Italian recipe. (In fact, a similar dish, sabanigh bi snobar wa sbeeb, *is popular among Middle Easterners.) Sicilian Jews or perhaps Sephardim brought the recipe to northern Italy, where it became a specialty of the Roman and Venetian ghettos. In the latter, cooks also prepared fried patties using the same ingredients.*

This dish would typically be part of a Friday night dinner, along with pane del sabato *(egg bread) and* riso del sabato *(Sabbath saffron rice), or served on Rosh Hashanah accompanied with* fagioli conditi *(Italian Green Bean Salad, page 105) and* finocchi alla giuida *(Italian Braised Fennel, page 251).*

3 pounds spinach, stemmed and washed well
    but not dried
About ¹/₂ teaspoon table salt or 1 teaspoon
    kosher salt
¹/₄ cup olive oil
1 large onion, chopped
¹/₄ cup pine nuts
¹/₄ to ¹/₂ cup golden raisins or dried currants
Ground black pepper to taste
Dash of freshly grated nutmeg (optional)

1. Heat a large dry pot over medium heat. Add the spinach, with just the water clinging to it, and ¼ teaspoon of the table salt or ½ teaspoon of the kosher salt. Cover and cook over medium heat until just wilted, about 5 minutes. Transfer to a colander or a large sieve and let drain.

2. In a large pot, heat the oil over medium heat. Add the onion and sauté until soft and translucent, about 5 minutes. Add the pine nuts and sauté until lightly colored, about 2 minutes.

3. Add the spinach, raisins, the remaining ¼ teaspoon table salt or ½ teaspoon kosher salt, pepper, and, if using, the nutmeg. Cook, stirring frequently, until most of the liquid evaporates, about 5 minutes. Serve immediately.

VARIATION

Italian Spinach with Garlic (*Spinaci Salatai*): Omit the onion and raisins. Add 2 cloves garlic to the hot oil and sauté until golden but not burnt, about 3 minutes, then discard the garlic.

INDIAN CURRIED SPINACH

(*Tarka Saag*)

6 TO 8 SERVINGS

The Baghdadis of Calcutta used spinach with more frequency than did their non-Jewish neighbors. Indian Jews, however, did adopt their neighbors' love of spices, which found their way into the cuisine, as exemplified by this dish.

A tarka is a mixture of hot ghee or oil and spices. The essential oils in the spices are fat solvents, and the heat contributes to the release of flavors. This dish is commonly accompanied with rice.

¼ cup *ghee* (Indian Clarified Butter, page 51) or vegetable oil
1 large onion, chopped
2 to 3 cloves garlic, minced
1 (1-inch) piece fresh ginger, minced (about 2 tablespoons)
1 teaspoon black cumin seeds or ½ teaspoon ground cumin
½ teaspoon fennel seeds or 1½ teaspoons ground coriander
3 pounds spinach, stemmed, washed, and dried
1 teaspoon seeded and minced jalapeño or other small hot green chili
1 teaspoon ground turmeric
About 1 teaspoon table salt or 2 teaspoons kosher salt
Ground black pepper to taste
Pinch of cayenne
1 tablespoon fresh lemon juice (optional)

1. In a karai (woklike Indian pan), wok, or large heavy pot, melt the ghee over medium heat. Add the onion, garlic, and ginger and sauté until soft and translucent, about 5 minutes. Add the cumin and fennel seeds and sauté for 1 minute.

2. Add the spinach, chili, turmeric, salt, pepper, and cayenne and toss to coat. Cover and cook, stirring occasionally, until the spinach is tender, about 15 minutes. If using, stir in the lemon juice. Serve warm or at room temperature.

VARIATION

Indian Curried Spinach with Cheese (*Saag Panir*): Substitute 1 cup *panir* (Indian White Cheese, page 49) or other mild fresh crumbly cheese for the lemon juice at the end of Step 2, gently stirring it in. Serve warm.

Sephardic Spinach Patties

(*Keftes de Espinaca*)

ABOUT 16 PATTIES

Among my favorite spinach dishes are these simple but delicious patties. Even spinach haters can't resist them, especially when they're splashed with a little fresh lemon juice; fresh juice does make a major difference in taste. Onions add a sweet flavor and textural complexity. These patties are traditional on Passover and Rosh Hashanah, corresponding to the emergence of the early and late spinach crops.

3 tablespoons olive oil or vegetable oil

1 large onion, chopped

2 to 4 cloves garlic, minced (optional)

2 pounds fresh spinach, stemmed, cooked, chopped, and squeezed dry, or 20 ounces thawed frozen chopped spinach, squeezed dry

About 1 cup matza meal or fine dried bread crumbs

About $^3/_4$ teaspoon table salt or 1 $^1/_2$ teaspoons kosher salt

Ground black pepper to taste

$^1/_2$ teaspoon freshly grated nutmeg or $^1/_2$ teaspoon cayenne (optional)

3 large eggs, lightly beaten

Vegetable oil for frying

Lemon wedges for serving

1. In a large skillet, heat the olive oil over medium heat. Add the onion and, if using, the garlic and sauté until soft and translucent, about 5 minutes. Remove from the heat and add the spinach, matza meal, salt, pepper, and, if using, the nutmeg. Stir in the eggs. If the mixture is too loose, add a little more matza meal. The mixture can be stored in the refrigerator for a day.

2. Shape the spinach mixture into patties 3 inches long and 1 $^1/_2$ inches wide, with tapered ends. In a large skillet, heat a thin layer of oil over medium heat. In batches, fry the patties, turning, until golden brown, about 3 minutes per side. Drain on paper towels. Serve warm, accompanied with lemon wedges.

Sephardic Spinach Patties with Cheese
(*Keftes de Espinaca con Queso*): Add 1 cup
(4 ounces) shredded Muenster, Swiss, Gouda, or
Cheddar cheese; or ¹/₄ cup grated kefalotyri or
Parmesan cheese.

Sephardic Spinach Patties with Walnuts
(*Keftes de Espinaca con Muez*): Substitute
¹/₂ to 1 cup finely chopped walnuts for the matza meal.

Italian Spinach Patties (*Polpettine di Spinaci*):
Add ³/₄ cup raisins soaked in white wine for 30 minutes, then drained, and ³/₄ cup toasted pine nuts (see
page 22).

N O T E   To reheat the spinach patties, place in a
large skillet, add 1¹/₂ cups Vegetable Stock (page 115),
and simmer over low heat for about 5 minutes.

GREEK SPINACH AND CHEESE CASSEROLE

(*Sfoungato*)

6 TO 9 SERVINGS

Sfoungato, or sfougato *(from the Greek word for
"sponge,"* sfoggos, *and the Ladino equivalent,* esponga*),
is also called* quajado de espinaca *in Greece,* sabanigh b'jiben *("spinach with cheese") in Syria, and*
almodrote *in Turkey. Sfoungato is descended, if not
in essence at least in name, from* ova spongia, *the
ancient Roman omelet mentioned by Apicius. The
Romans, however, were acquainted neither with
spinach nor baked vegetable casseroles. The combination of a vegetable, cheese, and egg in a casserole is
a characteristic feature of Sephardic cookery. Spinach
is one of the most popular of these dishes, of which
there are numerous variations, including those layered with mashed potatoes, topped with "nests" of
cheese, and baked with a crust like a pie.*

*Among many Sephardim from Greece, spinach
and cheese casserole is a nostalgic comfort food,
bringing back memories of a grandmother spreading
the cleaned fresh spinach over a tray to dry in the sun
before chopping it up. Today, cooks tend to use a salad
spinner and paper towels to dry spinach and sometimes, for a last-minute dish, even substitute frozen
spinach. In any case, too much moisture will result in
a soggy texture. The cheeses used in the dish vary
depending on preference and what is in the refrigerator. Serve large pieces of this lightly marbled casserole as an entrée, medium portions as a side dish, or
small squares as an appetizer.*

2 tablespoons vegetable oil or butter

1 onion, chopped, or 4 scallions, sliced

2 pounds fresh spinach, stemmed, washed, and
    coarsely chopped, or 20 ounces thawed frozen
    chopped spinach, drained

1/2 cup chopped fresh dill, 1 tablespoon chopped
    fresh mint, or 1/4 teaspoon freshly grated
    nutmeg (optional)

1 cup (8 ounces) farmer cheese

1 cup (5 ounces) crumbled feta cheese

1 cup (4 ounces) shredded kashkaval, Muenster,
    Gouda, yellow Cheddar, or Swiss cheese

4 large eggs, lightly beaten

About 1/2 teaspoon table salt or 1 teaspoon
    kosher salt

About 1/4 teaspoon ground black pepper

TOPPING:

About 3 tablespoons grated aged kashkaval
    or Parmesan cheese for sprinkling

1/4 cup unsalted butter or 3 tablespoons
    vegetable oil

2 cups plain yogurt mixed with 1 tablespoon
    dried mint (optional)

1. Preheat the oven to 350°F. Grease a 9-inch square baking dish.

2. In a large skillet, heat the oil over medium heat. Add the onion and sauté until soft and translucent, about 5 minutes. Add the spinach and cook until wilted and dry, about 5 minutes. If using, stir in the dill. Set aside.

3. Combine the cheeses, eggs, salt, and pepper. Stir in the spinach mixture. Spread in the prepared

pan. Sprinkle with the 3 tablespoons kashkaval cheese and dot with the butter. The casserole can be stored in the refrigerator for up to 1 day.

4. Bake until golden brown, about 45 minutes. Let stand for at least 5 minutes before serving. Serve warm or at room temperature, topped with dollops of the yogurt-mint mixture, if desired.

VARIATIONS

Double the recipe and bake in a 9-by-13-inch pan.

Sephardic Zucchini and Cheese Casserole (*Sfoungato con Calavassa*): Substitute 4 cups shredded zucchini (about 1 1/2 pounds), sprinkled lightly with salt, drained in a colander for 30 minutes, and squeezed to press out the excess liquid, for the spinach.

Greek Baked Spinach with Cheese Nests (*Sfongo/Fongos*): Omit the cheeses. Mix the spinach with only 1 egg and spread the spinach mixture in a 9-by-13-inch baking pan. Combine 2 cups (10 ounces) crumbled feta cheese or 2 cups (8 ounces) shredded kashkaval, Muenster, or Cheddar cheese, 6 lightly beaten eggs (or 3 eggs and 1 cup mashed potatoes), and a dash of black pepper. Using the back of a large spoon, make 6 equidistant indentations in the spinach, divide the cheese mixture among the indentations, and bake as above.

Balkan Spinach Pie (*Inchusa di Spinaka*): Increase the eggs to 5. Line two 8-inch pie plates with Sephardic Oil-Butter Pastry (page 177), Sephardic Oil Pastry (page 177), or Sephardic Yogurt Pastry (page 178). Divide the spinach mixture between the 2 pies, cover with a top layer of pastry, crimp the edges to seal, and bake in a preheated 350°F oven until golden brown, about 45 minutes.

❖ SQUASH ❖

The Cucurbitaceae family of vegetables can be divided into two groups: one, which includes gourds, cucumbers, and melons, is native to the Old World; the other, which includes pumpkins and squashes, comes from Central and South America. Most of the Old World gourds were originally inedible, utilized primarily as containers and musical instruments or for medicinal purposes and fuel. On the other hand, ancient Native American farmers bred a wide range of squashes that became, along with corn and beans, staples of their diet. What a surprise, then, for Europeans to discover gourdlike squashes and pumpkins that they could actually eat!

Indeed, squash proved among the most initially popular imports brought to Europe from the Americas, as attested by numerous paintings and scientific accounts of the vegetables by the middle of the sixteenth century. Jews of the Mediterranean in particular straightaway embraced squash, both the hard and the tender types, incorporating them in a wide range of dishes, including soups, stews, salads, patties, and casseroles.

Seasonal references to squash have less to do with the vegetable's actual seasonality than with its culinary use: "Winter" squash is mature squash, with a hard rind; and "summer" squash is immature, with thin, edible skin. Summer squashes are succulent and mildly flavored. The cylindrical, dark green variety, known by its Italian name, zucchini, is far and away the most popular of the summer squashes. The preferred variety in the Middle East is the *cousa*, or *koosa* (such as the Magda variety), called *kishu* in Israel, a small light green squash with a white, nutty flesh that is shorter and stouter and, therefore, better for stuffing and pickling, than zucchini. There are also various yellow hybrids.

What You Should Know: Look for firm summer squash with a shiny exterior. Avoid those with a dull rind or soft spots. Older squash (larger than 8 ounces) has more and tougher seeds and more water than immature ones. Summer squash consists of up to 95 percent water. To extract some of the moisture before sautéing, toss the sliced or grated squash with salt (1 teaspoon table salt or 2 teaspoons kosher salt for every pound of cut-up squash) and let stand in a colander for 30 minutes; rinse and pat dry before cooking. You won't find zucchini cooked with garlic in Mediterranean dishes, as it can dampen the squash's sweetness. Summer squash blends especially well with eggplant, so the two are frequently paired together in vegetable stews throughout the Mediterranean region. The varieties of summer squash can generally be used interchangeably.

TURKISH ZUCCHINI WITH TOMATOES

(*Calavassa con Tomat*)

6 TO 8 SERVINGS   Ⓓ OR Ⓟ

Most Turkish Jews enjoy this green squash cooked with tomatoes and olive oil at least once and frequently more times a week throughout most of the summer. The squash bounty usually lasts until after Sukkot, at which time its reappearance is eagerly awaited until the following summer. Calavassa, the Ladino word for "squash" is also slang for a "dullard" (the frequency of vegetable references in the language reflect the Sephardic passion for vegetables).

This characteristic Turkish-Jewish dish is sometimes called bocaditos de calavassa; bocaditos *literally means "little mouths" in Spanish, referring to the bite-sized pieces. Omit the lemon juice if serving cold. This dish is frequently accompanied with rice.*

> 3 tablespoons olive oil
> 1 large onion, chopped
> 1 pound plum tomatoes, peeled, seeded, and coarsely chopped (see page 291), about 2¹/₂ cups
> ¹/₄ cup water
> 1 teaspoon sugar
> About 1 teaspoon table salt or 2 teaspoons kosher salt
> Ground black pepper to taste
> 3 tablespoons fresh lemon juice (optional)
> 2 pounds small *cousa* squash, zucchini, or yellow squash, peeled and cut into chunks or thickly sliced
> ¹/₄ cup chopped fresh parsley or dill
> Yogurt for garnish (optional)

1. In a large saucepan, heat the oil over medium heat. Add the onion and sauté until soft and translucent, about 5 minutes. Add the tomatoes, water, sugar, salt, pepper, and, if using, the lemon juice. Bring to a boil, cover, reduce the heat to low, and simmer, stirring occasionally, until softened, about 15 minutes.

2. Add the squash, cover, and simmer until tender, about 10 minutes. Stir in the parsley and garnish with yogurt, if using. Serve warm or at room temperature.

VARIATIONS

Sephardic Green Beans with Tomatoes (*Fijon Verde con Tomat/Fassoulia*): Substitute 2 pounds trimmed green beans for the squash.

Turkish Spinach with Tomatoes (*Espinaca Kotcha*): Substitute 3 pounds stemmed spinach for the squash.

Middle Eastern Stuffed Zucchini in Yogurt Sauce

(Koosa Mahshi bil Leben)

6 SERVINGS D

The prevalent Middle Eastern way to stuff squash is to hollow out the whole squash (ma'oorah in Arabic) to form little tubes using a naqqara (a thin long-handled scoop). A melon baller or apple corer is a good substitute. Proficient corers know just when to make a sharp, quick twisting motion near the end, disengaging the pulp without damaging the sides or bottom. The labor and skill involved in this method of stuffing squash is certainly more intensive than simply halving them in the Sephardic way (medias de calavassa in Ladino), however, the effort is necessary in order to cook the whole squash submerged in a sauce in the Middle Eastern fashion. Because it is time consuming, whole stuffed squash are usually reserved for special occasions. Then, the women of the household gather with relatives and friends to prepare the squash, chatting and joking, turning a tedious chore into good-spirited fun.

Middle Easterners prepare several versions of stuffed zucchini. This one is served with a refreshing minty yogurt sauce that complements the delicately sweet squash. (For a nondairy meal, substitute a tomato sauce.) Yogurt made from sheep or goat's milk rather than cow's milk gives a less sharp taste to the sauce, which is preferred in the Middle East. In this vegetarian version, chickpeas and pine nuts add interesting textural and flavor contrasts to the rice and soft squash. The rice expands and absorbs flavor from the squash during the relatively lengthy cooking. Syrians might serve the latter version for a Rosh Hashanah dinner, alongside silka (chard), lubiya (black-eyed peas), salata (salad), and riz (white rice). Serve this dish as a main course or side dish with salads and bread.

6 *cousa* squash or thick zucchini,
    each 5 to 6 inches long

STUFFING:

1 cup long-grain rice, soaked in cold water
    to cover for 1 hour, drained, and rinsed

1 cup cooked chickpeas

1/4 cup olive oil or butter, melted

1 onion, chopped (optional)

1 tablespoon pine nuts (optional)

1/2 teaspoon dried mint, crushed, or 1/2 teaspoon
    ground allspice and 1/4 teaspoon ground
    cinnamon

About 1 teaspoon table salt or 2 teaspoons
    kosher salt

Ground black pepper to taste

YOGURT SAUCE:

1 tablespoon cornstarch

1/4 cup water

3 cups plain yogurt

1 tablespoon dried mint, crushed

About 1 teaspoon table salt or 2 teaspoons
    kosher salt

1/4 teaspoon sugar

2 to 3 cloves garlic, mashed (optional)

1. Cut the stem off each squash. Using a naqqara, melon baller, or apple corer, scoop out the pulp from the stem end to form a hollow tube straight through, leaving the sides and bottom intact. Or, slit the squash lengthwise without cutting all the way through and scoop out the pulp. Use the pulp in a separate dish or add it to soups or salads.

2. To make the stuffing: In a medium bowl, combine the rice, chickpeas, oil, onion, pine nuts, mint, salt, and pepper. Fill the zucchini three-quarters full with the stuffing, leaving room for expansion. Arrange in a single layer in a large pot or roasting pan and sprinkle any excess filling on top. Add water to cover and place an ovenproof plate on top to weigh down the squash.

3. Bring to a boil over medium-high heat. Cover tightly with a lid or aluminum foil, reduce the heat to low, and simmer on the stove top or bake in a preheated 350°F oven until the squash and rice are tender, about 45 minutes. Drain, returning the squash to the pan. Save the cooking liquid to add to a vegetable stock.

4. To make the sauce: In a medium saucepan, combine the cornstarch and water; stir to blend. Stir in the yogurt. Bring to a low boil, stirring constantly, over medium heat. Reduce the heat to low and simmer, stirring constantly but gently, for 2 minutes. Add the mint, salt, sugar, and, if using, the garlic.

5. Pour the sauce over the zucchini. Simmer over low heat or bake at 350°F, uncovered, until heated through, about 10 minutes. Serve warm.

VARIATION

Middle Eastern Stuffed Zucchini with Tomato Sauce (*Koosa Mahshi bil Benadora*): Omit the yogurt sauce. Heat 1 tablespoon olive oil in a large saucepan, add 3 to 4 minced cloves garlic, and sauté until they begin to color, about 2 minutes. Add 28 ounces peeled, seeded, and chopped plum tomatoes (about 4 cups), 3/4 teaspoon salt, 1/2 teaspoon sugar, and a pinch of black pepper and simmer for 15 minutes. Substitute for the water in Step 2 and cook as above serving the squash in the sauce.

❧ TOMATOES ❧

Tomato, the mildly acidic, pulpy South American fruit, first arrived in Spain in 1523, in Italy about two decades later, and in the rest of the southern Mediterranean shortly thereafter. It received a particularly enthusiastic reception in the Ottoman Empire, where it was incorporated into numerous stews, salads, and vegetable dishes. Sephardim also took to the tomato, combining it with onions and olive oil to form one of the classic bases for many of their recipes. Most Europeans, on the other hand, initially believed the tomato to be poisonous, the Italians calling it *mala insana* (Greek for "unhealthy fruit"), relegated the plant solely to ornamental use.

The earliest European record of tomato sauce appeared in Italy in 1692, while the first record of tomato sauce paired with pasta appeared nearly a century later. By the end of the eighteenth century, the tomato had gained widespread acceptance in Italy, reflected in the change of name for tomato from *mala insana* to *pomo dei Moro* ("apple of the Moors"), connoting its usage in Arab lands, and *pomodoro* ("golden apple"), connoting the yellow color of the original Mexican variety. The rest of the continent eventually followed Italy's lead, and the tomato emerged as a popular ingredient. Tomatoes remained taboo in the United States, however, for much longer. Thomas Jefferson credited Dr. John de Sequeyra, a Sephardic physician who settled in Williamsburg in 1745, with first importing tomatoes to Virginia, as well as persuading him that they were not only edible but also healthful.

Tomatoes add a unique distinction to cooking: a silky texture and a sweetness countered by acidity. Unfortunately, most store-bought fresh tomatoes—cultivated for their disease resistance, convenience in harvesting, and transportation and storage qualities—tend to be pale and tasteless. In addition, during handling, tomatoes are frequently subjected to temperatures below 55°F, which destroys the ripening enzyme, resulting in a woolly texture and a lack of flavor. (The red color of most store-bought tomatoes is produced by ethylene gas.) This has driven many people to the preferable options of growing their own, purchasing tastier imports from countries such as Israel, using tastier plum tomatoes, or using canned tomatoes.

What You Should Know: Do not refrigerate unripe tomatoes, which gives them poor texture and flavor. Leave unripe tomatoes, stem-end up, in a cool place out of direct sunlight until red and softened. Too much light softens tomatoes without sufficiently ripening them. If not subjected to temperatures below 55°F, pink tomatoes will ripen in 3 to 5 days, green ones in about a week. Use ripe tomatoes immediately, or if necessary refrigerate them for up to a few days to prevent spoilage.

To substitute canned: Use a 14.5-ounce can of crushed tomatoes for about 2 cups and a 28-ounce can for about 4 cups. (Check the ingredients to make sure that the contents are actually made from tomatoes and not tomato paste.)

NOTE To peel tomatoes: Very ripe tomatoes can be peeled without blanching. Run the blade of a dull knife (such as a butter knife) over the entire surface, cut out the stem end, then pull off the skin. To peel younger tomatoes, cut an "X" at the bottom of the fruit and drop in boiling water for 15 to 30 seconds, then immediately plunge into a bowl of ice water to stop the cooking. The skin will easily peel off.

To seed tomatoes: Cut them in half horizontally, hold upside down, and gently squeeze to remove the seeds and juice, while leaving the pulp.

To make tomato purée: In a blender or food processor, process peeled and seeded tomatoes until smooth.

SEPHARDIC CHEESE-STUFFED TOMATOES

(*Tomat Reyenado de Queso*)

6 SERVINGS

My grandmother remembered that her Romanian relatives used to wrap homemade soft cheese in cheesecloth and hang it over a bucket to drain for a day, then use it in dishes such as this Balkan favorite, stuffed vine-ripened tomatoes. Some cooks substituted the sharper kashkaval for the pot cheese. In either case, the cheese was commonly mixed with feta to provide a tang, but not enough to overwhelm the fruitiness of the tomatoes. Sometimes the top of the stuffed tomato is first dipped into egg, then flour, before frying, a characteristic Sephardic practice. This simple dish is easy, attractive, and delicious.

6 ripe tomatoes (about 6 ounces each)
Salt for sprinkling

STUFFING:

1 cup (4 ounces) shredded kashkaval, Cheddar, Swiss, or other sharp firm cheese; or 1 cup (8 ounces) farmer or pot cheese
1 cup (5 ounces) crumbled feta cheese or mashed potatoes
2 large eggs, lightly beaten
Ground black pepper to taste

Olive oil or vegetable oil for frying
About 1/2 cup water

1. Cut a small slice off the bottom of the tomatoes so they stand upright. Cut off the stem ends. Carefully scoop out and discard the seeds and pulp. Pat the insides of the tomatoes dry with paper towels. Sprinkle the insides lightly with salt and invert on paper towels to drain for about 30 minutes.

2. To make the stuffing: In a medium bowl, combine the cheeses, eggs, and pepper. Stir to blend. Spoon the stuffing into the tomatoes, mounding slightly.

3. In a large, heavy saucepan or skillet, heat a thin layer of oil over medium heat. Place the tomatoes, filling-side down, in the pan and fry until browned, about 3 minutes.

4. Invert the tomatoes and pour in the water. Bring to a boil, cover, reduce the heat to low, and simmer until the tomatoes are tender but not mushy, about 15 minutes. Serve warm.

VARIATIONS

Baked Stuffed Tomatoes (*Tomat Reyenado de Queso*): After Step 2, place the stuffed tomatoes in a baking dish, without the water, and bake in a preheated 375°F oven until tender, about 20 minutes, then place under a broiler until the tops are browned.

Greek Cheese-Stuffed Tomatoes (*Tomatates Yenas de Queso*): Add 1 teaspoon dried mint and ¼ teaspoon grated nutmeg to the stuffing.

SEPHARDIC RICE-STUFFED TOMATOES

(*Tomat Reyenado*)

8 SERVINGS

The use of rice pilaf as the stuffing signifies the Turkish origins of this dish. For an appetizer, substitute plum tomatoes for the large ones.

8 large, firm red or green tomatoes
(about 8 ounces each)

STUFFING:
3 tablespoons olive oil or vegetable oil
1 onion, chopped
1 cup long-grain rice
Reserved tomato pulp, above
2 cups water
¼ cup chopped fresh parsley
1 tablespoon chopped fresh mint or 1 teaspoon
    dried mint, crushed
1 teaspoon sugar
About 1 teaspoon table salt or 2 teaspoons
    kosher salt
Ground black pepper to taste
2 to 3 tablespoons dried currants or raisins (optional)
2 to 3 tablespoons pine nuts (optional)

SAUCE:
2 tablespoons olive oil
1 tablespoon fresh lemon juice
1 tablespoon granulated or packed brown sugar
    (optional)

1. Preheat the oven to 350°F.

2. Cut a small slice off the bottom of the tomatoes so they stand up straight. Cut off the stem end. Carefully scoop out the seeds and pulp, discarding the seeds and reserving the pulp.

3. To make the stuffing: In a medium, heavy saucepan, heat the oil over medium heat. Add the onion and sauté until soft and translucent, about 5 minutes. Add the rice and sauté until well coated and opaque, about 3 minutes. Add the reserved pulp, water, parsley, mint, sugar, salt, pepper, and, if using, the currants and pine nuts. Bring to a boil, cover, reduce the heat to low, and simmer until the liquid is absorbed, about 15 minutes.

4. In a large baking dish or ovenproof skillet, combine all the sauce ingredients. Spoon the stuffing into the tomatoes, mounding it slightly. Arrange in a single layer in the dish or pan and cover.

5. Bake until tender, about 40 minutes for large tomatoes, 20 to 30 minutes for plum tomatoes. Serve hot or at room temperature, drizzled with the sauce.

VARIATIONS

Substitute 1 tablespoon chopped fresh dill and $1/2$ teaspoon dried thyme for the mint. Or, substitute $3/4$ teaspoon ground cinnamon and $1/4$ teaspoon ground allspice for the mint. Or, omit the currants, pine nuts, and mint and add $3/4$ cup (4 ounces) crumbled feta cheese to the cooked rice. Syrians add a little tamarind sauce to the rice stuffing, or fill the tomatoes with cooked okra.

Turkish Rice-Stuffed Tomatoes (*Zeytinyagli Domates Dolmasi*): In place of the sauce, substitute 1 cup water, $1/3$ cup olive oil, 1 tablespoon tomato paste, and $1/2$ teaspoon table salt or 1 teaspoon kosher salt.

Sephardic Mixed Stuffed Vegetables (*Reyenados/Masasha*): Reduce the tomatoes to 2 and add 2 seeded, deribbed (white removed), and parboiled yellow or green bell peppers, 2 hollowed (leave several outer layers) and parboiled for 10 minutes large onions, and 2 halved and cored large zucchini.

TURNIPS

Turnips didn't always have a lackluster reputation. One of the world's first recorded recipes, found on four-thousand-year-old Sumerian tablets, is for turnips: "No meat is needed. Turnips. Boil water. Throw fat in. Add onion, dorsal thorn [an unknown seasoning], coriander, cumin, and kanasu [a legume]. Squeeze leek and garlic and spread juice over dish. Add onion and mint." As recorded recipes would have been intended for the upper class, turnips must have been considered a choice food. But as time passed, the turnip became relegated to poor man's food and animal fodder. A Talmudic statement reads: "Woe to the house where the turnip is common." Finally, with the potato's arrival in Europe in the 1700s, the turnip's role faded further. In the Middle East, turnips remain relevant primarily as pickles and in stews.

What You Should Know: Turnips have a sharp flavor and coarse texture. They come in numerous shapes, sizes, and colors, with white turnips tending to be sweeter than red ones. Fresh young turnips less than 2 inches in diameter are eaten raw in salads; larger, more mature ones should be cooked or pickled. Choose firm blemish-free roots. White turnips larger than 2 inches tend to be pithy. Fall and winter are the best seasons for tasty turnips. Turnips should be peeled or they will be bitter.

The rutabaga, also called yellow turnip and swede, is large and round—a firmer, hardier relative of the turnip, with an orange-yellow flesh, tan skin, and a violet neck. Use interchangeably with turnips. Rutabagas are very hard and usually sold waxed. Peel, then cut into pieces to cook.

BUKHARAN TURNIPS WITH CHICKPEAS

(Sholgom va Nuikhat)

4 TO 5 SERVINGS   Ⓓ

Most Bukharans, who never developed a taste for the American potato, profess a lingering fondness for this venerable vegetable, many preferring the white-skinned varieties. Turnips, frequently combined with other vegetables, play a prominent role in Uzbekistani cooking, the greens being cooked for an extended time and used as a salad or side dish. Fresh young turnips are even used raw in salads. This is served as a salad or side dish.

    1 onion, peeled
    3 turnips, peeled and quartered
    2 large carrots, cut into 2-inch pieces
    1 1/2 cups cooked chickpeas
    1/2 cup plain yogurt or sour cream
    Salt to taste
    Ground black pepper to taste

1. In a large pot of lightly salted boiling water, parboil the onion for 1 minute. Remove the onion, cut in half, then cut into slices.

2. Add the turnips and carrots to the water and cook until tender, about 10 minutes. Drain, saving the cooking liquid for soup stock. Cut the vegetables into 1/2-inch cubes.

3. In a large bowl, combine the turnips, carrots, onions, and chickpeas. Add the yogurt, salt, and pepper and toss to coat.

VEGETABLE STEWS

❧ · ❧

Vegetable stews made with very little or no meat date back to prehistory, serving as one-dish meals capable of feeding a large group. At times, these dishes featured a single starring vegetable, but more typically they contained several as a way of stretching a few ingredients and creating complexity. Vegetable stews remain the basis of various forms of cookery, including Indian curries and Ethiopian *wots*.

Early Old World stews commonly consisted of various combinations of turnips, parsnips, cabbage, gourds, and seasonal greens, flavored with onions, garlic, and various herbs. Dried legumes, such as fava beans, chickpeas, and split peas, were frequently added for complementary nutrition; these ingredients predominated throughout the winter. The appearance of the Indian eggplant in Persia (now Iran) around the fourth century C.E.. led to its inclusion in stews throughout the Persian and then Muslim worlds, but rarely in Europe. Among the Inquisition's supposed signs of Jewish cooking were vegetarian eggplant stews, including *berenjenas con cebolla* (eggplant with onions) and *berenjenas con huevos* (eggplant with eggs). Shortly after tomatoes arrived in Spain and, in the sixteenth century, Asia Minor, people began adding them to vegetable stews, sometimes along with other South American imports—peppers, squash, and green beans—with eminently pleasing results. These vegetable stews spread throughout the Middle East and the Mediterranean, the most famous in the West unquestionably being the Provençal ratatouille, the name deriving from the French *touiller* (from the Latin *tudiculare*), meaning "to stir" or "crush." Nonetheless, ratatouille arrived in that region relatively late in history, as it was first recorded in the early twentieth century. Arabs and Sephardim had already been enjoying versions for centuries.

What You Should Know: There is no single way to prepare vegetable stew. According to some cooks, each vegetable should be fried separately, then combined with the others in a tomato sauce for a final simmering. Other renditions call for cooking the ingredients together all at once; some layered, others mixed. Most vegetable stews are actually better when made in large quantities and reheated the next day, the flavors having an opportunity to meld and mellow. Middle Eastern vegetable stews tend to be cooked until all of the ingredients are very soft; any sign of crispness is a sign of a bad cook. Turks generally add a little lemon juice and always lots of olive oil. Vegetable stews are usually served with rice, bulgur, or, in northwest Africa, with couscous, and in Romania with *mamaliga* (Romanian Cornmeal Mush, page 379), providing a light main course or a flavorful side dish.

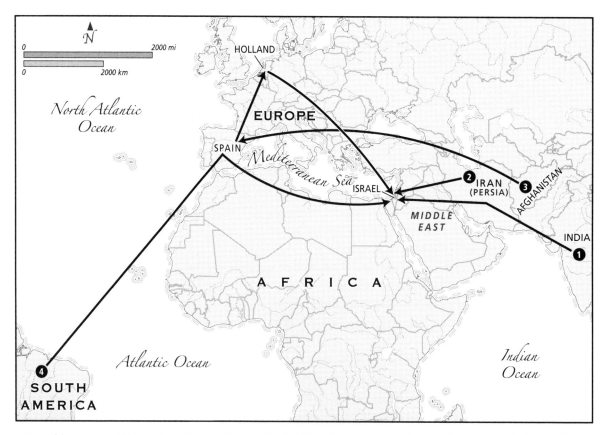

Vegetable Routes: *The variety of vegetables used in Old World stews grew along with the arrival of vegetables in the region. Indigenous Middle Eastern vegetables include cabbage, lettuce, radishes, beets, turnips, celery, leeks, onions, and garlic. Numerous other vegetables reached the Middle East from across the globe, their introduction revolutionizing Old World Jewish cooking.* **1** *Indian vegetables: eggplant, cucumbers;* **2** *spinach from Iran (formerly Persia);* **3** *carrots, originating in Afghanistan and developed in Holland;* **4** *South American vegetables: tomatoes, potatoes, peppers, green beans, squash*

❧ OLIVE TREES AND HONEY ❧

ROMANIAN VEGETABLE STEW

(Guvetch)

6 TO 8 SERVINGS AS A SIDE DISH   Ⓟ

The Marks/Markowitz family (my father's family) came to the United States from the small towns of Jassy and Husi, Romania, in the 1880s, seeking safety and opportunity in the wake of the pogroms and persecutions that swept eastern Europe following the assassination of Czar Alexander II. Family members scattered from Miami to Massachusetts. Since 1929, one branch of the family has held an annual reunion in western Florida. The Marks family reunion typically consists of sixty or more relatives, ranging from infants to people over one hundred years old, a few having attended the original gathering. At each of these potluck events, one of the prominently featured dishes is guvetch, *a vegetable stew that is a classic of Romanian cooking.*

Guvetch can be traced back to the Turkish occupation of the Balkans beginning in the fourteenth century. The Turks introduced their vegetable stews to the region, including the baked stew called djuvec, *named after the earthenware vessel in which it was cooked. The native Romanians, who pronounced the dish* guvetch *(also spelled* yuvetch *and* ghivetch*), quickly took to the dish, which became one of the most popular of Romanian dishes.*

Authentic, guvetch *derives its flavor from the slow cooking of a variety of vegetables, allowing their flavors to meld together. The actual contents can vary, although it is characteristic of Romanian cookery to use plenty of garlic—in this instance both minced and whole. Summer stews (guvetch yaz) contain seasonal vegetables, such as eggplants, okra, peppers, tomatoes, and zucchini. Winter stews (guvetch kis) are predominantly made with winter squash and various root vegetables—carrots, celeriac, potatoes,* and turnips. Guvetch de riz *refers to stews cooked with rice.*

Although, as with most plebeian dishes, there is no definitive recipe, this is a typical Marks family guvetch *adapted from my grandmother's recipe. Serve with* mamaliga *(Romanian Cornmeal Mush, page 379) or rice. At dairy meals, it is usually accompanied with yogurt or sour cream.*

I large eggplant (about 1½ pounds), peeled
About 1 tablespoon plus 1 teaspoon table salt
    or 2 tablespoons plus 2 teaspoons kosher salt
1¾ pounds plum tomatoes, peeled, seeded, and
    coarsely chopped (see page 291), about 4 cups
I cup extra-virgin olive oil
4 onions, sliced
2 to 4 cloves garlic, minced
I pound green beans, trimmed, or 1 pound okra,
    trimmed
4 small zucchini or yellow squash or any
    combination, cut into chunks
2 green bell peppers, seeded, deribbed (white
    removed), and sliced
2 red bell peppers, seeded, deribbed (white
    removed), and sliced
4 to 8 whole cloves garlic
I to 2 large carrots, sliced (optional)
I small head cauliflower, cut into florets (optional)
Ground black pepper to taste
Pinch of sugar
I cup water

1. Cut the eggplant crosswise into 1-inch-thick slices, then into 1-inch-wide sticks, then into 1-inch cubes. Put in a colander or on a wire rack, sprinkle lightly with 1 tablespoon of the table salt or 2 tablespoons of the kosher salt, and let stand for at least 1 hour. (Moisture will appear on the surface, and the eggplant will become more pliable.) Rinse the eggplant under cold water, then press repeatedly

between several layers of paper towels until the slices feel firm and dry. The eggplant can be stored in the refrigerator for up to 4 hours.

2. Preheat the oven to 350°F. Oil a deep 4-quart casserole dish or ovenproof pot. Spread half of the tomatoes in the casserole.

3. In a large, heavy saucepan, heat $^1/_2$ cup of the oil over medium-high heat. Add the eggplant and sauté until lightly browned, about 8 minutes. Transfer the eggplant to the casserole.

4. Drain off any oil from the pan, add $^1/_4$ cup of the remaining oil, and heat over medium heat. Add the onions and minced garlic and sauté until soft and translucent, 5 to 10 minutes. Spread half of the onions over the eggplant in the casserole.

5. Combine the green beans, zucchini, bell peppers, garlic cloves, and, if using, the carrots and/ or cauliflower and place in the casserole. Top with the remaining onions, then the remaining tomatoes. Sprinkle with the remaining salt, the pepper, and sugar. Add the water, then the remaining $^1/_4$ cup oil.

6. Bake, uncovered, until the vegetables are tender and most of the liquid absorbed, about $1^1/_2$ hours. Serve warm, at room temperature, or slightly chilled.

VARIATIONS

Greek Vegetable Stew (Yachni de Verduras): Use a large pot to cook the stew. Reduce the garlic to 1 to 2 minced cloves and the water to $^1/_4$ cup. Add 3 tablespoons chopped fresh dill or 2 teaspoons dried oregano. In Step 5, stir together all the ingredients. Cover and simmer over very low heat, stirring occasionally, until soft, about 35 minutes.

Romanian Baked Vegetable Stew (Kapama): Omit the water. Cover the casserole with aluminum foil and bake in a preheated 350°F oven until tender, about $1^1/_2$ hours. Or, use the water and sprinkle the bottom layer of tomatoes with $^3/_4$ cup long-grain rice.

GEORGIAN VEGETABLE STEW

(Adzhapsandali)

6 TO 8 SERVINGS AS A SIDE DISH   Ⓟ

I was first introduced to Georgian cooking and culture as a college student in 1973 when I spent a summer doing social work with recent immigrants in Israel—many of them Georgian families. I immediately fell in love with the vibrancy of the flavors and the people. Until recently, I learned, most Georgian homes had an open fire in the center of the large communal room with a shwatzetzkhli (large copper pot) hung by a chain from the ceiling, in which various stews were simmered. Outside was a clay oven used to bake flat breads.

The stews, the main component of Georgian daily fare, used many vegetables, but none more than eggplant. Introduced by the Persians, eggplant subsequently became the Georgians' favorite vegetable, and the heart of Georgian summer stews, with other produce added according to their availability and the discretion of the cook. Georgian stews are also distinguished by the large amount of fresh herbs they use—always in a careful balance.

Adzhapsandali is served as a side dish, salad, or condiment, usually accompanied with yogurt.

2 eggplants (about 1 1/4 pounds each), peeled

About 1 tablespoon plus 1 teaspoon table salt
    or 2 tablespoons plus 2 teaspoons kosher salt

2 large boiling potatoes, peeled and cubed
    (optional)

3/4 cup olive oil or vegetable oil

2 large onions, sliced or chopped

3 to 4 cloves garlic, minced

2 tablespoons tomato paste

1 3/4 pounds tomatoes, peeled, seeded, and
    chopped (see page 291), about 4 cups

3 to 4 green bell peppers, seeded, deribbed
    (white removed), and sliced

3 to 4 carrots, chopped (optional)

About 1 teaspoon sugar

Ground black pepper to taste

1/4 cup chopped fresh basil

1/4 cup chopped fresh cilantro

1/4 cup chopped fresh spearmint or dill

1/4 cup chopped fresh flat-leaf parsley

About 1/2 teaspoon cayenne or hot paprika
    (optional)

1. Cut the eggplants crosswise into 1-inch-thick slices, then into 1-inch-wide sticks, then into 1-inch cubes. Put in a colander or on a wire rack, sprinkle lightly with 1 tablespoon of the table salt or 2 tablespoons of the kosher salt, and let stand for at least 1 hour. (Moisture will appear on the surface, and the eggplant will become more pliable.) Rinse the eggplant under cold water, then press repeatedly between several layers of paper towels until the slices feel firm and dry. The eggplant can be stored in the refrigerator for up to 4 hours.

2. If using the potatoes, put them in a large saucepan and add cold water to cover. Add 1 1/4 teaspoons salt for every quart of water. Bring to a boil, cover, reduce the heat to medium-low, and simmer until nearly tender, about 20 minutes. Drain.

3. In a large saucepan, heat 1/2 cup of the oil over medium-high heat. Add the eggplant and sauté until lightly browned, about 5 minutes. Reduce the heat to medium-low and sauté until the eggplant is tender but still firm, about 10 minutes. Using a slotted spatula, transfer the eggplant to paper towels to drain and pour off any oil from the pan.

4. Heat the remaining 1/4 cup of the oil over medium heat. Add the onions and garlic and sauté until soft and translucent, 5 to 10 minutes. Add the tomato paste and stir until darkened, about 2 minutes. Return the eggplant to the pan and add the tomatoes, bell peppers, and the potatoes and/or carrots, if using. Stir in the sugar, the remaining 1 teaspoon table salt or 2 teaspoons kosher salt, and the pepper. Cover and simmer over low heat for about 20 minutes. Or, transfer the contents to an oiled 4-quart casserole and bake in a preheated 350°F oven for 40 minutes.

5. Stir in the basil, cilantro, mint, parsley, and, if using, the cayenne. Cover and cook until the vegetables are tender, about 10 minutes. Serve warm or at room temperature.

Turkish Lentil-Vegetable Stew

(Djuvec de Lenteja)

6 TO 8 SERVINGS AS A MAIN COURSE

I learned to make this dish from a pair of elderly Turkish sisters, Mathilde and Louise Nahum, living in Manhattan. As the two discussed making djuvec de lenteja *and other Turkish vegetable stews, they repeatedly apologized for not being able to show me the proper cookware. Their mother's Turkish earthenware pot, which gave its name to the stew, had cracked during the ocean passage and they could not locate another one like it in the United States. Ever since, they have had to make do with heavy-bottomed metal pots and what they consider inferior earthenware substitutes, with which, the sisters claim, they are unable to equal the taste of the food cooked in their mother's pot.*

This simple mélange of lentils and vegetables is representative of Turkish vegetarian cooking, which does not use a lot of spices, but relies on fresh ingredients and a few herbs for a subtle, yet satisfying flavor. The Nahum sisters serve this stew with bread and a green salad for a light lunch or dinner.

1 1/2 pounds (about 3 3/4 cups) dried brown, green, or red lentils, picked over and rinsed
1/4 cup olive oil or vegetable oil
1 large onion or leek, chopped
3 to 4 cloves garlic, minced
About 6 cups water
1 1/2 pounds boiling potatoes, peeled and cubed
1 pound carrots, sliced or finely chopped
1 bay leaf
About 1 1/4 teaspoons table salt or 2 1/2 teaspoons kosher salt
About 1/2 teaspoon ground black pepper
2 whole cloves or 1/2 teaspoon ground cloves (optional)
1 tablespoon chopped fresh thyme or 1 teaspoon dried thyme (optional)
6 ounces tomato paste, or 14 ounces plum tomatoes, peeled, seeded, and chopped (see page 291), about 2 cups
1 head cauliflower, cut into florets
1 pound green beans, trimmed
1/2 cup chopped fresh parsley and/or cilantro

1. Soak the lentils in warm water to cover for 2 hours. Drain.

2. In a large pot, heat the oil over medium heat. Add the onion and garlic and sauté until soft and translucent, about 5 minutes. Add the water, lentils, potatoes, carrots, bay leaf, salt, pepper, and, if using, the cloves or thyme, or both. Bring to a boil, cover, reduce the heat to low, and simmer until the lentils are tender, adding more liquid if necessary, about 15 minutes for red lentils, 30 minutes for green lentils, or 35 minutes for brown lentils.

3. Add the tomato paste, cauliflower, and green beans. Cover and simmer until tender, about 10 minutes. Garnish with the parsley. Serve hot.

OTTOMAN STEWS

Many stews from Turkey and the Balkans are named after the earthenware vessels in which they were originally cooked. These earthenware pots typified cooking throughout much of the biblical and Talmudic periods, when clay pots were arranged over horseshoe-shaped clay stands with the kindling underneath, and lit through the opening. When baked uncovered in the oven, a Turkish vegetable stew is cooked in a *guvetch* or *djuvec*, a large round clay baking pot. If cooked on top of the stove, the stew is made in a pot called a *yahni* or *yachni*. Other times, the stew's name refers to how the dish is made. A covered baked stew is called a *kapama*, from the Turkish *kapamak* ("to cover"). *Turlu*, the word for another baked stew, stems from the Turkish word for "mixture."

BUKHARAN VEGETABLE AND FRUIT STEW

(Dimlama)

5 TO 6 SERVINGS AS A SIDE DISH

The collapse of the Soviet Union and the subsequent rise in Islamic fundamentalism spurred a nearly complete exodus of the ancient Jewish communities of Uzbekistan and Tajikistan. Approximately thirty thousand of them settled in the Rego Park–Forest Hills area of Queens, New York. These Central Asian immigrants do not consider themselves Russians, like the large community in Brighton Beach, Brooklyn, but maintain a distinct culture. Many of them opened native food shops, restaurants, and bakeries along a stretch of 108th Street commonly called "Bukharan Broadway." Hence, all I need to do to explore this ancient cuisine is to take a subway ride from Manhattan to Queens. I was given this recipe, a synthesis of central Asian and Persian cooking, by one of the local members of the Bukharan community. The fruit imparts a refreshing fragrance and a tangy flavor. Serve with rice or noodles.

1/4 cup vegetable oil

2 large onions, chopped

2 carrots, thickly sliced

2 potatoes, peeled and diced

1 turnip, peeled and diced

2 large tomatoes, coarsely chopped

1 large quince, peeled, cored, and coarsely chopped (optional)

1 to 2 large tart apples, peeled, cored, and coarsely chopped

1/4 cup chopped fresh parsley, plus 2 tablespoons for garnish

1/4 cup chopped fresh cilantro, plus 2 tablespoons for garnish

About 1 teaspoon table salt or 2 teaspoons kosher salt

1. In a large, heavy saucepan, heat the oil over medium heat. Add the onions and sauté until soft and translucent, 5 to 10 minutes.

2. Add the carrots, potatoes, and turnip and sauté until well coated, about 2 minutes. Stir in the tomatoes, optional quince, apples, the 1/4 cup parsley, the 1/4 cup cilantro, and the salt. Add water to cover the mixture. Bring to a boil, cover, reduce the heat to low, and simmer until tender, about 45 minutes. Sprinkle with the 2 tablespoons parsley and cilantro. Serve warm.

CALCUTTA CURRIED VEGETABLES

(*Subzi*)

6 TO 8 SERVINGS AS A SIDE DISH

Subzi is the Hindi word for spiced cooked vegetables, called a "curry" in the West. It entails the Indian "wet" method of cooking vegetables, first sautéing them in oil or ghee, then simmering them in a little water to make a spicy sauce. Serve with rice or flat Indian breads, such as chapati.

1 eggplant (about 1¹/₄ pounds), peeled

About 2¹/₂ teaspoons table salt or 1 tablespoon
    plus 2 teaspoons kosher salt

2 each green and red bell peppers, seeded,
    deribbed (white removed), and cut into chunks

1 or 2 yellow bell peppers, seeded, deribbed
    (white removed), and cut into chunks (optional)

¹/₄ cup vegetable oil

1 large onion, chopped

1 tablespoon seeded and minced small
    hot green chilies

1 tablespoon minced garlic

1 tablespoon minced fresh ginger

1 teaspoon ground turmeric

2 green cardamom pods, bruised

2 whole cloves

1 bay leaf

4 boiling potatoes, peeled and cut into chunks

1 to 1¹/₂ pounds zucchini, cut into ¹/₄-inch-thick
    slices; or 8 ounces green beans, trimmed
    and cut into 2-inch pieces (optional)

1 pound tomatoes, peeled, seeded, and chopped
    (see page 291), about 2 cups

1 cup water

Ground black pepper to taste

2 tablespoons chopped fresh cilantro for garnish

1. Cut the eggplant crosswise into 1-inch-thick slices, then into 1-inch-wide sticks, then into 1-inch cubes. Put in a colander or on a wire rack, sprinkle lightly with 1¹/₂ teaspoons of the table salt or 1 tablespoon of the kosher salt, and let stand for at least 1 hour. (Moisture will appear on the surface, and the eggplant will become more pliable.) Rinse the eggplant under cold water, then press repeatedly between several layers of paper towels until the slices feel firm and dry. The eggplant can be stored in the refrigerator for up to 4 hours.

2. In a large pot of lightly salted boiling water, blanch the peppers for 3 minutes. Drain.

3. In a large saucepan, heat the oil over medium heat. Add the onion and sauté until soft and translucent, about 5 minutes. Add the chilies, garlic, ginger, turmeric, cardamom, cloves, and bay leaf and sauté for 2 to 3 minutes. Add the potatoes and sauté until lightly colored, about 2 minutes. Add the eggplant and bell peppers and stir-fry for 2 minutes. If using, add the zucchini.

4. Add the tomatoes, water, the remaining salt, and the pepper. Cover and cook over medium heat or bake in a preheated 425°F oven until the vegetables are tender, about 45 minutes. If the sauce is watery, uncover and cook until slightly thickened. Discard the cardamom pods, cloves, and bay leaf. Sprinkle with the cilantro. Serve warm or at room temperature.

VARIATION

Calcutta Spiced Vegetables (*Subzi*): Omit the chilies and ginger and add 2 teaspoons ground coriander and 1 teaspoon ground cumin. For a sweet-and-sour flavor, add 1 tablespoon fresh lemon juice and 1 teaspoon sugar.

ETHIOPIAN VEGETABLE STEW

(*Wot*)

5 TO 6 SERVINGS AS A SIDE DISH

A few years ago, I was asked to plan a special meal for the annual dinner of a Philadelphia Jewish organization. I developed an international menu featuring traditional Jewish food from around the world. Among the most popular dishes was this spiced Ethiopian wot *or stew. To prepare the* wot, *the kosher caterer assigned a Jamaican cook, who, after the trial run, announced, "Hey mon, we make the same thing in Jamaica, only with goat." I explained that in the Ethiopian Jewish communities, most dishes were vegetarian; chicken or meat (primarily goat, in fact) was generally reserved for special occasions. Serve with* injera *(pancake bread) or flat bread and* lab *(Ethiopian Cheese Spread, page 48) or yogurt.*

3 large onions, chopped

$^1/_2$ cup vegetable oil or peanut oil

6 to 8 cloves garlic, minced

1 to 3 teaspoons minced fresh ginger

$^1/_4$ teaspoon ground cardamom

$^1/_4$ teaspoon ground caraway seeds

$^1/_4$ teaspoon ground coriander

$^1/_4$ teaspoon crushed mustard seeds

3 carrots, thinly sliced

1 tablespoon tomato paste (optional)

1 cup water (if using tomato paste) or $^1/_2$ cup water mixed with $^1/_2$ cup tomato sauce

1 pound cabbage, cored and sliced (about 4 cups)

6 small new or boiling potatoes (about 1 pound), cubed

1 to 2 small hot green chilies, seeded and minced

1 teaspoon ground turmeric

1 small head cauliflower, cut into florets, or 8 ounces green beans, trimmed and cut into 1-inch pieces

About 1 teaspoon table salt or 2 teaspoons kosher salt

About $^1/_4$ teaspoon ground black pepper

5 to 6 hard-boiled eggs, peeled (optional)

1. In a large, dry saucepan over medium-low heat, cook the onions, stirring constantly, until they begin to soften, about 5 minutes.

2. Add the oil. When it begins to sputter, add the garlic, ginger, cardamom, caraway, coriander, and mustard seeds and sauté until fragrant, about 1 minute. Stir in the carrots and, if using, the tomato paste and sauté for 1 minute. Add $^1/_2$ cup of the water or $^1/_2$ cup of the tomato sauce mixture. Bring to a boil and cook, stirring constantly, until the liquid is reduced to the consistency of heavy cream, about 8 minutes.

3. Stir in the cabbage, potatoes, chilies, and turmeric. Cover and cook until the cabbage wilts slightly, about 3 minutes. Add the cauliflower, salt, and pepper. Cover and cook for 5 minutes.

4. Add the remaining $^1/_2$ cup water or the remaining $^1/_2$ cup tomato sauce mixture. Reduce the heat to low, cover, and simmer until the vegetables are tender and the sauce thickened, about 5 minutes. If using the eggs, pierce $^1/_2$-inch-deep holes over the surface of each with a toothpick, add the eggs to the stew, and turn gently in the sauce. Serve warm or at room temperature.

VARIATION

Milder Wot (*Aleecha*): Omit the chilies, caraway seeds, coriander, and mustard seeds. Add $^1/_8$ teaspoon ground cinnamon, $^1/_8$ teaspoon ground cloves, and $^1/_8$ teaspoon freshly grated nutmeg.

WOTS

WOTS

*W*ot (stew) is the national dish of Ethiopia, commonly cooked in a clay vessel over an open fire. *Aleecha,* or *alicha,* is a less spicy version. Ethiopian stews are typically fired up with chilies or a chili-based spice mixture called *berbere,* a combination of spices similar to that of Indian curries, derived from the ancient interaction between Ethiopia, Yemen, and Cochin, which resulted in the spread of Indian spice mixtures to eastern Africa. The unique method of roasting the onions in a dry skillet before adding fat helps to break them down completely, so that the onions actually help to thicken the sauce. Ethiopian stews are characteristically served by stacking a number of injera (pancake breads) on a large platter and spooning the stew over top. Diners then tear off pieces of bread, scooping up some of the stew.

TUNISIAN SAUTÉED VEGETABLES

(Keftaji)

4 SERVINGS AS A MAIN COURSE

After returning to New York from a recent trip to his homeland, a Tunisian expatriate I know complained to me that hamburgers, pizza, and other foreign fast food are supplanting traditional fare throughout North Africa. In response, he collected relatives' recipes for some of his favorite childhood foods, including keftaji, *to be able to prepare them whenever he felt the urge to recall his childhood and to preserve the recipes for his children. In this Tunisian specialty, which features Ottoman (the type of stew) and Sephardic (the method for cooking the eggs) influences, the vegetables are cooked separately, then married with a tomato sauce and topped either by meatballs, from which this dish's name derived, or a fried egg. In Tunisia,* keftaji *is served as a main course for lunch.*

TOMATO SAUCE:
$^1/_2$ cup water
3 tablespoons tomato paste
$^1/_2$ teaspoon ground coriander
About $^1/_2$ teaspoon table salt or 1 teaspoon
    kosher salt
About $^1/_4$ teaspoon ground black pepper
1 tablespoon red wine vinegar or fresh lemon juice

VEGETABLES:
1 pound boiling potatoes or peeled pumpkin,
    julienned or cut into $^1/_4$-inch thick slices
Salt
About 5 tablespoons olive oil
1 onion, sliced
1 pound zucchini, sliced
10 ounces red or green bell peppers, seeded,
    deribbed (white removed), and sliced

4 large eggs

About 4 teaspoons unsalted butter or margarine

Pinch of salt

1. To make the tomato sauce: In a small saucepan, combine the water, tomato paste, coriander, salt, and pepper. Simmer, stirring occasionally, until slightly thickened, about 10 minutes. Remove from the heat and stir in the vinegar.

2. Put the potatoes in a large saucepan and add water to cover. Add $1\frac{1}{4}$ teaspoons salt for every quart of water. Bring to a boil, cover, reduce the heat to medium-low, and cook gently until tender but not mushy, about 20 minutes. Drain.

3. In a large skillet, heat 2 tablespoons of the oil over medium-high heat. Add the onion and sauté until golden, 10 to 15 minutes. Using a slotted spoon, transfer the the onion to a heated large bowl and keep warm.

4. Add 2 tablespoons of the oil to the skillet, then the zucchini; sauté until tender, about 4 minutes. Using a slotted spoon, transfer the zucchini to the bowl with the onion.

5. Add the bell peppers to the skillet and sauté until tender, about 5 minutes. Transfer the peppers to the bowl with the other vegetables.

6. Add the remaining 1 tablespoon oil to the skillet, then the potatoes; cook over medium-high heat, stirring occasionally, until lightly golden, about 8 minutes. Add the potatoes to the bowl with the other vegetables, pour the tomato sauce over top, and toss to coat. Keep warm.

7. To fry the eggs: For each serving, crack an egg into a small bowl. Heat a small skillet over low heat for about 5 minutes. Add about 1 teaspoon of the butter and wait until the foam subsides, about 1 minute, then swirl to coat the skillet. Gently slide the egg into the pan. Drizzle about 1 teaspoon water around the outside edges of the egg. Cover and cook until the whites are set, about $2\frac{1}{2}$ minutes for a runny yolk, $3\frac{1}{2}$ minutes for a firm yolk. You can cook 2 eggs at the same time in a 9- or 10-inch skillet and, adding 1 tablespoon butter and 1 scant tablespoon water, all 4 eggs in a 12-inch skillet; if some of the edges run together, simply cut them to make individual servings.

8. Divide the vegetable mixture between serving dishes, top with a fried egg, and sprinkle with salt. Serve immediately.

NOTE The ideal fried egg has a white that is firm but not rubbery and a yolk that is thickened yet still at least slightly runny. The pan should be heated to the point where the white immediately sets up and neither runs nor immediately browns at the edges. Adding a little water and covering the skillet is a Sephardic cooking method that creates steam, which helps to eliminate rubbery whites.

MOROCCAN SPICY TOMATO AND PEPPER STEW WITH EGGS

(Shakshouka)

3 TO 4 SERVINGS AS A SIDE DISH   Ⓟ

I first discovered shakshouka *during a trip to Israel, sampling a particularly fiery rendition that required several cartons of yogurt to extinguish. There are many similar dishes around the world, and I've included several variations below. Most versions have only a slight kick, which I appreciate; you can even make one that uses only bell peppers for a very mild mixture. Anaheim chilies and hot paprika or harissa create a more pungent stew. Serve with pita bread or over rice.*

3 tablespoons olive oil or vegetable oil

I large onion, chopped

I to 2 cloves garlic, minced (optional)

4 green bell peppers or Anaheim chilies or any combination, seeded, deribbed (white removed), and diced or sliced

1 1/4 pounds plum tomatoes, peeled, seeded, and chopped (see page 291), about 3 cups

About 1/2 teaspoon table salt or I teaspoon kosher salt

1/4 teaspoon ground turmeric

2 to 6 teaspoons hot paprika, I to 2 tablespoons *harissa* (Northwest African Chili Paste, page 433), or 3 to 5 drops hot sauce (optional)

3 to 4 large eggs

1. In a medium skillet, heat the oil over medium heat. Add the onion and, if using, the garlic and sauté until soft and translucent, about 5 minutes. Add the peppers and sauté until crisp-tender, about 5 minutes. Add the tomatoes, salt, turmeric, and, for a more fiery stew, the hot paprika. Bring to a boil, reduce the heat to medium-low, and cook, stirring occasionally, until the tomatoes are softened, about 15 minutes.

2. With the back of a spoon, make 3 to 4 indentations in the stew. Carefully break the eggs, one at a time, into a small dish and slide one into each indentation. Cover the pan and cook over a low heat until the egg whites are set but the yolks are still soft, about 5 minutes. Or, divide the tomato mixture between 3 to 4 small baking dishes, make an indentation in the center of each, break in an egg, cover, and bake in a preheated 400°F oven until the eggs are set, about 10 minutes. Serve immediately.

VARIATIONS

Greek Tomato and Pepper Stew (*Armiko*): Omit the eggs. When the vegetables are soft, stir in 1/2 cup long-grain rice, cover, and simmer over low heat for 30 minutes.

Syrian Tomato and Pepper Stew with Eggs (*Beid b'Benadora/Tchatchouka*): Add with the tomatoes 1/2 cup cracked pitted green olives, 1 teaspoon ground cumin, and a pinch of sugar. This is commonly served with Syrian white cheese.

Tunisian Tomato and Pepper Stew with Eggs (*Shakshouka Tala*): Add 1 teaspoon ground cumin with the tomatoes or 1 1/2 teaspoons caraway seeds with the peppers.

Excellent version.
I made Syrian version.
Nice

    ✤ OLIVE TREES AND HONEY ✤

SHAKSHOUKA

Among the favorite stews of the Ottoman Empire was *saksuka* ("goatee"), consisting of various cooked vegetables and minced meat or sheep's liver. As *saksuka* evolved, the meat was generally eliminated, and new vegetables from America—tomatoes, peppers, and sometimes, potatoes—were added. Similar tomato-and-pepper-based stews, variously containing eggplant, artichoke hearts, cauliflower, fava beans, and summer squash, became standards in Turkey, Syria, Egypt, the Balkans, and the area where it enjoys the greatest popularity, the Maghreb. Related to the revamped *saksuka* was *menemen*, a tomato-and-pepper stew mixed with lightly beaten eggs and cooked like a thick omelet—named after a village located near the Turkish city of Smyrna (now Izmir).

When the Ottoman tomato-and-pepper stew reached northwest Africa, it was called *shakshouka*, or *chakhchouka*. The proportion of peppers to tomatoes and types of spices used differed greatly from cook to cook and place to place. Although most recipes are simply based on tomatoes and peppers, some used eggplant, zucchini, and other vegetables. Jewish tomato-based stews contain onions sautéed in olive oil, a characteristic Sephardic touch.

Most versions of *shakshouka* also feature eggs: Sometimes these are scrambled in the stew, as for the Turkish *menemen;* other times they are poached on top. Both of these methods of cooking eggs with vegetables date back among Sephardim to before the Expulsion for Spain. Tunisian Jews, in particular, became recognized for their numerous egg dishes, including *shakshouka*, which they prefer with more fire and spice than Moroccans, as well as a spicy omeletlike version using puréed peppers called *aijjah bil hrus*. Immigrants from northwest Africa brought *shakshouka* to Israel, where it was widely adopted, variously served as part of breakfast, a light lunch, or dinner. Without the eggs, *shakshouka* also appears as a part of a *meze* (appetizer assortment) or accompanied with rice or couscous as a side dish.

Moroccan Vegetable Stew for Couscous

(*Légumes pour le Couscous*)

6 TO 8 SERVINGS AS A MAIN COURSE

After I interviewed Michel Abehsera, a major figure in macrobiotics, for Kosher Gourmet Magazine, he offered to cook lunch for me. He made this stew over couscous, and it has since become one of my favorite dishes. According to Abehsera, "The secret to good health is to eat everything at a meal at the same time, not separately." Stews, of course, are ideal for this philosophy. Thus, this stew is a perfect representation of macrobiotic cooking, not to mention being naturally delicious. Other commonly added vegetables are artichoke hearts, cardoons, celery, fava beans, green peas, leeks, bell peppers, and chopped tomatoes. Smash some of the cooked chickpeas to produce a thicker sauce.

This dish would typically be served at a Moroccan Rosh Hashanah dinner accompanied with beet salad, carrot salad, spinach salad, and khboz *(anise bread). In the Maghreb, this stew is commonly served over a bed of couscous. Many Libyans, who lived under Italian colonial rule, substitute* acini de pepe *(pearl pasta) for the couscous. For a more fiery stew, drizzle with* harissa *(Northwest African Chili Paste, page 433).*

6 cups Vegetable Stock (page 115) or water
6 carrots, cut into chunks
3 onions, quartered
2 turnips, peeled and quartered
About 1 teaspoon table salt or 2 teaspoons kosher salt
2 (3-inch) sticks cinnamon or 1 teaspoon ground cinnamon
1/2 teaspoon saffron threads or ground turmeric
Dash of ground black pepper
1/2 head green cabbage, cored and shredded
1 butternut squash or 2 large sweet potatoes, peeled and cut into 2-inch pieces
3 zucchini, cut into chunks
2 cups cooked chickpeas
1/2 cup chopped fresh cilantro or parsley
Basic Steamed Couscous (page 413)
Onion-Raisin Topping for Couscous (page 414), optional

1. In a large pot, bring the stock to a boil. Add the carrots, onions, and turnips, then stir in the salt and spices. Return to a boil, cover, reduce the heat to low, and simmer for 30 minutes. Add the cabbage, squash, zucchini, and chickpeas and cook until the vegetables are tender, about 20 minutes. Stir in the cilantro.

2. Heap the couscous on a serving platter, make a well in the center, and fill with the vegetables. Arrange any remaining vegetables around the sides. Drizzle some of the cooking liquid over the couscous to moisten it, and pass the rest. Serve with the onion-raisin topping, if using.

VARIATION

For a sweeter stew: Add 2 to 3 tablespoons honey or sugar and/or 1/2 cup raisins. If desired, add 1/2 teaspoon ground ginger, 1/2 teaspoon freshly ground nutmeg, and 1/4 teaspoon ground cloves.

LEGUMES

❁ · ❁

Legumes comprise some of the most nutritious and flavorful foods in the vegetarian diet. Of more than fifteen thousand species of leguminous plants (vines and shrubs that produce a pod to encompass its seeds), only about twenty-two—including lentils, peas, chickpeas, haricot (common) beans, fava beans, soybeans, adzuki, black-eyed peas, mung beans, alfalfa, carob, and peanuts—are grown in any large quantity. In addition to protein, legumes are rich in vitamins and minerals. They are easy to grow and filling. Growing legumes also improves the soil by extracting nitrogen from the air, enhancing the soil for other crops.

The Bible mentioned three legumes: fava beans, chickpeas, and—at that time the most important—lentils. Black-eyed peas and several lesser-known pulses (the edible seeds of certain legumes), including lupine and vetch, arrived during the early Second Temple period (c. fourth century B.C.E.). These plants served as staples, for both humans and domesticated animals, in Israel as well as for many other ancient civilizations of the Old World. Indeed, the most prominent Roman families bore the names of legumes: Cicero (chickpeas), Fabius (fava beans), Lentulus (lentils), and Pisa (peas). The primary ways of preparing legumes was as stews and soups slow cooked in earthenware pots. In addition, the earliest cakes consisted of fried patties of mashed legumes sweetened with honey.

Ashkenazim in western Europe included legumes as a regular part of their diet, but, after migrating to eastern Europe, generally rejected them, moving to a diet consisting mostly of starches, dairy products, and a few vegetables. Among the exceptions were adding beans to Sabbath stews, preparing occasional bean soups, and using beans at certain symbolic occasions, such as serving chickpeas at a brit and lentils at a house of mourning. Otherwise, the consumption of legumes was commonly limited to periods of famine, when Ashkenazic rabbinic authorities even permitted their use during Passover.

In much of Sephardic and Middle Eastern Jewish cookery, beans and chickpeas, ancient symbols of plenty and renewal, are still common holiday dishes. On Rosh Hashanah, they are usually combined with other traditional foods, especially leeks, spinach, and carrots. Some Sephardim serve bean soups on Passover, since beans were a mainstay of the Hebrew diet in Egypt. As a meatless source of protein, bean dishes and soups are common fare in the Nine Days leading up to the fast of Tisha b'Av and for other dairy meals.

Throughout much of history, shortly after the harvest, groups of women would (and still do) customarily gather in a friend's house, encircle a mound of legumes, and sort though it to remove any dirt or stones, all the while chatting and sometimes singing.

What You Should Know: Legumes should be carefully picked over by spreading them in a single layer over a tray or baking sheet to look for and discard stones and clumps of dirt. Stored in a cool, dry place, dried legumes keep for more than a year.

❧ HARICOT BEANS ❧

Haricot, or common, beans follow only the soybean as the most important legume crop in the world. Originating somewhere in Central or South America, they were already being cultivated more than five millennia ago and had spread to North America thousands of years before the arrival of Columbus.

Originally, beans were used exclusively for their dried mature seeds: black, cannellini, cranberry, kidney, marrow, navy, pink, pinto, red, and so on, are all examples of these, with more than four thousand cultivars around today. Then, just over two thousand years ago, people began cultivating some haricot (the word stems from the Aztec word for bean, *ayacotl*, connoting its American origin) bean varieties for their green pods rather than their seeds, including green beans. Today, there are more than five hundred green bean cultivars in all sizes, shapes, textures, and colors. Columbus introduced the green bean to Europe in 1493 following his second voyage, and by the beginning of the seventeenth century green beans had spread throughout the Mediterranean.

More important to Europeans and Middle Easterners, however, were the mature dried haricot beans, which Hernando Cortes brought in 1528. They quickly spread across Europe and the Near East, becoming one of if not the only major source of protein in many areas. Due to the similarity of dried haricot beans to fava beans and green haricot bean to asparagus, these newcomers (unlike most other American imports) gained swift acceptance in Europe and were quickly adapted into native cuisines.

Along with two other American vegetables— potatoes and tomatoes—haricot beans, both dried and green, revolutionized the cookery of the Old

World. Green beans quickly became a common component of many stews and were also enjoyed on their own. The favorite Sephardic way of preparing green beans is in tomato sauce, sometimes with other common vegetables such as spinach and leeks. In Turkey and Greece, the beans are liberally doused in olive oil, while Persians cook them with rice or smother them in yogurt. In many Jewish communities, dried haricot beans supplanted fava beans and chickpeas in Sabbath stews, as well as various salads, spreads, and soups.

Haricot beans became particularly important in the Balkans. *Avicas*, or *fijones*, a thick white bean soup, was once a ubiquitous Friday night entrée, accompanied with various savory pastries and stuffed grape leaves, among the Jewish Greek community of Salonika. Leftover soup was often kept in the oven to simmer overnight, in the manner of a Sabbath stew, and then served for Sabbath lunch.

With the exception of *cholent* (Sabbath stew) and some soups, the Jews of central and eastern Europe rarely ate beans. Hungarians and Romanians, however, influenced by the lengthy Ottoman occupation of their countries and contact with Sephardim (who arrived with the Turks), developed an abiding affection for the newly introduced American beans, both dried and fresh. As a result, the cuisine of these two countries contains a number of legume dishes. The Ukrainians, more vegetable-accepting than Ashkenazim from Poland and the Balkans, adopted some of the neighboring Romanian bean fare, and even some Polish Jews eventually succumbed to the bean's charms. Nevertheless, most residents of Poland and the Balkan States for much of history steadfastly refused to eat most green vegetables or legumes.

MIDDLE EASTERN MASHED BEAN PÂTÉ

(*Salatet Ful Abiad*)

ABOUT 4 CUPS, OR 6 TO 8 SERVINGS

White bean salads, both whole and mashed, are popular throughout the Middle East. Most mashed-bean dishes are much thicker than the chickpea-based hummus. This version has the consistency of a pâté. As a result, a knife or spoon is recommended for serving it. The seasonings perk up the beans without overwhelming their flavor. Serve with pita bread or crackers.

> 10 ounces (1 1/2 cups) dried white or pinto beans, picked over, soaked for 8 hours in water to cover, and drained, or 4 cups canned white beans, drained
> 1 bay leaf
> 4 tablespoons olive oil
> 2 to 3 cloves garlic, minced
> About 1/3 cup fresh lemon or lime juice
> About 1/4 teaspoon cayenne or 8 drops hot sauce
> About 3/4 teaspoon table salt or 1 1/2 teaspoons kosher salt
> Paprika for garnish (optional)
> Chopped fresh parsley for garnish (optional)

1. If using dried beans, put the soaked beans and bay leaf in a large pot and add water to cover by 2 inches. Bring to a boil, reduce the heat to low, cover, and simmer until very tender, about 1 1/4 hours. Drain, discarding the bay leaf. Using a fork or spoon, or in a food processor, mash the beans.

2. In a large skillet, heat 3 tablespoons of the oil over medium heat. Add the garlic and sauté until lightly colored but not burnt, about 1 minute.

Add the beans, lemon juice, cayenne, and salt and cook, stirring, until the mixture is dry, 2 to 4 minutes.

3. Remove from the heat and stir in the remaining 1 tablespoon of the oil. Spoon into a bowl or crock, cover, and refrigerate for at least 3 hours and up to 2 days to allow the flavors to meld. Transfer to a serving plate and, if desired, sprinkle with the paprika and/or parsley.

VARIATIONS

Moroccan Bean Spread (*Bissara*): Add 2 teaspoons ground cumin with the beans.

Turkish Bean Spread (*Bakla Ezmesi*): Add 2 tablespoons chopped fresh dill in Step 3 with the remaining 1 tablespoon oil.

HUNGARIAN WHITE BEANS WITH SOUR CREAM

(Feher Bab)

5 TO 6 SERVINGS   Ⓓ

Sour cream is one of the principal ingredients in Hungarian cooking. It is essential in numerous Hungarian sauces, stews, soups, vegetable dishes, and pastries, imparting a touch of tartness and richness. In this recipe, Hungarians flavor the beans with another favorite, paprika, to produce a creamy, tangy dish. If the sauce is a little flat, stir in 1 tablespoon wine or cider vinegar.

1 pound (about 2⅓ cups) cannellini, navy, or other dried white beans, picked over, soaked for 8 hours in water to cover, and drained
1 bay leaf
2 tablespoons unsalted butter or vegetable oil
2 tablespoons unbleached all-purpose flour
1 teaspoon sweet Hungarian paprika
About ½ teaspoon table salt or 1 teaspoon kosher salt
Ground black pepper, to taste
½ cup sour cream

1. Put the soaked beans and bay leaf in a large pot and add water to cover by 2 inches. Bring to a boil, reduce the heat to low, cover, and simmer until very tender, at least 1¼ hours. Drain, reserving 2 cups of the cooking liquid to make the sauce.

2. To make the sauce: In a medium, heavy saucepan, melt the butter over medium heat. Add the flour and paprika and stir until bubbly, about 3 minutes. Gradually stir in the reserved cooking liquid and whisk vigorously until smooth. Add the beans, salt, and pepper and cook, stirring, until thickened, about 10 minutes.

3. Put the sour cream in a small bowl, gradually stir about ½ cup of the sauce into the sour cream, then stir the sour cream mixture into the pan and heat through. Serve warm.

VARIATION

Hungarian Green Beans in Sour Cream (*Tejfolos Zoldbab*): Substitute 2½ pounds green beans for the white beans. Trim and cut the beans into 1-inch pieces; blanch in salted boiling water until crisp-tender, about 5 minutes. Drain, reserving the cooking liquid to use in the sauce. Run the beans under cold water to stop the cooking and preserve the color. The beans can be left at room temperature for several hours and added with the salt and pepper to the sauce.

Sephardic White Beans with Leeks

(Avicas con Prassa)

5 TO 6 SERVINGS   Ⓟ

Cooking legumes with leeks and tomatoes is typical of Sephardic cuisine. Instead of the overly sweet American style of baked beans, I generally prefer this savory type, which, during the winter, I will often make in a slow cooker, adding the ingredients in the morning, then returning home hours later to a warm, hearty, and healthful meal made with little effort. Additionally, this recipe can be simmered or baked. Adjust the amount of lemon juice and sugar to personal preference. Serve the beans with plenty of fresh bread to sop up the caldo *(sauce), or over rice.*

I pound (about 2^1/$_3$ cups) cannellini, navy, or other dried white beans, picked over, soaked for 8 hours in water, and drained

I bay leaf

3 tablespoons olive oil or vegetable oil

3 to 4 leeks, sliced crosswise into ^{1}/$_2$-inch rings, washed, and drained

2 to 3 cloves garlic, minced

2 cups tomato sauce or I pound plum tomatoes, peeled, seeded, and chopped (see page 291), about 2^1/$_2$ cups, mixed with I tablespoon tomato paste

About I^1/$_2$ teaspoons table salt or I tablespoon kosher salt

Ground black pepper to taste

Pinch of sugar

Juice of I to 2 lemons (optional)

^{1}/$_4$ cup chopped fresh parsley or cilantro

1. Put the soaked beans and bay leaf in a large pot and add water to cover by 2 inches. Bring to a boil, reduce the heat to low, cover, and simmer until tender but not mushy, about 1 hour. Drain off most of the cooking liquid. Discard the bay leaf.

2. In a large, heavy saucepan, heat the oil over medium heat. Add the leeks and garlic and sauté until soft, about 5 minutes. Add the beans, tomato sauce, salt, pepper, sugar, and, if using, the lemon juice. Simmer, stirring occasionally, until the flavors meld, about 20 minutes. Or, cover and bake in a preheated 300°F oven, without stirring, until most of the liquid is absorbed, about 2 hours. (The long baking time yields a creamier texture and more intense flavors.) Stir in the parsley. Serve warm or at room temperature.

NOTE   White beans, the most popular type in the Balkans and Turkey, are generally seasoned sparingly in order not to overpower their delicate flavor.

VARIATIONS

Balkan White Beans in Tomato Sauce (*Yachini di Fijon Blanco*): Substitute 2 chopped onions for the leeks. Add 4 chopped stalks celery with the onions, and add 1 large bunch fresh spearmint and 5 whole allspice berries tied together in cheesecloth with the tomato sauce.

Romanian Baked Beans (*Gebakeneh Beblach*): Substitute 2 chopped onions for the leeks, omit the lemon juice, and increase the sugar to about 3 tablespoons.

Syrian White Beans in Tomato Sauce (*Fasuliya*): Substitute 2 chopped onions for the leeks, and add ^{1}/$_2$ to ^{3}/$_4$ teaspoon ground allspice (or 5 whole allspice berries), ^{1}/$_4$ teaspoon ground cinnamon, and a pinch of freshly grated nutmeg with the tomato sauce.

Dutch Brown Beans (*Shaknah*): Omit the tomatoes and, in Step 2, add 2 cups water and ^{1}/$_2$ cup honey or ^{1}/$_4$ cup molasses.

As American as Baked Beans

The Pilgrims did not come directly to Plymouth Rock from England, but spent a decade in Leyden in the Netherlands before seeking religious freedom in America in 1620. During their stay in Holland, the expatriates came in contact with the descendants of Sephardim who had fled Spain, a new experience for them as the Jews had been expelled from England in 1290 and would not be officially permitted to return until the mid-seventeenth century.

Being members of a fundamentalist sect, the Puritans observed Sunday as a day of rest and, therefore, refrained from cooking. Accustomed to the rather dull fare of their native England, they took a special interest in the exotic Sabbath dishes of the Jews, including long-simmered Sabbath bean stews such as *shkanah* (from an Arabic word meaning "hot"), made with dried fava beans, honey, and goose fat. In America, the immigrants substituted native white haricot beans for the fava beans, molasses for the honey, and bacon for the goose fat. The Pilgrims' synthesis of *shkanah* and American produce emerged as New England or Boston baked beans, a traditional Sunday dish that was placed in the oven on Saturday and left to simmer until after church services the following morning; thus, a descendant of an ancient Jewish stew became an American standard.

SEPHARDIC BEAN STEW

(*Hamin*)

6 TO 8 SERVINGS

Sabbath stew (hamin among Sephardim, cholent among Ashkenazim) is one of those dishes that people seem to either adore or disdain. Some people fail to appreciate its unique attributes, finding it old-fashioned and heavy. I count myself among the hamin*-lovers— unless it comes out dry, the fatal flaw of any Sabbath stew. Sephardic versions, with myriad variations, possess splendid nuances of flavor that I find appealing. This is a vegetarian version of the Sephardic Sabbath stew. For a spicy-sweet flavor, use the dates or sweet potatoes, or both.*

3 tablespoons vegetable oil

3 onions, sliced

14 ounces (about 2 cups) dried white beans or
   dried large lima beans; or a third each (²/₃ cup)
   white beans, lima beans, and dried chickpeas,
   picked over and rinsed

1 bay leaf

1 cup wheat berries, spelt berries, or barley

6 boiling potatoes, quartered; or 2 boiling potatoes,
   2 carrots, and 2 to 3 sweet potatoes, peeled
   and cut into large chunks

3 to 4 cloves garlic, minced

2 to 4 teaspoons ground cumin or 2 teaspoons
   cumin and 1¹/₂ teaspoons ground cinnamon

2 teaspoons ground turmeric

Ground black pepper to taste

About 9 cups water or 7 cups water mixed
   with 2 cups tomato sauce

About 1¹/₂ teaspoons table salt or 1 tablespoon
   kosher salt

4 to 5 dates, pitted and chopped (optional)

6 to 8 large eggs in shell, washed well (optional)

1. In a large pot, heat the oil over medium heat. Add the onions and sauté until soft and translucent, about 10 minutes. Remove from the heat and stir in the beans and bay leaf. In layers, add the wheat berries, then the potatoes. Sprinkle with the garlic, cumin, turmeric, and pepper.

2. Add enough water to cover by 2 inches. Bring to a boil, cover, reduce the heat to low, and simmer over medium-low heat until the beans are partially soft, about 1 hour.

3. Add the salt and more water to cover by 2 inches. For a sweet touch, add the dates. If using, put the eggs on top, pushing them into the liquid. Cover tightly. Place on a blech (a thin sheet of metal set over the range that acts as a heat diffuser) over very low heat or in a 200°F oven and cook overnight or for at least 8 hours. Serve warm.

VARIATIONS

Slow Cooker method: Combine all the ingredients in a 5-quart crockpot, cover, and cook on high for 8 to 10 hours.

Moroccan Wheat-Berry Rice Dumpling (*Kouclas*): In this version of the stew, the wheat berries are cooked separately in a cloth bag, preventing the ingredients from becoming completely mushy. Omit the wheat berries from the stew. Instead, combine ¹/₂ cup wheat berries, ¹/₂ cup brown rice, 1 tablespoon vegetable oil, a dash of paprika, and a pinch of salt. Tie in a cheesecloth square, leaving room for the grains to expand, and in Step 2, place in the center of the stew.

SABBATH STEWS

Like most people, Jews have always had a penchant for hot food, serving stews and casseroles on a regular basis. However, cooking, including rewarming, is one of the thirty-nine categories of work forbidden on the Sabbath. Therefore, cooks needed to develop ways to keep dishes warm not only for Friday night, but also for Saturday lunch without actively cooking them. As a solution, on Friday afternoon cooks would cover steampots with insulating materials or bury covered stewpots in dying embers of a fire to slowly (and passively) cook until the pot was retrieved for Saturday lunch. (The Talmud includes this act, called *tomnin et ha'hamin*, to "bury/cover the warm foods," in a list of the activities that a person must do before the onset of the Sabbath.) The contents of the ancient *hamin* were not stated, but they probably consisted of various grains and possibly legumes, items that were enhanced by the extensive cooking time.

Hot dishes gained particular importance in the eighth century C.E. when the Karaites, an antirabbinic sect in the Middle East, forbade the presence of any fire, light, or hot food during their version of the Sabbath. In the face of the intensity of this religious dispute, lighting the Sabbath candles and eating hot foods became not only an enhancement of the Sabbath, but also acts of affiliation with rabbinical tradition. Thereafter, the use and variety of hot Sabbath dishes widely expanded.

Unquestionably, the most popular and widespread hot Sabbath dish has long been a slow-simmered bean stew. In the tenth century, Sephardim began calling the dish *hamin*, or *hamim* (from the Hebrew word for "warm"), or, in southern Spain, *dafina*, or *adafina* (from the Arabic word for "covered" or "buried"). These stews were so identified with Jewish cooking that the Inquisition regarded anyone preparing such fare as suspect of practicing Judaism. In the Maghreb, these stews were called *skhina*, or *skhena* (from an Arabic word meaning "hot"), and *frackh* (Arabic for "happiness"); in Greece, sometimes *fijonicas* (from the Greek for "beans"); and in Iran, *khalebibi*. Ashkenazim also adopted *hamin*, renaming it *shalet*, or *cholent* (from the Old French for "warm"), the term first recorded circa 1246 in the book *Or Zarua* by Isaac ben Moses.

Originally, the stew pots were "buried" in hot ashes and insulating material to finish cooking and stay warm overnight. Later, in the Middle East, a *kanoun* (brazier) was frequently used. For the many households that did not possess a *kanoun*, on Friday afternoons, the husband, an older child, maid, or errand boy would haul the family's special earthenware *olla* (stew pot), the lid secured with wire latches or a flour-and-water paste, to the massive public oven. According to Jewish law, the food must be at least half cooked before the Sabbath. When all of the pots were assembled, the door was closed and sealed with clay, the entire collection to be left undisturbed overnight in the fading heat.

During the long, slow cooking process, the ingredients melded and permeated the dish, developing a distinctive complex flavor and a rich, creamy texture. On Saturday morning following synagogue services, the oven would be unlocked, the pots eagerly reclaimed by their owners, and the treasures hurried home for the Sabbath table. As the German poet Heinrich Heine (1797–1856) wrote in his poem "Prinzessin Sabbat" ("The Sabbath Princess"), "*Cholent* is the food of heaven … *Cholent* is the kosher ambrosia." Today, the pots are no longer "buried" in ashes, cooked on braziers, or baked in public facilities, but instead are usually baked in a home oven set to low, simmered in a slow cooker, or placed on a *blech* (a thin sheet of metal placed over the range top that serves as a heat diffuser) over very low heat to cook overnight. Otherwise, these stews are nearly identical to those prepared weekly for centuries by almost every Jewish community, from the large cities of Istanbul and Cairo to secluded towns in the mountains of central Asia and the Maghreb.

The precise components of the stews differ from region to region and family to family. Basic Sabbath stew consists of a mixture of beans and sometimes chickpeas along with a little fat. Many Sephardim include wheat berries or rice or a combination of both. Ashkenazim commonly add barley. Following their arrival from the Americas, potatoes, sweet potatoes, and red chilies or paprika all became popular stew additions, contributing new notes of texture and flavor. Some cooks add more complex components, like dumplings or *kishke* (grain sausages). In the Sephardic tradition, all of these stews contain *huevos haminados*, whole eggs that develop a brown color and creamy consistency during the cooking.

Sabbath stews reflect popular local seasonings and spice combinations. Italians might add a little sage to theirs, while an Indian stew is frequently seasoned with garam masala and fresh ginger. Hungarians, not surprisingly, add plenty of sweet paprika and Romanians put in ample garlic. Cinnamon and nutmeg or ground ginger are common in many Moroccan versions, which also use dates, honey, or quince preserves to impart an interesting depth of flavor and sweetness.

Unlike the European *cholent*, in which the ingredients are mixed together and served en masse, the components of the Sephardic *hamin* or *dafina* are frequently layered in the pot, then separated into different serving dishes. The eggs, usually peeled and put back in the pot for several minutes to absorb more flavor, are served first. Each diner individually seasons them with salt and ground cumin. The potatoes follow, served in a little cooking liquid. Then come the legumes and remaining cooking liquid in one bowl, the grains in another, and the dumpling in a third dish. In the Maghreb, the legumes were sometimes spooned over couscous left over from Friday dinner.

GEORGIAN RED BEANS IN SOUR PRUNE SAUCE

(Lobio Tkemali)

6 TO 8 SERVINGS

I truly enjoy Georgian food and always appreciate an invitation to a Georgian home for a meal. Georgians, however, do have a penchant for rather sour flavors, avoiding sugar in their cooking. This dish uses a favorite Georgian condiment, sour prune sauce, made from extremely tart Caucasian prunes. To Westerners more familiar with sweet-and-sour seasonings, the flavor may be unusual, but the sauce is also blended with an exotic mix of seasonings and paired with the mildly sweet, earthy flavor and creamy texture of red beans, yielding an intriguing result. Lobio tkemali is traditionally spread over a serving platter, garnished with red onion rings, and served as an appetizer or side dish accompanied with khachapuri (Georgian Pies, page 187) or flat bread.

Because tkemali, the traditional sour plum sauce, is rarely available outside of Georgia, this recipe uses a combination of prunes, vinegar, and tamarind or prune butter as an equivalent. Tamarind paste, also called concentrate, is available in Indian and Middle Eastern markets.

I pound (about 2¹/₃ cups) small dried red beans or kidney beans, picked over, washed well, and drained

I large onion, quartered

2 cloves garlic, halved

¹/₂ to I teaspoon red pepper flakes

2 bay leaves

I teaspoon table salt or 2 teaspoons kosher salt

PRUNE SAUCE:

9 to 10 pitted prunes

¹/₃ cup red wine or balsamic vinegar

5 tablespoons olive oil or vegetable oil

About I tablespoon tamarind paste or concentrate or 3 tablespoons unsweetened prune butter mixed with 3 tablespoons fresh lemon juice

2 to 3 cloves garlic, minced

¹/₂ to ³/₄ teaspoon ground coriander

¹/₂ teaspoon ground fenugreek

¹/₂ to I teaspoon red pepper flakes or cayenne pepper

About I¹/₄ teaspoons table salt or 2¹/₂ teaspoons kosher salt

About ¹/₈ teaspoon ground black pepper

¹/₃ cup chopped fresh cilantro

1. Combine the beans, onion, garlic, pepper flakes, and bay leaves in a large pot and add water to cover by 3 inches. Bring to a boil, cover, reduce the heat to low, and simmer until almost tender, about 1 hour and 45 minutes. Add the salt and continue simmering until very tender, about 15 additional minutes.

2. Drain the beans, discarding the onion, garlic, and bay leaves. Remove about 1 cup of the beans and mash until smooth. Stir the mashed beans into the whole beans. Let cool.

3. To make the sauce: In a small saucepan, simmer the prunes and vinegar over low heat until tender, about 15 minutes. Place in a food processor or blender, add the oil, tamarind, garlic, coriander, fenugreek, pepper flakes, salt, and pepper, and process until smooth. Add the cilantro.

4. Stir the prune sauce into the beans. Cover and refrigerate for at least 4 hours to allow the flavors to meld. Serve at room temperature.

Georgian Green Beans with Eggs

(Lobio Kverstkhi)

6 TO 8 SERVINGS   D OR P

Georgians often prepare fresh green beans by lightly marinating them in a subtle egg sauce. Some cooks vehemently assert that garlic overpowers the egg sauce's subtle flavor, while others insist it is necessary for the proper taste. This dish is a good example of green beans supplanting fava beans when they arrived from America. Originally, this dish was made only with fava beans, but green beans have become commonplace.

2 pounds green beans, trimmed and cut into
  1-inch pieces

3 tablespoons vegetable oil or *ghee* (Indian
  Clarified Butter, page 51)

2 onions, halved and thinly sliced

2 cloves garlic, minced (optional)

$^1/_4$ cup water

1$^1/_2$ teaspoons red wine vinegar

$^1/_2$ teaspoon turmeric or ground marigold petals
  (see Georgian Vegetable Salads, page 75)

About 1 teaspoon table salt or 2 teaspoons
  kosher salt

Ground black pepper to taste

$^1/_4$ cup chopped fresh cilantro

$^1/_4$ cup chopped fresh parsley

3 large eggs, lightly beaten

1. Cook the green beans in salted boiling water or steam over boiling water in a covered pot until crisp-tender, 6 to 7 minutes. Rinse under cold water to stop the cooking and drain.

2. In a large saucepan, heat the oil over medium heat. Add the onions and sauté until lightly golden, about 15 minutes. If using, add the garlic and sauté for 1 minute.

3. Add the beans and sauté until well coated, about 4 minutes. Add the water, vinegar, turmeric, salt, and pepper and cook, stirring occasionally, for about 10 minutes. Add the cilantro and parsley.

4. Stir a little of the hot cooking liquid into the eggs, then gradually stir the egg mixture into the beans. Cover and simmer over low heat until thickened, about 5 minutes. Do not boil. Serve immediately.

VARIATION

Omit the vinegar and add $^1/_2$ teaspoon ground coriander with the salt and $^1/_4$ cup chopped fresh basil with the cilantro.

SEPHARDIC GREEN BEANS WITH TOMATOES

(*Fasoulia*)

6 TO 8 SERVINGS   Ⓟ

The Middle Eastern preference for preparing beans is to cook them until they are mushy and serve them at room temperature, perhaps because they taste best this way in arid climates. Some of my Sephardic friends from the region insist that the relatively long cooking time develops the flavor. That said, I do not like the texture of cold overcooked beans and cook them only until crisp-tender and then enjoy them warm. Use olive oil if serving the fasoulia *cold, for extra flavor. If you like, serve with dollops of plain yogurt.*

3 tablespoons olive oil or vegetable oil

I yellow onion, chopped

3 to 4 cloves garlic, minced

14 ounces plum tomatoes, peeled, seeded, and chopped (see page 291), about 2 cups, or ¹/₂ cup tomato sauce

¹/₂ cup water

I teaspoon sugar

About I teaspoon table salt or 2 teaspoons kosher salt

Ground black pepper to taste

I tablespoon fresh lemon juice (optional)

2 pounds green beans, trimmed and cut into 2-inch pieces

1. In a large, heavy saucepan, heat the oil over medium heat. Add the onion and garlic and sauté until soft and translucent, about 5 minutes. Add the tomatoes, water, sugar, salt, pepper, and, if using, the lemon juice, and bring to a low boil.

2. Add the beans, cover, reduce the heat to low, and simmer, stirring occasionally, until they are crisp-tender, about 8 minutes, or very tender, about 25 minutes. Serve warm or at room temperature.

FASOULIA

*F*asoulia, also spelled *fasooleeye*, is the Arabic word for green bean. This dish, popular in Turkey and the Balkans, is also called *yachni di fijon verde* (Ladino for "green bean stew"), reflecting its Sephardic heritage. *Yachni* refers to a type of earthenware vessel as well as any stew cooked in it.

❧ Fava Beans ❧

Fava beans, *ful* in Arabic and *pul* in Hebrew—also known as broad, horse, and Windsor beans—are the seeds of a coarse annual vine possibly native to the eastern Mediterranean or the Afghanistan/Uzbekistan region. Before Columbus stumbled onto the Americas, the fava bean was the primary bean throughout much of the Old World, providing inexpensive food for the masses. Today, in America and much of Europe, the fava bean is practically nonexistent, except in the cookery of a few ethnic enclaves. On the other hand, it remains an important food in the Middle East and parts of southern Europe.

Fava beans grow in a pod 5 to 12 inches long containing 5 to 6 pale green or light brown beans that, when cooked, develop a nutty flavor and creamy texture. The three most prominent varieties are the large, whitish kidney-shaped European or Greek fava (*ful rumi* in Arabic), the medium-sized Upper Egyptian bean (*ful baladi*, literally "local/country bean"), and the small, round pigeon bean (not the same as pigeon pea). In Egypt, pigeon beans are called *ful hammam* (literally "bath fava"), probably referring to their being cooked over the fires of Egyptian public bathhouses, and are the customary type used for the classic Egyptian dish of stewed dried fava beans, *ful medame*. Medium-sized or small fava beans are generally preferred for stews; large ones are eaten whole for a *meze* (appetizer assortment). The large European fava is the type most available fresh in America. The cooking times of various varieties of fava beans differ greatly.

Fresh fava beans (*avas frescas* in Ladino and *ful akhdar* in Arabic) are available from April through early July. When young, the pods are 3 to 5 inches long, soft and tender, and have a velvety exterior; they can be eaten cooked or, when freshly picked, raw, along with the small beans inside. If the skins have turned creamy white and the beans are larger than $1/2$ inch, the skins should be removed after cooking; if the skins are still green, then you can leave them on. Once the pods fully mature (they are 6 to 12 inches long and have turned shiny and firm), they are too tough to eat; only the beans are consumed. One pound of fresh fava pods yields about 1 cup shelled beans.

Recalling that fava beans were a staple of the Israelites' diet during their stay in Egypt, fava bean dishes—most notably soups (called *bissara* in the Maghreb; Moroccan Bean Spread, page 312), rice with fresh fava beans, and dumplings cooked with fresh fava beans and artichoke hearts—became popular Sephardic Passover dishes. In the Maghreb, fresh fava beans were served over buttery couscous on Shavuot.

What You Should Know: Dried fava beans (*ful nabed*) and canned fava beans (which are cooked dried fava beans) can be found in specialty markets. If possible, buy dried fava beans labeled skinless. Note that dried fava beans have a very different flavor than fresh fava beans and are generally not interchangeable in recipes.

N O T E   To Skin Fresh Fava Beans: Put the beans into a large pot of boiling water, boil for about 45 seconds, drain, and drop into cold water. Using a fingernail, slit open the end where the bean was attached to the pod and squeeze out the bean.

To Skin Dried Fava Beans: Soak the beans in water to cover for at least 8 hours, then drain. Put the beans into a large pot of boiling water, boil about 10 minutes, strain, and gently squeeze out the beans.

Egyptian Slow-Simmered Fava Beans

(*Ful Medames*)

5 TO 6 SERVINGS ℗

Ful is a common dish throughout the Middle East, but adding hard-boiled eggs is a Jewish touch. To many Jews in Egypt, no Sabbath lunch was complete without ful medames *topped with eggs. Some families still eat it on a daily basis, typically accompanied with pita bread.*

3 quarts water

1 pound (about 2 cups) dried fava beans, preferably
    the small, round variety called pigeon beans
    (*ful hammam*); or large dried lima beans,
    such as gigantes, fordbooks, or butter beans,
    picked over, soaked for 12 to 24 hours in cold
    water, and drained

About $^1/_3$ cup olive oil or vegetable oil

About $^3/_4$ teaspoon ground black pepper

5 to 6 cloves garlic, minced (optional)

6 to 8 eggs in the shell, washed well

$^1/_3$ cup chopped fresh parsley or cilantro

About $^1/_4$ cup fresh lemon juice

About $1^1/_2$ teaspoons table salt or 1 tablespoon
    kosher salt

1. Bring the water to a boil in a large pot. Add the beans, return to a boil, cover, reduce the heat to medium-low, and simmer, stirring occasionally, for 30 minutes.

2. Stir in the oil, pepper, and, if using, the garlic. Add the eggs. Reduce the heat to low and simmer, stirring occasionally and adding more water if necessary, until the beans are very soft, about 2 hours or even overnight. The cooking time will vary according to the size and variety of the bean. Drain.

3. Remove the eggs. Peel, then quarter or chop. Set aside.

4. Some people prefer the beans whole, others slightly or completely mashed. If desired, mash one-third of the beans, then stir into the remaining beans. Add the parsley, lemon juice, and salt to the beans and toss to coat. (Egyptians commonly let individual diners add their own salt at the table.) Taste and adjust the seasoning. Divide the beans between serving bowls and top with the eggs. Serve warm or at room temperature.

VARIATIONS

To further flavor the *ful*, in Step 4 mix in a little mashed garlic, ground cumin, and olive oil or *ghee* (Indian Clarified Butter, page 51).

Iraqi *Ful*: Just before serving, sprinkle the beans lightly with dried mint.

Syrian *Ful*: In Step 4, add 1 to $1^1/_2$ teaspoons ground cumin and $^1/_4$ to $^1/_2$ teaspoon red pepper flakes or a pinch of Aleppo or cayenne pepper.

Yemenite *Ful*: Spoon about 2 tablespoons tahini (Middle Eastern Sesame Sauce, page 430) over each serving of beans.

FUL OF BEANS

In Egypt, *ful medames,* or *ful mudammas,* is practically the national dish, enjoyed by rich and poor alike. It can be found everywhere at any time of day—sold at fancy restaurants and special *ful* stores, and peddled by street vendors. The dish resembles the traditional *hamin* (Sabbath stew) that simmered overnight in dying embers to stay warm for Sabbath lunch, for the Jerusalem Talmud mentions a similar method for preparing fava beans in the town of Sepphoris. Even the dish's name reflects a similarity with *hamin: Medames* comes from the Coptic word for "buried," akin to the ancient Jewish practice of *tomnin et ha'hamin* ("burying the warm dishes") overnight in burning coals or insulating materials to serve hot for Sabbath lunch.

Today, *ful* is served by many Middle Eastern Jews as a breakfast dish, commonly accompanied with tomato-and-cucumber salads, black olives, and plenty of pita bread to sop up the sauce, as a side dish at lunch and dinner, as part of a *meze* (appetizer assortment), and for Sabbath lunch.

SYRIAN FRESH FAVA BEANS WITH YOGURT

(Ful Akhdar ma Laban)

4 TO 5 SERVINGS · D

The name Aleppo *derived from the Arabic word* haleb (milk), *referring to the abundance of the area's dairy products, which were primarily consumed in the form of* jiben (soft cheese) *and* leban (yogurt). *Both of these are still ubiquitous at breakfast and dinner, the traditional Middle Eastern dairy meals. (Lunch was the main meal of the day and the one to contain meat, for those who could afford it.) Mixing yogurt with vegetables is a common Middle Eastern practice, creating a tangy, silky sauce.*

Middle Eastern yogurt tends to be somewhat tarter and thinner than the commercial American brands, and indeed, many Syrians find American yogurt so bland that they insist on making it themselves. Therefore, adjust the amount of lemon juice in the sauce to your preference. This is one of the few recipes where fresh and canned fava beans are interchangeable, as they both are complemented by the yogurt sauce. If using tender, bright green young pods, cut them into 1-inch pieces and cook them with the beans.

1/4 cup olive oil or vegetable oil

2 onions or 6 to 8 scallions, chopped

2 to 3 cloves garlic, minced (optional)

2 pounds fresh fava beans, shelled and, if large and white, skinned; or about 3 cups canned fava beans, drained

1 1/2 cups water

1/4 cup chopped fresh cilantro or parsley

1 tablespoon sugar

SAUCE:

1 clove garlic

1/2 teaspoon table salt or 1 teaspoon kosher salt

1 cup plain yogurt, beaten until smooth

1 large egg, lightly beaten, or 1 1/2 teaspoons
    cornstarch dissolved in 1 1/2 teaspoons water

1 teaspoon packed brown or granulated sugar

About 1 teaspoon fresh lemon juice

About 1 tablespoon chopped fresh spearmint
    or 1 teaspoon dried

1 teaspoon ground mustard

1/2 teaspoon ground black pepper

Pinch of freshly grated nutmeg

1. In a medium, heavy saucepan, heat the oil over medium heat. Add the onions and, if using, the garlic and sauté until soft and translucent, 5 to 10 minutes. Stir in the beans, then the water, cilantro, and sugar. Bring to a boil, cover, reduce the heat to low, and simmer until tender, 10 to 20 minutes for small, young beans, 20 to 30 minutes for larger, older beans, or about 30 minutes for canned beans. Drain. Return the beans to the pot.

2. To make the sauce: Using the tip of a heavy knife or with a mortar and pestle, mash the garlic and salt into a paste. In a medium saucepan, combine the yogurt, egg, the garlic paste, sugar, lemon juice, mint, mustard, pepper, and nutmeg. Place over medium heat and, stirring constantly, bring to a simmer. (My friend's grandmother, who gave me this recipe, insisted that it was important to always stir in the same direction, and who am I to argue with tradition?) Reduce the heat to low and simmer, stirring constantly, until the yogurt begins to thicken, about 5 minutes.

3. Add the beans and simmer over low heat, stirring frequently, until heated through, about 5 minutes. Serve warm or cooled.

EGYPTIAN FAVA BEAN FRITTERS

(Tamiya)

ABOUT 40 PATTIES

Falafel, the famous chickpea fritter, is a direct descendant of this venerable Egyptian fava-based one. Falafel may be more popular, but some people prefer fritters made with the more flavorful fava beans. Do not substitute canned fava beans, which will result in an inappropriate texture. Middle Easterners favor their patties crisp on the outside and soft inside, with plenty of spice and garlic, and I concur. You can adjust the seasoning to your own taste.

1 pound (about 3 cups) dried fava beans,
    preferably the large variety and skinless

6 to 8 scallions, minced, or 1 onion, finely chopped

4 to 6 cloves garlic, crushed

1 cup chopped fresh cilantro or parsley,
    or 1/2 cup each

1 teaspoon baking powder

About 2 teaspoons ground coriander

2 teaspoons ground cumin

1/4 to 1/2 teaspoon cayenne pepper or red pepper
    flakes

About 1 1/2 teaspoons table salt or 1 tablespoon
    kosher salt

About 1/2 teaspoon ground black pepper

1/2 cup sesame seeds (optional)

Vegetable oil for deep-frying

1. Soak the beans in cold water to cover for at least 24 hours. Drain, reserving some of the soaking liquid, and pat dry with towels. If skinless beans are unavailable, rub to loosen the skins, then discard.

2. Grind the beans in a food mill or meat grinder. If neither appliance is available, process them in a food processor, but only until the beans form a paste. If blended too smoothly, the batter will tend to fall apart during cooking. Add the scallions, garlic, cilantro, baking powder, coriander, cumin, cayenne, salt, and pepper. If too thick, add a little of the reserved bean soaking liquid. Refrigerate until the batter is firm, at least 1 hour.

3. Shape the bean mixture into 1-inch balls. Flatten slightly and dip one side into the sesame seeds, if desired, in traditional Egyptian style.

4. In a large saucepan or deep skillet, heat at least 2 inches of oil over medium heat to 350°F.

5. Fry the patties in batches, turning once, until golden brown on all sides, about 5 minutes total. Using a wire-mesh skimmer or a slotted spoon, transfer to paper towels to drain. Keep warm in a 300°F oven while frying the remaining patties. Serve immediately as part of a meze (appetizer assortment), or in pita bread with a tomato-cucumber salad, tabbouleh (Middle Eastern Bulgur Salad, page 112), or pickles, drizzled with tahini (Middle Eastern Sesame Sauce, page 430).

VARIATION

Middle Eastern Chickpea Fritters (*Falafel*):
Soak 1 pound (2^1/$_2$ cups) dried chickpeas in water to cover for at least 12 hours and substitute for the fava beans. Or, use 8 ounces dried fava beans and 8 ounces dried chickpeas.

BEYOND FALAFEL

Beginning in the 1950s, Yemenite immigrants in Israel took up making falafel to earn a livelihood, utilizing the chickpea version common in the Levant, and transformed this ancient treat (the fava version originated among the Copts of Egypt) into the Israeli national street food.

Legume fritters are commonly stuffed into a pita with salad and accompanied with tahini sauce and the nontraditional Yemenite *z'chug* (chili sauce). Iraqi Jews use a different strategy by wrapping the fritters in a lavashlike bread called *lafah* or, in Jerusalem, *eshtanor*.

Today, these spicy croquettes, the Middle Eastern equivalent of fast food, are peddled by street vendors and at kiosks throughout Israel and all of the Levant. Professional *tamiya* and falafel makers use a special scooping device with a plunger to mold the 1-inch balls, but they are also easily formed by hand.

❧ BLACK-EYED PEAS ❧

There are a number of legumes in the category of field beans, the most well known in the West being the mung bean and its close relative, the black-eyed pea, also called the cowpea or crowder pea. Despite being labeled a pea, it is actually a bean. Black-eyed peas, possibly native to southern China or India, have been cultivated for more than five millennia. After arriving in Africa, they quickly emerged as an important crop and became commonly identified with that continent. Indeed, the Hebrew name for the dried black-eyed pea became *pol ha-mitzri* (Egyptian bean) and for the fresh pea, *pol loovi* (Libyan bean). Because the latter term is similar to the Hebrew for "to be many" and because legumes grow in profusion, the black-eyed pea became a traditional Rosh Hashanah food, a symbol of abundance and fertility.

Widely consumed in Israel in Talmudic times, black-eyed peas remain popular fare in only a few Jewish communities, particularly those from the Balkans, Ethiopia, Turkey, and Syria. Along with fava beans, black-eyed peas are one of the few legumes eaten both fresh and dried. Prepared either way, the seeds have an earthy, somewhat sweet flavor and are generally combined with other foods. Ethiopians commonly eat black-eyed peas with millet. In the eastern Mediterranean, the legume is typically partnered with rice. In the domains of the former Ottoman Empire, black-eyed peas are prepared as a salad or cooked with tomatoes and onions.

TURKISH BLACK-EYED PEAS WITH TOMATOES

(*Lubiya*)

4 TO 5 SERVINGS

There are many serendipitous similarities between the cuisine of the American south, where I grew up, and the cuisine of my Romanian roots: Both cultures are partial to highly spiced foods; both display a particular fondness for cornmeal, legumes, and okra; and both serve black-eyed peas on New Year's Day. My great-grandmother in Savannah, Georgia, who was renowned for her lemon meringue pie and benne wafers, also made black-eyed peas similar to this Turkish version. Tomato, onion, and garlic enhance the bean's savory, earthy flavor. Black-eyed peas, called lubiya, *or* loubia, *in Arabic and* fijones *in Ladino, are generally served as a side dish for dinner or for breakfast accompanied with rice or warm pita bread or corn bread to scoop up the sauce.*

> 10 ounces (about 1¹/₂ cups) dried black-eyed peas, picked over, soaked in cold water to cover for at least 4 hours, drained, and rinsed
> 3 tablespoons olive oil or vegetable oil
> 1 onion, chopped
> 2 to 4 cloves garlic, minced (optional)
> 1 tablespoon tomato paste
> 14 ounces plum tomatoes, peeled, seeded, and chopped (see page 291), about 2 cups, or 2 cups water mixed with 8 ounces tomato sauce
> About 1 teaspoon table salt or 2 teaspoons kosher salt
> ¹/₄ teaspoon sugar
> About ¹/₈ teaspoon ground black pepper

1. Put the peas in a large saucepan and add water to cover by 2 inches. Bring to a boil, reduce the heat to low, cover, and simmer until nearly tender, about 40 minutes. Drain, reserving 1/4 cup cooking liquid. (Use the remaining cooking liquid in a soup or stew.)

2. In a large saucepan, heat the oil over medium heat. Add the onion and, if using, the garlic and sauté until soft and translucent, about 5 minutes. Stir in the tomato paste and sauté until slightly darkened, about 2 minutes. Add the tomatoes, the reserved 1/4 cup cooking liquid, the salt, sugar, and pepper and bring to a boil.

3. Add the peas, cover, reduce the heat to low, and simmer, stirring occasionally and adding a little more water if necessary, until the peas are tender and the flavors meld, about 20 minutes. Serve warm.

VARIATIONS

Indian Black-Eyed Peas (*Lobia*): Omit the tomatoes and tomato paste. In Step 3, add with the peas 3 cups water, 1 tablespoon freshly grated ginger, about 1/2 teaspoon cayenne, and 1/4 teaspoon ground turmeric and cook for 40 minutes. Add 2 seeded and minced small hot green chilies, 4 teaspoons tamarind pulp, 3/4 teaspoon ground cumin, and 1/2 teaspoon garam masala and cook for another 20 minutes.

Sephardic Fresh Black-Eyed Peas (*Fijones Frescos*): Substitute 1 1/2 pounds shelled fresh or 10 ounces frozen black-eyed peas for the dried peas and omit the soaking and precooking in Step 1. Fresh black-eyed peas cook in about 45 minutes, frozen ones in about 25 minutes.

❧ CHICKPEAS ❧

The chickpea, which is not a pea but a legume, is believed to be a native of southeastern Turkey, where it was first cultivated, or of northern Persia. By the early Bronze Age, chickpeas were common throughout the Fertile Crescent, North Africa, India, and parts of Europe. Archaeologists have found chickpeas in Neolithic burial mounds as far north as Switzerland. The nutty-flavored chickpea is still a staple in much of the world, especially in India, where it is among the predominant legumes, utilized boiled, roasted, fried, and ground into flour.

In ancient Israel, chickpeas (*chamitz* or "sour" in Hebrew, denoting the sour taste of the plant's leaves and pods) trailed only lentils and fava beans in importance among legumes. Chickpeas were such prevalent fare among Sephardim that the authorities of the Spanish Inquisition considered them a sign of Jewish cooking, and people making chickpea stews were subject to arrest. Today, Sephardim use them in soups, Sabbath stews, and salads, and they also mix them with rice, bulgur, pasta, and various vegetables. Chickpeas constitute the main ingredient in two of the most well-known Middle Eastern dishes: hummus (chickpea purée) and falafel.

As with other legumes, chickpeas can be easily grown in abundance and so are an ancient symbol of fertility. In addition, the chickpea's round shape symbolizes the cycles of life and the year. Therefore, chickpeas are a common sight at parties celebrating a birth and are a traditional Rosh Hashanah food, a wish for a well-rounded year to come.

What You Should Know: Old chickpeas will not soften, no matter how long they are soaked and cooked, so check to see if there is a production date on the package and avoid those more than a year old.

MIDDLE EASTERN CHICKPEA DIP

(*Hummus bi Tahina*)

ABOUT 4 CUPS, OR 6 TO 8 SERVINGS

Long a staple in the Middle East, legumes are often prepared by being mashed into a smooth dip for bread. Unquestionably, the most popular and famous of these dips is hummus bi tahina (*Arabic for "chickpeas with sesame paste"*)*, more informally called* hummus. *Once a simple food for the impoverished, hummus is now ubiquitous at the* meze *table, by itself or in sandwiches. Serve with warm pita bread, crackers, or crudités.*

12 ounces (about 1 1/2 cups) dried chickpeas, picked over, soaked for 12 hours in water to cover, and drained, or 32 ounces canned chickpeas, drained and liquid reserved

About 1/2 cup tahini (Middle Eastern Sesame Sauce, page 430)

4 to 6 tablespoons fresh lemon juice

3 to 4 cloves garlic, minced

About 1 1/2 teaspoons table salt or 1 tablespoon kosher salt

Ground black pepper to taste

About 1/2 teaspoon ground cumin

1/8 teaspoon cayenne

Extra-virgin olive oil for drizzling

1/2 teaspoon paprika or ground sumac for garnish

3 tablespoons chopped fresh parsley or cilantro

1. If using dried chickpeas, put them in a large pot, add water to cover by 2 inches, bring to a boil, reduce the heat to low, cover, and simmer until tender, about 1 1/2 hours. Drain, reserving the cooking liquid.

2. In a food processor or using the back of a large spoon, mash the chickpeas. Add the tahini, 1/3 cup of the reserved cooking liquid or water, the lemon juice, garlic, salt, pepper, cumin, and cayenne and process until smooth. Add enough of the remaining cooking liquid to make a smooth, creamy paste with the consistency of mayonnaise. Store in the refrigerator for up to 3 days. To serve, spread the hummus on a serving plate and drizzle with olive oil. Sprinkle with the paprika or parsley, or both. Serve at room temperature.

MOROCCAN SPICY CHICKPEAS

(Tagine el Hummos)

6 TO 8 SERVINGS

The blend of spices typifies Moroccan seasoning, and transforms the dish's simple ingredients into a complex offering. This dish can be made in two ways, one that centers solely on the chickpeas, and one that incorporates vegetables to add more substance. Both versions are considered a side dish, but when served with couscous or rice they become a main course.

1 pound (about 2^1/$_2$ cups) dried chickpeas, picked over, soaked in water to cover for 12 hours, drained, and rinsed

3 tablespoons vegetable oil or olive oil

2 onions, chopped

2 to 3 cloves garlic, minced, or 2 small hot green chilies, seeded and minced

2 to 3 carrots, chopped (optional)

1 sweet potato, 1 pound seeded butternut squash, or 2 turnips, peeled and chopped (optional)

^{1}/$_4$ teaspoon cayenne

^{1}/$_4$ teaspoon ground cinnamon

^{1}/$_4$ teaspoon ground cumin

^{1}/$_4$ teaspoon ground ginger

^{1}/$_4$ teaspoon paprika

^{1}/$_8$ teaspoon saffron threads or ground turmeric

1^1/$_3$ pounds plum tomatoes, peeled, seeded, and chopped (see page 291), about 3 cups

About 1 teaspoon table salt or 2 teaspoons kosher salt

About ^{1}/$_4$ teaspoon ground black pepper

^{1}/$_4$ cup chopped fresh cilantro

^{1}/$_4$ cup chopped fresh parsley

Harissa (Northwest African Chili Paste, page 433), optional

1. Put the chickpeas in a large pot and add water to cover by 2 inches. Bring to a boil, cover, reduce the heat to low, and simmer until tender, about 1^1/$_2$ hours. Drain.

2. In a large skillet, heat the oil over medium heat. Add the onions and sauté for 1 minute. Add the garlic and, if using, the carrots and/or sweet potato and sauté until softened, about 10 minutes. Add the cayenne, cinnamon, cumin, ginger, paprika, and saffron and sauté for 1 minute. Add the tomatoes, salt, and pepper. Bring to a boil, cover, reduce the heat to low, and simmer, stirring occasionally, until the tomatoes liquefy into a sauce, about 20 minutes.

3. Add the chickpeas and cook, stirring occasionally, until slightly thickened, about 10 minutes. Stir in the cilantro and parsley. If desired, stir in *harissa* to taste. Serve warm or at room temperature.

VARIATIONS

For a more highly spiced dish, increase the cinnamon, cumin, and ginger to 1 teaspoon each and the cayenne to ^{1}/$_2$ teaspoon.

Moroccan Sweet-and-Sour Chickpeas (*Tagine el Hummos*): Simmer ^{1}/$_2$ cup chopped dates and 2 chopped preserved lemons in ^{1}/$_2$ cup water for 10 minutes and add with the tomatoes.

Moroccan Spicy Chickpeas and Fava Beans (*Tagine el Hummos wa Ful*): Reduce the cooked chickpeas to 3 cups (6 ounces or 1 cup dried) and add 3 cups cooked fava beans (6 ounces or 1 cup dried).

TUNISIAN CHICKPEAS WITH GREENS

(Tagine el Hummos)

Handwritten note: 1/6/14 Excellent. As is. Serve w/ table (harissa)

6 TO 8 SERVINGS ℗

Chickpeas, wheat, and barley, constitute the main-stays of the Tunisian diet, eaten at breakfast, lunch, and dinner. For millennia, almost every Tunisian soup and stew has contained chickpeas, commonly accented with cumin. In this dish, served on special occasions, a few basic, inexpensive ingredients are transformed into a richly flavored stew.

1 pound (about 2½ cups) dried chickpeas, picked over, soaked in water to cover for 12 hours, drained, and rinsed

2 tablespoons cumin seeds

20 whole peppercorns

2 small dried red peppers or 1 tablespoon *harissa* (Northwest African Chili Paste, page 433)

½ cup olive oil

2 (2-inch thick) slices French or Italian bread, crust removed

8 large cloves garlic

2 onions, chopped

2 tablespoons sweet paprika

1 cup water

2 tablespoons red wine vinegar

About 1 teaspoon table salt or 2 teaspoons kosher salt

1 pound fresh spinach, chard, or kale, stemmed

½ cup chopped fresh parsley

1. Put the chickpeas in a large pot and add water to cover by 2 inches. Bring to a boil, cover, reduce the heat to low, and simmer until tender, about 1½ hours. Drain.

2. Using a mortar and pestle or a spice grinder, grind the cumin, peppercorns, and peppers into a powder. If using harissa, stir into the ground spices.

3. In a large skillet, heat the oil over medium-high heat. Add the bread and 4 cloves of the garlic and cook until the bread is browned on both sides, about 2 minutes. Remove the bread and garlic. Tear the bread into pieces. In a food processor, blender, or with a mortar and pestle, process the bread and fried garlic until well blended.

4. In the same skillet, over medium-high heat, add the onions and sauté until soft and translucent, 5 to 10 minutes. Add the spice mixture and sauté for 5 minutes. (This helps to develop the flavors.) Add the remaining 4 cloves garlic and the paprika and stir for 30 seconds. Add the water, vinegar, and salt and bring to a boil, stirring.

5. Add the chickpeas, bread mixture, and spinach. (There might seem like a lot of spinach, but it will cook down.) Reduce the heat to medium and cook, stirring occasionally, until the spinach is tender and the sauce slightly thickened, about 10 minutes. Discard the garlic cloves and stir in the parsley. Serve warm.

VARIATIONS

Tunisian Chickpeas with Greens (*Tagine el Hummos***):** In this version, tomato paste is used to thicken the sauce instead of bread. Omit Step 3. Still add garlic in Step 4. In Step 5, add 2 tablespoons tomato paste with the spice mixture.

Tunisian Chickpeas with Vegetables (*Tagine el Hummos***):** Before adding the chickpeas, add 2 sliced carrots, 2 peeled and coarsely chopped potatoes, and 2 peeled and coarsely chopped turnips; cover and simmer for 10 minutes. Add with the chickpeas 1 cup cubed winter or summer squash, 2 seeded, deribbed (white removed), and sliced green bell peppers, and 2 seeded, deribbed (white removed), and sliced red bell peppers. This serves 5 to 6 as a main course.

ROMANIAN SWEETENED CHICKPEAS

(Tzimmes Nahit)

8 TO 10 SERVINGS AS A SIDE DISH ℗

Among Ashkenazim, chickpeas are traditional food at a shalom zachor *(celebration for a new son),* brit, *and on Purim. When most Ashkenazim eat chickpeas, variously called both* nahit *and* arbes *in Yiddish, they are generally served simply boiled with salt and pepper. This recipe features both sweet and peppery flavors, a combination popular in medieval times.*

> 1 pound (about 2½ cups) dried chickpeas,
>   picked over, soaked in cold water to cover
>   for 12 hours, drained, and rinsed
> 6 tablespoons shortening or vegetable oil
> ¼ cup unbleached all-purpose flour
> ¼ cup honey or packed brown sugar
> About 1½ teaspoons table salt or 1 tablespoon
>   kosher salt
> About 1 teaspoon ground black pepper

1. Put the chickpeas in a large pot and add water to cover by 2 inches. Bring to a boil, cover, reduce the heat to low, and simmer until tender, about 1½ hours. Drain, reserving 2½ cups of the cooking liquid.

2. In a large, heavy saucepan, melt the shortening over low heat. Stir in the flour and cook until bubbly, about 3 minutes. Add the honey and stir until lightly browned, about 2 minutes. Gradually stir in the 2½ cups reserved cooking liquid. Increase the heat to medium-high and bring to a boil, stirring constantly.

3. Add the chickpeas, salt, and pepper and cook, stirring frequently, until thickened, about 10 minutes. Serve warm.

❧ LENTILS ❧

The consumption of lentils stretches back before recorded history. In Roman times, however, lentils developed the standing of poor man's food and, in much of Europe, were considered something to avoid except during periods of famine. Arabs, on the other hand, viewed lentils as an energizer, and the legume flourished in Muslim cultures.

Lentils were a part of Jewish cookery from the onset, including the all-time most famous lentil dish, Jacob's red stew. They also used to make the biblical *ashishim*, a pressed cake made from ground roasted lentils mixed with honey and fried in oil. Lentils have a spherical shape with "no mouth" (no opening), symbolic of mourners who are required to be silent, and they are therefore traditional food in a house of mourning and before fasts. At the same time, like other legumes, they are a symbol of fertility and so are served on joyous occasions as well.

All lentils are members of the same species. Among their various colors—brown, dark green, orange, pinkish, and red—the brown variety (which actually ranges in color from olive green to brown) is the most prevalent one in the West. Brown lentils, which are unhulled, have a rather bland flavor and hold their shape well in cooking, making them best used in salads and stews. Green lentils, also unhulled, are firmer and take a little longer to cook than brown. Several varieties of very small, dark green lentils, called French lentils or *verte du Puy*, are renowned for their firm texture and considered a delicacy. Red lentils—called *massor dal* or *masur dal* in India—are usually hulled, revealing their bright reddish-orange interiors. Red lentils cook quicker than green varieties and, because they break down while cooking, are best for puréeing and using in soups. Red-brown lentils are unhulled red lentils; they have an earthier flavor than the hulled version and keep their shape better during cooking.

The somewhat bland, earthy flavor of lentils pairs well with garlic, tomato, and a wide variety of assertive herbs and spices. Sephardim generally use red lentils for soups and brown lentils for most other recipes. Syrians mix brown lentils with rice, bulgur, or noodles and use red lentils as a vegetarian substitute in meat dishes, such as *lahamagine* (Syrian Miniature Lentil Pizzas, page 159). Among the Bene Israel of Bombay, orange lentils (hulled red lentils), never red (unhulled) ones (which are associated with Jacob's wicked brother Esau), along with rice, formed the basis of most meals.

ETHIOPIAN LENTIL STEW

(Misir Wot)

5 TO 6 SERVINGS   D OR P

Legumes, especially lentils and split peas, constitute a considerable part of the Ethiopian diet; they are an important source of protein in that frequently impoverished land. Lentils are usually prepared as stews, like this one, well seasoned with a combination of spices more reminiscent of Indian cookery than African. A traditional spice mixture called berbere *adds extra fire. Some cooks insist on adding tomatoes for extra flavor, while others prefer the more pronounced earthy flavor of the lentils to shine. This stew is typically served as a main course with injera (Ethiopian flat bread), yogurt, and salads.*

6 cups water

1 pound (about 2 cups) brown or green lentils, picked over, rinsed, and drained

3 red or yellow onions, chopped

$^1/_2$ cup *ghee* (Indian Clarified Butter, page 51) or vegetable oil

2 to 3 cloves garlic, minced

2 to 3 teaspoons minced fresh ginger or 2 teaspoons cumin seeds

3 to 4 large green chilies, such as Anaheim or poblano

About 1 teaspoon table salt or 2 teaspoons kosher salt

Ground black pepper, to taste

$^1/_2$ to 2 teaspoons *berbere* (Ethiopian Chili Powder, page 437), optional

1. Bring the water to a boil in a large pot. Add the lentils (there should be enough liquid to completely cover them) and cook until they begin to get mushy, about 15 minutes. Set aside.

2. In a dry large skillet or saucepan over medium heat, cook the onions, stirring constantly, until they begin to soften, 2 to 3 minutes. Add the ghee, garlic, and ginger and sauté until fragrant, 2 to 3 minutes.

3. Add $^1/_2$ cup of the lentil cooking liquid, the chilies, the salt, pepper, and, for a fiery sauce, the *berbere* and cook, stirring constantly, until the chilies are softened, about 5 minutes.

4. Add the lentils and the remaining cooking liquid. Cover partially, reduce the heat to low, and simmer, stirring occasionally, until the lentils are tender and the sauce thickened, about 30 minutes. Taste and adjust the seasoning. Serve hot.

VARIATION

Ethiopian Lentil and Tomato Stew (*Misir Wot*): After Step 1, drain the lentils, reserving only 2 cups of the cooking liquid. In Step 3, add 3 cups seeded and chopped tomatoes and $^1/_2$ cup tomato paste.

Indian Lentils with Ginger and Lemon

(*Dal*)

6 TO 8 SERVINGS   Ⓓ OR Ⓟ

There are endless variations of Indian lentil stew. This version is redolent with fresh ginger and lemon. Dal is traditionally served in individual bowls; each diner eats part of it as a soup and then spoons the remainder over rice. Yellow lentils, called toovar dal *and* toor dal, *are actually kidney-shaped yellowish-brown pigeon peas and cook much quicker than brown lentils.*

1/4 cup *ghee* (Indian Clarified Butter, page 51)
    or vegetable oil

1 large onion, chopped

3 to 4 cloves garlic, minced

About 6 cups water

1 1/2 pounds (about 3 3/4 cups) brown or yellow
    lentils, picked over, soaked in cold water to
    cover for 2 hours, drained, and rinsed

4 teaspoons grated fresh ginger

2 tablespoons fresh lemon juice

About 1 1/4 teaspoons table salt or 2 1/2 teaspoons
    kosher salt

3/4 teaspoon grated lemon zest

About 1/2 teaspoon ground black pepper

1 (1-inch) piece cinnamon stick

1 bay leaf

Dash of cayenne or hot sauce

1/2 cup chopped fresh parsley or cilantro
    (optional)

1. In a large saucepan, melt the ghee over medium heat. Add the onion and garlic and sauté until soft and translucent, about 5 minutes.

2. Add the water, lentils, ginger, lemon juice, salt, zest, pepper, cinnamon, bay leaf, and cayenne. Bring to a boil, cover, reduce the heat to low, and simmer, adding more liquid if necessary, until the lentils are tender, about 20 minutes for yellow lentils and 40 minutes for brown lentils. Serve warm. If desired, garnish with the parsley.

VARIATION

Indian Curried Lentils (*Dal Kari*): Omit the lemon juice, zest, and cinnamon and add 2 teaspoons ground coriander, 1 teaspoon ground cumin, 1 teaspoon ground mustard, 1/2 teaspoon ground turmeric, and about 1/2 teaspoon red pepper flakes.

DAL

*D*al is the Hindi word for a split lentil, but it has evolved to mean a stewlike dish made from any legume. Few Indian meals would be considered complete without some type of dal, usually served as an accompaniment to a curry or spiced rice dish. Many Indian meals consist solely of dal and rice.

Dal made with split peas and pigeon peas, which generally break down into a thick sauce, is customarily served with bread, while dal made with lentils, which hold their shape, is generally accompanied with rice. Indian lentils are always zestfully seasoned, not only because of their ability to absorb flavors, but also to help overpower the bad breath that consuming too many of these legumes may produce.

CALCUTTA LENTIL FRITTERS

(*Vadas*)

ABOUT 15 FRITTERS   P

Following World War II, most of the Jewish community of Calcutta, once numbering around six thousand, emigrated, primarily to London. Another sizable group headed for Sydney. Today, fewer than forty Jewish families remain in Calcutta. During a trip to Australia in 1996, I met a few former Indian Jews who shared some of their recipes, including this one for red lentil vadas *(fritters), also called* piaju *(from a Hindi word for onion). While falafel, the famous chickpea fritter, is certainly the most well-known legume fritter, the Jews of Calcutta made their fritters with red lentils, giving them a pinkish interior. Since red lentils are somewhat bland, most of the flavor comes from the spices. They also make a version using split peas, which is slightly sweeter and has a slight green tinge.*

> 8 ounces (about 1 cup) red lentils or $^1/_2$ cup red
>   lentils and $^1/_2$ cup yellow lentils (*toovar dal*),
>   picked over, soaked in water to cover for
>   2 hours, drained, rinsed, and patted dry
> About $^3/_4$ teaspoon table salt or 1 $^1/_2$ teaspoons
>   kosher salt
> $^1/_2$ to $^3/_4$ teaspoon cayenne, or 1 small hot green
>   or red chili, seeded and minced
> $^1/_2$ teaspoon ground cumin or coriander
> About $^1/_2$ teaspoon ground black pepper
> 1 small onion, finely chopped
> $^1/_2$ to 1 teaspoon minced fresh ginger
> 2 to 3 tablespoons chopped fresh cilantro
> Vegetable oil for deep-frying

1. In a food processor, food mill, or meat grinder, grind the lentils with the salt, cayenne, cumin, and pepper. Add the onion, ginger, and cilantro.

2. In a large saucepan or deep skillet, heat at least 1$^1/_2$ inches oil over medium heat to 365°F.

3. In batches, drop the batter by heaping teaspoonfuls into the oil and fry until golden brown on all sides, about 5 minutes total. Using a wire-mesh skimmer or slotted spoon, transfer to paper towels to drain. Serve warm.

VARIATION

Calcutta Split Pea Fritters (*Filorees*): Substitute 1 cup split green peas for the lentils and omit the cumin.

SYRIAN LENTILS
WITH CHARD

(Adas bi Sili)

6 TO 8 SERVINGS   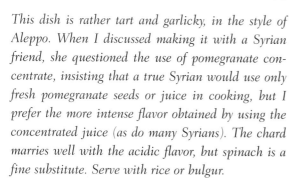

*This dish is rather tart and garlicky, in the style of
Aleppo. When I discussed making it with a Syrian
friend, she questioned the use of pomegranate concentrate, insisting that a true Syrian would use only
fresh pomegranate seeds or juice in cooking, but I
prefer the more intense flavor obtained by using the
concentrated juice (as do many Syrians). The chard
marries well with the acidic flavor, but spinach is a
fine substitute. Serve with rice or bulgur.*

    1/4 cup vegetable oil

    I large onion or leek, chopped

    4 to 8 cloves garlic, mashed

    About 6 cups water

    I pound (about 2 1/3 cups)) dried brown or red
        lentils, picked over, rinsed, soaked in water
        to cover for 2 hours, and drained

    I pound chard or fresh spinach, stemmed and
        shredded (about 9 cups), or 20 ounces thawed
        frozen chopped spinach, squeezed dry

    I bay leaf

    About 1 1/4 teaspoons table salt or 2 1/2 teaspoons
        kosher salt

    About 1/2 teaspoon ground black pepper

    I teaspoon ground cumin (optional)

    3/4 cup chopped fresh cilantro

    1/4 cup pomegranate concentrate (see page 22)
        and 2 tablespoons lemon juice, or about
        1/4 cup fresh lemon juice

1. In a large pot, heat the oil over medium
heat. Add the onion and garlic and sauté until soft
and translucent, about 5 minutes. Add the water,
lentils, chard, bay leaf, salt, pepper, and, if using,
the cumin. Bring to a boil, cover, reduce the heat to
low, and simmer until the lentils are tender, adding
more liquid if necessary, about 20 minutes for red
lentils or 40 minutes for brown lentils.

2. Add the cilantro, pomegranate concentrate,
and lemon juice mixture to taste and cook, uncovered, for about 5 minutes. Serve warm.

Middle Eastern Lentils and Rice

(*Mengedarrah*)

4 TO 6 SERVINGS D OR P

A Syrian friend attended college in Boston, his first extended stay away from home. His doting mother sent him a package every week generally containing two items: a large container of lentils and rice and a smaller container of fried onions to sprinkle over top. This food gift arrived like clockwork on Thursday to serve as dinner, and the remnants were finished for Friday and Saturday breakfast. One week, a strike delayed the package's arrival, and my friend performed poorly on a Friday morning exam, something he still attributes to a lack of lentils and rice. For many Middle Eastern Jews, that claim is no exaggeration, for lentils and rice constitute their ultimate comfort food.

Soaking for several hours helps to bring out the lentils' flavor and maintain their shape during cooking. Traditional accompaniments are yogurt and pita bread.

1/4 cup vegetable oil or *ghee* (Indian Clarified
  Butter, page 51)

2 large onions, halved and sliced into crescents

About 3 cups water

7 ounces (about 1 cup) brown or green lentils,
  picked over, rinsed, soaked in water to cover
  for 2 hours, and drained

About 1 teaspoon table salt or 2 teaspoons
  kosher salt

About 1/4 teaspoon ground black pepper

1 cup long-grain white rice, soaked in cold water
  to cover for 20 minutes and drained

1 to 2 tablespoons unsalted butter (optional)

1. In a medium saucepan, heat the oil over medium-high heat. Add the onions and sauté until golden brown, about 15 minutes. Remove half of the onions and let them cool. (Alternatively, you can remove all of the onions and use them all for the topping, or leave all of the fried onions in the saucepan to mix into the mengedarrah.)

2. Add 2 cups of the water to the saucepan and bring to a boil. Add the lentils, reduce the heat to low, and simmer, uncovered, until just tender but still firm, 15 to 20 minutes. Drain the cooking liquid into a measuring cup and add enough of the remaining 1 cup water to equal 2 cups, leaving the lentils in the saucepan.

3. Add the 2 cups liquid, salt, and pepper to the lentils and bring to a boil. Stir in the rice, return to a boil, cover, reduce the heat to very low, and simmer until the water is absorbed and the rice is tender, about 20 minutes. Do not remove the lid during cooking. Let stand, covered, for 10 minutes. Fluff with a fork. Transfer to a serving platter and, if using, dot with the butter. Top with the reserved fried onions. Serve warm or at room temperature.

VARIATIONS

The ratio of lentils to rice can be changed according to personal preference. Increase the rice to 2 cups, the reserved cooking liquid to 4 cups, and the salt to about 1 1/2 teaspoons. Or reduce the rice to 1/2 cup and reduce the reserved cooking liquid to 1 cup.

Syrian Lentils and Rice (*Mujadara*): Add 1/2 teaspoon ground allspice with the salt.

Egyptian Lentils, Rice, and Pasta (*Koshari*): In Step 3, after the rice is tender, stir in about 2 cups warm cooked elbow macaroni, *fideos* (coiled thin noodles), thin spaghetti broken into 2-inch pieces, or any combination. Transfer the lentil mixture to a serving platter, top with a little hot tomato sauce, and sprinkle the fried onions over the top.

Indian Lentils and Rice (*Khichri/Kitchree*): In Step 1, add to all the fried onions 2 teaspoons cumin seeds, 1 tablespoon minced small hot green chili, and 2 teaspoons minced fresh ginger. Sauté for about 2 minutes, then stir in 1 teaspoon ground turmeric and 1 (3-inch) cinnamon stick. Alternatively, add 1 1/2 teaspoons ground cumin and 1 teaspoon garam masala in Step 3 with the salt.

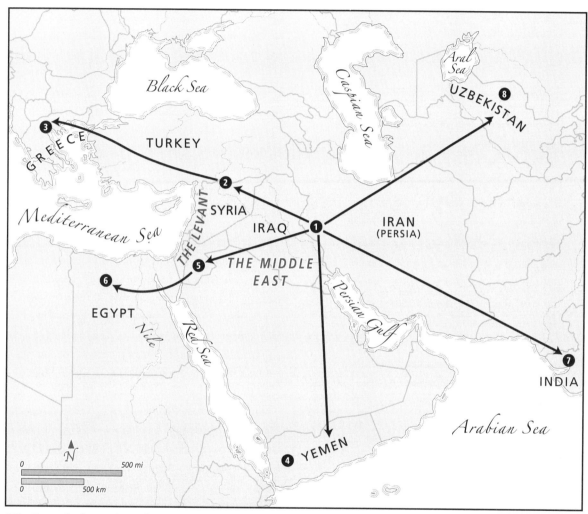

The Spread of Lentils and Rice: This popular dish spread across the Middle East and into India, the name varying from region to region. *1* kichree in Iraq, ados pol in Iran; *2* mengedarrah in Syria and Turkey; *3* mejedra in Greece; *4* enjadara in Yemen; *5* mujadara in the Levant; *6* koshari in Egypt; *7* kitchree in India; *8* jurot in Uzbekistan

MENGEDARRAH

After the Persians brought rice from India to central and western Asia, people began cooking this grain with vegetables, bulgur, noodles, and especially legumes. The medieval Arabic lentil and rice dish called *mengedarrah* became one of the most widespread and beloved dishes in the Muslim world.

The first record of *mengedarrah*, which literally means "having smallpox" in Arabic, referring to the dots of lentils in the white rice, appeared in the tenth century. Soon thereafter the dish was being served for both celebrations and working-class meals. Variations of the dish are called *mujadara*, or *megadara*, in the Levant, *mejedra* in Greece, and *enjadara* in Yemen. It is unknown whether the Persians brought the practice of mixing rice with lentils from India, where a similar dish is made. The Egyptian version, known as *koshari*, or *kushary*, first mentioned in the writings of Moroccan-born traveler Ibn Battuta (c. 1354), most certainly received its name from the Indian dish, *khichri* (Hindi for "hodgepodge").

Iraqis make the similar *kichree* with red lentils, cumin, and turmeric and top each serving with fried eggs. Bukharans substitute split mung beans for the lentils in *juroti*, a practice common in India as well.

❧ PEAS ❧

Peas, the seeds of an annual vinelike member of the Leguminosae family native to central Asia, were one of the earliest cultivated plants. Although there was no specific mention of peas in ancient Egyptian sources or in the Bible and Talmud, they were a staple in ancient Rome and later in medieval Europe. Until the sixteenth century, when varieties were developed that could be eaten fresh, peas were always dried, commonly used to make into thick soup.

Today, split peas remain popular in Ethiopian, Persian, and Indian cooking. Fresh peas are particularly popular in Italian, Balkan, and Syrian fare, often being cooked with or accompanied with rice. The familiar garden pea (green pea or English pea), usually considered a vegetable, is in season from April through June, and is best when picked young, since mature peas are tough. Garden peas come in many sizes, varying from the dwarf *petit pois* ("tiny pea" in French) to those almost $1/2$ inch in size.

What You Should Know: Choose fresh, bright green, well-filled pods. Fresh pods will squeak when rubbed together. Avoid those with large bulges, a sign that the pod houses older peas. Peas are best when freshly picked and cooked just before serving. Within 24 hours of picking, the sugar in peas begins turning to starch and the nutrients begin to fade. Frozen green peas, however, are usually packed within hours of picking, retaining their nutrients and freshness. Therefore, unless the fresh peas are almost straight from the farm, frozen ones generally taste better.

ETHIOPIAN SPLIT PEA PURÉE

(Yemesir Aleetcha)

4 TO 5 SERVINGS   Ⓓ or Ⓟ

Most of the Ethiopian Jews that I met in Israel during the late 1980s were undergoing the difficult experience of adjusting to a new life, foregoing much of their old ways. One aspect to which most tenaciously clung, however, was their native cuisine. Although today many Ethiopians have adopted Israeli eating habits, some still rely on injera (flat bread) and a vegetable- or legume-based wot (stew) as the basis of the two major meals of the day, breakfast and dinner. Ethiopians vary a limited diet of legumes and vegetables by altering the texture of the stews and adding a considerable amount of spices or chilies. Serve this stew with injera or pita bread and simple salads.

2 large red or yellow onions, chopped

1/4 cup vegetable oil or *ghee* (Indian Clarified
    Butter, page 51)

4 to 8 cloves garlic, mashed

1 teaspoon minced fresh ginger

3 cups water

1/2 teaspoon ground turmeric

About 3/4 teaspoon table salt or 1 1/2 teaspoons
    kosher salt

Ground black pepper to taste

1 small hot green chili, seeded and minced,
    or 2 teaspoons *chow* (Ethiopian Spice Paste,
    page 437); optional

1 cup (8 ounces) green or yellow split peas,
    picked over, rinsed, soaked in cold water to
    cover for 30 minutes, and drained

1. In a large, dry skillet or saucepan over medium-low heat, cook the onions, stirring constantly, until they begin to soften, about 5 minutes.

2. Add the oil. When it begins to sputter, add the garlic and ginger and sauté until fragrant, about 1 minute. Add the water, turmeric, salt, pepper, and, for a more fiery stew, the chili. Cover and bring to a boil.

3. Add the peas, return to a boil, cover partially, reduce the heat to low, and simmer, stirring occasionally and adding more water if necessary, until the peas are soft, about 40 minutes. Mash the peas. Serve warm.

VARIATIONS

Ethiopian Spicy Split Pea Stew (*Yemesir Wot*): Omit the chili and add with the water 1/2 teaspoon ground cardamom, 1/2 teaspoon ground turmeric, 1/4 teaspoon ground caraway seeds, 1/4 teaspoon ground coriander, 1/4 teaspoon crushed mustard seeds, 1/4 teaspoon paprika, and 1/8 teaspoon cayenne. Do not mash the peas.

Ethiopian Red Lentil Purée (*Kae Misr Aleetcha*): Substitute 1 cup red lentils for the peas, reducing the cooking time to about 20 minutes.

ITALIAN GREEN PEAS WITH ONIONS

(Piselli Alle Cipolle)

3 TO 4 SERVINGS

This dish, also called piselli in tegame *(stewed peas), needs little to enhance the natural sweetness of the peas.*

1/4 cup olive oil or vegetable oil

1 medium onion, chopped

2 pounds fresh green peas, shelled (about 2 cups), or 10 ounces (2 cups) frozen green peas

1/3 cup dry white wine or water

About 1 teaspoon table salt or 2 teaspoons kosher salt

1/4 teaspoon sugar

3 tablespoons chopped fresh parsley (optional)

In a large, heavy saucepan, heat the oil over medium heat. Add the onion and sauté until soft and translucent, about 5 minutes. Stir in the peas. Add the wine, salt, and sugar and simmer until tender, 5 to 10 minutes, depending on the age of the peas. If desired, sprinkle with the parsley.

INDIAN GREEN PEAS AND CHEESE

(Matar Panir)

4 SERVINGS

The sweet green peas complement the flavor and texture of the panir and the creamy curry sauce.

You can substitute packaged panir, sold in well-stocked markets, or even commercial mozzarella or unpasteurized queso blanco (Spanish white cheese) for the homemade cheese.

1/4 cup *ghee* (Indian Clarified Butter, page 51) or vegetable oil

1 large onion, chopped

2 to 3 cloves garlic, minced

1 teaspoon grated fresh ginger

1/2 teaspoon ground coriander

1/2 teaspoon garam masala

1/2 teaspoon ground turmeric

3 plum tomatoes, peeled, seeded, and chopped (see page 291), about 1 cup

About 1 1/2 teaspoons table salt or 1 tablespoon kosher salt

2 cups whey (from making the cheese balls) or water

1/2 teaspoon sugar

2 pounds fresh green peas, shelled (about 2 cups), or 10 ounces (2 cups) frozen green peas

Double recipe Middle Eastern Cheese Balls (page 49), or 8 ounces mozzarella or queso blanco, cut into 1-inch cubes

1/2 teaspoon cayenne pepper or red pepper flakes (optional)

1. In a large, heavy saucepan, melt the ghee over medium-low heat. Add the onion and sauté until golden, about 15 minutes. Add the garlic, ginger, coriander, garam masala, and turmeric and sauté until fragrant, about 1 minute.

2. Add the tomatoes and salt and simmer, stirring frequently, until the tomatoes liquefy, about 10 minutes. Add the whey and sugar and simmer for 5 minutes. Add the peas, cover, and simmer until nearly tender, about 5 minutes.

3. Add the cheese and cook, uncovered, until the cheese absorbs some sauce and softens, about 5 minutes. If desired, stir in the cayenne. Serve hot.

GRAINS

❀ · ❀

BY THE SWEAT OF YOUR BROW
YOU SHALL BRING FORTH BREAD.
—Genesis 3:19

As humans first began to settle and practice agriculture, grains replaced meat as the mainstay of the diet. No other food group is as nutritious and versatile as grains; they may be ground into flour for bread, pastries, pasta, and dumplings; fermented to make beer; or added whole to a host of soups, salads, side dishes, desserts, and fillings.

Since raw grain is inedibly hard and surrounded by an unpalatable hull, cooks initially roasted wild grains whole to soften them, usually—by sprinkling the grains on meat over a fire or on heated rocks, which simultaneously separated the kernel from the hull. Eventually, primitive cooks began to boil the parched grains in depressions of rocks heated by nearby campfires. The advent of pottery allowed bigger and more complex grain stews to be boiled, which could incorporate more foods, such as vegetables and legumes.

In due time, people began to crush grains between two stones to produce a meal that could be boiled more quickly than whole grains and yielded a smoother texture. When, early in human history, some of this pastelike gruel accidentally spilled into a campfire, the first rudimentary bread emerged from the ashes. Bread was tastier and more versatile than plain gruel, as well as more transportable. When wild yeast made its way into wheat dough it gave rise to leavened bread.

Not surprisingly, in light of grain's importance to the diet and economy of the ancient Middle East, the Bible frequently mentions various grains, primarily barley and wheat, which were both among the seven plants associated with Israel's blessing. Barley bread was the staple food in the Middle East until Roman times, when wheat supplanted it. Rice, too, gained prominence in the Middle East and parts of the Mediterranean following its introduction by the Persians, and quickly went on to become the most beloved grain in the region. On the other hand, wheat and rice were scarce and expensive in much of Europe, the people instead relying on barley, buckwheat, rye, and, after the advent of American produce, cornmeal.

From the onset, grains were essential to the daily Jewish diet as well as to holiday and ritual celebrations. In fact, some holidays revolved around

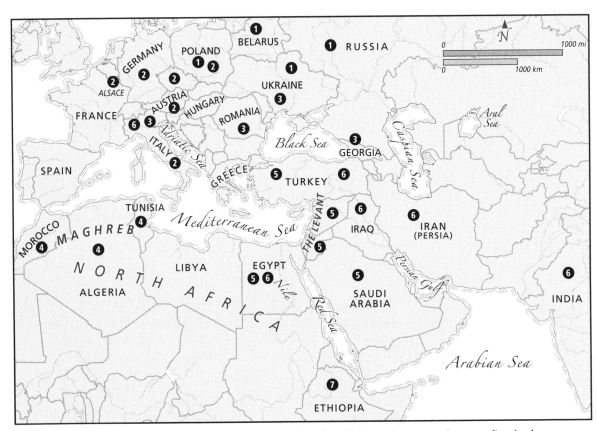

Primary Grains of the Regions: *1 buckwheat;* *2 wheat (noodles/pasta);* *3 corn (cornmeal);* *4 wheat (couscous);* *5 bulgur;* *6 rice;* *7 millet*

the appearance and growth of certain staple grains: Passover was connected with the ripening of the barley crop and Shavuot with the beginning of the wheat harvest. Today, grain cookery remains a significant part of both Sephardic and Ashkenazic traditions. All Sabbath and holiday meals commence with bread and usually entail a pastry or two. Sephardim commonly add whole-wheat grains to Sabbath and holiday dishes such as *hamin* (Sephardic Bean Stew, page 315) and stuffed vegetables. Rice is vital to Sephardic cooking, often symbolizing purity due to its white color. Sephardim traditionally eat rice on Shavout in the form of puddings. Ashkenazim use barley grains in *cholent*, soups, and kugels. In Georgia and Romania, cornmeal is often eaten in place of bread.

RICE

Rice, a native of Southeast Asia, is second only to wheat as the most widely cultivated cereal in the world. China and India have grown rice for more than five thousand years, and rice serves as the primary food of nearly half the human race. Rice spread westward to Persia more than twenty-three hundred years ago, where it became a beloved food incorporated into a wide variety of dishes. No other people have found as many uses and combinations for rice as the Persians, including *chelou* (plain steamed white rice) and *polo* (rice with various cooked ingredients), the latter being the origin of Turkish pilaf, Indian pilau, and Spanish paella.

Contact with the Persian Empire brought rice to Israel during the early Second Temple period (c. 200–300 B.C.E.), and by Roman times Israeli rice had become an important export—the Jerusalem

Talmud boasts: "There is none like it outside Israel." Suggestions in the Talmud for the blessing to offer over this grain include thanking God for creating "delicacies to delight the soul of every living being."

Each Middle Eastern Jewish community adopted the local rice varieties as well as the methods of preparing it. The Moors introduced rice to Spain in the eighth century, and it quickly became an integral part of Sephardic cuisine, being served practically every day in many households. By the tenth century, Egypt emerged as the largest producer of rice outside of the Far East. A favorite medieval Arabic way to eat rice was warm, with melted butter and sugar or milk. For meat meals, Jews substituted oil for butter and commonly added onions and garlic.

Although members of Alexander the Great's Indian campaign made note of rice, the grain reached Europe only during the Arab invasions at the beginning of the ninth century. Even after this, most Europeans treated rice with indifference—in general, the farther north in Europe, the less rice was used. Only in Italy and Spain did it become an important part of the cuisine, being used to create classic dishes such as risotto and paella. In the fifteenth century, rice was widely planted in the Po Valley of Italy and thereafter it rivaled wheat as the staple of the Lombardy region. Around that time, Sephardim fleeing the Expulsion from Spain introduced various Iberian rice dishes to Italy. Rice entered Ashkenazic cooking rather late and even then was only incorporated into a few dishes, primarily puddings and meat stuffings.

Rice remains a fundamental dish around the Mediterranean, prepared plain or flavored with herbs, chickpeas, orzo, or pine nuts. It is used as a filling for *dolmas* (stuffed vegetables), made into pilafs and puddings, and mixed with lentils to make *mengedarrah* (Middle Eastern Lentils and Rice, page 336), the classic Middle Eastern comfort food. Rice is regular Friday night fare among Middle Eastern Jews, who frequently color it yellow—the traditional Arabic sign of joy—with saffron or turmeric. The Bene Israel of Bombay add coconut and cardamom to their yellow rice. The Bene Israel serve *malida* (a sweetened rice, coconut, and fruit dish) at all festive occasions. Persians enjoy *nane berenji* (rice flour cookies) after important meals, and serve rice dishes at all special occasions. A characteristic of Sephardic cooking is that food should have contrast—in flavor, texture, and color, and this trait is reflected in many rice dishes, such as Sephardic Baked Rice with Chickpeas (page 345) and Sephardic Red Rice (page 347). Sephardim sauté rice in oil, unlike the Arabs who generally use clarified butter.

In the Near East, an important component of cooked rice is the browned (but not burnt) crust that forms along the bottom of the cooking vessel, called *tahdiq* in Persian and *a'hata* in Arabic. This crust is commonly crumbled and sprinkled over the soft rice once it is removed from the pot. In many households, the sound of a pot being scraped in the kitchen to remove the crust indicates that the rice was properly prepared. Crisp fried onion is another widespread Middle Eastern topping for rice.

RICE COOKING CHART

Type of Rice	Amount (Raw)	Liquid	Time	Yield (Cooked)
Long-grain white	1 cup	2 cups	18 minutes	3 cups
Long-grain brown	1 cup	2²/₃ cups	40 minutes	3¹/₂ to 4 cups
Parboiled	1 cup	2¹/₂ cups	20 minutes	3¹/₂ to 4 cups
Medium-grain white	1 cup	1¹/₂ cups	15 minutes	3 cups
Short-grain white	1 cup	1¹/₄ cups	17 minutes	2¹/₂ cups
Glutinous	1 cup	1 cup + 2 tablespoons	15 minutes	2¹/₂ cups

What You Should Know: A heavy pot will cook rice more evenly and precisely than one made of thin metal. The larger the quantity of rice, the lower the proportion of water, as the amount of evaporation is less. Soaking rice also reduces the cooking time. Adding sugar, salt, or an acid, such as lemon juice or tomatoes, to the rice slows the rice's ability to absorb the cooking liquid, thereby increasing the cooking time (25 minutes for a cup of long-grian rice) and giving the rice a firmer texture. Acids also affect the rice's color; for bright white rice, add a dash of lemon juice or vinegar to the water before cooking.

SEPHARDIC OVEN-COOKED RICE

(Arroz al Horno)

4 TO 5 SERVINGS

The Moors brought rice to Spain in the eighth century, the Arabic ar-ruzz *eventually giving rise to the Spanish word for rice,* arroz. *Since its arrival, most Spanish rice has been the nearly round short-grain type, which absorbs flavors easily and releases starch without disintegrating, unlike the firmer, fluffy long-grain varieties more common in the Persian and Ottoman Empires. Baking rice in a* cazuela *(casserole dish) or paella pan is an old Spanish cooking technique still common in modern Valencia, Spain's primary rice-growing region, as well as among some Sephardim.*

Cooking the rice in an oven (in a cazuela *or other pan) is a particularly useful method when preparing large amounts of rice or when you don't have time to watch the pot. It gives the rice a creamy texture, protects it against burning, and—in a low oven—keeps the rice warm for Sabbath dinner. This risottolike dish is traditionally served with salads, such as* michoteta *(Middle Eastern Mixed Vegetable Salad, page 89),* garvansos en salata *(Sephardic Chickpea Salad, page 109),* silka *(Sephardic Beet Greens, page 211), and tossed green salad, along with yogurt and crusty bread.*

¹/₄ cup olive oil or vegetable oil

2 onions, chopped

1¹/₂ cups short-grain rice, such as Valencia, Vialone, Carnaroli, or Arborio

3 cups boiling Vegetable Stock (page 115) or water

About 1 teaspoon table salt or 2 teaspoons kosher salt

¹/₄ teaspoon ground black pepper

¹/₄ cup chopped fresh parsley (optional)

1. Preheat the oven to 350°F.

2. In a cazuela, a large ovenproof saucepan, or flameproof 8-cup casserole dish, heat the oil over medium heat. Add the onions and sauté until soft and translucent, about 5 minutes. Add the rice and sauté until opaque, about 3 minutes. Pour the hot stock over the top. Stir in the salt, pepper, and, if using, the parsley. Bring to a boil.

3. Cover with a lid or aluminum foil and bake until the rice is tender and the liquid absorbed, about 40 minutes for white rice, 1 hour for brown rice. Remove from the oven and let stand, covered, for at least 10 minutes. Serve warm.

VARIATIONS

Sephardic Baked Rice with Chickpeas (*Arroz con Garvonsos al Horno*): At the end of Step 2, add 1 to 1¹/₂ cups cooked chickpeas and, if desired, ¹/₂ cup raisins.

Sephardic Baked Rice with Pine Nuts (*Arroz con Pinones*): Sauté ¹/₂ cup pine nuts in 3 tablespoons oil until golden brown and sprinkle over the top of the cooked rice.

Sephardic Baked Rice with Spinach (*Arroz con Spinaca al Horno*): At the end of Step 2, add 1¹/₂ to 2 pounds chopped stemmed spinach, 2 tablespoons fresh lemon juice, and ¹/₂ teaspoon sugar.

MIDDLE EASTERN YELLOW RICE

(Arroz con Azafran)

5 TO 6 SERVINGS   P

Medieval Arabic cooking utilized large amounts of saffron (zaffaran) to give food a yellow color, the traditional symbol of joy and happiness. This habit influenced not only Sephardim, but also Jews in Turkey, Yemen, and, beginning in the fifteenth century, Italy. For centuries, golden rice, called roz bi zaffaran *(rice with saffron) in Arabic,* riso col zafran *in Italian, and* arroz con azafran *or* arroz de Sabato *(Sabbath rice) in Ladino, has been a Friday night and holiday tradition in Sephardic and Middle Eastern communities.*

The seasonings, variety of rice, and cooking method vary slightly from region to region. Turmeric makes an inexpensive substitute for saffron and still provides a nice yellow color. This dish can either be simmered on a stovetop or baked in a cazuela or casserole. For special effect, this brightly colored rice is sometimes pressed into a ring mold or ramekins, inverted onto a serving platter, and sprinkled with coarsely chopped almonds or pistachios or toasted pine nuts. In some areas, cooks top the rice with a warm fruit and nut mixture, transforming a basic dish into something special.

$1/2$ teaspoon saffron threads or 1 teaspoon ground turmeric

3 tablespoons hot water

3 tablespoons vegetable oil

1 large onion or 10 scallions (white parts only), chopped

2 cups long-grain rice

4 cups Vegetable Stock (page 115) or water

About $1 1/2$ teaspoons table salt or 1 tablespoon kosher salt

FRUIT-AND-NUT TOPPING (OPTIONAL):

2 tablespoons vegetable oil

1 onion, chopped

1 cup sliced almonds

1 cup coarsely chopped pitted dates

$1/2$ cup golden raisins

1. If using the saffron, crumble it into a bowl or pound it into a powder in a mortar. Add the hot water and let it steep briefly.

2. In a large saucepan, heat the oil over medium heat. Add the onion and sauté until soft and translucent, about 5 minutes. If using the turmeric, add it now. Add the rice and stir until opaque, about 3 minutes.

3. To boil the rice, stir in the stock, saffron mixture, and salt, bring to a boil, cover, reduce the heat to low, and simmer until the rice is tender and the water absorbed, about 18 minutes. Remove from the heat and let stand, covered, for 10 minutes. Fluff with a fork. Or, to bake the rice, pour the sautéed onion and rice into a greased 8-cup casserole dish, add the boiling stock, saffron mixture, and salt, cover, and bake in a preheated 350°F oven until tender, about 40 minutes. Fluff with a fork.

4. To make the topping, if desired: In a medium skillet, heat the oil over medium heat. Add the onion and sauté until lightly golden, 10 to 15 minutes. Add the almonds, dates, and raisins, reduce the heat to low, and cook, stirring constantly, until heated through, about 10 minutes. Sprinkle over the top of the rice. Serve warm.

VARIATIONS

Iraqi Saffron Rice (*Ruz ib Asfor/Timman Azaffaran*): Grind together 2 teaspoons coriander seeds and 2 teaspoons cumin seeds. After sautéing the onion, add the spice mixture to the hot oil and sauté until fragrant, 1 to 2 minutes. Add with the rice ³/4 cup blanched almonds and ³/4 cup golden raisins or dried currants.

Kurdish Yellow Rice (*Ruz*): After sautéing the onion, add 2 teaspoons ground cumin and ³/4 teaspoon ground cardamom and sauté until fragrant, 1 to 2 minutes.

Sephardic Rice for Weddings (*Arroz de Bodas*): Although the name of this dish reflects its place at weddings, it is also served for other special occasions, too. After fluffing the rice in Step 3, stir in 1 cup seedless green grapes or golden raisins, ¹/4 cup toasted pine nuts or ¹/2 cup toasted slivered almonds, and ¹/2 cup chopped fresh parsley. Press into a well-greased 8-cup ring mold or bowl. Just before serving, place the mold in a large baking pan, add 1 inch hot water to the larger pan, and warm in a preheated 350°F oven until heated through, about 25 minutes. Remove the mold from the water bath and loosen the edges with a knife. Place a large serving plate on top, invert, and remove the mold.

Yemenite Yellow Rice (*Roz bi Zaffaran*): Add 3 to 4 minced cloves garlic with the onion. After sautéing the onion, add 2¹/2 teaspoons ground cumin and ¹/2 teaspoon ground black pepper and sauté until fragrant, 1 to 2 minutes.

SEPHARDIC RED RICE

(Arroz con tomat)

5 TO 6 SERVINGS

Although it is called Spanish Rice today, this rice dish, flavored and colored with a little tomato sauce, was until recently completely unknown in Spain. Rather, a similar dish was developed among Sephardim living in the Ottoman Empire following the arrival of the American tomato in the sixteenth century. Perhaps the Spanish designation comes because the Sephardim had come from Spain, or because they continued to name their recipes in Ladino, the traditional Sephardic form of Spanish. Indeed, Syrian Jews also call rice and tomato casseroles baked in the oven riz espanie (Spanish rice), since it was Sephardim who popularized the technique in the Middle East.

Whereas yellow saffron rice was customary for Sabbath and special occasions, red rice was found at many weekday meals as well as at some special-occasion meals, such as a Turkish Rosh Hashanah dinner. For extra flavor, some cooks add onion and garlic, but many like to eat it "plain." In many households, red rice, more common than plain white rice (arroz blanco), was such a staple that it would be served at both lunch and dinner.

2 cups long-grain white rice

3 tablespoons olive oil or vegetable oil

1 large onion, chopped (optional)

1 to 2 cloves garlic, minced (optional)

3 cups boiling water

1 cup tomato sauce, tomato purée, or smooth or chunky tomato salsa

About 1¹/2 teaspoons table salt or 1 tablespoon kosher salt

About ¹/4 teaspoon ground black pepper

About 1 teaspoon sugar (optional)

1. Wash the rice in lukewarm water until the water runs clear (this may require washing as many as 5 times), then soak in cold water to cover for at least 2 hours or up to 24 hours. Drain, rinse under cold running water, and drain again.

2. In a large, heavy saucepan, heat the oil over medium-low heat. If using, add the onion and garlic and sauté until soft and translucent, about 5 minutes. Add the rice and sauté until opaque, about 3 minutes.

3. Add the water, tomato sauce, salt, pepper, and, if using, the sugar. Bring to a boil, cover, reduce the heat to low, and simmer until the rice is tender and the liquid absorbed, 25 to 30 minutes. Or, place in a greased 8-cup casserole dish, cover, and bake in a preheated 350°F oven for about 50 minutes. Remove from the heat and let stand, covered, for about 10 minutes. Fluff with a fork. Serve warm.

N O T E The acid in tomatoes attracts water, slowing the rice's ability to absorb water and increasing the cooking time by about 10 minutes. Because the rice will absorb less water, it will have a firmer texture.

PERSIAN CRUSTY RICE

(Chelou)

6 TO 8 SERVINGS

No people have been more appreciative of the culinary possibilities of rice than the Persians. Their favorite cooking method involves soaking, parboiling, and then steaming long-grain rice to produce white rice with fluffy, separate, perfectly tender grains, called chelou. *Soaking and parboiling infuse the rice with moisture necessary for the final step of steaming.*

The rice is steamed in an oiled pan, which allows a crisp bottom crust to form, known as a tahdiq *(literally "bottom of the pan"). To many Persians, this is their favorite part of the dish. The preferred Persian rice is a long-grain variety called* domsiah *("black-tailed"). Look for it in ethnic markets, but basmati makes an acceptable substitute. The plain* chelou *is usually served with a stewlike gravy such as* khoreshe kavafs *(Persian Celery Stew, page 237), or simply with* turshi left *(Middle Eastern Pickled Turnips, page 59) and yogurt on the side.*

> 3 cups long-grain rice, such as domsiah or basmati
> 8 cups water plus 2 tablespoons
> 4 tablespoons table salt or 4 tablespoons kosher salt
> 2 tablespoons vegetable oil or melted margarine
> 1/4 teaspoon ground turmeric or pinch (about 20 threads) of saffron
> 1/2 teaspoon ground white pepper (optional)

1. Wash the rice in lukewarm water until the water runs clear (it may take as many as 5 times), then soak in cold water to cover for at least 2 hours or up to 24 hours. Drain, rinse under cold running water, and drain again.

2. In a large, heavy saucepan, bring the 8 cups water to a boil over medium heat and add the salt.

Add the rice and cook, stirring occasionally to prevent sticking, until al dente (tender but still firm), about 10 minutes; taste a few grains to see if the rice is soft enough. Drain, rinse under cold running water, and drain again.

3. In a large, heavy saucepan, heat 2 tablespoons of the oil over high heat. Stir in the turmeric, then the 2 tablespoons water and, if using, the pepper.

4. Spread half the rice over the turmeric mixture in the pan. Using the handle of a wooden spoon, poke 7 deep holes into the rice. (The holes vent the steam.) Drizzle with the remaining 2 tablespoons oil.

5. Place a kitchen towel or several layers of paper towels over the top of the pan. The towel is necessary to absorb the steam, preventing a mushy texture. Cover with the lid and cook over medium heat until steam appears, about 10 minutes. Reduce the heat to low and simmer until the rice is tender and the bottom crisp, about 30 minutes.

6. For easy removal of the crust, place the pot in a sink filled with 2 inches of cold water and let stand for 5 minutes. (Or, before beginning the dish, line the bottom of the pot with aluminum foil.) Be careful, as a cloud of steam will be released when you lift the lid. Invert the rice onto a large serving platter. Break the crust into large pieces and scatter over top. Or, mix 1 cup of the cooked rice with a pinch of saffron dissolved in 2 teaspoons hot water and sprinkle the yellow rice over the top of the remaining rice. Serve warm.

VARIATIONS

Potato or Onion Crust: In Step 3, cut 2 potatoes or onions into ¼-inch-thick slices and arrange in the bottom of the pan before adding the rice.

For a tender crust: Mix 1 cup parboiled rice with the turmeric/saffron and 2 tablespoons plain yogurt or 1 lightly beaten egg. Spread over the oil in the bottom of the pan, then top with the remaining rice.

For a smaller recipe that serves 4 to 5: Reduce the rice to 2 cups, but use the same amount of spices in the crust.

FILLED PERSIAN CRUSTY RICE

(*Polo*)

6 TO 8 SERVINGS

More elaborate chelou *are layered or, less frequently, mixed with vegetables or other ingredients, which impart some of their flavor into the rice during cooking. These dishes are called* polo *or* pulau.

> A choice of one Persian Crusty Rice filling
> (recipes on page 350)
> Persian Crusty Rice (previous recipe), prepared
> through Step 3
> 2 tablespoons vegetable oil or melted margarine

1. Prepare the desired Persian Crusty Rice filling.

2. Prepare the rice as in Persian Crusty Rice, spreading half the rice over the turmeric mixture. Scatter the filling over the bottom layer, leaving the edges uncovered, and mound the remaining rice over top. Or make several alternate levels of rice and filling, ending with rice. Using the handle of a wooden spoon, poke 7 deep holes into the rice. Drizzle with the 2 tablespoons oil.

3. Place a kitchen towel or several layers of paper towels over the top of the pan. Cover with the lid and cook over medium heat until steam appears, about 10 minutes. Reduce the heat to low and simmer

until the rice is tender and the bottom crisp, about 30 minutes.

4. For easy removal of the crust, place the pot in a sink filled with 2 inches of cold water and let stand for 5 minutes. (Or, before beginning the dish, line the bottom of the pot with aluminum foil.) Be careful, as a cloud of steam will be released when you lift the lid. Invert the rice onto a large serving platter. Break the crust into large pieces and scatter over top. Or, mix 1 cup of the cooked rice with a pinch of saffron dissolved in 2 teaspoons hot water and sprinkle the yellow rice over the top of the remaining rice. Serve warm.

PERSIAN CRUSTY RICE FILLINGS

Persian Rice with Green Beans (*Loobia Sabz Polo*): Use 1¹/₂ pounds cooked green beans cut into 1-inch pieces.

Persian Rice with Red Beans (*Loobia Polo*): Use 1¹/₂ cups cooked kidney or other red beans.

Persian Rice with Carrots and Beans (*Havij Loobia Polo*): Slice 3 carrots and cook in boiling water or steam until crisp-tender, 6 to 10 minutes. Mix with 1 cup cooked kidney or other red beans. If desired, mix with ¹/₂ teaspoon ground cinnamon.

Persian Rice with Lentils (*Adas Polo*): Instead of layering the rice with the filling, mix the rice with 1¹/₂ cups cooked brown lentils. If desired, add 2 cups pitted dates, 1 cup chopped dried apricots, or ¹/₂ to 1 cup dried currants or raisins.

Persian Rice with Lima Beans (*Baghala Polo*): Fava beans were the original legume added to this dish, but today the more common lima bean is generally used. Use 1 pound fresh or frozen baby lima beans or fava beans and 1 cup chopped fresh dill.

Persian Rice with Peas (*Nokhod Polo*): Cook 2 cups green peas until tender but not mushy, mix with 1 cup chopped fresh dill.

PERSIAN SWEET RICE

(*Shirin Polo*)

6 TO 8 SERVINGS

This flavorful dish is ubiquitous at Persian festive occasions, especially weddings. There are several variations, but the common denominators are rice, candied orange zest, and nuts. I prefer layering the rice with the orange-nut mixture to create delicious levels of flavor, but some people like to mix everything together before steaming. Others cook the rice first, then pass the warm orange-nut mixture alongside, allowing the diners to spoon some of it over their portions.

3 cups long-grain rice, such as domsiah or basmati
8 cups water
2 tablespoons table salt or 4 tablespoons kosher salt

FILLING:

1 cup finely slivered orange zest
2 cups water
2 cups sugar
Pinch of saffron threads or ground turmeric
³/₄ to 1 cup slivered almonds or ²/₃ cup almonds
    and ¹/₄ cup chopped pistachios
2 tablespoons rose water (optional)
¹/₄ teaspoon ground cardamom (optional)

4 tablespoons vegetable oil or melted margarine
¹/₄ teaspoon ground turmeric or pinch (about
    20 threads) of saffron
2 tablespoons water

1. Wash the rice in lukewarm water until the water runs clear (this may require washing as many as 5 times), then soak in cold water to cover for at least 2 hours or up to 24 hours. Drain, rinse under cold running water, and drain again.

2. In a large, heavy saucepan, bring the 8 cups water to a boil over medium heat and add the salt. Add the rice and cook, stirring occasionally to prevent sticking, until al dente (tender but still firm) about 10 minutes. Drain, rinse under cold running water, and drain again.

3. To make the filling: Fill a small saucepan with cold water. Add the orange zest, bring to a boil, drain, then repeat. In a medium saucepan, combine the zest, water, sugar, and saffron and stir over low heat until the sugar dissolves. Increase the heat to medium-high and bring to a boil. Reduce the heat to low and simmer until syrupy, about 20 minutes. Let cool, then stir in the nuts and, if using, the rose water and/or cardamom.

4. In a large, heavy saucepan, heat 2 tablespoons of the oil over high heat. Stir in the turmeric, then the 2 tablespoons water.

5. Spread one-third of the rice in the saucepan. Scatter half of the zest filling over top, cover with half of the remaining rice, then the remaining filling, and finally mound the remaining rice over top. Using the handle of a wooden spoon, poke 7 deep holes into the rice. Drizzle with the remaining 2 tablespoons oil.

6. Place a kitchen towel or several layers of paper towels over top of the pan. Cover with the lid and cook over medium heat until steam appears, about 10 minutes. Reduce the heat to low and simmer until the rice is tender and the bottom crisp, about 30 minutes.

7. For easy removal of the crust, place the pot in a sink filled with 2 inches of cold water and let stand for 5 minutes. (Or, before beginning the dish, line the bottom of the pot with aluminum foil.) Be careful, as a cloud of steam will be released when you lift the lid. Invert the rice onto a large serving platter. Break the crust into large pieces and scatter over the top. Serve warm.

VARIATIONS

Some cooks cut a piece of *lavash* (thin baked bread) to fit the pot and arrange it in the bottom of the pot before adding the rice to absorb any sugar that drips down, which could cause the crust to burn.

Persian Sweet Rice with Carrots (*Shirin Polo*): Heat $1/4$ cup vegetable oil in a large skillet, add 3 cups julienned carrots, and sauté until crisp-tender, about 5 minutes. Add to the syrup mixture and layer with the rice.

Persian Rice with Cherries (*Albaloo Polo*): Simmer 2 to 3 cups canned sour cherries with 1 cup sugar and $1/2$ cup cherry juice over medium heat for 30 minutes, then let cool and drain. Or soak 1 cup dried tart cherries or coarsely chopped dried apricots in warm water for 15 minutes, then drain. Add the cherries to the syrup mixture and layer with the rice.

PERSIAN RICE WITH PASTA

(Ruz ma Shayreeye)

5 TO 6 SERVINGS   Ⓟ

This dish, with its delicate color contrast between the light-colored rice and the darker orzo, originated in Persia. It is called aroz bi sheereya *in Syria,* roz bil shaghria *in Arabic, and* sha'aree *in India, where it is a traditional Simchat Torah dish. For the Sabbath, a little saffron or turmeric is frequently added to produce a yellow hue. At dairy meals, it is commonly served with yogurt. Frying the onion and rice in oil is a Jewish practice, permitting the dish to be served at a meat meal; the Arabs use clarified butter. Syrians usually garnish the rice with toasted pine nuts.*

> ¹/₄ cup vegetable oil
>
> 1 large onion, chopped
>
> 1 clove garlic, minced (optional)
>
> ¹/₄ cup orzo (rice-shaped pasta)
>
> 2 cups long-grain rice, such as domsiah or basmati
>
> 4 cups water
>
> About 1¹/₂ teaspoons table salt or 1 tablespoon kosher salt

1. In a medium saucepan, heat the oil over medium heat. Add the onion and, if using, the garlic and sauté until soft and translucent, about 5 minutes. Add the orzo and sauté until golden, about 3 minutes. Add the rice and sauté until opaque, about 3 minutes.

2. Add the water and salt. Bring to a boil, cover, reduce the heat to low, and simmer until the rice is tender but not mushy, about 18 minutes. Remove from the heat and let stand, covered, for about 10 minutes. Fluff with a fork. Serve warm.

VARIATIONS

Reduce the rice to 1 cup and increase the orzo to 1 cup and the water to 4¹/₃ cups.

Egyptian Rice with Vermicelli (*Roz bil Shaghria*): Substitute for the orzo ²/₃ cup 1-inch-long broken pieces of *fideos*, vermicelli, angel hair pasta, or other dried fine noodles. Add ¹/₂ teaspoon ground cinnamon and 6 coriander seeds to the rice before adding the water.

AZERBAIJANI RICE PILAF

(Plov)

5 TO 6 SERVINGS   Ⓓ OR Ⓟ

Azerbaijan is a small country that borders Russia and Georgia to the north and west and Turkey and Iran to the south. Similar to the cuisines of other areas once under Persian control, the cooking of Azerbaijan reflects a pronounced Persian influence, including their version of pilaf, plov. *Azerbaijanis agree that* plov *(pilaf) is their most important dish. Although rice is served on a regular basis,* plov *is reserved for special occasions, including weddings, funerals, and various family gatherings. It is customarily prepared in a tin-lined copper pot, which helps the flavorful bottom crust form, but you can use any heavy saucepan.*

A simple plov *is served as a side dish or with stews, such as* dimlama *(Bukharan Vegetable and Fruit Stew, page 301), while elaborate ones are featured as main courses or a grand finale, presented on a large platter. For a tart flavor,* plov *is sprinkled with ground sumac and, for dairy meals, accompanied with yogurt.*

RICE:

2¹/₂ cups basmati or other long-grain rice

2 tablespoons table salt or 4 tablespoons
   kosher salt

4 quarts water

¹/₄ cup vegetable oil or unsalted butter

¹/₄ cup water

4 large eggs, lightly beaten

3 to 4 tablespoons vegetable oil or melted butter

1. To prepare the rice: Wash the rice in luke-warm water until the water runs clear and drain. Place in a bowl and add cold water to cover by 1 inch. Stir in half of the salt and let soak for at least 1 or up to 3 hours. Drain and rinse under cold running water. (Soaking and rinsing the rice removes the excess starch that would make the kernels sticky, and shortens the cooking time.)

2. Bring the 4 quarts water to a boil over medium heat. Add the remaining salt. Gradually sprinkle in the rice. Cook, stirring occasionally to prevent sticking, until the rice is slightly al dente (tender but still firm), 5 to 7 minutes. Taste occasionally to see if the rice is ready. Drain, rinse under cold running water, and drain again.

3. To make the crust: In a large, heavy pot, heat the ¹/₄ cup oil and the ¹/₄ cup water over medium heat. Combine the eggs with 1¹/₂ cups of the rice and spread over the bottom of the pan. Mound the remaining rice on top. Using the handle of a wooden spoon, poke 7 deep holes into the rice mound. Drizzle with the oil.

4. Place a kitchen towel or several layers of paper towels over top of the pan. Cover with the lid and cook over medium heat until steam appears, about 10 minutes. Reduce the heat to low and simmer until the rice is tender and the bottom crisp, 40 to 60 minutes. Or, using an ovenproof pot, bake in a preheated 350°F oven for 1¹/₄ hours.

5. For easy removal of the crust, place the pot in a sink filled with 2 inches of cold water and let stand for 5 minutes. (Or, before beginning the dish, line the bottom of the pot with aluminum foil.) Be careful, as a cloud of steam will be released when you lift the lid. Invert the rice onto a large serving platter. Break the crust into pieces and scatter over the top. Serve warm.

VARIATIONS

Crumble 1 teaspoon saffron threads into 3 tablespoons warm water and let steep briefly. In Step 3, stir in 1 cup of the parboiled rice and sprinkle the saffron rice over the mounded remaining rice.

Azerbaijani Yogurt Crust for *Plov* (*Matsoni Kazmag*): For the crust, reduce the eggs to 2 and add ¹/₃ cup plain yogurt.

Azerbaijani Potato Crust for *Plov* (*Kartofli Kazmag*): Omit the eggs. In Step 3, after adding the oil and water, arrange 2 potatoes cut into ¹/₄-inch-thick slices in the bottom of the pot.

Azerbaijani Herb Pilaf (*Sabzi Plov*): In Step 3, mix 1¹/₂ cups chopped fresh parsley, 1 cup chopped scallions (white and light green parts only), ³/₄ cup chopped fresh dill, and ¹/₄ cup chopped fresh cilantro with the remaining rice before mounding in the pan.

THE KING OF AZERI CUISINE

I n Azerbiajan, there are more than one hundred kinds of rice pilaf (*plov*), all distinctive for their subtle tartness—produced with pomegranate juice, sour plums, dried lemons, sour cherries, and unripe grapes—or their slight sweetness—derived from fresh and dried fruits, such as apples, apricots, quinces, and raisins. The *plov* may also be accented with saffron, a spice that grows in the western part of Azerbaijan and is, therefore, less expensive there than in most places.

Unlike the Uzbeki and Persian styles of rice cookery, the rice and flavorings in Azerbaijan are usually prepared in separate pots, then combined for serving. The *kazmag*, or *gazmag*, the bottom crust, prevents the rice from burning and serves as a crunchy garnish. Basmati is the rice variety of choice. Leftover simple *plov* is used to make *kuku* (baked omelets).

BUKHARAN RICE PILAF WITH RAISINS AND NUTS
(Palov)

5 TO 6 SERVINGS

While cooks in Persian-influenced cultures make pilafs using long-grain rice, the signature pilafs in Uzbekistan feature a short-grain rice, which comes out slightly chewier and more sticky. Typical of Bukharan cookery, palov is sparsely seasoned and contains few or no pungent spices, allowing the flavors of the primary ingredients to blend and predominate. This is a simple vegetarian variation of the Uzbeki national dish, making use of a few basic ingredients of the region.

> 2 cups short-grain rice, such as Valencia, Vialone, Carnaroli, or Arborio; or long-grain rice
> 1/4 cup vegetable oil
> 1 pound carrots, julienned or coarsely grated
> 1 large onion, chopped
> 1/2 cup slivered almonds
> 1/2 cup golden raisins
> 2 tablespoons grated orange zest
> 1/2 teaspoon ground turmeric
> 3 3/4 cups boiling Vegetable Stock (page 115) or water
> 1 cup cooked chickpeas (optional)
> About 1 1/2 teaspoons table salt or 1 tablespoon kosher salt

1. Soak the rice in cold water to cover for 30 minutes. Drain, rinse under cold running water until the water runs clear, and drain again.

2. In a large, heavy pot, heat the oil over medium heat. Add the carrots and onion and sauté until softened, about 10 minutes. Add the almonds, raisins,

zest, and turmeric and sauté for about 3 minutes. Add the rice and sauté until opaque, about 3 minutes.

3. Add the stock and, if using, the chickpeas, increase the heat to medium-high, bring to a boil, and let boil for 1 minute. Add the salt, cover, reduce the heat to low, and simmer until the water is absorbed and the rice is tender, about 20 minutes. Remove from the heat and let stand, covered, for 10 minutes. Fluff with a fork. Serve warm.

VARIATION

Bukharan Mushroom Pilaf (*Palov s Gribami*): Omit the almonds, raisins, and orange zest. In Step 2, after the carrots and onions are softened, add 1½ pounds sliced fresh mushrooms and sauté until golden, about 15 minutes. If desired, add 1 seeded, deribbed (white removed), and coarsely chopped red bell pepper with the stock.

PALOV

Central Asia—encompassing Afghanistan, Kazakhstan, Turkmenstan, Tajikistan, and Uzbekistan—was once the site of the fabled Silk Road, along which the riches of the Orient traveled westward and cooking lore moved in both directions. The cooking of this vast expanse of mountains, plains, oases, and deserts was greatly influenced by its two powerful neighbors on either side, China and Persia. In light of the important role of rice in both those countries, it is not surprising to find it also a favorite in the lands in between. However, outside of a few rice-growing areas in central Asia, such as around the Caspian Sea, this grain tended to be expensive and therefore was reserved for special occasions and family gatherings.

One of the most beloved Uzbeki dishes is *palov*, or *pulov*, an adaptation of the Persian *polo*. Unlike the Persians, who usually layer the flavorings between the rice, Bukharans commonly mix all of the ingredients together in the pot. There are numerous variations of *palov*, made by adding different vegetables, legumes, and seasonings. Carrots and onions, vegetables that were and are readily available, are common in most versions.

While women prepare most of the meals in Uzbekistan, *palov* making became the domain of men. *Palov* was customarily cooked in a well-seasoned oval cast-iron pot, called a *kazan*, over a large fire or in a clay oven. The older the *kazan* (which is never washed with soap or scoured and so becomes seasoned over time), the better the *palov*. The *palov* is generally served at the end of the meal and traditionally eaten with the fingers. To honor guests in an Uzbeki home or even at a simple gathering of friends, the *palov* is customarily the center of the local hospitality ritual, *dastarkhan* (literally "tablecloth"), and accompanied with hot green tea sipped from a *piala* (special cup). To refuse to partake of a *palov* is to insult the host.

Bukharan Baked Rice and Fruit

(Savo)

5 TO 6 SERVINGS

Bukharan Jews developed a unique way of preparing rice, enclosing it in a linen bag (called a khalti *in Uzbekistan and similar to a* kouclas *in the Maghreb) and inserting the bag into a Sabbath stew to simmer slowly overnight. The constraints of the cloth prevent the rice from absorbing too much liquid and from becoming mushy or disintegrating during the extensive cooking time. Today, many Bukharans omit the bag and bake the rice in a casserole dish in the oven to serve warm for Sabbath dinner or lunch.*

This version features numerous fruits grown and beloved in Uzbekistan. During the long cooking time, the rice becomes very soft without becoming soggy and develops a crust on the bottom.

2 cups basmati or other long-grain rice

3 tablespoons vegetable oil

1 large onion, chopped

3 carrots, julienned or coarsely grated (optional)

3¹/₄ cups Vegetable Stock (page 115) or strained
    liquid from a fruit compote

About 1¹/₂ teaspoons table salt or 1 tablespoon
    kosher salt

1 teaspoon ground cinnamon

2 apples, cored and coarsely chopped

1 quince, cored and chopped (optional)

5 to 6 pitted prunes

4 to 5 pitted dates, coarsely chopped

2 to 3 tablespoons raisins

1. Soak the rice in cold water to cover for 30 minutes. Drain, rinse under cold running water until the water runs clear, and drain again.

2. Preheat the oven to 350°F.

3. In a flameproof 2- or 3-quart casserole or ovenproof pot, heat the oil over medium heat. Add the onion and sauté for 1 minute. If using, add the carrots. Sauté until the onion and carrots are softened, 5 to 10 minutes. Add the rice and sauté until opaque, about 3 minutes. Add the stock, salt, and cinnamon. Stir in the fruit and bring to a boil.

4. Cover and bake for 30 minutes, then reduce the heat to 225°F and continue baking, covered, until the rice develops a brown color, at least 3 hours or overnight. Serve warm.

INDIAN RICE PILAF

(*Pilau*)

5 TO 6 SERVINGS **D** OR **P**

In Calcuttan Jewish households, this pilau, *made with fragrant basmati rice and mouth-watering seasonings and garnished with raisins and nuts, was ubiquitous Friday night fare and was also common on various special occasions. Although most of that community has emigrated, many of the descendants still make* pilau *for every Sabbath. As is typical of Indian food,* pilau *has a lot of ingredients, but once you have them ready, the dish is fairly simple to make and cooks quickly. The majority of the heat in chilies comes from the membranes and seeds, so adjust the amount to your taste.*

- $^1/_4$ cup vegetable oil or *ghee* (Indian Clarified Butter, page 51)
- 3 to 4 green cardamom pods, crushed
- 1 (3-inch) stick cinnamon
- 3 to 4 whole cloves
- 1$^1/_2$ teaspoons cumin seeds
- 1 large onion or 10 scallions (white part only), chopped
- 1 tablespoon grated fresh ginger
- 1 to 3 small hot green chilies, seeded and minced
- 1 to 2 cloves garlic, minced
- 1 teaspoon ground turmeric or $^1/_2$ teaspoon saffron threads
- 2 cups basmati or other long-grain rice (not converted)
- 4 cups Vegetable Stock (page 115) or water
- About 1$^1/_2$ teaspoons table salt or 1 tablespoon kosher salt
- About $^1/_4$ teaspoon ground black pepper
- $^1/_4$ cup chopped fresh parsley
- $^1/_2$ cup toasted almonds for garnish (optional); see Note
- $^1/_2$ cup raisins for garnish (optional)

1. In a large saucepan or heavy flameproof casserole dish, heat the oil over medium heat. Add the cardamom, cinnamon, cloves, and cumin seeds and sauté until the cinnamon uncurls and the cloves begin to pop, about 1 minute. Add the onion, ginger, chilies, garlic, and turmeric and sauté until softened, about 5 minutes. Add the rice and stir until opaque, about 3 minutes.

2. Add the stock, salt, and pepper. Bring to a boil, cover, reduce the heat to low, and simmer until the rice is tender, about 18 minutes. Do not uncover during cooking. Remove from the heat and let stand, covered, for about 10 minutes. If any liquid remains, cook, uncovered, until evaporated. Fluff with a fork. Stir in the parsley and, if desired, garnish with the almonds and/or raisins. Serve warm.

VARIATIONS

For simpler seasoning: Omit the cinnamon stick, whole cloves, and cardamom pods. Add $^1/_2$ teaspoon ground cinnamon, $^1/_4$ teaspoon ground cardamom, and $^1/_8$ teaspoon ground cloves with the stock.

Vegetable *Pilau*: Before adding the stock, stir in 1 to 2 cups green peas, green beans, cauliflower florets, chopped carrots, or any combination.

NOTE To toast almonds, stir them in a dry heavy skillet over low heat until lightly browned, about 10 minutes, or spread them over a dry baking sheet and place in a preheated 350°F oven, shaking occasionally, until lightly browned, about 10 minutes.

INDIAN COCONUT RICE

(Nariyal Chawal)

5 TO 6 SERVINGS D OR P

Unsweetened coconut milk adds a richness and subtle flavor to the rice, while blending and mellowing the flavors of the dish. Because fresh coconut milk requires a long time to prepare (you can use canned coconut milk), the cooks in the Bene Israel community of Bombay served this dish only on the Sabbath and for personal celebrations. For a simpler topping, some cooks sprinkle grated coconut over the rice. Others mix a little grated coconut into the rice for extra flavor.

2 tablespoons *ghee* (Indian Clarified Butter, page 51) or vegetable oil

3 to 4 green cardamom pods, crushed

1 (3-inch) stick cinnamon, broken

3 to 4 whole cloves

2 to 3 bay leaves (optional)

2 to 3 small hot green chilies, seeded and minced (optional)

2 cups basmati or other long-grain rice, rinsed and drained

3 cups homemade or canned coconut milk (recipe follows) or 3¹/2 ounces (¹/2 block) coconut cream dissolved in 2³/4 cups water

1 cup water

1 tablespoon packed jaggery or brown sugar

About 1 teaspoon table salt or 2 teaspoons kosher salt

¹/2 teaspoon ground turmeric

NUT TOPPING (OPTIONAL):

¹/4 cup *ghee* or vegetable oil

²/3 cup raw slivered almonds

²/3 cup raw cashews

²/3 cup golden raisins

3 tablespoons grated coconut (optional)

1. In a medium, heavy saucepan, melt the ghee over medium heat. Add the cardamom, cinnamon, cloves, and, if using, the bay leaves and/or chilies and sauté until fragrant, about 30 seconds. Add the rice and stir until opaque, about 3 minutes.

2. Add the coconut milk, water, jaggery, salt, and turmeric. Bring to a boil, cover, reduce the heat to low, and simmer until the rice is tender and the liquid absorbed, about 20 minutes. Remove from the heat and let stand, covered, for about 10 minutes. Fluff with a fork. Serve warm as is or prepare the topping.

3. To make the optional nut topping: In a small, heavy saucepan, melt the ghee over medium heat. Add the almonds and cashews and sauté until golden, about 3 minutes. Stir in the raisins and, if using, the coconut. Sprinkle over the rice.

VARIATIONS

For simpler seasoning: Substitute ¹/4 to ¹/2 teaspoon ground cardamom, ¹/4 teaspoon ground cinnamon, and ¹/4 teaspoon ground cloves for the whole spices, adding them with the turmeric.

Indian Coconut Rice with Pigeon Peas (*Arroz con Guandu*): Omit the cardamom, cinnamon, and cloves and add 2 cups cooked pigeon peas with the coconut milk.

Indian Coconut Rice with Onions (*Nariyal Ka Bhat*): In Step 1, before adding the spices, add 2 thinly sliced onions and sauté until golden, about 15 minutes. Remove half of the onions and set aside. If desired, add 1 cup fresh or frozen green peas with the coconut milk. Cook as above. Sprinkle the cooked onions over the top instead of the nut topping.

NOTE Coconut cream comes commercially in 7-ounce blocks or in cans and needs to be dissolved in boiling water in order to equal coconut milk. Canned unsweetened coconut milk is usually thicker than fresh coconut milk (most contain thickeners, preservatives, and whitening agents), but can be substituted. Shake or stir coconut milk before using to mix in the cream. Do not confuse coconut milk or coconut cream with canned sweetened cream of coconut, a very thick, sugary liquid used in cocktails.

COCONUT MILK

ABOUT 2 CUPS

Coconut water is the liquid found inside fresh coconuts. Coconut milk is a thicker liquid made by steeping 1 part grated coconut meat in 1 part water. When the mixture is left standing, a thick, sweet cream (with a strong coconut flavor) separates and rises to the top. The cream is generally stirred back into the thinner liquid.

If fresh coconuts are unavailable, substitute unsweetened dried coconut or frozen shredded coconut. Coconut milk is best when fresh and used the same day it is made, as the delicate flavor deteriorates as it ages.

> 2 cups water
> 2 cups grated fresh, frozen, or unsweetened dried coconut

In a large saucepan, bring the water to a low boil. Stir in the coconut, remove from the heat, and let cool, stirring occasionally, for about 2 hours. Purée in a food processor or blender. Pour through a sieve lined with cheesecloth and set over a bowl, squeezing the cloth to extract the liquid. Cover and refrigerate for up to 2 days. Shake or stir before using.

INDIAN RICE AND VEGETABLE CASSEROLE

(Biryani)

6 TO 8 SERVINGS   Ⓓ OR Ⓟ

Besides the widespread pilau *(pilaf), Indian Jews also serve this rice casserole of Persian origin for celebrations and on holidays, especially during Sukkot, as the vegetables denote the harvest and the large dish is easy to carry outside to the sukkah. Biryani, a one-dish meal, contains a delicate balance of spices that accent the flavor of the basmati rice. Indian cookery incorporates a wealth of spices, but the flavorings have to be handled carefully. The yellow rice is cooked, layered with cooked vegetables, then just before serving it is baked in the oven. The types of vegetables are a matter of personal preference; some cooks also add any combination of white potatoes, sweet potatoes, carrots, green beans, and okra. If you like, serve with hard-boiled eggs and* raita *(yogurt salad) or plain yogurt.*

RICE LAYER:

3 tablespoons *ghee* (Indian Clarified Butter, page 51) or vegetable oil

2 cups white or brown basmati or other long-grain rice

4 cups water (5 cups for brown rice)

2 teaspoons ground turmeric

About 1 1/2 teaspoons table salt or 1 tablespoon kosher salt

VEGETABLE LAYER:

1/4 cup *ghee* or vegetable oil

1 large onion, chopped

1 1/2 teaspoons black or yellow mustard seeds

1 teaspoon poppy seeds

1 teaspoon ground coriander

1 teaspoon ground cumin

1 teaspoon ground turmeric

1/2 teaspoon ground cinnamon

1/4 to 1/2 teaspoon cayenne

3 small or 2 medium-small eggplants, peeled and diced, or 3 cups cauliflower florets

1 large zucchini, diced

1 large red or green bell pepper, seeded, deribbed (white removed), and diced

1 cup lima beans or green peas

2 cups tomato purée (see page 291), or 1 cup water mixed with 3 seeded and diced plum tomatoes

1 teaspoon sugar

About 1 teaspoon table salt or 2 teaspoons kosher salt

3/4 cup cooked or canned chickpeas (optional)

NUT MIXTURE:

1/4 cup *ghee* or vegetable oil

2/3 cup raw slivered almonds

2/3 cup raw cashews

2/3 cup golden raisins

1/4 cup chopped fresh cilantro for garnish

1. Preheat the oven to 350°F. Grease a 9-by-13-inch baking dish.

2. To make the rice layer: In a large, heavy saucepan, melt the ghee over medium heat. Add the rice and sauté until opaque, about 3 minutes. Add the water, turmeric, and salt. Bring to a boil, cover, reduce the heat to low, and simmer until the liquid is absorbed, about 18 minutes for white rice; about 40 minutes for brown rice.

3. To make the vegetable layer: In a large, heavy saucepan, melt the ghee over medium-high heat. Add the onion and sauté until soft and translucent, about 5 minutes. Add the mustard and poppy seeds and sauté until they begin to pop, about 30 seconds. Reduce the heat to low and stir in the coriander, cumin, turmeric, cinnamon, and cayenne.

4. Increase the heat to medium-high, add the eggplants, zucchini, and bell pepper, and sauté for 2 minutes. Stir in the lima beans, tomato purée, sugar, and salt. Bring to a boil, cover, reduce the heat to low, and simmer until the vegetables are crisp-tender, about 10 minutes. If using, add the chickpeas.

5. To make the nut mixture: In a small, heavy saucepan, melt the ghee over medium heat. Add the nuts and sauté until golden, about 3 minutes. Stir in the raisins. Remove from the heat.

6. Spread half of the rice in the prepared dish and top with the vegetable mixture. Combine the remaining rice with the nut mixture and spread over the vegetables.

7. Cover with a lid or aluminum foil and bake for 30 minutes. Sprinkle with the cilantro. Serve warm.

VARIATION

Omit the mustard seeds and poppy seeds and add 2 teaspoons freshly grated ginger with the other spices.

PERSIAN RICE AND EGGPLANT CASSEROLE

(Tahchin-e Badenjan)

6 TO 8 SERVINGS

Tah chin, a Farsi term meaning "arrange on the bottom," refers to a layered casserole. A tahchin could be layered with anything, from lamb and chicken to fish, but all use rice, usually mixed with yogurt. For dairy meals, Jews make versions with eggplant, spinach, mushrooms, or various combinations. Most tahchin involve creating a crisp rice bottom to keep the rice moist, while some instead use layers of eggplant. As is typical of Persian cooking, this dish is subtly rather than excessively spiced. This is commonly served with pita bread, turshi left (Middle Eastern Pickled Turnips, page 59), and yogurt.

I medium-large eggplant (about I 1/2 pounds),
   peeled
2 tablespoons table salt plus 1/4 teaspoon,
   or 4 tablespoons kosher salt plus 1/2 teaspoon
Olive oil or vegetable oil for frying
6 cups water
2 1/2 cups basmati or other long-grain rice, rinsed,
   soaked in warm water for 2 hours, and drained
6 tablespoons *ghee* (Indian Clarified Butter,
   page 51) or vegetable oil
I cup plain yogurt
3 large egg yolks, lightly beaten
1/4 teaspoon saffron threads, crushed,
   or 1/4 teaspoon ground turmeric
About 1/8 teaspoon ground white or black pepper
I 1/2 teaspoons ground cumin (optional)
1/2 teaspoon ground cinnamon (optional)
1/8 teaspoon ground cardamom (optional)
1/8 teaspoon ground cloves (optional)
1/8 teaspoon ground ginger (optional)

1. Cut the eggplant crosswise into $^1/_2$-inch-thick slices. Put in a colander or on a wire rack, sprinkle with $1^1/_2$ teaspoons of the table salt or 1 tablespoon of the kosher salt, and let stand for at least 1 hour. Rinse the eggplant under cold water, then press repeatedly between several layers of paper towels until the slices feel firm and dry. The eggplant can be covered and stored in the refrigerator for up to 4 hours.

2. In a large, heavy skillet, heat 3 tablespoons oil over medium heat. In batches, fry the eggplant, turning and adding more oil between the batches, until fork-tender and lightly browned, 3 to 5 minutes per side. Or, brush the eggplant slices lightly with oil and bake on an oiled baking sheet in a preheated 350°F oven until tender, about 15 minutes. Set aside.

3. In a medium saucepan, bring the water to a boil. Add $1^1/_2$ tablespoons of the table salt or 3 tablespoons of the kosher salt. Add the rice and cook, uncovered, until elongated and slightly softened, about 10 minutes. Do not overcook. Drain, rinse under cold water, and drain again.

4. Preheat the oven to 350°F. Spread 4 tablespoons ghee in an 8-cup round or rectangular casserole.

5. In a medium bowl, combine the yogurt, egg yolks, saffron, the $^1/_4$ teaspoon table salt or $^1/_2$ teaspoon kosher salt, the pepper, and optional spices. Stir in 2 cups of the rice. Spread the yogurt-rice mixture in the prepared casserole. Arrange the eggplant over the top, then cover with the remaining plain rice. Dot with the remaining 2 tablespoons ghee.

6. Cover with a lid or aluminum foil and bake until the bottom is golden brown, $1^1/_2$ to 2 hours. The longer you bake it, the thicker the tahdiq (crust) becomes. Let stand for 10 minutes before slicing. Loosen the edges of the tahchin with a knife, place a serving platter over top of the dish, invert, and remove the dish. Serve warm.

ITALIAN RICE CAKE

(*Bomba di Riso*)

6 TO 8 SERVINGS   D

Traditionally, Italian Jewish housewives tended to cook large batches of risotto for the Sabbath and holidays and then used the leftovers to make assorted dishes, most notably bomba di riso *and* arancini di riso *(croquettes; literally "little oranges"). The name* bomba *derives from the Italian word for "swelling," referring to the action of the pancake while frying.*

Bomba were traditionally made in a pan on the stove top rather than baked. With the popularization of the home oven, many cooks began baking the bomba *as a single large cake, a molded form of risotto, rather than frying it in a skillet. In either variation, the secret is using the right rice and cooking techniques. The rice in* bomba, *the same varieties used for risotto, is not cooked in the traditional manner, which eliminates the tedium of constant stirring. Serve this as a main course along with a tomato sauce, vegetable stew, or green salad, or as a side dish.*

5 cups Vegetable Stock (page 115) or water
$2^1/_2$ cups risotto rice, such as Carnaroli, Vialone, Arborio, or other short-grain varieties
About 2 teaspoons table salt or 4 teaspoons kosher salt
Pinch (about 20 threads) of saffron or $^1/_4$ teaspoon ground turmeric (optional)
4 large eggs, slightly beaten
$^1/_3$ cup grated Parmesan cheese
1 tablespoon unsalted butter
About $^1/_2$ teaspoon freshly grated nutmeg (optional)
4 cups (1 pound) shredded mozzarella cheese or 3 cups (12 ounces) shredded mozzarella and $1^1/_2$ cups (12 ounces) ricotta cheese

1. In a large saucepan, combine the stock, rice, salt, and, for a yellow color, the saffron. Cover and bring to a boil, about 5 minutes. Reduce the heat to low and simmer, without removing the lid, until the rice is tender, about 15 minutes. The cooking time depends on the age and type of rice. Spread over a flat tray and let cool.

2. Preheat the oven to 350°F. Grease an 8-cup baking dish or a 9-by-2½-inch ring mold.

3. In a large bowl, combine the rice, eggs, Parmesan, butter, and, if using, the nutmeg. Spread half of the rice mixture in the prepared dish, scatter with the cheese, and top with the remaining rice mixture. Or, mix the mozzarella and ricotta into the rice mixture instead of layering it.

4. Put the dish in a large baking pan and add about 1 inch of boiling water to the pan. Bake until set and golden, about 25 minutes. Run a knife along the inside of the dish to loosen the rice. Place a large serving platter over top, invert, and remove the dish. Serve warm.

VARIATION

Italian Large Rice Pancakes (*Bomba al Salto*): Increase the eggs to 8 and omit the Parmesan. Heat 2 tablespoons vegetable oil in a large skillet over low heat. Spread one-fourth of the rice mixture in the skillet, scatter with 2 cups (8 ounces) shredded mozzarella, and top with one-third of the remaining rice mixture. Cook until the bottom is golden, about 10 minutes. Invert the *bomba* onto a plate. Heat 2 additional tablespoons oil in the skillet, slide in the pancake, uncooked side down, and cook until golden, about 5 minutes. Repeat with the remaining ingredients. Makes 2 large pancakes.

N O T E Do not rinse the rice, as the starch is necessary to this dish.

RISOTTO

The Arabs introduced rice to Sicily during their occupation of that island. Later, in the sixteenth century, short-grain rice became widely planted in northern Italy and the people became avid rice consumers, especially the Jews, many of whom had grown up eating rice in Sicily before being exiled by the Spanish. Risotto originated in Lombardy and, by the nineteenth century, had spread throughout Italy, with every northern region of the country developing its own version. Although it is now featured at chic restaurants, risotto was once a comfort food largely consigned to family dinners as a way of using up leftover foods. It was usually served as a first course, made thick enough to be eaten with a fork. When dishes like *bomba* gained in popularity, people began making them in their own right, not merely as a means of utilizing leftovers.

ITALIAN RICE WITH BEETS

(Riso Rosso)

6 TO 8 SERVINGS

An Italian woman I met at a wedding shared the recipe for this pink-tinted pilaf with specks of bright red beets. She said that it was traditionally served in Italy only for Rosh Hashanah and Sukkot, when it made use of the new crop of beets. Today, with beets available year-round, this dish can be made more frequently. Serve warm as a side dish or at room temperature as a salad.

> 4 beets (about 1 pound), peeled and diced
>   or coarsely grated
> 1/4 cup olive oil or vegetable oil
> 1 large onion, chopped
> 2 cups long-grain rice
> 2 1/2 cups water
> 1 teaspoon grated lemon zest
> About 1 1/2 teaspoons table salt or 1 tablespoon
>   kosher salt
> About 1/4 teaspoon ground black pepper
> 1 tablespoon red wine vinegar
> 1/4 cup chopped fresh parsley (optional)

1. Put the beets in a medium saucepan, add cold water to cover, bring to a boil, reduce the heat to medium-low, cover, and simmer until tender, about 40 minutes. Drain, reserving 1 1/2 cups of the flavorful red cooking liquid.

2. In a large, heavy saucepan or flameproof casserole dish, heat the oil over medium heat. Add the onion and sauté until soft and translucent, about 5 minutes. Add the rice and stir until opaque, about 3 minutes.

3. Add the water, the 1 1/2 cups reserved beet juice, the zest, salt, and pepper. Bring to a boil,

cover, reduce the heat to low, and simmer until the water is absorbed and the rice is tender, about 18 minutes. Do not uncover during cooking.

4. Remove from the heat and let stand, covered, for 10 minutes. Fluff with a fork. Stir in the beets, the vinegar, and, if using, the parsley. The rice can be covered, refrigerated for up to 2 days, and reheated.

TURKISH RICE-STUFFED GRAPE LEAVES

(Yaprak Dolmasi)

ABOUT 40 SMALL ROLLS

Ancient Middle Eastern cooks ingeniously found a use for the otherwise wasted grape leaves—found in abundance among the numerous vineyards that dotted the countryside and urban gardens—by stuffing them with grains and simmering them in hot liquid until tender. Turkish Jews are particularly fond of vegetable-stuffed grape leaves, which can be used at both dairy or meat meals.

Spread by the Ottomans throughout their former domain, stuffed grape leaves are embraced in most of the countries bordering the Mediterranean. They are called yaprak dolmasi *in Turkey,* dolmades, *or dolmadakia yialandzi, and* yalandji dolma *in Greece,* dolma yalanchi *and* yalanchi sarma *in Armenia,* dolma bargh *in Iran,* yerba *in Syria, and* yaprakes finos *by Sephardim.*

This basic Turkish recipe contains elements common to all versions. Stuffed grape leaves make wonderful finger food, transforming even an otherwise plain meal into a special occasion. They are served as a side dish or, more frequently, as an appetizer with pita bread and sometimes plain yogurt or lemon wedges, in a fresh spinach salad, or as part of a meze *with* borekas *(Turkish Turnovers, page 176) and hummus (Middle Eastern Chickpea Dip, page 328).*

1 (1-pound) jar grape leaves or about 60 small
    or 40 medium fresh grape leaves

STUFFING:

2 tablespoons olive oil or vegetable oil

¼ cup pine nuts (optional)

2 onions, chopped

1 to 2 cloves garlic, minced (optional)

1 cup long-grain rice, rinsed and drained

About ¾ teaspoon table salt or 1½ teaspoons
    kosher salt

½ cup water

¼ cup chopped fresh parsley

About ½ cup dried currants (optional)

2 to 3 plum tomatoes, peeled, seeded,
    and chopped; optional

SAUCE:

About 1½ cups water

4 to 6 tablespoons fresh lemon juice

2 tablespoons extra-virgin olive oil

1 teaspoon sugar

About 1 teaspoon table salt or 2 teaspoons
    kosher salt

2 to 3 whole cloves garlic (optional)

1. If using preserved leaves, unroll, rinse under cold water, then soak in cold water to cover for 15 minutes. If using fresh grape leaves, blanch in boiling lightly salted water for about 5 minutes. (The most tender grapes leaves are picked in June; after blanching, they can be frozen for up to 6 months.) Drain and pat dry. Carefully cut off the stems.

2. To make the stuffing: In a large, heavy saucepan, heat the oil over medium heat. If using, add the pine nuts and sauté until golden, 2 to 3 minutes.

Using a slotted spoon, remove the nuts. Add the onions and, if using, the garlic and sauté until soft and translucent, 5 to 10 minutes. Add the rice and sauté until opaque, about 3 minutes. Stir in the salt and the ½ cup water, reduce the heat to low, and simmer until the liquid is absorbed, about 10 minutes. Add the parsley and, if using, the pine nuts, currants, and/or tomatoes. Let cool.

3. To assemble: Place the leaves on a flat surface, shiny-side down and vein-side up. On the small leaves, place 1 heaping teaspoon of the stuffing near the stem end; on the larger leaves, about 2 teaspoons. Carefully fold the leaf from the stem end to cover the stuffing. Fold the sides over, then roll up the leaf to make a neat package.

4. Cover the bottom of a heavy 3-quart saucepan with any extra leaves. Arrange the rolls, seam-side down, in layers in the prepared pan.

5. To make the sauce: In a medium bowl, combine the water, lemon juice, oil, sugar, salt, and, if using, the garlic. Pour over the stuffed grape leaves, adding more water if necessary to cover.

6. Weigh down the rolls with a heavy plate. Bring to a boil, cover, reduce the heat to low, and simmer until the rice and leaves are tender but not mushy, about 35 minutes. Let cool. Stuffed grape leaves will keep in the refrigerator for up to 1 week. Serve at room temperature or chilled.

VARIATIONS

Balkan Stuffed Grape Leaves (*Yaprakes*):
Add 3 tablespoons chopped fresh dill to the filling and 3 tablespoons chopped fresh dill to the sauce.

Syrian Stuffed Grape Leaves (*Yerba*): Add to the filling 2 to 3 tablespoons chopped fresh spearmint or 1 tablespoon dried mint, ½ teaspoon ground allspice, and ¼ teaspoon ground cinnamon. Add to the sauce 3 tablespoons *temerhindi* (Syrian Mock Tamarind Sauce, page 434) and 1 tablespoon sugar.

Sephardic Stuffed Grape Leaves with Beans (*Yaprakes con Avicas*): In Step 6, after cooking the grape leaves for 20 minutes, add 1¹/₂ cups cooked white beans.

Middle Eastern Rice-and-Lentil-Stuffed Grape Leaves (*Mihshee Wara Anib ma Adas*): Reduce the rice to ¹/₂ cup. Add 1¹/₂ cups cooked brown lentils, ¹/₃ cup chopped fresh spearmint or 3 tablespoons dried mint, ³/₄ teaspoon ground cumin, and ¹/₄ teaspoon ground allspice.

Middle Eastern Bulgur-and-Rice-Stuffed Grape Leaves (*Mihshee Wara Anib ma Bourghol*): Reduce the rice to ¹/₂ cup and add ¹/₂ cup bulgur soaked in warm water for 30 minutes and drained.

ASHKENAZIC BAKED RICE PUDDING

(*Reis Kugel*)

6 TO 9 SERVINGS   Ⓓ OR Ⓟ

Kugel, a rich baked casserole, is a mainstay of most Ashkenazic Sabbath, holiday, and special-occasion meals. There are numerous variations, as makes sense for a dish with a centuries-long heritage, and the dish is made in many countries including Germany, Austria, Hungary, Romania, Poland, Ukraine, and Lithuania. Ashkenazic Sweet Noodle Pudding (page 394) and potato kugel are arguably the two most popular versions, but also common and, at times, my favorite is rice kugel, a specialty of my Lithuanian grandmother. She usually added canned fruit cocktail, but I prefer using either dried or fresh fruit.

Rice kugel is served as both a side dish and, with extra sugar, as dessert. This adaptation of rice kugel has a somewhat firmer texture than some modern custardlike versions, which you can make by including dairy products.

4 cups water

About 2 teaspoons table salt or 4 teaspoons kosher salt

2 cups medium-grain or long-grain rice

¹/₂ cup (1 stick) unsalted margarine or butter

8 large eggs

³/₄ to 1 cup granulated or packed brown sugar

1 teaspoon vanilla extract

2 teaspoons grated lemon zest (optional)

³/₄ to 1 cup raisins, chopped dried apricots, or chopped pitted dates (optional)

About 1 teaspoon ground cinnamon for sprinkling

1. Preheat the oven to 350°F. Grease a 9-by-13-inch baking dish.

2. In a large saucepan, combine the water and 1¹/₂ teaspoons of the table salt or 3 teaspoons of the kosher salt. Bring to a boil and add the rice. Cover, reduce the heat to low, and simmer until the water is absorbed, about 18 minutes. Fluff with a fork. Add the margarine to the hot rice and let melt.

3. Meanwhile, in a medium bowl beat the eggs and sugar together until thick and creamy, about 5 minutes. Add the remaining ¹/₂ teaspoon table salt or 1 teaspoon kosher salt, the vanilla, and, if using, the zest. Stir in the rice and, if using, the raisins.

4. Pour into the prepared pan and sprinkle lightly with the cinnamon. Bake until golden brown, 50 to 60 minutes. Serve warm or at room temperature.

VARIATIONS

Custardy Rice Kugel: In Step 3, add 3 cups milk or 2 cups orange juice. Or add 12 ounces cottage cheese, 8 ounces softened cream cheese, and 1 cup milk. Or reduce the eggs to 4 and add 1 cup milk, 1 cup cottage or ricotta cheese, and ¹/₂ cup sour cream.

Brown Rice Kugel: Substitute 2 cups brown rice for the white rice, increase the water to 5 cups, and increase the rice cooking time to about 40 minutes.

Fruited Rice Kugel: Add ³/₄ cup raisins, 3 peeled, cored, and chopped apples, and ¹/₃ cup crushed pineapple.

Tahini Rice Kugel: Omit the butter and add ¹/₂ cup tahini (Middle Eastern Sesame Sauce, page 430) blended with 1 cup water.

KUGEL

The first kugels were adapted from medieval German savory steamed puddings, made from bread and cooked on top of the Sabbath stew. Although modern Americans associate puddings with a sweet, soft-textured dish, the word derives from the Old English *podding*, a boiled or steamed sausage made from grain mixtures, which was the original form of this dish. German Jews cooked a version of these grain puddings without sausage in their Sabbath stews.

Since the Sabbath grain puddings didn't use sausage casings, they were instead bound with eggs and shaped into balls, called *koogel* (German for "ball"). The only seasonings were salt and, when affordable, pepper—most of the flavor was absorbed from the stew.

Eventually, medieval Germans took to flavoring their steamed sausage-and-grain puddings with honey, spices, and dried fruit, and many Jews followed suit with their *koogels*, which they began cooking in a small, covered, round earthenware or metal dish placed inside the stew pot.

These humble puddings progressed toward new gastronomical heights around the fifteenth century, when eastern Europeans substituted noodles and, on Passover, matza for the grains. By the late sixteenth century, rice kugels (the Polish and Lithuanian pronunciation) emerged in eastern Europe, influenced by the Ottoman advances into Europe and the introduction of numerous Middle Eastern foods. In the mid-nineteenth century, potatoes were incorporated into the kugel repertoire and, in impoverished Poland, the potato kugel became the primary form of kugel, the expensive rice kugel being reserved for special occasions.

Beginning in the eighteenth century, in the regions where sugar beet factories were established (making sugar more affordable), Polish and Lithuanian Jews developed a preference for sweet (sometimes excessively sweet) noodle and rice kugels seasoned with cinnamon and containing raisins. In the twentieth century, innovative cooks also began making new (and healthier) kinds of savory kugels, adding various vegetables once unheard of in Europe, including broccoli, cauliflower, spinach, and zucchini.

Most kugels contain only a few ingredients, the common denominators being a starch base, eggs, and fat. If the dish lacks any of the basic ingredients, it is a casserole rather than a kugel.

WHEAT

Wheat was the preferred grain in biblical times, although barley was the predominant one. The primitive wheat varieties available four millenia ago were more difficult to grow, harvest, and thresh than barley and therefore wheat was a secondary crop. (Barley also made better beer.) In addition, primal wheat possessed a very low amount of gluten, and therefore breads made from it turned out flat and crumbly.

Wheat species, however, crossbreed frequently and easily in nature—there are now more than thirty thousand varieties of wheat. During the late Bronze Age, a type of ancient wheat called emmer spontaneously hybridized, leading to spelt and, more importantly, durum (from the Latin for "hard"), the firmest and most flavorful of all wheat species. By the biblical period, durum wheat was considered the finest of all wheats; the Bible mandated only ground and finely sifted durum (*solet*) for use in the Temple for making bread. However, due to its hardness, durum was primarily utilized whole for bulgur and coarsely ground to make porridges.

Emmer also spontaneously crossbred with a wild goat grass, giving rise to *aestivum*, sometimes called common wheat (the type we use today to make wheat flour), which was larger grained, higher yielding, easier to thresh, and more adaptable than its predecessors. *Aestivum* contains more starch and a higher level of gluten than durum or emmer, which allows it to produce the light texture and satisfying taste that the modern world associates with bread and the delicate flakiness of pastry. The Romans, in particular, favored *aestivum* and planted it in all of the territories under its dominion. Thus *aestivum*, common wheat, spread from its home in the Caspian plains to become the source of most modern flour and far and away the most important species of wheat. Nevertheless, durum remains popular in the Mediterranean and Middle East, used to make semolina, pasta, couscous, cracked wheat, and bulgur.

WHEAT BERRIES

Wheat berries are actual grains of wheat and are available in three main forms. Whole wheat berries are unprocessed, tan-colored whole grains of wheat with only the outer husk removed. Hulled wheat berries (also called shelled, or peeled, wheat), which lack the whole wheat's flavor, are white in color and stickier and softer when cooked. Wheat berries broken into pieces (coarse, medium, and fine) are called cracked wheat.

With a nutty flavor and chewy texture, wheat berries are delicious alone or mixed with other grains. They are also used in Middle Eastern soups, stews, like *hamin* (Sephardic Bean Stew, page 315), salads, casseroles, and puddings. Sweetened and mixed with fruits and nuts, they become a holiday dish called *kofyas* in Turkey, *assurei* (from an Arabic word for "ten") or *koliva* in Greece, and *korkoti* in Georgia. Because wheat berries resemble teeth, Middle Easterners customarily serve them at a party honoring a baby's first tooth. Wheat berries are available at natural foods stores and Middle Eastern groceries.

MIDDLE EASTERN
WHEAT BERRY STEW

(Harisa)

6 TO 8 SERVINGS

Harisa, *not the same thing as* harissa *(chili paste), is a hearty, slow-simmered stew or porridge made with wheat berries or cracked wheat that for many centuries has been served by Middle Easterners for Saturday Sabbath lunch. The extensive cooking time develops and melds the flavors, transforming a basic porridge into special fare.*

The cracked wheat or wheat berries may be left whole after cooking, or mashed to a pulp in the ancient manner for a smooth texture similar to (but more flavorful than) hot breakfast cereal (which after all is called cream of wheat!). Some versions of harisa *contain chickpeas and potatoes, some have spinach or other seasonal greens mixed in. A final light sprinkling of cinnamon is common. Although the original dish was made with lamb, Yemenites devised vegetarian versions that could be enjoyed with* samneh *(Middle Eastern Clarified Butter, page 51) and a drizzle of honey at dairy meals.*

- 3 tablespoons vegetable oil
- 3 large onions, sliced
- 1 tablespoon sweet paprika
- 1 tablespoon sugar
- About 2 teaspoons table salt or 4 teaspoons kosher salt
- Ground black pepper to taste
- 2 cups (1 pound) wheat berries or cracked wheat
- 1 to 3 cloves garlic
- 3 large sweet potatoes or 4 boiling potatoes, peeled and cubed, or 1/2 cup dried chickpeas (optional)
- 6 to 8 eggs in the shell, washed (optional)
- Ground cinnamon for sprinkling (optional)

1. In a large saucepan, heat the oil over medium heat. Add the onions and sauté until golden, about 15 minutes. Stir in the paprika, sugar, salt, and pepper. Add the wheat berries, garlic, and, if using, the potatoes. Add water to cover and bring to a boil. Cover, reduce the heat to medium-low, and simmer for 1 hour. Or, transfer to a casserole, cover, and bake in a 350°F oven for 1 hour.

2. Continue to simmer over medium-low heat or bake until the wheat berries are very tender and have a consistency that is neither dry nor very soupy, about 1 more hour, adding more water if necessary.

3. For the traditional, longer cooking method, if using eggs, arrange them in the top of the stew. Add more water to cover the stew. Tightly cover, place on a blech (a thin sheet of metal set over the range that acts as a heat diffuser) or place in a preheated 225°F oven and cook overnight. If baking in a casserole, bake in a 225°F oven overnight. The harisa should have the consistency of risotto or rice pudding, neither dry nor very soupy. Serve warm, sprinkled with a little cinnamon, if desired.

HARISA

For millennia, one of the staples of the Middle Eastern diet was a durum wheat porridge called *harisa*, from the Semitic *haras*, meaning "to break," referring to the crushed wheat. (This has nothing to do with the Maghrebi chili paste of the same-sounding name other than that both mixtures involve pounding.)

Jews devised their own form of *harisa* that could be served during the Sabbath. They would bury a pot of cracked or whole durum wheat berries in dying embers to slowly cook all night. Then, on Saturday morning, the mixture would sometimes be pounded into a creamy consistency by a non-Jewish maid or neighbor. Others would simply leave the wheat berries cracked or whole. The final step commonly consisted of a sprinkling of cinnamon.

By the seventh century C.E., the fame of Jewish *harisa* had spread to the highest reaches of Arab society. When a group of Yemenite Jews visited the Caliph Mu'awiya, ruler of the first Arabic-Islamic dynasty, the Umayyad, in his capital of Damascus, the first question he asked was whether they knew how to prepare the Jewish *harisa*, which he had sampled during a visit to Arabia (which included Yemen). The visitors obliged by preparing a batch for the grateful caliph.

Many Yemenite Jews continue to make *harisa* today for Sabbath lunch. The addition of fava beans and chickpeas to *harisa* during the early Middle Ages led to the emergence of the first Mediterranean Sabbath stew, *hamin*, or *dafina*, which by the eleventh century largely supplanted *harisa* as the predominant Sabbath dish. Nonetheless, even in thirteenth-century Spain, vendors commonly sold *harisa* from street corners.

In some households, non-Jewish cooks customarily still do the mashing on the Sabbath, only now they might use a food processor to achieve a creamy consistency. In the Sephardic manner, whole eggs are commonly cooked in the stew, then served alongside it for Sabbath lunch. In some instances, sugar is added at the table. On the other hand, Moroccans make a zesty Sabbath stew from wheat berries and red chilies called *orissa*.

✦ BULGUR ✦

More than four thousand years ago, Middle Easterners developed a special method for preparing whole grains (one of the first processed foods). After removing the chaff, they would boil the kernels in large pots for several hours until tender, then drain and sun-dry them on the flat roofs of houses. The dried kernels would then be crushed and sieved to separate various sizes. By far the favorite of these sun-dried grains was wheat groats, now commonly called bulgur (the Turkish pronunciation of the Arabic *burghul*). This form of wheat allows for easy preparation as well as much longer storage. The partial processing of the wheat berries imparts a delicate nutty flavor and soft, somewhat fluffy texture, while removing very little of the kernel's protein, vitamins, and minerals.

Sun-dried grains, especially bulgur, were a staple of ancient Mesopotamia and have been found in ancient Egyptian tombs. Persians adopted bulgur to make the classic cracked-grain porridge, *kashk*, which would later become kasha in Slavic lands. Bulgur remained a "poor man's dish" among Middle Eastern Jews, especially the very impoverished communities of Kurdistan and Yemen. It was commonly paired with other inexpensive foods, such as lentils, similar to the more upscale *mengedarrah* (Middle Eastern Lentils and Rice, page 336).

What You Should Know: Bulgur is available in natural foods stores and Middle Eastern groceries in three granulations: fine (also labeled No. 1), medium (also labeled No. 2), and coarse. The color varies depending on the type of wheat—red or white—and the preparation method. Most commercial bulgur is husked, the outer bran removed.

Bulgur is not the same as cracked wheat, which must be simmered in water to become edible. Bulgur is uniform in color, while cracked wheat is white inside. Fine- and medium-grain bulgur can generally be substituted for each other and can be prepared by simply soaking in liquid. When rehydrated, bulgur nearly triples in volume. Fine bulgur is generally used in salads, while medium is preferred for *kibbe* (Syrian Bulgur Torpedoes, page 372) and soups. The coarse type, wich requires a brief cooking period, is commonly used in pilafs, casseroles, stuffings, and stews.

[handwritten note: Super easy! Made Syrian style & Baked it.]

TURKISH BULGUR PILAF

(*Bulgur Pilavi*)

5 TO 6 SERVINGS ✿P

An elderly Turkish woman living in Manhattan gave me this simple recipe, which her mother had made at least once a week, and which is made in various ways throughout the Middle East. It is an everyday derivation of rice pilaf, as rice was frequently expensive and usually reserved for special occasions. The pilaf is further enhanced by adding various Middle Eastern standard foods and seasonings (see Variations). It is commonly accompanied with hard-boiled eggs and yogurt.

> 1/4 cup vegetable oil
>
> 1 large onion or 12 scallions, chopped
>
> 2 to 3 cloves garlic, minced (optional)
>
> 2 cups (12 ounces) coarse- or medium-grain bulgur
>
> 3 cups Vegetable Stock (page 115) or water
>
> About 1 teaspoon table salt or 2 teaspoons kosher salt
>
> About 1/4 teaspoon ground black pepper
>
> 1/4 to 1/2 cup chopped fresh parsley or chives

1. In a medium saucepan, heat the oil over medium heat. Add the onion and, if using, the garlic and sauté until soft and translucent, about 5 minutes. Stir in the bulgur and sauté until lightly colored, about 5 minutes.

2. Add the stock, salt, and pepper. Bring to a boil, cover, reduce the heat to medium-low, and simmer, stirring occasionally, until the bulgur is tender and the liquid is absorbed, about 20 minutes. Or prepare it in an ovenproof saucepan or transfer to a casserole, cover, and bake in a preheated 350°F oven for 40 minutes.

3. Remove from the heat and fluff the bulgur with a fork. Cover and let stand for 5 minutes. Stir in the parsley. The bulgur grains should be separate and fluffy but slightly chewy, not mushy. Serve warm.

VARIATIONS

In Step 2, add with the stock 1 1/2 cups cooked chickpeas, 1 1/2 cups cooked lentils, 8 ounces sautéed mushrooms, or 1 1/2 cups mixed dried fruits (raisins, apricots, and dates) and almonds.

Bulgur Timbales: Pack 2/3 to 1 cup of the bulgur mixture in an oiled timbale mold or custard cup and invert onto a serving plate. Repeat to make about 6 servings.

Persian Lemon Bulgur Pilaf (*Bourghol im Limon*): Add 1 1/2 teaspoons grated lemon zest with the water.

Syrian Bulgur Pilaf (*Bourghol Pilav*): This was a popular dish in Aleppo to serve on Thursday night—usually a dairy meal before the Sabbath. Cooked chickpeas were commonly added for extra flavor, texture, and nutrition. Add 1 teaspoon dried thyme or 1/2 teaspoon ground allspice and 1 teaspoon ground cumin with the water. If desired, just before serving, stir in 1 cup *jiben* (Syrian White Cheese, page 50), pot cheese, or farmer cheese or serve the cheese over the top. (Syrians historically used halloumi cheese, a firm, very salty type that is frequently soaked overnight in cold water before using.)

SYRIAN BULGUR TORPEDOES

(*Kibbe Nayeh*)

ABOUT 20 *KIBBE*　　

It is impossible to have a conversation on food with a Syrian without at least one mention of kibbe, *the national dish of Syria and Lebanon.* Kibbe (*a distortion of the Persian word* kebab, *or "form into a ball"*) *refers to a variety of meat preparations, most containing bulgur. The meat and bulgur mixture is spread over a platter or formed into torpedoes. A variation,* kibbe nabilseeyah, *consists of ground bulgur shaped into torpedoes, stuffed, and fried.*

In this Jewish variation, cooks shape vegetarian bulgur salad into torpedoes and skip the filling and frying. Kibbe are often served, alone or as part of a meze (appetizer assortment), with tahini (Middle Eastern Sesame Sauce, page 430), or with lemon wedges.

2 cups (12 ounces) fine-grain bulgur

6 tablespoons vegetable oil

2 onions, finely chopped

1/4 cup tomato paste

1 cup dried red lentils, rinsed and drained

2 cups water

6 to 8 scallions, minced

1 cup chopped fresh parsley

3 to 4 plum tomatoes, peeled, seeded, and minced (see page 291)

1 small green bell pepper, seeded, deribbed (white removed), and minced

1 small red bell pepper, seeded, deribbed (white removed) and minced

About 2 to 3 teaspoons ground cumin

About 2 teaspoons table salt or 4 teaspoons kosher salt

Pinch of Aleppo or cayenne pepper

1. Put the bulgur in a large bowl. In a large, heavy skillet, heat 2 tablespoons of the oil over medium heat. Add the onions and sauté until soft and translucent, 5 to 10 minutes. Stir in the tomato paste. Stir this mixture into the bulgur.

2. In a medium saucepan, combine the lentils and water. bring to a boil, partially cover, reduce the heat to low, and simmer, stirring frequently, until the lentils are tender, about 20 minutes. Stir the hot lentils and cooking liquid into the bulgur. Let cool.

3. Add the remaining 4 tablespoons oil, the scallions, parsley, tomatoes, bell peppers, cumin, salt, and Aleppo pepper. Cover and refrigerate for at least 30 minutes or up to 5 days.

4. One to two hours before serving, shape into cylinders 3 inches long and 1 inch wide, with tapered ends, and arrange on a serving platter.

SYRIAN GROUND BULGUR CASSEROLE

(Kibbe bil Seniyeh)

6 TO 8 SERVINGS

In kibbe bil seniyeh ("in a tray"), the filling is sandwiched between layers of the bulgur shell mixture. The dish is commonly baked in a round pan and cut into diamonds like baklava. The ingredients are usually ground with a mortar and pestle, but a food processor makes the task easier. This is a Jewish vegetarian version of baked kibbe, featuring a mushroom filling instead of the more traditional ground meat. It is commonly served with tahini sauce (Middle Eastern Sesame Sauce, page 430) or yogurt.

FILLING:

3 tablespoons vegetable oil

2 onions, chopped

I to 2 cloves garlic, minced

I pound button mushrooms, chopped

$^1/_4$ cup pine nuts

About $^1/_2$ teaspoon table salt or I teaspoon kosher salt

Ground black pepper to taste

SHELL:

I$^1/_2$ cups (9 ounces) fine-grain bulgur

4$^1/_2$ cups cold water

I onion, very finely chopped or puréed

$^1/_2$ cup unbleached all-purpose flour

I tablespoon vegetable oil or I large egg, lightly beaten

About I$^1/_2$ teaspoons table salt or I tablespoon kosher salt

About $^1/_2$ teaspoon ground black pepper

I teaspoon ground cumin and/or I teaspoon red pepper flakes (optional)

3 tablespoons vegetable oil or melted unsalted butter

1. Preheat the oven to 375°F. Grease a 9-inch round baking pan or deep dish pie plate.

2. To make the filling: In a large skillet, heat the oil over medium heat. Add the onions and garlic and sauté until soft and translucent, 5 to 10 minutes. Add the mushrooms and sauté until they release their liquid and it evaporates, about 10 minutes. Transfer the mushrooms to a food processor or blender and purée. Stir in the pine nuts, salt, and pepper.

3. To make the shell: Put the bulgur in a bowl, pour the water over it, and let soak for 30 minutes. Drain the bulgur in a sieve and press out any excess moisture with the back of a large spoon. Return to the bowl and stir in the onion, flour, oil, salt, pepper, and, if using, the cumin and/or pepper flakes. Process through a meat grinder or in a food processor to form a doughlike paste. Squeeze a little of the mixture together; if it does not hold together, add a little more flour.

4. Press half the shell mixture over the bottom of the prepared baking pan, spread with the mushroom mixture, and spread the remaining shell mixture over the top to cover. Cut all the way through the casserole to form wedges or the traditional diamond shapes. (This is the Middle Eastern style, leaving little bits on the edges.) Drizzle with the oil.

5. Bake until golden brown, about 55 minutes. Serve warm or at room temperature.

VARIATION

Syrian Rice *Kibbe* Shell (*Kibbe Ruz*): Soak 2 cups long-grain rice in 4 cups warm water overnight. Drain and pat dry. In a food processor, grind the rice with 1 teaspoon salt until smooth. Add 1 large egg. Substitute for the bulgur shell mixture.

❧ BARLEY ❧

Barley, possibly a native of northeast Africa, was arguably the world's first cultivated plant; only millet or einkorn may surpass it in antiquity. In much of the ancient world (throughout western and central Asia, most of Europe, and northern Africa), most people, young and old, urban and rural, primarily drank beer, which is made from barley, throughout the day, and ate bread made primarily from barley flour. Until the rise of precious metals and the invention of money, barley was the standard used to pay wages and rent.

Mentioned throughout the Bible, barley was one of the seven species associated with the land of Israel's blessing. The import of this grain was reflected in the Bible's record of a Midianite warrior's dream, in which barley—the most widely cultivated crop in Israel at that time—served as the symbol of his Israelite opponents and their agrarian lifestyle, opposing it to his own nomadic existence, symbolized by a tent. Its significance in ancient Israel can further be gleaned from a biblical injunction stating that the valuation of a field was to be determined according to the measurement of barley that could be sown in it. Although wheat was the preferred grain, barley served as the staple. Hence, in biblical times, when someone said bread, unless otherwise specified, they generally meant bread made from barley flour.

Shortly after the Roman conquest of the Levant, common wheat became the primary grain of the Middle East and barley was thereafter reduced to a poor man's food and animal fodder. However, barley remained the primary source of sustenance for the masses of southern Europe in the form of bread and porridge—a situation that only changed in the sixteenth century with the increased availability of other grains. In the wake of the improved technology and refined milling methods that followed the Industrial Revolution, wheat flour emerged as the most widely used type in Europe as well. The popularization of the potato in eastern Europe after 1840 led to the subsequent decline in the use of barley there.

Nevertheless, barley continues to play a role in the traditions of several Jewish communities. In the Balkans and Middle East, it goes into soups such as the Greek *sopa de cebada* (Greek Barley Soup, page 143) and the Armenian *spas* (Armenian Barley and Yogurt Soup, page 144), and in *belila* (sweetened barley), the latter a tradition on Rosh Hashanah and Sukkot. Eastern Europeans retain a particular fondness for this grain, often pairing it with mushrooms and incorporating it in such hearty fare as *cholent,* kugel, and thick soups, called *krupnik* in Poland and *kolish* in Ukraine.

What You Should Know: Whole barley is available in two forms: unpolished and pearl. Unpolished barley, also called hulled, pot, and Scotch barley, has had its outer husk removed. Pearl barley is further refined by steaming and polishing, a process that removes all of the bran. As a result, unpolished barley has a nuttier flavor and a sturdier and chewier texture than pearl barley. Unpolished barley, however, needs a long soaking time, while pearl barley requires no presoaking and about a fourth of the cooking time.

N O T E The advent of pasta in eastern Europe led to tiny barley-shaped dough bits called farfel, or barley farfel, frequently substituted for barley in this dish. Barley farfel is not to be confused with crumbled matza pieces, also called *farfel.*

ASHKENAZIC BARLEY WITH MUSHROOMS

(Gersht und Shveml)

5 TO 6 SERVINGS

I enjoy the nutty flavor and firm texture of barley. My mother would use it to make three specific dishes: cholent *(Sephardic Bean Stew, page 315), soup, and this old-fashioned eastern European grain dish. Barley with mushrooms can be eaten as a side dish or used to stuff bell peppers and cabbage leaves.*

1/4 cup vegetable oil
2 onions, chopped
2 carrots, minced
2 stalks celery, minced
2 to 3 cloves garlic, minced
8 ounces mushrooms, thinly sliced
1 cup (6 1/2 ounces) pearl barley
About 3 cups Vegetable Stock (page 115) or water
1 bay leaf
About 1 teaspoon table salt or 2 teaspoons kosher salt
Ground black pepper to taste

1. In a large saucepan, heat the oil over medium heat. Add the onions and sauté for 1 minute. Add the carrots, celery, and garlic and sauté until softened, about 10 minutes. Add the mushrooms and sauté until softened, about 5 minutes. Add the barley and stir to coat, about 1 minute.

2. Add the stock, bay leaf, salt, and pepper. Bring to a boil, cover, reduce the heat to low, and simmer, stirring frequently near the end, until the liquid is absorbed and the barley is tender, about 35 minutes. Serve warm. This dish can be prepared ahead and reheated, uncovered, in a 6-cup casserole in a preheated 350°F oven for about 25 minutes.

BUCKWHEAT

Buckwheat, a relative of rhubarb and sorrel, is a native of central Asia or Siberia, and it is still in those areas that much of its popularity resides. By the end of the Middle Ages, it had spread to western Europe, where it was most commonly ground into a flour. The Dutch introduced buckwheat to America by planting it in New Amsterdam in 1549, and the English name for the plant came from the Dutch *boekweit* ("beech wheat"), as the groats resemble the triangular beechnut. Buckwheat is botanically not a grain or a wheat but rather is the kernel of a fruit. However, since it shares most of a grain's properties and possesses the general nutritional breakdown of grains, it is usually categorized as one.

A sturdy plant that grows well in cooler climates and even in poor soil, buckwheat is ideally suited for Russia, Ukraine, and the Balkans, where, for centuries, along with dark bread, barley, and cabbage, it constituted the daily fare. Buckwheat was sometimes eaten at every meal in the form of groats, called kasha in Yiddish and in America and *grechnevoy* in Slavic lands (where the term *kasha* refers to any grain porridge).

In the middle of the nineteenth century, the rise in prominence of the potato in eastern Europe resulted in a marked decrease in the role of buckwheat in the Jewish diet, but this "grain" continues to be important in classic Ashkenazic cooking, most notably in *kasha varnishkes* (buckwheat with noodles) and in fillings for various foods.

Coating toasted kasha with a little egg before cooking is a characteristic Jewish technique intended to keep the groats separate and prevent the dish from becoming mushy. The favorite Jewish ways of using kasha, which is almost always flavored with sautéed onions, are mixing it with noodles or sautéed mushrooms, or as a pastry filling, most notably for knishes, pierogi, and strudels. Kasha's nutty flavor, which is more assertive than that of barley and wheat, complements bland foods, such as noodles and pastry, and pairs well with earthier fare, including cabbage and root vegetables.

What You Should Know: Buckwheat groats are available whole or ground into coarse, medium, and fine sizes; they are also sold plain or toasted, although most brands are now toasted. Toasting gives the beige cone-shaped groats a cocoa color, a more intense nutty flavor, and a crunchier texture. Unless you know that you will use toasted buckwheat relatively quickly, it is better to buy untoasted buckwheat and toast it yourself, as needed. (Toasting releases the natural oils, decreasing shelf life.)

Toasting Buckwheat: In a dry skillet over medium-high heat, toast the medium or coarse groats, stirring occasionally, until they are lightly browned and you smell the aroma, about 3 minutes.

VARNISHKES

In Ukraine, *varnishkes* referred to plain noodles and *vareniki* ("little boiled things") referred to filled noodles, both words coming from the Slavic *var*, meaning "to boil." The traditional Ukrainian way to shape noodles was to cut the pasta sheets into 1½-inch squares (called *plaetschen* in Yiddish), sometimes pinching together two opposite corners.

UKRAINIAN BUCKWHEAT AND NOODLES

(Kasha Varnishkes)

4 TO 6 SERVINGS   P

Kasha varnishkes, *once considered elaborate fare and served on Hanukkah, Purim, and other special occasions, is now a Jewish comfort food. I recently ordered it at a kosher restaurant in Denver, Colorado, only to be served a dish consisting primarily of* varnishkes *(noodles) with a disappointingly sparse sprinkling of kasha, possibly due to the high price of kasha in America. Ironically, this was historically quite the opposite in Europe, where inexpensive kasha constituted the bulk of the dish, supplemented lightly by the then-pricier noodles.*

Whereas kasha varnishkes *was originally made with noodle squares, today bow ties are the more prevalent form. In addition, while this dish was originally cooked in* schmaltz *(chicken fat) and chicken stock, using vegetable oil and vegetable stock makes this a lighter, vegetarian delight. Versatile* kasha varnishkes *goes with almost any entrée, but I enjoy it as a complete meal simply accompanied with cheese and a green salad.*

I large egg or egg white

I cup *kasha*, toasted

3 tablespoons vegetable oil

I large onion, chopped

2 cups boiling Vegetable Stock (page 115)
    or water

About I teaspoon table salt or 2 teaspoons
    kosher salt

Ground black pepper to taste

8 ounces bow tie pasta, *plaetschen* (pasta squares;
    see Egg Noodle Dough, page 392), or wide egg
    noodles

1. Lightly beat the egg in a small bowl, then add the kasha and stir until all the kernels are evenly coated.

2. In a heavy, 8-cup saucepan, heat the oil over medium heat. Add the onion and sauté until soft and translucent, about 5 minutes, or golden, about 15 minutes. Add the kasha and stir until each grain is separated, 2 to 3 minutes.

3. Add the boiling stock, salt, and pepper. Cover, reduce the heat to low, and simmer until the liquid is absorbed, 7 to 10 minutes.

4. Meanwhile, cook the noodles in a large pot of salted boiling water until tender, 7 to 10 minutes. Drain.

5. Fluff the kasha with a fork and stir in the noodles. Serve warm. For a slightly crunchy surface that contrasts with the soft noodles and kasha underneath, transfer to a greased 6- to 8-cup baking dish, top with 1 tablespoon melted butter or vegetable oil, and bake in a preheated 350°F oven until the top is lightly browned, about 15 minutes.

VARIATIONS

Ukrainian Kasha with Mushrooms (*Kasha mit Shveml*): Omit the noodles. In Step 2, before adding the *kasha,* add 8 ounces to 1 pound sliced mushrooms to the softened onions and sauté until tender, about 5 minutes.

Ukrainian Kasha with Sour Cream (*Kasha Paprikas*): Omit the noodles. In Step 3, before adding the liquid, stir 2 teaspoons sweet paprika into the *kasha* mixture. After fluffing the kasha in Step 5, stir in about $1/3$ cup sour cream.

❧ CORNMEAL ☙

The word *corn*, in England has historically been a generic term for any major grain (corn beef refers to the "grain"-sized salt used to pickle the meat). In North America, corn refers more specifically to Indian corn, what the English named maize. Shortly after Columbus's first voyage, Spanish explorers introduced corn, a native crop of southern Mexico, to Europe, and Portuguese vessels began shipping it from the Americas.

The Ottoman Turks, who preferred wheat and contemptuously rejected eating the new grain themselves, introduced the less-expensive corn to territories in Africa and the Balkans. Venetian and Dutch merchants quickly grasped the commercial potential of this American import and began peddling it, mainly in cornmeal form, throughout Europe. As usual with a new food, Jews, who were generally excluded from the guilds and owning land, frequently served as the middlemen for promoting and selling cornmeal. Thus, cornmeal generally entered the Jewish kitchen before that of most other Europeans, in a few areas becoming the predominant grain.

Corn, with its short growing period and lack of need to be threshed and winnowed, proved much less expensive and problematic than wheat or even barley, and was tastier and more versatile than the latter. Although corn did not fare very well in the climes of northern Europe, the milder conditions in the middle proved ideal for growing the new grain.

Today, corn is the third most planted field crop globally, following only wheat and rice, although only a very small percent of corn is consumed fresh (most of it is used for animal feed and processed into oil, syrup, starch, cold cereals, cornmeal, and various other things). Cornmeal can be adapted in numerous ways, including porridges (such as polenta and *mamaliga*), *gnocchi* (Italian dumplings), breads, soufflés, and even desserts.

What You Should Know: Cornmeal is ground whole untreated dried field corn kernels, and ranges in texture from fine to coarse. Stone-ground cornmeal, also called water-ground, is crushed by water-powered millstones, producing a coarser yet softer-textured meal. Whole-grain cornmeal is any cornmeal milled with the bran, germ, and endosperm; it is more perishable than cornmeal with the germ removed and should be stored in the freezer or refrigerator. (Some stone-ground cornmeal is also whole grain.) Although cornmeal without the germ has a longer shelf life, it lacks much of the flavor and nutrition of the whole-grain meal. To test if cornmeal contains the germ, pinch some of it. If it holds together, it contains at least some of the germ; if it falls apart, there is no germ.

The primary difference between white and yellow cornmeal is that the latter contains a larger amount of natural beta carotene due to the variety of corn. Otherwise, there is no perceptible difference in taste, texture, or nutrition between dishes made from either color meal.

GEORGIAN CORN CAKES

(Mchadi)

4 MEDIUM OR 8 SMALL PANCAKES P

Mchadi, *unleavened cornmeal pancakes, are a common sight at Georgian meals, where they are served as an accompaniment to a large variety of dishes, including stews and beans, and are used to scoop up gravy. Originally, the cakes were cooked in an ungreased earthenware skillet called a* ketsi *over hot coals, but a cast-iron skillet can be used. These sconelike cakes are similar to American johnnycakes and hoe cakes. Mchadi should be firm, to serve as a base for stews and other accompanying foods or as a substitute for bread. For the proper texture, use coarse-ground cornmeal. Serve with a vegetable stew, beans, cheese, plain yogurt, or butter.*

2 cups (8 ounces) coarse-ground cornmeal,
   preferably stone-ground
About ¹/₂ teaspoon table salt or I teaspoon
   kosher salt
About I¹/₂ cups water

1. In a medium bowl, combine the cornmeal and salt. Gradually stir in enough water to form a soft, sticky batter that can be formed into a ball. Cover and let stand for 10 minutes to soften the cornmeal, adding a little more water if necessary.

2. Divide batter into fourths or eighths. Wet your hands and shape into ¹/₂-inch-thick oval patties.

3. Heat a large cast-iron skillet over medium-low heat. (If you don't have a seasoned cast-iron skillet, heat a thin layer of vegetable oil in a metal or nonstick skillet.) Put the ovals in the skillet, cover, and cook, turning, until golden brown, about 5 minutes on each side. Keep warm in a 200°F oven for up to 1 hour until ready to serve. Serve warm.

ROMANIAN CORNMEAL MUSH

(Mamaliga)

ABOUT 7 CUPS,
OR 6 TO 8 SERVINGS   D OR P

Mamaliga *is the quintessential nostalgia food for a Romanian, memorialized in one of the most famous songs of the Yiddish theater, "Romania, Romania!" My older Romanian relatives remember* mamaliga *being made the old-fashioned way, stirred for an extensive time in a large copper pot over a low fire, and they insist that that is the only way to achieve the proper flavor. Having neither a copper pot nor the time and energy to cook* mamaliga *for hours, I find that about 20 minutes of cooking produces a superb flavor and texture.*

7 cups water
About 2¹/₂ teaspoons table salt or 5 teaspoons
   kosher salt
2 cups (8 ounces) medium- or coarse-ground
   cornmeal, preferably stone-ground
¹/₄ to ¹/₂ cup (¹/₂ to I stick) unsalted butter
   or margarine (optional)

1. In a large, heavy pot, bring the water to a boil over medium heat. Add the salt. Using a wooden spoon or whisk, add the cornmeal by releasing it from your fist in a slow, steady stream, stirring constantly to prevent lumps. (It can take up to 10 minutes to add all the cornmeal.) Cook, stirring constantly, until bubbly and slightly thickened, about 5 minutes. (Be careful, as the mush will occasionally sputter and can burn you. This is where a long-handled spoon comes in handy.)

2. Reduce the heat to low and simmer, stirring frequently, until creamy and thick and the mixture

begins to pull away from sides of the pan, about 20 minutes.

3. Remove from the heat. Dip a wooden spoon into cold water and use it to scrape the mamaliga from the sides and toward the center of the pot. (The mamaliga can be covered at this point and kept warm for up to 20 minutes to serve fresh. For soft mamaliga, stir in the butter and serve warm.

4. For firm mamaliga, place the pot over medium heat and let stand without stirring until the steam loosens the mamaliga from the bottom, 1 to 3 minutes.

5. Pour the hot mamaliga onto a wooden board at least 18 inches wide, or an inverted large baking sheet lined with parchment paper (dab a little mamaliga on the bottom corners to hold the paper in place), or a large serving platter. Spread into a rectangle $1/2$ to 1 inch thick and flatten the surface with the back of a wet spoon. Let stand until set, at least 2 hours.

6. Using thin kitchen twine or unflavored dental floss, cut into rectangles or squares. Use the slices like bread, as a bed for a stew or sauce, or fry in a little butter or margarine.

For a softer texture: Increase the water to 8 cups.

For a creamier texture: Reduce the water to 4 cups and add 4 cups milk.

Romanian Fried Cornmeal Mush (*Mamaliga Prajita*): Pour the mush into a greased 9-by-5-inch loaf pan and refrigerate until firm, at least 8 hours. Remove from the pan and cut into $1/2$-inch-thick slices. Fry in a little butter or oil, turning, until browned, about 5 minutes per side. If desired, serve with sour cream, yogurt, or jam. The slices can also be dipped into 3 lightly beaten eggs, then into 3 cups grated Parmesan cheese or cornmeal before frying. Some of my relatives commonly make a double batch of *mamaliga* and serve half of it warm, then pour the remaining porridge into a loaf pan for a different meal.

Romanian Cornmeal Mush with Cheese (*Mamaliga cu Bryndza*): Reduce the amount of salt in the main recipe to about $1^{1}/2$ teaspoons table salt or 1 tablespoon kosher salt. In Step 4, remove the *mamaliga* from the heat, add 1 cup (5 ounces) crumbled *bryndza* or other feta cheese; or 2 cups (8 ounces) shredded kashkaval, Cheddar, Muenster, or Monterey jack cheese; or $2/3$ cup (2 ounces) grated Parmesan cheese, and stir until melted. Serve warm as a porridge, or pour into a greased 8-cup baking dish or 9-by-5-inch loaf pan and bake in a preheated 350°F oven until lightly browned on top, about 20 minutes. Serve warm. For dinner, *bryndza* and *mamaliga* are sometimes accompanied with wine, always red, classically Moldavian dry Codru, Negru, Romaneshti, and Taraclia.

Romanian Baked Cheese-Layered Cornmeal Mush (*Mamaliga cu Lapte*): Spread one-third of the mush in a greased 8-cup baking dish, top with 1 cup (4 ounces) shredded kashkaval, Cheddar, Muenster, or Monterey jack cheese. Spread with half of the remaining mush, then another 1 cup cheese, and finally with the remaining mush. Drizzle with 2 tablespoons olive oil or melted butter and bake in a preheated 350°F oven until set and lightly browned on top, about 20 minutes.

Mamaliga

Since the time of the Etruscans, the peasants of the Italian and Balkan Peninsulas subsisted on grain porridges called *puls*, most notably of barley and millet, which were cheaper and easier to make than bread. After the Romans subdued the northern part of the Balkan Peninsula in 106 C.E., then called Dacia and now known as Romania, they shifted the staple of the diet of the native population to *puls*, which remained the region's primary form of sustenance for centuries.

Thus, in the sixteenth century when other conquerors, the Ottoman Turks, brought cornmeal to the Balkans for the peasants (keeping the preferred wheat for themselves), the new grain readily fit into the lifestyle. By the beginning of the eighteenth century, versatile and inexpensive cornmeal had replaced the traditional grains for the masses of Romania and northern Italy.

It is probable, due to the Turkish control of the Balkans, that cornmeal mush first became widespread in Romania before achieving that status in Italy. Indeed, Italians originally called corn *grano turco* (Turkish grain) and *sorgo turco* (Turkish sorghum). Whichever country came first, this hearty porridge—called *mamaliga* ("food of gold") in Romania, polenta ("grain meal," related to *puls*) in Italy, *puliszka* in Hungary, *kulesha* in Ukraine, and *gomi* in Georgia—became the staple of this stretch of land.

Preparing cornmeal mush became a daily morning ritual in Romanian and northern Italian households, complete with its own equipment and traditions. A special concave copper or cast-iron cauldron called a *ceaun* (*paiolo* in Italy) was typically set on a *pirostrii* (iron tripod) or hung from a chain in the center (hearth) of the main room. There, housewives followed the traditional ritual: Rising very early, they boiled water over an open wood fire, added the right amount of salt to the pot, then very gradually dribbled in a calculated measure of cornmeal, while continuously stirring, customarily in only one direction, with a *melesteu* (*bastoni* or *bastoncino* in Italy), a special 1-inch-thick long-handled wooden stick.

If the cornmeal is added too quickly or cooks at too high a temperature, it will seize up, resulting in a gummy texture and raw flavor. Constant stirring is necessary for even cooking and to prevent the dreaded lumps, whimsically called *shikshalach* in Yiddish. After all of the cornmeal was successfully doled into the pot, the porridge was continuously stirred over low heat until thickened, the long, slow cooking producing a smooth, creamy texture and sweet flavor. *Mamaliga* that is cooked for too short a time tends to be coarse, bitter, and not tender. The lower the proportion of liquid and the longer the cooking time, the firmer the texture. Romanian mush tends to be softer than the dense-style polenta preferred in the Veneto region of Italy.

When the steaming mass had achieved the desired consistency, bowls of the soft, hot mush were served for breakfast. The cauldron was hauled across the room and its remaining contents poured onto a special smooth wooden board called a *madia* (in Italy, polenta was poured onto the same board used to make pasta, called a *spianatoia*), and the thick mixture, which firms as it cools, was cut using a string or wire. Soft foods, such as goat cheese, unbaked cinnamon rolls, and *mamaliga*, tend to stick to knives, but a long piece of dental floss or twine held taut pulls through easily and straight.

Mamaliga was traditionally and is still served for breakfast, lunch, and dinner, variously in the form of a warm porridge, a casserole, in croquettes, and sliced as a bread substitute. There are numerous variations and ways of serving the basic *mamaliga*. Some cooks enhance it by stirring in cheese or buttermilk, while many prefer the pure corn flavor. For breakfast, it is usually served hot with butter, sour cream, yogurt, kashkaval cheese, honey, or fruit preserves. For lunch, slices of fresh *mamaliga* are served with a stew, such as *guvetch*, or cooked beans, helpful for both transporting the food and sopping up the sauce. Leftover slices are commonly fried. Dinner might consist of slices of *mamaliga*, along with a green salad, served with a selection of raw or fried onions, scallions, cheese, and sour cream, the firm pieces of mush performing like bread.

Ironically, cornmeal mush, once a peasant dish, has recently become popular fare in chic restaurants, as it melds with many flavors, both delicate and robust. Avoid buying the exorbitantly priced products labeled "polenta." Instead, use a medium-grind cornmeal, preferably stone-ground. Too finely ground a meal produces a gummy texture; too coarse produces a gritty texture. Salt is necessary not only for flavor but also to slow the cooking of the starch, ensuring that the outer part of the grain does not overcook before the inner part is done. "Instant polenta" lacks the flavor and texture of the real thing.

DUMPLINGS AND PASTA

❦ · ❦

Boiling balls or strips of dough in a liquid may, in hindsight, seem an obvious culinary technique. In actuality, it was a revolutionary idea. Before the Middle Ages, European dough dishes were fried or baked, not cooked in water. Then, in medieval Italy, a new dough-based food began appearing, the dumpling.

Early medieval Italian records mention "*maccheroni*" (from the Italian for "paste"), referring not to pasta but to dumplings made from "bread paste" and boiled in stews and soups as a way to extend those dishes as well as to utilize stale bread. By the twelfth century, Italians had introduced these rudimentary bread dumplings to southern Germany, where they were called *knodel* (akin to Old High German *knoto*, "knot"), the dumplings then moving to northern Germany, where they were called *kloese*, or *klosse*. Later, they spread across Europe, becoming known as *knedliky* in Czech, quenelles in French, and *knaidel* or *knaidlach* in eastern Yiddish.

Rabbi Meir of Rothenburg (1215–93), the supreme Ashkenazic rabbinical authority of his time, wrote of the consumption of dumplings, so they must have been well ensconced in the Jewish kitchens of his native southern Germany by the thirteenth century. Before the popularization of the potato in northeastern European communities in the nineteenth century, dumplings along with other starch dishes (dark breads, gruels, kugels, and pancakes) formed the bulk of the diet and became signature elements of Ashkenazic cuisine. On the other hand, boiled dumplings were rarely, if ever, found among Sephardic and Middle Eastern Jews (except those living in Iraq and Iran), who preferred to eat fried and baked pastries.

Beginning in the fourteenth century, as Italy and then other parts of Europe moved out of the Middle Ages, flour, including semolina, was increasingly substituted for the bread in dumplings. The dumplings often consisted of loose, rudimentary batters, such as the German *einlauf* ("run-in") and *ribbles* ("to rub"), the Austrian *nockerlach* ("little thumps"), and the Bavarian *spaetzle* ("little sparrows"). The batter was dropped, cut, or squeezed directly into boiling broth or water, producing dumplings that were lighter but much more fragile and therefore less versatile than rolled and dried pasta.

Soon, larger, more substantial flour dumplings became widespread—sometimes filled with chopped cooked vegetables or pieces of fruit as an efficient way to stretch limited resources or use up leftovers. In late spring and summer, seasonal soft cheese was commonly incorporated into dumplings. Before long, during the eight days of Passover, housewives, searching for ways to feed their family using the limited ingredients permitted and available during the holiday, incorporated matza meal into their dumplings, resulting in one of the Ashkenazic crowning culinary triumphs, *matse knaidlach* (matza balls). In the eighteenth century, potatoes and cornmeal became popular dumpling components. Today, central Europeans remain the world's most dumpling consumers.

Pasta, on the other hand (boiled dough that, unlike dumplings, has been kneaded and rolled, giving it greater strength and elasticity), appeared relatively late in the West. It originated in China, then it was recorded in the fifth century in central Asia, in the tenth century in Spain and Sicily, in the thirteenth century in mainland Italy, and in the fourteenth century in central and eastern Europe.

Once reaching the West, however, noodles became an integral element of cookery, both an everyday and celebration food. In the Middle East, noodles were originally added as an extender to soups and stews or sweetened with sugar as a dessert. Later, they were mixed with legumes and rice or added to omelets. By the tenth century, the Arabs had introduced noodles to Spain, and they quickly found a place in the Sephardic kitchen, where their culinary uses expanded with the addition of cheese and a variety of savory sauces. The generic Ladino term *macaron* was applied to all dried pasta, while *fila* was generally used for fresh egg noodles.

The first mention of noodles in a European Jewish source outside of Spain appeared in the writings of the Italian rabbi Kalonymous ben Kalonymous (1286–1328), who included macaroni and *tortelli* in a list of twenty-seven dishes served at a fantasy Purim feast. Soon, Italians began developing various complex and sophisticated pasta dishes, including those intended for serving on the Sabbath and holidays. Italian Jews, when adding cheese, used water instead of the then prevalent meat broth to cook the pasta, producing a daintier dish. In other instances, bread crumbs were substituted for Parmesan cheese. By the fourteenth century, noodles had reached the German Jewish kitchen. Within a century, *lukshen* (eastern Yiddish for "noodles") had become a mainstay in eastern Europe, introduced to the populace either by the Tartars, who overran the area beginning in 1240, or by German Jews from their contact with Polish Jews.

Sephardim, who prefer serving rice for special occasions, generally use fewer noodles, primarily employing them in simple baked dishes with cheese or a tomato sauce. On the other hand, noodles became ubiquitous at Ashkenazic Sabbath, holiday, and wedding tables, most notably in soups and kugels. Filled pasta, such as the Italian *tortelli*, eastern European kreplach, Sephardic *calsones*, and Bukharan *manti* became traditional holiday fare.

❧ DUMPLINGS ❧

Basic dumplings are simple doughs, with the kind of starch used varying from region to region. Adding fat to the dough produces a more tender texture; using semolina or matza meal in place of regular flour results in a lighter dumpling, as does adding eggs or baking powder. Some dumplings are flavored with herbs or cheese, others with sugar or fruit. The amount of liquid in the dumpling varies slightly depending on the moistness in the starch.

When making dumplings, always cook one test dumpling completely to ensure the consistency is right. If it falls apart, add a little extra flour or other starch to the dough or check that the water is not boiling too rapidly, which would cause the dumpling to break apart. If the dumpling is too heavy, add a little more liquid or egg white to the dough.

Use a large, broad pot to cook dumplings, allowing room for expansion. Avoid crowding the dough balls in the pot. Always add dumplings to plenty of gently boiling liquid, boil briefly to set the batter, then reduce the heat to a simmer. Too rapid a boil will cause soft doughs to disintegrate or the eggs to toughen. The dumplings can be cooked directly in a soup or stew or simmered in water and added to the soup later. Dumplings cooked in soups and stews absorb flavors from the liquid, while slightly thickening the liquid with the starches they release. Dumplings meant to expand during cooking (usually containing yeast or baking powder) are simmered covered and without lifting the lid, while most others, especially those that are similar to pasta (such as German *spaetzle* and Hungarian *galuska*) and cheese dumplings, are cooked uncovered. Although the batter can be (and sometimes should be) prepared ahead of time and refrigerated, dumplings are usually best when cooked just before serving.

Plain dumplings possess little intrinsic flavor, but often serve as a starting point for other flavors; top them with butter, grated cheese, tomato sauce, or gravy for a hearty side dish or appetizer. Or, float them on top of a bowl of soup or stew for a first or main course.

CZECH BREAD DUMPLINGS

(*Houskove Knedliky*)

ABOUT 12 DUMPLINGS

Zdenka Langer, an elderly member of my synagogue and a proud Czech, was renowned for her goulash, schnitzels, and numerous dumpling dishes made from longtime family recipes. She claimed that the writer Franz Kafka frequented her parents' home in Prague to eat her grandmother's dumplings. I can attest that, although Czech food can be rather heavy, Mrs. Langer's dumplings were always light, illustrating why Czechoslovakia was considered the dumpling capital of the world. For bread dumplings, Mrs. Langer maintained that the best results call for lean yeast bread containing no fat, eggs, or sweetener, and that the bread should not be too old, or a stale flavor would dominate.

The basis of these dumplings is a bread paste prepared in one of two ways: either by making bread crumbs or by soaking slices of bread in liquid, then mashing them into a paste. They are commonly served with a stew and some form of cabbage: braised, sweet-and-sour, soup, or sauerkraut.

4 cups cubed day-old lean yeast bread, such as
  water challah, French bread, or Italian bread,
  without the crust
$1/4$ cup vegetable oil or unsalted butter, softened
1 onion, minced
$1/4$ to $1/2$ cup finely chopped fresh parsley, chives,
  or sage
3 large eggs
1 tablespoon milk or water
1 teaspoon caraway seeds or dash of ground
  cloves, ground ginger, or freshly grated nutmeg
About 1 teaspoon table salt or 2 teaspoons
  kosher salt
About $1/4$ teaspoon ground black pepper

1. Preheat the oven to 300°F. In a food processor, grind the bread to form coarse crumbs. Spread over a large baking sheet and bake, stirring occasionally, until dry, about 20 minutes. Let cool. Alternatively, soak the bread in cold water to cover until soft but not mushy, about 5 minutes. Drain. Squeeze out the excess liquid.

2. In a medium skillet, heat the oil over medium heat. Add the onion and sauté until soft and translucent, about 5 minutes. Add the parsley and stir until wilted, about 30 seconds. Let cool.

3. In a medium bowl, beat together the eggs and milk. Stir in the bread crumbs or soaked bread and mash into a loose paste. Add the onion mixture, caraway, salt, and pepper and stir with a fork until well blended and the consistency of a soft dough. (Do not do this in a food processor, as it will become too smooth.) If the mixture is too loose, stir in 1 to 2 tablespoons unbleached all-purpose flour. Cover and let stand at room temperature for 1 hour.

4. Bring a large pot of lightly salted water to a gentle boil. Using 2 moistened soup spoons or your hands moistened with water, form the batter into 1-inch balls. Drop the dumplings into the water, stirring gently to prevent sticking. (Do not crowd the dumplings. If your pot is big enough, you can cook all of the dumplings at once, but for most contemporary pots, it is best to do this in 2 batches.) Cover, reduce the heat to low, and simmer until the dumplings are firm, about 15 minutes. Using a slotted spoon, transfer to a bowl. Serve immediately.

KNEDLIKY

It is a rare Czech meal that fails to include some sort of dumpling, either in soup, as a side dish, or even for dessert. Czech dumplings may be made from bread, flour, semolina, potatoes, matza, cheese, liver, or even sweet bread dough. Bread dumplings are the most ancient form, designed to utilize stale leftover loaves. Bread dumplings are somewhat lighter than the other prominent Czech potato dumpling. Some cooks mix a little semolina into the dough for firmness, but this also produces a heavier dumpling. Dumplings are commonly eaten with a spoon; by tradition, no Czech will cut up a dumpling with a knife, as this is said to spoil the flavor (although I haven't been able to tell the difference).

GERMAN FRIED DUMPLINGS WITH FRUIT

(Schnitzelkloese)

6 TO 8 DUMPLINGS   D OR P

Germans commonly simmered dumplings (often containing fruit) in stews for weekday meals or slow cooked them in Sabbath stews or tzimmes (vegetable and fruit stews). These dumplings were whimsically called Shabbos ganif ("Sabbath thief") because they stole flavor from the liquid in which they were cooked. Soon, some cooks began cooking the dumplings with fruits without the stew to create a different flavor.

I adapted this recipe from a pair of 1960s Israeli cookbooks, one of which called for adding 8 ounces of chopped suet (beef fat) to the batter and frying the dumplings in chicken fat. The other source offered a lighter version, more appropriate for a vegetarian book. Schnitzel, the German word for "little cut," generally refers to any breaded and fried boneless meat. Here, it denotes that the dumplings are fried before being baked in a pan of water. As the name kloese *indicates, the dish is from northern Germany. These dumplings were traditionally made on Friday and baked overnight in a low oven to serve warm for Sabbath lunch alongside a Sabbath stew or other main course, or sprinkled with additional sugar and eaten as dessert.*

2 cups unbleached all-purpose flour

1/4 cup sugar

1 tablespoon baking powder

About 1/2 teaspoon table salt or 1 teaspoon kosher salt

Dash of ground ginger or freshly grated nutmeg

3/4 cup (6 ounces) vegetable shortening or margarine, chilled

About 1/2 cup water or milk

Margarine or vegetable oil for frying

2 to 4 cups (12 ounces to 1 1/2 pounds) coarsely chopped mixed dried fruit, such as apples, apricots, dates, peaches, pears, and prunes

1. Preheat the oven to 200°F. Grease a deep 3- to 4-quart heatproof casserole.

2. In a medium bowl, combine the flour, sugar, baking powder, salt, and ginger. Using your fingertips, a pastry blender, or 2 dinner knives, cut the shortening into the flour mixture to the size of coarse crumbs. Stir in enough water to make a dough thick enough to mold. Do not overmix.

3. Using 2 moistened soup spoons or your hands moistened with water, form the batter into 6 to 8 equal portions and form into balls.

4. In a large skillet, melt the margarine over medium heat. Add the dumplings and fry, turning, until browned on all sides, about 6 to 8 minutes.

5. Place in the prepared casserole. (For a sweeter dish, sprinkle with 1/4 to 1/2 cup additional sugar.) Add the fruit and boiling water to cover. Tightly cover the dish and bake for at least 4 hours or preferably overnight. Serve warm.

CENTRAL EUROPEAN CHEESE DUMPLINGS

(Topfenknodel)

ABOUT 16 DUMPLINGS,
5 TO 6 SERVINGS   D

A distant relative of mine, originally from the Polish-German-Czechoslovakian border area (previously part of the Austrian Empire), was an exceptional cook but refused to share her recipes, claiming that either the dish would not turn out as good as hers did, in which case she would be blamed, or it would be as good or better, in which case her own cooking skills would be diminished. Among her repertoire were light, slightly tangy cheese dumplings. No one, however, ever wrangled the real recipe from her. Fortunately, I found a number of cooperative cooks who were more than willing to share their recipes with me.

These popular dumplings are called topfenknodel *in Austria and Germany,* turos gomboc *in Hungary,* syrove knedliky *in Czech, and* kluski *in Poland.* Topfen, *also called quark in German, is a thick, slightly tangy central European curd cheese popular for making dumplings, spreads, and toppings. Since* topfen *is generally unavailable in America, a little cream cheese is added to the pot cheese to approximate the original texture and flavor. You can substitute farmer cheese for the pot cheese, but first wrap it in several layers of paper towels, then let it drain for about 10 minutes to extract some of the excess moisture. Do not use cottage cheese, which contains too much liquid and is too firm. My grandmother served savory cheese dumplings on Shavuot as an appetizer, accompanied with sour cream or browned bread crumbs (2 cups fresh bread crumbs sautéed in 6 tablespoons butter until golden), or a sweetened version as dessert.*

1¾ cups (14 ounces) pot or soft goat cheese
¼ cup (2 ounces) cream cheese or mascarpone, softened
¼ cup grated onion
1 teaspoon table salt or 2 teaspoons kosher salt
2 large eggs, lightly beaten
2 tablespoons unsalted butter, softened
About ¾ cup semolina flour, farina (not quick-cooking), or matza meal

1. In a food processor or blender, or with an electric mixer, combine the cheeses, onion, and salt. Add the eggs and beat until smooth. Beat in the butter, 1 tablespoon at a time. Stir in enough of the semolina to produce a firm dough. (Getting the moisture level right so that the batter holds together in your hand is the tricky part.) Cover and refrigerate for at least 2 hours or overnight. (The semolina absorbs moisture from the batter and firms it.)

2. Bring a large pot of lightly salted water to a gentle boil. Using 2 moistened soup spoons or your hands moistened with water, form the batter into 1½-inch balls.

3. Drop the dumplings in the water in batches and stir gently to prevent sticking. Reduce the heat and simmer, uncovered, until they expand and rise to the surface, about 15 minutes. Using a slotted spoon, transfer to a bowl. Serve warm. To keep warm or reheat, place in a 200°F oven.

VARIATIONS

Austrian Jam-Filled Cheese Dumplings (*Gefulte Topfenknodel*): In the dumpling batter, omit the onion and add 3 to 5 tablespoons sugar and, if desired, 1 to 2 teaspoons grated lemon zest. Press a deep indentation into the cheese balls, fill with about

¼ teaspoon *lekvar* (prune butter) or other jam (about ¼ cup total), and press the dough around the filling to enclose. Cook as above. Serve with sweetened whipped cream, cinnamon sugar, or jam.

Romanian Cheese-Cornmeal Dumplings (Papanush): Omit the onion and substitute ½ to ¾ cup fine-grind yellow cornmeal for the semolina.

HUNGARIAN POTATO DUMPLINGS

(*Shlishkes*)

6 TO 8 SERVINGS   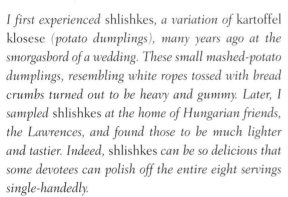

I first experienced shlishkes, *a variation of* kartoffel klosese *(potato dumplings), many years ago at the smorgasbord of a wedding. These small mashed-potato dumplings, resembling white ropes tossed with bread crumbs turned out to be heavy and gummy. Later, I sampled* shlishkes *at the home of Hungarian friends, the Lawrences, and found those to be much lighter and tastier. Indeed,* shlishkes *can be so delicious that some devotees can polish off the entire eight servings single-handedly.*

After the potato became popular in Europe in the nineteenth century, numerous versions of potato dumplings appeared. Shlishkes, *similar to the Italian* gnocchi di patate, *were once usually reserved for Hungarian and eastern European special occasions, as they required a bit of time to prepare. The secret to potato dumplings is to use a starchy potato and to keep the amount of flour to a minimum. Too much flour produces a heavy dumpling; too little flour produces mushy or unstable dumplings. Bread crumbs provide a nondairy substitute for grated cheese as a topping. Without the bread crumbs, the dumplings are commonly* served with goulash and other stews or simply tossed with melted butter and sometimes grated Parmesan cheese.

> 3 pounds unpeeled baking (russet) potatoes, scrubbed
> 1 tablespoon table salt or 2 tablespoons kosher salt
> 1 tablespoon vegetable shortening or oil
> 2 large eggs, lightly beaten
> About 3 cups unbleached all-purpose flour
>
> **TOPPING:**
> ½ cup (1 stick) unsalted butter or margarine
> 1½ cups fresh bread crumbs
> Salt to taste
> 1 tablespoon sweet or hot paprika (optional)

1. Put the potatoes in a large pot and add cold water to cover by 1 inch and 1 teaspoon of the table salt or 2 teaspoons of the kosher salt. Bring to a low boil over high heat, reduce the heat to medium-low, and simmer until fork-tender in the center, about 25 minutes. Do not overcook. (Overcooking breaks down the starch cells, resulting in a gummy texture.) Drain.

2. While still warm, peel the potatoes, then press through a potato ricer and stir in the shortening, or return to the warm pot and mash with the shortening. You should have about 6 cups. Transfer the potatoes into a large bowl. Blend in the eggs and the remaining salt. Let cool.

3. Add just enough flour to the potatoes to make a soft dough that holds together. The amount of flour will vary based on the moisture in the potatoes and humidity in the air.

4. Divide the dough into 6 pieces. On a lightly floured surface, roll each piece into a ½-inch-thick rope. Cut each rope into 1-inch-long pieces and dust with flour. Shlishkes may be prepared to this point, arranged in a single layer on a baking sheet, and

refrigerated for up to 4 hours or covered and frozen for up to 2 months. Do not thaw before cooking, but slightly increase the cooking time.

5. To a large pot of salted boiling water, add the dough pieces in batches, stirring gently to prevent sticking. Reduce the heat to a low boil and cook, uncovered, until the dumplings float to the surface and become firm, about 5 minutes. (To test if the dumplings are done, cut one in half. If the center is dry, it is done.) Transfer to a colander and drain. Shlishkes may be prepared to this point a day ahead and stored in a large bowl of cold water.

6. To make the topping: In a large, heavy skillet, melt the butter over medium heat. Add the bread crumbs, salt, and, if using, the paprika and stir to blend. Add the shlishkes and sauté until the bread crumbs are golden brown and coat the dumplings. Alternatively, toss the boiled shlishkes with the melted butter, then with the bread crumbs, spread over a baking sheet, and bake in a preheated 400°F oven until golden brown, 10 to 12 minutes. Serve immediately.

VARIATIONS

Lighter *Shlishkes*: Omit the eggs, increase the oil to 2 tablespoons, and reduce the flour to about $2^{1}/4$ cups. Reduce the cooking time to about 3 minutes.

Fruit *Shlishkes*: On a lightly floured surface, roll out the dough into a $^{1}/4$-inch-thick rectangle, cut into 3-inch rounds (about 16), place a pitted prune or dried apricot in the center of each round, fold over the edges, and press to seal. Cook as in Step 5.

 PASTA AND NOODLES

The terms *pasta* (derived from the Greek "to sprinkle," originally referring to a barley gruel sprinkled with salt) and *noodles* (from a German word for an enriched grain mixture formed into long, thin rolls and forcefed to geese) are interchangeable, although the latter usually encompasses these dishes from central Europe and the Far East, while pasta refers to Italian versions.

In Europe, pasta is made from two main kinds of dough: semolina dough, made from coarse durum wheat flour mixed with water, and egg dough, made from finely ground flour mixed with eggs. The texture and taste of the two differ greatly. Semolina pasta has a more pronounced wheat flavor and is easier than egg dough to manipulate into myriad shapes, an attribute that would eventually become an art form in southern Italy. This pasta was the predominant form in Sicily and the southern Mediterranean, an area that for more than two millennia grew ample durum wheat. In the warm climate, the water-based pasta could be dried and stored for long periods of time without spoilage. Egg pasta predominated in northern Italy and most of Europe, which primarily produced common wheat. The dough is generally used fresh, rolled into thin, elastic sheets that are then cut. Not coincidentally, the widespread usage of egg noodles in Europe corresponded to the emergence of widespread chicken raising and the resultant availability and relative low cost of eggs.

Thanks to the regular interaction between the Jewish communities of Franco-Germany and Italy, egg noodles probably reached Ashkenazim by the fourteenth century, several centuries before the food became popular among non-Jewish Germans. Ashkenazim from western and central Europe called egg noodles *vermesel* (related to the Latin vermicelli, "little worms," referring to a dish consisting of fried strips of dough) and, later, *frimsel*. On the other hand, by the sixteenth century, Ashkenazim in eastern Europe adopted the term *lukshen*, derived from the Farsi word for noodles, *lakshah* ("slippery"), suggesting a Persian connection. Whatever they were called, egg noodles became an important component of Ashkenazic cooking and, in eastern Europe, soon surpassed dumplings in import.

Nevertheless, Ashkenazim never developed the same faculty of shaping and saucing their pasta as the Italians and Sephardim. Ashkenazic noodle dishes are basic, homey, and filling. Ashkenazim commonly grated the fresh dough into small pellets called *farfel* (Yiddish for "fallen away") or cut it into various fundamental shapes, most notably *plaetschen* (squares), *fingerhuetchen* (thimbles), and the relatively late *shpaetzlen*, or *farfalle* (from the Italian for "butterfly," referring to pasta squares pinched in the middle).

At dairy meals, noodles were commonly flavored with a little butter or curd cheese or served with scrambled eggs. Eastern Europeans also mixed noodles with the predominant Slavic grain, buckwheat, to create the classic *kasha varnishkes* (Ukranian Buckwheat and Noodles, page 377). By the fifteenth century, soup with noodles replaced *verimselish* (fried dough strips in honey) as the first course for the Ashkenazic Friday evening dinner, a role it still retains. Kreplach (Eastern European Cheese-Filled Pasta Triangles, page 408) and *pirogen*, filled pasta, were reserved for special occasions, most notably at the meal before Yom Kippur and on Purim and Shavuot.

What You Should Know: Although pasta and noodles in all shapes and sizes are now readily available in stores, some people still craft their own. Egg noodles and fresh egg pasta are relatively easy to make at home with a rolling pin, while fresh semolina pasta often requires a machine.

The secret to preventing pasta from sticking during cooking is simple: Cook it in plenty of rapidly boiling water (at least 6 cups water for every 4 ounces of pasta) and stir right after adding the pasta to the water. Just before placing the noodles in the water, add a generous $1/2$ teaspoon table salt or 1 teaspoon kosher salt for every 4 cups of water. Many Italians insist that the cooking water "should be salty like the sea." Without salt, the pasta tastes flat. Do not add oil to the cooking water, or it will coat the starch on the pasta, preventing the sauce from adhering. Do not overcook pasta; the preferable consistency is al dente (literally "to the tooth"), firm to the bite, with neither a raw core nor a gumminess or mushiness.

Fresh pasta cooks much faster than dried pasta, in 30 seconds to a few minutes, depending on the thinness and shape. The best way to determine doneness is to taste the pasta. Unless otherwise directed, do not rinse pasta, which removes the thin layer of starch on the surface that helps the sauce to adhere. For saucing noodles, a general rule is the wider the noodle, the heartier the sauce; the narrower the noodle, the more delicate the sauce. In any case, the best pasta dishes use just enough sauce to enhance the pasta, not overwhelm its flavor.

Egg Noodle Dough

(Lukshen)

ABOUT 1 POUND DOUGH

In the words of an old Yiddish proverb, "Love is grand, but love with lukshen *is even better." For several centuries, noodle making was a weekly ritual in many Jewish households. The dough was mixed by hand on a large wooden cutting board. (Wood provides more control while incorporating the eggs into the flour.) A little flour was sprinkled over the board, then the dough was gradually rolled as thinly as possible—typically, with a detached broom handle. The pasta sheet was then rolled up and sliced into the desired shape. (The predominant all-purpose Ashkenazic cutting instrument was a half-moon-shaped knife called a* hockmesser, *or a* mezzaluna *by Italians.) The strips were hung over the broomstick and chairs or scattered over a floured cloth to dry, a step that prevents the noodles from clumping together in the cooking water.*

Fresh egg noodles, though admittedly less convenient than store-bought brands, do taste better. The presence of eggs results in a firm, elastic dough and a rich, tender, flavorful noodle. If the dough is too dry, it will be difficult to roll out. As a general rule of thumb, use 4 ounces (about $^3/_4$ cup) flour for every large egg. Variations in egg size, flour moisture, and humidity, however, can slightly alter the measurements. When making dough in an electric pasta machine, add a little olive or vegetable oil (about $1^1/_2$ teaspoons for $2^1/_4$ cups of flour) to increase the dough's elasticity, making it easier to extrude. Humidity makes noodle dough harder to work with, so novices should not try it on rainy days.

> About $2^1/_2$ cups unbleached all-purpose flour
>
> 3 large eggs, at room temperature
>
> 1 teaspoon table salt or 2 teaspoons kosher salt

1. To make the dough by hand: Sift the flour onto a pasta board or another flat surface and make a well in the center. Put the eggs and salt in the well. Using the tips of your fingers or tines of a fork, lightly beat the eggs. Gradually work the flour into the eggs, always working from the sides of the flour (without breaking the walls, which lets the eggs seep out), until the mixture holds together, about 3 minutes.

To make the dough in a food processor: In the work bowl, pulse the flour and salt together. With the machine on, add the eggs through the feed tube and process until the dough forms a soft ball that cleans the sides of bowl, about 30 seconds. If the dough is too sticky, blend in a little more flour, 1 tablespoon at a time; if too dry, add a little water, $^1/_2$ teaspoon at a time.

2. Bring any remaining flour over the dough to cover it and form into a ball. Put the dough on a lightly floured surface and knead until smooth and elastic, about 10 minutes by hand; about 3 minutes if using a food processor. Wrap in plastic wrap and let rest at room temperature for 1 hour or in the refrigerator for at least 30 minutes or up to 4 hours. If the chilled dough becomes too firm to work, let stand at room temperature for 30 minutes.

3. To roll the dough by hand: Divide the dough into 2 to 4 pieces and dust lightly with flour. Cover the other pieces with plastic wrap or an inverted bowl and set aside. Place on a lightly floured surface and press with the palm of your hand to flatten into a $^1/_4$-inch-thick square. Roll out the dough using a rolling pin, pushing the dough away from you, then rotating it a quarter turn and pushing again, until as thin as possible, at least a $^1/_8$-inch thickness for noodles and a $^1/_{16}$-inch thickness for filled pasta. Repeat with the remaining dough.

To roll the dough with a pasta machine: Set the machine on the widest setting (No. 1) and run the dough through the rollers. Dust lightly with flour, fold lengthwise into thirds, and run through the rollers again. (This kneads the dough.) Repeat folding lengthwise and rolling until the dough is smooth, elastic, and dry, twice more. If the dough becomes too long to be manageable, cut it in half and proceed separately with each piece, covering the unused piece with plastic wrap. Reset the machine to the next narrowest setting. Lightly flour the dough and run through the machine without folding. Continue running through the machine on increasingly narrower settings until reaching the desired thickness, the narrowest setting on a machine with 6 settings, or the next to the narrowest on a machine with 8 settings.

4. To shape the noodles: Hang the dough sheets on a pasta rack or place on lightly floured towels until they begin to feel dry but are still supple, about 5 minutes. The drying time will vary according to the thickness of the dough and climatic conditions. Lightly dust the dough sheets with flour. Starting from a short side, roll up jelly-roll style. Cut crosswise into strips between $^1/_8$ inch (thin) and $^1/_2$ inch (fat) wide. Unroll the dough strips, arrange in a single layer on cloth towels or hang over a clean pole or broom handle, and let stand until dry, at least 1 hour. Store in an airtight container or plastic bag at room temperature for up to 2 days or in the freezer for up to 1 month.

ALSATIAN FRIED NOODLES

(*Frimsel*)

3 TO 4 SERVINGS D OR P

The Alsatian love of noodles, generally prepared rather simply, such as in this common Friday night dish, reflects a German influence on the culture.

8 ounces fresh or dried thin egg noodles
3 tablespoons unsalted butter or margarine
About $^1/_4$ teaspoon table salt or $^1/_2$ teaspoon kosher salt
Ground black pepper to taste
$^1/_4$ cup vegetable oil

1. Bring a large pot of water to a rapid boil and add salt. Add the noodles, stirring briefly to prevent sticking. Cook until tender, about 30 to 60 seconds for fresh noodles; 3 to 5 minutes for dried. Drain.

2. Melt the butter in a large skillet over medium heat. Add two-thirds of the noodles and season with the salt and pepper. Cook, stirring constantly, until coated and heated through, about 3 minutes. Spoon onto a hot serving plate and keep warm.

3. Add the oil to the skillet. Add the remaining noodles and cook, stirring frequently, until crisp and golden brown, 5 to 10 minutes. Sprinkle over top or stir into the buttered noodles. Serve warm.

VARIATIONS

Add some sesame seeds, poppy seeds, caraway seeds, cinnamon, or nutmeg in Step 2.

Noodle Ring: Toss all of the cooked noodles with the butter, pack into a $5^1/_2$-cup ring mold, place the mold into a larger baking dish, add boiling water to reach halfway up the side of the mold, and bake in a preheated 375°F oven for 20 minutes. Invert onto a serving platter.

ASHKENAZIC SWEET NOODLE PUDDING

(Lukshen Kugel)

9 SERVINGS · D OR P

Some foods transcend time and place and become representations of a culture. For Ashkenazim, noodle kugel is one. These beloved baked puddings have long been a common sight on Ashkenazic Sabbath and holiday tables and at various life-cycle events, such as brits, bar mitzvahs, and weddings, with any leftovers served cold the following day.

Originally, kugels were savory, always containing eggs to bind the noodles and commonly seasoned with the predominant Ashkenazic flavoring, onion. Cooks developed their own preferences in the type of noodle, some insisting on fine noodles and others favoring a medium or wide size. Noodle kugels could be baked alongside the cholent *(Sabbath stew) or cooked with schmaltz in a covered skillet on top of the fire. For dairy meals, butter was substituted for the chicken fat and curd cheese was frequently added, or, for a custardlike texture, sour cream was used.*

Then in 1802, the first factory to refine sugar beets was established in Silesia, Germany (now Poland), and soon additional ones were built in various other parts of central and eastern Europe, many operated by Jews. In those areas near sugar beet refineries, particularly Poland and parts of Germany, the price of sugar plummeted, and as with many other Ashkenazic foods, the inhabitants began sweetening their noodle kugels. Meanwhile, in places such as Hungary and Galicia, sugar remained expensive and kugels stayed savory. Although some of my Hungarian friends insist that a zaltz-un-feffer *(salt-and-pepper) kugel is the true recipe, I nevertheless prefer my noodle kugel the way my mother and grandmothers made it: rather sweet with the occasional bite of fruit. When I sample a piece,*

not only am I transported by the taste but also by nostalgia, its essence conjuring up many happy occasions.

I pound fresh or dried medium or fine egg noodles
$^1/_2$ cup (I stick) unsalted butter or margarine
6 large eggs, lightly beaten
$^2/_3$ to I cup sugar or $^1/_2$ cup sugar and $^1/_2$ cup honey
I teaspoon vanilla extract
$^1/_2$ teaspoon ground cinnamon or I tablespoon orange marmalade
About I teaspoon table salt or 2 teaspoons kosher salt
About $^3/_4$ cup raisins, chopped dried apricots, or chopped mixed dried fruit (optional)
About $^3/_4$ cup chopped almonds, hazelnuts, or walnuts (optional)
Additional ground cinnamon for sprinkling

1. Preheat the oven to 350°F. Grease a 9-by-13-inch baking dish.

2. Bring a large pot of water to a rapid boil and add salt. Add the noodles, stirring briefly to separate. Return to a boil and cook, stirring occasionally, until al dente (tender but firm), 30 to 60 seconds for fresh fine noodles or 3 to 5 minutes for dried fine noodles, 2 to 3 minutes for fresh medium noodles or 7 to 10 minutes for dried medium noodles. Drain. Add the butter and toss until it is melted and blended.

3. In a large bowl, beat together the eggs, sugar, vanilla, cinnamon, and salt. Stir in the noodles and, if using, the raisins and nuts. Pour into the prepared pan, leveling the top with a spoon. Sprinkle with the cinnamon.

4. Bake until golden brown, about 1 hour. Serve warm or at room temperature. Store in the refrigerator for up to 1 week. Noodle kugel freezes well. To freeze, slightly underbake the kugel (about 45 minutes), let cool, wrap securely in freezer wrap, and

store for up to 1 month. Thaw the kugel and bake in a preheated 350°F oven for about 15 minutes. Fully baked kugels can also be frozen for up to a month but are best served cold.

NOTE If the dried fruit is not moist, soak it in warm water to cover for 25 minutes, then drain.

VARIATIONS

For a custard texture: Increase the eggs to 8 and add 1 cup (8 ounces) softened cream cheese and 2 cups milk, or 1 cup milk and 1 cup apricot nectar.

Soufflé Noodle Kugel: Separate the eggs and add the yolks as above. Beat the egg whites until stiff but not dry and fold into the noodle mixture.

Noodle Kugel with Apples (*Zeesih Lukshen Kugel mit Apfels*): Add 3 to 6 peeled, cored, and chopped or coarsely grated tart apples tossed with 3 tablespoons fresh lemon juice. Alternatively, add 2 cups applesauce, 1 teaspoon fresh lemon juice, and, if desired, 1/2 cup sour cream.

Sweet Noodle-Cheese Kugel (*Zeesih Lukshen un Kaese Kugel*): Add 2 cups (1 pound) farmer cheese, ricotta, or small-curd cottage cheese and 2 cups (16 ounces) sour cream or 1 cup (8 ounces) softened cream cheese. Or, add 1 cup (8 ounces) farmer or cottage cheese, 1 cup (8 ounces) sour cream, and 1/2 cup (4 ounces) cream cheese.

Galician Salt-and-Pepper Noodle Pudding (*Zaltz-un-Feffer Lukshen Kugel*): Omit the sugar, cinnamon, and raisins. Increase the table salt to about 2 teaspoons or the kosher salt to about 3 1/2 teaspoons and add about 1 teaspoon ground black pepper or to taste and 2 to 3 chopped onions sautéed in 1/2 cup vegetable oil (instead of the butter) until soft and translucent.

SEPHARDIC TOASTED NOODLES

(*Fideos Tostados*)

6 TO 8 SERVINGS

This recipe, featuring fried noodles and tomatoes, is one of the most common Sephardic ways of preparing pasta, so popular that it is frequently called simply fideos. *The noodles are first sautéed in oil, then simmered in enough liquid to soften, like risotto and paella. Many Sephardim serve* fideos *for Sukkot dinner accompanied with eggplant casserole and* fasoulias (*green beans*). *My friend Emily Levy garnishes this dish with diced avocados and, at dairy meals, dollops of yogurt or sour cream. Sephardim love this dish reheated. To reheat, cover and bake in a preheated 300°F oven for about 25 minutes.*

21 ounces plum tomatoes, peeled, seeded, and chopped (see page 291), about 3 cups

About 1 teaspoon sugar

About 1 teaspoon table salt or 2 teaspoons kosher salt

About 1/4 teaspoon ground black pepper

1 tablespoon minced onion (optional)

1 tablespoon minced green bell pepper (optional)

4 cups Vegetable Stock (page 115) or water

1/2 cup olive oil or vegetable oil

1 pound dried *fideos* (fine coiled noodles; do not break apart) or 1 pound dried angel hair pasta, broken into 1-inch pieces

1/3 cup chopped fresh cilantro or parsley (optional)

1. Put the tomatoes, sugar, salt, pepper, and, if using, the onion and bell pepper in a medium saucepan, cover, and simmer over low heat, stirring

occasionally, until tender, about 15 minutes. Stir in the stock.

2. In a large saucepan, heat the oil over medium heat. Add the noodles and fry until golden brown on both sides, about 5 minutes. Using a slotted spoon, transfer the noodles to a bowl. Alternatively, instead of frying the noodles, put the fideos in a 9-by-13-inch baking pan, brush both sides with the oil, and bake in a preheated 350°F oven, turning once halfway through, until golden brown on both sides, about 15 minutes.

3. Transfer the tomato mixture to the large saucepan and bring to a boil. Add the noodles to the pan, cover tightly, reduce the heat to low, and simmer, stirring occasionally to prevent sticking and to break up the coils, about 15 minutes. Or, bake, covered and stirring occasionally, in a pre-heated 350°F oven for about 25 minutes.

4. Uncover and continue cooking or baking, stirring frequently, until the liquid is absorbed and the noodles are tender. If using, sprinkle with the cilantro. Serve warm.

VARIATIONS

Sephardic Noodles with Beans and Spinach (*Fideos con Fijones*): In Step 2, before returning the noodles to the pan, stir in 2 cups cooked and drained white or black beans and 1 to 2 cups chopped cooked spinach.

Sephardic Noodles with Cheese (*Fideos con Queso*): Just before serving, sprinkle the dish with 1 1/2 cups (about 6 ounces) coarsely shredded mild firm white or yellow cheese or 1/2 cup grated Parmesan cheese.

FIDEOS

The prevailing Sephardic form of pasta is *fideos* (also spelled *fidellos* and *fideyos* and, in Greece, *fideikos*), a word derived from the Arabic word *fidawsh* ("to swell, or grow," as the noodles expand in boiling water). An import from North Africa, *fideos* were recorded in Spain as early as the thirteenth century. For generations thereafter, women would gather together to sit and chat while churning out an enormous batch of egg pasta to be stored for an extended period.

In some places, among Sephardim, this was done on the fast day of Tisha b'Av, providing a productive way to pass the time and make use of the warm weather for drying the pasta. Each woman would roll pieces of dough between her thumb and forefinger, creating very thin, inch-long tear-shaped noodles, called *sheriya* in Arabic. The noodles were sun-dried on large metal sheets, then stored in metal containers.

Dried *fideos*, available in Middle Eastern stores, consist of very fine coils of noodles, similar to angel hair pasta. Originally, these noodles were utilized only as an extender for soups, a role they continue to play. *Fideos* are also boiled and served as a side dish for stew, baked with cheese, topped with various sauces, or simply tossed with a little butter, salt, and pepper.

ITALIAN COLD PASTA WITH TOMATOES

(Tagliolini col Pomadori)

5 TO 6 SERVINGS

In 1516, the Venetians established the first imposed Jewish sector in Europe, called a ghetto, *named after the foundry next to which this Jewish area was located. There were soon walled-in Jewish sections throughout most of the Italian states, and from these ghettos— caused by the isolation—come some of the most authentic Jewish dishes. During the sixteenth century, many Conversos (forcibly converted Jews) who had managed to escape from Spain and Sicily traveled to northern Italy, where they introduced new culinary uses for the tomato, resulting in the first Jewish-Italian tomato dishes. In this one from Venice, meant for Sabbath lunch, the pasta is tossed with a tomato sauce and served at room temperature.*

SAUCE:

1/4 cup olive oil

1 onion, chopped

2 to 3 cloves garlic, minced

1 to 2 jalapeño chilies, seeded and minced,
  or 1/8 teaspoon cayenne (optional)

2 pounds ripe plum tomatoes, peeled, seeded, and
  chopped (see page 291), about 4 cups

1 to 3 teaspoons sugar

1 to 2 tablespoons red wine vinegar

1/4 cup chopped fresh parsley

About 1 1/2 teaspoons table salt or 1 tablespoon
  kosher salt

Ground black pepper to taste

Egg Noodle Dough (page 392), rolled and cut
  1/8 inch wide, or 1 pound fresh or dried
  tagliolini/taglierini or other thin egg noodles,
  such as linguine

1. To make the sauce: In a large saucepan, heat the oil over medium heat. Add the onion, garlic, and, if using, the chilies and sauté until soft, about 5 minutes. Add the tomatoes, sugar, vinegar, and, if using, the cayenne, and simmer, stirring occasionally, until the tomatoes begin to soften, about 15 minutes. Stir in the parsley, salt, and pepper. Set aside.

2. Bring a large pot of water to a rapid boil and add salt. Add the noodles, stirring briefly to separate. Return to a boil and cook, stirring occasionally, until al dente (tender but firm), 2 to 3 minutes for fresh pasta, 7 to 10 minutes for dried. Drain.

3. Pour the sauce over the noodles and toss to coat. Let cool. Serve at room temperature.

VARIATION

If you prefer fresh tomatoes prepared like a salsa, do not cook the sauce. Instead, omit the onion, mix the remaining sauce ingredients together, and let stand at room temperature for about 2 hours before tossing with the noodles.

NOTE *Tagliolini*, also called *taglierini*, are thin, flat noodles, commonly about 1/8 inch wide—slightly flatter and thinner than linguine. They are usually served with thin, lightly flavored sauces or vegetable-based sauces. If you cannot find them, substitute the slightly thicker linguine.

Italian Cold Pasta in Egg-Lemon Sauce

(Tagliolini con Brodo Brusca)

5 TO 6 SERVINGS

For many centuries, Italians ate only hot pasta. When Italian Jews wanted pasta on the Sabbath, however, it was necessary to find versions that would taste good at room temperature, and thus emerged the first cold pasta salads. This pasta dish comes from the ghetto of Pitigliano in southern Tuscany, which was established in 1608. It is usually served cold for Saturday lunch, but is also featured at the meal before Yom Kippur, providing extra carbohydrates and protein for the fast. The intensity of the lemon flavor heightens when served at room temperature. You can omit the flour to make a lighter but less stable sauce.

SAUCE:

2 large eggs

2 large egg yolks

About ¹/₃ cup fresh lemon juice

2 tablespoons unbleached all-purpose flour,
    or 1 tablespoon cornstarch

About 1 teaspoon table salt or 2 teaspoons
    kosher salt

2 teaspoons sugar (optional)

2 cups boiling Vegetable Stock (page 115)
    or water

Egg Noodle Dough (page 392), rolled and cut
    ¹/₈ inch wide, or 1 pound fresh or dried
    tagliolini/taglierini or other thin egg noodles,
    such as linguine

¹/₄ cup extra-virgin olive oil

2 tablespoons chopped fresh parsley for garnish
    (optional)

1. To make the sauce: In a nonreactive 4-cup saucepan, beat together the eggs, egg yolks, and lemon juice. In a small bowl, whisk a little of the egg mixture into the flour to make a paste, then stir the paste back into the egg mixture. Add the salt and, if using, the sugar. (The ingredients can also be combined in a blender.)

2. Gradually beat in the hot stock. Cook over medium-low heat, stirring constantly with a wooden spoon or whisk, until smooth and thickened to the consistency of a thin mayonnaise, about 8 minutes. Do not boil. Remove from the heat and continue to stir for 1 minute. Pour into a bowl, press a piece of plastic wrap against the surface, and let cool. (The sauce can be stored in the refrigerator for up to 3 days.)

3. Bring a large pot of water to a rapid boil and add salt. Add the noodles, stirring briefly to separate. Return to a boil and cook, stirring occasionally, until al dente (tender but firm), 2 to 3 minutes for fresh pasta, 7 to 10 minutes for dried. Drain. Toss the noodles with the oil and let cool for at least 30 minutes.

4. Mix the noodles with the sauce. If using, sprinkle with the parsley. Serve at room temperature.

SEPHARDIC BAKED NOODLES WITH CHEESE

(Fila con Queso)

This dish was among several that I was offered while interviewing a Sephardic family in Brooklyn. As with many cooks, the elderly woman, the Greek-born grandmother of the family, never used recipes but relied on her senses and instincts instead, a technique she called a ojo ("with the eye"). Her "handful" certainly differed from mine. So, as she added "a pinch of this" or "a handful of that," I caught it in a small bowl and measured it to determine a more exact quantity.

Unlike Italian pasta-and-cheese casseroles (or American macaroni and cheese), this Sephardic version, also called pastichio *by the Greeks, uses eggs as the thickening agent rather than a starch, giving it a custardlike texture. I prefer a combination of cheeses for added flavor complexity. You can substitute 1 pound ziti, elbow macaroni, or spaghetti for the noodles.*

Egg Noodle Dough (page 392), rolled and cut $1/4$-inch wide, or 1 pound fresh or dried medium egg noodles

SAUCE:

4 large eggs, lightly beaten

$1/2$ cup milk or light cream

$3/4$ cup (6 ounces) cream cheese, $3/4$ cup crumbled feta cheese, and $1/4$ cup (1 ounce) shredded kashkaval cheese; or 2 cups (1 pound) farmer cheese and 1 cup (8 ounces) softened cream cheese; or 1 cup (4 ounces) grated aged kashkaval or other sharp hard cheese

About $1/2$ teaspoon table salt or 1 teaspoon kosher salt

Ground white or black pepper to taste

1 tablespoon unsalted butter (optional)

1. Preheat the oven to 350°F. Grease a 9-by-13-inch baking dish.

2. Bring a large pot of water to a rapid boil and add salt. Add the noodles, stirring briefly to separate. Return to a boil and cook, stirring occasionally, until al dente (tender but firm), 2 to 3 minutes for fresh pasta, 7 to 10 minutes for dried. Drain.

3. To make the sauce: While the noodles are cooking, in a large bowl, beat together the eggs and milk. Add the cheeses, salt, and pepper. Stir in the pasta.

4. Pour into the prepared pan. If using, dot with the butter. Bake until set and golden brown, about 30 minutes. Serve warm.

Syrian Pasta with Eggplant

(*Macarona ib Berenja*)

4 TO 6 SERVINGS   P

Until recently, Syrians in America commonly substituted spaghetti for the prevalent forms of Middle Eastern pasta, such as sheriya (fine noodles), as they were unavailable. As a result, many Old World dishes took on a new look in the West, such as this one, which combines spaghetti with a zesty eggplant sauce.

The sauce can be flavored with a little fire by using chilies. Adding the pepper flakes early in the cooking diffuses the fire throughout the entire dish; stirring them in near the end results in sporadic bites of fire dispersed in the sauce. In the Middle East, pasta dishes are served as a main course or side dish, never in the Italian manner as a first course.

I eggplant, peeled
About 2 teaspoons table salt or 4 teaspoons
    kosher salt

SAUCE:

$^{1}/_{2}$ cup olive oil or vegetable oil
5 to 6 cloves garlic, minced
14 ounces tomatoes, peeled, seeded, and chopped
    (see page 291), about 2 cups
About I teaspoon table salt or 2 teaspoons
    kosher salt
About $^{1}/_{4}$ teaspoon ground black pepper
I tablespoon capers, I minced small dried red
    pepper, or about $^{1}/_{4}$ teaspoon red pepper
    flakes

2 tablespoons chopped fresh parsley
I pound thin spaghetti (spaghettini)

1. Cut the eggplant crosswise into 1-inch-thick slices, then into 1-inch-wide sticks, then into 1-inch cubes. Put in a colander or on a wire rack, sprinkle lightly with the salt, and let stand for at least 1 hour. (Moisture will appear on the surface, and the eggplant will become more pliable.) Rinse the eggplant under cold water, then press repeatedly between several layers of paper towels until the slices feel firm and dry. The eggplant can be stored in the refrigerator for up to 4 hours.

2. To make the sauce: Heat $^{1}/_{4}$ cup of the oil in a large skillet over medium heat. Add the garlic and sauté until fragrant, about 30 seconds. Add the tomatoes, salt, pepper, and capers. Cover, reduce the heat to low, and simmer, stirring occasionally, for 20 minutes.

3. In a large, heavy saucepan, heat the remaining $^{1}/_{4}$ cup oil over medium heat. Add the eggplant and sauté until lightly browned, about 8 minutes. Add the eggplant to the tomato sauce and simmer until tender, about 20 minutes. Stir in the parsley.

4. While the eggplant is simmering, bring a large pot of water to a rapid boil and add salt. Add the pasta, stirring briefly to separate. Return to a boil and cook, stirring occasionally, until al dente (tender but firm), 8 to 10 minutes. Drain.

5. Place the pasta on a large serving platter, pour the eggplant sauce on top, and toss to coat. Serve warm.

Syrian Tiny Pasta with Chickpeas

(*Keskasune*)

6 TO 8 SERVINGS   Ⓓ OR Ⓟ

This is one of the most ancient Middle Eastern pasta dishes, combining tiny pasta with the area's favorite legume, chickpeas. The result is filling, hearty, nutritious fare. It is also a traditional Rosh Hashanah dish, the round pasta and chickpeas representing life, fertility, and prosperity. Adjust the proportion of chickpeas to pasta according to personal preference.

3 1/2 cups water

1/4 cup vegetable oil

2 onions, chopped

2 cups (1 pound) *keskasune* (*acini de pepe*) pasta

1 to 2 cups cooked or canned chickpeas

About 1 teaspoon table salt or 2 teaspoons kosher salt

Ground black pepper to taste

1/4 cup unsalted butter (optional)

2 tablespoons grated Parmesan cheese (optional)

1. In a medium saucepan, bring the water to a boil. Meanwhile, heat the oil in a large, heavy saucepan over medium heat. Add the onions and sauté until soft and translucent, 5 to 10 minutes. Add the keskasune and sauté until golden brown, about 5 minutes.

2. Add the boiling water, chickpeas, salt, and pepper to the pasta. Bring to a boil, cover, reduce the heat to low, and simmer until the liquid is absorbed, about 20 minutes. For a creamy texture, add the butter and cheese and stir until melted. Serve warm.

VARIATION

Syrian Tiny Pasta with Cheese (*Keskasune bi Jiben*): Omit the chickpeas. Spoon the cooked pasta mixture into a greased casserole, sprinkle with 1 1/2 to 2 cups (6 to 8 ounces) shredded Muenster or Monterey jack cheese, and bake in a preheated 350°F oven until the cheese melts, about 8 minutes.

KESKASUNE PASTA

The Turks and Arabs never developed the wealth of pasta shaping or saucing of the Italians, and their pasta generally comes in only a few basic shapes, including *keskasune,* which looks like and is named after couscous, but is made from a dough like other pastas. *Acini de pepe* (Italian for "peppercorn"), also called "pearl pasta," is the Italian equivalent of *keskasune* and is available in grocery stores. Syrians serve the pasta without sauce, generally simply flavored with a little salt and maybe pepper and, at dairy meals, sometimes sprinkled with cheese. Browning the pasta in oil helps to keep each grain firm and separate.

FILLED PASTA

Whereas egg noodles were commonly served as everyday fare and as additions to festive dishes, filled pasta, being more labor-intensive and perishable, was generally reserved in most communities only for special occasions. Like other noodle dishes, the concept of filled pasta originated in the Far East and gradually made its way to western Asia and then Europe. The nomadic Turks, originating in Mongolia, migrated to the steppes of central Asia, then in the tenth century into the area of Bukhara before gradually advancing into the part of western Asia bearing their name, bringing with them many Chinese and central Asian foods, including a filled pasta called *manti*, or *tabak borek*. Considering that the appearance of the Turkish *manti* predates the advent of any other filled pasta in the Mediterranean region, it may have been the inspiration for the various comparable European pastas, such as the Sephardic *saltinoshes* and Italian *tortelli*. Similarly, it is probable that the Tartars, Mongolian tribes who overran Ukraine beginning in 1240 with the sacking of Kiev, introduced noodles and *manti* to eastern Europe, leading to the Polish *pierogi*, Ukrainian *vareniki*, and Ashkenazic kreplach. After leaving college for graduate school, I rented an apartment and began to cook for myself. While shopping in a local market for my first Sabbath meal prepared on my own, I became interested in some kreplach (remembering the light, flavorful ones my mother made) until I noticed the hefty price. So I decided to make them from scratch. Although my first kreplach turned out rather well, admittedly too many of them opened up during cooking, due to my faulty technique. I subsequently learned the two secrets to making filled pasta: pressing out as much air as possible from the center, and completely sealing the edges.

What You Should Know: The dough for delicate filled pasta must be rolled into a very thin sheet, even thinner than for most noodles, thin enough to discern the outline of your hand through it. If the dough is *too* thin, the filling will burst through; if too thick, the pasta will be pasty. To prevent sticking, roll out the dough on a lightly floured surface. Be sure to brush any excess flour from the tops of the sheet before filling them.

Have the filling ready to go and properly seasoned before rolling out the pasta, and be prepared to fill it as soon as possible, as the dough quickly dries out once rolled. If cracks start to appear on the edges of the dough sheet, cover it with a damp towel. (If the dough becomes too dry, it will not seal.) Use a little cold water as "glue" along the edges to seal. To avoid puncturing, it is preferable to move the thin sheets by draping them over your wrists rather than using your fingers.

For pasta triangles, cut the dough into squares, spoon a little filling in the center, brush the edges with water, and fold over to form a triangle, pressing out as much air as possible. For round pasta, place a dough sheet on a flat surface, evenly space the filling at the desired intervals, brush the uncovered dough around the filling with water, cover with a second dough sheet, and press around the mounds of filling to remove any air. The amount of filling and how closely it is spaced determines the size of the pasta. For ravioli, place mounds consisting of about 2 teaspoons filling 1 inch apart, with a $1/2$-inch border. Don't pile up the filling; this will stretch the dough, resulting in breaks. Cut the pasta using a sharp knife, pastry wheel, pizza cutter, or biscuit cutter. Press the edges with the tines of a fork or your fingers to seal. (If the pasta envelopes immediately rise to the top of the cooking water, it means too much air was left in the center.)

Line a baking tray with parchment paper or waxed paper and sprinkle with semolina, cornmeal, or flour to absorb the moisture. Arrange the filled pasta, without touching each other, on the tray, cover with a towel, and let stand until dry, about 1 hour. Or, refrigerate, uncovered, for up to 1 day.

If not cooking within a day, freeze the filled pasta by placing them on baking sheets, place in the freezer to harden, then transfer to plastic bags to store. Do not thaw, but add an extra 5 minutes to the cooking time.

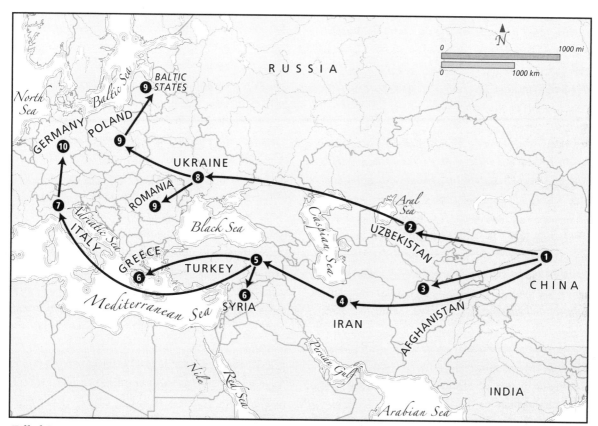

Filled Pasta Route: *Filled pasta originated in China and spread throughout much of Asia and Europe.*
1 Jiaodze (wonton); 2 Manti; 3 Manty; 4 Gushe barreh (or manti); 5 Manti; 6 Calsones; 7 Tortelli/ravioli;
8 Vareniki; 9 Pierogi/kreplach; 10 Maultaschen

BUKHARAN STEAMED FILLED PASTA

(Manti)

24 LARGE FILLED DUMPLINGS   Ⓓ OR Ⓟ

The Mongols of northern China developed a number of boiled and steamed noodle dishes, including a steamed filled bun called man tu *("savage's head," possibly referring to its crimped edges). This dish eventually evolved into a dumpling similar to the modern wonton. When the dumpling traveled to neighboring lands, it was called* mandu *in Korea,* mantu *in Afghanistan, and* manti *in Uzbekistan. Today, Bukharans serve* manti *for special occasions or when they simply desire a favorite comfort food.*

While visiting a Bukharan home in Queens, I watched as the housewife cooked a large batch of these dumplings in the multilevel steamer she had brought with her from Uzbekistan a decade before. The manti are served as a main course, generously sprinkled with freshly ground black pepper and slathered in a garlicky yogurt sauce or, for a nondairy meal, in Vegetable Stock (page 115). The yogurt sauce is also served with fried pancakes (chalpakee), *stuffed vegetables* (oshee), *and rice dishes.*

YOGURT SAUCE:

2 to 4 cloves garlic

About ¹/₂ teaspoon table salt or 1 teaspoon kosher salt

2 cups plain yogurt

¹/₄ cup chopped fresh cilantro or spearmint

Egg Noodle Dough (page 392), prepared through Step 3 and rolled out very thin, or 24 (about 6 ounces) round or square wonton or gyoza wrappers

Choice of *manti* filling (recipes follow)

Ground black pepper to taste

1. To make the sauce: Using the tip of a heavy knife or with a mortar and pestle, mash together the garlic and salt into a paste. Stir into the yogurt. Add the cilantro. Cover and refrigerate for at least 6 hours.

2. Using a pastry cutter, cut 4-inch rounds from the dough, or using a knife, cut into 4-inch squares.

3. To assemble the manti: Spoon 2 tablespoons filling into the center of each dough round, wet the edges of the dough with water, bring up the sides of the dough around the filling, and pinch together at the top. If using the dough squares, spoon 2 tablespoons filling into the center, wet the edges of the dough with water, fold one end over the filling to form a triangle, and press the edges to seal.

4. To steam: Oil the bottom of a flat metal basket steamer and bring 2 inches of water to a boil in the bottom of the steamer. To use a bamboo steamer: Put the steamer in a wok or pan and add water to reach about 1 inch from the bottom of the steamer, then put a lightly oiled heatproof plate in the basket. Add the manti in a single layer without touching, cover tightly, and steam for 20 minutes. If using a multilevel bamboo steamer, reverse the two compartments halfway through cooking. Transfer the manti to a warm plate, cover, and keep warm until ready to serve. Repeat to steam any remaining manti.

5. Sprinkle the manti with the pepper and serve warm, with the yogurt sauce.

VARIATION

Turkish *Manti*: Turkish *manti* tend to be smaller and are baked rather than steamed. Arrange the *manti* from Step 3 in a single layer in a greased baking pan and bake, uncovered, in a preheated 400°F oven until golden brown, about 25 minutes. Add 2 cups Vegetable Stock (page 115) and continue baking until tender, about 15 minutes. Serve with the yogurt sauce.

Bukharan Squash Manti Filling

(Osh Kovok Manti)

MAKES ABOUT 3 CUPS

3 tablespoons vegetable oil

2 onions, chopped

2 pounds winter squash, such as butternut, peeled, seeded, and grated

About $^1/_2$ teaspoon table salt or 1 teaspoon kosher salt

About $^1/_2$ teaspoon ground black pepper

About $^1/_2$ teaspoon ground cumin

$^1/_2$ teaspoon ground turmeric

In a large saucepan, heat the oil over medium heat. Add the onions and sauté until soft and translucent, 5 to 10 minutes. Add the remaining ingredients and cook, stirring frequently, until the squash breaks down and forms a uniform mass, about 15 minutes. Let cool.

Bukharan Potato Manti Filling

(Churchvara Manti)

MAKES ABOUT 3 CUPS

1 pound unpeeled baking potatoes, scrubbed

1 teaspoon table salt or 2 teaspoons kosher salt

$^1/_4$ cup unsalted butter or vegetable oil

2 onions chopped

Ground black pepper to taste

1. Put the potatoes in a large pot, add cold water to cover by 1 inch, then add $^1/_2$ teaspoon of the table salt or 1 teaspoon of the kosher salt. Bring to a low boil, reduce the heat to medium-low, and simmer until fork-tender, about 25 minutes. Drain.

2. While still warm, peel the potatoes, then process through a food mill or ricer. Or, return the potatoes to the warm cooking pot and mash with a potato masher, heavy whisk, or pastry blender over medium-low heat. You should have about 2 cups.

3. In a large skillet, melt the butter over medium heat. Add the onions and sauté until golden, about 15 minutes. Remove from the heat and stir in the potatoes, the remaining salt, and the pepper. Let cool.

ITALIAN PUMPKIN-FILLED PASTA

(Tortelli de Zucca)

ABOUT 40 FILLED DUMPLINGS

In Italy, tortelli *is used as a generic term for filled and folded pieces of pasta that are poached in boiling water, although as its name (meaning "rounds") suggests, it originally referred to filled pasta rounds. The term* ravioli, *derived from the Italian* raviolo *("little turnip") or* rabiole *("items of little value"), generally applies to pasta filled by being topped with a second piece of dough.*

These pumpkin-filled envelopes, popular in many Italian Jewish communities, were a particular specialty of Mantua in Lombardy. I was given two diverse sets of instructions for preparing the pumpkin filling for this pasta. A gracious housewife from Milan insisted that the filling must be earthy and savory, with some cheese perhaps mixed in for a dairy meal, but on no account should it ever contain any sweetener. An Italian chef working in Manhattan, on the other hand, informed me that his secret was adding a hint of sweetness with some crushed almond cookies (amaretti) as well as the Parmesan. I will leave it for you to decide between those experts. In any case, pumpkin and winter squash were historically autumn and winter fillings—their sweetness and round shape making them a perfect Rosh Hashanah dish—and also suited for Sukkot menus.

FILLING:

2 pounds cheese pumpkin, sugar pumpkin, or
   butternut squash, peeled, seeded, and diced,
   or 16 ounces pure-pack canned pumpkin
I large egg, lightly beaten
I large egg yolk
$^1/_2$ cup grated Parmesan cheese, $^1/_3$ cup crushed
   amaretti, or $^1/_4$ cup ground blanched almonds
About $^1/_4$ teaspoon table salt or $^1/_2$ teaspoon
   kosher salt
About $^1/_8$ teaspoon ground black pepper
$^1/_8$ teaspoon freshly grated nutmeg
I to 2 teaspoons sugar (optional)

Egg Noodle Dough (page 392), prepared through
   Step 3 and rolled out very thin, or 34 (about
   8 ounces) round wonton or gyoza wrappers
$^1/_4$ cup unsalted butter or margarine

1. To make the filling: Steam the pumpkin over boiling water in a covered steamer until tender, about 15 minutes. Purée the pumpkin in a food processor or food mill, then transfer to a medium saucepan and cook, stirring frequently, until dry. You should have about 2 cups. Or, use the canned pumpkin and simmer in a saucepan over medium-high heat, stirring with a wooden spoon, for about 5 minutes to remove any metallic flavor. Let cool. Stir in the remaining filling ingredients.

2. Cut the dough into 3-inch rounds. Gather the scraps and reroll.

3. On the dough rounds, place 1 tablespoon filling in the center, wet the edges of the dough with water, and fold in half over the filling to make half-moons, pressing out any air. Crimp the edges to seal. Place on a lightly floured surface, cover with a towel, and let stand until the dough begins to feel dry but is still supple, about 30 minutes. (At this point, the tortelli can also be frozen for up to 1 month. Do not thaw, but add an extra 5 minutes to the cooking time.)

4. Bring a large pot of water to a rapid boil and add salt. Add the tortelli in batches and cook, stirring occasionally with a wooden spoon to prevent sticking, until they float to the surface, about 7 minutes. Using a slotted spoon, transfer to paper towels to drain. Top with the butter and let melt. Serve warm.

VARIATIONS

Italian Pumpkin-Filled Ravioli (*Ravioli de Zucca*): Place 1 dough sheet on a lightly floured surface, evenly space 1 heaping teaspoon filling at $2^1/_2$-inch intervals, and brush the dough around the filling with cold water. Cover with a second dough sheet, press around the mounds to remove any air, and, using a biscuit cutter or pastry wheel, cut into 3-inch squares or rounds. Crimp the edges with the tines of a fork to seal.

Italian Spinach-Filled Pasta (*Tortelli de Spinaci*): Spinach makes an appearance beginning in the spring, providing a traditional Purim treat, and reappears in the fall to become a Rosh Hashanah dish. Substitute the spinach filling from the Venetian Spinach Pasta Roll (page 407), for the pumpkin filling.

VENETIAN SPINACH PASTA ROLL

(Rotolo di Pasta con Spinaci)

9 TO 12 SERVINGS   Ⓟ

One of the earliest Italian Jewish pasta dishes consisted of large pasta squares mixed with cooked spinach, a vegetable that first appeared in Italy in the thirteenth century. As food grew more sophisticated, chefs began rolling the spinach and other fillings into large pasta sheets (sfoglia)*, then poaching the rolls.*

Robert Stearn, a former chef at a Manhattan kosher Italian restaurant who passed along this impressive Tuscan dish to me, cooked it in a fish poacher, advising that the pan must be new or thoroughly cleaned, as the pasta should not taste fishy. He suggested as an alternative using doubled large disposable aluminum foil pans. I have also made this in a wide, well-cleaned pot, and it turned out fine. If your pots are too small, cut the roll in half and poach the two smaller rolls. Chef Stearn also strongly recommended using only freshly grated nutmeg, since this spice begins to lose its strength shortly after grating. Serve the pasta slices as an elegant appetizer, side dish, or even a main course, if desired, with a spicy tomato sauce or sage butter.

FILLING:

1/4 cup olive oil

1 onion, chopped

3 tablespoons pine nuts, toasted (see page 22); optional

2 pounds spinach, stemmed, cooked, chopped, and squeezed dry (about 4 cups)

1 large egg, lightly beaten

About 3/4 teaspoon table salt or 1 1/2 teaspoons kosher salt

Ground black pepper to taste

About 1/4 teaspoon freshly grated nutmeg

1/2 recipe (8 ounces) Egg Noodle Dough (page 392), prepared through Step 2

1. To make the filling: In a large skillet, heat the oil over medium heat. Add the onion and sauté until soft and translucent, about 5 minutes. If using, stir in the pine nuts. Add the spinach and sauté for 1 minute. Let cool. Stir in the egg, salt, pepper, and nutmeg.

2. Roll out the dough into a very thin rectangle, about 8 by 14 inches. Spread evenly with the filling, leaving 1-inch borders. Starting from a long side, roll up jelly-roll style. Wrap securely in cheesecloth, a kitchen towel, or plastic wrap and tie the ends.

3. Bring a large wide pot or fish poacher of water to a rapid boil and add salt. Carefully submerge the pasta roll in the water and boil until tender, about 20 minutes. Remove from the water.

4. Let stand at least 15 minutes before slicing. Unwrap and cut into 1-inch slices. Serve warm or at room temperature.

VARIATIONS

To rewarm the *rotolo*: Cut crosswise into 1-inch slices. Place, cut-side down, in a 9-by-13-inch baking dish, cover with a pasta sauce or sprinkle with 1/2 cup grated Parmesan cheese, and bake in a preheated 350°F oven until heated through, about 20 minutes.

Venetian Spinach and Cheese Pasta Roll (*Rotolo di Pasta con Spinaci e Formaggi*): Reduce the spinach to 2 1/2 cups (about 1 1/2 pounds fresh) and add 1 cup drained (overnight) ricotta cheese and 1/2 cup grated Parmesan or Romano cheese. In Italy, this was usually made with goat's milk ricotta; when using the now common versions made from cow's milk, add some freshly grated Parmesan to boost the flavor.

ITALIAN PASTA ROLLS

(Masconod)

6 TO 8 SERVINGS   D

This ancient Jewish dish bears an obvious similarity to the better-known cannelloni ("little channels") as well as the Sicilian pastry cannoli. Masconod is a common Jewish festival dish, especially at Sukkot and Shavuot. Some versions use cinnamon sugar instead of pepper ($1/2$ cup sugar mixed with 1 teaspoon ground cinnamon), a combination with Parmesan that some people find incongruous. I actually enjoy the contrast of sweet and pungent.

Egg Noodle Dough (page 392), prepared through
   Step 3 and rolled out very thin
$2^2/3$ cups (8 ounces) grated Parmesan cheese
1 teaspoon ground black pepper
2 to 3 tablespoons unsalted butter, melted

1. Cut the dough into about twenty 4- or 5-inch squares. Cover with a towel or plastic wrap and let stand until the dough begins to feel dry but is still supple, about 30 minutes.

2. Bring a large pot of water to a rapid boil and add salt. Add the pasta squares in batches and cook until al dente (tender but firm), about 5 minutes. Drain, rinse with cold water, and drain again.

3. Preheat the oven to 350°F. Grease a 9-by-13-inch casserole.

4. In a small bowl, stir the Parmesan and pepper together. Place the pasta squares on a flat surface and spread 1 heaping tablespoonful of the cheese mixture along one edge of pasta. Roll up jelly-roll style. Place, seam-side down, in a single layer in the prepared casserole. Drizzle with the butter and sprinkle with any remaining cheese mixture.

5. Bake until golden brown, about 30 minutes. Serve warm.

EASTERN EUROPEAN CHEESE-FILLED PASTA TRIANGLES

(Kaese Kreplach)

ABOUT 34 SMALL FILLED DUMPLINGS   D

Kreplach, from the Old French crespe *("curly" or "wrinkled"), originated in twelfth-century France as* krepish, *a piece of meat encased in pastry and fried. When Ashkenazim began moving eastward in Slavic lands, cheese was sometimes substituted for the meat, and after the introduction of pasta to eastern Europe in the fourteenth century, the dish evolved into a boiled dumpling. Filled pasta required a lot of effort (*potchka *in Yiddish) and therefore kreplach was generally reserved for special occasions and four specific holidays: Yom Kippur Eve, Hoshanah Rabbah, Purim, and Shavuot. Mystics compared the wrapping of dough with the divine envelopment of mercy and kindness demonstrated on Yom Kippur.*

Hoshanah Rabbah (the seventh day of Sukkot) is regarded as the day on which the verdicts of judgment that were decided on Yom Kippur are sealed, and accordingly, traditional Yom Kippur Eve foods are served on Hoshanah Rabbah. In kabbalistic tradition, Yom Kippur is compared with the seemingly unrelated holiday of Purim, as the similarity in names is viewed as no coincidence (PURim and kipPUR—pur is Hebrew for lots). Thus, a parallel was drawn between the physical lots of Purim cast by Haman and the metaphysical lots of Yom Kippur. On Purim, kreplach, sometimes filled with cherry, plum, or strawberry preserves, also represent the three-cornered hat ascribed to Haman. (Despite the fact that Persians never wore tricornered hats; such headwear only becoming popular in Europe around 1690.) Making food shaped like various parts of the body was in line with a widespread custom of symbolically eating some part of

Haman and thereby erasing his name. Fruit-filled kreplach are sometimes called varenikes, *the Ukrainian term for filled pasta.*

Although kreplach in general never achieved the same prominence in America as ravioli or wontons, hearty cheese versions became a mainstay of Catskills hotels and Jewish dairy restaurants. Cheese kreplach, commonly topped with melted butter or sour cream, are customary on Shavuot and other important dairy occasions, and were in some families an occasional weekday treat during the spring and summer when cheese was plentiful. Some people like to fry the cooked cheese kreplach for a crisp, caramelized surface that contrasts with the smooth filling.

FILLING:

2 cups (1 pound) farmer or pot cheese

1 large egg, lightly beaten

2 to 3 tablespoons sour cream

2 to 4 tablespoons fresh bread crumbs
   or matza meal

About $^1/_4$ teaspoon table salt or $^1/_2$ teaspoon
   kosher salt

About 3 tablespoons sugar (optional)

3 tablespoons raisins or 1 teaspoon grated lemon
   zest (optional)

Egg Noodle Dough (page 392), prepared through
   Step 3 and rolled out very thin, or 34 square
   wonton or gyoza wrappers (about 8 ounces)

$^1/_2$ cup (1 stick) unsalted butter or 1$^1/_2$ cups
   sour cream

1. To make the filling: In a large bowl, combine all the filling ingredients.

2. Cut the dough into 2$^1/_2$-inch squares. Place 1 teaspoon filling in the center of each square. Lightly brush the edges with water to moisten and fold over to form a triangle, pressing out any air. Pinch the edges or press with the tines of a fork to seal.

3. Place on a lightly floured surface, cover with a towel, and let stand until the dough begins to feel dry but is still supple, about 30 minutes. The kreplach may be refrigerated for up to 2 days or frozen for up to 8 months. To freeze, arrange in a single layer on a floured baking sheet, freeze until solid, then transfer to plastic bags. Do not thaw before cooking, but increase the cooking time by about 5 minutes.

4. Bring a large pot of water to a rapid boil and add salt. Add the kreplach in several batches and cook, stirring occasionally to prevent sticking, until they rise to the surface and become just tender, about 7 minutes. Using a slotted spoon, transfer to a colander to drain. Serve warm topped with the butter or accompanied with the sour cream.

VARIATIONS

Toss the poached kreplach with 1 cup fresh bread crumbs browned in $^1/_4$ cup butter.

Arrange the poached kreplach in a greased baking pan, lightly sprinkle with sugar, and bake in a preheated 350°F oven until golden brown, about 30 minutes.

Sephardic Filled Pasta

(Calsones)

ABOUT 30 FILLED DUMPLINGS   Ⓓ OR Ⓟ

Many years ago, I spent a Shavuot dinner with a Syrian family in the Flatbush section of Brooklyn. Instead of the cheese blintzes or kreplach found at an Ashkenazic Shavuot, this meal featured a pasta dish called calsones, *derived from* calzone, *the Italian stuffed turnover. The hostess insisted that the best filling for* calsones *was made with* myzithra *(fresh sheep's milk cheese), which imparts a slightly nutty flavor, while her sister-in-law maintained that a milder cheese, such as Muenster, was more appropriate. While both are good, I find the sheep's milk cheese more interesting, but to let you decide, I provided both different cheese fillings as well as a spinach option. Calsones are commonly accompanied with yogurt.*

> Egg Noodle Dough (page 392), prepared through
>   Step 3 and rolled out very thin
> Choice of *calsone* filling (recipes follow)
> $^1/_2$ cup (1 stick) unsalted butter or margarine
> Salt to taste

1. Cut the dough rectangle into $2^1/_2$-inch rounds. Place 1 teaspoon of the filling in the center of each round and fold over to form a half-moon, pressing out any air. Pinch the edges to seal. To make an optional ring shape, wrap the half-moon around a forefinger and pinch the two corners together.

2. Place on a lightly floured surface, cover with a towel, and let stand until the dough begins to feel dry but is still supple, about 30 minutes. The calsones may be covered and refrigerated for up to 2 days or frozen for up to 8 months. To freeze, arrange in a single layer on a floured baking sheet, freeze until solid, and transfer to plastic bags. Do not thaw before cooking, but add an extra 5 minutes to the cooking time.

3. Bring a large pot of water to a rapid boil and add salt. Add the calsones in batches, and cook, stirring occasionally to prevent sticking, until they rise to the surface and are just tender, about 7 minutes. Using a slotted spoon, transfer to a colander to drain. Toss the hot calsones with the butter and salt. Serve warm.

CALSONE FILLINGS

Cheese Calsone Filling

(Gomo de queso)

MAKES ABOUT 2 CUPS

> 1 cup (8 ounces) soft goat, ricotta, or farmer
>   cheese (see Note)
> 1 cup (3 ounces) grated Parmesan cheese
>   or 1 cup (4 ounces) shredded mozzarella
>   or halloumi
> 1 large egg, lightly beaten
> About $^1/_2$ teaspoon table salt or 1 teaspoon
>   kosher salt
> Ground white or black pepper to taste
> $^1/_4$ cup chopped fresh parsley or basil (optional)

In a large bowl, combine all the ingredients and stir to blend.

VARIATION

Use the 1 cup shredded mozzarella or halloumi and add $^1/_2$ cup ($1^1/_2$ ounces) grated Parmesan and $^3/_4$ cup (6 ounces) softened cream cheese.

NOTE   For pasta fillings, Middle Easterners commonly use homemade *jiben beida* (a mild white cheese), *myzithra,* or *anthotiro* (fresh sheep's milk cheese), which can occasionally be found in Middle Eastern and some specialty stores. A combination of Parmesan and ricotta or farmer cheese can be substituted for the latter.

Syrian Cheese Calsone Filling

(Calsones bil Jiben)

MAKES ABOUT 2 CUPS

2 cups (8 ounces) shredded Muenster cheese

1 large egg, lightly beaten

$1/8$ teaspoon baking powder

In a medium bowl, combine all the ingredients and stir to blend.

Spinach Calsone Filling

(Gomo de Espinaca)

MAKES ABOUT 2 CUPS

3 tablespoons olive oil or vegetable oil

2 onions, chopped

2 cloves garlic, minced (optional)

2 pounds fresh spinach, stemmed, cooked, chopped, and squeezed dry, or 20 ounces thawed frozen chopped spinach, squeezed dry

2 large eggs, lightly beaten

About $1/2$ teaspoon freshly grated nutmeg

About $3/4$ teaspoon salt

Ground black pepper to taste

$2/3$ cup pine nuts, toasted (see page 22), optional

In a heavy, medium skillet, heat the oil over medium heat. Add the onions and, if using, the garlic and sauté until soft and translucent, 5 to 10 minutes. Add the spinach and cook until the liquid evaporates. Let cool. Stir in the remaining ingredients.

CALSONES

Originally, the famous Italian calzone consisted of a long slice of sausage wrapped in the lean yeast dough used to make pizza and focaccia, the dish resembling the baggy long pants (*calzone*) worn by the men of Naples. Eventually, it evolved into the now-common half-moon-shaped pastry. When the Spanish overlords of southern Italy expelled its Jews in 1492, many went to northern Italy, while others headed for the liberal opportunities offered by the Ottoman Empire. There, the name of the bread pastries was applied by the Jewish refugees to similarly shaped local half-moon pasta envelopes, a popular dish at dairy meals. In Aleppo, Syria, the *calsones*, or *kalsonnes*, were commonly mixed with wide noodles, providing the main course for Thursday dinner, traditionally a dairy meal before the Sabbath. In Crete, they are deep-fried in olive oil and served warm or cooled.

❧ Couscous ❧

By the eleventh century, utilizing the venerable African practice of steaming foods in woven baskets, the Berbers—pre-Arab northwest African tribes—developed a process of steaming semolina granules called *seksu* in Berber and *kuskusu* in Arabic (the names were probably derived from the Arabic *kaskasa*, for "to pound" or "to make small"). The same word designates the various stews that are served with the pasta. Although the method for preparing homemade couscous has changed very little since then, the variety of stews served with it has grown dramatically.

Historically, couscous was made at home by hand. Unlike most pasta, couscous is not kneaded into a dough. Instead, *smeed* (finely crushed semolina) is placed in a *gsaa* (a large shallow earthenware or wooden bowl), gradually sprinkled with salty water and semolina flour, and stirred in a circular motion or rubbed with the right hand. The starch accumulates around the semolina granules to form progressively larger balls. The couscous is then shaken through a series of three sieves (*ghurbal*) with progressively smaller holes into a round woven basket (*tbak*) to produce grains of a uniform consistency. The entire process generally takes a group of three women most of the day to accomplish, but couscous is made in sufficient quantities to last for quite a while and is generally only done two or three times a year. Finally, the couscous is spread over a white sheet to dry in the sun for about four or five days, depending on the humidity. Inexpensive, nutritious, filling, and capable of being stored for more than a year, couscous, simply topped with sour milk and butter or with an elaborate stew, has long served as daily fare throughout the Maghreb.

Jews, a major presence in northwest Africa since at least Roman times, have been making couscous for more than a thousand years, and it is ingrained in their lifestyle. Moroccan, Tunisian, and Algerian Jews serve couscous with a beloved stew, usually accompanied with several salads, every Friday night, on the festivals, and for all special occasions. Most cooks make an extra-large quantity for Friday night in order to serve the leftover grains with the following day's *dafina* (Sabbath stew). The couscous stew for Rosh Hashanah, called *couscous aux sept legumes*, customarily contains seven symbolic vegetables, seven being a fortuitous number as Rosh Hashanah falls on the first day of the seventh month and the world was created in seven days. The dessert couscous for Rosh Hashanah is sprinkled with pomegranate seeds or small grapes. On Sukkot, a large assortment of vegetables, especially sweet potatoes, are added to the stew as a sign of the harvest. On special occasions, the couscous may be colored with saffron or topped with a garnish of warm poached quinces. For grand public affairs, such as weddings and bar mitzvahs, fine-grain couscous (*seffa*) is sweetened, mounded into a large pyramid, sprinkled with cinnamon, topped with dried fruits and nuts, and garnished with *datils rellenos* (stuffed dates), the sweetness denoting happiness.

What You Should Know: Most of the couscous available in the West comes in the form of fine grains processed through steaming under tremendous pressure, thereby transforming it into "instant" couscous, which requires no additional steaming or lengthy cooking, but only soaking in hot water. Instant couscous, available in grocery stores, can be substituted for the unprocessed medium-grain variety found at Middle Eastern groceries and some natural foods stores, particularly for dessert couscous, although it is not as light and fluffy. "Noninstant" couscous is available in bulk in most Middle Eastern groceries and some natural foods stores. Israeli couscous, also called *maghribiyya*, is toasted large pasta balls; it must be cooked and cannot be substituted for standard couscous.

In the Maghreb, both the grains and the stew are traditionally made in a *couscousière*, a two-compartment barrel-shaped vessel with a stewing pot (*tanjra* or *ikineksu*) on the bottom and an uncovered perforated steamer (*kiskis*) on top; the granules absorb some of the flavors of the stew below as they steam. A flour-water paste or dough rope is commonly wrapped around the juncture of the top and bottom parts of the *couscousière* to prevent the steam from escaping and to direct all of the hot air toward the couscous. A steamer or colander set over a large, deep pot can be substituted for the *couscousière*, but be sure to secure the juncture with dampened cheesecloth or a flour paste. After rehydrating instant couscous, some cooks additionally steam it for fluffier granules.

After steaming, the granules are customarily fluffed up and heaped onto a deep-sided serving platter. Moroccans typically arrange the vegetables on top of the couscous and pour the broth from the stew over the dish to moisten the grains. Algerians generally present the couscous, vegetables, and broth in separate serving dishes and let the individual diners combine them. Each region developed its own style of couscous stew, and every cook boasts a slightly different variation, adding a distinctive combination of spices, vegetables, fruits, and other ingredients. The resulting couscous can be fiery or sweet; it can contain an assortment of meats, poultry, or fish or be vegetarian. Tunisians prefer spicier, more robust stews; Moroccans tend to use plenty of spices, but subtly and with finesse. Algerians typically add tomatoes. Savory stews are generally accompanied with a fiery chili paste called *harissa*, which should be used sparingly by neophytes. At a Maghrebi feast, couscous with stew is rarely served as a main course, but in accord with the Middle Eastern style of hospitality, hosts offer the couscous as a meal's finale to ensure that the meal has produced *shaban* (complete satisfaction).

BASIC STEAMED COUSCOUS

ABOUT 9 CUPS

Although this double-steaming method may seem complicated and takes about an hour from start to finish, it is actually not difficult and generally coincides with making the stew. The result is much lighter and fluffier than instant couscous. One of my favorite ways to enjoy couscous is with Moroccan Vegetable Stew for Couscous (page 308).

> 1 pound (about 2⅔ cups) couscous, preferably medium grain (not instant)
> 2 cups cold water
> 1 tablespoon olive oil or vegetable oil
> 1 cup water mixed with about 1 teaspoon table salt or 2 teaspoons kosher salt

1. Put the couscous in a bowl, sprinkle with the cold water, drain, and let stand for 15 minutes. The granules will swell a little. Drizzle with the oil and stir with a fork or your fingers to separate the granules.

2. Bring a stew or water to a gentle boil in the bottom of a couscousière or a large pot with a steamer. (If the holes in the steamer are too large to hold the couscous, line it with cheesecloth.) Place the steamer

section in the pot at least 4 inches above the boiling stew or water. (If steam escapes from the sides of the steamer, secure a dampened piece of cheesecloth or a flour paste around the rim.) Gradually add the swollen couscous, forming a mound, and steam, uncovered, for 15 minutes. (Overcooking the couscous results in sticky pasta that bonds together.)

3. Spread the couscous over a large platter or baking sheet, breaking up any large clumps. Sprinkle with the 1 cup salted water and stir with a fork or your fingers to separate the granules and evenly distribute the salted water. Let rest for at least 15 minutes. The couscous can be covered with paper towels or a damp cloth and set aside at room temperature for up to 8 hours until ready for the final steaming.

4. Return the top part of the steamer to the pot, resealing the rim with cheesecloth, if necessary. Carefully return the couscous to the steamer, forming a mound. Steam, uncovered, until the couscous is heated through and tender but not mushy, about 20 minutes. (Tasting is the best way to determine doneness.) Heap the couscous onto a warm serving platter and stir with a fork to separate the granules.

COUSCOUS WITH ONION-RAISIN TOPPING

(*Couscous bil Basal wa Sbeeb*)

6 TO 8 SERVINGS   Ⓓ OR Ⓟ

In Marrakech and Tangiers, a seaport in northern Morocco located directly across from Gibraltar with a pronounced Spanish influence, locals top couscous with a sweet mixture of caramelized onions and raisins. It is usually served as a topping for blander, more substantial stews and saffron-accented couscous.

ONION-RAISIN TOPPING:

1 1/2 cups raisins
5 large onions, sliced
1 1/2 cups Vegetable Stock (page 115) or water
1 cup honey or sugar
1/2 cup (1 stick) unsalted butter or vegetable oil
2 teaspoons ground cinnamon
About 1 teaspoon table salt or 2 teaspoons kosher salt
1/2 teaspoon ground black pepper or 1 teaspoon ground ginger
1/2 teaspoon powdered saffron or ground turmeric

Basic Steamed Couscous (page 413)
Moroccan Vegetable Stew for Couscous (page 308) or other stew (optional)

1. To make the topping: Soak the raisins in cold water to cover for 1 hour. Drain.

2. In a large saucepan, combine the onions and 2½ cups water, cover, bring to a boil and cook for 5 minutes. Drain well.

3. Return the onions to the saucepan and add the stock, honey, butter, cinnamon, salt, pepper, and saffron. Bring to a boil, reduce the heat to medium-low, and simmer, uncovered, for 5 minutes.

4. Add the raisins, cover, and simmer for 30 minutes. Uncover and cook, stirring frequently, until the liquid evaporates and the sauce thickens. You will have about 6 cups.

5. Heap the couscous on a serving platter, make a well in the center, and fill with the onion-raisin topping. If desired, top with a stew. Serve warm.

VARIATION

Almond Topping: Sauté 1 cup (5½ ounces) blanched whole almonds in ⅓ cup *samneh* (Middle Eastern Clarified Butter, page 51) over medium heat until golden brown, then sprinkle over the onion-raisin topping.

[handwritten note: 2/22/15 As couscous should be → Use less salt. Steam real couscous. (Steaming it a pain. Takes 1 hour)]

DJERBA COUSCOUS WITH GREEN HERBS

(Fawwar)

6 TO 8 SERVINGS

Tabil, *a combination of coriander, caraway, chilies, and garlic, is the predominant Tunisian spice mixture (tabil was originally an Arabic word for "coriander"). In this dish from Djerba, a small island off the southeast coast of Tunisia, herbs and a cooling Tunisian Cucumber and Pepper Relish (page 416) add extra layers of flavor to the couscous. Buttermilk is usually served as a drink with this dish to help balance the fire of the chilies.*

> 8 ounces scallions, leeks (white and light green parts only), or any combination chopped (about 2 cups)
>
> 8 ounces parsley, stemmed and chopped (about 2 cups)
>
> 8 ounces fresh fennel leaves, dill, or a combination, chopped (about 2 cups)
>
> ½ cup chopped fresh celery leaves
>
> ½ cup olive oil
>
> 2 large onions, chopped
>
> 4 to 5 cloves garlic, minced
>
> ¼ cup tomato paste
>
> 2 large red bell peppers, seeded and deribbed (white removed), 1 coarsely chopped and 1 sliced
>
> 1 to 2 small hot green chilies, seeded and minced
>
> 2 teaspoons sweet paprika
>
> About 1½ teaspoons red pepper flakes
>
> About 2 teaspoons table salt or 4 teaspoons kosher salt
>
> 1 teaspoon ground caraway seeds
>
> 1 to 2 teaspoons ground coriander seeds
>
> Ground black pepper to taste
>
> 1½ cups water
>
> Basic Steamed Coucous (page 413)

1. Put the scallions, parsley, fennel, and celery leaves in the top of a couscousière or a steamer over boiling water and steam for 30 minutes. Let cool, then squeeze out the moisture.

2. In a large skillet or heavy saucepan, heat the oil over medium heat. Add the onions and garlic and sauté until soft and translucent, 5 to 10 minutes.

3. Add the tomato paste and stir until slightly darkened, about 1 minute. Stir in the bell peppers, chilies, paprika, pepper flakes, salt, caraway, coriander, and pepper. Add the water, bring to a boil, cover, reduce the heat to low, and simmer for 15 minutes. Remove the bell pepper slices (not the chopped bell pepper) and reserve. Meanwhile, finish preparing the couscous.

4. Pour the spice mixture and herbs over the couscous and toss to coat. Spoon onto a serving platter and arrange the bell pepper slices on top. Serve warm accompanied with the cucumber and pepper relish.

Tunisian Cucumber and Pepper Relish

(*Falfal bil Labid*)

ABOUT 4 CUPS   P

Tunisians commonly serve this relish with couscous.

> 2 cucumbers, peeled, seeded, and diced
> 2 red bell peppers, seeded, deribbed
>   (white removed), and diced
> 1 teaspoon table salt or 2 teaspoons kosher salt
> 2 tablespoons fresh lemon juice

In a medium bowl, combine the cucumbers and peppers. In a small bowl, stir the salt into the lemon juice to dissolve. Pour the salted juice over the vegetables and toss to coat. Cover and let stand at room temperature for at least 8 hours.

THE JEWS OF DJERBA

According to legend, a family of priests, survivors of the destruction of the First Temple in 586 B.C.E., fled to the site of an ancient Phoenician trading post on the island of Djerba, carrying with them the Temple's cornerstone or a door. The relic, claimed to have healing properties, was placed in the walls of El Ghriba ("the wondrous one") Synagogue located on the island.

Djerba has one of the oldest extant Jewish communities in the Diaspora, having endured for several thousand years, despite three major persecutions: by the Almohads in the twelfth century, the Spanish in 1519, and the Nazis in 1943. In 1946, there were still nearly five thousand Jews, consisting overwhelmingly of Cohanim (Jewish priests), living on Djerba. Today, about one thousand Jews remain, most working as silversmiths.

Once a year, however, the numbers swell as thousands of Jews of Tunisian descent, primarily now living in France and Israel, make an annual pilgrimage to the island for the holiday of Lag b'Omer. The visitors light candles, solicit a blessing from the rabbis, greet relatives and friends, and raise funds to support the ancient community. Nearby, vendors sell various native foods, especially the national favorite, *brik* (Tunisian Potato-Filled Pastry, page 198).

EGGS

❦ · ❦

Eggs gained a prominent role in cooking relatively late in history. Eggs, primarily from geese, ducks, and quail, were very seldom called for in ancient Greek recipes, and in Rome, even among the wealthy, they were used rather sparingly, being reserved for special occasions. Eggs are rarely mentioned in the Bible and then only in reference to being gathered from the wild. Even after people learned how to raise fowl, most species laid just enough eggs to maintain a healthy flock, leaving little surplus to be eaten. Only with the widespread breeding of the prolific chicken, an animal never mentioned in the Bible, could any sizable number of the eggs be eaten without threatening the reproductive cycle.

By the end of the Second Temple period, chicken eggs were becoming increasingly commonplace in the Middle East. Nevertheless, they remained a luxury. Even with all of the improvements in poultry raising, disease prevented growers from bunching too many birds in one location until after 1956, when vaccines became available to minimize poultry illnesses; chickens and eggs then became inexpensive for the first time in history.

The fowl of choice for early Ashkenazim a thousand years ago was the goose, both for its rich flavor and relative ease of raising. Eggs were a specialty item, appearing at important occasions such as the Passover Seder or a child's first day of school. In the fifteenth century, corresponding to a European meat shortage, chickens emerged as the most important food animal for Ashkenazim. Subsequently, most central and eastern European Jewish families kept at least a few chickens in their yard or in coops, which provided a regular supply of eggs. It was also at that time that eggs began appearing in Ashkenazic Sabbath bread (challah). Over the ensuing five centuries, chicken eggs played a significant role in Ashkenazic cookery, providing much of the protein. Egg dishes range from simple Polish *eier mit tzibbeles* (scrambled eggs with onions) to the sophisticated Alsatian *tarte aux oignons* (onion tart). Eggs were essential for classic Ashkenazic fare, such as *gehakte eier* (egg salad), kugels (baked puddings), *knaidlach* (dumplings), *triflach* (egg drops for soup), *lukshen* (noodles), latkes (pancakes), and blintzes (crepes).

In Muslim Spain and the southern Mediterranean, chickens remained popular, but tended to be more expensive than meat and were generally reserved for special occasions. Sephardim, however, ate eggs on a regular basis, developing some fairly sophisticated egg dishes, such as *huevos haminados* ("roasted" eggs), *fritadas* (omelets), *agristada* (egg-lemon sauce), *huevos de Haman* (Purim pastry encasing hard-boiled eggs), and a host of casseroles and baked goods.

During the Middle Ages, as eggs gained wider convention in the kitchen, they also took on various symbolic meanings and usage. In Jewish tradition, eggs are cited as the only food that becomes harder as it is cooked, while the eggshell is both paradoxically resilient yet fragile. Thus, it is symbolic of Jewish history as well as of fertility and life and death. Hard-boiled eggs are customarily served at all somber occasions, including the meals preceding major fasts and *Seudat Havra'ah* (the meal following a funeral). A roasted hard-boiled egg is used at the Passover Seder to commemorate the Chagiga, the festival sacrifice in the Temple that can no longer be offered. Many Ashkenazim start the Seder meal with hard-boiled eggs in salt water, while Sephardim feature the ubiquitous *huevos haminados*, both customs derived from the Roman practice of starting feasts with eggs.

OMELETS

Omelets provided a great way to use leftover food and abundant seasonal produce by mixing them with a few eggs, then frying the batter in a skillet, providing tasty, versatile, and filling home fare. Unlike French- and American-style omelets, in which eggs envelop a small amount of filling, Middle Eastern and Mediterranaean omelets emphasize the flavorings more than the eggs, usually containing just enough eggs to hold everything together.

The two primary types of Middle Eastern and Mediterranean omelets include small disk-shaped fritters—called *edgeh*, or *ijjet,* in Syria, *edjeh* in Persia and Iraq, *eggah* in Morocco, and *aijjah* in Tunisia—made by dropping egg mixtures by spoonfuls into hot oil, then browning both sides. The other type of omelet, a much less labor-intensive method, is a large egg cake called a frittata ("fried dish") by Italians, *fritada* by Sephardim, *tortilla* by Spaniards, *sfogato* (from the Greek for "sponge") by Greeks, *maquda*, or *marcoude*, by Tunisians, *kuku* by Iranians, and *chizhipizhi* by Georgians.

Syrian Omelets

(Edgeh)

ABOUT TEN 3-INCH OMELETS (P)

Many Syrians, both children and adults, consider these small omelets their favorite of all foods. Arabic-style small omelets are customarily fried in enough oil to produce a fritterlike exterior. Some cooks omit the bread crumbs for a more custardy texture, while others add a little more bread crumbs or flour, producing a pancakelike consistency. Various vegetables are generally mixed in, producing a more substantial dish. In many Middle Eastern households, edgeh *are served any time there are a lot of leftovers, especially on Sundays, using up the remains of the Sabbath meals, and are generally accompanied with a salad. Because* edgeh *can be served hot or cold, they are also common on the Sabbath and at picnics.* Edgeh *are featured as appetizers, frequently accompanied with yogurt, sometimes packed into pita bread as a sandwich, and on special occasions such as a bar mitzvah.*

- 4 large eggs, lightly beaten
- 1 small onion or 2 to 3 scallions (white and light green parts), finely chopped
- About 1 tablespoon fine fresh bread crumbs, matza meal, or unbleached all-purpose flour (optional)
- About 1/2 teaspoon table salt or 1 teaspoon kosher salt
- 1/4 teaspoon ground allspice
- About 1/2 cup vegetable oil for frying

1. In a medium bowl, combine the eggs, onion, bread crumbs, salt, and allspice. Stir to blend.

2. In a large, heavy skillet, heat about 1/2 inch oil over medium heat. In batches, drop the mixture by 2 tablespoonfuls and flatten slightly to form 1/4-inch-thick patties about 3 inches in diameter. Fry, turning once, until golden, about 2 minutes per side. The omelets can be kept warm on an oven-proof platter in a low oven for up to 30 minutes. Serve warm or at room temperature.

3. To reheat, arrange in a single layer on a baking sheet, cover with aluminum foil, and place in a preheated 350°F oven until heated through, about 12 minutes.

VARIATIONS

Lebanese Mint Omelets (*Ijjet Nana*): Add 3 tablespoons chopped fresh spearmint.

Syrian Artichoke Omelets (*Edgeh Ashok*): Add 4 cooked and chopped artichoke hearts.

Syrian Cauliflower Omelets (*Edgeh Zahra*): Add about 2 cups cooked and chopped cauliflower.

Syrian Cheese Omelets (*Edgeh Jiben*): Add 1 1/2 cups grated cheese, such as kashkaval, Muenster, or Parmesan.

Syrian Parsley Omelets (*Edgeh Ba'adoonis*): Add 1 cup chopped fresh parsley. Or, add 1/4 cup chopped fresh parsley, 1/2 cup chopped fresh spearmint or cilantro, and 1/4 teaspoon ground cumin.

Syrian Squash Omelets (*Edgeh Koosa*): Add 2 peeled, seeded, and coarsely grated zucchini (about 2 cups). Or, add 1 peeled, seeded, and diced large zucchini and 1/2 cup (2 ounces) grated cheese.

Large omelets (i.e., frittata)   Small omelets   Large and small omelets

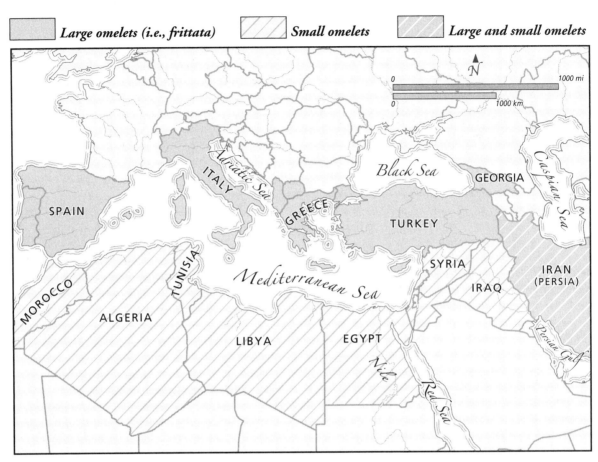

The Prevalence of Large and Small Omelets: *Countries influenced by the Italian frittata tend to make large, skillet-sized omelets. Arabic-influenced countries follow the Arabic style of cooking small, fried omelet patties. Persians enjoy both.*

IRAQI NOODLE OMELETS

(Edjah Shiriyya)

ABOUT EIGHT 4-INCH OMELETS

This dairy omelet, also spelled ijjet, *is popular with Iraqis during the Nine Days before the fast of Tisha b'Av and for other dairy meals. These are most commonly fried as individual pancakes but are also baked as a whole cake, as in the variation below.* Edjah *is commonly accompanied with yogurt or jam.*

- I pound very fine dried egg noodles or broken angel hair pasta
- 6 large eggs, lightly beaten
- I to I¹/₂ cups grated or shredded cheese, such as kashkaval, kefalotyri, Muenster, Cheddar, or Gouda
- About ³/₄ teaspoon table salt or I¹/₂ teaspoons kosher salt
- Ground white or black pepper to taste
- I¹/₂ teaspoons caraway seeds (optional)
- 2 to 3 tablespoons oil or butter for frying

1. In a large pot of salted boiling water, cook the noodles until al dente (tender but firm), 3 to 5 minutes. Do not overcook. Drain, rinse under cold water, and drain again.

2. In a large bowl, toss the noodles with the eggs, cheese, salt, pepper, and, if using, the caraway.

3. In a large, heavy skillet, heat a thin layer of oil over medium-low heat. In batches, drop the noodle batter by ¹/₂ cupfuls to form 4-inch pancakes. Or, use 2 tablespoons batter for 3-inch pancakes. Fry, turning once, until golden brown, about 2 minutes per side. The omelets can be kept warm on an ovenproof platter in a low oven for up to 30 minutes. Serve warm.

VARIATION

Middle Eastern Baked Noodles (*Macarona al Horno*): Spoon the pasta mixture into a greased 9-by-13-inch baking dish or two 9-inch pie plates and bake in a preheated 375°F oven until firm and golden brown, 20 to 30 minutes. Let stand for 5 minutes before cutting into wedges.

TUNISIAN POTATO OMELETS

(Aijjah Patata)

ABOUT TWELVE 3-INCH OMELETS P

Aijjah *is an example, among many others, of the Arabs bringing a Near Eastern dish,* edjeh, *to Africa where it was given a Maghrebi flavor, here enlivened with chilies and tomatoes. These are generally fried only as individual pancakes and not as a large cake. Tunisians commonly serve these omelets with yogurt or* harissa.

- 3 tablespoons vegetable oil
- I pound boiling potatoes, peeled and diced
- I onion, chopped (optional)
- ¹/₄ cup water
- I tablespoon tomato purée or 2 tomatoes, seeded and chopped (see page 291)
- I clove garlic, mashed
- About I¹/₂ teaspoons *harissa* (Northwest African Chili Paste, page 433), or I jalapeño chili, seeded and minced
- 4 large eggs, lightly beaten
- I tablespoon fine fresh bread crumbs, matza meal, or unbleached all-purpose flour
- About ¹/₂ teaspoon table salt or I teaspoon kosher salt
- Vegetable oil for deep-frying

1. In a large skillet, heat the 3 tablespoons oil over medium heat. Add the potatoes and, if using, the onion, and stir until well coated. Reduce the heat to medium-low and cook, stirring occasionally, until tender, about 15 minutes.

2. Combine the water, tomato purée, garlic, and harissa and stir into the potatoes. Remove from the heat and let cool. Stir in the eggs, bread crumbs, and salt.

3. In a large, heavy skillet or saucepan, heat at least $^1/_2$ inch oil over medium heat. In batches, drop the mixture by 2 tablespoonfuls and flatten slightly to form $^1/_4$-inch-thick patties about 3 inches in diameter. Fry, turning once, until golden, about 2 minutes per side. The omelets can be kept warm on an ovenproof platter in a low oven for up to 30 minutes. Serve warm or at room temperature.

PERSIAN CARROT OMELETS

(*Havij Edjeh*)

ABOUT TWELVE 3-INCH OMELETS D OR P

These lightly sweet omelets are a signature dish of Persian cuisine. Persian omelets, fried in only enough fat to prevent sticking, tend to have a softer exterior than their Arabic counterparts. Unlike the Persian kuku, *which can be fried as either a large cake or individual pancakes or baked as a large cake, edjeh are fried only as individual pancakes. Persian cooks often add dates to dishes to provide a pleasant sweet note, making this versatile dish suitable as either a side dish or a dessert. These omelets are usually served with yogurt or jam.*

4 large eggs

About $^1/_2$ teaspoon table salt or 1 teaspoon kosher salt

3 tablespoons unsalted butter or vegetable oil

2 onions, chopped

12 ounces carrots, grated (about 2 cups)

$^1/_2$ cup chopped pitted dates

$^1/_3$ cup dried currants or raisins

2 tablespoons fresh lemon juice

Vegetable oil or butter for frying

1. In a medium bowl, beat the eggs with the salt until blended. Set aside.

2. In a large skillet, melt the butter over medium heat. Add the onions and sauté for 1 minute. Add the carrots and sauté until softened, 5 to 10 minutes. Add the dates, currants, and lemon juice. Stir into the egg mixture.

3. In a large, heavy skillet, heat a thin layer of oil over medium heat. In batches, drop the mixture by 2 tablespoons and flatten slightly to form $^1/_4$-inch-thick patties about 3 inches in diameter. Fry, turning once, until golden, about 2 minutes per side. The omelets can be kept warm on an ovenproof platter in a low oven for up to 30 minutes. Serve warm or at room temperature.

VARIATION

Persian Carrot and Potato Omelets (*Sib Zamini Havij Edjeh*): Omit the dates, currants, and lemon juice and add 2 potatoes cooked in boiling water until knife-tender, then cooled, peeled, and coarsely grated, and $^1/_4$ teaspoon ground black pepper.

PERSIAN HERB OMELET

(*Kukuye Sabzi*)

4 TO 6 SERVINGS

Kuku is a popular Persian egg "pie" packed with herbs and vegetables. The word kuku *resembles the Farsi name for a native bird (*kuku *probably derived from the sound of the bird's call), which is how this egg-based dish ended up being named for a bird. Kukuye sabzi, the most popular variation of the Persian omelet, makes use of various seasonal fresh greens and herbs, the common denominator being spinach, demonstrating how a mix of strong, typically Persian seasonings will mellow when cooked with eggs. Since* kukuye sabzi *can be served warm or at room temperature, it often graces the Iranian Sabbath table as a side dish or part of a* meze *(appetizer assortment), but never as a main course. Kuku is found at such diverse occasions as a Purim feast or in a house of mourning, egg and greens representing the life cycle and renewal. It is also a traditional Hanukkah dish, fried in plenty of oil and served with rice or stews.*

There are cooks who use a larger amount of spinach and those who omit the parsley. Some use a combination of herbs, while others limit the flavorings to only dill. One woman chops all of the vegetables together in a food processor, while another insists on doing everything by hand. Some make them thicker, others thinner and slightly drier. To be honest, they are all tasty, but I prefer the more complex flavor of several herbs.

This dish is most commonly fried as a large cake, but it is also fried as individual pancakes or baked as a whole cake, as in the variations below. Kuku is commonly accompanied with yogurt.

4 tablespoons vegetable oil

2 onions, chopped, or 2 cups finely chopped leeks

8 ounces spinach, stemmed and finely chopped (about 2 cups)

1 to 2 cups finely chopped celery or leaf lettuce

1/2 cup finely chopped scallions (green parts only)

1 cup minced fresh flat-leaf parsley

1/4 cup chopped fresh dill

1/4 cup chopped fresh spearmint or cilantro, or 1/2 cup minced snipped chives (optional)

1/4 to 1/2 cup (1 to 2 ounces) chopped walnuts or grated kasseri or Parmesan cheese (optional)

4 teaspoons unbleached all-purpose flour

About 1 teaspoon table salt or 2 teaspoons kosher salt

About 1/2 teaspoon ground black pepper or freshly grated nutmeg

1/2 teaspoon ground turmeric

6 large eggs, lightly beaten

1. In a heavy 10-inch skillet, heat 2 tablespoons of the oil over medium heat. Add the onions and sauté until soft and translucent, 5 to 10 minutes. Add the spinach, celery, and scallions and sauté for 2 minutes. Transfer to a large bowl. Add the parsley, dill, mint, and, if using, the walnuts to the spinach mixture. Add the flour, salt, pepper, and turmeric. Stir in the eggs.

2. In the same skillet, heat the remaining 2 tablespoons oil over medium heat. Add the egg mixture, cover, and cook until the bottom is set but the top is still uncooked, about 5 minutes.

3. Loosen the edges of the omelet and slide it onto a large platter. Place the skillet over the platter and carefully invert. Continue cooking over medium heat until the bottom (former top) is set and lightly browned, about 5 minutes. Slide onto the serving platter and cut into wedges. Serve warm or at room temperature.

ASHKENAZIC EGG SALAD WITH FRIED ONION

(Gehakte Eier mit Tzibbles)

ABOUT 2 CUPS, OR 4 TO 5 SERVINGS

Should egg salad be flavored with raw or sautéed onions? This has been an ongoing question for years at my synagogue, being good-naturedly debated at the weekly Sabbath afternoon meal (shalosh seudot in Hebrew) when one version or the other is served at the table. The easier version—made with sharp raw onions and mayonnaise—appears more frequently. Nevertheless, for an egg-salad aficionado, the extra effort required to brown the onions is more than worthwhile; the sweet caramelized onions contrast deliciously with the mild eggs. Either way, egg salad makes a tasty appetizer, light entrée, or sandwich filling. Serve with crackers, matza, or slices of dark bread or challah.

6 large eggs in the shell

1¹/₂ teaspoons table salt or 3 teaspoons kosher salt

3 tablespoons vegetable oil

2 onions, chopped

2 tablespoons chopped fresh parsley or dill

Ground black pepper to taste

Lettuce leaves for garnish

Your choice of cucumber, tomato slices, or black olives for garnish

1. Bring a large pot of water to a boil. Using a slotted spoon, gently place the eggs in the pot and add 1 teaspoon of the table salt or 2 teaspoons of the kosher salt. Immediately reduce the heat to low and simmer for 12 minutes for medium eggs, 14 minutes for large eggs, or 15 minutes for extra-large eggs. Or, place the eggs in a single layer in a saucepan, add cold water to cover by about 1 inch, cover, bring to a boil, add the salt, turn off the heat, and let stand, covered, 12 minutes for medium eggs, 15 minutes for large eggs, and 18 minutes for extra-large eggs. Immediately drain and place in ice water or under cold running water until completely cooled. Store the eggs in the shell in the refrigerator for up to 1 week. Peel the eggs, place them in a large bowl, then coarsely chop or mash them.

2. In a large skillet, heat the oil over medium heat. Add the onions and sauté until lightly golden, 10 to 15 minutes. Stir the onions into the eggs. Add the parsley, the remaining ¹/₂ teaspoon table salt or 1 teaspoon kosher salt, and the pepper. For a chunky texture, stir until the mixture just holds together; for a smoother texture, blend well. Cover and refrigerate until ready to serve.

3. For individual portions, arrange scoops of the egg salad on a bed of lettuce and garnish with cucumber, tomato, or olives.

N O T E   Avoid cooking eggs over high heat; this produces rubbery whites and green rings around the yolks.

VARIATIONS

You can further vary the flavor and texture by stirring in additions, such as ¹/₂ to 1 cup chopped celery, sautéed mushrooms, chopped cooked green beans, chopped walnuts, and/or finely chopped bell pepper.

Raw Onion Egg Salad: For a more pungent flavor, omit the oil, use raw onions or substitute 6 to 8 chopped scallions, then stir about ¹/₄ cup mayonnaise into the egg mixture. Yemenites prepare a zesty version, adding chopped sour pickles and minced red chilies. For an unorthodox version, stir in a little caviar and a dash of lemon juice.

Hungarian "Jewish" Eggs (*Zsido Tojas*): Sauté the onions until soft and translucent, 5 to 10 minutes. Add 1 tablespoon sweet paprika and about 2 tablespoons prepared mustard with the salt.

Georgian Eggs in Walnut Sauce (*Kvertskhshi Nigvzis Satsebelit*): Although Georgians are not generally egg eaters, they do prepare Persian-style omelets called *chizipizhi* and serve hard-cooked eggs drenched in *bazha*, the country's favorite walnut sauce, which is enhanced with a medley of spices and herbs. Cut the hard-boiled eggs into quarters, arrange on a serving platter, and pour 1 1/2 cups bazha (Georgian Walnut Sauce; page 432) over top.

ASHKENAZIC EGG SALAD

Around the end of the eleventh century, Franco-German Jews developed the custom of eating hard-boiled eggs and salted raw onions, separately, during the Sabbath. At some point, the two foods came together in the form of a chopped-egg salad. There was no mayonnaise then; instead the chopped eggs were bound with a little schmaltz (poultry fat) and sometimes mixed with *gribenes* (chicken cracklings). This dish became even more popular in eastern Europe, where chickens provided an abundance of eggs. Today, egg salad remains popular for such light meals as a *kiddush* (Sabbath morning buffet), a *shalosh seudot* (Sabbath afternoon meal), and various life-cycle events, usually without the schmaltz and cracklings and commonly bound with mayonnaise.

SEPHARDIC "ROASTED" EGGS

(*Huevos Haminados*)

12 SERVINGS

I initially encountered this intriguing dish at my first Sephardic Sabbath lunch, when the hostess passed around a plate of brown eggs in the shell. I proceeded to peel mine thinking they were simply brown-shell eggs, only to find the interior brown colored as well. I wondered whether something had gone horribly wrong in the cooking, but as everyone else was devouring their eggs, I took a hesitant first bite and discovered a flavor and tender texture that I'd never tasted before.

The combination of a long cooking time and cooking the eggs with onion skins or sometimes coffee gives them a russet brown color, creamy texture, and subtle nutty flavor. The onion skins also cradle and protect the eggs during cooking. A little oil is commonly spread over the top to help prevent the water from evaporating, but when mixed into the water it produces pretty, mottle-colored eggs. Haminados are frequently served with borekas *(Turkish Turnovers, page 176) or sometimes* hummus *(Middle Eastern Chickpea Dip, page 328).*

> Brown skins from 12 onions, rinsed if dirty (about 4 cups)
> 12 large eggs in the shell (without any cracks)
> 1 teaspoon table salt or 2 teaspoons kosher salt
> About 3 tablespoons olive oil or vegetable oil

1. Arrange the onion skins in the bottom of a 4- to 6-quart pot or flameproof casserole and place the eggs on top. Add the salt, then add water to cover by at least 2 inches. Bring to a boil, drizzle with the oil, and cover with a lid or aluminum foil. Simmer over very low heat or transfer to a preheated 200°F oven and cook for at least 8 hours or preferably 12 hours.

2. Remove the eggs from the cooking liquid, rinse, and pat dry. Serve warm or at room temperature. Store in cold water in the refrigerator for up to 4 days. To reheat, place in boiling water for 3 to 5 minutes.

Cook the eggs in a slow cooker set on the lowest temperature for 12 hours.

For a darker brown color: Omit the onion skins and oil and add $1/2$ cup strong brewed coffee or 2 tablespoons ground coffee.

HAMINADOS

*H*uevos haminados (*haminados* is derived from the Hebrew word for "warm") is so closely identified with Sephardic culture that during the Spanish Inquisition, the presence of slow-cooked whole eggs with onion skins was considered a sign of Jewish cooking. Early in the development of Sephardic culture, women would bury the eggs alongside their Sabbath stew in the embers of a fire to bake overnight. Some North African and Calcutta Jews still prepare the eggs this way, covering them in sand and baking them in a low oven overnight. Eventually, Sephardim developed an easier technique: simmering or baking the eggs in water along with onion skins, usually saved from the previous week's cooking. The result was delicious hard-boiled eggs that looked as if they'd been roasted.

Haminados are ubiquitous to nearly all Sephardic celebrations and life-cycle events. They are served as the first course of the Passover Seder and cooked in Sephardic Sabbath stews. Because of the similarity of the word *hamin* to Haman, the villain of the Scroll of Esther, *haminados* became a traditional Purim food, and many Sephardim prepare pastries encasing hard-boiled eggs to represent Haman in jail. Cooks usually make *haminados* in large batches, ensuring leftovers, to be added to salads, beans, and vegetable stews during the following week.

SYRIAN EGGS WITH RHUBARB

(Beid bi Rhubarber)

3 TO 4 SERVINGS

Throughout much of my childhood, my parents grew various vegetables on our land in Virginia and West Virginia, including rhubarb. During rhubarb season, my mother would make compotes and pies, always adding plenty of sugar. Therefore, like most Western- ers, I learned to eat rhubarb sweet.

My Syrian friends, however, enjoy the natural tartness of rhubarb, evident in this lightly sweetened or sometimes unsweetened dish. Such thick, tart sauces have long played a role in Roman, Persian, and east- ern Arabic cookery, which originally featured a sour- grape sauce called agra. *Sour grapes were later replaced with the more fresh- and earthy-tasting rhubarb— once it arrived from Siberia—and the mildly acidic tomato from the New World, which can be substi- tuted for the rhubarb in this dish.*

Rhubarb stalks, 12 to 18 inches long, are tender and pink when young; older, very thick stalks are stringy and acidic, with a mottled red and green color, and should be avoided. Rhubarb grown in green- houses, which is increasingly common in the West, is less red, stringy, and acidic and has a milder flavor than that grown outdoors. Field-grown rhubarb is available from April through July; hothouse stalks are usually in the market from January through June. To store rhubarb, wrap in paper towels and place in a plastic bag in the refrigerator for up to 1 week. Rhubarb also freezes well, and many grocery stores carry it in 1-pound bags in the frozen food section.

This unusual dish, neither an omelet nor quite scrambled eggs, combines streaks of the tangy rhubarb sauce with the mild eggs. Some cooks stir the rhubarb sauce into scrambled eggs, resulting in a looser texture.

In either case, it is served warm for breakfast or lunch, alone or over toast or rice, and commonly served with Syrian white cheese, which has the consistency of a thick ricotta cheese, and apricot preserves.

4 firm, crisp stalks rhubarb (about 12 ounces total), preferably no more than 1 inch wide
2 tablespoons vegetable oil
2 cloves garlic, minced
1 to 3 tablespoons sugar
6 large eggs
About $^1/_2$ teaspoon table salt or 1 teaspoon kosher salt
Pinch of ground black pepper or ground allspice
$^1/_4$ to $^1/_2$ teaspoon dried mint, crumbled

1. Rinse the rhubarb stalks in cold water. Trim the base and leaves, the latter being toxic. If very fibrous, remove the strings by peeling from one end downward. Cut the stalks into 1-inch pieces. (You should have about 2 cups.)

2. In a large skillet, heat the oil over medium heat. Add the garlic and sauté until lightly colored but not burnt, about 30 seconds. Add the rhubarb and sugar, cover, and simmer, stirring occasionally, until the rhubarb is tender and breaks down, about 15 minutes.

3. In a medium bowl, beat the eggs with the salt and pepper until blended. Gently stir into the rhubarb to marbleize but not to completely blend, cover, and cook until set, about 3 minutes. Slide onto a serving platter and sprinkle with the mint. Serve hot.

VARIATION

Syrian Eggs with Tomatoes (*Benadora bi Beid*): Substitute 4 cups peeled, seeded, and chopped tomatoes (see page 291) for the rhubarb.

SAUCES AND SEASONINGS

❧ · ❧

Sauces provide moisture, texture, and supporting or balancing flavors to many dishes. Seasonings or flavorings (in powder, paste, or liquid form) provide complexity to foods both during cooking and before eating. The word "sauce" is derived from the Latin *salsus* ("salted"), a reference to the predominant flavor of early sauces. The mark of medieval sauces was an overpowering amount of spices, unlike modern sauces that are intended to complement rather than mask the taste of food. Sauces and condiments prominent on Jewish tables, like other foods, reflect the societies in which the communities developed. The few popular Ashkenazic sauces consisted primarily of basic flavors, most notably mushroom and sweet and sour; the foremost condiments were *chrain* (horseradish) and mustard. Sephardim developed a larger repertoire and lighter, more sophisticated sauces, such as egg-lemon, tomato, and fish roe. In the Middle East, tahini sauce (made from sesame seeds) and, after the introduction of produce from South America, chili sauces became essential in certain areas, such as *harissa* in northwest Africa and *z'chug* in Yemen.

The key to most sauces and condiments is spices. In the ancient world, most of the important spices—particularly pepper, cinnamon, cloves, nutmeg, and ginger—were grown in eastern Asia. Since spices store well and are relatively light, they lend themselves to being transported. No matter which way they traveled, scarcity and shipping costs meant that most spices in Europe were expensive and, all too frequently, fought over. As a result, spice trading served as one of the primary movers of history. In the eleventh century, Crusaders discovered exotic seasonings during their voyages to the Holy Land, and the continuous flow of soldiers

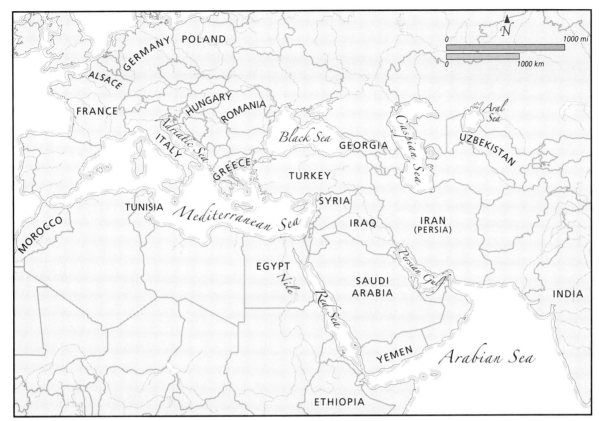

Predominant Seasonings: Alsace, France *(anise, nutmeg, cinnamon, ginger);* **Germany** *(poppy seeds, caraway);* **Poland** *(dill);* **Hungary** *(paprika);* **Romania** *(garlic, cumin, coriander);* **Greece** *(oregano, thyme, mint, fennel);* **Italy** *(basil, oregano, rosemary, saffron);* **Morocco** *(cumin, coriander, paprika, ginger, preserved lemon);* **Tunisia** *(coriander, caraway, chile);* **Egypt** *(sesame, coriander, cumin);* **Ethiopia** *(chilies, cardamom, cinnamon, cloves, coriander, ginger);* **Georgia** *(coriander, marigold petals, fenugreek);* **Uzbekistan** *(cumin, coriander);* **Turkey** *cumin, cinnamon, saffron);* **Lebanon** *(sesame, thyme, sumac);* **Syria** *(allspice, Aleppo chile, cumin, tamarind);* **Iraq** *(cumin, saffron, turmeric, dried lemon);* **Iran (Persia)** *(turmeric, mint);* **Yemen** *(chilies, fenugreek, cilantro);* **India** *(pepper, cardamom, cinnamon, coriander, turmeric, mustard seeds, ginger)*

and pilgrims during the following two centuries produced a taste among Europeans for Middle and Far Eastern spices, sparking the revival of the spice trade and European cookery.

Most locales developed their own characteristic flavor combinations and distinctive blends of spices used to flavor dishes, such as the Ethiopian *berbere*, the Georgian *khmeli suneli* (literally "mixture of aromas"), the Moroccan *ras-el-hanout* (literally "head of the shop"), the Turkish and Syrian *bharat*, the Tunisian *tabil*, and the Yemenite *hawaij*.

Although spice mixtures were commonly available in local bazaars, Jews, in order to avoid bugs or other kosher rule conflicts, traditionally ground their own at home, adapting the medleys to suit their tastes and preferences.

MIDDLE EASTERN SESAME SAUCE
(*Tahini/Tarator bi Tahini*)

ABOUT 1 ³/4 CUPS   Ⓓ OR Ⓟ

Tahini (from the Arabic "to grind"), also called tahina *and, in some areas,* rashi, *is a thick paste made from grinding sesame seeds. It originated as a by-product of sesame-oil production, but emerged as a beloved food in its own right. Today, tahini can be purchased at most Western supermarkets. Cans impart a slight metallic taste to the paste, so those brands sold in glass jars are preferable. Tahini contains no emulsifiers and will separate during storage; simply stir before using. Although the name of this sauce, popular in the Middle East as a dip, salad dressing, and sauce for falafel, is officially* tarator bi tahini *(sesame sauce), it is usually shortened to* tahini. *Use yogurt for a sharper sauce.*

> 1 cup tahini (sesame seed paste; see page 431), stirred well before using
> ¹/4 to ¹/2 cup fresh lemon juice
> 1 to 2 cloves garlic, mashed
> About ³/4 teaspoon table salt or 1 ¹/2 teaspoons kosher salt
> About ¹/2 cup water or plain yogurt

In a medium bowl, combine the tahini, lemon juice, garlic, and salt. Using a fork or spoon, blend until smooth. Add enough water to make a sauce of pouring consistency.

VARIATION

Yemenite Parsley Salad (*Baldonseyia*): Yemenites serve tahini at almost every meal, providing both flavor and necessary nutrition. Increase the water to about 1 cup and stir in 2 cups minced fresh parsley. If desired, drizzle with a little olive oil.

In an electric coffee mill or a blender, process white (hulled) sesame seeds with a little sesame or peanut oil until smooth and the consistency of peanut butter. Store in an airtight container in a cool, dry place for up to 3 months. Do not refrigerate, which hardens the paste.

Egg-Lemon Sauce

(Agristada)

ABOUT 2¹/₂ CUPS

Sephardic cooks, unable to use dairy products to thicken meat sauces and stews, substituted a nondairy egg-based sauce called salsa agresta *or* agristada. *Originally, this Spanish sauce was made with* agresto *(verjuice, from the Latin meaning "wild"), an acidic and fruity juice made from unripe grapes, which gave the sauce its name. The acid, besides contributing flavor, slows the coagulation of proteins in the eggs, reducing the chances of curdling while exposed to heat, and aids in the emulsification. From Roman times and throughout the Middle Ages, verjuice and wine vinegar served as the predominant souring agents in many parts of Europe. After lemons became prevalent in the West— in North Africa and Spain in the thirteenth century and in most of Europe in the eighteenth century— they generally replaced the harder-to-find* agresto. *(Vinegar is too sharp and bitter for this sauce.)*

The few medieval Mediterranean locales noted for citrus cultivation corresponded to sizable Jewish populations, partially due to the Jewish practice of growing citron (etrog) trees for the Sukkot holiday. Hence, citrus fruits emerged as an integral component of Mediterranean Jewish cooking. As early as the

thirteenth century, a rabbi from the central Italian town of Viterbo mentioned lemon juice, although this fruit was not yet grown in Italy, as an ingredient in Sabbath foods. Following the Expulsion from Spain in 1492, refugees brought salsa agresta *eastward, where the lemon version was called* brodo brusco *or* bagna brusca *in Italy,* avgolemono *in Greece, and* beda b'lemune *in Syria.* Agristada *serves a role similar to that of mayonnaise in the West, accompanying mild-flavored foods such as fried or poached fish, stuffed cabbage, rice, fried cauliflower, or plain white bread.*

2 large eggs
2 large egg yolks
About ¹/₃ cup fresh lemon juice
2 tablespoons unbleached all-purpose flour,
   1 tablespoon cornstarch, or 2 tablespoons
   matza cake meal
About 1 teaspoon table salt or 2 teaspoons
   kosher salt
2 teaspoons sugar (optional)
2 cups boiling Vegetable Stock (page 115) or water

1. In a nonreactive 4-cup saucepan, beat together the eggs, egg yolks, and lemon juice. In a small bowl, whisk a little of the egg mixture into the flour to make a paste, then stir the paste back into the egg mixture. Add the salt and, if using, the sugar. (The ingredients can also be combined in a blender.)

2. Gradually beat in the hot stock. Cook over medium-low heat, stirring constantly with a wooden spoon or a whisk, until smooth and thickened to the consistency of a thin mayonnaise, about 8 minutes. Do not boil. Remove from the heat and continue to stir for 1 minute. Pour into a bowl, press a piece of plastic wrap against the surface, and let cool. (The sauce can be stored in the refrigerator for up to 3 days.)

GEORGIAN WALNUT SAUCE

(*Bazha*)

ABOUT 1 CUP

Arguably, no group loves walnuts more than Georgians, who add them to almost any dish. This ardor manifests itself in dozens of walnut sauces—originally adapted from Persian cuisine. The most versatile of these sauces is bazha, *a rich uncooked, slightly tart mixture enlivened with a medley of garlic, spices, and herbs. Georgians like to add a little fenugreek for a touch of bitterness. For a more fiery filling, use the pepper flakes. Adjust the amount of vinegar for the degree of potency. The thickness of* bazha *varies according to the nature of the dish: A thicker sauce is used for pkhali (salads); a thinner sauce for smothering foods, such as eggs, poultry, and fish. Typical of Georgian taste, this uncooked sauce is slightly tart, as sweeteners are not used in their cooking.*

1 cup (4 ounces) walnut pieces

1 small onion, chopped

3 to 4 cloves garlic, minced

About $^1/_2$ teaspoon table salt or 1 teaspoon kosher salt

About 2 tablespoons red wine vinegar or $^1/_4$ cup pomegranate juice

3 to 4 tablespoons chopped fresh cilantro

$^1/_4$ to $^1/_2$ teaspoon ground coriander

$^1/_4$ to $^1/_2$ teaspoon cayenne pepper, hot paprika, or red pepper flakes

$^1/_4$ teaspoon ground turmeric or $^1/_2$ teaspoon ground dried marigold petals

$^1/_4$ teaspoon ground fenugreek (optional)

About $^1/_4$ cup water

Using a mortar and pestle or a food processor, grind the walnuts, onion, garlic, and salt into a paste. Stir in the vinegar, cilantro, coriander, cayenne, turmeric, and fenugreek. Add enough water to make a sauce with the consistency of heavy cream. Let stand at room temperature for at least 1 hour. The sauce will thicken as it stands. Cover and refrigerate for up to 3 days. If too thick, stir in a little more water.

WALNUTS

Walnuts are one of the oldest foods. Exploration of the Shanidar Caves in northern Iraq revealed human consumption of walnuts in prehistoric times. According to Pliny and other Romans, walnuts reached Greece and Rome by way of Persia. The Romans in turn spread the walnut throughout Europe, and eventually the nut found its way into nearly every country on the continent. Rabbinic literature is replete with references to walnuts, describing their characteristics in great detail. Walnut branches, along with those of palms and pines, were preferred for the fire of the altar in the Temple. In Talmudic times, walnut shells were tossed in front of a bride and groom as a sign of fruitfulness and prosperity. Today, some Jewish communities still use walnuts to make the Passover *charoset* and a variety of baked goods.

NORTHWEST AFRICAN CHILI PASTE

(Harissa)

ABOUT 1 1/3 CUPS

The Spanish occupied part of Tunisia from 1535 until the Turks conquered the region in 1574, and they may have introduced many New World foods—including chilies—to the region during that period. Harissa (from the Arabic "to break"), a scorching-hot, oily chili paste, is traditionally drizzled over a host of Moroccan and Tunisian dishes, including couscous, soups, vegetables, salads, and in Israel, falafel. (Try adding a little to the dressing for Moroccan orange and black olive salad.) It should be used sparingly by the faint of heart.

- 5 ounces (about 18) assorted dried hot red chilies, such as ancho, arból, cayenne, guajillo, New Mexico, and pequín, stemmed, slit lengthwise, and seeded
- 4 to 5 cloves garlic, chopped
- About 1/2 teaspoon table salt or 1 teaspoon kosher salt
- 2 to 3 tablespoons olive oil, plus more for covering paste

1. Put the chilies in a bowl and add hot water to cover. Let soak until softened, about 30 minutes. Drain.

2. In a food processor, blender, or mortar and pestle, purée the chilies, garlic, and salt. Add 2 to 3 tablespoons oil to make a smooth, thick paste. Transfer to a jar, cover with a thin layer of additional oil, and store in the refrigerator for up to 1 month.

VARIATIONS

Moroccan *Harissa*: Add 1 tablespoon ground cumin, or 1 1/2 teaspoons ground cumin and 1 teaspoon ground coriander.

Tunisian *Harissa*: Add 1 1/2 teaspoons ground caraway and 1 1/2 teaspoons ground coriander.

HOW HOT IS THAT CHILI?

Determining a chili's piquancy is no easy matter, because even chilies of the same variety can differ in intensity. A general rule of thumb is that the smaller chilies are, the hotter they tend to be, and chilies with pointed tips and broad shoulders tend to be hotter than those with rounded, blunt tips. Color is also a sign: Yellowish-orange veins are another indication of fire; brighter colors are more fiery; and reds are milder than greens. Each variety of chili has special characteristics: The mild ancho gives a raisiny, sweet flavor; cayenne produces a very hot sauce; guajillo imparts smoky, slightly sweet notes; New Mexico has an earthy, slightly acidic flavor; and pequín is extremely hot. A good combination of chiles for *harissa* is 12 New Mexico or Anaheim chilies, 3 ancho or pasilla chilies, and 1 arból, cayenne, cascabel, guajillo, or pequín chili. This is a relatively mild version of *harissa*; for more heat, increase the amount of arból, cayenne, cascabel, guajillo, or pequín chilies.

POMEGRANATE CONCENTRATE

(Hamoud er Rumman)

ABOUT ¹/₂ CUP

To preserve pomegranates' pleasant tart taste year-round, Middle Eastern cooks long ago learned to boil down the juice into a thick, conservable syrup. Juice cooked to the consistency of maple syrup is called pomegranate syrup. However, most versions reduce the juice to a molasses consistency—a thick, dark purple sweet-and-sour syrup variously known as pomegranate concentrate, pomegranate molasses, rob-e anar *in Persian,* nasrahab *in Georgian, and* hamoud er rumman, *or* dibs rumman, *in Arabic. Pomegranate molasses is not the same as grenadine, which contains a significant amount of sugar. Some brands of pomegranate concentrate do add sugar and/or lemon juice to adjust the sweetness, but most are made from pure pomegranate juice. Pomegranate concentrate is widely used in Iran, Iraq, Turkey, and Georgia, often in combination with garlic, cilantro, parsley, and tomato sauce to give a tart flavor to stews and savory fillings. Add a little to vinaigrettes, marinades, relishes, stuffed vegetables, and even vodka martinis. It will keep at room temperature for at least a year, and almost indefinitely in the refrigerator. Pomegranate concentrate is also available in Middle Eastern stores.*

2 cups unsweetened pomegranate juice

In a small saucepan, boil the pomegranate juice over medium heat, stirring occasionally, until reduced to about ¹/₂ cup, about 1 hour. It will darken. Let cool, then pour into a sterilized jar. Seal and store in the refrigerator almost indefinitely.

VARIATION

Add ¹/₃ cup fresh lemon juice and ¹/₃ cup sugar.

SYRIAN MOCK TAMARIND SAUCE

(Temerhindi)

ABOUT 3 CUPS

Syrians love tart flavors, and will commonly add tamarind sauce and lemon juice to their stews, sauces, and salads, sometimes in lip-puckering amounts. (One friend's grandmother always carries a lemon with her, just in case a dish requires some extra zest.) Temerhindi, also called ourt, *is a sweet-tart concentrate of tamarind pulp, lemon juice, and sugar, the amount of sweetness being based on personal preference. It provides the sweet-and-sour note in numerous Syrian dishes.*

Tamarind sauce is available in Middle Eastern and Greek stores, but some Syrians make their own, while many others use this mock version when tamarind is unavailable. Others, particularly Jews from Damascus, substitute the slightly tarter pomegranate concentrate. You can also substitute a mix of 2 tablespoons prune butter and 2 tablespoons apricot butter for an equal amount of tamarind sauce.

2¹/₂ cups (20 ounces) unsweetened prune juice
1¹/₂ cups (17 ounces) prune butter
1¹/₂ cups fresh lemon juice
1¹/₂ cups packed dark brown sugar
2¹/₄ teaspoons sour salt

In a large nonreactive pot, combine all the ingredients. Bring to a boil over high heat, reduce the heat to medium-low, and gently boil, uncovered, stirring occasionally with a wooden spoon, until thickened to the consistency of apple butter, about 2¹/₂ hours. Remove from the heat and let cool. Pour into sterilized jars, seal, and store in the refrigerator for up to 6 months.

Substitute 2¹/₂ pounds (about 10 cups) prunes for the prune butter and juice. Place in a large pot with cold water to cover, bring to a boil, reduce the heat to low, and simmer until soft, about 20 minutes. Pit the prunes, discarding the pits. Purée the pulp and cooking liquid in a blender or food processor until smooth. Simmer with the other ingredients until thickened, about 30 minutes.

TAMARIND (*TAMIR HINDI*)

The tamarind, or "date of India" in Arabic, is the fruit of an Indian evergreen tree, and was traditionally used to cure indigestion and constipation. Before lemons reached the Middle East—first recorded in the early tenth century in an Arabic book and widespread in the southern Mediterranean within two centuries—tamarind served as the primary souring agent in cooking, a role it maintains in India and Syria. While high in sugar, the tamarind is also a highly acidic fruit, with a flavor similar to a combination of apricots and prunes. Each 2- to 8-inch long reddish-brown pod encases up to 10 glossy seeds surrounded by a sticky, tart, brown pulp. The pulp is used to make jams, candies, marinades, and sauces, including Worcestershire. Although tamarind pods are rarely available in the United States except in Latino or Indian markets, the fruit is sold as concentrated pulp or in dried blocks, which must be softened in liquid before using.

MIDDLE EASTERN "HYSSOP" MIXTURE

(Za'atar)

ABOUT ³/4 CUP

This Middle Eastern spice mixture, named for an Arabic word for hyssop, holds a particular prominence in the Levant, where cooks use it to add an herbal-lemony-nutty flavor to various salads and vegetables, sprinkle it over labni (*Middle Eastern Yogurt Cheese, page 48*), *and mix it with olive oil to make a dip for warm pita bread.*

¹/4 cup brown sesame seeds
1 cup dried Syrian oregano, or ²/3 cup dried thyme and ¹/3 cup dried wild or sweet marjoram
2 to 4 tablespoons ground sumac or 1 tablespoon grated lemon zest
About ¹/2 teaspoon table salt or 1 teaspoon kosher salt (optional)

1. In a dry skillet, toast the sesame seeds over medium heat, shaking the pan frequently, until lightly golden, 2 to 3 minutes. Transfer to a bowl and let cool.

2. In a spice or coffee grinder or with a mortar and pestle, process the sesame seeds, oregano, sumac, and, if using, the salt into a fine powder. Store in an airtight container in a cool, dry place for up to 4 months.

HYSSOP

The plant currently called hyssop (*hyssopus officinalis*), a native of southern Europe, is so bitter that it is rarely used in cooking. The hyssop (*eizov*) referred to in the Bible is wild *za'atar* (*Origanum syriacum*), known variously in English as white oregano, Syrian oregano, and Lebanese oregano. However, due to overexploitation, this grayish-green member of the mint family has become a protected plant in Israel, carrying a large fine if picked. Consequently, most commercial brands labeled *za'atar* substitute another relative, thyme, or a mixture of cultivated herbs for the real thing.

ETHIOPIAN CHILI POWDER

(Berbere)

ABOUT ¹/₂ CUP

Berbere reflects the Arabic and Indian influences on Ethiopian cookery. Cardamom, cinnamon, nutmeg, and allspice add a sweet counterbalance to the fire of the chilies and peppercorns. Berbere *refers both to ground dried red chilies and to the classic Ethiopian spice mixture that includes them. The first time I sampled a dish seasoned with* berbere*, the Ethiopian cook had added a prodigious amount. My mouth stung for hours. Fortunately, most cooks employ the mixture more conservatively, allowing the flavors to emerge more gently.*

4 dried red chilies, such as arból, cayenne, guajillo, pequín, and sanaam or 1 to 2 tablespoons cayenne or hot paprika

1 tablespoon black peppercorns

1 teaspoon cardamom pods

1 teaspoon coriander seeds

1 teaspoon fenugreek seeds

1 teaspoon ground ginger

¹/₂ teaspoon ground cinnamon

¹/₂ teaspoon freshly grated nutmeg

¹/₄ teaspoon ground allspice

¹/₄ teaspoon ground cloves

1. If using whole chilies, stir them in a dry skillet over medium heat until darkened and warm but not burnt. Remove from the heat and let cool. Remove and discard the stems and seeds. If using cayenne pepper, combine with the other ground ingredients in Step 3.

2. In a dry skillet over medium heat, stir the peppercorns, cardamom, coriander, and fenugreek until lightly browned, about 3 minutes.

3. In a spice grinder or coffee grinder, process the chilies, toasted spices, and all the remaining spices into a fine powder. Store in an airtight container in a cool, dry place for up to 2 months.

VARIATIONS

Substitute ¹/₂ teaspoon ground cardamom, ¹/₂ teaspoon ground black pepper, ¹/₄ teaspoon ground coriander, and ¹/₈ to ¹/₄ teaspoon ground fenugreek for the whole seeds.

Ethiopian Spice Paste (*Chow*): Add about ¹/₃ cup water.

Milder Ethiopian Spice Mixture (*Quamam*): Omit the chilies and fenugreek and add a pinch of ground turmeric. *Quamam* is usually added near the end of cooking.

YEMENITE CHILI PASTE

(Z'chug)

ABOUT 2 CUPS   Ⓟ

Yemenite cuisine is a fiery one, dominated by chilies, cumin, and cilantro. Yemenites contend, supported by medical documentation, that the fire in their dishes helps to cleanse the body, and it is difficult to argue with them as they are usually free of the afflictions of Western society, such as high blood pressure, high cholesterol levels, and diabetes. The predominant Yemenite condiment is a fiery green chili paste, z'chug, often served with crushed tomatoes or diluted with a little hilbeh *(fenugreek paste) or tahini (Middle Eastern Sesame Sauce, page 430) to soften the potency. Traditionally, the chilies are pounded with garlic in a mortar or on a flat stone, then the spices mixed in, but a blender makes the process easier. Yemenites use this in numerous dishes, including* hilbeh *(Yemenite Fenugreek Relish, page 80) and Sephardic Red Lentil Soup (page 133). Add a little z'chug to stews, salads, and sauces, or serve with bread.*

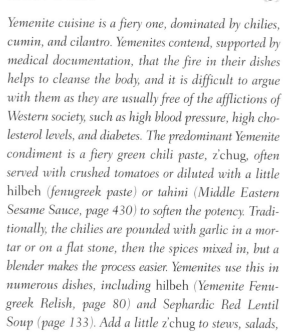

8 ounces small hot green chilies, such as chilaca, habanero, jalapeño, and New Mexico, seeded and puréed (about 1 cup)

1 1/2 cups chopped fresh cilantro, or 1 cup chopped fresh cilantro and 1 cup chopped fresh parsley

4 to 5 cloves garlic, crushed

3 to 5 green cardamom pods or 1/4 to 3/4 teaspoon ground cardamom

1 teaspoon ground cumin or caraway seeds

1 to 2 teaspoons ground black pepper

About 1 teaspoon table salt or 2 teaspoons kosher salt

2 tablespoons olive oil or 3 tablespoons fresh lemon juice (optional)

With a mortar and pestle or in a blender, grind all the ingredients together to produce a paste. Store, covered, in the refrigerator for up to 2 months.

VARIATION

Yemenite Red Chili Paste (Shatta): This is slightly milder and fruitier than *z'chug*. Substitute fresh red chilies, such as cayenne, serrano, surefire, and thai for the green chilies.

GLOSSARY

❧ · ❧

adafina: Also *dafina*. Sephardic Sabbath stew.

afikoman: A piece of the middle matza of the Passover Seder eaten at the end of the meal.

Ashkenazim: Jews who originated in Alsace but spread eastward to Germany and especially eastern Europe.

bar mitzvah: "Son of the commandment." A boy reaching the age of thirteen and the ceremony commemorating that event.

bat mitzvah: "Daughter of the commandment." A girl reaching the age of twelve and the ceremony commemorating that event.

beracha: A benediction/blessing.

brit milah: Circumcision ceremony.

bulgur: Steamed or boiled, then dried wheat groats.

challah: Sabbath bread.

chametz: Leavened grain products, prohibited during Passover.

·*charoset*: A fruit and nut mixture symbolizing mortar, used at the Passover Seder.

couscous: A Maghrebi dish of tiny semolina wheat grains, as well as any stew served with it.

couscousière: A special double-decker pot for making couscous.

desayuno: Spanish for "breakfast," but in the Sephardic sense connoting a casual brunch, typically on the Sabbath.

dolmas: Middle Eastern stuffed vegetables.

etrog: Citron, used in the Sukkot ritual of the Four Species.

fideos: Sephardic thin noodles.

Hagaddah: "Telling." The text of the Passover Seder.

hamin: Sephardic Sabbath stew.

Hamotzi: Blessing over bread.

harissa: A scorching-hot oily chili paste from northwest Africa.

Havdallah: Service held to usher out the Sabbath.

hilbeh: Yemenite fenugreek relish.

huevos haminados: Sephardic brown-colored hard-boiled eggs.

hummus: Middle Eastern dip of mashed chickpeas and tahini.

injera: Ethiopian pancake bread.

karpas: "Green." A vegetable representing spring and renewal, included on the Seder plate.

kasha: Toasted buckwheat groats.

keftes: Middle Eastern fried patties.

kibee: A distortion of the Persian word *kebab* ("form into a ball"), encompassing a variety of meat and bulgur dishes that constitute the national dish of Syria and Lebanon.

Kiddush: "Sanctification." A blessing over a cup of wine, symbolizing joy and fruitfulness, sanctifying the Sabbath and holidays.

kitniyot: "Legumes." A variety of non-*chametz* foods eschewed by Ashkenazim on Passover.

kosher: "Fit." Food prepared according to Jewish law.

kosher l'Pesach: Food kosher for Passover use.

kosher salt: Coarse additive-free salt.

kugel: Ashkenazic starch-based baked pudding.

labni: Middle Eastern strained yogurt (yogurt cheese).

Levant, the: The land on the eastern Mediterranean, encompassing Israel, Lebanon, Syria, and Turkey.

lokshen: Egg noodles in Yiddish.

lulav: Palm branch used in the Sukkot ritual of the Four Species.

Maghreb, the: Arabic for "setting sun." The Mediterranean coastal strip of northwest Africa, consisting of Morocco, Algeria, Libya, and Tunisia.

maror: "Bitter herbs" eaten at the Passover Seder.

matza: Unleavened bread, the only type permitted during Passover.

matza meal: Ground matza. Matza cake meal is very finely ground matza.

meze: Middle Eastern and Balkan appetizer assortment.

milchig: Foods containing dairy products.

Mishnah: "Teaching." Early codification of the oral tradition by Rabbi Judah Hanasi (c. 200 C.E.) serving as the basis of the Talmud.

Mizrachim: "Easterners." Generic term for Jews who are neither Ashkenazic or Sephardic.

pareve: Foods neither dairy nor meat.

phyllo: Paper-thin pastry dough.

pita: Middle Eastern flat bread sometimes called pocket bread.

Seder: "Order." The ceremonial dinner and service held on the first two nights of Passover commemorating the Exodus from Egypt.

Sephardim: Jews who originated in Spain or Portugal.

Seven Species: Term for the seven agricultural products for which the land of Israel is blessed: wheat, barley, wine, figs, pomegranates, olive oil, and honey.

Shalosh Seudot: "Third Meal." Third meal of the Sabbath served late on Saturday afternoon.

Sukkah: "Booth." Temporary dwelling for the Sukkot holiday.

tahini: Paste made from ground sesame seeds.

Talmud: Whenever the word *Talmud* appears by itself, it refers to the Babylonian version. Compilation of commentary on the Mishnah by the rabbinic authorities of Persia and Babylonia (from the second to end of the fifth century C.E.), and the primary sourcebook of Jewish tradition. There is also the Jerusalem Talmud containing the teachings of Israeli scholars.

Teimanim: Yemenite Jews.

wot: Ethiopian stew.

Yom Tov: "Good day." Jewish holiday.

z'chug: Yemenite chili paste.

INDEX

❦ · ❦